Shanghai

"All you've got to do is decide to go
and the hardest part is over.

So go!"

TONY WHEELER, COFOUNDER – LONELY PLANET

THIS EDITION WRITTEN AND RESEARCHED BY
Kate Morgan,
Helen Elfer, Trent Holden

Contents

(left) **Tiánzǐfáng p94**
Shopping in the French Concession's traditional alleyways.

··

(above) **Oriental Pearl TV Tower p146** Vertiginous views from atop.

··

(right) **Jade Buddha Temple p130** Stone lion detail.

··

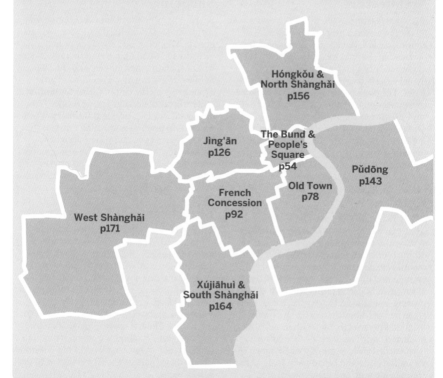

Welcome to Shànghǎi

Shànghǎi: few cities in the world evoke so much history, excess, glamour, mystique and exotic promise in name alone.

Architecture

Shànghǎi is home to the world's second-tallest tower and a host of other neck-craning colossi. But it's not all sky-scraping razzmatazz. Beyond the crisp veneer of the modern city typified by Pǔdōng, you can lift the lid to a treasure chest of architectural styles. The city's period of greatest cosmopolitan excess – the 1920s and '30s – left the city with pristine examples of art deco buildings. And there's more: from Jesuit cathedrals, Jewish synagogues and Buddhist temples to home-grown *lòngtáng* (laneway) and *shíkùmén* (stone gate) housing, Shànghǎi's architectural heritage is like none other.

Cuisine

Thirty years ago Shànghǎi's dour restaurant scene was all tin trays and scowling waiting staff, with international food confined to the dining rooms of 'exclusive' hotels. Today the mouth-watering restaurant scene is varied, exciting and up to the minute – and Shànghǎi has its own Michelin dining guide in 2017, proving just how far the city has come. Food is the hub of Chinese social life. It's over a meal that people catch up with friends, celebrate and clinch business deals, and spend hard-earned cash. Some of your best memories of the city could be culinary, so do as the Shanghainese do and make a meal of it.

Shopping

Bearing in mind that Chinese shoppers constitute up to 47% of the global luxury-goods market, shopping is rarely done in half-measures in Shànghǎi. Retail therapy is one way of spending new money and the Shanghainese aren't called 小资 (*xiǎozī* – 'little capitalists') by the rest of China for nothing, especially at the luxury end of things. But it's not all Prada, Gucci and Burberry. There are pop-up boutiques, bustling markets, cool vintage shops and young designer outlets. Beyond clothing you're also spoiled for choice, whether you're in the market for antiques, ceramics, art, Tibetan jewellery... whatever is on your shopping list.

Entertainment & the Arts

Běijīng often hogs the limelight as China's cultural nexus but, for what is essentially a town of wheelers and dealers, Shànghǎi is surprisingly creative. Many art galleries are exciting, offering a window onto contemporary Chinese concerns, while nightlife options have exploded. Acrobatics shows are always a favourite and you might grab the chance to catch some Chinese opera. Shànghǎi's music and club scene is vibrant: from unpretentious jazz and indie venues to all-night hip-hop and electro dance parties, the city swings with the best of them.

Why I Love Shànghǎi

By Kate Morgan, Writer

From the architectural landmarks lining the Bund and the rickety charm of the Old Town to the leafy backstreets of the former French Concession, Shànghǎi is a city that just begs for wandering. And eating. I love that you can slurp a bowl of hand-pulled noodles or bite into soupy *xiǎolóngbāo* dumplings for next to nothing, then splurge on cocktails and fusion fare while gazing out from a rooftop bar on the Bund, over the Huángpǔ River to Pǔdōng's space-age night scene. Shànghǎi's roller-coaster backstory is as decadent as it is debauched, but these days there is a palpable energy and confidence that the city is on the rise...again.

For more about our writers, see p320

Top: Chinese opera performer (p237)

Shànghǎi's
Top 13

The Bund *(p56)*

1 The Bund is mainland China's most iconic concession-era backdrop, Shànghǎi's standout spectacle and a source of intense local pride. A gorgeous curve of larger-than-life heritage architecture, the buildings here may be dwarfed by the city's modern high-rises, but they carry a gravity that simply can't be matched. A monument to the unbridled pursuit of wealth, the Bund was unsurprisingly left to languish during the communist years, but China's economic renaissance has restored its standing among the city's panoramas.

◉ *The Bund & People's Square*

Architecture *(p241)*

2 It's hard to talk about Shànghǎi without references to skyscrapers, the defining architectural style of the city. Pǔdōng towers are forever scaling new heights; the newest addition, the Shànghǎi Tower, even eclipses the sun at certain angles. There's nowhere else in mainland China quite like it. But Shànghǎi is no one-trick pony and the sheer diversity of architectural styles is hugely impressive. Wandering the city neighbourhoods takes you past art deco marvels, concession-era villas, Buddhist temples and neoclassical beauties. RIGHT: PǓDŌNG SKYLINE

◉ *Architecture in Shànghǎi*

PETER STUCKINGS/GETTY IMAGES ©

Dining in the French Concession

(p100)

3 An incomparable melange of regional Chinese restaurants, stylish Shanghainese eateries, international dining and no-frills street food, the French Concession is the epicentre of the city's culinary revolution. On a single strip you might find explosively hot Sichuanese, a Hong Kong–style diner, Shanghainese seafood and MSG-free noodles – venture just a little bit further and you can travel to the end of the Middle Kingdom and back.

RIGHT: STREET-FOOD STALL, TIÁNZǏFÁNG (P94)

✕ *French Concession*

JON ARNOLD/GETTY IMAGES ©

ANTON_IVANOV/SHUTTERSTOCK ©

Markets (p90)

4 Shànghǎi's air-conditioned malls can be a haven on a hot day, but if you want to see locals in their true shopping element, drop by a market. Get your haggling hat on and your elbows out – among all the jostling and banter, endless fakes and tricks of the trade, you might just find exactly what you're looking for. Don't forget: prices aren't fixed. In the Old Town, roll up your sleeves in the South Bund Fabric Market or cast a shrewd eye over the goods at the Fúyòu Antique Market.

LEFT: MARKET AT THE TEMPLE OF THE TOWN GOD (P82)

🔒 **Old Town**

Yùyuán Gardens (p80)

5 Yùyuán Gardens – in Shànghǎi's Old Town – is one of the nation's best examples of traditional Chinese gardens. With its ponds, trees, flowers, bridges, pavilions and harmonic compositions, Yùyuán Gardens encourages contemplation and reflection – elusive moods in today's frantic Shànghǎi. It's a popular place, though, so get here early in the day while it's still quiet. After exploring, join the hectic throb of shoppers in the attached bazaar, an excellent place to pick up skilfully made handicrafts and keepsakes.

⊙ **Old Town**

Jade Buddha Temple (p130)

6 While Shànghǎi and materialism fit together like hand and glove, the city's connection to spiritual matters can seem more tenuous, to say the least. Despite first impressions, however, the city harbours a strong affection for religious tradition, best observed in the main courtyard of this century-old Buddhist temple, which witnesses a continual stream of worshippers throughout the day. Housed on the top floor of a rear building is the temple's centrepiece and crowd-puller, a 1.9m-high statue of Sakyamuni crafted from pure Burmese jade.

👁 *Jìng'ān*

Toasting the Town (p43)

7 The heady promise of lipstick-smudged martini glasses and flashing neon lights doesn't always match expectations in Shànghǎi, one-time city of sin, but there's no doubt that the place loves to party and have a drink or two. With everything on offer from cocktails at slick rooftop bars lining the Bund and secret speakeasy-style spots in the French Concession to craft-beer breweries and intimate wine bars, whatever your tipple you'll have no trouble finding plenty of ways to toast the town.

🍷 *Drinking & Nightlife*

EXPOSE/SHUTTERSTOCK ©

8

M50 (p128)

8 Shànghǎi has traditionally eschewed the arts in favour of more commercial pursuits, but the escalating value of Chinese artwork has led to the emergence of a busy gallery scene. Located in former cotton mills, the industrially chic M50 is the city's main creative hub and Shànghǎi's answer to the 798 Art District in Běijīng. Dozens of edgy galleries, a handful of studios and occasional events make this an absorbing place to wander. LEFT: WORK BY XU ZHEN, PRODUCED BY MADEIN COMPANY

👁 *Jìng'ān*

9

WGAISS/SHUTTERSTOCK ©

10

ZHAO JIAN KANG/SHUTTERSTOCK ©

GIFTOGRAPHY/SHUTTERSTOCK ©

Shànghǎi Museum (p61)

9 Shànghǎi has never been a city to bother with the rear-view mirror, and this obvious disregard for tradition is what most distinguishes it from the rest of the country. The one glaring exception, however, is the standout Shànghǎi Museum, an inspiring tribute to the path of beauty throughout the millennia, from ancient bronzes to gorgeous ceramic masterpieces from the Qing dynasty. Come here for Chinese landscape paintings, sea-green celadon jars, Buddhist statuary and a taste of a world that has since disappeared.

The Bund & People's Square

Hángzhōu's West Lake (p179)

10 Whiz down to Hángzhōu on the high-speed train in a shot but, whatever you do, take your time dawdling around willow-fringed West Lake, one of the nation's top sights. The most famous city lake in China, it's vast, placid and beautiful in equal measure, and best savoured in a very low gear. With its pagoda-capped hills to the north, picturesque causeways and lakeside gardens and parks, West Lake is even more spellbinding come nightfall, when couples walk languorously along its shores. Sundown provides spectacular photographs across the water to the setting sun. LEFT: ANCIENT PAVILION ON WEST LAKE

Day Trips from Shànghǎi

French Concession Fashion (p119)

11 In the early 20th century, Shànghǎi single-handedly shaped the image of the modern Chinese woman through calendar posters, which were printed in the millions and distributed throughout the rural hinterland and beyond. Ever since, it has worn the crown of China's most fashionable city, and there's no better place to get a feel for the latest trends than the French Concession. Browse boutiques for sequin-covered shoes, Tibetan-inspired jewellery, silky summer dresses and the hip new styles of a growing crop of local and international designers. TOP: SHOPPING IN TIÁNZǏFÁNG (P94)

French Concession

Lǐlòng & Lòngtáng *(p247)*

12 When Shànghǎi's superscale buildings leave you feeling totally dwarfed, get down to the city's traditional *lǐlòng* and *lòngtáng* lanes. Exploring this charming realm allows you to discover a more personable aspect to the city, so go slowly. This is where you can find Shànghǎi's homey and more intimate side: narrow alleys, classic three-storey buildings, a warm community spirit, history, heritage and a lethargic tempo entirely at odds with the roar of the main drag.

⊙ *Architecture in Shànghǎi*

ULLSTEIN BILD/GETTY IMAGES ©

PRASIT PHOTO/GETTY IMAGES ©

Zhūjiājiǎo *(p197)*

13 The nearest decent-sized water town to Shànghǎi, Zhūjiājiǎo is ideal for a day trip. Easily reached by bus, it offers quintessential traditional bridges, pinched lanes, ancient streets, hoary Qing-dynasty temples, waterside views and even some pretty fine cafes. It's fun losing your bearings, but Zhūjiājiǎo is small enough to mean you never get entirely lost. If you take to the water-town culture, you can carry on from Zhūjiājiǎo to other canal towns in neighbouring Jiāngsū province.

⊙ *Day Trips from Shànghǎi*

What's New

Fine Dining

Shànghǎi's fine dining continues to get more international imports with a crop of excellent new restaurants, some headed up by Michelin-star chefs, including Joël Robuchon (p72), Hakkasan (p73), 8½ Otto e Mezzo Bombana (p73) and Alan Wong's (p139). Famed dining guide Michelin has announced that Shànghǎi will be getting its very own guide in 2017.

Bulgari Hotel

After hotel openings in London, Bali and Milan, exclusive Bulgari turned its attention to an area north of Sūzhōu Creek near the Bund for its latest address, set for a 2017 opening. The modern Foster + Partners tower will be offset by the adjacent traditional Chinese Chamber of Commerce building, housing one of the hotel's restaurants. (www.bulgarihotels.com/en-us/shanghai)

Shànghǎi Disneyland

Opened in June 2016, the 3.9-sq-km Shànghǎi Disneyland – mainland China's first – will top kids' wish lists for many years to come. Located in Pǔdōng, it is served by its own metro station and has two themed hotels and a huge 40-hectare lake. (p147)

The Shànghǎi Metro

The Shànghǎi metro is the world's fastest-growing underground rail network, and recent developments continue to be a boon for visitors. There are plans to extend the network with nine new lines and an additional 250km, with work starting 2017. (p260)

Yuz Museum

Housed in the former hangar of the Longua Airport, this huge contemporary art space is an excellent addition to Shànghǎi's emerging art scene. It hosts world-class temporary exhibitions. (p168)

Aurora Museum

Bringing a culture hit to flashy Pǔdōng, the Aurora Museum houses a treasure trove of jade, porcelain and pottery, some dating back to the Neolithic period. (p148)

Shànghǎi Natural History Museum & Jìng'ān Sculpture Park

This museum's slick new home (p134) is set over five floors, exhibiting everything from the African Savannah to life-size mechanical dinosaurs. In the surrounding gardens is a new sculpture park (p135), where visitors can roam between the likes of giant ostriches that have their heads buried in the ground and a huge thatched fox.

Legoland Discovery Centre

Kids will get a kick out of the new Legoland Discovery Centre, where they can hone their Lego-building skills and speed-test Lego cars on the track. (p174)

Long Museum

Part of the West Bund art area development, the Long Museum displays contemporary art and Chinese artefacts in an impressively designed four-storey building by Chinese architect Liu Yichun. (p168)

Shànghǎi Tower

This colossal skyscraper – topping out at 632m – has redefined the Pǔdōng skyline. Gently corkscrewing into the Shànghǎi stratus, the twisting glass-clad tower contains the world's highest observation deck, entertainment venues, shopping outlets, offices, a luxury hotel and 'sky lobbies' bathed in natural daylight. (p148)

For more recommendations and reviews, see **lonelyplanet. com/shanghai**

Need to Know

For more information, see Survival Guide (p253)

Currency

Rénmínbì (RMB); basic unit is the yuán (¥).

Language

Mandarin, Shanghainese

Visas

Needed for all visits to Shànghǎi except transits of up to 144 hours.

Money

ATMs are widespread and generally accept Visa, MasterCard, Cirrus and Maestro cards. Most operate 24 hours.

Mobile Phones

Using a mobile phone is most convenient. Skype (www.skype.com) and Viber (www.viber.com) are useful for cheap or free calls. You won't get far communicating with anyone in China unless you have the WeChat app (also known as Weixin).

Time

China Standard Time/Běijīng Time (GMT/UTC plus eight hours)

Wi-fi

Available in most bars, cafes, restaurants and hotels.

Daily Costs

Budget: Less than ¥400

➡ Dorm bed: ¥75–90

➡ Double room from ¥200 (per person)

➡ Cheap hole-in-the-wall restaurants, food markets and street food: ¥50

➡ Bike hire, metro or other transport: ¥20–30

➡ Museums: some have free entry

➡ Sundries: ¥40–60

Midrange: ¥400–¥1300

➡ Double room in a midrange hotel: ¥350–650 (per person)

➡ Lunch and dinner in decent local restaurants: ¥150–200

➡ Entertainment: ¥80

Top End: More than ¥1300

➡ Double room in a top-end hotel: from ¥650 (per person)

➡ Lunch and dinner in excellent restaurants: ¥300 and up

➡ Shopping at top-end boutiques: ¥300

Advance Planning

Three months before Book a room at popular hotel accommodation.

One month before Book tables for well-known restaurants; check listings on entertainment sites such as SmartShanghai (www.smartshanghai.com) and City Weekend (www.cityweekend.com.cn) for art exhibitions, live music, festivals and shows, and book your tickets.

A few days before Check the weather and pollution index (http://aqicn.org/city/shanghai).

Useful Websites

➡ **Lonely Planet** (lonelyplanet.com/shanghai) Destination information, hotel bookings, traveller forum and more.

➡ **City Weekend** (www.cityweekend.com.cn/shanghai) Comprehensive listings website of popular expat magazine. News stories can be weak.

➡ **Shanghaiist** (www.shanghaiist.com) Excellent source of news and reviews.

➡ **Smart Shanghai** (www.smartshanghai.com) Quality listings website with forum.

WHEN TO GO

Summer is peak season but it's hot and sticky with heavy rain; spring and late September to October are optimal. Winter is cold and clammy.

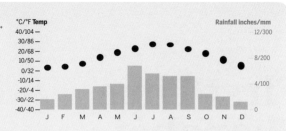

Arriving in Shànghǎi

Pǔdōng International Airport
The superfast Maglev (p254) train runs to Longyang Rd metro stop on line 2 (eight minutes, ¥50); from there you can catch the metro into central Shànghǎi. Metro line 2 also runs right from the airport passing through central Shànghǎi (45 minutes, ¥7 to People's Square). A taxi to the Bund will cost around ¥160 and take approximately one hour.

Hóngqiáo International Airport Terminal 2 (where most flights arrive) is connected to downtown Shànghǎi by metro lines 2 and 10 (30 minutes to People's Square). A taxi to the Bund will cost around ¥100 and take approximately 45 minutes.

For much more on **arrival** see p254

Money-Saving Tips

Shànghǎi isn't cheap and costs can mount up. Here are some tips to help your yuán go further.

➤ **Target happy hour** Buy one and get one free, usually from 5pm to 8pm – this can be crucial when paying ¥35-plus for a small bottle of beer.

➤ **Take the metro** It's cheap, efficient, fast, and goes almost everywhere (but doesn't run late at night).

➤ **Haggle** If prices aren't displayed, haggling is often the *lingua franca*, especially in markets (but not in department stores or shops).

➤ **Stay visa-free** For transit stays of 144 hours and less, there's no need to fork out for a visa.

For much more on **getting around** see p259

Sleeping

From ultrachic, carbon-neutral boutique rooms and sumptuous five-star hotels housed in glimmering towers to grand heritage affairs and snappy, down-to-earth backpacker haunts, the range of accommodation is just what you would expect from a city of this stature.

Useful Websites

➤ **Lonely Planet** (lonelyplanet.com/china/shanghai/hotels) Hotel bookings and forum.

➤ **CTrip** (http://english.ctrip.com) An excellent online agency, good for hotel bookings.

➤ **eLong** (www.elong.net) Hotel bookings.

For much more on **sleeping** see p201

TOURIST INFORMATION

Shànghǎi has about a dozen or so rather useless **Tourist Information & Service Centres** (旅游咨询服务中心, Lǚyóu Zīxún Fúwù Zhōngxīn; p270) where you can at least get free maps and (sometimes) information. **Shanghai Information Centre for International Visitors** (Map p303; ☎021 6384 9366; Xīntiāndì South Block, Bldg 2, Lane 123, Xingye Rd; 兴业路123弄新天地南里2号楼; ⊙9.30am-9.30pm; Ⓜ Xintiandi) is one of the most useful.

First Time Shànghǎi

For more information, see Survival Guide (p253)

Checklist

➡ Ensure your passport is valid for at least six months past your arrival date.

➡ Organise your visa.

➡ Check airline baggage restrictions.

➡ Check your vaccinations are up to date.

➡ Get a pre-trip dental check-up.

➡ Arrange for appropriate travel insurance.

➡ Inform your debit-/credit-card company you're heading away.

What to Pack

➡ Sunscreen and sunhat in summer

➡ Insect repellent to keep mosquitoes at bay

➡ Good walking shoes – Shànghǎi's concrete distances can become foot-numbing

➡ Phrasebook with Chinese characters – English is spoken fitfully

➡ An electrical adaptor

➡ Any prescribed drugs you may need

➡ Earplugs for hotel rooms with paper-thin walls

Top Tips for Your Trip

➡ The Shànghǎi metro will be your best friend: fast, efficient, cheap, punctual and extensive.

➡ Taxis are widespread and great value for short hops.

➡ For budget accommodation, stick to Pǔxī, not Pǔdōng.

➡ Plan your time – the metro system is excellent but criss-crossing Shànghǎi can eat into your time. Instead, choose just one or two neighbourhoods to explore in a day. For our suggested itineraries, see p22.

➡ If you've only a few days, stick to the city's core districts of the Bund, People's Square, the French Concession and Jìng'ān, with a foray or two to Pǔdōng.

What to Wear

Shànghǎi is a fairly casual destination, so you can wear what you want most of the time, although more modest dress is required for temple and mosque visits. For fancy dinners, smart-casual should be all that's required – no restaurant will insist on jackets or ties. Winters are clammy, draining and cold, so warm clothing is crucial; summers are hot, humid and long, with epic downpours. An umbrella won't go astray in either season.

Be Forewarned

To most visitors, Shànghǎi feels very safe, and crimes against foreigners are rare. If you have something stolen, you must report the crime at the district Public Security Bureau (PSB, 公安局, Gōng'ānjú) office and obtain a police report.

Visitors to the Bund, East Nanjing Rd, People's Square and elsewhere can be targeted by scams that leave them out of pocket, often involving visits to teahouses where the victim is left with the bill.

For full details, see p268.

Credit Cards

Credit cards are more readily accepted in Shànghǎi than in other parts of China. Most tourist hotels will accept major credit cards (with a 4% processing charge) such as Visa, Amex, MasterCard, Diners and JCB, as will banks, upper-end restaurants and tourist-related shops. Credit hasn't caught on among most Chinese, and most local credit cards are in fact debit cards. Always carry enough cash for buying train tickets and for emergencies.

For more information on Money, see p267.

Bargaining

Haggling is de rigueur (and a common language between foreigners and Chinese vendors) in markets where goods do not have a clearly marked price, but not in department stores or high-street shops. Don't be afraid to come in really low, but remain polite.

Tipping

➡ **Restaurants** Never tip at budget eateries; some (midrange and up) restaurants will levy a service charge, so check your bill first.

➡ **Bars** No need to tip in bars or clubs.

➡ **Hotels** Porters at midrange and high-end hotels may expect around ¥5 per bag.

➡ **Taxis** No need to tip.

Street vendor selling fruit

Etiquette

➡ Chinese people rarely kiss each other upon greeting, but shaking hands is fine.

➡ If visiting a local person's home, take off your shoes.

➡ If you smoke, offer your cigarettes around.

➡ Don't stick your chopsticks vertically into your bowl of rice.

➡ At dinner, it's polite to ensure the person sitting next to you has enough to eat and to replenish their glass.

➡ Avoid large, expansive physical gestures.

Guided Tours

➡ **Big Bus Tours** (p261) & **City Sightseeing Buses** (p261) Double-decker open-bus tours.

➡ **Insiders Experience** (p261) Fun motorbike-sidecar tours.

➡ **Newman Tours** (p261) Themed guided walks.

➡ **BOHDI** (p259) Night-time cycling tours and trips.

➡ **China Cycle Tours** (p261) City and rural tours in Shànghǎi and Sūzhōu.

Language

Outside of city hotels, English is not widely spoken. You'll be able to get by in tourist areas, but it's useful to learn a few basic phrases. Some restaurants may not have English menus. To help decipher written Chinese, a Pleco app (www.pleco.com) or phrasebook is useful.

For more information, see Language (p274).

Getting Around

For more information, see Transport (p254)

Metro

Quickest way to travel around town. The extensive system runs from 5.30am to 10.30pm or 11pm. Tickets are cheap; trains run regularly and with few delays.

Taxi

Cabs are affordable, plentiful and the way to go for short hops around town or trips late at night.

Bus

Slow-going on Shànghǎi's congested roads and difficult for non-Chinese speakers to use but can be useful if you get the hang of them.

Bicycle

Handy for sightseeing around smaller neighbourhoods; not so useful for large distances.

Ferry

Great for crossing the Huángpǔ River.

Walking

The central areas of town can be explored on foot; moving between Shànghǎi's sprawling expanses is hard going.

Car Hire

Because of restrictions, paperwork and an undeveloped rental network, self-drive is generally not an option, but cars with drivers can be hired.

Key Phrases

Chūzūchē (出租车) Taxi

Dìtiě (地铁) Literally the 'underground railway'; this is what the Chinese call the Shànghǎi metro – it's shorthand for *dìxià tiělù* (地下铁路; underground railway)

Dìtiězhàn (地铁站) Metro station

Dùchuán (渡船) Ferry

Gōnggòng qìchē (公共汽车) Public bus

Gōnggòng qìchēzhàn (公共汽车站) Bus stop

Jiāotōng Kǎ (交通卡) Transport Card

Piào (票) Ticket

Qǐng gěi wǒ fāpiào (请给我发票) Please give me a receipt

Shǒubānchē/Mòbānchē (首班车／末班车) First/last train (or bus)

Zìxíngchē (自行车) Bicycle

Key Routes

Metro line 1 Runs from Fujin Rd in the north, through Shànghǎi Railway Station and People's Square, along Middle Huaihai Rd, through Xújiāhuì and Shànghǎi South Railway Station to Xīnzhuāng in the south.

Metro line 2 Runs from East Xujing in the west via Hóngqiáo Railway Station and Hóngqiáo International Airport, passing through Jìng'ān, People's Square, East Nanjing Rd and the Bund district and on to Longyang Rd, the site of the Maglev terminus, before terminating at Pǔdōng International Airport in the east.

Metro line 10 Runs from Hóngqiáo Railway Station in the west through Hóngqiáo International Airport to the French Concession, the Old Town, the Bund area and Hóngkǒu, and terminating at Xinjiangwancheng.

How to Hail a Taxi

➡ Look for a taxi with an illuminated light behind the windscreen.

➡ Hail it from the street by raising your arm. Drivers should pull over when they see you.

➡ You can also catch a taxi from a taxi rank.

➡ Have your destination written out in Chinese or use your mobile phone to have your hotel concierge translate for you in the event of communication problems.

TOP TIPS

➡ If you're in town for more than a week, invest in a Transport Card.

➡ There's no need to tip taxi drivers.

➡ Cars can still turn when the green man is lit at crossings, so stay alert.

➡ Combine taxi trips and metro journeys to get around Shànghǎi quickly.

➡ If taking a taxi, have your destination written down in Chinese or take your hotel business card with you (if you don't speak Chinese).

➡ Try to have some coins for the metro ticket machines, as notes sometimes don't work.

➡ Forget about hiring a car.

When to Travel

➡ Rush hour (*gāofēng shíjiān*) is roughly from 7.30am to 9.30am and 5pm to 7pm on working days, when millions of people are on the move. The metro and buses are packed out and empty taxis can be hard to find.

➡ Taxis are in short supply when one of Shànghǎi's summer downpours inundates town.

➡ The pricier taxi night-rates run from 11pm to 5am.

Etiquette

➡ Passengers should stand on the right when using escalators in metro stations but this is frequently ignored; prepare for a mass of people and get your elbows out.

➡ Hand over your bag to be scanned at the security check at metro stations. A lot of locals ignore the request, but it's good form to oblige.

➡ Have your ticket or Transport Card ready when leaving the station. Locals go through the barriers without breaking pace. Transport Cards are swiped while single-fare tickets are fed into the machine, where they are retained.

➡ Wait for passengers to disembark the metro and buses before boarding at marked embarkation points.

➡ Address taxi or bus drivers as *sījī* ('driver').

Tickets & Passes

➡ The Transport Card is a handy smartcard on which you can store credit for use on the metro, in taxis, on most buses and on some ferries. Swipe the touchpad at both ends of your metro journey, but only once for bus journeys. You won't save money, but you will be spared queuing or hunting for change. A refundable deposit of ¥20 is required.

➡ Plastic tickets can also be used on the metro, and you can use cash on buses (drop coins into the slot on entering or pay the conductor) and in taxis. The taxi driver will ask if you want to use cash (*xiànjīn*) or a card (*kǎ*).

➡ Buy Transport Cards or top up credit at the service counter in metro stations and at numerous convenience stores and banks.

For much more on **getting around** see p259 ➡

TRAVEL AT NIGHT

The metro stops early, so you could be left high and dry from roughly 10.30pm. Buses 300 to 399 are night buses, but buses in general are not easy to use if you don't know Chinese. Taking a taxi is your best and fastest option; cabs are usually plentiful. Note that the more expensive taxi night-rate operates between 11pm to 5am. Shànghǎi's public transport is generally safe at night; as anywhere though, use common sense.

Top Itineraries

Day One

The Bund & People's Square (p54)

 Follow the sweep of architectural pomp along the **Bund** and savour the art deco grandeur of the **Fairmont Peace Hotel**, before walking along the riverside promenade to view the **Pǔdōng** skyline across the river. Art lovers can swoop upon the **Rockbund Art Museum**, while architecture fans enjoy the highlights of **Yuanmingyuan Road**. Head west along East Nanjing Rd past shoppers to **People's Square**.

Lunch Lost Heaven (p71): all the flavours of far-off Yúnnán province.

The Bund & People's Square (p54)

Immerse yourself in the collection of the **Shànghǎi Museum** before weighing up the **Shànghǎi Urban Planning Exhibition Hall** or discovering a pocket of greenery in People's Park. For views, shoot up in the lift to the lobby of the JW Marriott on the 38th floor of **Tomorrow Square**.

Dinner Jiājiā Soup Dumplings (p73): some of the city's best *xiǎolóngbāo*.

Pǔdōng (p143)

Hop on the metro (or a sightseeing bus) from People's Square to Lùjiāzuǐ to wander round the walkway in front of the **Oriental Pearl TV Tower**. Select between the observation towers of the **Shànghǎi Tower**, **Jīnmào Tower** and the **Shànghǎi World Financial Center**, or settle for evening cocktails at **Flair**.

Day Two

French Concession (p92)

 Peruse the architecture and boutiques of **Xīntiāndì** and explore the **Shíkùmén Open House Museum** for a lowdown on *shíkùmén* (stone-gate house) architecture before watching artists at work at the **Shànghǎi Arts & Crafts Museum** or taking a seat to watch locals relaxing in French-designed **Fùxīng Park**.

Lunch Crystal Jade (p105): Cantonese and Shanghainese dim sum.

French Concession (p92)

Admire the dazzling glass creations at the **Liúli China Museum** before disappearing among **Tiánzǐfáng's** warren of lanes. Boutique window-shop around Tiánzǐfáng; take your hat off to the collection in the **Propaganda Poster Art Centre**; and hunt down contemporary art at **Art Labor** and **Leo Gallery**.

Dinner Jian Guo 328 (p107): homestyle Shànghǎi on a fab menu.

The Bund & People's Square (p54)

 Finish up the day in style, sipping cocktails and dining on the **Bund**, but most of all enjoy the mind-altering neon views. Select from a long list: **Glam**, **Pop**, **Long Bar**, **Bar Rouge** or **Shook!** – or don your best threads for views, booze and moves at **M1NT**. Die-hard traditionalists can lend an ear to the jazz band in the **Fairmont Peace Hotel Jazz Bar**.

Day Three

Old Town (p78)

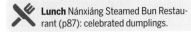 Reach the Old Town's **Yùyuán Gardens** early in the day, before the crowds arrive. Sift through the handicrafts on sale in the **Yùyuán Bazaar** before tracking down bargain collectables along **Old Street** and **Fúyòu Antique Market**. Head east past **Dǒngjiādù Cathedral** to the **Cool Docks** for its fetching blend of *shíkùmén,* riverside warehouse architecture and views.

 Lunch Nánxiáng Steamed Bun Restaurant (p87): celebrated dumplings.

Jìng'ān (p126)

Weave some Buddhist mystery into your afternoon at the **Jade Buddha Temple** before sprinkling contemporary art into the mix at the fascinating galleries of **M50**. Wander around the **Jìng'ān Sculpture Park** and the excellent **Shànghǎi Natural History Museum** or explore the **Jìng'ān Temple** before seeking out the *lǐlòng* lanes of the **Bubbling Well Road Apartments** and shopping along West Nanjing Rd.

Dinner Fu 1088 (p139): fine Shànghǎi cuisine in dapper villa surrounds.

French Concession (p92)

Round off your day in some of Shànghǎi's best bars, all handily located in the French Concession: chill out at **Bell Bar**; seek out craft beers along **Yongkang Road** or at **Boxing Cat Brewery**; sink a drink in the garden of **Cotton's** or corner your perfect cocktail at **Speak Low**.

Day Four

Xújiāhuì & South Shànghǎi (p164)

Spend the morning admiring the former Jesuit sights of Xújiāhuì, in particular **St Ignatius Cathedral** and the **Tousewe Museum**. Pay your respects at the Buddhist **Lónghuá Temple & Pagoda**; the green-fingered can explore the foliage of the **Shànghǎi Botanical Gardens**.

Lunch Hóng Làjiāo Xiāngcàiguǎn (p169): spicy Húnán fare; friendly atmosphere.

Hóngkǒu & North Shànghǎi (p156)

Pay a visit to the **Ohel Moishe Synagogue** and the surrounding former Jewish neighbourhood; walk up **Duolun Road Cultural Street**; track down some of the neighbourhood's best architecture and relax in **Lu Xun Park**. In the late afternoon, head back south to the North Bund area of Hóngkǒu, near the Bund.

Dinner Guǒyúan (p160): super spice-infused dishes from Húnán.

Pǔdōng (p143)

Get haggling at the **AP Xīnyáng Fashion & Gifts Market** before closing time, or get a handle on local history at the **Shànghǎi History Museum**. Follow up with an evening walk along the **Riverside Promenade**, followed by cocktails and a jacuzzi at **Vue** bar.

If You Like...

Views

The Bund Walk the promenade for views of Pǔdōng's soaring skyline on one side and concession-era magnificence on the other. (p56)

Shànghǎi Tower The world's highest observation deck in Shànghǎi's tallest tower. (p148)

Flair An outdoor terrace gives this sky-high Pǔdōng bar the wow factor. (p154)

Oriental Pearl TV Tower Brave the glass-bottomed floor for staggering views. (p146)

JW Marriott Tomorrow Square Zip aloft to the 38th-floor lobby for stupendous vistas over People's Square. (p205)

Cloud 9 This cool bar at the top of the Jīnmào Tower is a great alternative to the observation decks. (p155)

West Lake Hángzhōu's main attraction is the very definition of classical beauty in China. (p179)

Modern Architecture

Shànghǎi Tower Adding a glass twist to the Pǔdōng skyline, this 632m-high skyscraper is a breathtaking colossus. (p148)

Tomorrow Square The People's Square supertower could easily double as the headquarters for a sci-fi corporation. (p66)

Jīnmào Tower No longer the tallest, but still one of the city's most graceful buildings. (p148)

JON ARNOLD/GETTY IMAGES ©

Fùxīng Park, French Concession (p96)

China Art Museum The upturned red pyramid was the symbol of the 2010 World Expo. (p149)

Oriental Art Center Way out in Pǔdōng, this classical-music venue was designed to resemble the five petals of a butterfly orchid. (p155)

Shànghǎi Grand Theatre The curving eaves of this theatre recall traditional Chinese architectural design. (p75)

Oriental Pearl TV Tower Not so subtle perhaps, but this poured-concrete tripod remains a Shànghǎi icon. (p146)

Museums

Shànghǎi Museum Extraordinary overview of traditional Chinese art through the millennia, from ancient bronzes to Qing dynasty ink paintings. (p61)

Sūzhōu Museum Local artefacts – jade, ceramics and carvings – housed in a gorgeous contemporary building. (p189)

Shànghǎi History Museum Fun and accessible introduction to old Shànghǎi. (p148)

Shànghǎi Urban Planning Exhibition Hall The highlight here is an incredible scale model of the megalopolis c 2020. (p66)

Shànghǎi Natural History Museum Get up close to dinosaur fossils in this striking new location. (p134)

Shànghǎi Arts & Crafts Museum Watch craftspeople at work. (p99)

Shíkùmén Open House Museum Peek inside a *shíkùmén* house. (p96)

Aurora Museum Provides a culture hit in Pǔdōng with a treasure trove of antiquities. (p148)

Temples & Churches

Jade Buddha Temple Shànghǎi's most active Buddhist temple. (p130)

Língyǐn Temple Hángzhōu's main Buddhist temple, with a remarkable series of cliff-side carvings. (p182)

Chénxiānggé Monastery This Old Town temple shelters a gorgeous effigy of the Buddhist goddess of compassion. (p82)

Confucius Temple A tranquil spot with old trees and a Sunday book market, located in an atmospheric part of the Old Town. (p86)

Jìng'ān Temple Recently rebuilt downtown Buddhist temple fashioned from Burmese teak. (p129)

Ohel Moishe Synagogue One-time heart of Shànghǎi's Jewish ghetto, now home to the Jewish Refugees Museum. (p159)

Lónghuá Temple & Pagoda The oldest and largest monastery in the city. (p167)

Temple of the Town God Shànghǎi is one of the few cities in China whose Taoist town god weathered the vicissitudes of the 20th century. (p82)

Dǒngjiādù Cathedral Shànghǎi's oldest church, established by Spanish Jesuits in 1853. (p87)

Shéshān Basilica Magnificently crowning a hilltop southwest of the city. (p200)

Art Deco Architecture

Fairmont Peace Hotel Built as the legendary Cathay Hotel, this is the best surviving example of art deco style in Shànghǎi. (p206)

For more top Shànghǎi spots, see the following:
➡ Eating (p33)
➡ Drinking & Nightlife (p43)
➡ Entertainment (p45)
➡ Shopping (p47)

Rockbund Art Museum Straight from the deco textbook, with some Chinese ingredients. (p64)

Park Hotel The tallest building in Shànghǎi until the 1980s and an early inspiration for IM Pei. (p206)

Embankment Building An art deco landmark now housing rental holiday apartments. (p160)

Art Deco Artsy boutique in the M50 complex containing a trove of period furnishings. (p142)

Cathay Theatre Catch a movie in this original 1930s French Concession theatre. (p119)

Broadway Mansions A classic 1934 apartment block north of Sūzhōu Creek that today houses a deco-style hotel. (p162)

Art Galleries & Art Museums

M50 Former manufacturing space now housing the largest collection of art galleries in the city. (p128)

Propaganda Poster Art Centre Collection of 3000 original posters from the golden age of Maoist propaganda. (p98)

Beaugeste Superb photography gallery tucked away in Tiánzǐfáng. (p97)

Shànghǎi Gallery of Art Conceptual Chinese art on the Bund. (p65)

Leo Gallery Works by young Chinese artists. (p100)

Art on the Bund Collection of art galleries in the backstreets of the Bund showcasing contemporary Chinese and international artists. (p65)

Mínshēng Art Museum Excellent line-up of contemporary Chinese art exhibits. (p174)

China Art Museum Former World Expo China Pavilion reconfigured as a mammoth five-floor art museum, Pǔdōngside. (p149)

Long Museum Contemporary art and Chinese artefacts in an imposing building designed by Chinese architect Liu Yichun. (p168)

Yuz Museum World-class contemporary art gallery housed in the former hangar of Longhua Airport. (p168)

Massages & Spas

Dragonfly Long-time favourite with private rooms and soothing atmosphere. (p124)

Subconscious Day Spa Ecofriendly spa with traditional massage and yoga classes. (p124)

Double Rainbow Massage House Let the visually impaired masseuses work out the knots. (p124)

Green Massage A range of massages in a calming environment. (p124)

Street Food

Qībǎo Sample barbecued squid or indulge in sweet dumplings: Qībǎo corners the market for Shànghǎi street food. (p173)

Yunnan Road Food Street One of the best strips for unpretentious regional Chinese restaurants. (p71)

Huanghe Road Food Street Near People's Park, this strip has some big traditional restaurants, but it's most famous for its dumplings. (p71)

Yùyuán Bazaar It's crowded and overpriced, but famous spots such as Nánxiáng Steamed Bun Restaurant make it a can't-miss option. (p80)

Markets

AP Xīnyáng Fashion & Gifts Market The city's largest market sells everything from tailor-made clothes to counterfeit bags. (p155)

South Bund Fabric Market Have a suit, dress or blouse tailor-made for a song. (p90)

Ghost Market At the Fúyòu Antique Market on Sundays, sellers from the countryside hawk their wares. (p90)

Yùyuán Bazaar The ultimate Shànghǎi souvenir market in the Old Town: slightly tacky and extremely crowded, but always entertaining. (p80)

Boutique Shopping

Spin Imaginative ceramics from a new generation of designers. (p141)

Dòng Liáng Hip threads from some of the best local designers. (p122)

Brocade Country Jewellery, clothing and handicrafts from the Miao of Guìzhōu province. (p123)

Annabel Lee An elegant shop that specialises in embroidery and sells accessories in silk, linen and cashmere. (p76)

OOAK Concept Boutique Three small floors of inspiring jewellery and good-looking clothing designs for women. (p122)

Lolo Love Vintage For all your vintage needs. (p122)

Culture Matters Come here to pick up the latest canvas-shoe styles. (p122)

Chouchou Chic Kids' clothes from a joint French-Chinese brand. (p121)

Urban Tribe Local fashion label inspired by the ethnic groups of China and Southeast Asia. (p121)

Free Stuff

M50 Shànghǎi's best-known arts enclave. (p128)

Shànghǎi Museum Arguably the best museum in China – showcases the craft of a millennia. (p61)

Fùxīng Park A delightful spot to escape the city heat and traffic noise. (p96)

The Bund The trail of art deco and neoclassical buildings makes this one of the country's great city strolls. (p56)

Tiánzǐfáng A charming tree-lined pocket of traditional *lòngtáng* alleys, interspersed with wi-fi cafes, cool bars and restaurants, art shops and excellent small boutiques. (p94)

Power Station of Art Modern large-scale installations and design shows in a disused power station. (p82)

Liu Haisu Art Gallery Houses a collection of Liu Haisu's beautiful paintings, as well as contemporary art from around the world. (p174)

CY Tung Maritime Museum Learn all about the astonishing 15th-century explorer Zheng He. (p167)

Month By Month

January

The Western New Year is greeted wildly in bars citywide.

⭐ Western New Year

Lónghuá Temple (p167) has excellent New Year (元旦, Yuándàn) celebrations, with dragon and lion dances. On 1 January the abbot strikes the bell 108 times while the monks beat on gongs and offer prayers for the forthcoming year.

February

Preparations for the festive Chinese New Year are under way as hundreds of millions of people get ready to journey home. If you plan to travel, book tickets well in advance.

⭐ Chinese New Year

Commonly called the Spring Festival (春节, Chūn Jié), Chinese New Year is the equivalent of Christmas. Families get together to feast on dumplings, vegetate in front of the TV, hand out *hóngbāo* (red envelopes stuffed with money) and take a week-long holiday. New Year's Eve fireworks can be a chaotic but good show. The festival traditionally commences on the first day of the first moon of the traditional lunar calendar (28 January 2017, 16 February 2018, 5 February 2019).

⭐ Lantern Festival

Lantern Festival falls on the 15th day of the first lunar month (11 February 2017, 2 March 2018, 19 February 2019). Families make *yuán xiāo* (also called *tāng yuán;* delicious dumplings of glutinous rice with sweet fillings) and sometimes hang paper lanterns. It's a colourful time to visit Yùyuán Gardens.

⭐ Valentine's Day

Valentine's Day (情人节, Qíngrén Jié) is taken seriously by Shànghǎi suitors as an occasion for a massive blowout: it's the chance to buy their true love that Cartier wristwatch or diamond ring, or a bunch of 11 roses.

March

March in Shànghǎi is usually grey, cold and clammy, though hints of spring often appear by the month's end.

☆ JUE Festival

Two-week arts-and-music festival (www.juefestival.com) held in both Shànghǎi and Běijīng. One of the best times of the year for music lovers and creative types.

☆ Shànghǎi International Literary Festival

To counter Shànghǎi's drift towards philistinism, this highly popular festival for book lovers is staged in Glam (p74) in March or April, with a range of famous names in attendance.

⭐ Birthday of Guanyin

The Buddhist goddess of mercy celebrates her birthday (观世音生日, Guānshìyīn Shēngrì) on the 19th day of the second lunar month (16 March 2017, 4 April 2018, 25 March 2019).

April

Spring is springing, and transport and hotels are booked solid on Tomb Sweeping Day, now extended into a long weekend.

✹ Tomb Sweeping Day

Qīngmíng Jié (清明节) public holiday is held every 4 or 5 April, when more than six million Shanghainese visit the graves of their dearly departed relatives.

✹ Lónghuá Temple Fair

The two-week fair (龙华寺庙会, Lónghuá Sìmiào Huì) at Lónghuá Temple (p167) coincides with the blossoming of the local peach trees and kicks off on the third day of the third lunar month (30 March 2017, 18 April 2018, 7 April 2019).

☆ Formula One (F1)

The slick Shànghǎi International Circuit has hosted F1's Chinese Grand Prix every year since 2004. The race (www.formula1.com) usually comes to town for three days in mid-April.

May

The thermometer is starting to rocket as the month kicks off with the busy Labour Day holiday period.

✹ Labour Day

On 1 May, the whole of China gears up for a hard-earned three-day holiday.

June

The sweltering summer heat kicks in and rainfall in Shànghǎi hits its peak.

✹ Dragon Boat Festival

This public holiday (端午节, Duānwǔ Jié) is celebrated on the fifth day of the fifth lunar month (30 May 2017, 18 June 2018, 7 June 2019) with boat races along the Huángpǔ River, Sūzhōu Creek and Diànshān Lake.

☆ Shanghai International Film Festival

With screenings at various cinemas around Shànghǎi, this festival (www.siff.com) brings a range of international and locally produced films to town.

July

Shànghǎi sweats it out under a summer sun and the streets are awash with school kids on holiday.

✹ West Lake Lotuses in Bloom

Hángzhōu's lovely West Lake (p179) offers a stunning combination of long summer nights and full pink lotus blooms. The first West Lake Lotus Festival was in 2013.

September

The tail end of summer, this is one of the best times to visit as temperatures drop from August highs, although rainfall is still abundant.

✹ Mid-Autumn Festival

The Mid-Autumn Festival (中秋节, Zhōngqiū Jié) is the time to give and receive delicious moon cakes. The festival, now a one-day public holiday, takes place on the 15th day of the eighth lunar month (4 October 2017, 24 September 2018, 13 September 2019).

✹ International Qiántáng River Tide Observing Festival

The most popular time to witness the surging river tides sweeping at up to 40km/h along the Qiántáng River at Yánguān, outside Hángzhōu, is during the Mid-Autumn Festival, although you can catch the wall of water during the beginning and middle of every lunar month.

✹ Sūzhōu Silk Festival

Sūzhōu's silk festival brings exhibitions devoted to silk history and production, and silk merchants showing off their wares to crowds of thousands.

October

The week-long National Day holiday beginning 1 October wreaks havoc and it's best to avoid travelling. Book your hotel well in advance.

✘ Hairy Crabs

Now's the time to sample delicious dàzháxiè (hairy crabs) in Shànghǎi. They're at their best between October and December.

(Top) Lantern Festival (p27)
(Bottom) Performers at the Lónghuá Temple Fair (p28)

☆ Shanghai Biennale

Held once every two years, this popular international arts festival (www.shanghai biennale.org) takes place on the former World Expo grounds.

November

Autumn's last gasp before winter begins.

☆ China Shanghai International Arts Festival

A month-long program (www.artsbird.com) of cultural events in October and November, which includes the Shanghai Art Fair, a varied program of international music, dance, opera and acrobatics, and exhibitions of the Shanghai Biennale.

🏃 Shanghai International Marathon

Usually held on the last Sunday of November, this annual event (www.shmara thon.com) attracts around 20,000 runners. It starts at the Bund and also includes a half-marathon.

December

Shànghǎi winters are generally unpleasant, with temperatures cold enough to chill you through, but rarely low enough for snow.

🎊 Christmas

Not an official Chinese festival, Christmas (圣诞节, Shèngdàn Jié) is nevertheless a major milestone on the commercial calendar, and Shànghǎi's big shopping zones sparkle with decorations and glisten with fake snow.

With Kids

Shànghǎi may not top most kids' holiday wish lists, but that may change with the new Shànghǎi Disney Resort park in Pǔdōng now adding a must-see attraction to the city. There are also several other Shànghǎi sights to keep the family entertained.

Need to Know

➡ **Admission** In general, 1.4m (4ft 7in) is the cut-off height for children's tickets. Children under 0.8m (2ft 7in) normally get in for free.

➡ **Schedule** Holidays and weekends naturally see traffic peak, but in China 'crowded' takes on a new meaning. Try to schedule visits for weekdays if possible.

➡ **Info** For more information on events and activities, see *That's Shanghai* (http://online. thatsmags.com/city/shanghai) or *City Weekend* (www.cityweekend.com.cn/shanghai).

Acrobatics Shows

An evening with the acrobats – either at Shànghǎi Circus World (p163) or the Shànghǎi Centre Theatre (p141) – will certainly keep most kids (not to mention adults, too) entertained, with plate spinning, contortionism and even daredevil motorcycle feats performed to the *Star Wars* theme music.

Museums

Shànghǎi Natural History Museum
Kids'll love this new-look museum (p134) with its dinosaur fossils, taxidermied animals, live reptiles and butterfly house.

Shànghǎi History Museum
Waxworks and interactive exhibits make this museum (p148) fun for everyone.

Shànghǎi Science & Technology Museum
There are loads of things for kids to explore at this museum (p149), from volcano and space exhibits to sports activities and robots that can solve Rubik's cubes before your eyes. It also has IMAX and 4D theatres.

Amusement & Water Parks

Shànghǎi Disneyland
Set to suck in Chinese tots and young kids nationwide, this is mainland China's first Disney Resort (p147). Expect epic queues.

Legoland Discovery Centre
Until the actual Legoland hits the city (plans are in the works), this discovery centre (p174) will keep little Lego fans satisfied. Learn Lego building skills and check out mini Shànghǎi Land made from millions of Lego pieces.

Happy Valley
An amusement park (p200) with scores of roller coasters, dive machines and other heart-thumping rides, plus mellower attractions for younger kids and a water park.

Dino Beach
This water park (p177) boasts Asia's largest wave pool and is a fun-filled way to beat the summer heat.

Maglev
You might want to save this trip for your first or last day in Shànghǎi, heading from or to Pǔdōng International Airport, but a trip on the hovering Maglev train (p254) is thrilling (for all ages).

Like a Local

On the surface Shànghǎi appears more Western than anywhere else in China, bar Hong Kong. But don't be fooled by appearances – even if the Shanghainese are known for their flings with things foreign, engaging in local life quickly exposes a culture that is deeply Chinese.

Eat Like a Local

This is actually a little trickier than it sounds. If you're wondering how you could not eat like a local, you only need to step into a Western restaurant or bar any night of the week – in Shànghǎi, temptations to stay in your comfort zone are everywhere. Eating Shanghainese-style may require an initial leap of faith (you want me to eat *what*?), but be brave and travel your taste buds: with specialties such as freshly pulled noodles, braised pork belly and quick-fried shrimp, you won't regret it.

Practise Taichi

Head out to the nearest park in the early morning and look for a group that seems to be moving in slow motion. That's the martial art of taichi (*tàijíquán* is its full name), and if you want to try to follow along, you'll usually be welcomed. You may not learn much if you're just in town for a few days, but you can kick-start a new interest. If you're in Shànghǎi for the long haul, there are plenty of places to study. Taichi can be knackering, and some styles – such as Chen style – are seriously gruelling, even if you're 100% fit. The elderly in China generally are admirably active and supple.

Learn Chinese

True, you won't be yacking with locals in Mandarin overnight, but learning the basics – or at least trying to – will take you a long way. It's also great for your ego: you only need to master a handful of words before receiving lavish compliments about your language skills. On that note, it's good form to return the compliment when someone speaks to you in English.

If you've been hankering to learn some Shanghainese, well, we won't discourage you, but try to get Mandarin down first.

Get on the Bus

The abundance of cheap taxis makes it all too easy to steer clear of public transport, but hopping on a bus is actually the best way to become part of the local fabric and you can see what's above ground. You will also be a rarity, as most *lǎowài* (foreigners) avoid the bus because it's challenging to use, but it's true Shànghǎi. A sense of adventure (and the name of your destination written down in Chinese) are helpful.

Shop Till You Drop

The Shanghainese are Olympian shoppers. It doesn't matter whether you prefer the see-and-be-seen of megamalls or browsing in independent boutiques, creating your own individual style – no matter how crazy the look – is an essential part of Shanghainese identity. Guys, take note: many Shanghainese women expect their boyfriends to accompany them on shopping excursions and, just as importantly, to carry their purse or handbag.

For Free

Shànghǎi can dig serious holes in your wallet. And with inflation and yuán appreciation, it's only going to become a pricier destination. But there are some options for those on a budget or who just want to save cash.

Museums & Galleries

Shànghǎi Museum

Shànghǎi's premier museum (p61) walks you through the pages of Chinese history via sumptuous art forms such as porcelain and landscape painting. The number of daily visitors is limited, so don't show up too late.

Power Station of Art

Inventive and thought-provoking art and design exhibitions are hosted in this vast former power station (p82) near the Huángpǔ River.

Bund History Museum

Located beneath the Monument to the People's Heroes at the north end of the Bund, this museum (p64) introduces the history of the area through a selection of old photographs and maps.

M50

M50 (p128) is the largest complex of modern-art galleries in Shànghǎi, housed in an industrial setting.

Liu Haisu Art Gallery

Moved to a new location in 2016, this excellent museum (p174) houses a collection of Liu Haisu's beautiful paintings, as well as contemporary art from around the world.

CY Tung Maritime Museum

Get the lowdown on the astonishing 15th-century explorer Zheng He at this museum (p167).

Communist Heritage

Make sure you have your passport with you as you may need it to gain access to the Site of the 1st National Congress of the CCP (p96), Zhou Enlai's Former Residence (p96) and the Former Residence of Mao Zedong (p130).

Walks

The Bund

The Bund (p56) is the first port of call for most visitors to Shànghǎi. Thankfully, strolling the promenade and peeking inside the historic buildings doesn't cost a cent. Restaurants and bars here are mostly upmarket.

Walking Tours

Follow one of our walking tours as they guide you around the backstreets and historic neighbourhoods of the Bund, Old Town, French Concession and Jìng'ān.

Parks

Shànghǎi's parks, many of which are free, are great for people-watching. There is almost always something going on, whether it's people practising qì gōng or taichi, playing chess or holding impromptu music concerts.

Traditional braised pork and rice dish (p36)

Eating

Brash, stylish and forward-thinking, Shànghǎi's culinary scene typifies the city's craving for foreign trends and tastes. As much an introduction to regional Chinese cuisine as a magnet for talented chefs from around the globe, Shànghǎi has staked a formidable claim as the Middle Kingdom's hottest dining destination.

NEED TO KNOW

Price Ranges

The following price ranges refer to a main course.

$ Less than ¥60

$$ ¥60–160

$$$ More than ¥160

Opening Hours

In general, the Chinese eat earlier than Westerners. Restaurants serve lunch from around 11am to 2pm and then often close until 5pm, when the dinner crowd starts pitching up. They then carry on serving until 11pm. Smaller restaurants are more easygoing, so if you're hungry out of hours they're often happy to accommodate you, though you may be dining alone.

Ordering

Many places have English and/or picture menus, although they aren't always as comprehensive (or comprehensible) as the Chinese version. In any case, if you see a dish on someone else's table that looks absolutely delicious, just point at it when the waiter comes – no one will think you're being rude.

Tipping

Tipping is not done in the majority of restaurants. High-end international restaurants are another matter; while tipping is not obligatory, it is encouraged. Hotel restaurants automatically add a 15% service charge.

Reservations

At high-end restaurants or smaller places, it's sometimes necessary to book a week or more ahead, particularly if you want a decent table with a view. Otherwise, a couple of days in advance is fine.

Shanghainese Cuisine

Shànghǎi cuisine has been heavily influenced by the culinary styles of neighbouring provinces. Many of the techniques, ingredients and flavours originated in the much older cities of Yángzhōu, Sūzhōu and Hángzhōu. Broadly speaking, dishes tend to be sweeter and oilier than in other parts of China. Spiciness is anathema to Shànghǎi cooking.

Dumplings served in a bamboo steamer

The eastern provinces around the Yangzi River delta produce China's best soy sauces, vinegars and rice wines, and the method of braising (known as 'red cooking'), using soy sauce and sugar as a base, was perfected here. As a general rule, the regional cuisine emphasises the freshness of ingredients – as with Cantonese food – using sauces and seasonings only to enhance the original flavours. Look out for the characters 本帮菜 (běnbāngcài) on restaurant shopfronts and in menus, which refers to authentic Shànghǎi homestyle cooking.

DUMPLINGS

Dumplings are the easiest way to become acquainted with Shanghainese cuisine. The city's favourite dumpling is the xiǎolóngbāo (小笼包, 'little steamer buns'), copied everywhere else in China but only true to form here. Xiǎolóngbāo are normally bought by the lóng (笼, steamer basket) and dipped in vinegar. They're simple, delicious, and have no annoying bones or unusual ingredients that might otherwise deter the naturally squeamish. There's an art to eating them, though, as they're full of a delicious but scalding gelatinous broth: the trick is to avoid both burning your tongue and staining your shirt (not easy), while road-testing your (shaky?) chopstick skills.

Tradition attributes the invention of the dumpling – filled with pork, or in more upmarket establishments with pork and crab – to Nánxiáng, a village north of Shànghǎi city.

Another Shanghainese speciality is shēngjiān (生煎), scallion-and-sesame-

(Top) Locals buy breakfast at a street stall in the Old Town
(Right) *Dàzháxiè* (hairy crabs; p36)

seed-coated dumplings that are fried in an enormous flat-bottomed wok, which is covered with a wooden lid. These are also pork-based; again, watch out for the palate-scorching, scalding oil, which can travel.

On the sweet side are *tāng yuán* (汤圆; also known as *yuán xiāo*), small glutinous rice balls crammed with sweet fillings such as black-sesame paste or red-bean paste. They're traditionally eaten during the Lantern Festival and are utterly delectable. You can find them easily in Qībǎo at any time of year and are not hard to find anywhere in Shànghǎi, especially in small hole-in-the-wall places.

FISH & SEAFOOD

The city's position as a major port at the head of the Yangzi River delta means that you'll find plenty of fish and seafood, especially crab, river eel and shrimp. The word for fish *(yú)* is a homonym for 'plenty' or 'surplus', and fish is a mandatory dish for most banquets and celebrations. Types commonly appearing on Shànghǎi's menus include *guìyú* (Mandarin fish), *lúyú* (Songjiang perch), *chāngyú* (pomfret) and *huángyú* (yellow croaker). Fish is usually *qīngzhēng* (steamed) but can be stir-fried, pan-fried or grilled. Squirrel-shaped Mandarin fish is one of the more famous dishes from Sūzhōu.

Dàzháxiè (hairy crabs) are a Shànghǎi speciality between October and December. They are eaten with soy, ginger and vinegar and downed with warm Shàoxīng rice wine. The crab is thought to increase the body's yin, or coldness, and so rice wine is taken lukewarm to add yang.

CLASSIC DISHES

Some of the most common Shanghainese dishes:

Smoked fish (熏鱼, *xūn yú*) This cold appetiser is gingery sweet and absolutely succulent when prepared correctly.

Drunken chicken (醉鸡, *zuìjī*) Another cold appetiser that consists of steamed chicken marinated overnight in Shàoxīng rice wine.

Braised pork (红烧肉, *hóngshāo ròu*) The uncontested king of Shanghainese home-cooking, this dish consists of tender, fatty pieces of pork stewed in sweet soy sauce.

Crystal shrimp (水晶虾仁, *shuǐjīng xiārén*) They may not look like much, but these quick-fried shrimp undergo an elaborate preparation that results in a unique texture that's both crispy and tender.

Lion's head meatball (狮子头, *shīzi tóu*) A large creamy meatball made of crab and minced pork, often presented as a single serving.

Crab and tofu casserole (蟹粉豆腐, *xièfěn dòufu*) Another dish that emphasises texture, this is a good way to indulge in crab without over-the-top prices.

Sichuanese

One of China's most famous regional cuisines, Sìchuān cooking relies on six basic tastes, which can be combined together to form more than 20 distinct flavours, including 'numbing spicy', 'sour spicy', 'fish-flavour spicy' and 'chilli-oil spicy'. A key ingredient of Sichuanese cuisine is the Sìchuān peppercorn (花椒, *huājiāo*), which stimulates a characteristic tingling sensation (known as

---

CHEAP EATS

Shànghǎi's restaurants are in a whole other ballpark when compared to the rest of China – meal prices here exceed Běijīng and, to top it off, the portions are smaller. Thankfully, you can still eat cheaply if you know where to look. Malls are always a good place to begin; they may lack atmosphere, but you will always find food inside – check the basement or top floors. The larger malls are best as they often have decent food courts.

Street food is another sure thing, though in some neighbourhoods tiny restaurants and backstreet stalls can be hard to find. Look for corner noodle shops (面馆, *miànguǎn*) or dumpling vendors – popular stalwart chains include Yang's Fry Dumplings, Jiājiā Soup Dumplings, Wúyuè Rénjiā and Ajisen – and there are also a handful of top places to discover that are popular with Shànghǎi diners (but virtually unknown to foreign foodies without a tip-off). When in doubt, head to one of the official food streets for a good selection of restaurants that won't empty your wallet.

More and more restaurants catering to office workers offer good-value weekday lunch specials – to take advantage, ask for a *tàocān* (套餐).

má) when eaten. Although spices dominate, the key to a good meal, as with all Chinese cuisines, is to balance the different flavours, so even those who don't like it hot will find something to savour.

Sichuanese cuisine uses ingredients that are inexpensive and relatively easy to find, hence a lot of restaurants across China – particularly tiny family-run places – have incorporated the standards in their menus. Look for classics such as *gōngbǎo jīdīng* (kung pao chicken), *mápó dòufu* (mapo tofu), *yúxiāng qiézi* (fish-flavoured eggplant), *huíguōròu* (twice-cooked pork) and *dàndàn miàn* (dandan noodles). In Shànghǎi, one of the most popular Sichuanese dishes is a giant bowl of tender pieces of catfish or frog suspended in hot chilli oil.

Hunanese

Known as *xiāngcài* (湘菜) in Chinese, Hunanese is another chilli-driven cooking tradition from China's wholesome heartland province of Húnán. It differs from Sichuanese cooking notably in its use of fresh chilli peppers (Sìchuān cuisine often makes use of chilli paste), which is ladled liberally onto many dishes. The heat from the peppers helps to expel moisture from the body, combating high humidity in summer. Chicken, frog, freshwater fish and pork are key ingredients; some of the all-time classics include *zīrán páigǔ* (cumin spare ribs), *gānguō tuǐròu* (smoked-pork drypot) and *máo shì hóngshāo ròu* (Mao Family braised pork).

Cantonese

Cantonese cuisine shares some similarities with Shànghǎi cuisine, notably light seasoning, an emphasis on natural flavours and lots of seafood (海鲜, *hǎixiān*). The Cantonese believe that good cooking does not require much flavouring, for it is the *xiān* (natural freshness) of the ingredients that mark a truly high-grade dish. Hence the near obsessive attention paid to the freshness of ingredients in southern cuisine.

Many of the smartest restaurants in Shànghǎi (often located in hotels) are Cantonese, though these cater primarily to Hong Kong tourists and businesspeople. The Cantonese restaurants that are most popular among everyday Shanghainese are entirely different; these are based on Hong Kong–style cafeterias known as *chá cāntīng* (tea restaurants). Tea restaurants have a

casual, downmarket atmosphere that's somewhat similar to an American diner, and feature an incredibly eclectic menu that ranges from Cantonese comfort food (beef with oyster sauce) to Italian pasta, Malaysian curries, sandwiches and an endless array of rice and noodle dishes.

The other famous tradition associated with Cantonese cuisine is, of course, dim sum (点心, *diǎnxīn*), which is served in a number of places in Shànghǎi, often incorporating local specialities (eg *xiǎolóngbāo*) in addition to Cantonese standards.

Muslim

Most of Shànghǎi's Muslim restaurants are run by Uighurs – Central Asians from Xīnjiāng, in China's far northwest. A refreshing alternative to the seafood and sweetness of Shanghainese cuisine, Xīnjiāng dishes involve lots of mutton (though chicken and fish dishes are available), peppers, potatoes, cumin and delicious naan bread. Charcoal-grilled lamb kebabs are the staple here. It's not unusual for Uighur restaurants to offer evening performances of some kind (usually karaoke-style singing and dancing).

JOESAYHELLO/SHUTTERSTOCK ©

Dim sum dishes

Shànghǎi's other main Muslim food vendors are tiny noodle stalls that specialise in *lāmiàn* (hand-pulled noodles), which are made fresh to order and can be served either in broth or fried.

Street Food

Shànghǎi's street food is excellent and usually quite safe to eat. It generally consists of tiny dumpling and noodle shops along with vendors selling snacks such as *cōngyóu bǐng* (green onion pancakes), *bāozi* (steamed buns), *chòu dòufu* (stinky tofu) and *dìguā* (baked sweet potatoes). The city's food streets are also great places to browse for snacks. Try the following destinations:

➡ Yunnan Rd (p71)

➡ Huanghe Rd (p71)

➡ Qībǎo (p173)

Hotpot

A hugely popular winter meal is *huǒguō* (hotpot), and several chain restaurants corner the market. There are two varieties of hotpot: Sìchuān and Mongolian. A typical Sìchuān version is the circular *yuānyāng* hotpot, cleaved into hot (red) and mild (creamy coloured) sections, into which you plunge vegetables and meats. Plucking the cooked chunks from the broth, diners dip them in different sauces before consuming. It's a sweat-inducing experience that's best done with a group but can refreshingly be done solo in fast-food-style hotpot restaurants. Mongolian hotpots differ in both appearance and flavour. These are typically a brass pot with a central stove and a ring-like bowl of non-spicy broth, into which are dropped thin slices of lamb and vegetables. Again, they are accompanied by sauces.

International

Shànghǎi is a destination for both global superchefs and less-established international talents trying to make a mark, so some fantastic meals can be found. Many restaurants are not averse to importing local ingredients and flavours; it's not exactly fusion cuisine, but it's not something you're likely to get back home either.

Much lower down the food chain are Shànghǎi's pubs and breweries, which are seriously happening dining destinations, for their convivial atmosphere and huge serv-

Shànghǎi street-food stall

ings of comfort food. Expect burgers, pasta, Southern fried classics and countless sandwich variations. Slick, cool cafe-restaurant chains such as Element Fresh and Baker & Spice serve an inventive and wide range of international and Asian cuisine to a largely young and dapper clientele.

Vegetarians

Chīzhāi (吃斋, vegetarianism) became something of a snobbish fad in Shànghǎi in the 1930s, when it was linked to Taoist and Buddhist groups. Growing middle-class values and attention to healthy living have encouraged a minor revival, although nothing like the zealous vegetarian and vegan populations in countries such as the UK or the USA. Beyond Buddhist dictates, very few Chinese give up meat for ethical reasons. But there is a growing band of vegetarian restaurants in Shànghǎi, and monasteries all have good meat-free restaurants.

The Chinese are masters at adding variety to vegetarian cooking and, to the bemusement of Western vegetarians, like to create so-called 'mock meat' dishes. Not only is it made to taste like any meaty food you could possibly think of, it's also made to resemble it; dishes can be made to look like everything from fish to spare ribs and chicken nuggets.

Etiquette

Strict rules of etiquette don't apply to Chinese dining; table manners are relaxed and get more so as the meal unfolds and the drinks flow. Meals commence in Confucian fashion – with good intentions, harmonic arrangement of chopsticks and a clean tablecloth – before spiralling into total Taoist mayhem, fuelled by incessant toasts with *báijiǔ* (hard liquor) or beer and furious smoking all round. Large groups, in particular, wreak havoc wherever they dine, with vast quantities of food often strewn across and under the table at the end of a meal.

A typical dining scenario sees a group of people seated at a round table, often with one person ordering on everyone's behalf. At Chinese restaurants, group diners never order their own dishes, but instead a selection of dishes embracing both *ròu* (meat) and *cài* (vegetables) are chosen for everyone to share. At large tables, dishes are placed on a lazy Susan, so the food revolves to each diner, occasionally knocking over

Top: Fresh and preserved eel prepared and sold street-side

Middle: A typical Shànghǎi meal, including greens, soup and dumplings

Bottom: Servers dish up steaming-hot street food

TIM DRAPER/GETTY IMAGES ©

Meat, vegetable and rice dish

full glasses of beer and causing consternation. Rice normally comes at the end of the meal. If you want it before, just ask.

The mainland Chinese dig their chopsticks into communal dishes, although some dishes are ladled out with spoons. Don't worry too much about your chopstick technique, especially when chasing that slippery button mushroom around your plate; many Chinese are equally fazed by knives and forks.

COOKING SCHOOLS

Learn how to make your own *xiǎolóngbāo* (小笼包, 'little steamer buns') dumplings at the following Shànghǎi institutions.

The Kitchen At... (p125) Great culinary school offering courses in regional Chinese and Western cuisines; good for both long-term residents and short-term visitors.

Chinese Cooking Workshop (p125) Learn different Chinese cooking styles from dim sum to Sichuanese. It also offers market tours and courses for kids.

Service

If there's one thing that drives foreigners in Shànghǎi crazy, it's the service. To be fair, some waiters really are completely disorganised and indifferent, but the underlying problem here is twofold: first, Chinese and Westerners have completely different expectations when it comes to what constitutes good service; second, overcoming the language barrier is no trifling matter. Remember that many waitstaff will only have a minimal command of English (if they speak it at all) and, unless you are able to hold your own in Mandarin, there will inevitably be a few mix-ups and scowling faces somewhere along the way. Occasionally a waiter will be so intimidated by a non-Chinese-speaking customer that they will, unfortunately, completely ignore you, especially if it's a busy night. If you're having trouble, shout out *Fúwùyuán!* (Waiter!) loudly – don't be shy – and someone will usually appear.

If you're eating at a smaller place without a menu, be sure to clarify the total price *before* you finalise your order. If you don't use the wrapped serviette that is often dropped on your table and you are charged for it, ask for it to be deducted from the bill.

Eating by Neighbourhood

➡ **The Bund & People's Square** (p70) You'll find everything here, from superchefs to food streets.

➡ **Old Town** (p87) The place to try Shànghǎi's famous dumplings.

➡ **French Concession** (p100) The epicentre of Shànghǎi dining.

➡ **Jìng'ān** (p135) Popular vegetarian restaurants and sumptuous Chinese.

➡ **Pǔdōng** (p150) Where to come for dinner with a view.

Lonely Planet's Top Choices

Yang's Fry Dumplings (p73) Simple, soupy and oh-so-good.

El Willy (p89) Tasty tapas and paellas with Bund views.

Table No 1 by Jason Atherton (p89) Modern European flavours in a casual communal atmosphere.

Din Tai Fung (p138) Glorified street food from the renegade province.

Lost Heaven (p109) A taste of paradise, from Yúnnán with love.

Fú Hé Huì (p175) Gastronomic vegetarian set menu in elegant surrounds.

Best by Budget

$

Yang's Fry Dumplings (p73) The fried dumpling king, with branches scattered around town.

Jian Guo 328 (p107) Shanghainese homestyle, crammed with flavour, rammed with diners.

Guǒyúan (p160) For the full spectrum of fiery Húnán flavours.

Co. Cheese Melt Bar (p135) Gourmet toasties with homemade pickles and hot sauces.

Hóng Làjiāo Xiāngcàiguǎn (p169) Smoky, spicy Húnán flavours.

$$

Dǐ Shuǐ Dòng (p105) French Concession shrine to fiery Hunanese cuisine.

Commune Social (p139) Tasty tapas from UK celebrity chef, Jason Atherton.

Lost Heaven (p109) Delicious Yunnanese in atmospheric surrounds.

Jesse (p108) The best of Shanghainese home-cooking.

$$$

Fú Hé Huì (p175) Gastronomic vegetarian in a period villa setting.

T8 (p106) Molecular cuisine in a renovated *shíkùmén* in stylish Xīntiāndì.

Mr & Mrs Bund (p72) French bistro fare on the Bund.

Ultraviolet (p71) Conceptual dining in a secret location.

Best by Cuisine

Sichuanese

Yúxìn Chuāncài (p70) Past masters in the spicy-yet-numbing Sìchuān culinary arts.

Sichuan Folk (p150) You could eat here twice a day and still want more.

South Beauty (p150) Magnificent, rich and flavoursome, with tip-top views to boot.

Cantonese

Cha's (p104) Perennially popular old-school Canto fixture off Huaihai Rd.

Xian Yue Hien (p110) Delicious, dainty dim sum, in an exquisite setting.

Hakkasan (p73) High-end dim sum in dark-wood decor.

Southeast Asian & South Asian

Pho Real (p109) *Pho* the real thing and a neat ambience, this is your place.

Vedas (p111) Sublime and aromatic Indian cuisine.

Coconut Paradise (p110) Sugar, spice and all things nice at this Thai joint.

Food Fusion (p106) Fantastic and affordable Malaysian cuisine.

Cyclo (p137) Fresh-flavoured Vietnamese.

Uighur

Xīnjiāng Restaurant (p170) Go the whole hog with an entire lamb roast.

Yàkèxī (p136) Spangly Jìng'ān Xīnjiāng fixture for skewers, noodles and all things mutton.

Xībó (p109) The upmarket Xīnjiāng choice, with a French Concession address.

Best Shanghainese

Jian Guo 328 (p107) Classic MSG-free cooking and an outstanding menu.

Jesse (p108; Xīnjíshì) Standout Shànghǎi home-cooking and a class act.

1221 (p175) Modern, smart, long-standing and unfailingly good.

Fu 1088 (p139) For a period villa atmosphere and lashings of sophistication.

Bǎoluó Jiǔlóu (p111) Everpopular and expanded to accommodate a deluge of diners.

Best Dumplings

Yang's Fry Dumplings (p73) Simply scrumptious.

Din Tai Fung (p105) Pricier than the street equivalent, but outstanding *xiǎolóngbāo*.

Nánxiáng Steamed Bun Restaurant (p87) Shànghǎi's most famous with round-the-block lines.

Bǎinián Lóngpáo (p175) Crab-filled dumplings in charming Qībǎo.

Jiājiā Soup Dumplings (p73) Humble spot serving some of the city's best *xiǎolóngbāo*.

Best Noodles

Jian Guo 328 (p107) Serves some of the best scallion oil noodles in the city.

Wèixiāng Zhāi (p104) Chow down with the locals at this no-frills spot.

Wúyuè Rénjiā (p88) Tasty Sūzhōu noodles in the Old Town.

Best Brunches

ElEfante (p111) Brunch alfresco in the courtyard from the Dumbo food truck.

Light & Salt (p138) Tuck into breakfast pizzas while overlooking the English garden.

On 56 (p154) Spend Sunday with free-flowing champagne.

Le Royal Méridien Shanghai (p207) One of the city's best brunches.

Mr & Mrs Bund (p72) Fill up on brunch with jugs of Pimms.

Best International

Commune Social (p139) Shànghǎi's tapas-lovers are buzzing big time so join the queue.

ElEfante (p111) Romantic and alluring dining environment meets superb Mediterranean food.

Co. Cheese Melt Bar (p135) Gourmet toasties and craft beer; a match made in heaven.

Light & Salt (p71) Contemporary European cuisine with Bund views.

Best Gastronomic

Mr & Mrs Bund (p72) With bundles of personality and an appealing casual vibe.

T8 (p106) Elegant and stylish Xīntiāndì heavyweight in the gastronomic league.

M on the Bund (p72) Still winning plaudits for its faultless Bund-side menu and lavish views.

Ultraviolet (p71) Two-to-three-month waiting list. Say no more.

Jean Georges (p73) French-Asian fusion in a temple to gastronomy.

Alan Wong's (p139) Celebrity chef dishes up a five-course degustation Hawaiian menu.

Best Cafes

Citizen Café (p112) Sip cocktails on the terrace overlooking Jinxian Rd.

Sumerian (p135) Top-notch coffee and tasty bagels.

Element Fresh (p138) Tasty smoothies, crisp salads and house-made hummus.

Baker & Spice (p108) For all things sticky, sweet, wholesome and appetising.

Best Vegetarian

Vegetarian Lifestyle (p138) Consistently tasty, wholesome, organic and MSG-free flavours.

Godly (p137) Buddhist ethos and flesh-free meat-look-alike dishes are its stock-in-trade.

Jen Dow Vegetarian Restaurant (p137) Three floors of goodness, slung out behind the Jìng'ān Temple.

Fú Hé Huì (p175) Eight-course gastronomic vegetarian menu in a private villa setting.

Drinking & Nightlife

Shànghǎi adores its lychee martinis and cappuccinos to go and, with dazzling salaries and soaring property prices leaving the streets sloshing with cash, there are more than enough bars and cafes to wet the lips of the thirsty white-collar set. There's a happening nightlife scene that keeps everyone – VIP or not – well entertained.

Bars

While bars today are predominantly frequented by expats and internationally minded locals, the race is on to capture the domestic market. In Běijīng a more populist approach rules, but Shànghǎi has stayed true to its roots: it's all about looking flash, sipping craft cocktails, boutique beer or imported wine, and tapping into the appetite for new trends. As might be expected, new bars pop up and disappear as fast as the money vanishes from your wallet, but the upside of the intense competition is weekly specials and happy hours (generally from 5pm to 8pm) that manage to keep things affordable.

Cafes

Cafe culture has long steeped Shànghǎi in caffeine and roasted coffee beans. Though decent teahouses can be as rare as hen's teeth in hip areas, single-origin espressos and lattes are all over the place, from well-known chains to independent coffee roasters. Also look out for street stalls selling *zhēnzhū nǎichá* (bubble tea), a fabulously addictive Taiwanese milk tea with tapioca balls, and all sorts of related spin-offs, such as hot ginger drinks or freshly puréed papaya smoothies.

Clubbing

Shànghǎi's clubs are mostly big, glossy places devoted to playing mainstream house, techno and hip-hop. The offerings are getting better, and each year sees at least one new opening that strives to go beyond mainstream expectations. Loads of big-name DJs are flying in, which has helped boost interest among the locals, although the crowds are still predominantly made up of Westerners, Hong Kong and Taiwanese expats, and young, rich Shanghainese. Unsurprisingly, high turnover is the name of the game; check the local listings for the latest up-to-date hot spots.

Drinking & Nightlife by Neighbourhood

➡ **The Bund & People's Square** (p74) The Bund serves up glamour and gorgeous views in equal measure.

➡ **French Concession** (p112) The East has a fine crop of cafes and bohemian boltholes; the West is the most alcohol-saturated stretch of the city, jostling with clubs, pubs and microbreweries.

➡ **Jìng'ān** (p139) Sports bars and a few divey faves.

➡ **Pǔdōng** (p154) It's all about the views in Pǔdōng.

PUB CRAWL SHANGHAI

Every Saturday at 9.30pm, this organised **pub crawl** (http://pubcrawlshanghai.com; ¥150) starts with an hour-long open bar (with free snacks) and progresses to a series of bars around town, with free shots and cut-price booze to follow. It's a great way to size up the Shànghǎi bar scene and make new friends. Sign up online.

NEED TO KNOW

Opening Hours

➡ Many bars offer full dining and lunch from 11am (earlier for weekend brunch). Bars only serving drinks open anywhere between 4.30pm and 8pm.

➡ Last call at bars is usually 1am; there's a handful serving till 4am or 5am.

➡ Clubs generally don't get going until 10pm and stay open until 2am on weekdays or 5am on weekends. Most close Sundays and Mondays.

➡ Some sports bars are open around the clock, depending on what time the big game is on.

Prices

Expect to spend roughly:
➡ ¥35 to ¥45 for bottled beer
➡ ¥70 to ¥90 for cocktails
➡ ¥30 to ¥35 for coffee
➡ ¥15 to ¥20 for tea and juice

Event Listings

➡ Smart Shanghai (www.smartshanghai.com)
➡ City Weekend (www.cityweekend.com.cn/shanghai)

Lonely Planet's Top Choices

Glam (p74) Iconic views, great drinks and a first-rate events line-up.

Bell Bar (p113) The place to kick back in Tiánzǐfáng.

Speak Low (p115) Speakeasy with expertly crafted cocktails.

Shelter (p115) Cold War relic turned underground dance floor.

Cotton's (p115) The French Concession villa that everyone wants to call home.

Best Views

Flair (p154) Awesome night-time panoramas from the terrace.

Vue (p162) Hop into the alfresco jacuzzi, but don't forget your swimsuit.

Sir Elly's Terrace (p74) Find 270-degrees-worth of the best views in town.

Cloud 9 (p155) Stunning views from the 87th floor of the Jīnmào Tower.

Best Brews

Boxing Cat Brewery (p115) Much-applauded three-floor microbrewery: the cat's pyjamas.

Kāibā (p141) For more draught craft beers and brews than you can shake a stick at.

Brew (p155) Putting Pǔdōng on the Shànghǎi ale map.

Tap House (p140) Brew house with 24 craft beers on tap in the cool Zhāng Garden complex.

Best Cocktails

El Cóctel (p115) Mixology central.

Constellation (p117) A galaxy of gorgeous cocktails from the hands of expert mixers.

Fennel Lounge (p117) Awesome drinks and a classy ambience.

Speak Low (p115) Japanese-influenced drinks in a speakeasy spot.

Tailor Bar (p139) Tailor-made cocktails to suit your tastes.

Best Design

Long Bar (p74) The Waldorf Astoria's re-creation of the legendary 34m-long Shànghǎi Club bar.

Bar Rouge (p74) Hip, supercrisp and stylish, with awesome views on tap.

Flair (p154) Japan's Super Potato–designed interior, almost as lovely as the view.

Senator Saloon (p115) 1920s Prohibition-style spot with dark-wood booths and pressed-metal ceilings.

Best Wine

Le Bordelais (p116) Top spot for Shànghǎi wine lovers.

Dr Wine (p115) Just what the doctor ordered.

Café des Stagiaires (p112) Fine wine is one of this bar's fortes.

Best Dives

Time Passage (p118) Rock-steady, unpretentious and a cut above the rest.

C's (p176) Graffiti-infested underground warren of cheap booze.

B&C (p141) Hugs from the owners and unlikely to break the bank.

Best Clubs

M1NT (p74) Shànghǎi all the way, with breathtaking views and sharks (the finned variety).

Dada (p114) When the grungy, indie-dive mood hits.

Shelter (p115) Underground lair in a reconverted bomb shelter.

⭐ Entertainment

Shànghǎi is no longer the decadent city that slipped on its dancing shoes as the revolution shot its way into town, but entertainment options have blossomed again over the past decade. Plug into the local cultural scene for a stimulating shot of gallery openings, music concerts and laid-back movie nights at the local bar.

Acrobatics

Shànghǎi troupes are among the best in the world. Spending a night watching them spinning plates on poles and tying themselves in knots never fails to entertain. *Era: Intersection of Time* is a hugely enjoyable and popular acrobatics, music, circus and dance show held nightly from 7.30pm to 9pm in the Shànghǎi Circus World (p163). Feats conclude with eight motorcyclists zipping around within a globe – it's a massive hit with kids.

Music

Back in the 1920s and '30s, Shànghǎi enjoyed a brief heyday in the jazz spotlight, when big-band swing was the entertainment of choice. It remains a popular genre and, even if you won't catch many household names, there are some surprisingly good musicians here and some excellent clubs.

Classical music is also big, with both local and international orchestras performing regularly. For traditional Chinese music, check out the programs at the Oriental Art Center (p155) or Shànghǎi Grand Theatre (p75).

Shànghǎi's rock scene continues to evolve, with a couple of great venues such as Yùyīntáng (p176) and MAO Livehouse (p118). A dedicated local following means that shows are often packed.

Chinese Opera

The shrill falsetto, crashing cymbals, expressive masks and painted faces of Běijīng opera are what most people have in mind when they think of Chinese opera, though the art form actually has a number of different styles. A local predecessor to Běijīng opera is the melodic Kūnjù or Kūnqǔ (Kun opera, from nearby Kūnshān), one of the oldest existing forms of Chinese opera, and best known for its 19-hour-long adaptation of the 16th-century erotic-love ghost story *The Peony Pavilion*. One of the few Kun opera troupes in the country is based in Shànghǎi.

The main problem with seeing a traditional opera in Shànghǎi is that there are no English surtitles and performances can be, well, quite lengthy. But the plot lines are relatively simple, which makes following the action not impossible. Nonetheless, before snatching up tickets for *A Dream of Red Mansions* at the Shànghǎi Grand Theatre, try the Běijīng opera highlights show in the Yìfū Theatre (p76) first.

Entertainment by Neighbourhood

➧ **The Bund & People's Square** (p75) Accessible entertainment: jazz, blues, classical music, ballet, soloists and Chinese opera.

➧ **French Concession** (p118) Stylish, eclectic choice for live rock, theatre, jazz and classical music.

➧ **Jìng'ān** (p141) For acrobatics and ballroom dancing.

➧ **Pǔdōng** (p155) Classical music, jazz, dance, opera and theatre, in a contemporary setting.

NEED TO KNOW

Tickets

➡ Tickets for all of Shànghǎi's performing-arts events can be purchased at the venues where the performances take place.

➡ Tickets are also available from Smart Ticket (www.smartshanghai.com/smartticket).

➡ **Shànghǎi Cultural Information & Booking Centre** (上海文化信息票务中心, Shànghǎi Wénhuà Xìnxī Piàowù Zhōngxīn; ☑021 6217 2426; www.culture.sh.cn; 272 Fengxian Rd; 奉贤路272号; ☺9am-5pm; Ⓜ Line 2, 12, 13 to West Nanjing Rd), which is directly behind the Westgate Mall on West Nanjing Rd, often has tickets available when other places have sold out.

Event Listings

➡ SmartShanghai (www.smartshanghai.com)

➡ City Weekend (www.cityweekend.com.cn/shanghai).

Lonely Planet's Top Choices

Shànghǎi Centre Theatre (p141) Spend an evening with the acrobats.

Shànghǎi Circus World (p163) Venue of the amazing acrobatics event *Era: Intersection of Time.*

Fairmont Peace Hotel Jazz Bar (p75) Swing with Shànghǎi's most famous – and oldest – jazz band.

Shànghǎi Grand Theatre (p75) Ballet, opera and classical music on the biggest stage in town.

Best Classical Venues

Yìfū Theatre (p76) Shànghǎi's leading venue for traditional Chinese opera.

Shànghǎi Grand Theatre (p75) The top venue in Shànghǎi, right in the heart of town.

Oriental Art Center (p155) The modern Pǔdōng choice for classical, jazz, dance, Chinese and Western opera.

Shànghǎi Concert Hall (p76) Classical concerts and local and international soloists.

Shanghai Culture Square (p119) State-of-the-art facility for musicals, drama, ballet and classical music.

Best Live-Music Venues

Cotton Club (p118) Long-established mainstay of the Shànghǎi blues and jazz scene.

Yùyīntáng (p176) Shànghǎi's premier indie venue, where the amps get cranked up to 11.

House of Blues & Jazz (p75) For all your Bund-side blues and jazz needs.

MAO Livehouse (p118) At the heart of Shànghǎi's international and local live-music circuit.

Best Cinemas

Cathay Theatre (p119) Classic art deco picture-house decorating the corner of Middle Huaihai Rd and South Maoming Rd.

UME International Cineplex (p119) Right at the heart of the action in Xīntiāndì.

Shànghǎi Film Art Centre (p176) The principal venue for the Shanghai International Film Festival.

Best Chinese Opera & Theatre

Yìfū Theatre (p76) Sit with local opera-goers and enjoy the classics.

Pearl Theatre (p163) For drama, cabaret and more in a fantastic old theatre building.

Dàguān Theater (p155) Spiffing Pǔdōng theatre with cutting-edge equipment.

Píngtán Museum (p194) Live performances of Sūzhōu's musical storytelling.

IFC Mall, Pǔdōng (p155)

🛍 Shopping

Shànghǎi's runaway property market and thrusting economy have filled pockets citywide: Shànghǎi shoppers buy up big-time. While locals have a passion for luxury goods and designer labels, it's not all about Gucci, Prada and Louis Vuitton. Whether you're after boutique threads, a set of snappy heels, Chinese antiques, handmade ceramics or a period poster from the Mao era, Shànghǎi is an A to Z of shopping.

Boutiques

The French Concession's bijou boutiques are where the most interesting finds are hidden. Given the sheer number of tiny shops, though, it can be hard to separate the good from the not so good. Start with recommended shopping strips to get a feel for local fashion before crossing town for a specific store. Keep in mind that unless you are petite finding the right size can be difficult.

Tailor-Made Clothes

For clothing that's the perfect size, the Old Town fabric markets may be the solution. All manner of textiles can be found, from synthetic to silk and cashmere. Compare fabric and prices at different stands to ensure no one is blatantly ripping you off. Suits, trousers, shirts, dresses and scarves can be made at such places in as little as 24 hours (expect to pay extra), though a one-week turnaround is more realistic. For traditional Chinese qípáo (cheongsam) and jackets, head to South Maoming Rd.

NEED TO KNOW

Opening Hours

Most shops open from 10am to 10pm daily, though government-run stores often close at 6pm while smaller boutiques may not open until noon. Yùyuán Bazaar and other markets are best visited early in the day.

Customs

Technically, nothing older than approximately 200 years can be taken out of China, but you'd be lucky to corner any genuine antiques that old in Shànghǎi. If buying a reproduction, make sure the dealer provides paperwork declaring it's not an antique. Dealers should also provide the proper receipts and paperwork for any antique items. Keep these along with the dealer's business card, just in case.

Phrases to Know

➜ *Duōshao qián?* (多少钱) – How much?

➜ *Tài guì le!* (太贵了) – Too expensive!

➜ *Tài xiǎo* (太小) – Too small.

➜ *Tài dà* (太大) – Too big.

➜ *Bù yào* (不要) – I don't want it.

Counterfeits

'In Shànghǎi, everything can be faked except for your mother', or so the saying goes. Counterfeit goods are ubiquitous; even if you've set out to buy a genuine item, there's no guarantee that's what you're going to get. Antiques in particular are almost always reproductions: the best advice is to buy something because you like it, not because you think it has historic value.

DVD stores and fake markets are drawcards for visitors and can make for a fun browse, but remember that although your purchases might not cost much (provided you're a decent bargainer), they most likely break international copyright law, and they may soon fall apart.

Bargaining

In Shànghǎi markets, haggling over prices is standard practice. Most common is for the vendor to punch a price into a calculator and hand it hopefully to you for inspection. You then laugh theatrically and tap in 10% to 25% of their price, before looking the vendor in the eye. The seller shakes their head, emits a dismissive cry, adjusts the price a bit and hands the calculator back to you. This goes on until the price drops by at least 50%. At some touristy places, like Yùyuán Bazaar, vendors will go as low as 25% of the original price. But at stores where a discount is not normally offered, you may only get 10% or 20% off.

It often pays to smile, shrug and walk away to a nearby stall selling exactly the same thing. Most times the vendor will chase you down and get you to agree to a deal. Bear in mind, though, that the point is to achieve a mutually acceptable price and not to screw the vendor into the ground. It's always best to smile, which will help keep negotiations light even if you don't ultimately agree on a sale.

If negotiating in pidgin Chinese, be very careful of similar-sounding numbers: 14 (十四; *shísì*) and 40 (四十; *sìshí*); and 108 (一百零八; *yībǎilíngbā*) and 180 (一百八; *yībǎibā*). These offer great potential for misunderstanding, deliberate or otherwise.

Shipping

Most reputable shops will take care of insurance, customs and shipping for larger items, but find out first exactly what the dealer covers. Separate charges may materialise for handling, packaging, customs duty and quarantine, driving the shipping charges above the price of the item. Also consider how much it will cost to get the goods from the destination shipping port to your home.

Shipping clothing, curios and household items on your own is generally not a problem. China Post (中国邮政; Zhōngguó Yóuzhèng) has an excellent packing system for airmailing light items.

Shopping by Neighbourhood

➜ **The Bund & People's Square** (p76) Luxury togs, gifts, accessories and East Nanjing Rd.

➜ **Old Town** (p90) Fabric and antique markets plus an abundance of souvenirs.

➜ **French Concession** (p119) Hip boutiques, shoe shops, vintage, jewellery, ceramics, malls and *shíkùmén* alleyway shopping.

➜ **Jìng'ān** (p141) Upmarket malls, designer shopping, funky ceramics and knock-offs.

➜ **Pǔdōng** (p155) Big-name malls and fakes.

Lonely Planet's Top Choices

Tiānshān Tea City (p176) For all the tea in China...head to tea city.

Old Street (p90) All your souvenir needs, from calendar posters to Mao-era kitsch.

Spin (p141) Take home beautiful ceramic teacups and dinnerware.

AP Xīnyáng Fashion & Gifts Market (p155) The mother of all fake markets.

Amy Lin's Pearls (p142) Fresh- and saltwater pearls at unbeatable prices.

Best Souvenirs & Antiques

Fúyòu Antique Market (p90) Delve into this sprawling market for a diamond or two from the rough.

Art Deco (p142) Choice selection of furniture from Swinging Shànghǎi's deco age.

Yùyuán Bazaar (p80) A compendium of Middle Kingdom knick-knacks, souvenirs and gifts.

1930 (p123) Art deco lighting and vintage treasure.

Best Markets

Shíliùpù Fabric Market (p90) Bundles of affordable silks and all manner of fabrics.

South Bund Fabric Market (p90) Stuffed with fabric stalls.

AP Xīnyáng Fashion & Gifts Market (p155) Shànghǎi's premier bonanza for knock-offs; a sprawling mass of bargains.

Best Tea

Tiānshān Tea City (p176) Three floors crammed with tea and accessories.

Huìfēng Tea Shop (p121) Great little store with friendly service and a good range of tea.

Zhēnchálín Tea (p119) Taste-test your way around this store in Tiánzǐfáng.

Xiao Ye Tea Shop (p142) Pick up one of the cakes of *pǔ'ěr* tea lining the walls.

Best Pottery & Ceramics

Spin (p141) Beautiful store with a stunning range of Chinese ceramics.

Happy Clay (p122) Tiny shop with stacked shelves of handmade dinnerware in pastels.

Design Commune (p141) Showroom of designer homewares run by interior-design duo Neri & Hu.

Blue Shànghǎi White (p76) For beautifully made Jǐngdézhèn porcelain teaware.

Best Art

Shànghǎi Museum Art Store (p76) A cut above the rest, with quality porcelain and some great books.

Propaganda Poster Art Centre (p98) The cream of Mao-era agitprop, before it became kitsch.

Best Local Fashion

Annabel Lee (p76) Elegant array of silk, linen and cashmere accessories, just off the Bund.

Xīntiāndì Style (p121) Host of stylish boutiques, all under one roof.

Dòng Liáng (p122) High-end designer boutique showcasing the best of local designers.

Urban Tribe (p121) Ethnic-inspired natural-fabric clothing and excellent handmade jewellery.

Explore Shànghǎi

SHÀNGHǍI'S
TOP SIGHTS

Neighbourhoods at a Glance

❶ The Bund & People's Square p54

Shànghǎi's standout landmark is the Bund, a grandiose curve of colonial-era buildings lining the western bank of the Huángpǔ River. It's the first stop for visitors, and the historic architecture houses a profusion of exclusive restaurants, bars, shops and hotels.

Running perpendicular from the waterfront is East Nanjing Rd – a maelstrom of shoppers, department stores and neon lighting – which eventually runs into the city's heart, People's Square. The de facto centre of town, this large open space is studded with museums and fenced in by skyscrapers.

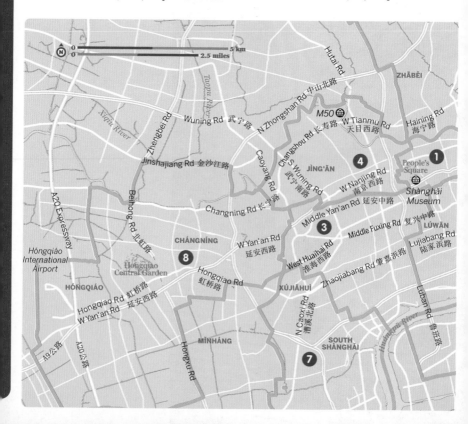

② Old Town p78

The original city core and the sole part of Shànghǎi to pre-date the 1850s, the Old Town is a favourite with visitors hoping to glimpse 'traditional' China. Many of the older buildings have been replaced with modern apartment blocks, but there are still more temples here than in the rest of the city combined, and pockets are impregnated with atmosphere and shabby charm.

③ French Concession p92

The city's most stylish side, the former French Concession is where the bulk of Shànghǎi's disposable cash is splashed. The low-rise, villa-lined leafy backstreets are perfectly geared to shopping, dining and entertainment, but a brood of museums makes the former concession – now a handsome melange of several distinct neighbourhoods – a cultural experience as well.

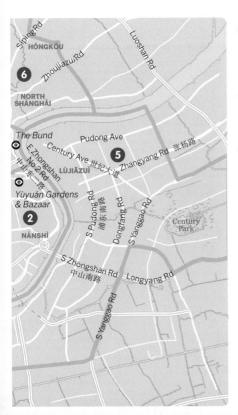

④ Jìng'ān p126

North of the French Concession ranges the vibrant commercial district of Jìng'ān, an expat-friendly domain anchored on bustling West Nanjing Rd, and defined by its abundance of period architecture, malls, top-end hotels and enticing *lòngtáng* architecture. The grittier railway-station area isn't far from the city's most famous Buddhist temple and happening art enclave.

⑤ Pǔdōng p143

Pǔdōng is new Shànghǎi, sprawling east with seemingly infinite high-rises and skyscrapers from the Huángpǔ River's far bank. A dazzling cosmos of high-altitude five-star hotels, banks, Maglev trains, giant TV screens and, less glamorously, faceless residential towers, set to a backdrop of roaring traffic and construction work.

⑥ Hóngkǒu & North Shànghǎi p156

Hóngkǒu envelops north Shànghǎi from Sūzhōu Creek and the Bund. It's a relatively unpolished domain of old lanes, working-class textures and heritage architecture. A former American- and later a Japanese-controlled concession, Hóngkǒu is undergoing gradual (sometimes lavish) redevelopment, especially close to Sūzhōu Creek.

⑦ Xújiāhuì & South Shànghǎi p164

An extension of the French Concession, Xújiāhuì's interesting Jesuit heritage and prestigious Jiāotōng University contrast spectacularly with oversized shopping centres dominating its main intersection. There's a handful of decent neighbourhood restaurants, street-food stalls around the university and smart mall-dining options.

⑧ West Shànghǎi p171

Heading west, the residential and office towers, conference centres and busy highways of Shànghǎi's suburban districts stretch to the horizon. Focal points include Hóngqiáo's airport and railway station, art galleries and day trips to the old canal town of Qībǎo.

NEIGHBOURHOODS AT A GLANCE

The Bund & People's Square

THE BUND | PEOPLE'S SQUARE

Neighbourhood Top Five

1 **The Bund** (p56) Strolling along the promenade, and capturing Pǔdōng lighting up through a martini glass.

2 **Shànghǎi Museum** (p61) Loading up on Chinese culture's greatest hits at this world-class museum.

3 **High Dining** (p72) Indulging at some of Shànghǎi's signature Bund restaurants, such as Mr & Mrs Bund, with showstopping views as standard.

4 **East Nanjing Rd** (p64) Plunging into the neon-lit swell of this famous pedestrianised road.

5 **Rockbund Art Museum** (p64) Catching up with the latest trends in contemporary Chinese art along the 'Art on the Bund' precinct.

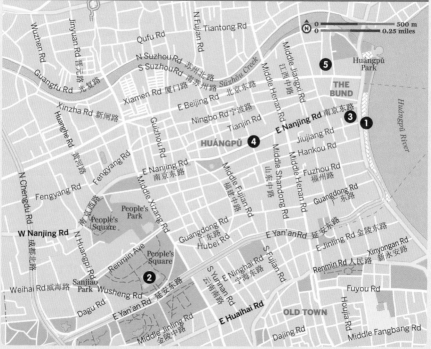

For more detail of this area see Map p296 ➡

Explore: The Bund & People's Square

Shànghǎi's definitive spectacle, the grand sweep of the riverside Bund (外滩, Wàitān) is a designer retail and dining strip; it's *the* address in town for the city's most exclusive boutiques, restaurants and hotels. The best strategy is just to stroll, weighing up the bombastic neoclassical contours with the pristine geometry of Pǔdōng over the water.

The streets west from the waterfront morph instantly into a less salubrious commercial district housed in the uncleaned shells of concession-era buildings, mixed with newer skyscrapers and office towers. Yet even the most casual of wanders yields sudden architectural gems.

Continuing west is People's Square (人民广场), a swathe of open space boxed in by towers. The de-facto city centre, it's the address of a host of museums, entertainment venues, malls, a park and the city hall. Much less austere than Běijīng's Tiān'ānmén Sq, People's Square is free of the rigid geometry and supervision of the capital's better-known rectangle, with musicians serenading pockets of intense crowds.

Linking the Bund with People's Square is East Nanjing Rd, once China's most famous shopping street. Mostly pedestrian, it's a bonanza of department stores, neon signs, determined English-speaking girls latching on to foreign men (and getting kickbacks from the cafes they drag their victims to), incessant offers of massage, and hawkers flogging replica watches and gimmicky toys. If you don't mind melees, it's a fun saunter.

Local Life

➡**Dumplings** Sample *shēngjiān* at Yang's Fry Dumplings (p73) or *xiǎolóngbāo* at Jiājiā Soup Dumplings (p73) or Nánxiáng Steamed Bun Restaurant (p70).

➡**Museum-hopping** Spend a rainy day checking out the museums at People's Square.

➡**Shopping** Join the throngs on East Nanjing Rd, crowding into malls or angling for discounts in the subterranean stalls around People's Square metro station.

Getting There & Away

➡**Metro** The Bund is a 10-minute walk east from the East Nanjing Rd stop (lines 2 and 10). People's Square, one of the city's busiest stations, is served by lines 1, 2 and 8.

➡**Pedicab** Drivers hang out in side streets along the Bund and charge ¥10 (total) to Yùyuán Gardens.

➡**Bund Sightseeing Tunnel** Runs from the Bund to Pǔdōng under the Huángpǔ River.

➡**Tourist Train** Runs the length of East Nanjing Rd's pedestrianised section (tickets ¥5), from Middle Henan Rd to Shànghǎi No 1 Department Store.

Lonely Planet's Top Tip

Avoid the young people posing as out-of-town students who ply the main tourist drags (East Nanjing Rd, the Bund), engaging visitors in conversation. They seem friendly enough. You help them take their picture, chat about China and they invite you to a traditional tea ceremony. It sounds welcoming, but don't do it. You'll get the tea all right, but you'll also get a bill for US$100 or more.

Best Places to Eat

➡ Lost Heaven (p71)
➡ Yang's Fry Dumplings (p73)
➡ Mr & Mrs Bund (p72)
➡ Yúxìn Chuāncài (p70)
➡ M on the Bund (p72)

For reviews, see p70 ➡

Best Places to Drink

➡ Long Bar (p74)
➡ M1NT (p74)
➡ Barbarossa (p75)
➡ Glam (p74)
➡ Pop (p74)

For reviews, see p74 ➡

Best Places to Shop

➡ Annabel Lee (p76)
➡ Sūzhōu Cobblers (p76)
➡ Shànghǎi Museum Art Store (p76)
➡ Shànghǎi No 1 Food Store (p76)
➡ Blue Shànghǎi White (p76)

For reviews, see p76 ➡

TOP SIGHT
THE BUND

Symbolic of colonial Shànghǎi, the Bund was the city's Wall St, a place of feverish trading and fortunes made and lost. Originally a towpath for dragging barges of rice, it was gradually transformed into a grandiose sweep of the most powerful banks and trading houses in Shànghǎi, and it has remained the first port of call for visitors since passengers began disembarking here over a century ago. Today, however, it's the extravagant bars and restaurants and the hypnotising views of Pǔdōng that pull crowds.

Promenade

The Bund offers a host of things to do, but most visitors head straight for the riverside promenade to pose for photos in front of Pǔdōng's ever-changing skyline. The area is essentially open around the clock, but it's at its best in the early morning, when locals are out practising taichi, or in the early evening, when both sides of the river are lit up and the romance of the waterfront reaches a crescendo. The promenade begins at Huángpǔ Park; you can follow it 1km to the Bund's south end at the Meteorological Signal Tower.

Huángpǔ Park

China's first public **park** (黄浦公园, Huángpǔ Gōngyuán; Map p296; Ⓜ Line 2, 10 to East Nanjing Rd) was laid out in 1886 by a Scottish gardener shipped out to Shànghǎi especially for that purpose. The park achieved lasting notoriety for its apocryphal 'No dogs or Chinese allowed' sign. Located at the northern end of the Bund, the park's anachronistic Monument to the People's Heroes (p64) hides the entrance to the Bund History Museum (p64), which contains a collection of old maps and photographs.

DON'T MISS

➡ The promenade
➡ Fairmont Peace Hotel
➡ Hongkong & Shanghai Bank Building
➡ Dining or drinks with a view

PRACTICALITIES

➡ 外滩, Wàitān
➡ Map p296, G3
➡ 3 East Zhongshan No 1 Rd; 3 中山东一路
➡ Ⓜ Line 2, 10 to East Nanjing Rd

Jardine Matheson

Standing at No 27 on the Bund is the former head-quarters of early opium traders **Jardine Matheson** 怡和洋行, Yí Hé Yángháng; Map p296; 27 East Zhongshan No 1 Rd; 中山东一路27号; ⓜ Line 2,10 to East Nanjing Rd), which went on to become one of the most powerful trading houses in Hong Kong and Shànghǎi. Also known as EWO, it was the first foreign company to erect a building on the Bund – in 1851. It later invested in China's earliest railways and cotton mills, and even operated a popular brewery. The current building replaced the original and was completed in 1922. In 1941 the British Embassy occupied the top floor, facing the German Embassy across the road in the Glen Line Building, at No 28. Jardine Matheson now holds the House of Roosevelt, which is quite possibly China's largest wine cellar and bar.

Bank of China

Originally established in 1897, the **Bank of China** (中国银行, Zhōngguó Yínháng; Map p296; 23 East Zhongshan No 1 Rd; 中山东一路23号; ⓜ Line 2, 10 to East Nanjing Rd), at No 23, relocated its headquarters from Běijīng to Shànghǎi in the 1920s, undergoing a major transformation from state bureaucracy to a market-driven business. Although the bank has occupied this address since 1923, the present building was only begun in 1935 and was originally designed to be the tallest building in the city at 33 storeys high. The Sino-Japanese War interrupted construction and it finally opened in 1942, its front door guarded by a magnificent pair of art deco lions.

Fairmont Peace Hotel

Lording it over the corner of East Nanjing and East Zhongshan Rds is the most famous building on the Bund, the landmark Fairmont Peace Hotel (p206), constructed between 1926 and 1929. It was originally built as Sassoon House, with Victor Sassoon's famous Cathay Hotel on the 4th to 7th floors. It wasn't for the hoi polloi; the guest list ran to Charlie Chaplin, George Bernard Shaw and Noel Coward, who penned *Private Lives* here in four days in 1930 when he had the flu. Sassoon himself spent weekdays in his personal suite on the top floor, just beneath the green pyramid. The building was renamed the Peace Hotel in 1956.

Pop in to savour the wonderful art deco lobby and magnificent rotunda, or lend an ear to the old jazz band (p75) in the evenings. It's also possible to arrange an hour-long tour (¥100) of the premises through the Peace Gallery (p64) a small, museum-like space displaying intriguing hotel memorabilia, hidden up a flight of stairs near the main entrance. It's recommended you book a half-day in advance.

WHAT'S IN A NAME?

The Bund gets its Anglo-Indian name from the embankments built up to discourage flooding (a *band* is an embankment in Hindi). There's some debate over how to say the word, though given its origins, it's likely the correct pronunciation is 'bunned', not 'booned'.

The Bund's monumental art deco and neoclassical facades presented an imposing – if strikingly un-Chinese – view for those arriving in the busy port. For a glimpse of how it might have looked, take a river cruise (p77) departing from the docks in either Pǔxī or Pǔdōng.

SHÀNGHǍI CLUB

The Shànghǎi Club, at No 2 on the Bund, originally had 20 rooms for residents, but its most famous accoutrement was its bar – at 34m it was said to be the longest in Asia. Once one of the most exclusive spots in the city, the building lost considerable face in the 1990s when a KFC set up inside in the foyer, but it found redemption with the opening of the Waldorf Astoria (p206).

The Bund

The best way to get acquainted with Shànghǎi is to take a stroll along the Bund.

This illustration shows the main sights along the Bund's central stretch, beginning near the intersection with East Nanjing Rd.

The Bund is 1km long and walking it should take around an hour.

Head to the area south of the Hongkong & Shanghai Bank Building to find the biggest selection of drinking and dining destinations.

Hongkong & Shanghai Bank Building (1923)

Head into this massive bank to marvel at the beautiful mosaic ceiling, featuring the 12 zodiac signs and the world's (former) eight centres of finance.

Custom House (1927)

One of the most important buildings on the Bund, Custom House was capped by the largest clock face in Asia and 'Big Ching', a bell modelled on London's Big Ben.

OSTILL / SHUTTERSTOCK ©

SEAN PAVONE / SHUTTERSTOCK ©

Former Bank of Communications (1947)

Bund Public Service Centre (2010)

TOP TIP

The promenade is open around the clock, but it's at its best in the early morning, when locals are out practising taichi, or in the early evening, when both sides of the river are lit up and the majesty of the waterfront is at its grandest.

North China Daily News Building (1924)

Known as the 'Old Lady of the Bund'. The *News* ran from 1864 to 1951 as the main English-language newspaper in China. Look for the paper's motto above the central windows.

Fairmont Peace Hotel (1929)

Originally built as the Cathay Hotel, this art deco masterpiece was *the* place to stay in Shànghǎi and the crown jewel in Victor Sassoon's real-estate empire.

JON ARNOLD / GETTY IMAGES ©

Former Chartered Bank Building (1923)

Reopened in 2004 as the upscale entertainment complex Bund 18; the building's top-floor Bar Rouge is one of the Bund's premier late-night destinations.

GREG ELMS / GETTY IMAGES ©

Russo-Chinese Bank Building (1902)

Former Bank of Taiwan (1927)

Former Palace Hotel (1906)

Now known as the Swatch Art Peace Hotel (an artists' residence and gallery, with a top-floor restaurant and bar), this building was completed in 1908 and hosted Sun Yatsen's victory celebration in 1911 following his election as the first president of the Republic of China.

PHILIPPE LOPEZ / AFP / GETTY IMAGES ©

1906

THE SWATCH ART PEACE HOTEL

Bank of China (1942)

This unusual building was originally commissioned to be the tallest building in Shànghǎi but, probably because of Victor Sassoon's influence, wound up being 1m shorter than its neighbour.

Custom House

The **Custom House** (自订的房子; Zì Dìng De Fángzi; Map p296; 13 East Zhongshan No 1 Rd; 中山东一路13号; Ⓜ Line 2, 10 to East Nanjing Rd, exit 1), established at this site in 1857 and rebuilt in 1927, is one of the most important buildings on the Bund. Capping it is Big Ching, a bell modelled on London's Big Ben. Clocks were by no means new to China, but Shànghǎi was the first city in which they gained widespread acceptance and the lives of many became dictated by a standardised, common schedule. During the Cultural Revolution, Big Ching was replaced with loudspeakers that blasted out revolutionary songs ('The East is Red') and slogans. Look for the socialist realism plaque outside its front door, depicting scenes from the 'liberation' of Shànghǎi.

Hongkong & Shanghai Bank Building

Adjacent to the Custom House, the **Hongkong & Shanghai Bank Building** (HSBC Building, 汇丰大厦; Map p296; 12 East Zhongshan No 1 Rd; 中山东一路12号; Ⓜ Line 2, 10 to East Nanjing Rd) was constructed in 1923. The bank was first established in Hong Kong in 1864 and in Shànghǎi in 1865 to finance trade, and soon became one of the richest in Shànghǎi, arranging the indemnity paid after the Boxer Rebellion. The magnificent mosaic ceiling inside the entrance was plastered over until its restoration in 1997 and is therefore well preserved. Photography is not allowed inside.

Three on the Bund

When it opened in 2004, **Three on the Bund** (外滩三号, Wàitān Sān Hào; Map p296; 3 East Zhongshan No 1 Rd; 中山东一路3号; Ⓜ Line 2, 10 to East Nanjing Rd) became the strip's first lifestyle destination and the model that many other Bund edifices followed. Upscale restaurants and bars occupy most floors, along with the conceptually minded Shànghǎi Gallery of Art (p65).

Gutzlaff Signal Tower

The **signal tower** (外滩信号台, Wàitān Xìnhào Tái; Map p296; 1 East Zhongshan No 2 Rd; 中山东二路1号; ☺ 10am-5pm; Ⓜ Line 2, 10 to East Nanjing Rd, exit 3) was built in 1907 to replace the wooden original as well as to serve as a meteorological relay station for the tireless Shànghǎi Jesuits. In the early 1950s it was commandeered as a riverboat police station, and in 1995 the entire edifice was shunted 22.4m to its present location.

TOP SIGHT
SHÀNGHĂI MUSEUM

One of the world's premier repositories of Chinese art, the Shànghăi Museum celebrates one masterpiece after another while guiding visitors through the pages of Chinese history. Whether you prefer the meditative beauty of a landscape painting or the crafted perfection of a Song dynasty bowl, the luxurious curves of a Ming chair or the expressive face of a Nuo mask, this is the one museum in Shànghăi you must not miss.

Ancient Chinese Bronzes Gallery

On the ground floor is one of the museum's star attractions, a collection of ancient bronzes, some of which date back to 2200 BC. Many visitors are unfamiliar with this early aspect of Chinese art and for this reason the exhibit may seem less appealing than others, but Asian art enthusiasts should make a point of stopping by this unrivalled collection.

These bronzes were created during a long shamanistic period that saw the development of ancestor worship and ritual – two facets of life that would go on to dominate Confucianism.

Their diversity of shapes and versatility is striking, revealing the significance of bronze in important rituals and, later, everyday life. Objects range from wine bottles, jars and goblets to weapons and two-toned bells, once China's chief musical instrument. The most important ritual bronzes were *dĭng* (three- or four-legged food vessels used for cooking and serving) – one highlight in the collection is an enormous 10th-century *dĭng* weighing 200kg. Look for inscriptions on the vessels and you'll be able to witness the early evolution of Chinese writing.

DON'T MISS

➡ Ancient Chinese Bronzes Gallery
➡ Ancient Chinese Ceramics Gallery
➡ Chinese Painting Gallery
➡ Minority Nationalities Art Gallery

PRACTICALITIES

➡ 上海博物馆, Shànghăi Bówùguăn
➡ Map p296, C6
➡ www.shanghai museum.net
➡ 201 Renmin Ave; 人民大道201号
➡ free
➡ ⊙9am-5pm, last entry 4pm
➡ 🚻
➡ Ⓜ Line 1, 2, 8 to People's Square

ARCHITECTURAL INSPIRATION

Before you enter the museum, admire the exterior of the building. Designed to recall an ancient bronze *dǐng* (a three-legged cooking vessel), the building also echoes the shape of a famous bronze mirror from the Han dynasty, exhibited within the museum.

The audio guide is well worth the ¥40 (¥400 deposit, or your passport). It highlights particularly interesting items as well as offering good gallery overviews and general background information.

CALLIGRAPHY GALLERY

Chinese characters, which express both meaning as a word and visual beauty as an image, are one of the most fascinating aspects of the Chinese language. While the full scope of the 3rd-floor Calligraphy Gallery may be unfathomable for those who don't read Chinese, anyone can enjoy the purely aesthetic balance of Chinese brush artistry.

Decoration is an intrinsic element of the beauty of ancient bronzes. The most common design is the stylised animal motif, depicting dragons, lions and the phoenix. This was replaced in the 10th century BC by zigzags (representing thunder) and cloud designs, and later by geometric shapes. As bronzes lost their ritual significance, decorative scenes from daily life made an appearance. Later still, stamped moulds, lost wax techniques and piece moulds enabled designs to become ever more complex.

When appreciating the bronzes, remember that they would have originally been a dazzling golden colour. Oxidisation has given them their characteristic dull green patina.

Ancient Chinese Sculpture Gallery

On the ground floor, exhibits in the Ancient Chinese Sculpture Gallery range from the funeral sculptures of the Qin and Han dynasties to the predominantly Buddhist sculptures of the following centuries, which were heavily influenced by the Indian and Central Asian styles that came to China via the Silk Road. If you're interested in Buddhism and the various representations of Bodhisattvas, disciples and fierce-looking *lokapalas* (Buddhist protectors), it's certainly worth a visit. Note that the sculptures displayed were almost all painted, but only scraps of pigment survive.

Ancient Chinese Ceramics Gallery

On the 2nd floor, the Ancient Chinese Ceramics Gallery is one of the largest and most fascinating galleries in the museum. The exhibits include so much more than the stereotypical blue-and-white porcelain that many think of when they hear the word 'China'. Even if you don't consider yourself a fan, this is one gallery that everyone should at least take a look at.

It begins with 6000-year-old pottery excavated from just outside Shànghǎi before leapfrogging ahead to the figurines of Han times; the *sāncǎi* (polychrome) pottery of the Tang; the marvellously diverse and elegant tableware of the Song; and the sea-green celadon jars, Yíxīng teapots and vast collection of porcelain produced under the Ming and Qing. The highlight is undoubtedly the porcelain from the famed pottery town of Jǐngdézhèn in Jiāngxī province, where you'll see an evolution in techniques, design and colours, from underglazes of iconic cobalt blue to blood red.

Don't worry if you don't know your 'ewer with overhead handles in *dòucǎi*' from your 'brush-holder with *fěncǎi* design' – it's all part of a luxurious learning curve. Look out for the 'celadon vase with ancient bronze design' and the delightful Ming dynasty white-glazed porcelain statues of Guanyin, the goddess of mercy. Angled mirrors beneath each piece reveal the mark on the foot. A reproduction kiln and workshop is located at the end of the gallery.

Chinese Painting Gallery

On the 3rd floor, the Chinese Painting Gallery leads visitors through various styles of traditional Chinese painting, with many works dwelling on idealised landscapes. At first glance many appear to be similar, but upon closer inspection you'll realise that there is a vast array of techniques used to depict the natural world. There are some true masterpieces here, from painters such as Ni Zan (1301–74), Wang Meng (1308–85) and Wu Wei (1459–1508). Although works are rotated regularly, the Ming collection is generally regarded as containing the best selection of paintings. Scroll paintings are 'read' from right to left.

Minority Nationalities Art Gallery

Save something for the Minority Nationalities Art Gallery on the 4th floor, which introduces visitors to the diversity of China's non-Han ethnic groups, totalling (officially) some 9% of the country's population. Displays focus mainly on dress: from the salmon fish-skin suit from Hēilóngjiāng and the furs of the Siberian Oroqen, to the embroidery and batik of Guìzhōu's Miao and Dong, the Middle Eastern satin robes of the Uighurs and the wild hairstyles of the former slave-owning Yi. Handicrafts and artefacts include intricate masks, Miao silverware and Yi lacquer work.

Other Galleries

The **Ancient Chinese Jade Gallery** reveals the transformation of jade use from early mystical symbols (such as the *bì*, 'jade discs', used to worship heaven) to ritual weapons and jewellery. Exhibit 414 is a remarkable totem, with an engraved phoenix carrying a human head. Bamboo drills, abrasive sand and garnets crushed in water were used to shape some of the pieces, which date back more than 5000 years.

When it comes to the **Coin Gallery**, it's tempting to keep moving. But do look for the *bànliáng* coins, standardised during the Qin dynasty, which are pierced with a hole so they could be carried by string. Some older coins are shaped like keys or knives.

Offering a change of pace, the **Ming & Qing Furniture Gallery** features rose and sandalwood furniture of the elegant Ming dynasty and heavier, more baroque examples from the Qing dynasty. Several mock offices and reception rooms offer a glimpse of wealthy Chinese home life. An interesting exhibit are the models unearthed from an officer's tomb discovered in the 1960s, which show examples of Ming dynasty furniture.

Although obscure, the **Seal Gallery** on the 3rd floor provides a fascinating glimpse into the niche art form of miniature carving. Seals (chops) are notable both for the intricacy of their design and the special script used on the underside, which is known to only a handful of artisans and calligraphers. Look for the two orange soapstone seals that feature incredibly detailed landscapes in miniature.

 **SIGHTS**

THE BUND & PEOPLE'S SQUARE SIGHTS

◉ The Bund

THE BUND   ARCHITECTURE
See p56.

PEACE GALLERY   MUSEUM
Map p296 (和平收藏馆, Hépíng Shōucángguǎn;
Fairmont Peace Hotel, 20 East Nanjing Rd; 南京东
路20号费尔蒙和平饭店; ⊙10am-7pm; Ⓜ Line 2,
10 to East Nanjing Rd) **FREE** This intriguing little museum, in essence a long room stuffed
with period objects and photos relating
to the colourful history of the Peace Hotel
(p206), is an absorbing and atmospheric diversion. Head through the first entrance to
the hotel off East Nanjing Rd (walking west
from the Bund) and it's upstairs on the right.
Hour-long tours (¥100) of the hotel are run
through here at 10.30am and 2.30pm.

BUND HISTORY MUSEUM   MUSEUM
Map p296 (外滩历史纪念馆, Wàitān Lìshǐ
Jìniànguǎn; ⊙9am-4pm Mon-Fri; Ⓜ Line 2, 10 to
East Nanjing Rd, exit 7) **FREE** Beneath the Monument to the People's Heroes, this underground museum has some interesting info
and photos on the history of the Bund. It's a
good starting point before setting off to explore the promenade's colonial architecture.

MONUMENT TO THE
PEOPLE'S HEROES   MONUMENT
Map p296 (人民英雄纪念碑, Rénmín Yīngxióng
Jìniànbēi; Ⓜ Line 2, 10 to East Nanjing Rd, exit 7)
Up from Huángpǔ Park, this anachronistic
monument stands above the Bund History
Museum (p64). Its socialist realism friezes
depict the postwar triumphs of communism
in Shànghǎi. Come here early in the morning for excellent photo ops as locals perform
taichi to the backdrop of Pǔdōng's skyline.

FORMER BRITISH
CONSULATE   HISTORIC BUILDING
Map p296 (英国驻上海总领事馆, Yīngguó Zhù
Shànghǎi Zǒng Lǐngshìguǎn; 33 East Zhongshan
No 1 Rd; 33 中山東路 1 號; Ⓜ Line 2, 10 to East
Nanjing, exit 7) The original British Consulate was one of the first foreign buildings
to go up in Shànghǎi in 1852, though it was
destroyed in a fire and replaced with the
current structure in 1873. Now renovated, it
is used as a financiers' club and restaurant,
No 1 Waitanyuan (p72), which serves high
tea. Also within the grounds are the former

Consul's Residence (1884) – now a flagship
Patek Philippe store – and several century-
old magnolia trees.

YUANMINGYUAN RD   AREA
Map p296 (圆明园路, Yuánmíngyuán Lù; Ⓜ Line
2, 10 to East Nanjing Rd) Like a smaller, more
condensed version of the Bund, the pedestrianised, cobblestone Yuanmingyuan Rd
is lined with a mishmash of colonial architecture. Running parallel with the Bund,
just one block back, the road features some
fine examples of renovated red-brick and
stone buildings dating from the 1900s.
Look for the art deco YWCA Building (No
133) and Chinese Baptist Publication building (No 209), the ornate 1907 red-brick Pan-
ama Legation building (No 97) and the 1927
neoclassical Lyceum Building.

ROCKBUND ART MUSEUM   MUSEUM
Map p296 (RAM, 上海外滩美术馆, Shànghǎi
Wàitān Měishùguǎn; www.rockbundartmuseum.
org; 20 Huqiu Rd; 虎丘路20号; adult/child
¥30/15; ⊙10am-6pm Tue-Sun; Ⓜ Line 2, 10 to
East Nanjing Rd) Housed in the magnificent former Royal Asiatic Society building
(1932) – once Shànghǎi's first museum –
this world-class gallery behind the Bund
focuses on contemporary Chinese and international art, with rotating exhibits year-
round and no permanent collection. One of
the city's top modern-art venues, the building's interior and exterior are both sublime.
Check out the unique art deco eight-sided
bāguà (trigram) windows at the front, a
fetching synthesis of Western modernist
styling and traditional Chinese design.

The interior is all textbook deco lines and
curves, including the fine staircase. Head to
the rooftop terrace for excellent views, despite the hulking form of the Peninsula Hotel blocking out much of Lùjiāzuǐ. Admission
includes a free coffee from the top-floor cafe.

EAST NANJING ROAD   AREA
Map p296 (南京东路, Nánjīng Dōnglù; Ⓜ Line 2,
10 to East Nanjing Rd) Linking the Bund with
People's Square is East Nanjing Rd, once
known as Nanking Rd. The first department stores in China opened here in the
1920s, when the modern machine age –
with its new products, automobiles, art deco
styling and newfangled ideas – was ushered
in. A glowing forest of neon at night, it's no
longer the cream of Shànghǎi shopping, but
its pedestrian strip remains one of the most
famous and crowded streets in China.

ART ON THE BUND

Scattered among the Bund's elegant heritage architecture are numerous small contemporary galleries that together form an interesting little art precinct. It's a more refined scene than the gritty M50 art district, with the galleries set within beautiful historic buildings, many of which were formerly banks. Its centrepiece is the world-class Rockbund Art Museum (p64).

For a map of the galleries in the area, pick up the self-guided walking map *Art on the Bund*, or get in touch with Ming Ming from AroundSpace to arrange a tour. Shanghai Detour (www.shanghai-detour.org) also has a very handy art map you can download.

BANK (银行, Yínháng; Map p296; www.mabsociety.com; 1st Fl 59 Xiangang Rd; 香港路59号1楼; ⏰10.30am-6.30pm Tue-Sun; Ⓜ Line 2, 10 to East Nanjing Rd) **FREE** Hidden down a side street without fanfare is this wonderful contemporary gallery in a dilapidated former bank union building (c 1929). Set up by a New Yorker, BANK holds shows every two months, exhibiting all art forms by a mix of local and international young, emerging and big-name artists.

AroundSpace (周围艺术画廊, Zhōuwéi Yìshù Huàláng; Map p296; www.aroundspace. gallery; 33 Middle Sichuan Rd; 四川中路33号; ⏰10.30am-6pm Tue-Sun; Ⓜ Line 2, 10 to East Nanjing Rd) **FREE** Like several other gallery buildings in the area, the 1932 art deco building housing AroundSpace was formerly a Chinese bank. Its classy gallery space holds several exhibitions concurrently, specialising in emerging and established Chinese contemporary artists.

PearlLam Galleries (珍珠林画廊, Zhēnzhū Lín Huàláng; Map p296; www.pearllam.com; 181 Middle Jiangxi Rd; 中间江西路181号; ⏰10.30am-7pm; Ⓜ Line 2, 10 to East Nanjing Rd) **FREE** The Shànghǎi branch of this international contemporary gallery is set up in an old bank dating from 1936. With a mix of Chinese and international abstract artists, it's definitely worth popping in to see what's showing. There's also another exhibition space in the somewhat creepy basement.

Shànghǎi Gallery of Art (外滩三号沪申画廊, Wàitān Sānhào Hùshēn Huàláng; Map p296; www.shanghaigalleryofart.com; 3rd fl, Three on the Bund, 3 East Zhongshan No1 Rd; 中山东一路三号三楼; ⏰10am-7pm; Ⓜ Line 2, 10 to East Nanjing Rd) **FREE** Take the lift up to the 3rd floor of Three on the Bund to this neat, minimalist art gallery showcasing current highbrow and conceptual Chinese art. It's all bare concrete pillars, ventilation ducts and acres of wall space; there are a couple of divans on which you can sit and admire the works on view.

Art + Shanghai (艺术 + 上海, Yìshù + Shànghǎi; Map p296; ☑021 6333 7223; www.art plusshanghai.com; 191 South Suzhou Rd; 苏州南路191号; ⏰10am-7pm Tue-Sun; Ⓜ Line 2, 10 to East Nanjing Rd) **FREE** This riverside gallery showcases mainly local artists and offers a good insight into the state of the Chinese art scene.

BUND SIGHTSEEING TUNNEL　　TUNNEL
Map p296 (外滩观光隧道, Wàitān Guānguāng Suìdào; 300 East Zhongshan No 1 Rd; 中山东一路300号; one way/return ¥50/70; ⏰8am-10pm; Ⓜ Line 2, 10 to East Nanjing Rd) A 647m voyage with entertainment including budget effects, garish lighting and dreadful props, the Bund Sightseeing Tunnel is a transport mode guaranteed to get you to Pǔdōng in an altered state. Stepping from the trains at the terminus, visitors are visibly nonplussed, their disbelief surpassed only by those with return tickets. Departures are every 15 minutes; the ride takes five minutes.

For those not wanting to endure such kitsch, take the public ferry, which costs a fraction of the price and from which you can enjoy the views.

⦿ People's Square

MOORE MEMORIAL CHURCH　　CHURCH
Map p296 (摩尔纪念教堂, Mó'ěr Jìniàn Jiàotáng; 316 Middle Xizang Rd; 316 中间西藏路; Ⓜ Line 1, 2, 8 to People's Square, exit 14) Designed by notable Hungarian architect Ladislaus Hudec, the Moore Memorial Church (c 1931) is a standout red-brick Christian edifice east of People's Square. During WWII it was used as a headquarters of the Japanese military police. During the Cultural Revolution it

became a high school, before reverting to a church in 1979. It's only open to the public for Sunday worship.

SHÀNGHǍI MUSEUM MUSEUM
See p61.

SHÀNGHǍI URBAN PLANNING EXHIBITION HALL MUSEUM

Map p296 (上海城市规划展示馆, Shànghǎi Chéngshì Guīhuà Zhǎnshìguǎn; www.supec.org; 100 Renmin Ave, entrance on Middle Xizang Rd; 人民大道100号; adult/child ¥30/15; ◷9am-5pm Tue-Sun, last entry 4pm; ⓂLine 1, 2, 8 to People's Square, exit 2) Set over five levels, this modern museum covers Shànghǎi's urban planning history, tracing its development from swampy fishing village to modern-day megacity. Its mix of photography, models, and interactive multimedia displays keeps things entertaining. The 1st floor covers the city's rise, including the establishment of the international settlement, and profiles its colonial architecture and *shíkùmén* (stone gate) housing. The most popular feature is on the 3rd floor – a visually stunning model showing a detailed layout of this megalopolis-to-be, plus an impressive Virtual World 3D wraparound tour.

The 4th floor is a bit more niche, covering themes of transport and sustainability, but all is well presented. There's a small

---

SHÀNGHǍI MARRIAGE MARKET

Despite the rise in popularity of online dating sites around the world, in People's Park locals prefer a more traditional – albeit unconventional – matchmaking approach. From around midday each Sunday (and some Saturdays), elderly parents convene on behalf of their unmarried children to help find them a life partner – often without the knowledge of the child themselves! Wandering the park you'll encounter large gatherings of hopeful parents sitting in rows with opened umbrellas. On closer inspection each is pinned with an attachment stating their child's age, height, weight, zodiac sign, career details and, occasionally, photos, among other stats for the perspective suitor's parents to inspect. Tourists are welcome to wander through, however it's best to respect their privacy by not taking close-range photography.

---

cafe on the 5th floor overlooking People's Park. Audio guides are ¥20, but exhibits are generally well-captioned. The 2nd floor shows temporary exhibits.

Upon exiting you'll find yourself in 'Old Shanghai Street', a re-creation of 1930s Shànghǎi, complete with vintage cars, historical photographs and a cobble-stone walkway that leads to a modern underground shopping plaza.

SHÀNGHǍI MUSEUM OF CONTEMPORARY ART MUSEUM

Map p296 (上海当代艺术馆, Shànghǎi Dāngdài Yishùguǎn, MOCA Shànghǎi; www.mocashanghai.org; People's Park; 人民公园; adult/student ¥50/25; ◷10am-6pm; ⓂLine 1, 2, 8 to People's Square) Nonprofit MOCA has an all-glass home to maximise natural sunlight (when it cuts through the clouds), a tip-top location in People's Park and a fresh, invigorating approach to exhibiting contemporary art. Exhibits are temporary only; check the website to see what's on. On the top floor there's a light-filled restaurant and bar with a terrace; there's a ¥20 discount for ticket holders.

PEOPLE'S PARK PARK

Map p296 (人民公园, Rénmín Gōngyuán; ◷6am-6pm, to 7pm Jul-Sep; ⓂLine 1, 2, 8 to People's Square) Occupying the site of the colonial racetrack (which became a holding camp during WWII), People's Park is a green refuge from Shànghǎi's fume-ridden roads. It's home to the Shànghǎi Museum of Contemporary Art, pond-side bar Barbarossa (p75), and a small children's fairground, and is overlooked by the towering form of Tomorrow Square, the old British racecourse club building and the art deco classic Park Hotel. It's the site of the Shànghǎi marriage market.

TOMORROW SQUARE NOTABLE BUILDING

Map p296 (明天广场, Míngtiān Guǎngchǎng; 399 West Nanjing Rd; 南京西路399号; ⓂLine 1, 2, 8 to People's Square) This stupendous tower seizes the Shànghǎi zeitgeist with dramatic aplomb. Resembling a sci-fi corporation headquarters, the stratospheric building is given further lift by the stylistic awkwardness of nearby rivals. The foyer of the JW Marriott Tomorrow Square hotel debuts on the 38th floor – pop up to put People's Square in proper perspective.

PARK HOTEL HISTORIC BUILDING

Map p296 (国际饭店, Guójì Fàndiàn; www.theparkhotelshanghai.com; 170 West Nanjing Rd; 南京

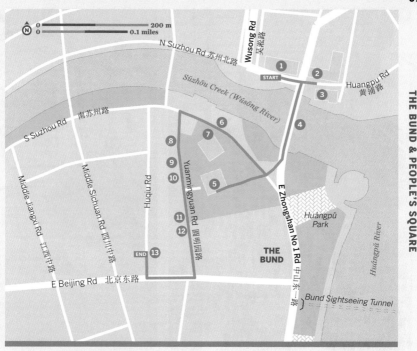

🏃 Neighbourhood Walk
The North Bund

START BROADWAY MANSIONS
END ROCKBUND ART MUSEUM
LENGTH 800M; 45 MINUTES

Begin in Hóngkǒu, where the American Settlement was established in 1848. First stop, the 1934 Orwellian brick pile ❶ **Broadway Mansions** (p162), originally an apartment block that later became a favourite with military officers and journalists for its commanding views over the harbour. The Japanese occupied the building from 1937 until the end of WWII. Not far away is ❷ **Astor House Hotel** (p213), opened in 1846. It was Shànghǎi's most prestigious hotel until the completion of the Cathay in 1929, and from 1990 to 1998 its Peacock Ballroom found new employment as the Shànghǎi Stock Exchange. Across the street is the original ❸ **Russian Consulate** (p263), still in use today. Head south over ❹ **Wàibáidù Bridge** (1906), the first steel bridge in China, over which trams used to glide.

Cross the street to the grounds of the ❺ **former British Consulate** (p64), built in 1873. The original building (1852) was one

of the first foreign buildings in Shànghǎi but went up in an 1870 conflagration. Continue west past the ❻ **former Shànghǎi Rowing Club** (1905) – note the old filled-in swimming pool next door, with grass in the lanes – and ❼ **former Union Church** (1886) to reach lavishly restored Yuanmingyuan Rd. This street was once home to several godowns – buildings that served as both warehouses and office space. These buildings were shared by traders and missionaries, such as the ❽ **China Baptist Publication Society**, whose Gotham-esque offices at No 187 (1932) were designed by the prolific Ladislaus Hudec.

Further along is the Italian Renaissance ❾ **Lyceum Building** (1927), the multi-denominational ❿ **Associate Mission Building** (1924; No 169); the ornate deco brick-and-stone ⓫ **YWCA Building** (1932; No 133); and the red-brick ⓬ **Yuanmingyuan Apartments** (No 115). Turn right onto East Beijing Rd, and right again on Huqiu Rd to end the tour at the Royal Asiatic Society Building (1933). Once Shànghǎi's first museum, it now houses the ⓭ **Rockbund Art Museum** (p64).

1. East Nanjing Road (p64)
Shànghǎi's famous pedestrianised shopping strip continues to draw huge crowds.

2. The Bund (p56)
The Bund Bull by Arturo Di Modica is a feature piece along the city's waterfront promenade.

3. Shànghǎi Museum (p61)
One of the world's premier repositories of Chinese art, this museum celebrates one masterpiece after another.

4. Pǔdōng Skyline (p242)
Bars and restaurants along the Bund offer stunning views of Pǔdōng's skyscraper architecture.

西路170号; Ｍ Line 1, 2, 8 to People's Square, exit 8)
Designed by Hungarian architect Ladislaus
Hudec and erected as a bank in 1934, the
Park Hotel was Shànghǎi's tallest building until the 1980s, when shoulder-padded
architects first started squinting hopefully
in the direction of Pǔdōng. Back in the days
when building height had a different meaning, it was said your hat would fall off if you
looked at the roof.

GREAT WORLD ARCHITECTURE

Map p296 (大世界, Dà Shìjiè; cnr East Yan'an &
Middle Xizang Rds; 延安东路西藏中路的路口;
Ｍ Line 1, 2, 8 to People's Square) At the corner
of East Yan'an Rd and Middle Xizang Rd
stands the building of the former Great
World, a place for acrobats and nightlife
stars that was opened in 1917 to rival the
existing New World on Nanjing Rd. In the
1930s it was taken over by the gangster
Pockmarked Huang and became a six-floor
house of ill-repute before its eventual reha-
bilitation under the communists during the
Mao years.

EATING

**A Bund address is the crown jewels in
Shànghǎi, luring international superchefs and hotel restaurants vying for
mainland China's first Michelin star.
While the settings are often spectacular
and the views are knockout, there's less
diversity and charm here than in the
French Concession. Many local eateries
are in malls or designated food streets;
try Huanghe Rd or Yunnan Rd for an old-
school Shànghǎi atmosphere.**

✕ The Bund

★ YÚXÌN CHUĀNCÀI SICHUAN $

Map p296 (渝信川菜, Yú Xìn Chuāncài; ☑ 021 6361
1777; 5th fl, Huasheng Tower, 399 Jiujiang Rd; 九江
路399号华盛大厦5楼; dishes ¥20-98; ⊙ 11am-
2.30pm & 5-9.30pm; ☎; Ｍ Line 2, 10 to East Nanjing Rd) At the top of Shànghǎi's best Sìchuān
restaurants, Yúxìn is a dab hand in the art of
blistering chillies and numbing peppercorns.
All-stars include the 'mouth-watering chick-
en' starter (口水鸡; *kǒushuǐ jī*), or opt for the
simply smoking spicy chicken (辣子鸡; *làzi
jī*), the crispy camphor tea duck (half/whole
¥38/68) or catfish in chilli oil.

SHÀNGHǍI GRANDMOTHER SHANGHAI $

Map p296 (上海姥姥, Shànghǎi Lǎolao; ☑ 021
6321 6613; 70 Fuzhou Rd; 福州路70号; dishes
¥25-150; ⊙ 10.30am-9.30pm; Ｍ Line 2,10 to East
Nanjing Rd) This packed eatery is within
easy striking distance of the Bund and
cooks up all manner of home-style dishes.
You can't go wrong with the classics here:
braised aubergine in soya sauce, Grandmother's braised pork, crispy duck, three-
cup chicken and *mápó dòufu* (麻婆豆腐;
tofu and pork crumbs in a spicy sauce)
rarely disappoint.

DINING PLUS CAFE $

Map p296 (就餐者优先, Jiùcān Zhě Yōuxiān; 166
Middle Sichuan Rd, cnr Fuzhou Rd; 四川中路166
号在福州路的路口; dishes from ¥52; ⊙ 8am-
10pm Mon-Fri, 9am-10pm Sat & Sun; Ｍ Line 2,
10 to East Nanjing Rd) This stylish open-plan
cafe is a perfect place to take a break from
sightseeing along the Bund. The menu is
comprised of Western fare such as burgers,
pasta dishes and wraps (including smoked
duck fajitas). The real highlight, however, is
the rooftop deck with outlooks over heritage buildings; a great place for a coffee or
reasonably priced draught beer. It also does
a contemporary-style high tea, costing ¥128
for two people.

NÁNXIÁNG STEAMED BUN RESTAURANT DUMPLING $

Map p296 (南翔馒头店, Nánxiáng Mántou Diàn;
3rd fl, Shànghǎi No 1 Food Store, 720 East Nanjing Rd; 南京东路720号上海市第一食品商
店3楼; 8 dumplings from ¥18; ⊙ 9.30am-9pm;
Ｍ Line 1, 2, 8 to People's Square, exit 19; Line 2, 10
to East Nanjing Rd) The purveyors of some of
Shànghǎi's best-loved dumplings have several branches around town, and this is one
of the less crowded.

TOCK'S MONTREAL DELI CANADIAN $

Map p296 (www.facebook.com/TocksMontreal
Deli; 221 Middle Henan Rd; 河南中路221号;
mains from ¥45; ⊙ 11am-11pm; Ｍ Line 2, 10 to
East Nanjing Rd) Unsurprisingly, this is the
sole place in town serving Montreal-style
smoked meat, but Shànghǎi could sorely do
with more of them. The meat – spiced and
cured Australian beef, slow-smoked locally
– is gorgeously tender and each sandwich
comes with homemade fries, coleslaw and
a pickle. Canadian Moosehead lager and organic coffee is at hand for lubrication. Pou-
tine is also on the menu for ¥45.

SALON DE THÉ JOËL ROBUCHON   BAKERY $

Map p296 (卢布松茶室, Qiáo Lúbù Sōng Cháshì; www.joelrobuchon-china.com; Bund 18, 18 Zhongshan Rd; 中山东一路18号; sandwiches from ¥25, high tea 1-/2-persons ¥328/522; ⊘10am-9pm; Ⓜ Line 2, 10 to East Nanjing Rd) This reasonably priced patisserie by celebrity French-chef Joël Robuchon opened alongside Atelier (p72) in 2016. Grab tongs and a tray, and peruse the pleasing array of baguettes and salted butter brioches, then move on to the glass display of glistening èclairs, cakes and macarons. Grab a sandwich to go, or find a table in the elegant tea room in the lobby, where a French-influenced high tea is served.

★**LOST HEAVEN**   YUNNAN $$

Map p296 (花马天堂, Huāmǎ Tiāntáng; ☑021 6330 0967; www.lostheaven.com.cn; 17 East Yan'an Rd; 延安东路17号; dishes ¥50-160; ⊘11.30am-3pm & 5.30-10.30pm; Ⓜ Line 2, 10 to East Nanjing Rd) Lost Heaven might not have the views that keep its rivals in business, but why go to the same old Western restaurants when you can get sophisticated Bai, Dai and Miao folk cuisine from China's mighty southwest? Specialities are flowers (banana and pomegranate), wild mushrooms, chillies, Burmese curries, Bai chicken and superb *pǔ'ěr* teas, all served up in gorgeous Yúnnán-meets-Shànghǎi surrounds. The rooftop bar and lounge is a popular spot for a drink.

MERCATO   ITALIAN $$

Map p296 (市场, Shìchǎng; ☑021 6321 9922; www.jean-georges.com; 6th fl, Three on the Bund, 3 East Zhongshan No 1 Rd; 中山东一路3号6楼; mains ¥80-228; ⊘5.30-11pm; ☎; Ⓜ Line 2, 10 to East Nanjing Rd) Chef Jean-Georges Vongerichten's celebrated Italian restaurant has a stunning location by the Bund and a stylishly relaxed modern-rustic setting designed by Neri & Hu. The menu is based around shared plates, as well as affordable, generic tasting, wood-fired pizzas. Reserve ahead, especially for a window table. Go the complimentary tap water over exorbitantly priced bottled varieties.

★**LIGHT & SALT**   INTERNATIONAL $$$

Map p296 (光与盐, Guāng Yǔ Yán; ☑021 6361 1086; www.light-n-salt.com; 6th Fl YMCA Bldg, 133 Yuanmingyuan Rd; 圆明园路133号6楼; mains ¥167-330; set lunch 2-/3-course ¥158/188; ⊘noon-2.30pm & 6-10.30pm Mon-Fri, 11.30am-4pm & 6-10.30pm Sat & Sun; Ⓜ Line 2, 10 to East Nanjing Rd) In the elegant art deco former YMCA building, this classy yet casual restaurant is divided into different sections to suit many moods. Diners will appreciate smart leather booths, dining tables and an outdoor terrace with brilliant Bund views from which you can enjoy contemporary European-influenced mains. If you're needing a drink, check out quality cocktails at its speakeasy-style Library Distillery, or enjoy a coffee in the plant-filled cafe stocked with art and design books.

★**ULTRAVIOLET**   GASTRONOMY $$$

(紫外线, Zǐwàixiàn; www.uvbypp.cc; dinner from ¥5000; ⊘dinner Tue-Sat; Ⓜ Line 2, 10 to East Nanjing Rd) You've probably paired food and wine before, but what about coupling an illuminated apple-wasabi communion wafer

---

PEOPLE'S SQUARE FOOD STREETS

These streets are lined with an amazing variety of Chinese restaurants, each with its own speciality.

Huanghe Road Food Street (黄河路美食街, Huánghé Lù Měishí Jiē; Map p296; Ⓜ Line 1, 2, 8 to People's Square) With a prime central location near People's Park, Huanghe Rd covers all the bases from cheap lunches to late-night post-theatre snacks. You'll find large restaurants, but Huanghe Rd is best for dumplings – get 'em fried at Yang's (p73) or served up in bamboo steamers across the road at Jiājiā Soup Dumplings (p73).

Yunnan Road Food Street (云南路美食街, Yúnnán Lù Měishí Jiē; Map p296; Ⓜ Line 1, 2, 8 to People's Square; Line 8 to Dashijie) Yunnan Rd has some great speciality restaurants and is just the spot for an authentic meal after museum-hopping at People's Square. Look out for Shaanxi dumplings and noodles at No 15 and five-fragrance dim sum at **Wǔ Fāng Zhāi** (五芳斋; Map p296; 28 Yunnan South Rd; 云南南路28号; dumplings from ¥12; ⊘7am-10pm). You can also get *yán shuǐ yā* (salted duck; 盐水鸭) and steamed dumplings at **Xiǎo Jīn Líng** (小金陵; Map p296; 55 Yunnan South Rd; 云南南路55号; dumplings from ¥8; ⊘8am-9pm), plus Mongolian hotpot and Yunnanese.

IDENTITY & THE SHÀNGHǍI DIALECT

Older Shanghainese are highly conscious of the disappearance of the Shànghǎi dialect (Shànghǎihuà), under assault from the increased promotion of the Mandarin (Pǔtōnghuà) dialect and the flood of immigrant tongues. It's a deeply tribal element of Shànghǎi culture and heritage, so the vanishing of the dialect equals a loss of identity. Fewer and fewer young Shanghainese and children are now able to speak the pure form of the dialect; or can understand it only and prefer to speak Mandarin. Youngsters might not care, but older Shanghainese agonise over the tongue's slow extinction. The most perfectly preserved forms of Shànghǎihuà survive in rural areas around Shànghǎi, where Mandarin has less of a toehold. The Shanghainese may remind themselves of the Chinese idiom – *jiùde bù qù, xīnde bù lái* (旧的不去新的不来; 'If the old doesn't go, the new doesn't arrive') – but it may offer scant consolation.

with purple candles and a specially designed cathedral scent? Welcome to China's most conceptual dining experience. The evening's diners gather first at Mr & Mrs Bund for an aperitif before they're whisked away to a secret location.

The meal consists of 20 courses – each accompanied by a different sensory mood (sounds, scents and images). This is Paul Pairet's masterpiece, years in the making. Revolving around his signature mischievous creations, a dinner here is bound to be unlike anything you've ever experienced before.

Reservations must be made online; book months in advance.

★ MR & MRS BUND FRENCH $$$

Map p296 (先生及夫人外滩; Xiānshēng Jí Fūrén Wàitān; ☑021 6323 9898; www.mmbund.com; 6th fl, Bund 18, 18 East Zhongshan No 1 Rd; 中山东一路18号6楼; mains ¥160-800, 2-/3-course set lunch ¥200/250; ⊗11.30am-2pm Mon-Fri, 6-10.30pm Sun & Mon, 6pm-2am Tue-Sat; Ⓜ Line 2, 10 to East Nanjing Rd) French chef Paul Pairet's casual eatery aims for a space that's considerably more playful than your average fine-dining Bund restaurant. The mix-and-match menu has a heavy French bistro influence, reimagined and served up with Pairet's ingenious presentation. But it's not just the food you're here for: it's the post-midnight menu deal (two-/three-course meals ¥250/300), the bingo nights and the wonderfully wonky atmosphere. Ring the doorbell for entry.

Brunch (from 11am to 2.30pm on weekends) is another reason to visit, with jugs of Pimm's for ¥150.

★ M ON THE BUND EUROPEAN $$$

Map p296 (米氏西餐厅; Mǐshì Xīcāntīng; ☑021 6350 9988; www.m-restaurantgroup.com/mbund/home.html; 7th fl, 20 Guangdong Rd; 广东路20号7楼; mains ¥200-400, 2-course set lunch ¥188, weekend brunch 2-/3-courses ¥268/298; ⊗11.30am-2.30pm & 6-10.30pm; Ⓜ Line 2, 10 to East Nanjing Rd) M exudes a timelessness and level of sophistication that eclipses the razzle-dazzle of many other upscale Shànghǎi restaurants. The menu ain't radical, but that's the question it seems to ask you – is breaking new culinary ground really so crucial? Crispy suckling pig and tagine with saffron are, after all, simply delicious just the way they are.

The art deco dining room and 7th-floor terrace overlooking the Bund are equally gorgeous. It's also a heavenly spot for afternoon tea (from ¥88 to ¥138). Make reservations well in advance.

ATELIER DE JOËL ROBUCHON FRENCH $$$

Map p296 (☑021 6071 8888; www.joelrobuchon-china.com; Bund 18, 3rd fl, 18 East Zhongshan No 1 Rd; 中山东一路18号3楼; dishes from ¥300; ⊗5.30pm-11pm daily, 11.30-2pm Sat & Sun; ❋☏; Ⓜ Line 2, 10 to East Nanjing Rd) If Bund 18 wasn't already epicurean enough, the arrival of Michelin-starred, French chef Joël Robuchon's new restaurant confirms it so. Much the same as in his other luxury restaurants, this is definitely the place to treat yourself to classic French fare, heavy on butter and foie gras. The decor is dark hues of red and black, and is centred by Asia's supposedly largest teppanyaki bar.

NO 1 WAITANYUAN DESSERTS $$$

Map p296 (外滩源一号, Wàitān Yuán Yī Hào; ☑021 5308 9803; www.wtysh.com; 33 East Zhongshan No 1 Rd; h中山东一路33号; platter for 2 persons ¥288; ⊗high tea 2-5pm; Ⓜ Line 2, 10 to East Nanjing Rd) Nowhere's more fitting for a spot of high tea than the former British Consulate (p64). Enjoy cucumber sandwiches, scones and English breakfast tea overlooking the magnificent gardens with a Pǔdōng skyline backdrop. The three-tiered platters are loaded with gourmet cakes and finger sandwiches, served with antique silver cutlery and teapots. Reserve a day or two in advance to get a garden table.

Afterwards stroll the gardens to admire the architecture. Waitanyuan, an exclusive club, is also a restaurant that serves dim sum for lunch.

JEAN GEORGES FUSION $$$
Map p296 (法国餐厅, Fǎguó Cāntīng; ☑021 6321 7733; www.threeonthebund.com; 4th fl, Three on the Bund, 3 East Zhongshan No 1 Rd; 中山东一路3号4楼; lunch/dinner ¥298/698; ◷11.30am-2.30pm & 6-10.30pm; ☎; ⓂLine 2, 10 to East Nanjing Rd) Pitched somewhere between Gotham City and new Shànghǎi is the reboot of Jean-Georges Vongerichten's dimly lit, copper-appliquéd temple to gastronomy. The refurbished digs have been decked out by acclaimed designers Neri & Hu, yet the menu retains its classic French-Asian fusion dishes.

The same building houses Jean-George's Italian restaurant Mercato (p71), and CHi-Q modern Korean on the 2nd floor.

8½ OTTO E MEZZO BOMBANA ITALIAN $$$
Map p296 (☑021 6087 2890; www.ottoemezzobombana.com/shanghai; 6-7th fl 169 Yuanmingyuan Rd; 圆明园路169号6—7楼; mains ¥228-418, degustation menu ¥2000; ◷6-11pm; ⓂLine 2, 10 to East Nanjing Rd) Following Umberto Bombana's success in Hong Kong with the only three-star Michelin Italian restaurant outside Italy, he's now opened up in Shànghǎi. Homemade pastas are the standout, including a seafood cannelloni filled with a mix of blue lobster, snow crab and sea urchin. Housed in a 1920s heritage building overlooking the Bund, Otto features an outdoor terrace from which to enjoy the view. Reservations recommended.

HAKKASAN CANTONESE $$$
Map p296 (客家人, Kèjiā Rén; ☑021 6321 5888; www.hakkasan.com; 6th fl, Bund 18, 18 East Zhongshan No 1 Rd; 中山东一路18号5楼; mains ¥120-300; ◷5.30-11pm daily, 11am-3pm Fri-Sun; ⓂLine 2, 10 to East Nanjing Rd) The opening of the Shànghǎi branch of this acclaimed Cantonese restaurant sees the Bund add another culinary star to its belt. A former Michelin-star winning restaurant, it's all about high-end Chinese dim sum (such as jasmine-tea smoked pork ribs) and mains such as truffle roast duck. The decor is

dark with heavy woods, seductive lighting and intricate Chinese partitions – though it doesn't capitalise on its Bund views.

LOBBY, PENINSULA HOTEL BRITISH $$$
Map p296 (上海半岛酒店, Shànghǎi Bàndǎo Jiǔdiàn; http://shanghai.peninsula.com; 32 East Zhongshan No 1 Rd; 中山东一路32号; 1/2 persons ¥368/667; ◷2-6pm; ⓂLine 2, 10 to East Nanjing Rd) Afternoon heritage tea for visitors in smart-casual attire in the sumptuous Peninsula lobby is a decadent delight, with gorgeously presented scones, macaroons, clotted cream, jam, biscuits, tea, of course, and live piano tinklings. For ¥585, a glass of champers is thrown in.

People's Square

★YANG'S FRY DUMPLINGS DUMPLINGS $
Map p296 (小杨生煎馆, Xiǎoyáng Shēngjiān Guǎn; 97 Huanghe Rd; 黄河路97号; dumplings from ¥8; ◷6.30am-8.30pm; ⓂLine 1, 2, 8 to People's Square) The city's most famous place for sesame-seed-and-scallion-coated *shēngjiān* (生煎; fried dumplings) gets nil points for decor or service, but queues can stretch to the horizon as eager diners wait for scalding *shēngjiān* to be dished into mustard-coloured bowls. Watch out for boiling meat juices that unexpectedly jet down your shirt (and your neighbour's). Per *liǎng* (两; four dumplings) ¥8.

★JIĀJIĀ SOUP DUMPLINGS DUMPLING $
Map p296 (佳家汤包, Jiājiā Tāngbāo; 90 Huanghe Rd; 黄河路90号; 12 dumplings ¥25; ◷7am-10pm; ⓂLines 1, 2, 8) A fixture on Huanghe Road Food Street, this humble tiled restaurant is a real contender for one of Shànghǎi's best dumpling places, with juicy pork and crab *xiǎolóngbāo* served up in bamboo steamers. Expect a queue and to share a table.

ROOF 325 EUROPEAN $$
Map p296 (屋顶325, Wūdǐng 325; ☑021 6327 0767; www.roof325.com; 5th fl, 325 West Nanjing Rd; 南京西路325号原上海美术馆5楼; lunch from ¥105, dinner ¥165-455; ◷11am-12.30am; ⓂLine 1, 2, 8 to People's Square, exit 11) The former Shànghǎi Race Club building, and then the Shànghǎi Art Museum, today this grand colonial bluestone building is home to a rooftop restaurant-bar with splendid views overlooking People's Park. The menu is decent, with wagyu sirloin steaks and spicy seafood stew, but it's more about the

view and setting. It's a good spot for a sunset cocktail or high tea – served from 2.30pm to 5pm.

WÁNG BǍOHÉ JIǓJIĀ
SHANGHAI $$$

Map p296 (王宝和酒家; ☑021 6322 3673; 603 Fuzhou Rd; 福州路603号; dishes ¥22-200, set menu ¥450-800; ⊙11am-1.30pm & 5-9pm; MLine 1, 2, 8 to People's Square) More than 250 years old, this restaurant claims a fame that rests on its extravagant selection of crab dishes; its popularity reaches an apex during hairy-crab season (October to December). Most diners opt for one of the all-crabs-must-die banquets, but if you're new to hairy crab, you might want to give it a try elsewhere before 'shelling out' for an eight-course meal. Reserve.

🍷 DRINKING & NIGHTLIFE

🍷 The Bund

⭐ GLAM
LOUNGE

Map p296 (魅力, Mèilì; 7th fl, 20 Guangdong Rd; 广东路20号7楼; cocktails ¥80-100; ⊙5pm-late; MLine 2, 10 to East Nanjing Rd) The decor here is decidedly bohemian – full of art and curiosities – and its cool retro feel makes it one of the Bund's most atmospheric spots for a drink. Cocktail prices are accessible, as is the bar menu, ranging from truffle cheese toasties to soft-serve ice cream.

⭐ LONG BAR
BAR

Map p296 (廊吧, Láng Bā; ☑021 6322 9988; 2 East Zhongshan No 1 Rd; 中山东一路2号; drinks from ¥70; ⊙4pm-1am Mon-Sat, 2pm-1am Sun; 🛜; MLine 2, 10 to East Nanjing Rd) For a taste of colonial-era Shànghǎi's elitist trappings, you'll do no better than the Long Bar. This was once the members-only Shànghǎi Club, whose most spectacular accoutrement was a 34m-long wooden bar. Foreign businessmen would sit here according to rank, comparing fortunes, with the taipans (foreign heads of business) closest to the view of the Bund.

Now part of the Waldorf Astoria, the bar's original wood-panelled decor has been painstakingly re-created from old photographs. There's a good selection of old-fashioned cocktails as well as an oyster bar (and jazz, naturally).

M1NT
CLUB

Map p296 (☑021 6391 2811; www.m1ntglobal. com; 24th fl, Cross Tower, 318 Fuzhou Rd; 福州路318号24楼; ⊙9.30pm-late Wed-Sat; MLine 2, 10 to East Nanjing Rd) Exclusive penthouse-style club with knockout city views and snazzy fusion food but not a lot of dance space. Dress to impress or you'll get thrown into the shark tank. No sports shoes etc.

POP
BAR

Map p296 (流行音乐, Liúxíng Yīnyuè; ☑021 6321 0909; www.threeonthebund.com; 7th fl, Three on the Bund, 3 East Zhongshan No 1 Rd; 中山东一路3号7楼; ⊙11am-late; MLine 2, 10 to East Nanjing Rd) On the top floor of Three on the Bund, Pop's splendid roof terrace is divided into multiple entities, all with choice views of Pǔdōng's hypnotising neon performance. There's always a crowd, whether they're here for the Miami art deco–themed cocktail bar or the Louisiana-style Whisper bar, specialising in American rye whiskeys and bourbon. There's also a stylish restaurant that channels a retro New York brassiere.

SHOOK!
BAR

Map p296 (6th fl, Bund 18, 23 East Zhongshan No 1 Rd; 中山东一路23号5楼; ⊙5pm-late; MLine 2, 10 to East Nanjing Rd) Sure, it's not quite as fashionable (or pretentious) as its neighbours, but that's not necessarily a bad thing: the views from Shook!'s rooftop are just as good, and it's a more laid-back spot to enjoy a slice of Shànghǎi's famed glamour without breaking the bank. Aim for happy hour (5.30pm to 7pm) for ¥50 cocktails.

SIR ELLY'S TERRACE
BAR

Map p296 (艾利爵士露台, Àilì Juéshì Lùtái; 14th fl, Peninsula Shanghai, 32 East No 1 Zhongshan Rd; 中山东一路32号半岛酒店14楼; cocktails ¥120; ⊙6pm-midnight Sun-Thu, to 1am Fri & Sat; 🛜; MLine 2, 10 to East Nanjing Rd) Offering some of Shànghǎi's best cocktails, shaken up with that winning ingredient: 270-degree views to Pǔdōng, over Sūzhōu Creek and down the Bund. Of course it's not cheap, but the views are priceless. The rooftop terrace opens from April to December.

BAR ROUGE
BAR

Map p296 (Rouge酒吧, Rouge Jiǔbā; ☑021 6339 1199; www.bar-rouge-shanghai.com; 7th fl, Bund 18, 18 East Zhongshan No 1 Rd; 中山东一路18号7楼; cover charge after 10pm Wed-Sat ¥100; ⊙6pm-late; MLine 2, 10 to East Nanjing Rd) Bar Rouge attracts a cashed-up party crowd

NO DOGS OR CHINESE

A notorious sign at Huángpǔ Park (p56), then called the Public Gardens, apocryphally declared 'No dogs or Chinese allowed'. Although this widely promoted notice never actually existed, the general gist of the wording hits the mark. A series of regulations was indeed posted outside the gardens listing 10 rules governing use of the park.

The first regulation noted that 'The gardens are for the use of the foreign community,' while the fourth ruled that 'Dogs and bicycles are not admitted.' Chinese were barred from the park (as expressed in the first regulation), an injustice that gave rise to the canard.

The bluntly worded sign has, however, become firmly embedded in the Chinese consciousness. Bruce Lee destroys a Shànghǎi park sign declaring 'No dogs and Chinese allowed' with a flying kick in *Fist of Fury* and Chinese history books cite the insult as further evidence of Chinese humiliation at the hands of foreigners. For a thorough academic examination of the subject, hunt down *Shanghai's 'Dogs and Chinese not Admitted' Sign: Legend, History and Contemporary Symbol* by Robert A Bickers and Jeffrey N Wasserstrom, published in the *China Quarterly*, No 142 (June 1995).

who come for the fantastic views from the rooftop terrace and the all-night DJ parties. The lipstick-red decor is slick and the crowd slicker, so ordinary mortals can sometimes struggle to get served on busy nights.

🍷 People's Square

★BARBAROSSA
BAR

Map p296 (芭芭露莎会所, Bābālùshā Huìsuǒ; www.barbarossa.com.cn; People's Park, 231 West Nanjing Rd; 南京西路231号人民公园内; ⏰11am-2am; 🛜; Ⓜ Line 1, 2, 8 to People's Square, exit 11) Set back in People's Park alongside a pond, Barbarossa is all about escapism. Forget Shànghǎi, this is Morocco channelled by Hollywood set designers. The action gets steadily more intense as you ascend to the roof terrace, via the cushion-strewn 2nd floor, where the hordes puff on fruit-flavoured hookahs. At night, use the park entrance just east of the former Shànghǎi Race Club building (上海跑马总会; Shànghǎi Pǎomǎ Zǒnghuì).

Happy hour (from 2pm to 8pm) is a good time to visit for two-for-one cocktails.

☆ ENTERTAINMENT

★SHÀNGHǍI GRAND THEATRE
CLASSICAL MUSIC

Map p296 (上海大剧院, Shànghǎi Dàjùyuàn; ☏021 6386 8686; www.shgtheatre.com; 300 Renmin Ave; 人民广场人民大道300号; ⏰box office 9am-8pm; Ⓜ Line 1, 2, 8 to People's Square) Shànghǎi's state-of-the-art concert venue

hosts everything from Broadway musicals to symphonies, ballets, operas, and performances by internationally acclaimed classical soloists. There are also traditional Chinese-music performances. Pick up a schedule at the ticket office.

FAIRMONT PEACE HOTEL JAZZ BAR
JAZZ

Map p296 (爵士吧, Juéshì Bā; ☏021 6138 6883; 20 East Nanjing Rd; 南京东路20号费尔蒙和平饭店; ⏰5.30pm-2am, live music from 7pm; Ⓜ Line 2, 10 to East Nanjing Rd) Shànghǎi's most famous hotel features Shànghǎi's most famous jazz band (starts at 7pm), a septuagenarian sextet that's been churning out nostalgic covers such as 'Moon River' and 'Summertime' since the dawn of time. There's no admission fee, but you'll need to sink a drink from the bar (draught beer starts at ¥70, a White Lady is ¥98).

The original band takes the stage from 7pm to 9.45pm; to get the pulse moving, a 'sultry female vocalist' does her bit from 9.45pm.

HOUSE OF BLUES & JAZZ
LIVE MUSIC

Map p296 (布鲁斯乐爵士之屋, Bùlǔsī Yuè Juéshì Zhīwū; ☏021 6323 2779; 60 Fuzhou Rd; 福州路60号; beer from ¥70; ⏰5pm-1am Tue-Sun; Ⓜ Line 2, 10 to East Nanjing Rd) Fittingly dark and divey, this vintage jazz and blues bar exudes plenty of class with its polished heavy wood decor. The house band delivers live jazz or blues from 9.30pm (10pm on Friday and Saturday) to 1am. Sunday night is a free-for-all jam. Entry is free if you're here to eat or drink; happy hour offers half-priced beers to 8pm.

The attached restaurant is set within an atmospheric dining room with an international menu and teppanyaki bar.

SHÀNGHĂI CONCERT HALL   CLASSICAL MUSIC
Map p296 (上海音乐厅, Shànghǎi Yīnyuè Tīng; ☑021 6386 2836; www.shanghaiconcerthall. org; 523 East Yan'an Rd; 人民广场延安东路523号; tickets ¥80-480; ⓜLine 1, 2, 8 to People's Square; Line 8 to Dashijie) A decade or so ago, the government shunted all 5650 tonnes of this classic 1930s building 66m away from busy East Yan'an Rd to a quieter parkside setting. It features smaller-scale concerts plus local and international soloists.

YÌFŪ THEATRE   CHINESE OPERA
Map p296 (逸夫舞台, Yìfū Wǔtái; ☑021 6322 5294; www.tianchan.com; 701 Fuzhou Rd; 人民广场福州路701号; tickets ¥30-280; ⓜLine 1, 2, 8 to People's Square) One block east of People's Square, this is the main opera theatre in town. The theatre presents a popular program of Běijīng, Kun and Yue (Shàoxīng) opera. A Běijīng opera highlights show is performed several times a week at 1.30pm and 7.15pm; pick up a brochure at the ticket office.

🛍 SHOPPING

The Bund is all about luxury shopping, while beneath People's Square, a maze of former bomb shelters has been transformed into a downmarket shopping centre known as D-Mall. Linking the two is East Nanjing Rd, which reached its peak as the most famous shopping strip in East Asia in the 1920s. An interesting alternative route running parallel to East Nanjing Rd is energetic Fuzhou Rd (福州路), lined with rows of century-old shops selling calligraphy brushes, ink, seals and patterned paper among other art supplies. A few blocks west are several bookshops and publishing houses.

★ SHÀNGHĂI MUSEUM ART STORE   GIFTS & SOUVENIRS
Map p296 (上海博物馆艺术品商店, Shànghǎi Bówùguǎn Yìshùpǐn Shāngdiàn; 201 Renmin Ave; 人民大道201号; ⓧ9.30am-5pm; ⓜLine 1, 2, 8 to People's Square) Attached to the Shànghǎi Museum and entered from East Yan'an Rd, this shop offers a refreshing change from the usual tourist tat. Apart from the excellent range of books on Chinese art and architecture (including many Shànghǎi-centric titles), there's a good selection of quality cards, prints and slides. The annex shop sells fine imitations of some of the museum's ceramic pieces, as well as scarves and bags.

★ ANNABEL LEE   FASHION & ACCESSORIES
Map p296 (安梨家居, Ānlí Jiājū; www.annabel -lee.com; No 1, Lane 8, East Zhongshan No 1 Rd; 中山东一路8弄1号; ⓧ10am-8pm; ⓜLine 2, 10 to East Nanjing Rd) This elegant shop sells a range of soft-coloured accessories in silk, linen and cashmere, many of which feature delicate and stylish embroidery. Peruse the collection of shawls, scarves, cushion covers, table runners and purses, evening bags and nighties. They also have men's silk pyjamas.

★ SŪZHŌU COBBLERS   FASHION & ACCESSORIES
Map p296 (上海起想艺术品, Shànghǎi Qǐxiǎng Yìshùpǐn; www.suzhou-cobblers.com; Unit 101, 17 Fuzhou Rd; 福州路17号101室; ⓧ10am-6.30pm; ⓜLine 2, 10 to East Nanjing Rd) Right off the Bund, this cute boutique sells exquisite hand-embroidered silk slippers, bags, hats and clothing. Patterns and colours are based on the fashions of the 1930s, and as far as the owner, Huang 'Denise' Mengqi, is concerned, the products are one of a kind. Slippers start at ¥650 and can be made to order.

★ SHÀNGHĂI NO 1 FOOD STORE   FOOD
Map p296 (第一食品商店, Dìyī Shípǐn Shāngdiàn; 720 East Nanjing Rd; 南京东路720号; ⓧ9.30am-10pm; ⓜLine 1, 2, 8 to People's Square, exit 19; Line 2, 10 to East Nanjing) Brave the crowds to check out the amazing variety of dried meats, mushrooms, ginseng, chicken feet and sea cucumber, as well as more tempting snacks including sunflower seeds, nuts, dried fruit, moon cakes and tea. Built in 1925 and redone in 2012, this used to be Sun Sun, one of Shànghǎi's big department stores. There are restaurants on the 3rd floor.

★ BLUE SHÀNGHĂI WHITE   CERAMICS
Map p296 (海晨, Hǎi Chén; ☑021 6352 2222; www.blueshanghaiwhite.com; Unit 103, 17 Fuzhou Rd; 福州路17号103室; ⓧ10.30am-6.30pm; ⓜLine 2, 10 to East Nanjing Rd) Just off the Bund, this little boutique is a great place to browse for a contemporary take on a traditional art form. It sells a tasteful selection of hand-painted Jǐngdézhèn porcelain teacups (from ¥150), teapots and vases, dis-

played together with the shop's ingeniously designed wooden furniture.

★FOREIGN LANGUAGES BOOKSTORE
BOOKS

Map p296 (外文书店, Wàiwén Shūdiàn; www.sbt. com.cn; 390 Fuzhou Rd; 福州路390号; ⊙10am-6.30pm; Ⓜ Line 2, 10 to East Nanjing Rd) Open since the 1950s, this monumental red-brick bookshop is Shànghǎi's best for English-language fiction, nonfiction and travel guides. There's also a stellar selection of Chinese cultural, cooking and language books. Kid's literature is on the 4th floor.

RUYEE LIFE GALLERY
CLOTHING

Map p296 (Ruyee 生活画廊, Ruyee Shēnghuó Huàláng; www.ninaino.cn; No 2, Lane 8, East Zhong-shan No 1 Rd; 中山东一路8弄2号; ⊙10am-10pm; Ⓜ Line 2, 10 to East Nanjing Rd) This boutique shop specialises in garments made of cash-mere from Inner Mongolia, with oh-so very soft jumpers, gloves, beanies, rugs and acces-sories. They also sell children's wear upstairs.

SILK KING
CLOTHING

Map p296 (真丝大王, Zhēnsī Dàwáng; ☑021 6321 1869; 136 East Nanjing Rd; 南京东路136号; ⊙10am-10pm; Ⓜ Line 2, 10 to East Nanjing Rd) The city's largest fabric chain is good for a quick browse to see a typical selection of Chinese prints and fabric designs. In-house tailors can make you a custom-fit qípáo (cheongsam), shirt or jacket in three to 10 days for around ¥2000. Twenty-four-hour rush jobs are also possible.

The shop is full of photos of past visiting heads of state and their partners.

DUŎYÚNXUĀN ART SHOP
ARTS & CRAFTS

Map p296 (朵云轩, Duǒyún Xuān; ☑021 6360 6475; 422 East Nanjing Rd; 南京东路422号; ⊙ground fl 9.30am-9.30pm, other floors to 5.30pm; Ⓜ Line 2, 10 to East Nanjing Rd) A multi-storey, traditional-looking building (look for the two enormous calligraphy brushes out-side) with an excellent selection of art and calligraphy supplies. The 2nd and 3rd floors house antiques as well as excellent calligra-phy and brush-painting galleries. You can get your own chop (seal) made here.

RAFFLES CITY
MALL

Map p296 (来福士广场, Láifúshì Guǎngchǎng; ☑021 6340 3600; 268 Middle Xizang Rd; 西藏中路268号; ⊙10am-10pm; Ⓜ Line 1, 2, 8 to People's Square) This seven-floor Singapore-owned mall is the most popular shopping destina-tion by People's Square, with everything from clothes to electronics and toys. Like most Shànghǎi malls, it's also a big-time dining destination: food courts, restau-rants and juice bars occupy the basement and upper levels.

🏃 SPORTS & ACTIVITIES

HUÁNGPǓ RIVER CRUISE
CRUISE

Map p296 (黄浦江游览, Huángpǔ Jiāng Yóulǎn; 219-239 East Zhongshan No 2 Rd; 中山东二路219-239号; tickets ¥120; ⊙11am-9.30pm; Ⓜ Line 2, 10 to East Nanjing Rd) The Huángpǔ River offers intriguing views of the Bund, Pǔdōng and riverfront activity. The night cruises are arguably more scenic, though boat traf-fic during the day is more interesting. Most cruises last 50 minutes.

Departures are from the docks on the south end of the Bund (near East Jinling Rd) or, less conveniently, from the Shíliùpǔ Docks (十六铺; Shíliùpǔ), a 20-minute walk south of the Bund. Buy tickets at the departure points or from the Bund **tourist informa-tion and service centre** (旅游咨询服务中心, Lǚyóu Zīxún Fúwù Zhōngxīn; Map p296; ⊙9.30am-9.30pm; Ⓜ East Nanjing Rd), beneath the Bund Promenade and opposite the intersection with East Nanjing Rd. Departure times vary.

MORNING EXERCISES ALONG THE BUND

Early risers wandering along the Bund are rewarded with the fascinating sight of locals doing their morning exer-cises, posed against the backdrop of Pǔdōng's skyline – there are brilliant photo opportunities to be had in the morning light.

You'll see myriad offbeat ways to get the circulation flowing, with everything from groups of taichi practitioners with synchronised hand fans, to those hon-ing their sword-wielding techniques, to bunny hopping down stairs or walking backwards along the promenade.

Kite flying is also a popular pastime. It's an impressive sight as middle-aged men take control of these magnificent crafts as they soar to stunning heights.

Aim to get here around 7.30am (or earlier) as things wind up around 9am.

Old Town

Neighbourhood Top Five

1 **Yùyuán Gardens & Bazaar** (p80) Zoning out from Shànghǎi's urban modernity in these gorgeous Chinese gardens.

2 **Old Town walking tour** (p83) Delving into traditional alleys and backstreets to uncover the city's past.

3 **Old Shànghǎi Teahouse** (p90) Learning about traditional tea culture while sipping a fragrant brew.

4 **Temple of the Town God** (p82) Paying your respects to the diverse pantheon of divinities.

5 **Souvenir shopping** (p90) Picking up handmade treasures in the Old Town's markets.

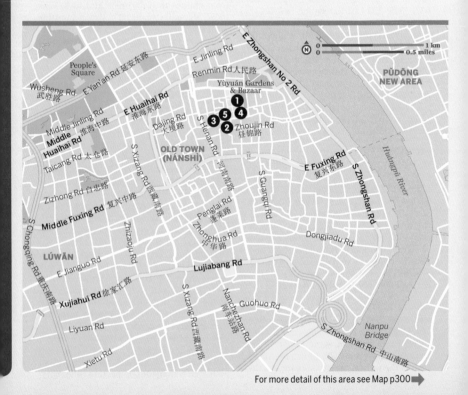

For more detail of this area see Map p300 ➡

Explore: Old Town

Known to locals as Nánshì (南市; literally 'Southern City'), the Old Town is the most traditionally Chinese area of Shànghǎi, along with Qībǎo. Long a concoction of old-fashioned textures, tatty charm and musty temples, the neighbourhood's central positioning and lucrative real estate potential have been mined by developers, squeezing out the old for the new. For glimpses of old Shànghǎi (that of the Chinese, not the foreigners), however, explore the surviving Old Town backstreets with their narrow, pinched and crowded lanes, dark alleys and overhanging laundry.

The oval layout of the Old Town follows the footprint of its old 5km-long city walls, flung up to defend against marauding Japanese pirates. The 16th-century city wall was eventually torn down in 1912, but its outline remains along Renmin and Zhonghua Rds.

Temple buffs will adore the area's modest Confucian, Taoist, Buddhist, Christian and Muslim shrines, but most visitors are here to capture the traditional Chinese charms of the Yùyuán Gardens.

East of the Old Town, the riverside Cool Docks and South Bund 22 have brought some pizzazz to formerly run-down areas, attracting a steady stream of deep-pocketed diners and drinkers to smart bars and restaurants.

Local Life

➧**Lanes** Jostle with Shànghǎi locals wandering along the pinched Old Town back lanes.

➧**Chinese medicine** Forage for the best panaceas at the Tóng Hán Chūn Traditional Medicine Store (p91).

➧**Religious devotion** Fathom the profound Buddhist mysteries of the Chénxiānggé Monastery (p82).

➧**Markets** Haggle for all you're worth over fine silks alongside the Shanghainese in the South Bund Fabric Market (p90).

Getting There & Away

➧**Metro** Line 10 runs from East Nanjing Rd to the French Concession, passing under the Old Town. The Yuyuan Garden station is close to most sights. Line 8, which runs south from People's Square to the China Art Museum, intersects with line 10 at Laoximen (near the Confucian Temple), line 9 at Lujiabang Rd and line 4 at South Xizang Rd. Line 9 runs along the Old Town's southern edge and into Pǔdōng with a station at Xiaonanmen.

➧**Bus** Route 11 circles the Old Town, following Renmin and Zhonghua Rds; bus 66 travels along Henan Rd, connecting the Old Town with East Nanjing Rd.

Lonely Planet's Top Tip

Development has called in last orders for much of Shànghǎi's Old Town. The most intriguing areas to wander are well off the main drag: the alleys north of the Confucian Temple (old roads such as Zhuangjia St) retain their old flavour, as do some of the alleys off Dajing Rd (such as Changsheng St) and the western stretch of Dongjiadu Rd.

OLD TOWN

Best Places to Eat

➧ Kebabs on the Grille (p89)
➧ Nánxiáng Steamed Bun Restaurant (p87)
➧ el Willy (p89)
➧ Table No 1 by Jason Atherton (p89)

For reviews, see p87 ➧

Best Places to Shop

➧ Old Street (p90)
➧ South Bund Fabric Market (p90)
➧ Tóng Hán Chūn Traditional Medicine Store (p91)

For reviews, see p90 ➧

TOP SIGHT
YÙYUÁN GARDENS & BAZAAR

With its shaded corridors, glittering pools churning with carp, pavilions, pines sprouting wistfully from rockeries, whispering bamboo, jasmine clumps, potted flowering plants and stony recesses, the labyrinthine Yùyuán Gardens (豫园, Yùyuán) are a delightful escape from Shànghǎi's hard-edged, glass-and-steel modernity. The attached bazaar (豫园商城, Yùyuán Shāngchéng) is a treasure trove of handicrafts, souvenirs and snacking opportunities, but brace yourself for a powerful onslaught of visitors.

The Yùyuán Gardens

The Yùyuán Gardens were founded by the Pan family, who were rich Ming dynasty officials. The gardens took 18 years (from 1559 to 1577) to be nurtured into existence, only to be ransacked during the Opium War in 1842, when British officers were barracked here, and again during the Taiping Rebellion, this time by the French in reprisal for attacks on their nearby concession.

Today the restored gardens are a fine example of Ming garden design. The gardens are small, but seem much bigger thanks to an ingenious use of rocks and alcoves. Nonetheless, they were simply never designed to accommodate the number of visitors that descend daily, so prepare for considerable disruption to the harmonious feng shui.

A handy map depicting the layout of the gardens can be found just inside the entrance. As you enter, **Three Ears of Corn Hall** (三穗堂, Sānsuìtáng) is the largest of the halls in the gardens. Its wood doors and beams are carved with images of corn, rice, millet and fruit, all symbolising a bountiful harvest. The **rockeries** (假山, jiǎshān) attempt to recreate a mountain setting within the flatland of the garden, so that when combined with

DON'T MISS

→ Hall of Heralding Spring
→ Exquisite Jade Rock
→ Shopping and snacking in the bazaar

PRACTICALITIES

→ 豫园、豫园商城, Yùyuán & Yùyuán Shāngchéng
→ Map p300, B6
→ Anren St; 安仁街
→ high/low season ¥40/30
→ ⊘8.30am-5.15pm, last entry at 4.45pm
→ Ⓜ Line 10 to Yuyuan Garden

ponds (池塘, *chítáng*) they suggest the 'hills and rivers' (*shānshuǐ*) of China's landscapes. The largest rockery in the gardens is the **Great Rockery** (大假山, Dàjiǎshān), with its huge arranged stones, ranging west of the **Chamber of Ten Thousand Flowers** (万花楼, Wànhuālóu).

In the east of the gardens, keep an eye out for the **Hall of Heralding Spring** (点春堂, Diǎnchūn Táng), which in 1853 was the headquarters of the Small Swords Society, a rebel group affiliated to the Taiping rebels. To the south, the **Exquisite Jade Rock** (玉玲珑, Yù Línglóng) was destined for the imperial court in Běijīng until the boat carrying it sank outside Shànghǎi.

South of the Exquisite Jade Rock is the **inner garden** (内园, *nèiyuán*), where you can also find the beautiful **stage** (古戏台, *gǔxìtái*) dating from 1888, with a gilded, carved ceiling and fine acoustics, as well as the charming **Hall for Watching Waves** (观涛楼, Guāntāo Lóu).

Spring and summer blossoms bring a fragrant and floral aspect to the gardens, especially in the luxurious petals of its *Magnolia grandiflora,* Shànghǎi's flower. Other trees include the luohan pine, bristling with thick needles, and willows, towering ginkgos, cherry trees and beautiful dawn redwoods.

The Bazaar

Next to the Yùyuán Gardens entrance rises the Mid-Lake Pavilion Teahouse (p90), once part of the gardens and now one of the most famous teahouses in China. The zigzag causeway is designed to thwart spirits, who can only journey in straight lines.

Surrounding all this is the restored bazaar area, where scores of speciality shops and restaurants – including the Nánxiáng Steamed Bun Restaurant (p87) – jostle over narrow laneways and small squares in a mock 'ye olde Cathay' setting. There are some choice gift-giving ideas in the souvenir shops, from painted snuff bottles to silhouette cuttings from paper and leather, delightful Chinese kites, embroidered paintings and clever palm-and-finger paintings.

At the heart of the melee, south of the Yùyuán Gardens exit (Map p300), is the venerable Temple of the Town God (p82), dedicated to the protector of the city of Shànghǎi. Any city in China with any sense of history should have a temple to their town god, and it is always located within the old quarter.

DAWN REDWOODS

Among the trees and foliage at the Yùyuán Gardens are dawn redwoods (Metasequoia), a towering and elegant fine-needled deciduous tree dating to the Jurassic period and growing up to 60m. Once considered extinct, a single example was discovered in 1941 in Sìchuān province. Three years later, a small stand of the trees was located, from which the tree was disseminated (around China and the globe).

More than a thousand visitors stream into the gardens daily, so go early; arrive at midday and you'll be wedged in the entrance with camera-toting tour groups. Weekends are also overpowering. Aim to give yourself at least an hour or two to explore the garden.

WIND & WATER

The Yùyuán Gardens are devised with the central precept of feng shui (literally 'wind water') in mind. The main gate is south-facing to maximise the *yángqì* (male, positive energy); all rockeries and ponds are deliberately arranged to maximise positive '*qì*'; and the undulating 'dragon walls' in the gardens bring good fortune.

◉ SIGHTS

That elusive sense of an olden-days Shànghǎi can be glimpsed through the sights of this neighbourhood: the temples, Yùyuán Gardens and old *shíkùmén* lanes

YÙYUÁN GARDENS & BAZAAR
GARDENS, BAZAAR

See p80.

CHÉNXIĀNGGÉ MONASTERY
BUDDHIST TEMPLE

Map p300 (沉香阁, Chénxiāng Gé; 29 Chenxiangge Rd; 沉香阁路29号; ¥10; ⊙7am-5pm; MLine 10 to Yuyuan Garden) Sheltering a community of dark-brown-clothed monks from the Chénhǎi (Sea of Dust) – what Buddhists call the mortal world, but which could equally refer to Shànghǎi's murky atmosphere – this lovely yellow-walled temple is a tranquil refuge. At the temple rear, the **Guanyin Tower** guides you upstairs to a glittering effigy of the male-looking goddess, Guanyin herself (p88), within a resplendent gilded cabinet.

Carved from *chénxiāng* wood (Chinese eaglewood) and seated in *lalitasana* posture, head tilted and with one arm resting on her leg, this version is a modern copy – the original disappeared during the Cultural Revolution.

At the front, the **Hall of Heavenly Kings** (天王殿; Tiānwáng Diàn) envelops four gilded Heavenly Kings (each belonging to a different compass point) and a slightly androgynous form of Maitreya. Muttered prayers and chanted hymns fill the **Great Treasure Hall** (大雄宝殿; Dàxióng Bǎodiàn), where a statue of Sakyamuni (Buddha) is flanked by two rows of nine *luóhàn* (arhats).

TEMPLE OF THE TOWN GOD
TAOIST TEMPLE

Map p300 (城隍庙, Chénghuáng Miào; 9 Yùyuán Bazaar, off Middle Fangbang Rd; 豫园商城方浜中路; ¥10; ⊙8.30am-4.30pm; MLine 10 to Yuyuan Garden) Chinese towns traditionally had a Taoist temple of the town god, but many fell victim to periodic upheaval. Originally dating to the early 15th century, this particular temple was badly damaged during the Cultural Revolution and later restored. Note the fine carvings on the roof as you enter the main hall, which is dedicated to Huo Guang, a Han dynasty general, flanked by rows of effigies representing both martial and civil virtues.

Exit the hall north and peek into the multi-faith hall on your right, which is dedicated to three female deities: Guanyin (Buddhist), Tianhou and Yanmu Niangniang (Taoist). Gazing fiercely over offerings of fruit from the rear Chengghuang Hall is the red-faced and bearded town god himself. Also note the Tàisuì Hall where worshippers pay respects to divine figures representing each year of the Chinese zodiac.

FǍZÀNGJIǍNG TEMPLE
BUDDHIST TEMPLE

Map p300 (法藏讲寺, Fǎzàngjiǎng Sì; 271 Ji'an Rd; 吉安路271号; suggested donation incl incense ¥5; ⊙7.30am-4pm; MLine 8, 10 to Laoximen) This simple but very active temple is curiously accessed from the west, rather than the south, where the entrance to Buddhist temples usually lies. The restored main hall encloses a large modern statue of Sakyamuni, seated lily-top between two walls glinting with gilded *luóhàn* (arhats).

Other lesser halls shelter a trinity of golden Buddhist effigies and there's a small shrine to the Buddhist god of the underworld, Dizang Wang. A handy vegetarian restaurant (from 9am to 9pm) is right next door for karmic sustenance.

POWER STATION OF ART
GALLERY

(上海当代艺术博物馆, Shànghǎi Dāngdài Yìshù Bówùguǎn; Lane 20 Huayuangang Rd; 花园港路200号; ⊙11am-7pm Tue-Sun, last entry 6pm; MLine 4, 8 to South Xizang Rd) FREE The vast Power Station of Art in the disused Nánshì Power Plant holds modern large-scale installations, design shows and other temporary exhibitions, some quite provocative. It also hosts the Shànghǎi Biennale.

COOL DOCKS
ARCHITECTURE

Map p300 (老码头, Lǎomǎtóu; www.thecooldocks.com; 479 South Zhongshan Rd; 中山南路479号; MLine 9 to Xiaonanmen) The riverside Cool Docks consist of several *shíkùmén* (石库门; stone-gate houses) surrounded by red-brick warehouses, near (but not quite on) the waterfront. Now full of restaurants and bars and all lit up at night, the Cool Docks' isolated positioning (it lacks the central location and transport connections of Xīntiāndì in the French Concession) has hobbled ambitions. Although high-profile and trendy restaurant, bar and hotel openings have helped give it a much-needed lift, it remains an entertainment backwater.

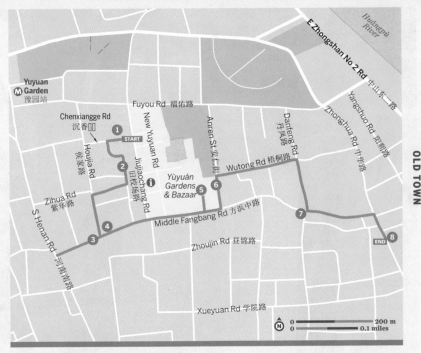

Neighbourhood Walk
Walking Old Town

START CHÉNXIĀNGGÉ MONASTERY
END SHÍLIÙPÙ FABRIC MARKET
LENGTH 1KM; TWO HOURS

Begin by visiting the charming
1 Chénxiānggé Monastery (p82) on
Chenxiangge Rd, a Buddhist retreat from
the surrounding clamour.

Filled with newly found serenity, exit the
temple and weave south down
2 Wangyima Alley (王医马弄), a small,
typical Old Town alley immediately facing
you. Follow the alley, then turn west along
Zhongwangyima Alley (中王医马弄) before
turning south onto Houjia Rd.

Wander along Middle Fangbang Rd –
once a canal and also known as **3 Old
Street** (p90) – and browse for Tibetan jewellery, teapots and prints of 1930s poster
advertisements. Alternatively, break for a
pot of refreshing oolong tea at the **4 Old
Shànghǎi Teahouse** (p90).

Head east down Old Street, passing the
Yùyuán Bazaar, to pay your respects to the

red-faced town protector at the **5 Temple
of the Town God** (p82).

Upon exiting, continue east down Middle
Fangbang Rd and then turn north onto
6 Anren St. Wend your way past the outdoor mah-jong and Chinese chess matches,
then turn east onto Wutong Rd and then
south on Danfeng Rd, a pinched lane frequently dressed with hanging washing. Note
the lovely old doorways on Danfeng Rd, such
as the carved red-brick gateway at No 193.

Exit Danfeng Rd, turning east onto
Middle Fangbang Rd at the old **7 stone
archway** (四牌楼, sì páilou). Stroll down
the boisterous shopping street, filled with
snack stands, clothing shops and booming
stereo systems. As long as the eastern part
of town remains standing over the next few
years, there will be plenty of little alleys to
explore here, particularly off to the south.
When you reach the end of Middle Fangbang Rd, cross Zhonghua Rd (which marks
the eastern boundary of the old city wall) to
the **8 Shíliùpù Fabric Market** (p90) for a
tailor-made shirt, dress or jacket.

上海文庙

1. Confucius Temple (p86)
This modest and charming temple to Confucius is cultivated with beribboned trees, magnolias and birdsong.

2. Yùyuán Gardens (p80)
A delightful escape from the city's hard-edged modernity, the stunning gardens are home to one of the most famous teahouses in China.

3. Temple of the Town God (p82)
This Taoist temple was badly damaged during the Cultural Revolution but has since been restored for visiting worshippers.

3

BÁIYÚN TEMPLE
TAOIST TEMPLE

Map p300 (白云观, Báiyún Guàn; 239 Dajing Rd; 大境路239号; ¥5; ⏱8am-4.30pm; Ⓜ Line 8 to Dashijie) The port-red and recently built Taoist Báiyún (White Cloud) Temple is fronted by an entrance with twin eaves and separated from Dàjìng Pavilion, a preserved section of the city walls, by Dajing Lane. As it is not a historical temple, it has little heritage value.

SUNNY BEACH
BEACH

Map p300 (老码头阳光沙滩, Lǎomǎtou Yángguāng Shātān; ☎133 1167 3735; South Zhongshan Rd; ¥50; ⏱10am-10pm; Ⓜ Line 9 to Xiaonanmen) Life's a beach, even in the middle of Shànghǎi. If the sun comes out, pop down to this small but amusing artificial strip of sand right by the river and north of the Cool Docks. There you'll find a backdrop of Lùjiāzuǐ, a limited bar, deckchairs, beach volleyball and Frisbee. Keep your expectations fairly low.

CONFUCIUS TEMPLE
CONFUCIAN TEMPLE

Map p300 (文庙, Wén Miào; 215 Wenmiao Rd; 文庙路215号; adult/student ¥10/5; ⏱9am-5pm, last entry 4.30pm; Ⓜ Line 8,10 to Laoximen) A modest and charming retreat, this well-tended temple to Confucius is cultivated with maples, pines, magnolias and birdsong. The layout is typically Confucian, its few worshippers complemented by ancient and venerable trees, including a 300-year-old elm. The main hall for worshipping Confucius is **Dàchéng Hall** (大成殿; Dàchéng Diàn), complete with twin eaves and a statue of the sage outside.

The towering **Kuíxīng Pavilion** (Kuíxīng Gé) in the west is named after the god of the literati. Originally dating to 1294, when the Mongols held sway through China, the temple moved to its current site in 1855, at a time when Christian Taiping rebels were sending much of China skywards in sheets of flame. In line with Confucian championing of learning, a busy secondhand market of (largely Chinese-language) books is held in the temple every Sunday morning (admission ¥10; open from 7am to 3pm). There are some genuine finds.

DÀJÌNG PAVILION
HISTORIC SITE

Map p300 (大境阁, Dàjìng Gé; 259 Dajing Rd; 大境路; ¥5; ⏱9am-5pm; Ⓜ Line 8 to Dashijie) Dating from 1815, this pavilion contains the only preserved section of the 5km-long city walls. Also within the pavilion is a small Guandi temple, which found a new calling as a factory during the Cultural Revolution. In the middle sits the fiery-faced Guandi, with an equally fierce God of Wealth to his left and Yuexia Laoren (月下老人) to his right.

ⓘ NAVIGATING SHÀNGHǍI ON FOOT

Unlike in other Chinese cities where street signs are in Chinese (sometimes accompanied by pinyin), all street signs in Shànghǎi display the name of the road in Chinese script and its English translation. We use road names as they appear on street signs, to aid navigation on foot. But we also list road names in Chinese to assist you in your journey around town.

By far the majority of roads in Shànghǎi are affixed with the word *lù* (路), which means 'road', as in Huashan Lu (Huashan Rd). Occasionally the word *jiē* (街) is used, which means 'street', as in Menghua Jie (Menghua St). The other convention you may see is *dàdào* (大道), which means 'avenue' or 'boulevard', as in Renmin Dadao (Renmin Ave). Alleys are called *lòng* (弄) or *lǐ* (里).

Many road names are also compound words that place the road in context with others in the city, by using the points of the compass. These include:

➡ *běi* – 北 (north)

➡ *nán* – 南 (south)

➡ *dōng* – 东 (east)

➡ *xī* – 西 (west)

➡ *zhōng* – 中 (middle)

So, Nanjing Donglu (南京东路) literally means East Nanjing Rd, while Huaihai Zhonglu (淮海中路) means Middle Huaihai Rd. Other words you may see are *huán* (环; ring, as in ring road) and numbers, such as Ruijin Erlu (瑞金二路), or Ruijin No 2 Rd.

MOUNTAIN-WATER GARDENS

Classical Chinese gardens can be an acquired taste: there are no lawns, few flowering plants, and huge misshapen rocks strewn about. Yet a stroll in the Yùyuán Gardens (p80), and the gardens of Sūzhōu, is a walk through many different facets of Chinese civilisation, and this is what makes them so unique. Architecture, philosophy, art and literature all converge, and a background in some basics of Chinese culture helps to fully appreciate the garden design.

The Chinese for 'landscape' is *shānshuǐ* (山水), literally 'mountain-water'. Mountains and rivers constitute a large part of China's geography, and are fundamental to Chinese life, philosophy, religion and art. So the central part of any garden landscape is a pond surrounded by rock formations.

This also reflects the influence of Taoist thought. Contrary to geometrically designed formal European gardens, where humans saw themselves as masters, Chinese gardens seek to create a microcosm of the natural world through an asymmetrical layout of streams, hills, plants and pavilions (they symbolise humanity's place in the universe – never in the centre, just a part of the whole).

Symbolism works on every level. Plants are chosen as much for their symbolic meaning as their beauty (the pine for longevity, the peony for nobility); the billowy rocks call to mind not only mountains but also the changing, indefinable nature of the Tao (the underlying principle of the universe in Taoist thought); and the names of gardens and halls are often literary allusions to ideals expressed in classical poetry. Painting, too, goes hand in hand with gardening, its aesthetics reproduced in gardens through the use of carefully placed windows and doors that frame a particular view.

Finally, it's worth remembering that gardens in China have always been lived in. Generally part of a residence, they weren't so much contemplative (as in Japan) as they were a backdrop for everyday life: family gatherings, late-night drinking parties, discussions of philosophy, art and politics – it's the people who spent their leisure hours there that ultimately gave the gardens their unique spirit.

You can climb up to the restored battlements. A small calligraphy museum is adjoined to the pavilion.

DŎNGJIĀDÙ CATHEDRAL
CHURCH

Map p300 (董家渡教堂, Dǒngjiādù Jiàotáng; 185 Dongjiadu Rd; 董家渡路185号; [M]Line 4 to Nanpu Bridge) Just outside the Old Town and once known as St Francis Xavier Church, this magnificent whitewashed cathedral is Shànghǎi's oldest church, built by Spanish Jesuits in 1853. A splendid sight, the church was located within a famously Catholic area of Shànghǎi and is generally open if you want to view the well-kept interior (ring the bell at the side door).

PEACH GARDEN MOSQUE
MOSQUE

Map p300 (小桃园清真寺, Xiǎotáoyuán Qīngzhēnsì; 52 Xiaotaoyuan Rd; 小桃园路52号; ⊙8am-7pm; [M]Line 8, 10 to Laoximen; Line 10 to Yuyuan Garden) Originally dating to 1917, this famous mosque is the main place of worship for Shànghǎi's Muslims.

🍴 EATING

The Yùyuán Gardens area is hardly a dining destination in itself, but if you're visiting the Old Town you needn't go hungry. There's snack food a-plenty and several famous old restaurants, while a collection of upmarket and stylish choices in South Bund 22 and the Cool Docks makes it easy to tie in the area's sights with dinner and drinks by the river. For all manner of Chinese snacks, try the stalls in the Yùyuán Bazaar. The Old Town also bursts with food streets, such as Shouning Rd where chilli-oiled crayfish, grilled squid, dumplings, stinky *dòufu* (tofu), flat breads and roast duck converge in a formidable aroma.

NÁNXIÁNG STEAMED BUN RESTAURANT
DUMPLING $

Map p300 (南翔馒头店, Nánxiáng Mántou Diàn; 85 Yuyuan Rd, Yùyuán Bazaar; 豫园商城豫园路85号; 12 dumplings on 1st fl ¥22; ⊙1st fl 10am-9pm, 2nd fl 7am-8pm, 3rd fl 9.30am-7pm; [M]Line 10 to Yuyuan Garden) Shànghǎi's most famous dumpling restaurant divides the purists,

GUANYIN, GODDESS OF MERCY

Encountered in Buddhist temples across Shànghǎi and China, the Bodhisattva Guanyin is the Buddhist Goddess of Mercy. Her full name is Guanshiyin (观世音; literally 'Observing the Cries of the World'), but she is also called Guanzizai, Guanyin Dashi and Guanyin Pusa, or, in Sanskrit, Avalokiteshvara. Known as Kannon in Japanese, Guanyam in Cantonese and Quan Am in Vietnamese, she is one of the most recognisable figures in Buddhism. Her mission is to offer sympathy to the world, from a wellspring of infinite compassion, and she is most revered by female worshippers.

Guanyin can often be found at the very rear of the main hall, facing north (most of the other divinities, apart from Weituo, face south). She typically has her own little shrine and stands on the head of a big fish, holding a lotus in her hand, with attendant luóhàn (arhats) and children in a montage behind her. On other occasions, she has her own hall, often towards the rear of the temple, as in Shànghǎi's Chénxiānggé Monastery (p82). Sometimes, she is worshipped within her very own temple.

The goddess is also the presiding divinity on the island of Pǔtuóshān off the coast of Zhèjiāng, a site of great veneration for Buddhists and one of China's four sacred Buddhist mountains.

In ancient Chinese effigies, the goddess was male rather than female, and can sometimes be found seated lalitasana, a lithe and relaxed regal posture where one of Guanyin's feet typically rests on, or near, the thigh of the other leg.

Guanyin can appear in many forms, often with just two arms, but sometimes in a multiarmed form or with a fan of arms behind her in the famous 1000-hand form (Qiānshǒu Guanyin). The 11-faced Guanyin, the fierce horse-head Guanyin, the Songzi Guanyin (literally 'Offering Son Guanyin') and the Dripping Water Guanyin are just some of her myriad manifestations. She was also a favourite subject for déhuà glazed porcelain figures, which are very elegant and either snow white or creamy. Examples exist in the Shànghǎi Museum (p61).

who love the place, from the younger crowd, who see an overrated tourist trap. Decide for yourself how the xiǎolóngbāo rate, but lines are long and you won't even get near it on weekends. There are three dining halls upstairs, with the prices escalating (and crowds diminishing) in each room.

The takeaway deal (including crab meat) is comparable to what you pay elsewhere for xiǎolóngbāo, but the queue snakes halfway around the Yùyuán Bazaar.

ELEMENT FRESH SANDWICHES $
Map p300 (新元素, Xīnyuánsù; www.element fresh.com; 6th fl, Fraser Residence, 228 South Xizang Rd; 西藏南路228号6楼; breakfast from ¥38, meals ¥60-100; 🔊; ⓂLine 8 to Dashijie) Handy Old Town outpost of the health-conscious chain dedicated to pick-me-up breakfasts, crisp salads, sandwiches, and feel-good juices and smoothies.

WÚYUÈ RÉNJIĀ NOODLES $
Map p300 (吴越人家; 234 Fuyou Rd; 福佑路234号; mains ¥15-25; ◷9am-8.30pm; ⓂLine 10 to Yuyuan Garden) Right next to KFC north of the Yùyuán Gardens, this upstairs place

doesn't look particularly appealing but it serves typical Old Town fare and it's a well-known family name in Shànghǎi. They serve up excellent, filling bowls of Sūzhōu noodles. Choose between tāng (soupy) and gān (dry) noodles; in either case, the flavouring comes on a side plate.

Try the mixed noodles with shredded beef (¥20) or the spicy meat noodles in red oil (红油腊肉面; hóngyóu làròu miàn; ¥13). Ask for the English picture menu.

SŌNGYUÈLÓU CHINESE $
Map p300 (松月楼; ☎021 6355 3630; 23 Bailing Rd; 百灵路23号; dishes from ¥10; ◷9am-9pm; 🔊; ⓂLine 10 to Yuyuan Garden) Dating to 1910, this place has cheap eats, such as wonton (馄饨汤; húntún tāng; ¥10), and veggie options, including tofu masquerading as meat (such as black-pepper beef noodle soup, ¥35). Upstairs has an English menu, and spotless tablecloths, and comes with a price hike. Downstairs is a Mandarin-only, busy, canteen-style affair where you order first, get a receipt and then a share table with fellow diners.

★EL WILLY   SPANISH $$

Map p300 (☑021 5404 5757; www.elwillygroup.com; 5th fl, South Bund 22, 22 East Zhongshan No 2 Rd; 中山东二路22号5楼; mains from ¥65, 3-course set menus ¥168; ☺11am-2.30pm & 6-10.30pm Mon-Sat; Ⓜ Line 10 to Yuyuan Garden) Ensconced in the stunningly converted South Bund 22, bright, vivacious, bubbly and relocated from the French Concession, Willy Trullas Moreno's fetching and fun restaurant is a more relaxed counterpoint to many other overdressed Bund operations. Seasonally adjusted scrumptious tapas and paellas are Willy's forte, paired with some serene Bund views beyond the windows. Chopsticks encourage the communal Chinese dining approach.

★KEBABS ON THE
GRILLE   INDIAN $$

Map p300 (☑021 6152 6567; No 8, Cool Docks, 505 South Zhongshan Rd; 中山南路505号老码头8号; mains ¥55-135, set lunches 11am-2pm Mon-Fri ¥48; ☺11am-10.30pm; Ⓜ Line 9 to Xiaonanmen) This immensely popular and busy Cool Docks restaurant is a genuine crowd-pleaser, and has alfresco seating by the pond outside. The Boti mutton (barbecued lamb pieces) is adorable. There's a delicious range of tandoori dishes, live table-top grills, vegetarian choices, smooth and spicy daal options, plus an all-you-can-eat Sunday brunch (¥150). Another central branch can be found west of **People's Square** (在格栅烤肉串; Zài Gézhà Kǎoròu Chuàn; Map p296; ☑021 3315 0132; 227 North Huangpi Rd, inside Central Plaza; 黄陂北路227号; dishes ¥50-125, set lunch ¥48-58; ☺11am-10.30pm; Ⓜ Line 1, 2, 8 to People's Square, exit 11).

★TABLE NO 1 BY
JASON ATHERTON   EUROPEAN $$$

Map p300 (☑021 6080 2918; www.tableno-1.com; The Waterhouse at South Bund, 1-3 Maojiayuan Rd; 毛家园路1-3号; mains ¥148-268; ☺lunch & dinner; ☎; Ⓜ Line 9 to Xiaonanmen) On the ground floor of the Waterhouse (p208) by the Cool Docks, British chef Jason Atherton's Table No 1 fits in perfectly with the distressed industrial-chic theme. A low-key cocktail bar gives way to a deceptively casual dining room where candlelit wooden tables are arranged in communal dining style. A short selection of modern European dishes make up a beautifully considered menu.

Sharing options are also available.

NAPA WINE BAR AND
KITCHEN   FUSION $$$

Map p300 (Bund 22, 22 East Zhongshan No 2 Rd; 中山东二路22号; mains ¥168-288, set menus from ¥398; ☺noon-2.30pm & 6-11pm Tue-Fri, noon-4pm & 6-11pm Sat & Sun, 6-11pm Mon; Ⓜ Line 2, 10 to Nanjing East Road) One of Shànghǎi's go-to addresses for fine dining, Napa plates up beautifully presented gastronomic dishes in an elegant Bund setting. The food combines elements of Asian and Western cuisines, and, as the name suggests, there's a strong emphasis on wine pairing. A good choice for a serious splurge.

CHAR   STEAK $$$

Map p300 (恰餐厅; Qià Cāntīng; ☑021 3302 9995; www.char-thebund.com; 29th-31st fl, Hotel Indigo, 585 East Zhongshan No 2 Rd; 中山东二路585号29-31楼; steaks from ¥438-2188; ☺12pm-12.30am; ☎; Ⓜ Line 9 to Xiaonanmen) Housed in Hotel Indigo (p208), Char is a wildly pricey steakhouse sensation. Park yourself on a sofa against the window or in a comfy chair facing Lùjiāzuǐ for optimum views. Or keep one eye on the open kitchen to see how your Tajima Wagyu rib-eye steak, grilled black cod or seafood tower is coming along. There's a choice of six different steak knives. Book ahead.

The views continue in spectacular fashion from the terrace of the supremely chilled-out upstairs bar.

🍷 DRINKING & NIGHTLIFE

There are plenty of late-night, boozy restaurants, but the Old Town isn't really the place to come for bars and clubs.

CHAR BAR   BAR

Map p300 (恰酒吧; Qià Jiǔbā; www.char-thebund.com; 30th fl, Hotel Indigo, 585 East Zhongshan No 2 Rd; 中山东二路585号30楼; ☺4.30pm-1am; Ⓜ Line 9 to Xiaonanmen) This stretch of the Bund is ideal for a rooftop bar and Char ticks all the boxes. The outdoor terrace has some of the finest views over the Huángpǔ River across to the thrilling neon lights of Pǔdōng. Inside, intimate tables are filled with noisy drinkers dressed to the nines.

Drinks are as pricey as you'd expect (cocktails start at ¥95), but for a taste of textbook Bund glamour, it's worth the splurge.

MID-LAKE PAVILION TEAHOUSE　TEAHOUSE
Map p300 (湖心亭, Húxīntíng; Yuyuan Bazaar; 豫园商城; tea ¥50; ⏰8am-9pm; Ⓜ Line 10 to Yuyuan Garden) Next to the entrance to the Yùyuán Gardens is the Mid-Lake Pavilion Teahouse, once part of the gardens and now one of the most famous teahouses in China, visited by Queen Elizabeth II and Bill Clinton, among others. The zigzag causeway is designed to thwart spirits (and trap tourists), who can only travel in straight lines.

The wonderfully lengthy menu recommends suitable brews to drink in each season and the tea is served elegantly with tiny nibbles.

OLD SHÀNGHǍI TEAHOUSE　TEAHOUSE
Map p300 (老上海茶馆, Lǎo Shànghǎi Cháguǎn; ☏021 5382 1202; 385 Middle Fangbang Rd; 方浜中路385号; tea from ¥45; ⏰9am-9pm; Ⓜ Line 10 to Yuyuan Garden) A bit like the attic of an eccentric aunt, this wonderfully decrepit 2nd-floor teahouse, overlooking the throng of Old Street (p90), is a temple to the 1930s, with music on scratched records, period typewriters, aged photos, an old fireplace, sewing machines, electric fans, an ancient fridge, oodles of charm and tea, of course.

🛍 SHOPPING

Although not originally set up as a shopping district, Yùyuán Bazaar has become exactly that. All souvenirs can be found here or on the bordering Old Street (Middle Fangbang Rd), which itself is stuffed with tourist paraphernalia and kitsch, and blasted with shrill techno spliced with Chinese opera, children's ditties and random music. You can find anything from Chinese kites to walking sticks, fans and delightful kitsch. The Shíliùpù Fabric Market and the South Bund Fabric Market are both fine places to go in search of inexpensive fabric or to have a dress or shirt tailor-made.

⭐**OLD STREET**　GIFTS & SOUVENIRS
Map p300 (老街, Lǎo Jiē; Middle Fangbang Rd; 方浜中路; Ⓜ Line 10 to Yuyuan Garden) This renovated Qing dynasty stretch of Middle Fangbang Rd is lined with specialist tourist shops, spilling forth with shadow puppets, jade jewellery, embroidered fabrics, kites, horn combs, chopsticks, *zǐshā* teapots, old advertising posters, banknotes, Tibetan jewellery, the usual knock-off Mao memorabilia, reproduction 1930s posters, old illustrated books and calligraphy manuals, and surreal 3D-dazzle kitten photos.

Since the closure of the long-standing Dongtai Road Antique Market, some interesting items show up in these shops, but it's best not to assume anything is a genuine antique.

⭐**SOUTH BUND FABRIC MARKET**　CLOTHING
Map p300 (南外滩轻纺面料市场, Nán Wàitān Qīngfǎng Miànliào Shìchǎng; 399 Lujiabang Rd; 陆家浜路399号; ⏰8.30am-6pm; Ⓜ Line 4 to Nanpu Bridge) This old building with more than 100 stalls is one of the best and easiest fabric markets for tourists as many of the stallholders speak a little English. Dresses and suits can be chosen from pattern books or copied from pictures and made up in a dizzying range of fabrics.

Cashmere and wool coats, curtains, suits and leather jackets can all be made to order for a fraction of the price you might spend elsewhere. Take your time when negotiating a price and examining the materials to make a good purchase. If you're not confident tackling the market alone, great **shopping tours** (www.shoppingtoursshanghai.com; half-day tours from ¥800; ⏰group tours run Mon, Wed & Fri) are available.

SHÍLIÙPÙ FABRIC MARKET　CLOTHING
Map p300 (十六铺面料城, Shíliùpù Miànliào Chéng; ☏021 6330 1043; 2 Zhonghua Rd; 中华路2号; ⏰8.30am-6pm; Ⓜ Line 9 to Xiaonanmen) Having silk shirts, dresses and cashmere coats tailor-made for a song is one of Shànghǎi's great indulgences. This three-storey building, one of several fabric markets in the city, is conveniently located near the Yùyuán Bazaar. It's a cheaper source of silk than many shops, with prices around ¥200 per metre.

There are many types of fabric here in addition to silk, from wool and velvet to synthetic, but the quality of the material varies, so shop around. Allow at least three days or more for orders, to give time for amendments to be made.

FÚYÒU ANTIQUE MARKET　ANTIQUES, SOUVENIRS
Map p300 (福佑工艺品市场, Fúyòu Gōngyìpǐn Shìchǎng; 459 Middle Fangbang Rd; 方浜中路459号; ⏰9am-5.30pm; Ⓜ Line 10 to Yuyuan Garden) There's a permanent antique market here on the 1st and 2nd floors, but the place

SEDUCTION & THE CITY

Shànghǎi owes its reputation as the most fashionable city in China to calendar posters, the print runs of which once numbered in the tens of millions. Distribution of these – given out as bonus gifts, a practice that began at the Shànghǎi racecourse in the late 1890s – reached from China's interior to Southeast Asia.

The basic idea behind the posters – associating a product with an attractive woman to encourage subconscious desire and consumption – today sounds like Marketing 101, but in the early 20th century it was revolutionary. Calendar posters not only introduced new products to Chinese everywhere, their portrayal of Shànghǎi women – wearing make-up and stylish clothing, smoking cigarettes and surrounded by foreign goods – set the standard for modern fashion that many Chinese women (trapped in rural lives with little freedom and certainly no nearby department stores) would dream of for decades.

Today, reproduction posters are sold throughout the Old Town for as little as ¥10, though finding a bona fide original is quite a challenge. For an in-depth look at calendar posters and Shànghǎi's role in modern China, see Wen-Hsin Yeh's *Shanghai Splendor*.

really gets humming for the **Ghost Market** on Sunday at dawn, when sellers from the countryside fill up all four floors and then some. The range is good, but there's a lot of junk, so you need a shrewd eye if you don't want to pay too much over the odds. Use your best haggling skills.

TÓNG HÁN CHŪN TRADITIONAL MEDICINE STORE
MEDICINE

Map p300 (童涵春堂, Tóng Hán Chūn Táng; ☑021 6355 0308; 20 New Yuyuan Rd; 豫园新路20号; ⊙9am-9pm; ⓂLine 10 to Yuyuan Garden) An intriguing emporium of elixirs, infusions and remedies, this place has been selling Chinese medicinal cures since 1783. There's a vast range here, including modern medications, but it's all labelled in Chinese and little English is spoken, so take along a translator. On the 3rd floor, traditional Chinese medicine doctors offer consultations (you'll need an appointment).

SPORTS & ACTIVITIES

UNTOUR SHANGHAI
FOOD & DRINK

(http://untourshanghai.com; per person ¥450) See a whole new side to the Old Town on an evening Night Markets Food Tour. Gregarious and knowledgeable guides introduce you to the city's vibrant scene through a walk around neighbourhood alleys famous for their street food.

Stops at sizzling stalls and neon-lit restaurants give you the chance to sample everything from chilli-oil–soaked crayfish to deep-fried water snake (butchered right there on the roadside), all washed down with beer and *báijiǔ* (a face-numbing spirit). It's a fantastic way to learn about the diverse flavours and cooking styles within China. Dumpling and breakfast tours are also available.

French Concession

FRENCH CONCESSION EAST | FRENCH CONCESSION WEST

Neighbourhood Top Five

1 **Tiánzǐfáng** (p94) Weaving through a forest of shoppers' elbows in the charming *shíkùmén* (stonegate house) warren.

2 **Xinle and Fumin Roads** (p120) Shopping for fashion and homewares in the boutiques along these strips.

3 **Jian Guo 328** (p107) Savouring home-style Shanghainese cuisine.

4 **Xīntiāndì** (p95) Moseying around the interior of a *shíkùmén* house.

5 **Speak Low** (p115) Finding the secret portal to some of the city's best cocktails.

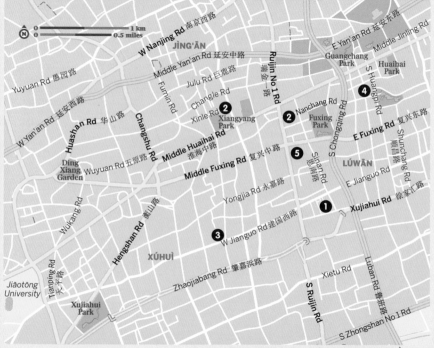

For more detail of this area see Maps p302 and p306 ➡

Explore: French Concession

The French Concession is Shànghǎi sunny side up; it's the city at its coolest, hippest and most elegant. Once home to the bulk of Shànghǎi's adventurers, revolutionaries, gangsters, prostitutes and writers – ironically many of them weren't French – the former concession (also called Frenchtown) is the most graceful part of Pǔxī. Shànghǎi's erstwhile reputation as the 'Paris of the East' owes a big debt to this neighbourhood's tree-lined avenues, 1920s mansions and French-influenced architecture.

The concession's leafy backstreets and European disposition make exploration a delight. Most first-time visitors start off in Xīntiāndì, which offers an all-in-one introduction to the local *shíkùmén* (stone-gate house) architecture alongside alluring dining and shopping options. South from here is the former concession's other big draw: Tiánzǐfáng, a less-polished warren of lanes and arty boutiques that can keep you wandering (often lost) indefinitely.

The French Concession's real attraction is not sightseeing. Like Shànghǎi itself, the area thrives on its endless quest for sophistication. Its tirelessly inventive restaurant and bar scene, coupled with pop-up boutiques, cool cafes and diverse entertainment options, means that you should come prepared to expand your tastes – just make sure you have cash to spend.

Local Life

➡ **Lǐlòng & Lòngtáng** Slip down some of Shànghǎi's most charming alleyways for a glimpse of the homely rhythms of community life.

➡ **Foot massages** Sink into an armchair (maybe catch some Hong Kong action on the tube) and have your tension kneaded away.

➡ **Snacks** Dumplings, noodles, haute cuisine, Sìchuānese, Húnánese, stinky tofu and lychee ice cream – no matter when or where, you'll find something to eat (and a local at your elbow).

Getting There & Away

➡ **Metro lines 1 and 10** Main lines serving the French Concession area, both running east–west past Xīntiāndì. Line 1 continues on to People's Square, while line 10 serves the Old Town and East Nanjing Rd (the Bund). The two lines meet at the South Shaanxi Rd metro stop.

➡ **Metro line 9** At the southern edge of the concession, line 9 serves Tiánzǐfáng.

➡ **Metro line 7** North–south line providing a handy link between the French Concession and the Jìng'ān neighbourhood; it connects with line 1 at Changshu Rd and line 9 at Zhaojiabang Rd.

Lonely Planet's Top Tip

Although most expats use the colonial-era term 'French Concession', the name means little to most Shanghainese. Locals call much of the eastern area Lúwān (卢湾) or Huángpǔ (黄浦), while the area west of South Shaanxi Rd is known as Xúhuì (徐汇), a district that extends southwest into Xújiāhuì. If you're in Shànghǎi for more than a short visit, it's worth familiarising yourself with these official district names. The literal Chinese for the historic French Concession is Fǎzūjiè (法租界).

✕ Best Places to Eat

➡ T8 (p106)
➡ Jian Guo 328 (p107)
➡ Lost Heaven (p109)
➡ Dī Shuǐ Dòng (p105)

For reviews, see p100 ➡

🍷 Best Places to Drink

➡ El Cóctel (p115)
➡ Speak Low (p115)
➡ Boxing Cat Brewery (p115)
➡ Dr Wine (p115)

For reviews, see p112 ➡

🛍 Best Places to Shop

➡ Tiánzǐfáng (p94)
➡ Pīlìngpǎlāng – Anfu Lu (p122)
➡ Dòng Liáng (p122)
➡ OOAK Concept Boutique (p122)

For reviews, see p119 ➡

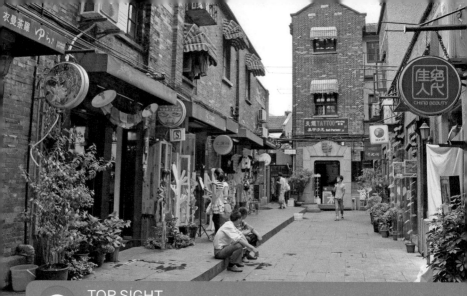

TOP SIGHT
TIÁNZǏFÁNG

A shopping complex housed within a grid of traditional alleyways, Tiánzǐfáng is probably the most accessible, authentic, charming and vibrant example of Shànghǎi's trademark traditional back-lane architecture. A community of design studios, local families, cafes and boutiques, it's a much-needed counterpoint to Shànghǎi's megamalls and dwarfing skyscrapers, but it can get crowded.

Galleries

There are three main north–south lanes (Nos 210, 248 and 274) criss-crossed by irregular east–west alleyways, which makes exploration disorienting and fun. Most shops and boutiques are slim and bijou. One gallery to seek out is Beaugeste (p97), which has thought-provoking contemporary photography exhibits. It's open by appointment only on weekdays.

Just outside the complex on Taikang Rd, an enormous peony bloom covers the exterior of the Liúli China Museum (p97), dedicated to the art of glass sculpture.

Shopping & Drinking

Shopping is the main driver in Tiánzǐfáng. The recent explosion of creative start-ups makes for some satisfying finds, from local fashion brands to Běijīng-style messenger bags, vintage glasses and experimental perfumes. Stalls flogging mass-produced souvenir dross have inevitably pitched up, so you'll need to hunt for the genuine boutiques; but rest assured, they're still here.

Elsewhere, a cool band of bars, cafes and restaurants – such as Kommune (p105), Bell Bar (p113) and I Love Shanghai (p114) – make for the ideal pit stop to refuel.

DON'T MISS

➡ Boutique browsing
➡ Liúli China Museum
➡ An evening drink at an alleway cafe

PRACTICALITIES

➡ 田子坊
➡ Map p302, E6
➡ www.tianzifang.cn
➡ Taikang Rd; 泰康路
➡ Ⓜ Dapuqiao

TOP SIGHT
XĪNTIĀNDÌ

With its own namesake metro station, Xīntiāndì has been a Shànghǎi icon for a decade or more. An upscale entertainment and shopping complex modelled on traditional *lòngtáng* (alleyway) homes, this was the first development in the city to prove that historical architecture makes big commercial sense. Elsewhere that might sound like a no-brainer, but in 21st-century China, where bulldozers are always on standby, it came as quite a revelation.

Well-heeled shoppers and alfresco diners keep things lively until late. If you're looking for a memorable meal, to wet your whistle in a dapper bar or to browse through some of Shànghǎi's more fashionable boutiques, you're in the right spot.

Exploring the Complex

The heart of the complex, cleaved into a pedestrianised north and south block, consists of largely rebuilt traditional *shíkùmén* (stone-gate houses), brought bang up-to-date with a stylish modern spin. But while the layout suggests a flavour of yesteryear, don't expect too much historical magic or cultural allure. Xīntiāndì doesn't nurture a lived-in charm, or the creaking, rickety simplicity of Shànghǎi's Old Town. Beyond the two sights located in the north block – the eye-opening Shíkùmén Open House Museum (p96), which reveals the interior of a well-to-do *shíkùmén* household, and the Site of the 1st National Congress of the CCP (p96) – it's best for strolling the pretty alleyways and enjoying a summer evening over drinks or a meal.

Serious shoppers – and diners – will eventually gravitate towards the malls at the southern tip of the south block. Beyond the first, which holds three top-notch restaurants on the 2nd floor – Din Tai Fung (p105), Crystal Jade (p105) and Shànghǎi Min (p106) – is the Xīntiāndì Style (p121) mall, showcasing local brands and chic pieces at the vanguard of Shanghainese fashion.

DON'T MISS

➜ Shíkùmén Open House Museum
➜ Alfresco dining
➜ Window-shopping

PRACTICALITIES

➜ 新天地
➜ Map p302, G2
➜ www.xintiandi.com
➜ 2 blocks between Tai-cang, Zizhong, Madang & South Huangpi Rds; 太仓路与马当路路口
➜ Ⓜ South Huangpi Road, Xintiandi

⊙ SIGHTS

⊙ French Concession East

XĪNTIĀNDÌ
AREA

See p95.

SHÍKÙMÉN OPEN HOUSE MUSEUM
MUSEUM

Map p302 (石库门屋里厢, Shíkùmén Wūlǐxiāng; Xīntiāndì North Block, Bldg 25; 太仓路181弄新天地北里25号楼; adult/child ¥20/10; ⊙10.30am-10.30pm; ⓂSouth Huangpi Rd, Xintiandi) This two-floor exhibition invites you into a typical *shíkùmén* (stone-gate house) household, decked out with period furniture. The ground-floor arrangement contains a courtyard, entrance hall, bedroom, study and lounge. There's a small kitchen to the rear and natural illumination spills down from *tiānjǐng* (light wells) above. The small, north-facing wedge-shaped *tíngzijiān* (pavilion) room on the landing, almost at the top of the stairs between the 1st and 2nd floors, was a common feature of *shíkùmén*, and was often rented out.

The main bedrooms are all on the 2nd floor, linked together by doors, and there is an exhibition room displaying artworks depicting daily life in those days.

SITE OF THE 1ST NATIONAL CONGRESS OF THE CCP
HISTORIC BUILDING

Map p302 (中共一大会址纪念馆, Zhōnggòng Yīdàhuìzhǐ Jìniànguǎn; Xīntiāndì North Block, 76 Xingye Rd; 兴业路76号; ⊙9am-5pm; ⓂSouth Huangpi Rd, Xintiandi) FREE On 23 July 1921, the Chinese Communist Party (CCP) was founded in this French Concession building (then 106 rue Wantz). In one fell swoop this unassuming *shíkùmén* block was transformed into one of Chinese communism's holiest shrines. Beyond the communist narcissism, there's little to see, although historians will enjoy ruminating on the site's historic momentousness.

SUN YATSEN'S FORMER RESIDENCE
HISTORIC BUILDING

Map p302 (孙中山故居, Sūn Zhōngshān Gùjū; ☎021 5306 3361; 7 Xiangshan Rd; 香山路7号; adult ¥20, child over 6 yrs & seniors ¥10, audio guide ¥20; ⊙9am-4pm; ⓂSouth Shaanxi Rd, Xintiandi) Sun Zhongshan predictably receives the full-on hagiographic treatment at this shrine to China's *guófù* (国父; father of the nation). A capacious exhibition hall next door further pampers his memory and serves as a full-on prelude to his pebble-dash 'Spanish-style' home.

Once you get to his house proper – where he lived on what was rue Moliere from 1918 to 1924 – you need to pop transparent shower caps over your shoes to protect the threadbare carpets. Don't forget to catch the lovely garden, where a *Magnolia grandiflora* flowers deliciously in summer.

FÙXĪNG PARK
PARK

Map p302 (复兴公园, Fùxīng Gōngyuán; ⊙6am-6pm; ⓂSouth Shaanxi Rd, Xintiandi) This leafy spot with a large lawn, laid out by the French in 1909 and later used by the Japanese as a parade ground in the late 1930s, remains one of the city's more enticing parks. There is always plenty to see here: the park is a refuge for the elderly and a practising field for itinerant musicians, chess players, people walking backwards and slow-moving taichi types.

Heavily shaded by big-leafed *wutong* trees, it's a choice place to take a seat and escape the summer sun; there's even a popular kids' playground. Wreathed in the laughter of children, the huge stony-faced busts of Karl Marx and Friedrich Engels gaze out from a seemingly redundant epoch, and nobody seems to notice. The park stays open until 8pm during the summer months.

ST NICHOLAS CHURCH
CHURCH

Map p302 (圣尼古拉斯教堂, Shèngnígǔlāsī Jiàotáng; 16 Gaolan Rd; 皋兰路16号; ⓂSouth Shaanxi Rd) A short walk west along Gaolan Rd from Fùxīng Park is rewarded by the distinctive shape of the vacant, and now derelict, St Nicholas Church, one of Shànghǎi's small band of Russian Orthodox houses of worship, built to service the huge influx of Russians who arrived in Shànghǎi in the 1930s.

Dating from 1934, the church has a typically varied CV, ranging from shrine to washing-machine factory to French restaurant. It was spared desecration during the Cultural Revolution by a portrait of Mao Zedong, hung strategically from the dome. The building is not open to the public.

ZHOU ENLAI'S FORMER RESIDENCE
HISTORIC BUILDING

Map p302 (周恩来故居, Zhōu Ēnlái Gùjū; ☎021 6473 0420; 73 Sinan Rd; 思南路73号; ⊙9am-5pm, last entry 4pm; ⓂSouth Shaanxi Rd, Xintiandi) FREE In 1946, Zhou Enlai, the much-loved (although some swear he was even

SHÀNGHǍI SHÍKÙMÉN & LǏLÒNG

Visitors should definitely take the time to seek out some *shíkùmén* (stone-gate house) and *lǐlòng* (alleyway) architecture while in Shànghǎi. Not only is the architecture stunning – a combination of English terrace housing with Chinese feng shui sensibilities – but these alleyways also offer an insight into the lives and ways of the local community. Sadly, this type of community has almost disappeared in Shànghǎi as a lot of the housing has been demolished over the years, though there are still some examples you can take a look at:

Cité Bourgogne (步高里, Bùgāo Lǐ; Map p302; cnr West Jianguo Rd & South Shaanxi Rds; 建国西路陕西南路的路口; MJiashan Rd) Not far from Tiánzǐfáng in the French Concession, Cité Bourgogne is an excellent example of a *shíkùmén lǐlòng* neighbourhood and it has been relatively well preserved. You can wander through the lane, though be respectful of residents' privacy. You might find locals hanging out laundry, chatting or playing cards.

Zhāng Garden (p130) In Jing'an, this is a beautiful example of *shíkùmén* architecture.

Shanyin Road Wander down Shanyin Rd in the Hongkou district for some fine examples at Nos 41 to 50, Lane 180. If the gate is open, the guard may let you have a stroll through.

more sly than Mao) first premier of the People's Republic of China, lived briefly in this former French Concession Spanish villa. Zhou was then head of the Communist Party's Shànghǎi office, giving press conferences and dodging Kuomintang agents who spied on him from across the road.

After wandering through the home, carry on into the charming garden and discover Zhou's Buick (a replica) in the garage.

TIÁNZǏFÁNG   AREA
See p94.

LIÚLI CHINA MUSEUM   MUSEUM
Map p302 (琉璃艺术博物馆, Liúli Yìshù Bówùguǎn; ☑021 6461 3189; www.liulichina museum.com; 25 Taikang Rd; 泰康路25号; adult/child under 18 yrs ¥20/free; ◎10am-5pm Tue-Sun) Founded by Taiwanese artists Loretta Yang and Chang Yi, the Liúli China Museum is dedicated to the art of glass sculpture (*pâte de verre* or lost-wax casting). Peruse the collection of ancient artefacts – some of which date back more than 2000 years – to admire the early artisanship of pieces such as earrings, belt buckles and even a Tang dynasty crystal *wéiqí* (go) set.

The collection transitions fluidly to more contemporary creations from around the world, before moving on to Yang's serene Buddhist-inspired creations, including a sublime 1.6m-high, 1000-armed

Guanyin, which was modelled on a Yuan dynasty mural in the Mògāo Caves near Dūnhuáng.

On the ground floor is the Luili cafe and a shop selling *liúli* crystal, where you can snag an attractive glass bracelet for around ¥1500.

BEAUGESTE   GALLERY
Map p302 (比极影像, Bǐjí Yǐngxiàng; ☑021 6466 9012; www.beaugeste-gallery.com; 5th fl, No 5, Lane 210, Taikang Rd; 泰康路210弄5号520室 田子坊; ◎10am-6pm Sat & Sun; MDapuqiao) **FREE** One of Shànghǎi's top galleries, this small space is concealed high above the street-level crowds. Curator Jean Loh captures humanistic themes in contemporary Chinese photography, and his wide range of contacts and excellent eye ensure exhibits are always both moving and thought-provoking. Note that the gallery is open by appointment only during the week.

REN WEIYIN ART
GALLERY   GALLERY
Map p302 (www.renweiyinart.com; Blg 3, Lane 210, Tianzifang; 泰康路210弄; ◎10am-6pm; MDapuqiao) **FREE** This gallery exhibits around 150 paintings by one of China's most well-known post-impressionists, Ren Weiyin. In 1961 his studio was forcibly closed and he was sent to a forced labour camp. He spent most of his life as a shoe repairman. His daughter opened this gallery to showcase her father's work and life.

THE SOONG FAMILY

The Soongs probably wielded more influence and power over modern China than any other family. The father of the family, Charlie Soong, grew up in Hǎinán and, after an American evangelical education, finally settled in Shànghǎi. He began to print bibles and money, becoming a wealthy businessman and developing ties with secret societies, during which time he became good friends with Sun Yatsen (Sun Zhongshan). Charlie had three daughters and a son.

Soong Ailing – said to be the first Chinese girl in Shànghǎi to own a bicycle – married HH Kung, the wealthy descendent of Confucius, Bank of China head and later finance minister of the Republic of China. Soong Meiling (May-ling) became the third wife of Chiang Kaishek (Kuomintang leader and future president of the Republic of China) in 1928. She went to the USA during the Japanese occupation of China and fled to Taiwan with Chiang after the communist victory. Much to the disapproval of her father, Soong Qingling (more commonly known as Song Qingling) married Sun Yatsen, 30 years her elder, studied in Moscow and was the only member of the family to live in China after 1949, until her death in 1981. TV Soong, Charlie's only son, served as the Republic of China's finance minister and premier, becoming the richest man of his generation.

Mainland Chinese say that of the three daughters, one loved money (Ailing), one loved power (Meiling) but only one loved China (Qingling). Among them, the siblings stewed up a heady brew of fascism and communism.

Song Qingling died in Běijīng and is buried at the Song Qingling Mausoleum in Shànghǎi. Her sister Meiling declined the invitation to return to China to attend her funeral; she died in the USA in October 2003, aged 105.

SHÀNGHǍI MUSEUM OF PUBLIC SECURITY   MUSEUM

(上海公安博物馆, Shànghǎi Gōng'ān Bówùguǎn; ☑021 6472 0256; 518 South Ruijin Rd; 瑞金南路 518号; ◎9am-4.30pm Mon-Sat, last entry 4pm; ⓂDapuqiao) FREE It may sound turgid and dull, but this museum deals out an ace or two from an otherwise humdrum hand of traffic control and post-Liberation security milestones. The gold pistols of Sun Yatsen and 1930s gangster Huang Jinrong are worth hunting down amid the fine collection of Al Capone–style machine guns and pen-guns. Look out for the collection of hand-painted business cards once dispensed by the city's top *jìnǚ* (prostitutes).

MOLLER HOUSE   HISTORIC BUILDING

Map p302 (马勒别墅, Mǎlè Biéshù; 30 South Shaanxi Rd; 陕西南路30号; ⓂSouth Shaanxi Rd) One of Shànghǎi's most whimsical buildings, the Scandinavian-influenced Gothic peaks of the Moller House could double as the Munsters' holiday home. Swedish owner and horse-racing fan Eric Moller owned the Moller Line, a shipping firm. Previously home to the Communist Youth League, the building now houses a hotel, the **Héngshān Moller Villa** (衡山马勒别墅饭店; Héngshān Mǎlè Biéshù Fàndiàn; Map p302; ☑021 6247 8881;

www.mollervilla.com; 30 South Shaanxi Rd; 陕西 南路30号; r from ¥1500, feature room ¥3800; ✳@☎; ⓂSouth Shaanxi Rd). Building No 2 is a recent extension, copied in similar style.

Fanciful perhaps, legend attests that a fortune teller warned Moller that tragedy would befall him on the house's completion, so the tycoon dragged out its construction (until 1949). Moller clung on for a few more years before dying in a plane crash in 1954.

CHRIST THE KING CHURCH   CHURCH

Map p302 (君王天主堂; Jūnwáng Tiānzhǔtáng; cnr Julu & Maoming Rds; ◎hours vary) The Christ the King Church, built in 1928, was originally located on Changle Rd in the French Concession. Now situated on the corner of Julu and Maoming Rds, it can be visited for a look-see inside.

⊙ French Concession West

PROPAGANDA POSTER ART CENTRE   GALLERY

Map p306 (宣传画年画艺术中心, Xuānchuánhuà Niánhuà Yìshù Zhōngxīn; ☑021 6211 1845; www.shanghaipropagandaart.com; Room B-0C, President Mansion, 868 Huashan

Rd; 华山路868号B-0C室; ¥20; ⊙10am-5pm; Ⓜ Shanghai Library) If phalanxes of red tractors, bumper harvests, muscled peasants and lantern-jawed proletariats fire you up, this small gallery in the bowels of a residential block should intoxicate. The collection of original posters from the 1950s, '60s and '70s – the golden age of Maoist poster production – will have you weak-kneed at the cartoon world of anti-US defiance. The centre divides into a showroom and a shop selling posters and postcards.

Once you find the main entrance, a guard will pop a small business card with a map on it into your hands and point the way. Head around the back of the apartment blocks to Building 4B and take the lift or stairs to the basement. It's a good idea to phone ahead (they speak some English) before heading out here to make sure it's open. The exhibition rounds off with a collection of cigarette posters from the 1920s.

SHANGHAI CAMERA HISTORY MUSEUM
MUSEUM

Map p306 (300 Anfu Rd; 安福路300号; ⊙10am-10pm Tue, Wed, Fri-Sun, last admission 9.30pm; Ⓜ Changshu Rd) FREE One for diehard vintage camera fans, this museum displays cameras from the 20th century, including old folding cameras from the 1920s and '30s as well as a collection of retro Polaroid cameras. The museum focuses on the well-known Shànghǎi brand, Seagull, but you'll also find international brands such as Nikon and Leica. There's a quiet cafe on the 2nd floor with photography books and magazines to flick through.

SHÀNGHǍI ARTS & CRAFTS MUSEUM
MUSEUM

Map p302 (上海工艺美术博物馆, Shànghǎi Gōngyì Měishù Bówùguǎn; ☑021 6431 4074; www.shgmb.com; 79 Fenyang Rd; 汾阳路79号; ¥8; ⊙9am-5pm, last entry 4pm; Ⓜ Changshu Rd) Repositioned as a museum, this arts and crafts institute displays traditional crafts such as needlepoint embroidery, paper cutting, lacquer work, jade cutting and lantern making. Watch traditional crafts being performed live by craftspeople and admire the wonderful exhibits, from jade, to ivory to ink stones and beyond. The 1905 building itself is a highlight, once serving as the residence for Chen Yi, Shànghǎi's first mayor after the founding of the Chinese Communist Party (CCP).

After exploring the lovely garden, head up the steps to a host of splendid ivory and boxwood carvings on the 1st floor, where divine (Guanyin) and semidivine (Mao Zedong) beings are displayed; also look out for the exquisite ivory spider hanging from a web. Further displays include opera costumes and Shànghǎi dough modelling, while among the goods for sale you can grab goldfish lanterns (from ¥60) or some intricate paper cuttings (剪纸; *jiǎnzhǐ*).

RUSSIAN ORTHODOX MISSION CHURCH
CHURCH

Map p302 (东正教圣母大堂, Dōngzhèngjiào Shèngmǔ Dàtáng; 55 Xinle Rd; 新乐路55号; Ⓜ South Shaanxi Rd) Built in 1934, this lovely blue-domed church was designed for the huge influx of Russian worshippers to Shànghǎi in the 1930s.

SONG QINGLING'S FORMER RESIDENCE
HISTORIC BUILDING

Map p306 (宋庆龄故居, Sòng Qìnglíng Gùjū; ☑021 6474 7183; www.shsoong-chingling.com; 1843 Middle Huaihai Rd; 淮海中路1843号; adult/child ¥20/¥10; ⊙9am-4.30pm; Ⓜ Jiaotong University) Built in the 1920s by a Greek shipping magnate, this quiet building became home to Song Qingling, wife of Dr Sun Yatsen, from 1948 to 1963. Size up two of her black limousines (one a gift from Stalin) in the garage and pad about the house, conjuring up sensations of yesteryear from its period furnishings. The highlight is the gorgeous garden, with tall magnolias and camphor trees towering over a delightful lawn, where Song entertained guests with conversation and tea.

A few personal belongings are also on display in the house, including autographed books from American journalists Edgar Snow and Agnes Smedley, and a collection of old photographs depicting the Soong sisters (p98) and various heads of state.

WUKANG ROAD TOURIST INFORMATION CENTRE
ARCHITECTURE

Map p306 (武康路旅游咨询中心, Wǔkāng Lù Lǚyóu Zīxún Zhōngxīn; 393 Wukang Rd; 武康路393号; ⊙9am-5pm; Ⓜ Shanghai Library) On one of the area's best-preserved streets, this centre displays scale-model concession buildings, photos of historic Shànghǎi architecture and maps for self-guided walking tours of Wukang Rd. It's in the former residence of Huang Xing (1874–1916), a revolutionary who cofounded the Republic of China together with Sun Yatsen. Note the fantastic art deco extension to the south along Wukang Rd.

FERGUSON LANE
AREA

Map p306 (武康庭, Wǔkāng Tíng; www.fergu sonlane.com.cn; 378 Wukang Rd; 武康路378号; MShanghai Library, Jiaotong University) On those rare days when Shànghǎi's skies are cloud-free, the chic Ferguson Lane court-yard fills up in the blink of an eye with boutique browsers, latte lovers and brunch fanatics. Centered around a 1920s villa, the small art deco complex houses an art gal-lery, a couple of shops and a few tempting eateries including the Coffee Tree (p109), Azul (p111) and Farine (p107). It sits on his-toric Wukang Rd and is a lovely place to wander.

CHINESE PRINTED BLUE NANKEEN EXHIBITION HALL
MUSEUM

Map p306 (中国蓝印花布馆, Zhōngguó Lán Yìnhuābù Guǎn; ☑021 5403 7947; No 24, Lane 637, Changle Rd; 长乐路637弄24号; ◎9am-5pm; MChangshu Rd) FREE Head down the lane and through courtyards until you see blue cloth drying in the yard. Origi-nally produced in Jiāngsū, Zhèjiāng and Guìzhōu provinces, this blue-and-white cotton fabric (sometimes called blue calico) is similar to batik, and is coloured using a starch-resist method and indigo dye bath. This museum and shop displays and sells items made by hand, from the cloth right down to the buttons.

Started by Japanese artist Kubo Mase, it has been in business for decades, takes pride in quality and does not give discounts.

LEO GALLERY
GALLERY

Map p306 (狮语画廊, Shīyǔ Huàláng; ☑021 5465 9278; www.leogallery.com.cn; 376 Wukang Rd; 武康路376号; ◎11am-7pm Tue-Sun; MShanghai Li-brary, Jiaotong University) FREE Spread across two buildings in the charming Ferguson Lane complex (p100), the Leo Gallery focus-es on works by young Chinese artists.

COMMUNITY CHURCH
CHURCH

Map p306 (☑021 6437 6576; 53 Hengshan Rd; 衡山路53号; MHengshan Rd) Shànghǎi's largest and most popular, this nondenominational ivy-cloaked church was built in 1924. There are no cheesy Chinese Catholic frills and the church lawn is a gorgeous expanse of green, while the lush tangle of plant life adds to the sense of pleasant refuge.

ART LABOR
GALLERY

Map p306 (☑021 3460 5331; www.artlabor gallery.com; Bldg 4, Surpass Court, 570 Yongjia Rd; 永嘉路570号4号楼; ◎10am-7pm Mon-Fri, noon-6pm Sat & Sun; MHengshan Rd) FREE An independent gallery representing a balance of Chinese and international artists, both emerging and established.

BA JIN'S FORMER RESIDENCE
HISTORIC BUILDING

Map p306 (巴金故居, Bājīn Gùjū; 113 Wukang Rd; 武康路113号; ◎10am-4.30pm Tue-Sun; MShanghai Library) FREE This charming lit-tle pebble-dash residence with a delightful garden wouldn't look out of place in a leafy London suburb. It's where the acclaimed author Ba Jin (1904–2005) lived from 1955 to the mid-1990s. Ba was the author of doz-ens of novels and short stories (including *Random Thoughts* and *Family*). His house today contains a collection of old photos, books and manuscripts.

Many of his works were published dur-ing the peak of his career in the 1930s. Like many intellectuals, he was persecuted mercilessly during the Cultural Revolution, during which time his wife died after being denied medical treatment. Passport may be needed for entry.

✖ EATING

The French Concession is where it's at when it comes to dining. No matter what you crave, you'll probably find it here from gastronomic fusion fare, wild Yúnnán mushrooms and sushi to tongue-tingling Sìchuān, wood-fired pizzas and hand-pulled noodles. Taojiang Rd, Dongping Rd, Fumin Rd and Xīntiāndì are the main culinary hot spots in town, and with dozens of choices between them, you'd have to eat out every night for a year to try them all.

✖ French Concession East

★Ā DÀ CÓNGYÓUBǏNG
SHANGHAI $

Map p302 (阿大葱油饼; 2, Lane 159, South Maoming Rd; 茂名南路159弄2号; cóngyóubǐng ¥5; ◎6am-3pm Thu-Tue; MSouth Shaanxi Rd) *The* very definition of a hole-in-the-wall, Ā Dà Cóngyóubǐng is a takeaway spot with a long queue of hungry locals (a one hour

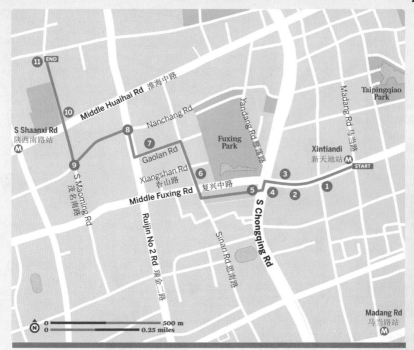

🏃 Neighbourhood Walk
French Concession Stroll

START XINTIANDI METRO STATION
END OKURA GARDEN HOTEL SHANGHAI
LENGTH 2.5KM; 75 MINUTES

Begin walking west on Middle Fuxing Rd (formerly rue Lafayette), first passing the red-brick Italianate **①All Saint's Church** (1925), then the **②Park Apartments** (1926) and smaller private villas fronted by palm trees, which date to the same era. On the northern side of Middle Fuxing Rd at No 512 is the **③Former Residence of Liu Haisu** (1896–1994), a 20th-century artist who revolutionised traditional Chinese art by introducing Western painting styles. Opposite, at the corner with South Chongqing Rd, is the **④Dubail Apartment Building** (1931), the one-time home of US journalist and communist sympathiser Agnes Smedley (1892–1950).

Turn into **⑤Sinan Mansions**, a complex of luxurious 1920s private villas built south of French Park (now Fùxīng Park) and renovated as an upscale lifestyle destination; today it houses numerous cafes and restaurants (and ultraexclusive short-term residences to the south). Exit on Sinan Rd (route Massenet) and walk north to **⑥Sun Yatsen's Former Residence** (p96), where the father of modern China lived from 1918 to 1924. On Gaolan Rd (route Cohen) is the Russian Orthodox **⑦St Nicholas Church** (p96), built in 1934 in dedication to the murdered tsar of Russia.

From Gaolan Rd, turn right into Rujin No 2 Rd, then left on to **⑧Nanchang Road** (rue Vallon), a shopping strip where you'll find boutiques selling jewellery, shoes, antiques and clothing. Turn right onto **⑨South Maoming Road** (route Cardinal Mercier), another shopping hot spot that specialises in *qípáo* (figure-hugging Chinese dresses) and other Chinese-style clothes. Across busy Huaihai Rd stands the landmark art deco **⑩Cathay Theatre** (p119), built 1932, beyond which, along South Maoming Rd, is the **⑪Okura Garden Hotel Shanghai**, originally constructed as the French Club (Cercle Sportif Français) in 1926. Take the eastern entrance and the stairs to columns capped with stunning deco nude reliefs, concealed during the Cultural Revolution.

1. Xīntiāndì (p95)

An upscale entertainment and shopping complex modelled on traditional *lòngtáng* (alleyway) homes.

2. Shíkùmén Architecture (p247)

Xīntiāndì's architecture consists largely of rebuilt traditional Shànghǎi *shíkùmén* (stone-gate houses).

3. Tiánzǐfáng (p94)

A shopping complex housed within a grid of traditional alleyways, Tiánzǐfáng is an accessible and authentic example of laneway architecture.

4. Shíkùmén Open House Museum (p96)

This two-floor exhibition invites you into a typical *shíkùmén* household, decked out with period furniture.

wait is not unheard of), serving the tastiest of that crispy Shànghǎi snacking stalwart: *cōngyóubǐng* (spring-onion pancake). You can get them all over town, but this simple place frequently edges into Top 10 lists (as voted by local diners).

Follow the aroma down the small alley, which actually leads off Nanchang Rd near the intersection of South Maoming Rd.

★ CHA'S
CANTONESE $

Map p302 (查餐厅, Chá Cāntīng; ☏021 6093 2062; 30 Sinan Rd; 思南路30号; dishes ¥32-58; ☺11am-1.30am; ⓜSouth Shaanxi Rd) This crammed Cantonese diner does its best to teleport you to 1950s Hong Kong, with old-style tiled floors, retro stained-glass and whirring ceiling fans to set the scene. You'll need to wait to get a table, so use the time wisely and peruse the extensive menu of classic comfort food (curries, sweet-and-sour pork, stir-fried beef in sweet sauce, pineapple buns) in advance.

EAST
ASIAN $

Map p302 (☏021 6467 0100; www.east-eatery. com; Tiánzǐfáng, No 39, Lane 155, Middle Jianguo Rd; 建国中路155弄39号田子坊; bao 1/3 pieces ¥12/30, dishes from ¥50; ☺11am-11pm; ☎; ⓜDapuqiao Rd) Set in a lane house in bustling Tiánzǐfáng, East is a smart eatery split between a casual street food cafe and an upstairs restaurant. The cafe serves noodle soups and Tawain's favourite steamed bun snack, *bao* (steamed bun sandwich), in bamboo steamers with a choice of fillings from pulled pork and confit duck to grilled tofu steak. Upstairs dishes up a creative fusion of Chinese, Korean and Japanese flavours in share plates.

WÈIXIĀNG ZHÁI
NOODLES $

Map p302 (味香斋; 14 Yandang Rd; 雁荡路14号; noodles ¥10; ☺6am-9pm; ⓜSouth Huangpi Rd, Xintiandi) The reason to come to this no-frills local spot is to do as the locals do and scoop up a bowl of *májiàng miàn* (麻酱面; savoury sesame noodles). At just ¥10 for a bowl of hand-pulled noodles with this rich sesame paste, it's the reason Wèixiāng Zhái is consistently packed. Pay at the counter and clip your ticket to your table.

DIǍN SHÍ ZHÁI XIǍO YÀN
SHANGHAI $

Map p302 (点石斋小宴; ☏021 5465 0270; 320 Yongjia Rd; 永嘉路320号; dishes from ¥32; ☺11am-2pm & 5.30-9.30pm; ⓜSouth Shaanxi Rd, Jiashan Rd) Shànghǎi cuisine can be

cloyingly sweet when improperly prepared, but this elegant restaurant hits the mark with its delicate flavours. It has a wonderful range of cold appetisers and seafood dishes. Be sure to look out for the excellent Zhèjiāng dishes, including Shàoxīng drunken chicken and individual portions of tender *dōngpō ròu* (stewed pork fat).

LÁNXĪN CĀNTĪNG
SHANGHAI $

Map p302 (兰心餐厅; 130 Jinxian Rd; 进贤路130号; dishes ¥12-65; ☺10am-10pm; ⓜSouth Shaanxi Rd) Some of the best Shanghainese kitchens are holes in the wall along Jinxian Rd. These aren't the domain of international superchefs; they're unpretentious and family run – the last of a dying breed. Winning dishes include the classic *hóngshāo ròu* (红烧肉; braised pork), the delectable *gānshāo chāngyú* (干烧鲳鱼; quick-fried pomfret fish) and *xiǎopái luóbo tāng* (小排萝卜汤; spare-rib-and-radish soup).

For total immersion, order up a bottle of warm *huáng jiǔ* (黄酒; traditional Chinese wine). No reservations, no English and cash only.

FĒNGYÙ SHĒNGJIĀN
DUMPLINGS $

Map p302 (丰裕生煎; 41 Ruijin No 2 Rd, cnr Nanchang Rd; 瑞金二路41号; dishes from ¥5; ☺6am-8.30pm; ⓜSouth Shaanxi Rd) If you thought Shànghǎi dining was all white linen tablecloths, steaming hand towels and perfectly formed waitresses in cheongsam clutching gold-embossed menus, think again. Chow down on fine *xiǎolóngbāo* (dumplings; ¥6), *shēngjiān* (生煎; fried dumplings; ¥5) and *miàntiáo* (noodles; ¥8) with the hardworking proletariat at Fēngyù, where plastic trays, fixed furniture and zero English rule.

Pay at the entrance and join the queue.

BANKURA
JAPANESE $

Map p302 (万藏, Wànzàng; ☏021 6215 0373; 344 Changle Rd; 长乐路344号; noodles ¥30-55, lunch sets ¥39; ☺11.30am-2pm & 5.30pm-late; ⓜSouth Shaanxi Rd) Pull up a seat at this underground Japanese noodle bar, where the focus is on soba (thin buckwheat noodles, often served cold) and udon (thick wheat noodles, often served in broth) choices, as well as delectable extras such as grilled shiitake mushrooms, curried shrimp and fried-eel rice bowls.

In the evening, the drinks menu – *shōchū* (Japanese distilled spirit made from grains) cocktails and plum wine – provides further incentive to drop by.

DÀ MÁO CÓNGYÓUBǏNG
SHANGHAI $

Map p302 (大毛葱油饼; 213 Hefei Rd; 合肥路213号; cóngyóubǐng from ¥3.50; ⏰6am-6pm; Ⓜ Xintiandi) Delightfully scrummy, crisp and flavoursome spring-onion pancakes (葱油饼; *cóngyóubǐng*) are the speciality at this ramshackle hole-in-the-wall snack point that sees regular lines of customers. It's *dìdào* (authentic), old school and on the money. Takeaway only.

FUNK A DELI
CAFE $

Map p302 (www.funkadeli.com; 46 Yongkang Rd; 永康路46号; mains from ¥45; ⏰11am-late; ☎; Ⓜ South Shaanxi Rd) Funk a Deli brings Italian flair to bar-stuffed Yongkang Rd, serving panini sandwiches with imported cheese and meats along with Italian wine and Peroni beer. Stop by for a Campari aperitif or glass of prosecco.

★ DÌ SHUǏ DÒNG
HUNANESE $$

Map p302 (滴水洞; ☎021 6253 2689; 2nd fl, 56 South Maoming Rd; 茂名南路56号2楼; dishes ¥25-128; ⏰11am-1am; Ⓜ South Shaanxi Rd) Until the chilled lagers arrive, the faint breeze from the spreading of the blue-and-white tablecloth by your waiter may be the last cooling sensation at Dì Shuǐ Dòng, a rustic upstairs shrine to the volcanic cuisine of Húnán. Loved by Shanghainese and expats in equal measure, dishes are ferried in by sprightly peasant-attired staff to tables stuffed with enthusiastic, red-faced diners.

The claim to fame is the Húnán-style cumin-crusted ribs, but there's no excuse not to sample the *làzi jīdīng* (fried chicken with chillies), the excellent Húnán-style fried crab in claypot or even the classic boiled frog. Cool down with plenty of beers and crowd-pleasing caramelised bananas for dessert.

SOUTHERN BARBARIAN
YUNNAN $$

Map p302 (南蛮子, Nánmánzi; ☎021 5157 5510; 2nd fl, Gourmet Zone, 56 South Maoming Rd; 茂名南路56号生活艺术空间2楼; dishes ¥25-118; ⏰11am-2pm & 5-10pm; Ⓜ South Shaanxi Rd) Despite the alarming name, there's nothing remotely barbaric about the food here. Instead, you get fine MSG-free Yúnnán cuisine served by friendly staff in a laid-back (though somewhat noisy) atmosphere. It's hard to fault any of the dishes but the goat's cheese is unmissable, and the stewed beef and mint casserole is almost as good, as is the incomparable 'grandmother's mashed potatoes'.

It's essential to make room for the chicken wings too, which come covered in a seriously addictive secret sauce. To top it off, there's an impressively long imported beer list. You can also enter at 169 Jinxian Rd.

YÈ SHÀNGHǍI
SHANGHAI $$

Map p302 (夜上海; ☎021 6311 2323; Xīntiāndì North Block, 338 South Huangpi Rd; 黄陂南路338号新天地北里; dishes ¥68-188, set lunch menu ¥88; ⏰11.30am-2.30pm & 5.30-10.30pm; Ⓜ South Huangpi Rd, Xintiandi) Yè offers sophisticated, unchallenging Shanghainese cuisine in classy Xīntiāndì surroundings. The drunken chicken and smoked fish starters are an excellent overture to local flavours; the crispy duck comes with thick pancakes and the sautéed string beans and bamboo shoots dish doesn't disappoint either. An affordable wine list gives it a further tick.

DIN TAI FUNG
DUMPLING $$

Map p302 (鼎泰丰, Dǐng Tài Fēng; ☎021 6385 8378; www.dintaifung.com.cn; Xīntiāndì South Block, 2nd fl, Bldg 6; 兴业路123弄新天地南里6号楼2楼; 10 dumplings ¥60-96; ⏰10am-midnight; Ⓜ South Huangpi Rd, Xintiandi) One of the many branches of Taiwan's most famous chain, where the dumplings are fantastic and the service classy, but it does come with a price tag. It's on the 2nd floor, inside the Xīntiāndì mall. Reserve.

CRYSTAL JADE
DIM SUM $$

Map p302 (翡翠酒家, Fěicuì Jiǔjiā; ☎021 6385 8752; Xīntiāndì South Block, 2nd fl, Bldg 6; 兴业路123弄新天地南里6号楼2楼; dim sum ¥20-42; ⏰11am-10.30pm; Ⓜ South Huangpi Rd, Xintiandi) One of Xīntiāndì's long-standing success stories, Crystal Jade can still draw lines out the door. What separates it from other dim sum restaurants is the dough: dumpling skins are perfectly tender; steamed buns come out light and airy; and the freshly pulled noodles are just plain delicious. Go for lunch, when both Cantonese and Shanghainese dim sum are served.

The long communal table is good for solo diners. You'll find Crystal Jade on the 2nd floor of the mall.

KOMMUNE
CAFE $$

Map p302 (公社, Gōngshè; ☎021 6466 2416; www.kommune.me; Tiánzǐfáng, The Yard, No 7, Lane 210, Taikang Rd; 泰康路210弄7号田子坊; meals from ¥77; ⏰9am-midnight; ☎; Ⓜ Dapuqiao Rd) The original Tiánzǐfáng cafe, Kommune is a consistently bustling hang-out providing an

EATING ORGANIC

The organic movement in China has only recently sprouted, but it has quickly spread in Shànghǎi. With the quality of produce and manufactured products in China becoming increasingly dubious, there's been enough negative publicity (generated by the discovery of bean sprouts being soaked in a banned chemical solution at local markets, glass noodle samples that contained aluminium, and mutated eggs that bounced 'like ping-pong balls') that Shanghainese are starting to get interested. A number of organic farms have started up on the city's outskirts in recent years. The following restaurants specialise in local organic ingredients:

Organic Kitchen (p110)

Green & Safe (p107)

Hunter Gatherer (p108)

Vegetarian Lifestyle (p106)

essential pit stop when exploring the area. There's outdoor seating, all-day big breakfasts, sandwiches, burgers and curries on the menu, along with good coffee and something stronger.

SHÀNGHǍI MIN   SHANGHAI $$

Map p302 (小南国, Xiǎo Nán Guó; ☑400 820 9777; Xīntiāndì South Block, 2nd fl, Bldg 6; 兴业路123弄新天地南里6号楼2楼; dishes ¥35-198; ⏰11am-10pm; Ⓜ South Huangpi Rd, Xintiandi) Even with the smart banquet halls and classy presentation, this is still one of Shànghǎi's more affordable (and delicious) chains. First-rate dishes include tofu and crab casserole, lion's head meatballs, pork trotters braised for six hours and the usual run of Shanghainese dumplings and noodles. Finish off with sweet rice dumplings in osmanthus juice. Located in the Xīntiāndì mall.

GǓYÌ HÚNÁN
RESTAURANT   HUNANESE $$

Map p306 (古意湘味浓, Gǔyì Xiāngwèinóng; ☑021 6249 5628; 87 Fumin Rd; 富民路87号; dishes ¥38-128; ⏰11am-2pm & 5.30-10.30pm; Ⓜ Jing'an Temple, Changshu Rd) Gǔyì is a fine Húnán choice for a romantic dinner. It has a classy atmosphere equalled by a comprehensive menu, which includes great huǒguō (hotpot; from ¥48) featuring beef, chicken, crab or frog and delectable cumin ribs.

Reserve a couple of days in advance.

VEGETARIAN LIFESTYLE   CHINESE $$

Map p302 (枣子树, Zǎozishù; ☑021 6384 8000; www.jujubetree.com; 77 Songshan Rd; 嵩山路77号; dishes ¥30-85; ⏰11am-9.30pm; ☑; Ⓜ South Huangpi Rd) Head into a courtyard off Songshan Rd to find a branch of this popular vegetarian restaurant, where organic, MSG-free and oil-light dishes are the order of the day. No alcohol is served.

KABB   AMERICAN $$

Map p302 (凯博西餐厅, Kǎibó Xīcāntīng; ☑021 5465 3856; www.kabbsh.com; Xīntiāndì North Block, Bldg 5; 太仓路181弄新天地北里5号楼; mains ¥65-125; ⏰7am-1am; 🛜; Ⓜ South Huangpi Rd, Xintiandi) This smart Xīntiāndì grill serves authentic American-portioned comfort food (sandwiches, burgers and burritos). The outdoor cafe-style seating is particularly popular for a slower-paced weekend brunch, when the menu stretches to French toast with bananas and eggs Benedict.

FOOD FUSION   MALAYSIAN $$

Map p302 (融合, Rónghé; ☑021 6385 3906; 8th fl, Parkson Plaza, 918 Middle Huaihai Rd; 淮海中路918号百盛8楼; dishes ¥38-168, lunch sets from ¥38; ⏰10am-10pm; Ⓜ South Shaanxi Rd) Up on the 8th floor of the Parkson Plaza you'll find this hopping Malaysian option. Join the thronging office workers filling the lift and ascend to aromas of coriander, star anise, nutmeg, cinnamon and ginger. Crowd-pleasing classics include *rendang* beef, chilli-flecked laksa (coconut curry noodle soup), fish curry, *roti canai* and Nonya desserts.

★T8   FUSION $$$

Map p302 (☑021 6355 8999; http://t8-shanghai.com; Xīntiāndì North Block, Bldg 8; 太仓路181弄新天地北里8号楼; mains ¥238-598, set lunch weekdays ¥158; ⏰11am-2.30pm & 6.30-10.30pm; Ⓜ South Huangpi Rd, Xintiandi) T8 aims to seduce, which it does exceptionally well. Catalan chef Jordi Servalls Bonilla is at the helm, bringing a preference for molecular cuisine with dishes such as *tataki* of sesame-crusted tuna and foie gras millefeuille (a layered pastry cake). The renovated grey-brick *shíkùmén* with striking feng shui–driven entrance is the perfect setting.

The dark, warm interior is decorated with antique Chinese cabinets and a carved wooden screen. Reserve ahead.

✕ French Concession West

★ JIAN GUO 328   SHANGHAI $
Map p302 (建国, Jiànguó; ☑021 6471 3819; 328 West Jianguo Rd; 建国西路328号; mains ¥22-58; ⊗11am-2pm & 5-9.30pm; Ⓜ Jiashan Rd) Frequently crammed, this boisterous narrow two-floor MSG-free spot tucked away on Jianguo Rd does a roaring trade on the back of excellent well-priced Shanghainese cuisine. You can't go wrong with the menu; highlights include the deep fried duck legs, aubergine casserole, scallion-oil noodles and yellow croaker fish spring rolls. Reserve.

★ SÌCHUĀN CITIZEN   SICHUAN $
Map p302 (龙门阵茶屋, Lóngménzhèn Cháwū; ☑021 5404 1235; 30 Donghu Rd; 东湖路30号; dishes ¥26-98, set lunch ¥38-68; ⊗11am-10.30pm; ☎; Ⓜ South Shaanxi Rd) The subdued evening lighting and welcoming service concocts a warm and homely atmosphere at this popular outpost of Sìchuān cuisine in Shànghǎi. The extensive photo menu is foreigner friendly and includes a sizeable vegetarian selection. The *dan dan* noodles are textbook spicy while the pork wontons in hot oil (¥10) are spot on.

Not all dishes hit the *chuāncài* (川菜; Sìchuān food) nail on the head, though, and the *mápó dòufu* (tofu and pork crumbs in a spicy sauce; ¥26) is wide of the mark. Quench it all with a large bottle of Budweiser for ¥30 or one of the great cocktails. Service can be slow at busy times.

★ SPICY JOINT   SICHUAN $
Map p302 (辛香汇, Xīnxiānghuì; ☑021 6470 2777; 3rd fl, K Wah Center, 1028 Middle Huaihai Rd; 淮海中路1028号嘉华中心3楼; dishes ¥12-60; ⊗11am-10pm; ☎; Ⓜ South Shaanxi Rd) If you only go to one Sìchuān joint in town, make it this one, where the blistering heat is matched only by its scorching popularity. Dishes are inexpensive by the city's standards; favourites include massive bowls of

spicy catfish in hot chilli oil, an addictive garlic-cucumber salad, smoked-tea duck and chilli-coated lamb chops.

Be forewarned that the wait can be excruciatingly long at peak times; you'll need a mobile number to secure a place in the queue.

AL'S DINER   AMERICAN $
Map p306 (☑021 5465 1259; www.eatatalsdiner.com; 204 Xinle Rd; 新乐路204号; mains ¥35-85; ⊗9am-midnight; Ⓜ South Shaanxi Rd, Changshu Rd) Al's is a smart casual spot bringing you classic American diner dishes (biscuits and gravy, tuna melt, clam chowder) and hangover favourites (fried kimchi chicken, all-day egg breakfasts, burgers). The small space is consistently packed; just try to get near it on a Sunday. Don't miss dessert thanks to on-site Gracie's (p108) ice cream.

BOOM BOOM BAGELS   BAKERY, CAFE $
Map p306 (www.boomboombagels.com; 39 Anfu Rd; 安福路39号; bagels ¥35-58; ⊗6.30am-10pm; ☎; Ⓜ Changshu Rd) Bagel bar isn't a combo you hear often but it's certainly working for Boom Boom. They boil their bagels fresh every day before piling them with toppings such as smoked pulled pork with BBQ slaw, or tuna melt with crispy bacon. By day, match it with a Sumerian (p135) coffee; by night opt for craft beer on tap or cocktails.

GREEN & SAFE   INTERNATIONAL $
Map p306 (☑021 5465 1288; 6 Dongping Rd; 东平路6号; mains from ¥48; ⊗8am-midnight; Ⓜ Changshu Rd) 🌿 Expat favourite Green & Safe is the closest thing you'll get to Whole Foods in Shànghǎi. Head upstairs to the inviting loft-style restaurant with open kitchen to try free-range meat from the company's farm (juicy burgers, racks of lamb). Happy hour runs from 4pm to 6pm and 9pm to midnight, with ¥28 beer and wine. Stock up on bottles of organic wine, fresh produce, pastries, sustainable chocolate and ecofriendly bathroom products from the downstairs organic shop-cafe.

FARINE   BAKERY, CAFE $
Map p306 (http://farine-bakery.com; Ferguson Lane, 378 Wukang Rd; 武康路378号1楼; pastries & cakes from ¥18; ⊗7am-8pm Mon-Thu, to 10pm Fri-Sun; Ⓜ Shanghai Library, Jiaotong University) It can be hard to find a seat on the outdoor terrace facing Wukang Rd at this *boulangerie* during the weekend crush hour.

Choose a quieter off-peak moment to sink some well-executed pastries, sandwiches, fantastic breads (baked with imported stone-ground flour) and coffee at this eye-catching Ferguson Lane spot. There is another small branch in the IFC Mall (p155), Pǔdōng.

LA CRÊPERIE
FRENCH $

Map p306 (☑021 5465 9055; www.lacreperie. com.cn; 1 Taojiang Rd; 桃江路1号; mains from ¥55, weekend brunch ¥128-158; ◎11am-11pm; ⓂChangshu Rd) This appetising slice of Brittany in Shànghǎi is a great stop-off for expertly made, delicious savoury or sweet crêpes (from ¥52) and galettes (from ¥72), with matching lighthouse salt and pepper shakers, lovely cider and homely service.

MIA'S YÚNNÁN KITCHEN
YUNNAN $

Map p306 (香所云南菜, Xiāngsuǒ Yúnnán Cài; ☑021 5403 5266; 45-47 Anfu Rd; 安福路45-47号; mains ¥35-68; ◎11am-10pm; ⓂChangshu Rd) On balance, Shànghǎi has more popular Yúnnán restaurants, but intimate Mia's offers a more homely and rustic French Concession ambience, with lashings of wild vegetables including Jizong mushrooms and spicy fern. The fried goat's cheese is spot on. Finish it off with lemongrass tea or a pot Yúnnán rose tea (¥25 pot for two).

HUNTER GATHERER
HEALTH FOOD $

Map p306 (悦衡食集, Yuè Héng Shíjí; ☑021 5461 0552; www.behuntergatherer.com; 106, 308 Anfu Rd; 安福路308号; bowls from ¥48; ◎10am-10pm; ⓢ; ⓂChangshu Rd) ✑ Split between a downstairs produce shop and upstairs cafe-shop, Hunter Gatherer is all about organic farm-to-table food. The cafe is a light, bright space where you can tuck into salad bowls and wraps filled with ingredients such as quinoa, roasted veg, goji berries, antibiotic-free chicken and chopped kale. To drink, choose from fresh juices and smoothies, or go the organic Yúnnán coffee or black sesame chai latte.

The shop sells imported goods from jars of hot pickles to old-style sodas (sweetened with cane sugar) and sustainable chocolate.

GRACIE'S
ICE CREAM $

Map p306 (☑021 5465 1259; www.icecream bygracies.com; 204 Xinle Rd; 新乐路204号; single scoops ¥30; ◎9am-midnight; ⓂSouth Shaanxi Rd, Changshu Rd) Gracie's tempts from the back of Al's Diner (p107) with her home-made ice cream in hard-to-resist flavours of miso caramel, London fog (inspired by Earl Grey), salted Oreo, and black sesame and honey. Available in small takeaway cups or cones (¥30) or larger take-home tubs (¥90).

BAKER & SPICE
CAFE $

Map p306 (www.bakerandspice.com.cn; 195 Anfu Rd; 安福路195号; sandwiches & salads from ¥50; ◎6am-10.30pm; ⓢ; ⓂChangshu Rd) Whether you're craving a healthy sit-down lunch or a takeaway treat, Baker & Spice has you covered. The long wooden communal table suits solo diners while couples and groups natter away at tables spread out in this bright and airy bakery-cafe. Everything comes lovingly presented: sandwiches on dense, fibre-rich bread; quinoa and kale salads; muffins; pains-au-chocolate; tartines; cakes; and sizeable vanilla custard Berliners.

PAIN CHAUD
BAKERY, CAFE $

Map p302 (☑021 5424 9630; 29-31 Yongkang Rd; 永康路29-31号; pastries from ¥14; ◎8am-10pm; ⓢ; ⓂSouth Shaanxi Rd) On a strip best known for its nightlife, chic bakery/cafe Pain Chaud gives good reason to get here earlier in the day. Join the queue drooling over the display and trying to decide what to get by the time they reach the white-aproned staff at the counter; not easy with delectable chocolate eclairs, croissants, and baguettes stuffed with cheese staring at you.

GRAPE RESTAURANT
SHANGHAI $

Map p302 (葡萄园酒家, Pútáoyuán Jiǔjiā; ☑021 5404 0486; 55 Xinle Rd; 新乐路55号; dishes ¥18-78; ◎11am-midnight; ⓂSouth Shaanxi Rd) This long-standing fave from the 1980s still serves up reliable and inexpensive Shanghainese in its bright premises beside the old Russian Orthodox church. Try the crab dishes – you won't find them any cheaper.

★JESSE
SHANGHAI $$

Map p306 (吉士酒楼, Jíshì Jiǔlóu; ☑021 6282 9260; www.xinjishi.com; 41 Tianping Rd; 天平路41号; dishes ¥28-188; ◎11am-4pm & 5.30pm-midnight; ⓂJiaotong University) Jesse specialises in packing lots of people into tight spaces, so if you tend to gesture wildly when you talk, watch out with those chopsticks. This is Shanghainese home-cooking at its best: crab dumplings, jujubes (red dates) stuffed with glutinous rice, Grandma's braised pork and plenty of fish, drunken shrimp and eel.

★**LOST HEAVEN** YUNNAN **$$**
Map p306 (花马天堂, Huāmǎ Tiāntáng; ☑021 6433 5126; www.lostheaven.com.cn; 38 Gaoyou Rd; 高邮路38号; dishes ¥48-96; ⏱11.30am-1.30pm & 5.30-10.30pm; Ⓜ Shanghai Library) Located on a quiet street in Shànghǎi's most desirable neighbourhood, Lost Heaven is stylish and atmospheric with subdued red lighting and a giant Buddha dominating the main dining area. The Yúnnán food is delicately flavoured and nicely presented, although purists may bemoan the way some dishes, such as the Dali chicken, aren't as spicy as they should be. The Yúnnán vegetable cakes come with a salsa-like garnish and make a fantastic starter.

There are a few branches around town, including one on the Bund (p71). Reserve.

DĪ SHUǏ DÒNG HUNANESE **$$**
Map p306 (滴水洞; ☑021 6415 9448; 5 Dongping Rd; 东平路5号; dishes ¥25-128; ⏱10am-12.30am; Ⓜ Changshu Rd) This branch of the spicy Húnán favourite isn't the most popular but it's less crowded than others and the menu's equally good.

TEPITO MEXICAN **$$**
Map p306 (291 Fumin Rd; 富民路291号; ⏱noon-1.30pm Mon-Fri, to 11.30pm Sat & Sun; Ⓜ Changshu Rd, South Shaanxi Rd) Tepito brings authentic Mexican food to Shànghǎi (no Tex-Mex!), headed up by chef Edgar Hernandez from Mexico City, in a glaringly bright upmarket cantina space. While the food can be a bit hit-and-miss, standouts include the kingfish *tiradito* (similar to a ceviche) and *carnitas taquitos* (crispy baked rolled tortillas) filled with tender pork. The front terrace is popular for knocking back strong margaritas.

LIQUID LAUNDRY AMERICAN **$$**
Map p302 (☑021 6445 9589; www.theliquidlaundry.com; 2nd fl, Kwah Centre, 1028 Middle Huaihai Rd; 淮海中路1028号2楼; mains ¥48-128; ⏱11am-midnight Sun-Wed, to 2am Thu-Sat; ☎; Ⓜ South Shaanxi Rd) With bow-tied 'mixologists', subway-tiled walls and exposed warehouse piping, Liquid Laundry will have you thinking you've just walked off the elevator into NYC. This vast gastropub/cocktail bar offers several options – wood-fired pizza at the counter, American bourbon whiskeys in the lounge area, rotisserie chicken with homemade hot sauce to a backdrop of shiny brewery vats, and 15 craft beer taps.

COFFEE TREE CAFE **$$**
Map p306 (Ferguson Lane, 376 Wukang Rd; 武康路376号; mains ¥68-108; ⏱8.30am-10pm Mon-Fri, 9am-10pm Sat & Sun; ☎; Ⓜ Shanghai Library) Full of well-heeled diners come weekend brunch time, this cafe in Ferguson Lane is a pleasant spot for a coffee. Sit on the patio in the sun-filled courtyard out front, ringed by well-composed brickwork and verdant foliage. The brunches are deservedly popular; you can fill yourself up with two courses and a bottomless coffee for ¥138.

XĪBÓ CENTRAL ASIAN **$$**
Map p306 (锡伯新疆餐厅, Xībó Xīnjiāng Cāntīng; ☑021 5403 8330; www.xiboxinjiang.com; 3rd fl, 83 Changshu Rd; 常熟路83号3楼; mains ¥38-128; ⏱noon-2.30pm & 6pm-midnight; Ⓜ Changshu Rd) Trust Shànghǎi to serve up a stylish Xīnjiāng joint, because this isn't the type of place you're likely to find out in China's wild northwest. But who's complaining? When you need a mutton fix, beef skewers or some spicy 'big plate chicken', Xībó will do you right (and the restaurant donates healthily to charities in west China).

PHO REAL VIETNAMESE **$$**
Map p306 (☑021 5403 8110; www.phorealgroup.cn; 166 Fumin Rd; 富民路166号; pho from ¥50; ⏱11am-2pm & 5.30-10pm; Ⓜ Changshu Rd, Jing'an Temple) This pint-sized eatery does a brisk trade in *pho* (beef noodle soup flavoured with mint, star anise and cilantro), spring rolls and *bahn mi* (Vietnamese baguette). There's a vegetarian *pho* for non meat-eaters too. Round it all out with a chilled Saigon lager (¥38). It only seats about 20, with no reservations, so pitch up early and prepare to wait.

There's another branch of Pho Real located at 1465 Fuxing Rd (p110), which does accept reservations.

GARLIC TURKISH **$$**
Map p306 (www.garlicshanghai.com; 698 Yongjia Rd; 永嘉路698号; mains from ¥78; ⏱6-11.30pm Mon-Fri, noon-midnight Sat & Sun; Ⓜ Hengshan Rd) The ancestral homeland of much of China's northwestern Uighur cuisine, Turkish food gets a swish French Concession revamp at smart Garli. The *hunkar begendi* ('Sultan's Favorite' tandoori lamb with charcoal-grilled aubergine; ¥160) is delightful and typical of the rich flavours coursing through an ample menu.

Book ahead for weekends.

There's a strong showing of Turkish wines plus, for feasting families, a downstairs kids' zone with PlayStation.

ORGANIC KITCHEN
CAFE $$

Map p306 (☑021 6418 3220; www.organic kitchenshanghai.com; 57 West Fuxing Rd; 复兴西路57号; mains from ¥50, breakfast sets ¥50-68; ⊙8am-10pm; 🛜🍴; Ⓜ Shanghai Library, Changshu Rd) 🍃 A cosy white-brick-walled cafe, the Organic Kitchen focuses on health-conscious comfort food, and the menu stretches from all-day breakfast sets and salads to falafel wraps, quinoa burgers, Indian curries and banana muffins. There's a long list of freshly squeezed juices and smoothies.

HAIKU
JAPANESE $$

Map p306 (隐泉之语, Yǐnquán Zhī Yǔ; ☑021 6445 0021; 28b Taojiang Rd; 桃江路28号乙; maki rolls ¥70-140; ⊙11am-2pm & 5.30-10pm; Ⓜ Changshu Rd) The name of the game at Haiku is 'let's see how many different things we can fit into a maki roll'. The Dynamite roll wraps up raw tuna with a killer spicy sauce, while the Moto-roll-ah is a deep-fried spicy tuna, snow crab and avocado combo. Can't make up your mind? Pimp My Roll may be the one for you – it's loaded with everything. Reserve.

XIAN YUE HIEN
DIM SUM $$

Map p306 (申粤轩酒楼, Shēnyuèxuān Jiǔlóu; ☑021 6251 1166; www.syx-dx.com; 849 Huashan Rd; 华山路849号; dim sum ¥17-28; ⊙11am-2.30pm & 5-10pm; Ⓜ Shanghai Library) The Dǐng Xiāng Garden, originally built for the concubine of a Qing dynasty mandarin, is reserved for retired Communist Party cadres, so to peek behind the undulating dragon wall, you need to dine here. At the pointy end, seafood dishes can get very expensive, but the real draw is the dim sum, served overlooking the lawn on mornings and afternoons.

Afternoon tea is served from 2.30pm to 5pm. Reserve ahead.

PĪNCHUĀN
SICHUAN $$

Map p306 (品川, ☑400 820 7706; 47 Taojiang Rd; 桃江路47号; dishes ¥49-119; ⊙11am-2pm & 5-10pm; Ⓜ Changshu Rd) The telltale blend of chillies and peppercorns here is best summed up in two words: là (辣; spicy) and má (麻; numbing). Even though Pīnchuān has hit the upscale button repeatedly in the past few years, this is still a fine place to experience the tongue tingling of Sìchuān cooking. Try the popular sliced beef in hot chilli oil served in a big glass bowl. Reserve.

COCONUT PARADISE
THAI $$

Map p306 (椰香天堂, Yēxiāng Tiāntáng; ☑021 6248 1998; 38 Fumin Rd; 富民路38号; dishes ¥68-188; ⊙11.30am-2pm & 5.30-10pm; Ⓜ Jing'an Temple) Coconut Paradise is a tropical delight, its lush garden seating and dimly lit interior making for a decidedly romantic venue. Curries, fish salads and *tom yung goong* soup will bring back memories of days spent lazing around in northern Thailand, and by the end of the meal, you might even forget you're in Shànghǎi. No MSG. Reserve a few days ahead.

PHO REAL
VIETNAMESE $$

Map p306 (☑021 6437 2222; www.phorealgroup. cn; 1465 Fuxing Rd; 复兴中路1465号; pho from ¥50; ⊙11am-2pm & 5.30-10pm Mon-Fri, 11am-3.30pm & 6-10pm Sat & Sun; Ⓜ Changshu Rd) Sit at the wooden counter or grab a table at this handy branch of the Vietnamese *pho* restaurant. Takes reservations.

CH2 BY WHISK
CAFE $$

Map p306 (☑021 5404 7770; 1250 Middle Huaihai Rd; 卢湾区淮海中路1250号; mains & desserts both from ¥55; ⊙10am-11.30pm; 🛜; Ⓜ Changshu Rd) Tucked away down a recess off Middle Huaihai Rd, CH2 (formerly Whisk) dishes up an addictive line of luxurious desserts, such as chocolate tarts, brownie cheesecake and mousse, along with a popular Italian menu. The decor is a little bit Euro glam but when the lights dim in the evening, it's a romantic spot. It's a crucial stop for chocaholics.

NEPALI KITCHEN
NEPALESE $$

Map p306 (尼泊尔餐厅, Níbó'ěr Cāntīng; ☑021 5404 6281; www.nepalikitchenshanghai.com; No 4, Lane 819, Julu Rd; 巨鹿路819弄4号; mains ¥45-85; ⊙11am-2pm & 6-10.30pm Mon-Fri, 11am-3pm & 6-11pm Sat, 11am-3pm Sun; Ⓜ Jing'an Temple, Changshu Rd) Reminisce about that Himalayan trek over a plate of Tibetan *momo* (dumplings) or a *choila* (spicy chicken) amid prayer flags in this homey, lodge-like place. For a more laid-back meal, take your shoes off and recline on traditional cushions, surrounded by colourful *thangkas* and paper lamps.

Both the set lunch and dinner are a good bet, from ¥55, with a choice of vegetarian or meat sets.

GLO LONDON
BRITISH $$

Map p306 (☏021 6466 6565; www.glolondon.com; 1 South Wulumuqi Rd; 乌鲁木齐南路1号; mains from ¥98, 2-/3-course set lunch ¥88/110; ⊗11am-10.30pm; MChangshu Rd, Hengshan Rd) This four-storey affair wants to be everything to everyone, and, amazingly enough, it seems to be working. The 1st floor is a coffee specialist cafe, Coffee Academics, while the slick 2nd floor (the Gastro Grill) serves the greatest hits of British cuisine – from tandoori lamb chops to beer-battered cod (and chips). The swish Glo Wine Bar (p118) occupies the 3rd floor.

There's a rooftop terrace BBQ spot that opens from May to October (5pm to late).

BĂOLUÓ JIŬLÓU
SHANGHAI $$

Map p306 (保罗酒楼; ☏021 6279 2827; 271 Fumin Rd; 富民路271号; dishes ¥58; ⊗11am-late; MChangshu Rd, Jing'an Temple) Gather up some friends to join the Shanghainese at this expanded, highly popular Fumin Rd venue. It's a great place to get a feel for Shànghǎi's famous buzz. Try the excellent baked eel (保罗烤鳗; *bǎoluó kǎomán*) or pot-stewed crab and pork.

VEDAS
INDIAN $$

Map p306 (维达斯, Wéi Dá Sī; www.vedascuisine.com; 3rd fl, 83 Changshu Rd; 常熟路83号3楼; mains from ¥88; ⊗11.30am-2pm & 5.30-10.30pm; ☏; MChangshu Rd) Vedas hides the sterility of its modern tower-block setting with good-looking woodwork, warm service and a generous menu of full-flavoured Indian dishes. The delightful Bombay prawn curry (¥88) is piquant and creamy in equal measure, while the basmati rice is cooked to perfection and arrives in steaming abundance. Vegetarians will find much to coo about. Set meals are good value and the naan is tip-top.

SIMPLY THAI
THAI $$

Map p306 (天泰餐厅, Tiāntài Cāntīng; ☏021 6445 9551; www.simplythai.com.cn; 5c Dongping Rd; 东平路5号C座; dishes ¥58-180; ⊗11am-11pm; MChangshu Rd) This popular branch of Shànghǎi's favourite Thai has a tree-shaded patio, perfect for alfresco dining. Expect reasonably priced classics such as green and red curries, tom yum soup and fiery green papaya salad.

DA MARCO
ITALIAN $$

Map p306 (大马可餐厅, Dàmǎkě Cāntīng; ☏021 6210 4495; www.damarco.com.cn; 103 Dong Zhu'anbang Rd, inside Parklane blg; 东诸安浜路103号; pasta & pizza ¥68-88, mains ¥108-168; ⊗noon-11pm; ☏; MJiangsu Rd) This homey spot is one of the most popular Italian restaurants in town and remains a steal after 15 years in business (an eternity in Shànghǎi). Menu highlights include pear and Gorgonzola pizza and sea bass baked in salt, as well as a selection of Italian cheeses and, of course, classic tiramisu. Reserve.

ELEMENT FRESH
CAFE $$

Map p302 (新元素, Xīnyuánsù; ☏021 6279 8682; 4th fl, K Wah Centre, 1028 Middle Huaihai Rd, 淮海中路1028号嘉华中心4楼; sandwiches & salads ¥48-128, dinner from ¥168; ⊗9am-11pm; ☏☏; MSouth Shaanxi Rd) This sleek and good-looking branch of the health-conscious eatery is a cool choice, with an inviting bar area and a largely faultless menu of big salads, cleansing juices and hearty soups.

★ELEFANTE
MEDITERRANEAN $$$

Map p302 (☏021 5404 8085; www.el-efante.com; 20 Donghu Rd; 东湖路20号; lunch set ¥128, weekend brunch from ¥198; ⊗11.30am-3pm & 6-10.30pm Mon-Fri, 11am-3pm Sat & Sun; MSouth Shaanxi Rd) Willy Trullas Moreno's ElEfante sits squarely at the heart of the French Concession – in the same spot as his first venture – with a choice patio and romantic 1920s villa setting. Its tantalising Mediterranean menu, with tapas-style dishes, has pronounced Spanish and Italian inflections, and has local gastronomes buzzing.

On weekends in summer you'll often find the Dumbo food truck parked in the patio hosting the city's most well-known chefs cooking up tasty brunches.

AZUL
TAPAS $$$

Map p306 (☏021 5405 2252; www.azultapaslounge.cn; 8th fl, 378 Wukang Rd; 武康路378号8楼; tapas ¥48-128, weekend brunch ¥158-178; ⊗11am-midnight; ☏; MShanghai Library, Jiaotong University) Peruvian restaurateur Eduardo Vargas specialises in hip fusion food slanted towards South American flavours. On the top floor of the art deco Ferguson Lane complex – complete with lovely terrace – Azul keeps the tapas tradition going strong with temptations that run from prawn ceviche tostadas (marinated raw prawns on a toasted tortilla) to reinvented standards such as *patatas bravas*.

Get stuck into free-flowing margaritas for ¥100 per person, midday to 5pm weekends. Reserve.

KAGEN
TEPPANYAKI $$$

Map p306 (隐泉源铁板烧, Yīnquán Yuán Tiěbǎnshāo; ☑021 6433 3232; 28d Taojiang Rd; 桃江路28号丁; all-you-can-eat-&-drink teppanyaki ¥328; ⏰5.30-11pm Mon-Thu & Sun, 11.30am-midnight Fri & Sat; Ⓜ Changshu Rd) Opened by the folks at Haiku (p110) next door, super-sleek Kagen offers excellent value all-you-can-eat-and-drink teppanyaki. Wagyu beef, tiger prawns and foie gras are some of the finer ingredients on the menu, and quality sushi, sashimi, sake and wine are all part of the buffet deal. It also offers an à la carte menu. Reserve.

SHINTORI NULL II
FUSION $$$

Map p306 (新都里无二店, Xīndūlǐ Wú'èr Diàn; ☑021 5404 5252; 803 Julu Rd; 巨鹿路803号; dishes ¥80-160, tasting menu ¥380; ⏰6-10.30pm; Ⓜ Jing'an Temple) The industrial-chic interior here resembles a set from a Peter Greenaway film, from the eye-catching open kitchen to the sleek staff running around like an army of ninjas. The dishes (Peking duck rolls, cold noodles served in an ice bowl, beef steak on *pǔěr* leaves) are excellent, but they maintain the minimalist theme, so make sure to order enough. Reserve.

YONGFOO ELITE RESIDENCE
CHINESE $$$

Map p306 (雍福会, Yōngfú Huì; www.yongfooelite.com; 200 Yongfu Rd; 永福路200号; set menu dinner from ¥780; ⏰11.30am-midnight) Although this 1930s residence was once members-only, it's since opened to the general public as a restaurant – great news, because the decor is absolutely stunning. Take time out for afternoon tea or return later for dinner and drinks to fully appreciate the antique-strewn setting, which includes a gorgeous carved archway from Zhèjiāng in the garden.

🍷 DRINKING & NIGHTLIFE

Home to the largest concentration of bars and cafes in Shànghǎi, the French Concession offers drinkers a choice between elegant bars housed in colonial-era villas, speakeasy-style spots, craft beer breweries and expat-friendly sports pubs. The small strip of Yongfu Rd between West Fuxing and Wuyuan Rds is lined with bars and clubs, while a crop of beer bars has sprung up on Yongkang Rd.

🍷 French Concession East

★ CITIZEN CAFÉ
CAFE

Map p302 (天台餐厅, Tiāntái Cāntīng; 222 Jinxian Rd; 进贤路222号; ⏰11am-12.30am; 🐿; Ⓜ South Shaanxi Rd) Decked out with Chesterfield seating, dark-wood-panelled walls, whirring ceiling fans and small lamps, this feels like a snug private gentlemans' club by day and romantic candlelit hideaway come sundown. Weekday lunch sets (11am to 2pm) are great value where you can recharge with a club sandwich, fries and a latte for ¥45. The small 2nd-floor terrace is a great spot for sipping cocktails while watching street scenes unfold.

★ CAFÉ DEL VOLCÁN
CAFE

Map p302 (www.cafevolcan.com; 80 Yongkang Rd; 永康路80号; espressos ¥26, flat whites ¥36; ⏰8am-8pm Mon-Fri, 10am-8pm Sat & Sun; 🐿; Ⓜ South Shaanxi Rd) Tiny Café del Volcán offers a pit stop from the bustle of bar-heavy Yongkang Rd. The minimalist cafe has just a few wooden box tables sharing the space with the roasting machine. The coffee here is excellent and its signature beans come from the owner's coffee plantation in Guatemala – in the family for 120 years – while other single-origin beans are from Ethiopia, Kenya, Panama and Yùnnàn.

★ CAFÉ DES STAGIAIRES
BAR

Map p302 (www.cafestagiaires.com; 54-56 Yongkang Rd; 永康路54-56号; mains from ¥45; ⏰10am-midnight; 🐿; Ⓜ South Shaanxi Rd) One of the original bars on buzzing Yongkang Rd, this hip oasis of Francophilia spills over with slightly zany Gallic charm. There's a coke bottle chandelier and a (French) geography lesson via the wine list: Languedoc, Provence, Côte du Rhône, Loire, Alsace, Bourgogne, Bordeaux and, *bien sûr*, Rest of the World. Each table is regularly stocked with addictive chilli peanuts.

If that's insufficient, sample the quality charcuterie, cheese and pizzas. Happy hour is 5pm to 8pm weekdays and 2pm to 6pm weekends, with great value wine at ¥20 per glass.

SEESAW
CAFE

Map p306 (因为新鲜所以特别, Yīnwèi Xīnxiān Suǒyǐ Tèbié; www.seesawcoffee.com; Rm 101, 433 Yuyuan Lu; 愚园路433弄101单元; coffee from ¥38; ⏰8.30am-7pm Mon-Fri, 9.30am-7.30pm

Sat & Sun; 🛜; Ⓜ Line 2, 7 to Jing'an Temple) Well hidden down a car park off Yuyuan Rd, Seesaw is a must for coffee aficionados seeking out single-origin beans. It's not cheap, but they roast on-site and coffees are prepared by expert baristas doing V-60 pourovers, siphon, six-hour cold brews and espresso. They directly source green beans from Africa, the Americas and locally in Yùnnàn. There are cakes but no meals.

Call ahead for its cupping sessions, held at 7pm on Thursday evenings. There are several branches of Seesaw located across town, including one next to the **Muji flagship shop** (Map p302; www.seesawcoffee.com; 755 Middle Huaihai Rd; 黄浦区淮海中路755号; ⊙9am-10pm Mon-Fri, 10am-10pm Sat & Sun; 🛜; Ⓜ South Shaanxi Rd) and a nearby cafe in Reel mall, across from Jing'an Temple (p129).

★ BELL BAR   BAR
Map p302 (http://bellbar.cn; Tiánzǐfáng, back door No 11, Lane 248, Taikang Rd; 泰康路248 弄11号后门田子坊; ⊙11am-2am Wed-Mon, 2pm-2am Tue; 🛜; Ⓜ Dapuqiao) This eccentric, unconventional boho haven is a delightful Tiánzǐfáng hideaway, with creaking, narrow wooden stairs leading to a higgledy-piggledy array of rooms and the tucked-away attic slung out above. Expect hookah pipes, mismatched furniture and a small, secluded mezzanine for stowaways from the bedlam outside. It's in the second alley (Lane 248) on the right.

DEAN'S BOTTLE SHOP   BAR
Map p302 (40 Yongkang Rd; 永康路40号; beers from ¥30; ⊙4-10pm Mon-Fri, 3-10pm Sat & Sun; Ⓜ South Shaanxi Rd) A great start to a trawl along the bars of Yongkang Rd, Dean's Bottle Shop is exactly that, with a few stools for stopping in to sample the products. There's a few beers on tap and a great selection of bottled craft beers from around the globe, including Moosehead lager, Young's double chocolate, Brooklyn lager and Magnum pear cider.

There's another shop on nearby Shaoxing Rd (p114).

UNION TRADING COMPANY   COCKTAIL BAR
Map p302 (64 Fenyang Rd; 汾阳路64号; cocktails from ¥80; ⊙6pm-late; Ⓜ Changshu Rd) Shànghǎi's cocktail-bar scene just goes from strength to strength thanks to bars like Union Trading Company. The long

wooden bar serves as a spot to sit and watch the bartenders do their thing using seasonal ingredients and a menu that changes every few months. The cocktail list is ambitious and inventive, though it doesn't always hit the mark. The entrance is on Middle Fuxing Rd.

HOP PROJECT   BAR
Map p302 (50 Yongkang Rd; 永康路50号; ⊙11am-late; Ⓜ South Shaanxi Rd) The Hop Project, run by an Australian, features Little Creatures pale ale and Mornington Peninsula brews from Down Under, along with Boxing Cat beers, a Tsingtao IPA and craft beer from Běijīng. Pair it with a gourmet sandwich melt courtesy of Co. Cheese (p135). Don't miss the pickleback shot – a shot of whiskey chased by a shot of homemade pickle juice (much better than it sounds).

BOXING CAT BREWERY   BREWERY
Map p302 (拳击猫啤酒屋, Quánjīmāo Píjiǔwū; www.boxingcatbrewery.com; Unit 26a, Sinan Mansions, 519 Middle Fuxing Rd; 复兴中路519号思南公馆26a; ⊙5pm-midnight Mon-Wed, 5pm-2am Thu, 3pm-2am Fri, 10am-2am Sat, 10am-midnight Sun; Ⓜ Xintiandi) This branch of Boxing Cat Brewery in the Sinan Mansions complex isn't as popular as its West Fuxing Rd outfit (p115), but it is a staple among Shànghǎi's beer-o-philes and features a strong showing of craft brews. The main downstairs bar area is more upmarket lounge than comfy pub; try to nab a seat at the bar.

VIENNA CAFÉ   CAFE

Map p302 (维也纳咖啡馆, Wéiyěnà Kāfēiguǎn; ☑021 6445 2131; 25 Shaoxing Rd; 绍兴路25号; ☺8am-10pm; ☎; MJiashan Rd) With a small sun-flecked conservatory at the rear, this European-style cafe does striped-wallpaper and round marble-top tables; it's ideal for unwinding with a Kafka, homemade Sacher torte and a coffee. Sign up for one of the breakfasts for endless caffeine on tap and nod off to the soft jazz accompaniment.

I LOVE SHANGHAI   BAR

Map p302 (我爱上海, Wǒ Ài Shànghǎi; Lane 1, 248 Taikang Rd; 泰康路248弄田子坊内1号后门; ☺6pm-late; MDapuqiao) Beloved Jing'an grungy dive bar, I Love Shanghai, has recently relocated to Tiánzǐfáng, bringing with it its combination of reasonably priced drinks and an often rowdy atmosphere.

DR BAR   BAR

Map p302 (博士酒吧, Bóshì Jiǔbā; Xintiandi North Block, Bldg 15, Lane 181, Taicang Rd; 新天地北里太仓路181弄15号楼; ☺5pm-1am; MSouth Huangpi Rd, Xintiandi) This neat bar is just what the doctor ordered: all in black and chrome; pupil-dilating minimalist cool. Note the almost obliterated Maoist slogans outside, on either side of the *shíkùmén* (stone-gate) door.

DEAN'S BOTTLE SHOP   BAR

Map p302 (www.deansbottleshop.cn; 37 Shaoxing Rd; 绍兴路37号; ☺1-10pm; MDapuqiao) This nirvana for lovers of the grain (and, to a lesser extent, grape) has row upon row of imported bottled bliss – Moosehead lager, Old Rasputin, tequila, rum, bourbon, widely sourced vino – all at bargain prices. With more than enough labels to test even the most well-travelled palates, it's more shop than bar, but you can sit down at the long communal table. It has a smaller shop nearby on Yongkang Rd (p113).

LÒUSHÌ   CAFE

Map p302 (陋室; 145 Nanchang Rd; 南昌路145号; ☺10am-8pm; ☎; MSouth Shaanxi Rd) At the back of the Ze Casa antique shop – cluttered with Shànghǎi antiques and collectibles, from the chairs you sit in to the art deco light fixtures and attractive furniture fashioned from recycled wood – is this homey cafe. It's a popular spot with laptop users for its free wi-fi, good coffee and quiet, comfy atmosphere.

SOLO CAFE   CAFE, BAR

Map p302 (☑021 5383 3370; 126 Nanchang Rd; 南昌路126号; ☺10.30am-1am Tue-Sun; ☎; MSouth Shaanxi Rd) Solo is a great little spot to stop off for a coffee or drink near Fùxīng Park (p96). Hanging beer bottles decorate the front wall entrance, where you can sit at street-front tables and watch the world go by. It sells craft beer by the bottle and has a great selection of Belgian beers. If you're feeling hungry, it also does light snacks, sandwiches and pizza.

DADA   CLUB

Map p306 (115 Xingfu Rd; 幸福路115号; ☺8pm-late; MJiaotong University) This friendly no-frills place stuffed away down an alley near Jiāotōng University is one of Shànghǎi's most popular dives, specialising in cheap drinks and popular weekend dance parties, with local and international DJs.

YY'S   BAR

Map p302 (轮回酒吧, Lúnhuí Jiǔbā; ☑021 6466 4098; basement, 125 Nanchang Rd; 南昌路125号; ☺6pm-4am; ☎; MSouth Shaanxi Rd) Once home to the Shànghǎi underground scene (way back in the 1990s), YY's has successfully remained on the fringes of the city's consciousness, without ever becoming too hip. Now relegated to the basement, it continues to attract an alternative crowd and has its own rough-edged appeal, which increases as night blurs into dawn.

SHÀNGHǍI SLOGANS

Unlike Běijīng and other towns and villages across China, Shànghǎi has largely scrubbed away its slogans (政治口号; *zhèngzhì kǒuhào*) from the Cultural Revolution, despite the city's once heady revolutionary zeal. In the French Concession, two almost vanished slogans decorate either side of the door to the minimalist Xīntiāndì saloon Dr Bar. An imposing and well-preserved scarlet slogan survives high up on the north wall of the **Huángpǔ Hotel** (黄浦饭店, Huángpǔ Fàndiàn; 106 Huangpu Rd; 黄浦路), not far from the Hyatt on the Bund in Hóngkǒu. The Maoist-era slogan is visible through the gate, but note that the hotel is for Chinese military and naval guests (foreigners not accepted), so be discreet when looking for it.

🍸 French Concession West

⭐SPEAK LOW
COCKTAIL BAR

Map p302 (📞021 6416 0133; 579 Middle Fuxing Rd; 复兴中路579号; ⏰6pm-1.30am Sun-Thu, to 2.30am Fri & Sat; Ⓜ) Speak Low is a standout in a city overrun with speakeasy-style bars. Once you find your way in through Ocho bar equipment shop, start with a drink on the 2nd floor; cocktails run ¥75 to ¥85. Then head upstairs (hint: find China and you'll find the entrance) to the intimate, seating-only bar for expertly crafted Japanese-influenced cocktails from ¥100.

Third-floor signature drinks include the Speak Low – made with Barcardi, matcha tea and sherry, served with chocolates – and the Ladybird, with shiso-infused tequila served in a wooden sake cup complete with plum salt rim.

⭐SENATOR SALOON
COCKTAIL BAR

Map p306 (📞021 5423 1330; www.senatorsaloon. com; 98 Wuyuan Rd; 五原路98号; ⏰5pm-1am Mon-Fri, to late Sat & Sun; Ⓜ Changshu Rd) From the team behind Sìchuān Citizen (p107) and Citizen Café (p112) comes this classy 1920's Prohibition Era–style cocktail bar in a quiet spot on Wuyuan Rd. Slink into a dark-wood booth under pressed metal ceilings and dim art deco lights to order a barrel-aged Negroni from waitstaff decked out in braces and bow ties. There's a long menu of American bourbon and whiskey rye-based cocktails, and excellent table service.

⭐BOXING CAT BREWERY
BREWERY

Map p306 (拳击猫啤酒屋, Quánjīmāo Píjiǔwū; www.boxingcatbrewery.com; 82 West Fuxing Rd; 复兴西路82号; ⏰5pm-midnight Mon-Wed, 5pm-2am Thu, 3pm-2am Fri, 10am-midnight Sat & Sun; 🛜; Ⓜ Shanghai Library, Changshu Rd) A deservedly popular three-floor microbrewery, with a rotating line-up of top-notch beers that range from the Standing 8 Pilsner to the Right Hook Helles. But that's not all – the omnipresent restaurateur Kelley Lee has paired Southern home cooking (gumbo, blackened fish tacos), burgers and beer snacks with the drinks. Come for a pint; stay for dinner.

⭐DR WINE
WINE BAR

Map p306 (葡萄酒博士, Pútáojiǔ Bóshì; 177 Fumin Rd; 富民路177号; ⏰11am-2am; 🛜; Ⓜ Jing'an Temple) Black-leather armchairs, salvaged *shíkùmén* brick walls and worn-in tables set the mood at this casual, two-storey wine bar on Fumin Rd. Wines are sold by both the glass (from ¥48) and bottle. Pair it with the usual French accompaniments – a cheeseboard (from ¥88) or charcuterie plate (saucisson, pâté etc, from ¥120) – and settle in for the night.

⭐EL CÓCTEL
BAR

Map p306 (📞021 6433 6511; 2nd fl, 47 Yongfu Rd; 永福路47号; ⏰5.30pm-late; Ⓜ Shanghai Library) What do you get when you cross an ever-inventive Spanish chef with a perfectionist bartender from Japan? El Cóctel, of course – a retro cocktail lounge that mixes up some damn fine drinks, but make sure you come with cash to spare. Like a lot of bars in the city, it can get very smoky, and if you don't reserve you might find it hard to get in.

⭐SHELTER
CLUB

Map p306 (5 Yongfu Rd; 永福路5号; ⏰9pm-4am Wed-Sat; Ⓜ Shanghai Library) The darling of the underground crowd, Shelter is a converted bomb shelter where you can count on great music, cheap drinks and a non-existent dress code. It brings in a fantastic line-up of international DJs and hip-hop artists; the large barely lit dance area is the place to be. Cover for big shows ranges from ¥30 to ¥100.

⭐COTTON'S
BAR

Map p306 (棉花酒吧, Miánhuā Jiǔbā; 📞021 6433 7995; www.cottons-shanghai.com; 132 Anting Rd; 安亭路132号; ⏰11am-midnight Sun-Thu, to 1am Fri & Sat; 🛜; Ⓜ Hengshan Rd, Zhaojiabang Rd) This excellent bar is perhaps the most pleasant spot in the concession to raise a glass. Ensconced in a converted 1930s villa, the bar's interior has cosy sofas and fireplaces to snuggle around in the winter, and a tiny outdoor terrace on the 2nd floor. The real draw, though, is the garden, which is intimate yet still big enough not to feel cramped.

The drinks and bar snacks, pizzas, burgers, salads and sandwiches are reasonably priced and the crowd is a good mix of locals and expats. You'll have to get here early on weekends to grab a table outside, or book ahead.

⭐APARTMENT
BAR

Map p306 (📞021 6437 9478; www.theapartment-shanghai.com; 3rd fl, 47 Yongfu Rd; 永福路47号; ⏰11am-late; 🛜; Ⓜ Shanghai Library) This trendy loft-style bar is designed to pull in the full spectrum of 30-something professionals, with a comfort-food menu; a dance space and lounge zone; a retro bar room; and topping it all, a rooftop terrace for views.

DR BEER
BREWERY

Map p306 (啤酒博士, Píjiǔ Bóshì; 83 Fumin Rd; 富民路83号; ☺5pm-2am; ⊗; MJing'an Temple, exit 9) Brewing its own beers on-site, the industrial-chic Dr Beer pulls its ales directly from the production vats that sit in a glass gallery behind the bar. It does six beers, including a very decent IPA and interesting seasonals such as ginger pale ale. Happy hour ¥35 pints runs 5pm to 8pm Monday to Thursday. There's pub food, plus DJs and live music on weekends.

UPTOWN RECORDS 'N BEER
BAR

Map p306 (131 Yongfu Rd; 永福路131号; ☺3pm-1am; MShanghai Library) Grab a craft beer from the fridge, plonk on a stool and listen to some tunes on the turntable from the excellent selection of vinyl at this shop/bar. Sip on a Saranac, Brooklyn east IPA, beer-Lao or Rogue while listening to the likes of King Khan & the BBQ Show, The Stooges, Blondie, John Cale, Roxy Music or Fats Domino. Bottled beers from ¥18 to ¥28.

1984 BOOKSTORE & CAFE
CAFE

Map p306 (11 Hunan Rd; 湖南路11号; ☺10am-9pm; ⊗; MShanghai Library) Big Brother might be watching but he'd be hard-pressed to find you in this hidden nook of a bookshop-cafe off Hunan Rd. There's no sign, just a metal gate, and you'll need to buzz to get in. Once inside, there is a cosy room with exposed brick walls and a fantastic outdoor courtyard garden; perfect for breakfast or a coffee stop.

It stocks a good range of English and Chinese books (yes, you can pick up a copy of *Nineteen Eighty-Four*), canvas tote bags and cute notebooks.

FUMI COFFEE
CAFE

Map p306 (215 Fumin Rd; 富民路215号; ☺8am-9pm; ⊗; MJing'an Temple) White concrete walls decorated with stovetop espresso makers leave no guessing as to what design-savvy Fumi is all about: good coffee. Single-origin beans are sourced from Colombia and Peru then roasted locally and brewed into the usual espresso, latte, cold drip, and filter coffees and the not-so-usual matcha

mocha, nitro brew (cold-drip extraction for 24 hours) and double espresso livened up with sparkling water.

Not sure what to order? Try the tasting combo of a piccolo, latte, filter and espresso (¥55 to ¥65).

DAGA BREWPUB
BREWERY

Map p306 (37 Ta'an Rd; 徐汇区泰安路37号; ☺10am-1am Mon-Thu, 11am-1am Fri-Sun; MJiao tong University) Beer enthusiasts should stop by Daga to sample the mostly Chinese craft beer on 18 rotating taps, including a Shànghǎi jasmine lager and wheat beers from Nánjīng. The brews are a bit hit and miss, but you can taste test before settling on an order. Exposed brick walls and comfort food (chilli dogs, beer-battered fish and chips) round out the warm pub atmosphere. Happy hour runs a generous midday to 8pm.

NACHBAR
CAFE, BAR

Map p306 (街坊, Jiēfāng; ☏021 6431 0868; 623 Yongjia Rd; 永嘉路623号; ☺11am-11pm; ⊗; MHengshan Rd) Intimate cafe/bar with vintage trinkets, polished concrete and a foliage-covered exposed brick wall in a quiet spot on Yongjia Rd. Nachbar serves up good coffee and light meals by day and turns into the perfect spot for a cocktail on its rooftop terrace, complete with swing sweat, on warm summer evenings.

SHÀNGHǍI BREWERY
BREWERY

Map p306 (www.shanghaibrewery.com; 15 Dongping Rd; 东平路15号; ☺10am-2am Sun-Thu, to 3am Fri & Sat; ⊗; MChangshu Rd, Hengshan Rd) Hand-crafted microbrews, a big range of comfort food, pool tables and sport on TV... no surprise this massive two-storey hang-out heaves on Friday and Saturday nights, and is popular for Sunday arvo sessions. Try the Czech-style People's Pilsner or the Hong Mei Amber Hefeweizen, which start at a mere ¥25 during happy hour (from 2pm to 8pm).

LE BORDELAIS
WINE BAR

Map p302 (www.le-bordelais.com; 2nd fl, 301 Jiashan Rd; 嘉善路301号2楼; ☺11.30am-late; ⊗; MJiashan Rd) For Bordeaux wine enthusiasts, welcoming Le Bordelais is an affordable choice in a city increasingly dotted with wine bars. Knowledgeable staff are on hand for pointers, while a decent French bistro menu takes care of evening dining and weekend brunches.

TEA TASTING

It may be a rather clichéd choice, but there's no doubt that a Yíxīng teapot and a package of oolong tea makes for a convenient gift. But how do you go about a purchase?

Two things to remember: first of all, be sure to taste (品尝; *pǐncháng*) and compare several different teas – flavours vary widely, and there's no point in buying a premium grade if you don't like it. Tasting is free (免费; *miǎnfèi*) and fun, but it's good form to make some sort of purchase afterwards. Second, tea is generally priced by the *jīn* (斤; 500g), which may be more tea than you can finish in a year. Purchase several *liǎng* (两; 50g) instead – divide the list price by 10 for an idea of the final cost. Some of the different types of tea for sale include oolong (乌龙; *wūlóng*), green (绿; *lǜ*), flower (花茶; *huāchá*) and pu-erh (普洱; *pǔ'ěr*) – true connoisseurs have a different teapot for each type of tea.

Try the following shops:

Huìfēng Tea Shop (p121)

Yányè Míngchá (p123)

Tiānshān Tea City (p176)

Zhēnchálín Tea (p119)

ZEN CAFE
CAFE

Map p306 (钲艺廊, Zhēng Yìláng; www.zenlife store.com; 7 Dongping Rd; 东平路7号; ⏰10am-10pm Mon-Thu & Sun, 10.30am-10.30pm Fri & Sat; 🚇; Ⓜ Changshu Rd) Tucked away upstairs in the rafters of the Zen Lifestore design shop (p123), this lovely little cafe is well away from the Shànghǎi hurly-burly (although it can fill up). It's the perfect place for a quiet coffee or pot of tea, and it also serves cakes and light meals.

FENNEL LOUNGE
BAR

Map p306 (回香, Huí Xiāng; ☑021 3353 1773; 217 Zhenning Rd, entrance on Dongzhu'anbang Rd; 镇宁路217号; cocktails from ¥78; ⏰10am-late; 🚇; Ⓜ Line 2, 11 to Jiangsu Rd, exit 3) This classy cocktail lounge is divided into a dining room, a cosy living-type room with a tiny stage, and a lounge area featuring a sunken bar and casual seating. An impressive drinks list, skilled bar staff and an eclectic line-up of live acoustic performances on Friday and Saturday (everything from jazz and rock to traditional Chinese music) make it a favourite with hip, cashed-up 30-somethings.

LUCCA 390
CLUB

Map p306 (www.lucca.cc; 390 Panyu Rd; 番禺路390号; ⏰6pm-late; 🚇; Ⓜ Jiaotong University) One of the only LGBT clubs in Shànghǎi, Lucca 390 (formerly 390 Bar) was opened up by the team at Shànghǎi Studio. The club is divided into several sections, with dance floors, bars and food on offer. It also hosts a number of events throughout the year.

ENOTERRA
WINE BAR

Map p306 (☑021 5404 0050; www.enoteca.com. cn; 53-57 Anfu Rd; 安福路53-57号; ⏰10am-2am; 🚇; Ⓜ Changshu Rd) Wine bars have hit Shànghǎi big time. With its convivial atmosphere and affordable wines by the glass and bottle, Enoterra was the first to provide a winning formula. There's a definite focus on French wines but there's a good selection of New World wines as well. Cheese boards and meals are also served. Happy hour (4pm to 8pm daily) is excellent value with half-price glasses of wine.

CONSTELLATION
BAR

Map p302 (酒池星座, Jiǔchí Xīngzuò; ☑021 5404 0970; 86 Xinle Rd; 新乐路86号; ⏰7pm-2am; Ⓜ South Shaanxi Rd) The bow-tied staff at the Japanese-run Constellation take their drinks seriously – you're not going to get any watered-down cocktails here. A choice selection of whiskies, Van Gogh prints on the walls and overhead black lights make this a classy yet appealingly eccentric place. Arrive early on Friday and Saturday nights as the place packs out.

PEOPLE 7
BAR

Map p306 (人间荧七, Rénjiān Yíngqī; ☑021 5404 0707; 803 Julu Rd; 巨鹿路803号; ⏰11.30am-2pm & 6pm-midnight; Ⓜ Jing'an Temple, Changshu Rd) Getting into this superstylish bar is an achievement in itself. That's not because there's a door policy, but because the shiny steel doors only open if you insert your hand into one of the nine holes set into the wall. Once inside, there's a long steel bar on which to rest the oddly shaped glass your cocktail arrives in.

With white armchairs scattered throughout the dimly lit interior and bathrooms that are even harder to work out than the front door, this place could be oppressively trendy. But it isn't. It does affordable Chinese food, too.

GLO WINE BAR
BAR

Map p306 (www.glolondon.com; 1 South Wulumuqi Rd; 乌鲁木齐南路1号; ⏰5pm-2am Mon-Fri, 11am-2am Sat & Sun; Ⓜ Changshu Rd, Hengshan Rd) Glo London's wine bar is angling to become the neighbourhood's sophisticated option – no rowdy guys cheering on their favourite teams here. Instead you get candlelit tables and all the requisite pretty young things.

ABBEY ROAD
BAR

Map p306 (艾比之路, Àibǐzhī Lù; www.abbey road-shanghai.com; 3 Taojiang Rd; 桃江路3号; ⏰11am-midnight Mon-Fri, 9am-1am Sat & Sun; 📶 Ⓜ Changshu Rd) The cheap beer with classic rock combination works its stuff again, attracting plenty of regulars to this pub. Once the weather becomes nice, the tree-shaded outdoor patio adds the final ingredient to make this a favourite. There are large portions of comfort pub food too, and live music on Saturday afternoons from 4pm.

CAMEL
SPORTS BAR

Map p306 (www.camelsportsbar.com; 1 Yueyang Rd; 岳阳路1号; ⏰11am-2am Mon-Fri, 10am-2am Sat & Sun; Ⓜ Changshu Rd) The French Concession's go-to sports bar, Camel has pool tables, dartboards, foosball, big screens at all angles and nightly meal and drink offers, plus a big Tuesday quiz night. The bar often stays open until odd hours so that fans can catch that crucial 4am game.

EDDY'S BAR
BAR

Map p306 (嘉浓休, Jiānóng Xiūxián; 1877 Middle Huaihai Rd; 淮海中路1877号, 近天平路; ⏰8pm-2am; Ⓜ Jiaotong University) Shànghǎi's longest-running gay bar is a friendly place with a flash, square bar to sit around, as well as a few corners to hide away in. It attracts both locals and expats, but it's mostly for the boys rather than the girls. The entrance is on Tianping Rd.

BEAVER
BAR

Map p306 (28 Yueyang Rd; 岳阳路28号; ⏰5.30pm-late; Ⓜ Chengshan Rd, Hengshan Rd) For a grungy ambience, this chipped and bruised bar gets straight to the point, hoovering up no-nonsense beer hounds with affordable booze, an undemanding music menu tilted towards US rock, and table football.

TIME PASSAGE
BAR

Map p306 (昨天今天明天, Zuótiān Jīntiān Míngtiān; ☎21 6240 2588; No 183, Lane 1038, Caojiayan Rd; 曹家堰路1038弄183号; ⏰5pm-late; 📶 Ⓜ Jiangsu Rd) Time Passage has real staying power, clocking up around 20 years in the business of cheap beer and good music. Beyond its no-nonsense Gucci-free vibe – not a suit in sight – it's a relaxing, down-to-earth spot for an evening beer or a daytime coffee.

There's live music on Friday and Saturday nights, and a daily happy hour from 5.30pm to 7.30pm.

⭐ ENTERTAINMENT

SHANGHAI SYMPHONY ORCHESTRA HALL
CLASSICAL MUSIC

Map p306 (上海交响乐团, Shànghǎi Jiāoxiǎngyuè Tuán; www.shsymphony.com; 1380 Middle Fuxing Rd; 复兴中路1380号; Ⓜ Changshu Rd) Designed by architects Isozaki Arata and Yasushisa Toyota, and opening in 2014, this concert venue is now the home of the Shanghai Symphony Orchestra, which has been going strong since 1949. Small chamber music concerts are held most Friday evenings at affordable prices, but they do tend to sell out, so book in advance. Tickets can be bought at the venue box office or on the website.

MAO LIVEHOUSE
LIVE MUSIC

Map p302 (☎021 6445 0086; 3rd fl, 308 South Chongqing Rd; 重庆南路308号3楼; Ⓜ Dapuqiao) One of the city's best and largest music venues, MAO is a stalwart of the Shànghǎi music scene, with acts ranging from rock to pop to electronica. Check the website or Facebook page for schedules and ticket prices.

COTTON CLUB
LIVE MUSIC

Map p306 (棉花俱乐部, Miánhuā Jùlèbù; ☎021 6437 7110; www.thecottonclub.cn; 1416 Middle Huaihai Rd; 淮海中路1416号; ⏰7.30pm-2am Tue-Sun; Ⓜ Changshu Rd) Harlem it ain't, but this is still the best and longest-running bar for live jazz in Shànghǎi. It features blues and jazz groups throughout the week. Wynton Marsalis once stepped in to jam, forever sealing the Cotton Club's reputation as the top live-music haunt in town. The music gets going around 9 or 10pm.

SHÀNGHÃI CONSERVATORY OF MUSIC
CLASSICAL MUSIC

Map p302 (上海音乐学院, Shànghǎi Yīnyuè Xuéyuàn; ☑021 6431 1792; 20 Fenyang Rd; 汾阳路20号; ⊙ticket office 9am-8.30pm; ⓂSouth Shaanxi Rd) The auditorium here holds classical-music performances (Chinese and Western), usually on weekends at 7.30pm, and the musicians are often the stars of the future. You can buy tickets next door to the campus at Music Ticket; they also sell tickets to performances at other venues in the city.

SHANGHAI CULTURE SQUARE
THEATRE

Map p302 (上海文化广场, Shànghǎi Wénhuà Guǎngchǎng; 597 Middle Fuxing Rd; 复兴中路597号; ⊙box office 9am-7pm; ⓂSouth Shaanxi Rd) State-of-the-art theatrical facility with a focus on musicals, drama, ballet and classic traditional Chinese and international productions.

CATHAY THEATRE
CINEMA

Map p302 (国泰电影院, Guótài Diànyǐngyuàn; 870 Middle Huaihai Rd; 淮海中路870号; tickets from ¥40; ⓂSouth Shaanxi Rd) This 1932 art deco theatre is one of the cheaper and more centrally located French Concession cinemas. If you want to know if the film is in the original language, ask if it's the *yuánbǎn* (原版) version.

UME INTERNATIONAL CINEPLEX
CINEMA

Map p302 (国际影城, Guójì Yǐngchéng; www. ume.com.cn; Xīntiāndì South Block, 5th fl, Bldg 6; 新天地南里6号楼5楼; ⓂSouth Huangpi Rd) This thoroughly modern cinema complex at Xīntiāndì screens Hollywood and Chinese films, with half-price tickets before 7pm on Tuesdays and before midday on weekends.

KŪN OPERA HOUSE
CHINESE OPERA

(上海昆剧团, Shànghǎi Kūnjù Tuán; ☑021 6437 7756; 295 South Zhongshan No 2 Rd, South Shànghǎi; 中山南二路295号; ⓂDamuqiao Rd) Shànghǎi's Kun opera troupe has moved to a new home south of the city. There are usually monthly performances, but you'll have to call ahead for the schedule. No English.

🛍 SHOPPING

🛍 French Concession East

ZHĒNCHÁLÍN TEA
DRINKS

Map p302 (臻茶林, Zhēnchálín; No 13, Lane 210, Taikang Rd, Tiánzǐfáng; 泰康路210弄13号田子坊; ⊙10am-8.30pm; ⓂDapuqiao) From the entrance this looks like just another tea shop, but poke around inside and you'll find specially blended herbal teas from Ayako, a traditional Chinese medicine–certified nutritionist. Peruse the hand-wrapped *pǔ'ěr* teas and ceramic and crystal teaware while staff ply you with tiny cups of ginseng oolong and offer tasters of whatever takes your fancy to keep you lingering.

Bags of tea start at around ¥45.

TASTE
HOMEWARES

Map p302 (www.taste-shop.com; Rm 105, Bldg 3, 210 Taikang Rd; 泰康路210号150室3|号楼; ⊙12.30-8.30pm Tue-Sun; ⓂDapuqiao) With the meticulous presentation at this stylish concept store, you'd be forgiven for thinking you stepped into a museum. Every piece has been carefully curated, from the copper watering cans from England, French scented candles and beautiful charcoal ceramics to jewellery by Antik, and Merchant & Mills dressmaking scissors. Upstairs is an ultra cool cafe, and there are plans to open a restaurant across the road.

MUJI
DEPARTMENT STORE

Map p302 (無印良品, Wúyìn Liángpǐn; 755 Middle Huaihai Rd; 淮海中路755号; ⊙10am-10pm; ⓂSouth Shaanxi Rd) Muji fans will love Shànghǎi's flagship store (the largest in mainland China), spread over three floors and stocking everything from the usual stationery, travel goods, clothing and kitchenware to an aroma lab, furniture, cosmetics and books. There's even a design-your-own tote bag area, as well as a Muji cafe.

GIFT ZEN
GIFTS & SOUVENIRS

Map p302 (钲艺廊, Zhēng Yì Láng; www.zen lifestore.com; L130, Xīntiāndì Style, 245 Madang Rd; 马当路245号新天地時尚L130; ⊙10am-10pm; ⓂXintiandi) Small but serene shop with a highly browse-worthy collection of design-led gift ideas with a modernist slant, including Frank Lloyd-Wright style bookmarks, pieces from the V&A and Tate Modern in London and MoMA in New York,

BEST SHOPPING STRIPS

Looking for the best spots in Shànghǎi's French Concession to wander and window-shop? Around the South Shaanxi Rd metro station there are a few blocks that are a must for serious clothes shoppers. Afternoons and evenings are the best hours for browsing: some smaller shops don't open their doors until noon, but most stay open until 10pm.

Nanchang Road A good street for general browsing, with shoes, antiques, and men's and women's clothing.

Changle Road Young designers and emerging local brands have taken over a one-block stretch of Changle Rd, east of Ruijin No 1 Rd.

Xinle Road This two-block stretch has less-high-end fashion than Changle Rd but ultimately greater variety. Pop into Comme Moi (p123) for chic classic clothing.

South Maoming Road South of Huaihai Rd you'll find custom-tailored traditional women's clothing (such as qípáo; figure-hugging Chinese dress); north of Huaihai Rd there's tailored men's suits and dress shoes.

and some fabulous and eye-catching ceramics and cloisonné.

POTTERY WORKSHOP   CERAMICS

Map p302 (乐天陶社, Lètiān Táoshè; www.pottery workshop.com.cn; Tiánzǐfáng, 220 Taikang Rd; 泰康路220号田子坊; ⊙10.30am-6.30pm; Ⓜ Dapuqiao) Originally founded in Hong Kong, the Pottery Workshop is a community arts centre offering classes in ceramic design at their South Shaanxi Rd studio (p124). The diverse creations of the workshop's resident artists – including those in China's ceramics capital, Jǐngdézhèn – are on display in this shop at the entrance to Tiánzǐfáng.

IAPM MALL   MALL

Map p302 (http://www.iapm.com.cn/; 999 Middle Huaihai Rd; 淮海中路999号; ⊙10am-11pm; Ⓢ; Ⓜ South Shaanxi Rd) There is a mix of high-end designers (Stella McCartney, Alexander McQueen, Miu Miu, Prada) and younger casual brands such as Mango, Camper and Muji at this upscale mall, worth a look for the spectacular and well-considered interior design alone. You'll also find a branch of the supermarket city'super here, packed with imported goods.

YIZIDI   GIFTS & SOUVENIRS

Map p302 (煙纸店, Yān Zhǐ Diàn; Xīntiāndì North Block, Bldg 25; 太仓路181弄新天地北里25号楼; ⊙10am-10pm Mon-Thu & Sun, 10.30am-10.30pm Fri & Sat; Ⓜ South Huangpi Rd) It might be the tiniest shop imaginable but Yizidi – which is part of the Zen Lifestore (p123) group – manages to pack in a

number of great gifts and souvenirs, from hand-sewn brightly coloured slippers made in Shànghǎi to Saint John wind-up toys (robots, planes, cars).

GARDEN BOOKS   BOOKS

Map p302 (韬奋西文书局, Tāofèn Xīwén Shūjú; 325 Changle Rd; 长乐路325号; ⊙10am-10pm; Ⓢ; Ⓜ South Shaanxi Rd) The shelves are well-stocked at this bookshop-cafe-cum-gelato-bar, which features a great selection of novels, art books, cookbooks, language references, and books on Shànghǎi and China. Grab youreslf a book or two and then indulge in a scoop of black sesame ice cream (¥25).

SHANGHAI TANG   CLOTHING

Map p302 (上海滩, Shànghǎi Tān; www.shang haitang.com; Xīntiāndì North Block, Bldg 15; 太仓路181弄新天地北里15号楼; ⊙10am-11pm; Ⓜ South Huangpi Rd) Hong Kong–based Shanghai Tang flies the flag for the Middle Kingdom in the world of high-end fashion. The designs are classic Chinese with a twist, incorporating fluorescent colours, traditional motifs and luxury fabrics such as silk and cashmere into the clothes and accessories. More affordable items include slinky tops and scarves, but if you have to ask the price of an item here, you probably can't afford it.

SHÀNGHǍI 1936   CLOTHING

Map p302 (No 9, Lane 210 Taicang Rd; 泰康路210弄9号; ⊙10am-9pm; Ⓜ Dapuqiao) Specialists in tailor-made traditional Chinese clothing on the main lane in Tiánzǐfáng.

XĪNTIĀNDÌ STYLE
MALL

Map p302 (新天地时尚, Xīntiāndì Shíshàng; 245 Madang Rd; 马当路245号; ⊘10am-10pm; Ⓜ Xintiandi) Serious shoppers should make for Xīntiāndì Style, a high-end mall featuring a handful of Chinese and local designers including **Heirloom** (Map p302; www. heirloombags.com; 78 Xinle Rd; 新乐路78号; ⊘10am-10pm; Ⓜ South Shaanxi Rd), the Thing and Even Penniless (p121).

HUÌFĒNG TEA SHOP
DRINKS

Map p302 (汇丰茶庄, Huìfēng Cházhuāng; ☎021 6472 7196; 124 South Maoming Rd; 茂名南路124号; ⊘9am-9pm; Ⓜ South Shaanxi Rd) A friendly, reliable tea shop, which has loads of good-quality clay teapots and cups, and a great range of Chinese tea from oolong and green to flower and *pǔ'ěr*. Sample varieties and make your choice. Good-quality tea prices start from around ¥50 for 50g. Some English is spoken.

EVEN PENNILESS
FASHION & ACCESSORIES

Map p302 (Xīntiāndì Style, 245 Madang Rd; 马当路245号; ⊘10am-10pm) Set up by local designer Gao Xin, Even Penniless is famous for its minimal clean lines and deconstructed pieces in mostly black, white and grey tones.

CHOUCHOU CHIC
CLOTHING

Map p302 (喆缤豆小童生活馆, Zhébīndòu Xiǎotóng Shēnghuó Guǎn; www.chouchouchic. com; 164 South Shaanxi Rd; 陕西南路164号; ⊘10am-9pm; Ⓜ South Shaanxi Rd) French Chinese hybrid Chouchou Chic sells kids' clothes (up to age eight) that are infinitely cuter than what you find at the souvenir stalls. Most of the clothing is Western-style, but you can find some attractive floral-patterned fabrics and Chinese-style cotton dresses as well. Prices start at ¥148; the entrance is on Changle Rd.

There's another branch on **Taikang Rd** (Map p302; www.chouchouchic.com; No 5, Lane 248, Taikang Rd; 泰康路248弄5号; ⊘10am-9pm; Ⓜ Dapuqiao).

SHÀNGHǍI MUSEUM SHOP
GIFTS & SOUVENIRS

Map p302 (上海博物馆商店, Shànghǎi Bówùguǎn Shāngdiàn; 123 Taicang Rd; 太仓路123号; ⊘11am-6pm; Ⓜ South Huangpi Rd) A two-floor outpost of the excellent Shànghǎi Museum Art Store (p76), with a choice selection of ceramics, calligraphy brushes, jade and other collectibles.

URBAN TRIBE
CLOTHING

Map p302 (城市山民, Chéngshì Shānmín; www. urbantribe.cn; No 14, Lane 248, Taikang Rd; 泰康路248弄14号; ⊘10am-9.30pm; Ⓜ Dapuqiao) Urban Tribe is the only contemporary Shànghǎi label to draw inspiration from the ethnic groups of China and Southeast Asia. The collection of loose-fitting blouses, pants and jackets made of natural fabrics are a refreshing departure from the city's on-the-go attitude and usual taste for flamboyance. It also stocks a great selection of handmade silver jewellery and ceramics.

There's a branch on **West Fuxing Rd** (Map p306; www.urbantribe.cn; 133 West Fuxing Rd; 复兴西路133号; ⊘10am-10pm; Ⓜ Shanghai Library); don't miss it's lovely tea garden.

PCS
SHOES

Map p302 (Pop Classic Sneakers; 130 Nanchang Rd; 南昌路130号; ⊘1-10pm; Ⓜ South Shaanxi Rd) This tiny shoebox of a shop has a fantastic collection of men's canvas sneakers, all sold at unbeatable prices. Try on a pair of original Feiyues, Warriors or spruced-up Ospop worker boots.

HARVEST
CLOTHING

Map p302 (Rm 18, Bldg 3, Lane 210, Taikang Rd, Tiánzǐfáng; 泰康路210弄3号楼118室田子坊; ⊘9.30am-8pm; Ⓜ Dapuqiao) Miao embroidery from southwest China.

YÚNWÚXĪN
JEWELLERY

Map p302 (云无心; 142 Nanchang Rd; 南昌路142号; ⊘11.30am-9pm; Ⓜ South Shaanxi Rd) Drop by this incense-filled boutique to peruse the collection of handmade Tibetan-themed jewellery, fashioned from mother-of-pearl, red coral and turquoise.

SHANGHAI CODE
VINTAGE

Map p302 (上海密码, Shànghǎi Mìmǎ; No 9, Lane 274, Taikang Rd, Tiánzǐfáng; 泰康路274弄9号田子坊; ⊘1-9pm; Ⓜ Dapuqiao) This Tiánzǐfáng shop sells rows of vintage glasses frames from the 1940s to the 1990s, old watches and new designer sunglasses. Vintage frames kick off from around ¥300.

XĪNGGUĀNG PHOTOGRAPHY EQUIPMENT
PHOTOGRAPHY

(星光摄影器材城, Xīngguāng Shèyǐng Qìcái Chéng; 288 Luban Rd; 淮海中路288号; ⊘8am-7pm; Ⓜ Dapuqiao, Luban Rd) There are three main floors of photography equipment here. While prices vary (you need to bargain; no guarantees) there are some good buys awaiting among the cameras, lenses, tripods and bags. A real find is Shen-Hao (申豪) on the 4th floor, which sells its hard-to-find field cameras. There's a repair shop on the 3rd floor.

FÓ GUĀNG
ARTS & CRAFTS

Map p302 (佛光; 594 South Shaanxi Rd; 陕西南路594号; ⊙11am-8pm; Ⓜ Jiashan Rd) Permeated with the aroma of incense and sedated by Buddhist music, this tiny shop stocks Tibetan Buddhist mystery: statuettes, *dorjes* (*vajra*; from ¥400), *purbhas* (ritual daggers), jade amulets, pendants, bracelets and other accoutrements. The name literally means 'Light of the Buddha'.

AVOCADO LADY
FOOD & DRINKS

Map p306 (红峰副食品商店, Hóngfēngfù Shípǐn Shāngdiàn; 274 South Wulumuqi Rd; 乌鲁木齐南路274号; ⊙6am-10pm; Ⓜ Changshu Rd) If the eye-watering prices levied by some Shànghǎi importers of foreign foods and fruits drives you round the bend, join the scrum (literally) of expats at this small vegetable shop on South Wulumuqi Rd. There's fantastically priced bottles of wine piled up on the floor, avocados, mangoes, refrigerated imported cheeses, coffees, cereals and much more; it's crammed to the rafters with goods (and shoppers).

🏠 French Concession West

★ DÒNG LIÁNG
FASHION & ACCESSORIES

Map p306 (楝梁; ☑021 3469 6926; www.dongliangchina.com; 184 Fumin Rd; 富民路184號; ⊙noon-9pm; Ⓜ Changshu Rd, Jing'an Temple) For an up-to-the-minute look at what's hot in local fashion, head to this beautiful boutique housed in a converted villa. Showcasing new Chinese design talent, pieces don't come cheap. The offerings are some of the coolest fashion and accessory collections from designers such as Ms Min, Yifang Wan, Hefang and Comme Moi together in one studio. There is another branch nearby on Changle Rd.

★ CULTURE MATTERS
SHOES

Map p306 (15 Dongping Rd; 东平路15号; ⊙11am-9.30pm; Ⓜ Hengshan Rd, Changshu Rd) Sneaker freaks should stop by this small Dongping Rd shop to ogle its fine selection of cool Feiyue and Warrior trainers (originating in Shànghǎi in the 1920s as martial arts shoes). There are a few branches around

town including one at **Tai'an Rd** (Map p306; 20 Tai'an Rd;泰安路20号; ⊙11am-9.30pm; Ⓜ Jiatong University) and prices start at an incredible ¥60.

★ OOAK CONCEPT BOUTIQUE
JEWELLERY

Map p306 (OOAK设计师品牌概念店, OOAK Shèjìshī Pǐnpái Gàiniàndiàn; www.theooak.com; 30, Lane 820, Julu Rd; 巨鹿路820弄30号; ⊙11am-8pm; Ⓜ Jiashan Rd, Hengshan Rd) Tall and skinny OOAK ('One of a Kind') has three floors of inspiring jewellery; catchy and attractive modern clothing for women; and bags and shoes from a host of talented big-name and aspiring independent designers from Europe and far flung parts of the globe.

★ LOLO LOVE VINTAGE
VINTAGE

Map p306 (2 Yongfu Rd; 永福路2号; ⊙noon-9pm; Ⓜ Shanghai Library, Changshu Rd) There's rock and roll on the stereo and a huge white rabbit, stuffed peacock and plastic cactus outside this wacky shrine to vintage 1940s and 1950s glad rags, behind the blue steel door on Yongfu Rd. It's stuffed with frocks, blouses, tops, shoes, brooches and sundry togs spilling from hangers, shelves and battered suitcases.

There's a lovely garden out the front.

★ PÍLÌNGPĀLÁNG – ANFU LU
CERAMICS

Map p306 (噼呤啪啷; www.pilingpalang.com; 183 Anfu Rd; 安福路183号; ⊙10am-9.30pm; Ⓜ Changshu Rd) You'll find gorgeous vibrant-coloured ceramics, cloisonné and lacquer, in pieces that celebrate traditional Chinese forms while adding a modern and deco-inspired slant here at Pílìngpālàng. Tea caddies and decorative trays make for great gifts or souvenirs.

HAPPY CLAY
CERAMICS

Map p302 (Donghu Rd; 东湖路; small bowls & plates from ¥36; ⊙11am-9pm Tue-Sun; Ⓜ South Shaanxi Rd) Happy Clay's small shop has shelves stacked with cute, wonky, hand-made ceramic pieces (plates, mugs, bowls, chopstick holders) in a range of colours and at affordable prices; it's at the end of the alley by the restaurant ElEfante.

MADAME MAO'S DOWRY
CLOTHING, SOUVENIRS

Map p306 (毛太设计, Máotài Shèjì; ☑021 5403 3551; madamemaosdowry.com; 207 Fumin Rd; 富民路207号; ⊙10am-7pm; Ⓜ Jing'an Temple)

What better way to brighten up your hall than with a poster of jubilant socialist workers? Beyond the Cultural Revolution paintings and prints here at Madame Mao's, there's a collection of locally designed clothing, jewellery, ceramics and textiles – including cute *bāozi* (steamed bun) printed tea towels from Pinyin Press, and some fantastic cards.

COMME MOI FASHION & ACCESSORIES
Map p302 (☑021 5466 4689; www.commemoi. com.cn; 169 Xinle Rd; 新乐路169号; MSouth Shaanxi Rd) Fitted out by Shànghǎi-based designers Neri & Hu, and located in the art deco Donghu Hotel building, this is the flagship store of Comme Moi. Created by one of China's most successful supermodels, Lu Yan, the Comme Moi label features relaxed chic styles in classic muted tones.

YÁNYÈ MÍNGCHÁ DRINKS
Map p306 (严叶茗茶; 170 Fumin Rd; 富民路170号; ⊙9am-9pm; MJing'an Temple) A range of tea, a large selection of clay teapots and free tastings are a few reasons to stop by this shop on Fumin Rd. Limited English is spoken but the owner is very friendly and eager to help.

ZEN LIFESTORE HOMEWARES
Map p306 (钲艺廊, Zhēng Yìláng; 7 Dongping Rd; 东平路7号; ⊙10am-10pm Sun-Thu, 10.30am-10.30pm Fri & Sat; MChangshu Rd) A bright and often crammed little design shop, Zen Lifestore stocks Oriental bits and bobs, bone china decorative gifts and colourful ceramics from a range of designers, as well as items from New York's MOMA shop.

1930 VINTAGE, HOMEWARES
Map p306 (☑021 5465 3955; 25 Tai'an Rd; 泰安路25号; ⊙11am-7pm Thu-Tue; MJiaotong University) Take a poke through this delightful vintage furniture and lighting shop near Ferguson Lane (p100) to admire art deco lamps, Bauhaus furniture, decorative glass ashtrays, scalloped mirrors and many more treasures.

COTTAGE SHOP ACCESSORIES, VINTAGE
Map p306 (☑021 3416 0523; 170 Wulumqi Middle Rd; 乌鲁木齐中路170号; ⊙11am-8pm; MChangshu Rd) If you're in the market for an antique camera, bowler hat, vintage checked shirt, kerosene lamp or designer leather wallet, duck into the Cottage Shop and you won't be disappointed.

C'EST SI BON BY I.C.OLOGY HOMEWARES
Map p306 (www.i-c-ology.com/cest-si-bon.html; Room 1201, 376 Wukang Rd; 房间1201武康路376号; ⊙noon-6pm Tue-Fri, 10.30am-8pm Sat & Sun; MShanghai Library, Jiaotong University) A wander through the Ferguson Lane complex will bring you to this cute design and homewares shop filled with lifestyle products by local and international designers. It's a great spot for gifts, with products ranging from brass pens and rulers to printed linen by Pinyin Press, jewellery boxes made from recycled wood, scented candles, ceramics by Japanese designers and geometric-printed socks.

BROCADE COUNTRY FASHION & ACCESSORIES
Map p302 (锦绣坊, Jǐnxiù Fǎng; 616 Julu Rd; 巨鹿路616号; ⊙10am-7.30pm; MSouth Shaanxi Rd) Peruse an exquisite collection of minority handicrafts from China's southwest, most of which are secondhand (ie not made for the tourist trade) and personally selected by owner Liu Xiaolan, a Guìzhōu native. Items for sale include embroidered wall hangings (some of which were originally baby carriers), sashes, shoes and hats, as well as silver jewellery.

PARAMITA ARTS & CRAFTS
Map p306 (波罗蜜多西藏工艺品, Bōluómìduō Xīzàng Gōngyìpǐn; ☑021 6248 2148; http//:paramita.taobao.com; 850-851 Julu Rd; 巨鹿路850-1号; ⊙10am-9pm; MChangshu Rd, Jing'an Temple) If you can't make it to Tibet, at least swing by Paramita for its inspiring collection of souvenirs, including yak-bone amulets, masks, jewellery, framed mandalas and other Buddhist treasures from the Himalayas. It's a nonprofit organisation, founded to help Tibetans with minimal education find employment.

KAVA KAVA HOMEWARES
Map p306 (www.kavakavahome.com; 810 Julu Rd; 巨鹿路810号; ⊙10am-6pm; MJing'an Temple) Seriously good-looking modern but traditionally styled lacquer cabinets, chairs, tables and cabinets.

NEW WAVE HEARING FASHION & ACCESSORIES
Map p306 (纽波, Niǔ Bō; ☑English service line 137 6193 6837; www.newwave-hearing.com; Joy Tower, 15th fl, Rm C, 9 Zhenning Rd; 镇宁路9号九尊大厦15楼C座; MChangshu Rd) In case you forgot to pack a pair, this ear specialist stocks high-grade earplugs imported from the USA.

🏃 SPORTS & ACTIVITIES

★**DOUBLE RAINBOW
MASSAGE HOUSE**   MASSAGE
Map p302 (双彩虹保健按摩厅, Shuāng Cǎihóng Bǎojiàn Ànmó Tīng; ☎021 6473 4000; 45 Yongjia Rd; 永嘉路45号; 45/68/90 minutes ¥60/90/120; ⏰noon-midnight; Ⓜ South Shaanxi Rd) Perhaps Shànghǎi's best neighbourhood massage parlour, where the shared rooms have little ambience but the facilities are spotless and the prices are unbeatable. Choose your preference of soft, medium or hard, and the visually impaired masseuses here will have you groaning in agony in no time as they seek out those little-visited pressure points. Choose between traditional massage or a herbal foot bath, or try both.

DRAGONFLY   MASSAGE
Map p306 (悠庭保健会所, Yōutíng Bǎojiàn Huìsuǒ; ☎021 5403 9982; www.dragonfly.net.cn; 206 Xinle Rd; 新乐路206号; Chinese massage per 60/90 mins ¥188/¥282; ⏰10am-midnight; Ⓜ South Shaanxi Rd) One of the longest-running massage services in Shànghǎi, the soothing Dragonfly offers Chinese body massages, foot massages and Japanese-style shiatsu, in addition to more specialised services such as aroma oil massages, body scrubs and beauty treatments. Prices include a private room and a change of clothes. Reserve.

**POTTERY
WORKSHOP**   ART
Map p302 (乐天陶社, Lètiān Táo Shè; ☎021 6445 0902; www.potteryworkshop.com.cn; 1a, Lane 180, South Shaanxi Rd; 陕西南路180弄1号; courses from ¥1000; ⏰9am-5pm Mon-Fri, 10am-6pm Sat & Sun; Ⓜ South Shaanxi Rd) Originally founded in Hong Kong, the Pottery Workshop is a community arts centre offering classes in ceramic design catering to all levels. Classes are held 10am to 1pm on Tuesday and Friday, and 2pm to 5pm Saturday and Sunday. A course of four classes is ¥1000 and you can drop in to any class time that suits; weekends get busy, though, so opt for weekdays if you can.

Beginners will be taught how to hand build using the pinch, coil and slab methods before learning how to throw on the wheel. A set of tools is included in the price but there is an extra small fee for firing your works.

**SUBCONSCIOUS
DAY SPA**   MASSAGE
Map p306 (桑格水疗会所, Sāngkè Shuǐliáo Huìsuǒ; ☎021 6415 0636; www.subconscious dayspa.com; 183 Fumin Rd; 富民路183号; Chinese massage per 60/90 minutes ¥168/250; ⏰10am-midnight; Ⓜ Changshu Rd, Jing'an Temple) The scent of lemongrass fills the air as you enter this serene, ecofriendly spa, which uses locally sourced materials, organic oils and nontoxic plants. A veritable centre for mind-body rejuvenation, Subconscious offers an array of traditional massages, from *tuīná* (traditional) and hot-stone to Thai, as well as eight-person yoga classes and beauty treatments, such as manicures and waxing.

FLOWER FINGERS   BEAUTY SALON
Map p306 (花指闲, Huā Zhǐ Xián; ☎021 6433 4335; 344 Middle Wulumqi Rd; 乌鲁木齐中路344号; ⏰10am-11pm; Ⓜ Changshu Road) There's no shortage of nail salons in Shànghǎi but Flower Fingers is a favourite thanks to its great service and reasonable prices. The two-storey building has a rustic comfy atmosphere with soft reclining armchairs and free tea. Settle in for a foot massage (30 minutes, ¥68) while you get your nails filed, buffed and polished. Manicures start at ¥49, more for gel polish.

MANNA YOGA CENTER   YOGA
Map p302 (哈达瑜伽会所, Hādá Yújiā Huìsuǒ; ☎021 6218 0955; www.cnyoga.com; 1 South Maoming Rd; 茂名南路1号; classes from ¥168; Ⓜ South Shaanxi Rd) Next door to the Lóngwǔ Kung Fu Center, this is one of Shànghǎi's premier yoga spaces. Sign up for intro classes or a range of more advanced styles, from hatha and Bikram to ashtanga and Pilates. Classes in English are offered on Monday, Tuesday and Thursday. Check the website for schedules.

**LÓNGWǓ KUNG FU
CENTER**   MARTIAL ARTS
Map p302 (龙武功夫馆, Lóngwǔ Gōngfu Guǎn; ☎021 6287 1528; 3rd fl,1 South Maoming Rd; 茂名南路1号; 1/20 lessons ¥150/2400, 6 months ¥3600; Ⓜ South Shaanxi Rd) Brush up on your taekwondo *poomsae*, hone your Chinese kung fu skills or simply learn a few taichi moves to help slip aboard the bus at rush hour. The largest centre in the city, Lóngwǔ also offers children's classes on weekend mornings and lessons in English.

BEST MASSAGE & SPAS

In Shànghǎi, a body or foot massage will come far cheaper than you'd pay at home. Options range from neighbourhood foot-massage parlours – where everyone kicks back on an armchair and watches TV – to midrange and luxury hotel spas, which offer private rooms, a change of clothes and a wonderfully soothing atmosphere. The latter usually offer beauty treatments (waxing, manicures etc) as well. Just remember, traditional massage *(tuīná)* is not particularly gentle. As your masseuse might very well tell you: no pain, no gain. Our favourites:

Double Rainbow Massage House (p124)

Green Massage (p142)

Dragonfly (p124)

Subconscious Day Spa (p124)

GREEN MASSAGE　　MASSAGE
Map p302 (青籁养身, Qīnglài Yǎngshén; ☑021 5386 0222; www.greenmassage.com.cn; 58 Taicang Rd; 太仓路58号; Chinese massage 60/90/120 mins ¥228/342/456; ⊗10am-2am; ⓂSouth Huangpi Rd) Calming fragrances envelop guests at this plush midrange spa attached to the Casa Serena hotel, which offers traditional Chinese, hot stone, and aromatherapy massages along with spa services such as relaxing body scrubs and deep cleansing facials. Reserve.

CHINESE COOKING WORKSHOP　COOKING
Map p306 (www.chinesecookingworkshop.com; 108-109, 2 Dongping Rd; 东平路2号; courses from ¥150-200; ⓂHengshan Rd, Shanghai Library) Cook your own dumplings and wok dishes while you learn different Chinese cooking styles from dim sum to Sìchuān at this cooking school in the French Concession. It also offers private tours, market tours and courses for kids.

SHÀNGHǍI GǓQÍN CULTURAL
FOUNDATION　　ART
Map p306 (上海古琴文化会, Shànghǎi Gǔqín Wénhuà Huì; ☑021 6437 4111; 1801 Middle Huaihai Rd; 淮海中路1801号; 10 classes ¥1188; ⊗10am-9pm; ⓂShanghai Library) This cultural centre offers classes in a handful of traditional arts: Chinese ink painting, *wéiqí* (围棋; traditional game of go) and the *gǔqín* (古琴; seven-string zither). Drop by to visit the peaceful 1930s villa and garden and the students might give you a brief demonstration.

KITCHEN AT...　　COOKING
Map p302 (☑021 6433 2700; www.thekitchenat.com; 3rd Floor, Bldg 20, Lane 383, South Xiangyang Rd; 襄阳南路383弄20号3楼; ⓂJiashan Rd) Great culinary school offering courses in regional Chinese and Western cuisines; good for both long-term residents and short-term visitors.

HONGWU KUNGFU
CENTRE　　MARTIAL ARTS
Map p302 (☑137 0168 5893; www.shanghaikungfucentre.com; Room 311, 3rd fl, International Artists' Factory, No 3, Lane 210, Taikang Rd; 法租界泰康路210弄3号3楼311; 3-month courses ¥2400; ⓂDapuqiao) This centre runs English-language taichi classes on Thursdays and Sundays and *wǔshù* (martial arts) classes on Tuesdays and Sundays. Call for the latest schedules as they tend to change.

Jìng'ān

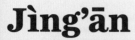

SOUTH JÌNG'ĀN | NORTH JÌNG'ĀN

Neighbourhood Top Five

1 Jade Buddha Temple (p130) Fathoming the fantastic at Shànghǎi's most sacred shrine.

2 M50 (p128) Catching up with the latest trends in the Chinese art world at this post-industrial art precinct.

3 Jìng'ān Sculpture Park (p135) Enjoying offbeat art installations while strolling through this art park.

4 Jìng'ān Temple (p129) Wandering this atmospheric temple, contrasted by a

modern skyscraper backdrop.

5 Shànghǎi Centre Theatre (p141) Catching local acrobats performing nightly at this venue.

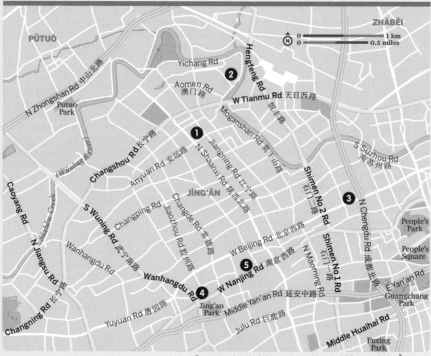

For more detail of this area see Maps p309 and p310

Explore: Jìng'ān

In the early days of the International Settlement, West Nanjing Rd was known as Bubbling Well Rd; its far western end was where city stopped and countryside began. By the swinging 1920s, the fields were being swallowed up by the rapidly expanding city, and Bubbling Well Rd was one of Shànghǎi's busiest and most exclusive streets. Apart from its name, not much has changed since then. The main thoroughfare of today's Jìng'ān district (静安), West Nanjing Rd is the address of some of the city's glitziest malls, high-end shops and five-star hotels.

Pǔdōng may have taller towers and the French Concession more charm, but this part of Jìng'ān is still the city's most exclusive neighbourhood. Even the skyscrapers here suggest harmony – a change from the disjointed skyline in other districts – while the traditional *lǐlòng* (alleyways) are unexpectedly well preserved. The heart of all the consumer action is the Shànghǎi Centre, a focal point both for tourists and the many expats who work in the district.

Head north of West Nanjing Rd and you're plunged into grittier, more authentic areas. The first stop on many tours of Jìng'ān is the Jade Buddha Temple. A short hike to the north are the M50 art galleries along Sūzhōu Creek. Good streets to explore for a taste of an authentic working-class Shànghǎi neighbourhood include the bustling Jiangning and North Shaanxi Rds.

Local Life

→ **Temple life** Join worshippers at the Jade Buddha (p130) and Jìng'ān Temples (p129), followed by a Buddhist vegetarian meal.

→ **Art** Admire contemporary Chinese art in edgy M50 (p128).

→ **Neighbourhood Life** Delve into the *lǐlòng* (alleyways) of the Bubbling Well Road Apartments on a walking tour (p131).

Getting There & Away

→ **Metro line 2** Runs parallel to West Nanjing Rd, stopping at People's Square, West Nanjing Rd, Jing'an Temple and Jiangsu Rd.

→ **Metro line 7** Runs north–south and interacts with line 2 at Jing'an Temple and line 1 at Changshu Rd in the French Concession.

→ **Metro line 13** When completed, will link Changshou Rd in north Jìng'ān with West Nanjing Rd.

Lonely Planet's Top Tip

Jìng'ān has some remarkably well-preserved *lǐlòng* (alleyways). The gentrified Bubbling Well Road Apartments are a great place to start exploration, and architecture buffs should also seek out the handful of lanes off Yuyuan Rd in the west of the district, particularly those at Nos 395 and 361, near the intersection with West Beijing Rd.

✖ Best Places to Eat

→ Commune Social (p139)
→ Jen Dow Vegetarian Restaurant (p137)
→ Yang's Fry Dumplings (p135)
→ Fù 1088 (p139)
→ Alan Wong's (p139)

For reviews, see p135 ➡

☐ Best Places to Drink

→ Dogtown (p139)
→ Tailor Bar (p139)
→ Mokkos Lamu (p140)
→ BeerGrdn (p140)
→ That One Place (p140)

For reviews, see p139 ➡

☐ Best Places to Shop

→ Spin (p141)
→ Jǐngdézhèn Porcelain Artware (p141)
→ Design Commune (p141)
→ Han City Fashion & Accessories Plaza (p142)
→ 10 Corso Como (p142)

For reviews, see p141 ➡

JÌNG'ĀN

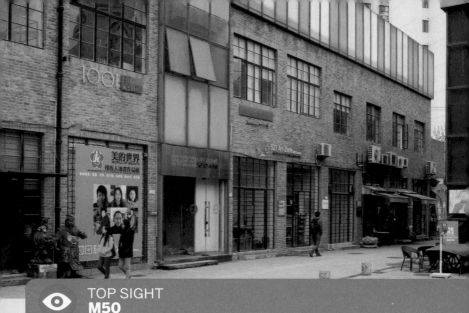

TOP SIGHT
M50

Shànghǎi may be known for its glitz and glamour, but it's got an edgy subculture too. The industrial M50 art complex is one prime example, where galleries have set up in disused factories and cotton mills, utilising the vast space to showcase contemporary Chinese emerging and established artists.

Exploring M50

It's worth spending a half-day poking around the galleries here. There are a lot of mass-produced commercial prints (especially in buildings 3 and 4), but also some challenging, innovative galleries and works. Most galleries open from 10am to 6pm; some close on Monday.

Galleries

Established galleries here include ShanghART (p134) with a big, dramatic space showcasing the work of some of the 40 artists it represents. Forward-thinking, provocative and entertaining island6 (p134) focuses on the collaborative works of Liu Dao, an art collective of painters, writers and multimedia artists who create edgy pieces in its on-site studio. Other notables include Sanzi's Sanzi Art (p134) and Yu Nancheng's Fish Studio (p134) – both local artists of international repute who marry traditional styles with a contemporary twist. For cutting-edge avant-garde works try Antenna Space (p134) or **Chronus Art Center** (CAC, 新时线媒体艺术中心, Xīn Shíjiàn Méitǐ Yìshù Zhōngxīn; Map p309; ☏021 5271 5789; www.chronusartcenter.org; Bldg 18, 50 Moganshan Rd; 莫干山路50号18号楼; ☉11am-6pm Wed-Sun). Across the road is **The Gallery** (画廊; Huàláng; Map p309; www.thegallery.com.cn; 87 Moganshan Rd; 莫干山路87号; ☉10am-6pm Tue-Sun), an art collective featuring innovative Chinese contemporary art and photography. For a hands-on experience, visit DN Club (p142) with its classes using vintage SLRs and a dark room for developing prints.

DON'T MISS

- ➡ ShanghART
- ➡ island6
- ➡ Antenna Space
- ➡ Moganshan Rd street art

PRACTICALITIES

- ➡ M50创意产业集聚区, M50 Chuàngyì Chǎnyè Jíjùqū
- ➡ Map p309, B2
- ➡ www.m50.com.cn/en
- ➡ 50 Moganshan Rd; 莫干山路50号
- ➡ free
- ➡ Ⓜ Line 3, 4 to Zhongtan Rd, exit 5; Line 1, 3, 4 to Shanghai Railway Station, exit 3

 **SIGHTS**

⊙ South Jìng'ān

JÌNG'ĀN TEMPLE   BUDDHIST TEMPLE

Map p310 (静安寺, Jìng'ān Sì; 1686-1688 West Nanjing Rd; 南京西路1686-1688号; ¥50; ⊙7.30am-5pm; Ⓜ Line 2, 7 to Jing'an Temple, exit 1) With the original temple dating back to AD 1216, the much-restored Jìng'ān Temple was here well before all the audacious skyscrapers and glitzy shopping malls. Today it stands like a shimmering mirage in defiance of West Nanjing Rd's soaring modern architecture; a sacred portal to the Buddhist world that partially, at least, underpins this metropolis of 24 million souls.

While the tinkle of wind chimes and burning of incense can't compete with blaring horns and car emissions, the temple still emits an air of reverence.

Constructed largely of Burmese teak, the temple has some impressive statues, including a massive 8.8m-high, 15-tonne silver Buddha in the main **Mahavira Hall** with 46 pillars; a 3.87m-high Burmese white-jade Sakyamuni in the side halls; and a 5 tonne Guanyin statue in the **Guanyin Hall**, carved from a 1000-year-old camphor tree. The temple still rattles away to the sounds of construction, while in the bunker beneath the main hall is an unfinished space, housing 18 glittering *luóhàn* (arhats), but little else. The complex has been designed to incorporate shops and restaurants around its perimeter (including a fantastic vegetarian restaurant at the rear), which stretches around the block. The ¥50 admission charge is steep for such a modest and thoroughly modern place of worship.

Khi Vehdu, who ran Jìng'ān Temple in the 1930s, was one of the most remarkable figures of the time. The nearly 2m-tall abbot had a large following as well as seven concubines, each of whom had a house and a car. During the Cultural Revolution the temple was stripped of its Buddhist statues and transformed into a plastics factory before burning to the ground in 1972.

Good times to visit include the Festival of Bathing Buddha (on the eighth day of the fourth lunar month) and at the full moon.

JÌNG'ĀN PARK   PARK

Map p310 (静安公园, Jìng'ān Gōngyuán; 1649 West Nanjing Rd; 南京西路1649号; Ⓜ Line 2, 7 to Jing'an Temple, exit 1) Across from Jìng'ān Temple, this pleasant landscaped garden is a nice little oasis in the city. Grab a fresh juice from a stall vendor and stroll past flowerbeds, public sculpture, a Chinese pavilion and pond, and a small rocky outcrop. This was the former site of Bubbling Well Road Cemetery before it was controversially relocated in 1954.

SHÀNGHĂI CHILDREN'S PALACE   ARCHITECTURE

Map p310 (少年宫, Shàonián Gōng; West Nanjing Rd; 南京西路; ♿; Ⓜ Line 2, 7 to Jing'an Temple, exit 1) A grand, white, two-storey 1920s building, the Shànghăi Children's Palace was formerly Kadoorie House, named after its wealthy Jewish owner. It's closed to the public, but architecture buffs can wander its grounds and still peek in the rooms of Elly Kadoorie's 1920s mansion, once the site of Shànghăi's most extravagant balls. As a reminder of Mao's vision for the palace, the building's stately lawn is dotted with socialist realism statues, and the facade is topped by a communist star. It still hosts activities for children.

FORMER RESIDENCE OF LIU CHANGSHENG   HISTORIC BUILDING

Map p310 (刘长胜上海故居, Liú Chángshēng Shànghăi Gùjū; www.jinganmuseum.org; 81 Yuyuan Rd; 愚园路81号; ⊙9-11.30am & 1-4.30pm Tue-Sun; Ⓜ Line 2, 7 to Jing'an Temple, exit 3) **FREE** Inside a red-brick villa, this museum details the rise of the Chinese Community Party (CPC). It's the former residence of underground CPC leader Liu Changsheng and, while predictably propaganda-filled, it's worth a short poke around to see historical photographs and a local interpretation of events leading to the 'liberation' of Shànghăi.

SALVADOR DALÍ SCULPTURE   PUBLIC ART

Map p310 (cnr West Nanjing & Changde Rds; 南京西路常德路的路口; Ⓜ Line 2, 7 to Jing'an Temple) On the corner of ritzy West Nanjing Rd sits *Nobility of Time*, a bronze sculpture created by Salvador Dalí, who constructed this signature dripping-clock piece in 1977.

MAO ZEDONG'S 1920 APARTMENT   HISTORIC BUILDING

Map p310 (上海毛泽东故居, Máozédōng Gùjū; 63 Anyi Rd; 安义路63号; ⊙9-11am & 1-4pm Tue-Sun; Ⓜ Line 2, 7 to Jing'an Temple, exit 7) **FREE** Though Mao Zedong only lived at this two-storey apartment for a few months in 1920, it's here the seeds were laid for the formation of the CCP. Within is a small museum displaying historical photographs, his personal belongings, a reproduction of his bedroom and short video on his life. While the facade is intact, the rest of the building has undergone a 21st-century makeover to incorporate Mao Space gallery.

MAO SPACE   GALLERY

Map p310 (MAO 空间; MAO Kōngjiān; 61 Anyi Rd; 安义路61号; ⊙11am-7pm Tue-Sun; M Line 2, 7 to Jing'an Temple, exit 7) **FREE** Located within the former short-term 1920s residence of Mao Zedong, this somewhat paradoxical pop-art gallery offers an intriguing insight to modern China's interpretation of Chairman Mao. The on-site MAOS shop is a good place to pick up some unique art pieces.

SHÀNGHĂI EXHIBITION CENTRE   ARCHITECTURE

Map p310 (上海展览中心, Shànghǎi Zhǎnlǎn Zhōngxīn; 1000 Middle Yan'an Rd; 延安中路1000 号; M Lines 2, 7 to Jing'an Temple, exit 8) **FREE** The hulking monolith of the Shànghǎi Exhibition Centre was built in 1955 as the Sino-Soviet Friendship Mansion – a friendship that soon turned sour and even regressed to the brink of war in the 1960s. The Stalinist-style architecture is based on St Petersberg's Admiralty Building, with neoclassical columns and a skeletal spire topped by a communist red star. Though located across from the Shànghǎi Centre, the best view is from the Yan'an Rd side, where the building is fronted by a stirring bronze socialist realist monument and red-star stained-glass windows.

OHEL RACHEL SYNAGOGUE   HISTORIC BUILDING

Map p310 (拉结会堂, Lājié Huìtáng; 500 North Shaanxi Rd; 陕西北路500号; M Line 2, 12, 13 to West Nanjing Rd) This synagogue was built by Jacob Sassoon in 1920, and was the first of seven synagogues built in Shànghǎi (only two remain). It was constructed in the Greek revival style, inspired by the Sephardic synagogues of London. Unfortunately, it's closed to the public.

FORMER RESIDENCE OF MAO ZEDONG   HISTORIC BUILDING

Map p310 (毛泽东旧居, Máo Zédōng Jiùjū; No 5-9, 120 North Maoming Rd; 茂名北路120弄5-9 号; ⊙9-11.30am & 1-4.30pm; M Line 2, 12, 13 West Nanjing Rd, exit 12) **FREE** The Great Helmsman Mao Zedong lived here in the latter half of 1924 with his second wife, Yang Kaihui, and

their two children at the time, Anying and Anqing. The residence has old photos and newspaper clippings on display, but for many foreigners the real highlight is the building itself, a beautiful example of *shíkùmén* (stone-gate house) architecture. The building is currently closed for renovations.

ZHĀNG GARDEN   ARCHITECTURE

Map p310 (张园, Zhāng Yuán; Taixing Rd; 泰兴路; M Line 2, 12, 13 to West Nanjing Rd) It's hard not to be impressed by the beautiful *shíkùmén* architecture of Zhāng Garden, down Taixing Rd, off West Nanjing Rd and west of Shimen No 1 Rd. What you see in Zhāng Garden today – mainly *shíkùmén* housing, a mix of two- and three-bay villas with tall entryways, handsome windows and hanging balcony pavilions – is merely a small portion of its former site. What survives is a sign of the wealth of its pre-1949 occupants.

Formerly known as Arcadia Hall, the site was first built in 1878 by a European merchant as a fairground for foreigners. It was acquired in 1882 by Zhang Shuhe, a wealthy Wúxī businessman, who later opened it up to the public. There was a huge garden, a dance hall, meeting rooms, a theatre for Chinese opera, a photography studio, a teahouse and restaurants. It later served as a location for political meetings and rallies against the Qing government.

Today, a single *shíkùmén* villa can house 20 or even 40 families, a mix of Shanghainese residents and migrant families from neighbouring provinces. It's easy to get lost in the alleys but don't worry – you'll find your way back to the main boulevard eventually.

◉ North Jìng'ān

M50   GALLERY

See p128.

JADE BUDDHA TEMPLE   BUDDHIST TEMPLE

Map p309 (玉佛寺, Yùfó Sì; cnr Anyuan & Jiangning Rds; 安远路和江宁路街口; high/low season ¥20/10; ⊙8am-4.30pm; M Line 7, 13 to Changshou Rd, exit 5) One of Shànghǎi's few active Buddhist monasteries, this temple was built between 1918 and 1928. The highlight is a transcendent Buddha crafted from pure jade, one of five shipped back to China by the monk Hui Gen at the turn of the 20th century. It's a popular stopover for tour buses, so be prepared for crowds. In February, during the Lunar New Year, the temple is very busy,

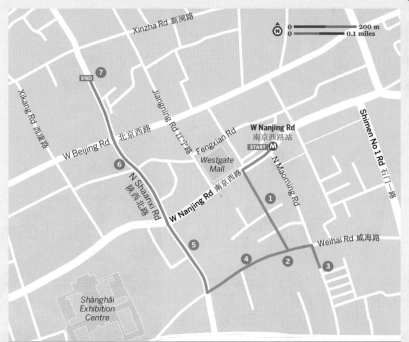

🏃 Neighbourhood Walk
Jìng'ān

START WEST NANJING RD METRO STATION
END OHEL RACHEL SYNAGOGUE
LENGTH 1.7KM; 1½ HOURS

Begin by walking through the **❶ Bubbling Well Road Apartments** (静安别墅, Jìng'ān Biéshù), which you can enter off West Nanjing Rd. One of the most delightful surviving new-style *lǐlòng* housing complexes in Shànghǎi, with three-storey red-brick houses built between 1928 and 1932, it's a great spot to catch daily residential life – people walking their dogs, playing cards or hanging out laundry to dry. Note how the architecture blends Chinese motifs with European-style terraced housing. Exit at the south end of the complex, which faces **❷ Sun Court**, a 1928 apartment block, and turn left onto Weihai Rd. Continue right onto North Maoming Rd and explore the lovingly preserved *shíkùmén* (stone-gate house) architecture of the **❸ Former Residence of Mao Zedong** (p130), where the 30-year-old Mao lived for several months in 1924.

Retrace your steps and return to Sun Court, continuing west down Weihai Rd and passing a **❹ tea shop** (p142) at No 686, with a fabulous collection of aged *pǔ'ěr* cakes lining the walls. Turn right onto North Shaanxi Rd, where you'll eventually get a glimpse of an enormous **❺ garden residence** (1918) at No 186, which once belonged to Wúxī native Rong Zongjing, one of Shànghǎi's most powerful industrialists. Rong Zongjing's nephew, Rong Yiren, was one of the rare individuals with a capitalist background to succeed in communist China, becoming vice mayor of Shànghǎi in 1957 and later vice-president of the PRC from 1993 to 1998.

Follow Shaanxi Rd north, past **❻ Grace Baptist Church** (怀恩堂, Huái'ēn Táng) at No 375, which was moved here in 1942. Continue north till you reach the Sassoon-built **❼ Ohel Rachel Synagogue** (p130) from 1920 at No 500, the first of seven synagogues built in Shànghǎi (only two remain). It is currently closed to the public but can be visited on tours with Shanghai Jews (www.shanghai-jews.com).

132

DIEGO GRANDI/SHUTTERSTOCK ©

JEFFREY GREENBERG/GETTY IMAGES ©

3

KATOOSHA/SHUTTERSTOCK ©

1. Shànghǎi Centre Theatre (p141)
The Shànghǎi Acrobatics Troupe has fun and popular performances at this theatre most nights.

2. Jìng'ān Temple (p129)
The restored temple with its roof of golden lions is a shimmering mirage contrasting with West Nanjing Rd's soaring modern architecture.

3. Jade Buddha Temple (p130)
This 20th-century temple features a pure jade Buddha and splendidly carved wooden *luóhàn* (arhats).

4. West Nanjing Road (p141)
Home to high-end Western fashion brands and luxury items, as well as Shànghǎi's most exclusive malls.

as some 20,000 Chinese Buddhists throng to pray for prosperity.

The first temple on your immediate left upon entering is the **Hall of Heavenly Kings**, holding the statues of the Four Heavenly Kings who each look upon the four cardinal points. Directly opposite is the twin-eaved **Grand Hall**, the temple's most significant building, where worshippers pray to the past, present and future Buddhas. Also within the Grand Hall are splendidly carved *luóhàn* (arhats), lashed to the walls with wires and a copper-coloured statue of Guanyin at the rear. Passing through the Grand Hall you'll reach a gated tranquil courtyard, where stairs lead up to the **Jade Buddha Hall**. The absolute centrepiece of the temple is the 1.9m-high pale-green jade Buddha, seated upstairs and carved from one piece. Photographs are not permitted. Walking further into the complex is the **Reclining Budda Hall**, which contains a small reclining white jade Buddha from Burma that's displayed in a glass cabinet.

The complex was renovated recently, which saw several halls demolished and re-placed with new buildings to the right of the entrance.

To get here, take Changshou metro station exit 5 and walk along Anyuan Rd, passing by a lively produce market and street-food vendors. A vegetarian restaurant is also within the temple complex around the corner.

SHANGHART GALLERY

Map p309 (香格纳画廊, Xiānggènà Huàláng; ☏021 6359 3923; www.shanghartgallery.com; Bldg 16 & 18, 50 Moganshan Rd; M50创意产业/16 和18号楼; ⊙10am-6pm; Ⓜ Line 3, 4 to Zhongtan Rd, exit 5; Line 1, 3, 4 to Shanghai Railway Station, exit 3) FREE An original M50 gallery (p128) and one of Shanghai's first contemporary art spaces, ShanghART is still going strong 20 years on. It's split into two galleries, both immense rooms displaying established local and international artists.

ISLAND6 GALLERY

Map p309 (六岛, Liù Dǎo; ☏021 6227 7856; www.island6.org; Bldg 6, 50 Moganshan Rd; 莫干山路50号; ⊙10am-7pm daily) One of the M50 art precinct's (p128) most forward-thinking, provocative and entertaining galleries. It focuses on the collaborative works of Liu Dao, an art collective of painters, writers and multimedia artists who create its edgy pieces in a studio on-site; it has a smaller gallery on the 1st floor of Building 7.

SĀNZĬ ART GALLERY

Map p309 (鳜子艺术, Sānzǐ Yìshù; www.sanziart. com; Room 4a-107, 50 Moganshan Rd; 莫干山路50 号4a–107房间; ⊙10am-6pm Tue-Sun; Ⓜ Line 3, 4 to Zhongtan Rd, exit 5; Line 1, 3, 4 to Shanghai Railway Station, exit 3) FREE This museum showcases the work of well-established Chinese artist Sanzi, who specialises in traditional Chinese art with a contemporary twist through the use of oils on canvas. He's also notable for his beautiful hand-painted Jǐngdézhèn ceramics. He's signed with acclaimed New York gallery Taglialatella (Warhol, Hirst, Koons).

FISH STUDIO GALLERY

Map p309 (鱼工作室, Yú Gōngzuò Shì; ☏021 6227 5102; www.yunancheng.com; Bldg 4, Room B-101, 50 Moganshan Rd; 莫干山路50号4号楼 房间B- 101; ⊙10.30am-5.30pm; Ⓜ Line 3, 4 to Zhongtan Rd, exit 5; Line 1, 3, 4 to Shanghai Railway Station, exit 3) FREE The gallery of Yu Nancheng, a Shànghǎi artist internationally renowned for his distinctive layered 3D oil paintings with iconic red images depicting traditional and modern China.

ANTENNA SPACE GALLERY

Map p309 (天线空间, Tiānxiàn Kōngjiān; ☏021 6256 0182; www.antenna-space.com/en; Bldg 17, 50 Moganshan Rd; 莫干山路50号17号楼202; ⊙11am-6.30pm Tue-Sun; Ⓜ Line 3, 4 to Zhongtan Rd, exit 5; Line 1, 3, 4 to Shanghai Railway Station, exit 3) FREE One of Shànghǎi's best galleries to take the pulse of China's avant-garde art scene, with a focus on new media works.

SITE OF COMMUNIST UNDERGROUND ORGANIZATION MUSEUM

Map p309 (中共地下党, Zhōnggòng Dìxià Dǎng; www.jinganmuseum.com/en; 339 Shanhaiguan Rd; 山海关路339号; ⊙9-11.30am & 1-4.30pm Tue-Sun; Ⓜ Line 2, 12, 13 to West Nanjng Rd, exit 1) FREE This red-brick *shíkùmén* building was used by the CCP in the early days for its underground secret meetings; the primary school within was a front for the covert gatherings. It's one of Shànghǎi's numerous CCP museums – all of which are aimed at party hardliners. It includes a few quirky interactive exhibits to lighten the mood.

SHÀNGHǍI NATURAL HISTORY MUSEUM MUSEUM

Map p309 (上海自然博物馆, Shànghǎi Zìrán Bówùguǎn; ☏021 6862 2000; www.snhm.org. cn; 510 West Beijing Rd; 北京西路510号; adult/teen/under 13 yr ¥30/12/free; ⊙9am-5.15pm Tue-Sun; Ⓜ Lines 2, 12, 13 to West Nanjng Rd)

Perhaps not quite on the same scale as the Smithsonian, Shànghǎi's new sleek space would nevertheless be a fitting choice for a *Night at the Museum* movie. As comprehensive as it is entertaining and informative, the museum is packed with displays of taxidermied animals, dinosaurs and cool interactive features. Its architecture is also a highlight, with a striking design that is beautifully integrated in its art-filled Jìng'ān Sculpture Park (p135) setting.

Spread over five levels, life-size creatures are the focal point throughout, with taxidermied (mostly realistic) animals, birds and reptiles, and models of soaring marine animals hanging spectacularly from the top floor. The African Savannah exhibit on the basement floor is a highlight, capturing all the drama of life on the plains with an epic full-wall animation feature screening on the hour.

Dinosaur fossils are well represented (including the indigenous Yunnanese 'Lufeng lizard'); these are interspersed with impressive life-like mechanical dinosaurs that move and roar.

The building's exterior spirals like a nautilus shell topped by a curved lawn embankment, Chinese-inspired water garden and vertical garden wall. Within, the main architectural feature is a 30m-high glass atrium, with a conical molecular-shaped glass 'cell wall' that floods the building with natural light. Symbolic of the living organisms within, its transparent core holds a tranquil courtyard garden with a pond full of plants, trickling waterfalls and rocky outcrops.

JÌNG'ĀN SCULPTURE PARK
SCULPTURE, GARDEN

Map p310 (静安雕塑公园, Jìng'ān Diāosù Gōngyuán; 128 Shimen 2nd Rd; 石门二路128号; ⊘6am-8.30pm; Ⓜ Lines 2, 12, 13 to West Nanjing Rd) FREE The attractive Jìng'ān Sculpture Park contains a mix of permanent and temporary pieces created by mainly international artists. The sculptures are scattered, making it a wonderful place to stroll and browse the thought-provoking abstract works, which are dappled with absurdity and humour. You'll find a massive thatched fox sitting on a shipping container, a cast-bronze family of lazing buffalo, and ostriches with their heads buried in the ground. In April the blossoming cherry trees are an attractive sight.

The impressive Shànghǎi Natural History Museum is also located here.

✖ EATING

✖ South Jìng'ān

★YANG'S FRY DUMPLINGS
DUMPLINGS $

Map p310 (小杨生煎馆, Xiǎoyáng Shēngjiān Guǎn; 2nd fl, 269 Wujiang Rd; 吴江路269号2楼; 4 fried dumplings from ¥8; ⊘10am-10pm; Ⓜ Line 2, 12, 13 to West Nanjing Rd, exit 4) A much-too-small outlet of this famous dumpling-house chain, specialising in delicious pork and prawn *shēngjiān*. Pass your receipt to the kitchen to collect your dumplings.

★SUMERIAN
CAFE $

Map p310 (苏美尔人, Sū Měi Ěr Rén; www.sumeriancoffee.com; 415 North Shaanxi Rd; 陕西北路415号; mains from ¥20; ⊘7am-8pm; 🗢; Ⓜ Line 2, 12, 13 to West Nanjing Rd, exit 1) Run by a bright and sunny team of staff, good-looking Sumerian packs a lot into a small space. The real drawcard here is the coffee – the cafe roasts its own single-origin beans sourced seasonally from Ethiopia, El Salvador and China. It does good pour-overs and lattes, as well as a nitro and eight-hour cold drip. The homemade bagels are also a standout, with a delicious selection of toppings and spreads.

CO. CHEESE MELT BAR
SANDWICHES $

Map p310 (32 Yuyuan East Rd; 愚园东路32号; sandwiches from ¥25; ⊘11.30am-10pm Tue-Thu & Sun, to 1am Sat; 🗢; Ⓜ Line 2, 7 to Jing'an Temple) A godsend for those with a hankering for the ultimate in Western comfort food, this joint is dedicated entirely to the humble grilled-cheese sandwich. Run by a Canadian expat, this intimate bar offers a selection of 20 gourmet cheese melts on sourdough, or build your own classic grilled cheese on white bread with a side of pickles and hot sauces.

There's an IPA and cider on tap, bottled craft beers and a good bar selection. Jars of homemade Polish pickles line the walls. Don't miss the signature pickleback – a shot of whiskey with briny pickle-juice chaser. If you want something different for a boozy brunch, try the alcoholic cereal served with Baileys milk.

YANG SONGFENG
NOODLES $

Map p310 (Shop M, 4th fl, Han City Fashion & Accessories Plaza, 480 West Nanjing Rd; 南京西路480号南政大厦B座4楼; noodles ¥12; ⊘9am-8.30pm; Ⓜ Line 2, 12, 13 to West Nanjing Rd, exit 1) It's a mere counter in a food court, but don't be put off: the Shànghǎi hand-pulled noodles

THE GREAT JEWISH FAMILIES

The Sassoon family consisted of generations of shrewd businesspeople from Baghdad to Bombay, whose achievements brought them wealth, knighthoods and far-reaching influence. Though it was David Sassoon who initiated cotton trading out of Bombay (now Mumbai), India, to China, and son Elias Sassoon who had the ingenuity to buy and build his own warehouses in Shànghǎi, it was Sir Victor Sassoon (1881–1961) who finally amassed the family fortune and enjoyed his wealth during Shànghǎi's heyday. Victor concentrated his energies on buying up Shànghǎi's land and building offices, apartments and warehouses; at one time he owned an estimated 1900 buildings in Shànghǎi. Victor left the city in 1941, returning only briefly after the war to tidy up the business, then he and his assets relocated to the Bahamas. He had plenty of romantic affairs but remained a bachelor until he finally married his American nurse when he was 70.

Today the Sassoon legacy lives on in the historic Fairmont Peace Hotel (p206) and Sassoon Mansion (known to Sassoon as 'Eve') – now the Cypress Hotel in Hóngqiáo – each the site of some infamously raucous Sassoon soirées. For one of his celebrated fancy-dress parties, he requested guests to come dressed as if shipwrecked.

The company of David Sassoon & Sons gave rise to several other notables in Shànghǎi, among them Silas Hardoon and Elly Kadoorie. Hardoon began his illustrious career as a night guard and later, in 1880, as manager of David Sassoon & Sons. Two years later he set out to do business on his own and promptly went bust. His second independent business venture in 1920 proved successful and Silas Hardoon made a name for himself in real estate. In his father's memory he built the Beth Aharon Synagogue near Sūzhōu Creek, which later served as a shelter for Polish Jews who had fled Europe. It has since been demolished. Once a well-respected member of both the French and International Councils, Hardoon became the subject of scandal when he married his Eurasian wife, Luo Jialing, and adopted several multicultural children. He then began to study Buddhism. His estate, including the school he had erected (now the grounds of the Shànghǎi Exhibition Centre), went up in smoke during the Sino-Japanese War. At the time of his death in 1931, he was the richest man in Shànghǎi.

Like Silas Hardoon, Elly Kadoorie began a career with David Sassoon & Sons in 1880, and he too broke away and amassed a fortune – in real estate, banking and rubber production. His famous mansion is the result of too much money left in the hands of an unreliable architect; after returning from three years in England, Kadoorie found a 19.5m-high ballroom aglow with 5.4m-wide chandeliers and enough imported marble to warrant the name Marble Hall. Architecture detectives can still visit the staircases and peek at the ballroom of the former mansion, once the site of Shànghǎi's most extravagant balls and now home to the Children's Palace (p129). Kadoorie died a year before the end of WWII; you can visit his mausoleum in the International Cemetery.

With their immense wealth, many Jewish families were pivotal in aiding the thousands of refugees who fled to Shànghǎi, principally Jewish refugees between 1933 and 1941. The Kadoorie family now resides in Hong Kong and is still involved in charity work.

are supreme. There's pork off the bone or hearty vegetables – perfect for restoring calories on a Jìng'ān shopping jaunt. The pork *bao* are also great for a quick snack.

PHO STORE
VIETNAMESE $

Map p310 (118 Xikang Rd; 西康路118号; dishes ¥25-80; ◎11am-9.45pm; MLine 2, 7 to Jing'an Temple, Line 2, 12, 13 to West Nanjing Rd) This vibrant hole-in-the-wall Vietnamese joint with pop art decorating its walls has a wonderful selection of hearty bowls of *pho* (noodle soup), vermicelli dishes, fresh *bahn mi*

(filled bread rolls) and rice-paper rolls filled with soft-shell crab. Try one of the delicious Southeast Asian–inspired cocktails infused with lemongrass, lychee and basil.

YÀKÈXĪ
XINJIANG $

Map p310 (亚克西; 379 Xikang Rd; 西康路379号; mains from ¥18; ◎11.30am-10pm; MLine 7 to Changping Rd, exit 2; Line 2, 12, 13 to West Nanjing Rd, exit 4) Not a single inch of wall space survives undecorated at this corner-side Xīnjiāng restaurant, and although the spangled, overblown interior only vaguely channels Kashgar, the food summons up the pungent aromas of China's mighty northwest. The staples – lamb kebabs (¥6 each), *shàozi* noodles (¥Y18), naan bread (¥6) – are tasty and filling. Uighur dancing shakes tail feathers from 7pm nightly (apart from Mondays).

CYCLO VIETNAMESE $

Map p310 (三轮车夫, Sānlúnchē Fū; ☑021 6135 0150; www.cyclorestaurant.com; 678 North Shaanxi Rd; 陕西北路678号; mains ¥40-80; ⊙11am-2.30pm & 6-10.30pm Mon-Fri, 11.30am-10.30pm Sat & Sun; Ⓜ Line 7 to Changping Rd, exit 2) Set up by a father and son duo, Cyclo – named after Vietnam's version of the local *sānlúnchē* (pedicabs) that infest Ho Chi Minh City and Hanoi – is spot on. It propels all the scrumptious flavours of China's southwesterly neighbour into Shànghǎi, with delicious spring rolls, *pho, banh mi,* Vietnamese salads and an unwavering focus on fresh ingredients. The decor is warm and homely with plenty of plants, but service can be slow.

NÁNXIÁNG STEAMED BUN RESTAURANT DUMPLING $

Map p310 (南翔馒头店, Nánxiáng Mántou Diàn; 2nd fl, 269 Wujiang Rd; 吴江路269号2楼; 4 dumplings ¥16; ⊙10am-10pm; Ⓜ Line 2, 12, 13 to West Nanjing Rd, exit 4) A not-too-busy branch of the famous Shànghǎi dumpling restaurant.

JEN DOW VEGETARIAN RESTAURANT CHINESE $

Map p310 (人道素菜小吃, Réndào Sùcài Xiǎochī; 153 Yuyuan Rd; 愚园路153号; noodles from ¥20, lunch/dinner buffet ¥178/198; ⊙9am-9pm, buffet 11.30am-2pm & 5.30-9pm; ☑; Ⓜ Line 2, 7 to Jing'an Temple, exit 1) Your body is a temple so treat it with respect by dining at this fab ground-floor meat-free eatery slung out behind the Jìng'ān Temple. You can slurp up a vast, tasty bowl of noodles densely sprinkled with crisp, fresh mushroom, bamboo shoots, cabbage and carrots for a mere ¥20 – it's a meal in itself.

Also at hand are vegetarian hotpots (¥55) and a host of other choices, plus Portuguese egg tarts and other baked delicacies at the door. Order fast-food-style from the counter. Upstairs, the smarter 2nd floor is a civilised choice with a Chinese and Western menu. The blistering and salty *mápó dòufu* (tofu and pork crumbs in a spicy sauce) hits the Sìchuān nail squarely on the head, with mushrooms in place of meat, while the sizzling seafood bake with

melted cheese is crisp and filling. Service is efficient; the only fly in the ointment is the Richard Clayderman musak.

The 3rd floor has a classy buffet, with creative vegetarian fare. Head here Monday evenings for the ¥130 all-you-can-eat feast.

CITY SHOP SUPERMARKET $

Map p310 (城市超市, Chéngshì Chāoshì; ☑400 811 1797; www.cityshop.com.cn; B1, Shànghǎi Centre, 1376 West Nanjing Rd; 南京西路1376号; ⊙8am-10pm; Ⓜ Line 2, 7 to Jing'an Temple; Line 2, 12, 13 to West Nanjing Rd) In the basement floor of the Shànghǎi Centre, this supermarket is the place to get all those imported goodies you just can't find anywhere else. It also has a bakery with a good choice of inexpensive sandwiches. There's free delivery for orders over ¥200.

PURE AND WHOLE VEGETARIAN $

Map p310 (純和整個, Chún Hé Zhěnggè; ☑021 5175 9822; www.pureandwhole.com; 98 Yanping Rd; 延平路98号; dishes ¥37-78; ⊙11.30am-10pm; ✳🅿☑; Ⓜ Line 2, 7 to Jing'an Temple, exit 2) When you've overdosed on dumplings, this popular vegetarian restaurant offers much-needed respite with detox salads, wholewheat wraps stuffed with tofu 'chorizo', chickpeas and avocado, or white-bean stews. It does cleansing juices and creative blended drinks. Grab a seat upstairs overlooking the main road.

GODLY CHINESE $

Map p310 (功德林, Gōngdélín; ☑021 6327 0218; www.shgodly.com; 445 West Nanjing Rd; 南京西路445号; dishes ¥16-88; ⊙11am-2pm & 5-9pm; ☑; Ⓜ Line 1, 2, 8 to People's Square) Shànghǎi's second-oldest vegetarian restaurant (opened in 1922), Godly never fails to perplex Western vegetarians – almost everything on the menu is prepared to resemble meat, down to sinewy textures and bony chunks. Don't worry though, the smoked beef and the fried chicken with sesame oil are actually made of tofu, no matter how convincing they look.

★HǍI DǏ LÃO HOTPOT $$

Map p310 (海底捞; ☑021 6258 9758; 3rd fl, 1068 West Beijing Rd; 北京西路1068号3楼; hotpot per person ¥100-120; ⊙10.30am-late; 🅿; Ⓜ Line 2, 12, 13 to West Nanjing Rd) This Sichuanese hotpot restaurant is all about service, and the assault begins the minute you walk in the door. Pre-dining options include complimentary shoeshines, manicures and

JÌNG'ĀN EATING

trays of fresh fruit; once you've actually sat down, the buzz of activity continues with the donning of matching red aprons and a YouTube-worthy noodle-stretching dance performance (order *lāo miàn;* 捞面).

DIN TAI FUNG
DUMPLINGS $$

Map p310 (鼎泰丰, Dǐng Tài Fēng; ☏021 6289 9182; www.dintaifung.com.tw/en; Shànghǎi Centre, 1376 West Nanjing Rd; 南京西路1376号; 10 dumplings ¥58-88; ◷10am-10pm; ◪; ⓂLine 2, 7 to Jing'an Temple, exit 1) Critically acclaimed dumplings and flawless service from Taiwan's most famous dumpling chain. Reserve ahead.

LIGHT & SALT
INTERNATIONAL $$

Map p310 (光与盐, Guāng Yǔ Yán; ☏021 5266 0930; www.light-n-salt.com; 407 North Shaanxi Rd; 陕西北路407号; dishes ¥90-350, set lunch 2/3 courses ¥157/187; ◷noon-midnight; ⓂLine 2, 12, 13 to West Nanjing Rd, exit 1) Located on a trendy strip of boutiques is the second branch of this classy-yet-casual bistro with big windows overlooking an English garden. The international menu changes seasonally, but expect the likes of marinated roast lamb rib, duck pie and roasted miso cod. The set lunches are popular, and weekend brunch includes breakfast pizza and Bloody Marys.

BULL & CLAW
SEAFOOD $$

Map p310 (公牛和爪, Gōngniú Hé Zhǎo; ☏021 6266 6819; www.thebullandclaw.com; 466 Xikang Rd; 西康路466号; mains ¥108-250; ◷11am-late; ✻⛾; ⓂLine 7 to Changping Rd, exit 2) This smart-casual restaurant catering to a well-heeled clientele lives up to its name with a menu specialising in steaks and lobster. The speciality is the half Nova Scotia lobster stuffed into a rosemary ciabatta (¥148), which goes superbly with one of the craft beers on tap. It's decked out in retro furniture, rustic heavy wood floorboards, white tiles and a vertical garden growing on the back wall.

LYNN
SHANGHAI $$

Map p310 (琳怡, Lín Yí; ☏021 6247 0101; 99-1 Xikang Rd; 西康路99-1号; dishes ¥65-300; ◷11.30am-10.30pm; ⓂLine 2, 7 to Jing'an Temple; Line 2, 12, 13 to West Nanjing Rd) Lynn offers consistently good, cleverly presented dishes in plush but unfussy surroundings. The lunch dim-sum menu offers a range of delicate dumplings, while for dinner there are more traditional Shanghainese dishes

such as eggplant with minced pork in a garlic-and-chilli sauce. More adventurous standouts include the sautéed chicken with sesame pockets and deep-fried spare ribs with honey and garlic.

Weekends feature ¥98 all-you-can-eat dim sum for brunch from 11.30am to 2pm. Reserve.

MÉILÓNGZHÈN
JIŬJIĀ
CHINESE $$

Map p310 (梅陇镇酒家; ☏021 6253 5353; No 22, Lane 1081, West Nanjing Rd; 南京西路1081号22弄号; dishes ¥25-120; ◷11am-2pm & 5-9pm; ⓂLine 2, 12, 13 to West Nanjing Rd, exit 1) This esteemed *lǎozìhào* ('old name') restaurant has been serving delighted diners since the 1930s. The menu mixes Sìchuān and Shanghainese tastes and ranges from the pricey (crab with tofu) to the more reasonable (fish slices with tangerine peel). The rooms once housed the Shanghai Communist Party headquarters, but are now bedecked in wood carvings, huge palace lamps and photos of foreign dignitaries.

ELEMENT FRESH
CAFE $$

Map p310 (新元素, Xīnyuánsù; ☏021 6279 8682; www.elementfresh.com; Shànghǎi Centre, 1376 West Nanjing Rd; 南京西路1376号; sandwiches & salads ¥45-98, dinner from ¥128; ◷7am-11pm; ⛾◪; ⓂLine 2, 7 to Jing'an Temple; Line 2, 12, 13 to West Nanjing Rd) Perennially popular, Element Fresh hits the spot with its tempting selection of healthy salads, pasta and noodle dishes (Western and Asian) and hefty sandwiches. Then there are the imaginative smoothies, big breakfasts, coffee and after-work cocktails.

GUMGUM
BURGERS $$

Map p310 (居姆居姆, Jūmǔ Jūmǔ; www.gumgum.cn; 60 Lane 273, Jiaozhou Rd; 胶州路273弄60号; mains from ¥68; ◷11am-10pm; ✻⛾; ⓂLine 2, 7 to Jing'an Temple, exit 2; Line 7 to Changping Rd) This hip little burger joint run by a local studio has an industrial decor that mixes splashes of old-school fluoro with skateboards on the wall. The fridge is full of bottled craft beers that pair well with the menu of inventive burgers and ribs.

VEGETARIAN LIFESTYLE
CHINESE $$

Map p310 (枣子树, Zǎozǐshù; ☏021 6215 7566; www.jujubetree.com; 258 Fengxian Rd; 奉贤路258号; dishes ¥28-80; ◷11am-9.30pm; ◪; ⓂLine 2, 12, 13 to West Nanjing Rd) The folks at this stylish restaurant are maximising meat-free goodness with organic vegetarian fare fashioned for the masses. There are loads of clever dishes, including soup served in a pumpkin, but the best are the sweet Wúxī 'spare ribs' (stuffed with lotus root, of course) and claypots galore. It's MSG-free and cooks go light on the oil. It's alcohol free.

★FU 1088 SHANGHAI $$$

Map p310 (福1088; ☎021 5239 7878; 375 Zhenning Rd; 镇宁路375号; ☷11am-2pm & 5.30-11pm; ⓜLine 2, 11 to Jiangsu Rd) In a 1930s villa, exclusive Fu 1088 has 17 rooms filled with Chinese antiques. Rooms are rented out privately, with white-gloved service and an emphasis on elegant Shanghainese fare with a modern twist such as shredded crab and drunken chicken. There's a minimum charge of ¥300 per person for lunch, and ¥400 for dinner, excluding drinks.

ALAN WONG'S HAWAIIAN $$$

Map p310 (黄志光的, Huángzhìguāng De; www.alanwongs.com; 2nd fl, Shanghai Centre, 1376 West Nanjing Rd; 南京西路1376号2楼; tasting dishes ¥68-400, 5-course menu ¥700; ☷11.30am-2pm & 5.30-10pm; ▣☏; ⓜLine 2, 7 to Jing'an Temple; Line 2, 12, 13 to West Nanjing Rd) Bringing a slice of Hawaii to China, celebrity chef Alan Wong's new Shanghai venture rides on the success of his acclaimed Honolulu restaurants. Here it's all about contemporary (Spam-free) Hawaiian cuisine, with fresh, traditional ingredients that incorporate Japanese, Korean and Chinese flavours. The five-dish degustation menu offers the likes of buttery poached lobster and twice-cooked soy-braised ribs.

Even if you're not dining, the blue neon-lit cocktail bar is a good reason to pop by, with a menu of original recipes expertly concocted from fresh fruit ingredients.

✖ North Jìng'ān

JADE BUDDHA TEMPLE VEGETARIAN RESTAURANT CHINESE $

Map p309 (玉佛寺素斋, Yùfó Sì Sùzhāi; 999 Jiangning Rd; 江宁路999号; dishes ¥22-58; ☷8am-6pm; ▣; ⓜLine 7, 13 to Changshou Rd, exit 5) Pull up a seat alongside the monks, nuns and lay worshippers for a vegetarian feast at this Buddhist banquet hall. On the menu are dumplings, noodles, hotpot and mock-meat dishes such as succulent soya Sichuan chicken.

CANS TEA & BOOK HOUSE SHANGHAI $

Map p309 (茶图书馆罐, Chá Túshū Guǎn Guàn; Room 105-2, Building 3, 50 Moganshan Rd; 莫干山路50号3号楼105-2 罐子书屋; mains ¥16-35; ☷10am-6pm; ⓜLine 3, 4 to Zhongtan Rd, exit 5; Line 1, 3, 4 to Shanghai Railway Station, exit 3) Within the entrance to M50 (p128), this art-book store serves great noodles (go the salted mustard green with tofu), dumplings and speciality teas.

★COMMUNE SOCIAL TAPAS $$

Map p309 (食社, Shíshè; www.communesocial.com; 511 Jiangning Rd; 江宁路511号; tapas ¥38-198, set-lunch menu 3/5 course ¥178/218; ☷noon-2.30pm & 6-10.30pm Tue-Fri, noon-3pm & 6-10.30pm Sat, to 3pm Sun; ⓜLine 7 to Changping Rd) A venture by UK celebrity chef Jason Atherton, this natty Neri & Hu–designed restaurant blends a stylish, yet relaxed, vibe with sensational tasting dishes, exquisitely presented by chef Scott Melvin. It's divided neatly into upstairs cocktail bar with terrace, downstairs open-kitchen tapas bar and dessert bar. It's the talk of the town, but has a no-reservations policy, so prepare to queue.

🍷 DRINKING & NIGHTLIFE

🍺 South Jìng'ān

★DOGTOWN BAR

Map p310 (狗镇, Gǒu Zhèn; 409 N Shaanxi Rd; 陕西北路409号; ☷4-10pm Mon-Fri, noon-11pm Sat & Sun; ⓜLine 2, 7 to Jing'an Temple; Line 2, 12, 13 to West Nanjing Rd) Run by the team from Sumerian (p135) next door, this pocket-sized bar is literally a streetside shack with a few stools at its bar, though most revellers stand on the pavement with beer in hand. It's a great place to get chatting to random strangers. For early starters, there's a free keg of Asahi going on weekends from noon until it runs out.

If that wasn't a sweet enough deal, Dogtown also serves homemade soft-corn tortilla tacos (from ¥15) and bagels. Note it's closed during the winter months.

TAILOR BAR COCKTAIL BAR

Map p310 (裁缝栏, Cáiféng Lán; ☎183 0197 7360; 4th Fl, 2 Huashan Rd; 华山路2号4楼; cocktails ¥90-150; ☷6.30pm-late; ⓜLine 2, 7 to Jing'an Temple) Set up by London-trained mixologist Eddie Yang, this swanky speakeasy is accessed via a nondescript lift next to a Chinese medicine shop. It lives up to its name with cocktails tailor-made to suit your tastes; there's no menu, so pick a few items and let the staff do their thing. During the day they serve coffee and there are good views of Jìng'ān Temple.

MOKKOS LAMU
BAR

Map p310 (1245 Wuding W Rd; 武定西路1245 号; ⊘7pm-2am; MLine 2, 11 to Jiangsu Rd, exit 5) Hidden away on a residential side street, Mokkos is a long-running local fave that specialises in nothing but *shōchū* (Japanese spirit made from grains). It's an intimate, jovial and welcoming bar where drinkers sit on stools around the curved bar lined with large, aesthetically pleasing *shōchū* bottles. There's a choice of wheat, rice or potato varieties, and it also does *shōchū* cocktails for ¥40.

There's a guitar on the wall for regular impromptu jams.

ROOSTER
BAR

Map p310 (公鸡, Gōngjī; www.roosterchina.com; 455 N Shanxi Rd; 陕西北路455号; ⊘11am-late; ☎; MLine 2, 12, 13 to West Nanjing Rd, exit 1) This stylish, casual expat bar buzzes with the after-work crowd who come here for happy hour. There are six craft beers on tap, affordable cocktails, and ¥25 glasses of wine (from 5pm to 8pm). There's a good choice of bar food, half-price wings on Tuesday and trivia nights on Sunday. Its original branch is at 51 Yongkang Rd.

BEERGRDN
BAR

Map p310 (啤酒花园, Píjiǔ Huāyuán; www.beergrdn.cn; 183 Jiaozhou Rd; 胶州路183号; ⊘7am-10.30pm; MLine 2, 7 to Jing'an Temple, exit 1) Inside the eco-chic Urbn (p211), this fashionable, laid-back bar is a good spot for a relaxed drink, with old-school arcade games and an attractive outdoor terrace. There's craft beer on tap (including their own IPA) and a good cocktail list; happy hour runs from 4pm to 8pm. It's a happening weekend brunch spot, and has a quality menu with items such as house-smoked fish and homemade ricotta.

THE SHED
SPORTS BAR

Map p310 (大棚, Dàpéng; ☑021 6237 6381; www.shedsh.com; 698 Shaanxi Bei Rd; 陕西北路698号; ⊘11am-late; ☎; MLine 7 to Changping

Rd, exit 2) A smarter than usual sports bar, the Shed is set up with multiple TVs showing live games across the globe. Drinks are reasonably priced and it's popular for Sunday roasts (especially with Brits), Wednesday wing nights and half-price food on Mondays.

TAP HOUSE
PUB

Map p310 (点击楼, Diǎnjī Lóu; 99 Taixing Rd; 泰兴路99号; ⊘11am-1am; ☎; MLine 2, 12, 13 to West Nanjing Rd, exit 4) Part of the trendy Zhāng Garden (p130) eating and drinking complex within an atmospheric *lòngtáng*, this brew house has 24 craft beers on tap. Food is also a highlight with southern BBQ dishes (mains from ¥65) including beef brisket marinated in Brooklyn lager. There's a rooftop terrace when the weather's nice. Its VPN-enabled wi-fi is handy.

THAT ONE PLACE
BAR

Map p310 (这一个地方, Zhè Yīgè Dìfāng; No 10, 273 Jiaozhou Lu; 胶州路273弄10号; ⊘11am-10pm; MLine 2, 7 to Jing'an Temple, exit 2; Line 7 to Changping Rd) Run by a long-term US expat, this cosy dive bar is hidden down an alleyway that's emerging as a hip little strip. It's all about affordable craft beer, with a focus on brews from the Pacific Northwest. It's a real local, and has the intimacy of hanging out in a mate's lounge room.

MY PLACE
RUIN BAR
BAR

Map p310 (我将毁灭吧, Wǒ Jiāng Huǐmiè Bā; 3rd fl, 1788 Xinzha Rd; 新闸路1788号3楼; ⊘6pm-late; MLine 2, 7 to Jing'an Temple, exit 2; Line 7 to Changping Rd) Rising from the ashes of I Love Shanghai (which relocated to Tiánzǐfáng), My Place was established by two regulars who wanted to keep a dive bar running for locals. There's pool, darts and cheap drinks – including the house rocket-fuel 'Weng Weng' challenge. It's located above the Singaporean restaurant Orchard CRC.

THE SPOT
BAR

Map p310 (位置, Wèizhí; ☑021 6247 3579; www.thespot.com.cn; 255 Tongren Rd; 铜仁路255号; ⊘11am-late; ☎; MLine 2, 7 to Jing'an Temple; Line 2, 12, 13 to West Nanjing Rd) Attracting a mixed crowd, the Spot is part bistro, part lounge bar with a DJ spinning tracks, but when push comes to shove, it's a sports bar best for catching live games. Check the website for the schedule. Happy hour runs until 8pm nightly.

KĀIBĀ
BAR

Map p310 (开巴; www.kaiba-beerbar.com; 479 Wuding Rd; 武定路479号; ⊙10am-late Mon-Fri, 2pm-late Sat & Sun; ☎; Ⓜ Line 7 to Changping Rd, exit 2) Beer-o-philes who have endured too many bottles of Shànghǎi's watery Reeb may do cartwheels at the Trappist brews and 20 craft beers on tap served up in this chilled, reclaimed concrete, wood and brick setting. There's also a decent menu of pub food.

🍸 North Jìng'ān

BANDU CABIN
CAFE

Map p309 (半度音乐, Bàndù Yīnyuè; ☑ 021 6276 8267; www.bandumusic.com; Bldg 11, 50 Moganshan Rd; 莫干山路50号11号楼; ⊙10am-6.30pm Sun-Fri, to 10pm Sat; Ⓜ Line 3, 4 to Zhongtan Rd, exit 5; Line 1, 3, 4 to Shanghai Railway Station, exit 3) With charmingly eclectic mismatched furniture, this laid-back cafe-cum-record-label serves up noodles, drinks and snacks, along with traditional Chinese music concerts every second Saturday at 7.30pm (¥80). Phone ahead on Friday to reserve seats. There's also a quality selection of Chinese folk-music CDs. It's across from ShanghART (p134).

B&C
BAR

Map p309 (公元前, Gōngyuán Qián; 685 Xikang Rd; 西康路685号; ⊙4pm-late; Ⓜ Line 7 to Changping Rd, exit 4) You get welcoming hugs from sociable co-owner Candy at this huge old-school bar. Prices are low – in dive territory – with pool and darts for those unable to just sit and yak barside, while Bon Jovi and Duran Duran transport everyone back to the good old days of big, bad hairstyles. It shares space with Detroit BBQ, which serves ribs and pulled pork.

☆ ENTERTAINMENT

★ SHÀNGHǍI CENTRE
THEATRE
ACROBATICS

Map p310 (上海商城剧院, Shànghǎi Shāngchéng Jùyuàn; ☑ 021 6279 8948; Shànghǎi Centre, 1376 West Nanjing Rd; 南京西路1376号; tickets ¥120-300; Ⓜ Line 2, 7 to Jing'an Temple) The Shànghǎi Acrobatics Troupe has popular performances here at 7.30pm most nights. It's a short but fun show and is high on the to-do list of most first-time visitors. Buy tickets a couple of days in advance from the ticket office on the right-hand side at the entrance to the Shànghǎi Centre.

🛍 SHOPPING

West Nanjing Rd is more upmarket than the eastern end. It's home to high-end Western fashion brands and luxury items, as well as Shànghǎi's most exclusive malls, such as Plaza 66. Behind People's Square is Dagu Rd, with a number of large DVD stores.

★ SPIN
CERAMICS

Map p310 (旋, Xuán; www.spinceramics.com; 360 Kangding Rd; 康定路360号; ⊙11am-8pm; Ⓜ Line 7 to Changping Rd, exit 2) High on creative flair, Spin brings Chinese ceramics up to speed with oblong teacups, twisted sake sets and all manner of cool plates, chopstick holders and 'kung fu' vases. Pieces are never overbearing, but trendily lean towards the whimsical, geometric, thoughtful and elegant. All are made by Shànghǎi designers in the famous pottery town of Jǐngdézhèn. Prices are reasonable – pick up contemporary (beautiful) spiral teacups for ¥70.

★ DESIGN COMMUNE
HOMEWARES

Map p309 (設計公社, Shèjì Gōngshè; www.thedesignrepublic.com; 511 Jiangning Rd; 江宁路511号; ⊙10am-7pm; Ⓜ Line 7 to Changping Rd) Run by esteemed interior-design duo Neri & Hu – the last word on everything tasteful in Shanghai – Design Republic has set up this multilevel showroom displaying products from acclaimed local and international designers. Within a beautiful red-brick building that was a former police headquarters (c 1909), here you'll encounter anything from Scandinavian furniture to designer glassware, ceramics and accessories.

JǏNGDÉZHÈN PORCELAIN ARTWARE
CERAMICS

Map p310 (景德镇艺术瓷器, Jǐngdézhèn Yìshù Cíqì; ☑ 021 6253 8865; 212 North Shaanxi Rd; 陕西北路212号; ⊙10am-9pm; Ⓜ Line 2, 12, 13 to West Nanjing Rd, exit 1) This is one of the best places for high-quality traditional Chinese porcelain. Blue-and-white vases, plates, teapots and cups are some of the many choices available. Credit cards are accepted, and overseas shipping can be arranged.

XINLELU.COM

CLOTHING

Map p310 (www.facebook.com/shopxinlelu; 414 North Shaanxi Rd; 陕西北路414号; ⊙11am-9pm; MLine 2, 12, 13 to West Nanjing Rd, exit 1) Local style mavens XinleLu.com have ventured into the offline world with this original showroom, displaying the best of their hand-picked bags, shoes and dresses from local designers.

10 CORSO COMO

FASHION & ACCESSORIES

Map p310 (www.10corsocomo.com; Wheelock Sq, 1717 West Nanjing Rd; 南京西路1717号; ⊙10am-10pm; MLine 2, 7 to Jing'an Temple) The first China branch of this glamorous Milan boutique incorporates the same model of 'slow shopping'. Over five floors there's a mix of men's and women's clothing, shoes, accessories, art books and design pieces. Its mainly international names, with a few Chinese designers. Head upstairs for its art gallery and cafe overlooking Jìng'ān Temple (p129), or to the champagne bar in the lobby.

XIǍOYÈ TEA SHOP

DRINKS

Map p310 (小叶名茶, Xiǎoyè Míng Chá; 686 Weihai Rd; 威海路686号; ⊙8am-8.30pm; MLine 2, 12, 13 to West Nanjing Rd) This tea store has a good collection of *pǔ'ěr* (aged fermented tea from Yúnnán) cakes and bricks lining the walls, as well as loose-leaf oolong, white and herbal teas. The back room also sells teapots and utensils.

AMY LIN'S PEARLS

JEWELLERY

Map p310 (艾敏林氏珍珠, Àimín Línshì Zhēnzhū; ☎139 1631 3466; www.amylinspearls.com; Room 30, 3rd fl, 580 West Nanjing Rd; 南京西路580号3楼30号; ⊙10am-8pm; MLine 2, 12, 13 to West Nanjing Rd, exit 1) It may be in a market known for fake goods, but Amy Lin's is the most reliable retailer of pearls of all colours and sizes. Freshwater pearls (from ¥80), including prized black Zhèjiāng pearls (from ¥1500) and saltwater pearls (from ¥200), are available here. Staff speak English and will string your selection for you. Jade and jewellery available, too.

HAN CITY FASHION & ACCESSORIES PLAZA

CLOTHING

Map p310 (韩城服饰礼品广场, Hánchéng Fúshì Lǐpǐn Guǎngchǎng; 580 West Nanjing Rd; 南京西路580号; ⊙10am-10pm; MLine 2, 12, 13 to West Nanjing Rd, exit 1) This unassuming building is a popular location to pick up knock-offs, with hundreds of stalls spread across four floors. Scavenge for bags, belts, jackets, shoes, suitcases, sunglasses, ties, T-shirts, DVDs and electronics. Prices are all inflated, so bargain hard.

ART DECO

ANTIQUES

Map p309 (凹凸家具库, Āotū Jiājù Kù; ☎021 6277 8927; www.aotuku.com/en; Bldg 7, 50 Moganshan Rd; 莫干山路50号7号楼; ⊙10am-6pm Tue-Sun; MLine 3, 4 to Zhongtan Rd; Line 1, 3, 4 to Shanghai Railway Station) For stylish period furnishings, stop by artist Ding Yi's gallery in the M50 complex (p128). His standout antique collection includes folding screens, art deco armoires, tables and chairs, and a few vintage poster girls on the walls to help cast that 1930s spell.

🏃 SPORTS & ACTIVITIES

DN CLUB

PHOTOGRAPHY

Map p309 (当年, Dāngnián; ☎021 6276 9657; Room 107, Bldg 17, 50 Moganshan Rd; M50创意产业17号楼107室; course ¥380; ⊙10am-6pm Tue-Sun; MLine 3, 4 to Zhongtan Rd, exit 5; Line 1, 3, 4 to Shanghai Railway Station, exit 3) For photo-developing courses and prints, pop into DN Club in the M50 complex (p128). They'll provide a vintage SLR for you to snap a roll of film, then you'll return to develop and enlarge the prints yourself in their darkroom. Otherwise you can take in your own film to develop. Bring your passport as a deposit.

GREEN MASSAGE

MASSAGE

Map p310 (青籁养身, Qīnglài Yǎngshén; ☎021 6289 7776; www.greenmassage.com.cn; 2nd fl, Shànghǎi Centre, 1376 West Nanjing Rd; 南京西路1376号2楼; massages & spa treatments ¥216-398; ⊙10.30am-midnight; MJing'an Temple or West Nanjing Rd) Soothing midrange spa with foot, *tuīná* (traditional massage) and shiatsu massages. Reserve. It's in both East and West buildings.

Pǔdōng

Neighbourhood Top Five

1 Oriental Pearl TV Tower (p146) Viewing Shànghǎi from low-orbit altitude through the glass-floored walkway.

2 Flair (p154) Sinking an evening alfresco cocktail and bathing yourself in Pǔdōng's neon glow.

3 Aurora Museum (p148) Getting a culture hit admiring ancient jade and porcelain treasures.

4 Riverside Promenade (p149) Taking a stroll and aiming your camera westwards as the sun sets over Pǔxī.

5 Shànghǎi History Museum (p148) Leafing through the colourful pages of the city's history.

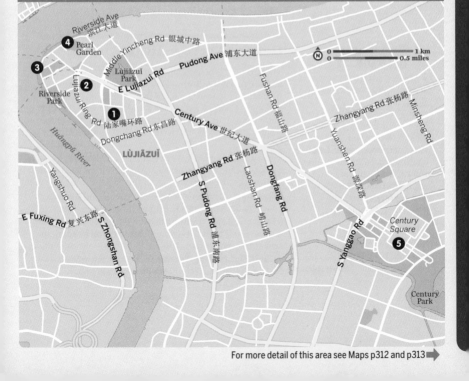

For more detail of this area see Maps p312 and p313 ➡

Lonely Planet's Top Tip

The best time to see Lùjiāzuǐ's modern architecture is during late afternoon or at twilight/early evening, especially during summer (the wide Pǔdōng roads make the sun merciless). Sky-high views from observation decks, bars and restaurants allow you to contrast day, dusk and evening views. Walk around the elevated walkway by the Oriental Pearl TV Tower for show-stopping evening visuals.

Best Places to Eat

→ Sichuan Folk (p150)
→ Yi Cafe (p154)
→ Yang's Fry Dumplings (p150)
→ Grand Cafe (p154)

For reviews, see p150 →

Best Places to Drink

→ Cloud 9 (p155)
→ Flair (p154)
→ 100 Century Avenue (p154)
→ Brew (p155)

For reviews, see p154 →

Best Places to Shop

→ AP Xīnyáng Fashion & Gifts Market (p155)
→ IFC Mall (p155)
→ Superbrand Mall (p155)

For reviews, see p155 →

Explore: Pǔdōng

With its neck-craning tourists, scurrying suits and dazzling evening neonscapes, Pǔdōng is a place name many Westerners know before setting foot in China. More than 1.5 times bigger than urban Shànghǎi, the economic powerhouse of the Pǔdōng New Area (浦东新区; Pǔdōng Xīnqū) swallows up the eastern bank of the Huángpǔ River.

The high-rise area directly across from the Bund is the Lùjiāzuǐ Finance and Trade Zone, where China's largest stock market (the Shànghǎi Stock Exchange) makes or breaks China's nouveau riche. There's no obvious focal point where people congregate, although a swirlpool of sightseers rotates around the elevated walkway by the Oriental Pearl TV Tower.

Opened in mid-2016, the Shànghǎi Disney Resort in Pǔdōng is already sucking in legions of thrill-seeking tots and young-at-heart.

Local Life

→**Shop** Flee the slick malls and make a beeline to the AP Xīnyáng Fashion & Gifts Market (p155) to haggle among local shoppers.

→**Take a ferry** Hop aboard the ferry across the Huángpǔ River with a scrum of Shànghǎi workers (and take your bike with you).

Getting There & Away

→**Metro** Line 2 powers through Lùjiāzuǐ, Century Ave and the Science & Technology Museum. Line 9 cuts through the southern part of the French Concession and on to Century Ave. Lines 4 and 6 also slice through Pǔdōng, all four lines converging at Century Ave. Other connections include metro lines 7, 8, 11 and the Maglev train.

→**Ferry** Runs regularly between Pǔxī and Pǔdōng for the six-minute trip across the river (¥2). It's a 10-minute walk to the Jīnmào Tower from the dock.

→**Bus** Both City Sightseeing Buses (p261) and Big Bus Tours (p261) have lines to Lùjiāzuǐ from Pǔxī.

→**Taxi** A taxi ride from the Bund will cost you around ¥30, as you'll have to pay the ¥15 tunnel toll heading eastwards.

→**Bund Sightseeing Tunnel** Travel underneath the Huángpǔ River in a tunnel dedicated to kitsch.

TOP SIGHT
SHÀNGHĂI WORLD FINANCIAL CENTER

Although trumped by the adjacent Shànghăi Tower as the city's most stratospheric building, the awe-inspiring 492m-high Shànghăi World Financial Center is an astonishing sight, even more so come nightfall when its 'bottle opener' top dances with lights.

There are three **observation decks** – on levels 94, 97 and 100 – each with head-spinningly altitude-adjusted ticket prices and wow-factor elevators thrown in. The top two (located at the bottom and top of the trapezoid) are known as Sky Walks. It's debatable whether the top Sky Walk (474m) is the best spot for Shang-high views, though. The hexagonal space is bright and futuristic, and some of the floor is transparent glass, but the lack of a 360-degree sweep – windows only face west or east – detracts somewhat. But you do get to look down on the top of the Jīnmào Tower, which might be worth the ticket price alone.

Access to the observation deck is on the west side of the building off Dongtai Rd; access to the Park Hyatt is on the south side of the building.

DON'T MISS

➡ Observation decks
➡ 100 Century Avenue

PRACTICALITIES

➡ 上海环球金融中心, Shànghăi Huánqiú Jīnróng Zhōngxīn
➡ Map p312, C3
➡ ☏ 021 5878 0101
➡ www.swfc-observatory.com
➡ 100 Century Ave; 世纪大道100号
➡ observation decks 94th fl adult/child ¥120/60, 94th, 97th & 100th fl ¥180/90
➡ ⏰8am-11pm, last entry 10.30pm
➡ Ⓜ Lujiazui

DIBROVA/SHUTTERSTOCK ©

ORIENTAL PEARL TV TOWER

This 468m-tall poured-concrete tripod tower is the most iconic contemporary building in the city, and its image is flashed around town on everything from postcards to T-shirts. Love it or hate it, the Deng Xiaoping–era design is inadvertently retro; a certain mix of sci-fi meets Soviet brutalist architecture.

To start your tour, take the lift to the 263m-high **Sightseeing Floor** for 360-degree views across to the Bund and its rising sprawl of heritage buildings. The highlight is the **Transparent Observatory** (259m), where you can peer way down through the glass-bottomed walkway (for acrophobes, you can opt out and walk on the inner ring of wooden floor). Don't miss the excellent Shànghǎi History Museum (p148) in the basement with its life-size models and realistic waxworks.

Other features of the tower include a **revolving restaurant** at 267m high (it takes two hours to complete one full 'orbit'), a **Space Capsule Sightseeing floor**, a 5D cinema and an indoor roller coaster to boot – all of which can be skipped, though good options if you have kids in tow.

DON'T MISS

➜ Transparent observatory
➜ Shanghai History Museum
➜ Boat tours on the Huángpǔ River from the Pearl Dock, next to the tower.

PRACTICALITIES

➜ 东方明珠广播电视塔, Dōngfāng Míngzhū Guǎngbō Diànshì Tǎ
➜ Map p312, B2
➜ ☏021 5879 1888
➜ 1 Century Ave; 世纪大道1号
➜ ¥160-220
➜ ⊙8am-10pm, revolving restaurant 11am-2pm & 5-9pm
➜ Ⓜ Lujiazui

TOP SIGHT
SHÀNGHĂI DISNEYLAND

After a decade of planning and diplomatic wrangling, the Magic Kingdom finally arrived in the Middle Kingdom in 2016, offering up a spectacular serving of Disney seasoned with a dash of Chinese culture. 'Main Street USA' has become the locally inspired yet rather sterile 'Gardens of the Imagination', and you can gnaw the ears off a steamed Micky Mouse pork bun at snack vendors throughout the park.

Much has been said about the queues; if you're serious about packing in all the big rides in a day, aim to arrive at least 30 minutes before the park opens, and play a tactical Fast Pass game (the longest lines are at Roaring Rapids, Soaring Over the Horizon and TRON). Alternatively, for groups of up to six, a cool ¥12,500 gets you a 'Premier Tour' with fast access to all the rides.

With younger kids you can take things at a more leisurely pace, and there are plenty of roving musical performances, costumed characters to meet and the excellent **parade** (3.30pm) and **fireworks display** (8.30pm), which don't require any waiting. The shows, too, are considerably easier to get into, particularly *Tarzan: Call of the Jungle*, a top-notch acrobatic performance in a blissfully air-conditioned arena.

DON'T MISS

➡ Mickey's Storybook Express
➡ Pirates of the Caribbean: Battle for the Sunken Treasure
➡ TRON Lightcycle Power Run
➡ 'Ignite the Dream' fireworks display
➡ *Tarzan: Call of the Jungle*

PRACTICALITIES

➡ 上海迪士尼乐园, Shànghǎi Díshìní Lèyuán
➡ ☏021 3158 0000
➡ www.shanghai disneyresort.com
➡ Shànghǎi Disney Resort, Pǔdōng
➡ adult/child 1.0-1.4m/ senior ¥499/375/375
➡ ⊙9am-9pm
➡ MDisney Resort

⊙ SIGHTS

**SHÀNGHĂI WORLD
FINANCIAL CENTER**   NOTABLE BUILDING
See p145.

**ORIENTAL PEARL
TV TOWER**   NOTABLE BUILDING
See p146.

**SHÀNGHĂI
DISNEYLAND**   AMUSEMENT PARK
See p147.

SHÀNGHĂI TOWER   NOTABLE BUILDING
Map p312 (上海中心大厦, Shànghăi Zhōngxīn Dàshà; www.shanghaitower.com.cn; cnr Middle Yincheng & Huayuanshiqiao Rds; ¥160; ⊙9am-9pm; MLujiazui) China's tallest building dramatically twists skywards from its footing in Lùjiāzuǐ. The 121-storey 632m-tall Gensler-designed Shànghăi Tower topped out in August 2013 and opened in mid-2016. The spiral-shaped tower houses office space, entertainment venues, shops, a conference centre, a luxury hotel and 'sky lobbies'. The gently corkscrewing form – its nine interior cylindrical units wrapped in two glass skins – is the world's second-tallest building at the time of writing. The observation deck on the 118th floor is the world's highest.

The twist is introduced by the outer skin of glass which swivels though 120 degrees as it rises, while atrium 'sky gardens' in the vertical spaces sandwiched between the two layers of glass open up a large volume of the tower to public use. The tower is sustainably designed: as well as providing insulation, the huge area of glass will vastly reduce electrical consumption through the use of sunlight. The tower's shape furthermore reduces wind loads by 24%, which generated a saving of US$58m in construction costs. Before the tower even went up, engineers were faced with building the 61,000m^3 concrete mat that would support its colossal mass in the boggy land of Pŭdōng.

Uppermost floors of the tower are reserved for that obligatory Shànghăi attraction – the world's highest skydeck above ground level – with passengers ferried skywards in the world's fastest lifts (64km/h), designed by Mitsubishi (and the world's tallest single-lift elevator). Visitors can gaze down on the both the Jīnmào Tower (p148) and Shànghăi World Financial Center (p145) below. A six-level luxury retail podium fills the base of the tower.

**SHÀNGHĂI HISTORY
MUSEUM**   MUSEUM
Map p312 (上海城市历史发展陈列馆, Shànghăi Chéngshì Lìshǐ Fāzhǎn Chénlièguǎn; ☑021 5879 8888; 1 Century Ave; 世纪大道1号, Oriental Pearl TV Tower basement; ¥35, English audio tour ¥30; ⊙8am-9.30pm; MLujiazui) The entire family will enjoy this informative museum with a fun presentation on old Shànghăi. Learn how the city prospered on the back of the cotton trade and junk transportation, when it was known as 'Little Sūzhōu'. Life-sized models of traditional shops are staffed by realistic waxworks, amid a wealth of historical detail, including a boundary stone from the International Settlement and one of the bronze lions that originally guarded the entrance to the HSBC bank on the Bund.

Some exhibits are hands-on or accompanied by creative video presentations. The city's transport history gets a look-in; you can size up an antique bus, an old wheelbarrow taxi and an ornate sedan chair.

AURORA MUSEUM   MUSEUM
Map p312 (震旦博物馆, Zhèn Dàn Bówùguǎn; ☑021 5840 8899; www.auroramuseum.cn; Aurora Building, 99 Fucheng Rd; 富城路99号震旦大厦; ¥60; ⊙10am-5pm Tue-Sun, to 9pm Fri, last entry 1hr before closing; MLujiazui) Designed by renowned Japanese architect, Andō Tadao, the Aurora Museum is set over six floors of the Aurora building and houses a stunning collection of Chinese treasures. Artefacts and antiquities on display include pottery from the Han dynasty; jade dating back from the Neolithic to the Qing dynasty; blue-and-white porcelain spanning the Yuan, Ming and Qing dynasties; as well as Buddhist sculptures from the Gandharan and Northern Wei period. Don't miss the jade burial suit of 2903 tiles sewn with gold wire.

JĪNMÀO TOWER   NOTABLE BUILDING
Map p312 (金茂大厦, Jīnmào Dàshà; ☑021 5047 5101; 88 Century Ave; 世纪大道88号; adult/student/child ¥120/90/60; ⊙8.30am-10pm; MLujiazui) Resembling an art deco take on a pagoda, this crystalline edifice is a beauty. It's essentially an office block with the high-altitude Grand Hyatt (p213) renting space from the 53rd to 87th floors. You can zip up in the elevators to the 88th-floor **observation deck**, accessed from the separate podium building to the side of the main tower (aim for clear days at dusk for both day and night views).

Alternatively, sample the same view through the carbonated fizz of a gin and tonic at Cloud 9 (p155) on the 87th floor of the Grand Hyatt (accessed on the south side of the building), and photograph the hotel's astonishing barrel-vaulted atrium.

M21: 21ST CENTURY MINSHENG ART MUSEUM
MUSEUM

(上海二十一世纪民生美术馆, Shànghǎi Èrshíyī Shìjì Mínshēng Měishù Guǎn; ☑021 6105 2121; www.21msms.com; 1929 Shibo Ave; 世博大道1929号; ◯10am-6pm Tue-Sun; Ⓜ China Art Museum) ䷀ Opened in 2014, this contemporary art museum is a sister gallery to the Minsheng Art Museum (p174) in Red Town. It occupies the former French Pavilion in the World Expo site and hosts exhibitions from China and overseas.

CHINA ART MUSEUM
MUSEUM

(中华艺术宫, Zhōnghuá Yìshùgōng; 205 Shangnan Rd; 上南路205号; ◯10am-6pm Tue-Sun, last entry 5pm; Ⓜ China Art Museum) ䷀ Set on the former site of the World Expo China Pavilion, this 160,000-sq-metre five-floor modern-art museum hosts some excellent international exhibitions and the inverted red pyramid building is a modern icon of Shànghǎi. On the downside, the permanent Chinese art collection is prosaic with lots of propaganda, and there's a lack of information, while the confusing layout will have you ripping your hair out trying to find a logical route. Any captions that do exist are clumsily translated.

If you need a snack or drink stop, there is a Jamaica Blue cafe and a Starbucks onsite. Otherwise, across the road is the River Mall, though, aside from Sichuan Folk (p150), the choice there is pretty limited.

HIMALAYAS MUSEUM
MUSEUM

Map p313 (喜玛拉雅美术馆, Xǐmǎlāyǎ Měishùguǎn; www.himalayasart.cn; Himalayas Center, 1188 Fangdian Rd; 喜玛拉雅中心芳甸路1188弄1号; free-40¥; ◯10am-6pm Tue-Sun; Ⓜ Huamu Rd) In the eye-catching Himalayas Center (attached to the Jumeirah Himalayas Hotel) and formerly the Zendai Museum of Art, this art gallery has become a fixture on the Pǔdōng art scene, with an emphasis on contemporary exhibitions in a modern art space.

SHÀNGHǍI OCEAN AQUARIUM
AQUARIUM

Map p312 (上海海洋水族馆; Shànghǎi Hǎiyáng Shuǐzúguǎn; ☑021 5877 9988; www.sh-aquarium.com; 1388 Lujiazui Ring Rd; 陆家嘴环路1388号; adult/child ¥160/110; ◯9am-6pm, last tickets 5.30pm; ⓦ; Ⓜ Lujiazui) Education meets entertainment in this slick and intelligently

PǓDŌNG TO PǓXĪ FERRY

To get to the **Cool Docks** in the South Bund area from Pǔdōng, consider taking the ferry (东复线; ¥2, every 10 to 20 minutes from 5am to 11pm) from the Dongchang Rd dock to the Fuxing Rd dock. For the Old Town and the Bund, hop on the ferry (东金线; ¥2, every 15 minutes from 7am to 10pm) to the Jinling Rd dock.

designed aquarium that children will love. Join them on a tour through the aquatic environments from the Yangzi River to Australia and South America, from the frigid ecosystems of the Antarctic to the flourishing marine life of coral reefs. The 155m-long underwater clear viewing tunnel has gobsmacking views. Feeding times for spotted seals, penguins and sharks are between 9.45am and 11.10am and 2.15pm and 3.40pm.

RIVERSIDE PROMENADE
WATERFRONT

Map p312 (滨江大道, Bīnjiāng Dàdào; Ⓜ Lujiazui) Hands down the best stroll in Pǔdōng. The sections of promenade alongside Riverside Ave on the eastern bank of the Huángpǔ River offer splendid views to the Bund across the way. Choicely positioned cafes look out over the water.

MERCEDES-BENZ ARENA
ARENA

(梅赛德斯奔驰文化中心, Méisàidésī Bēnchí Wénhuà Zhōngxīn; ☑hotline 400 181 6688; www.mercedes-benzarena.com; 1200 Shibo Ave; 世博大道1200号; Ⓜ China Art Museum) The galactically-styled UFO structure of the Mercedes-Benz Arena at the former World Expo site is a truly impressive building. It hosts big-name international bands and events, there's an ice-skating rink, a cinema and views over the area from the 6th floor Sky View deck.

SHÀNGHǍI SCIENCE & TECHNOLOGY MUSEUM
MUSEUM

Map p313 (上海科技馆, Shànghǎi Kējìguǎn; ☑021 6862 2000; www.sstm.org.cn; 2000 Century Ave; 世纪大道2000号; adult/student/child under 1.3m or 6yrs ¥60/45/free; ◯9am-5.15pm Tue-Sun, last tickets 4.30pm; Ⓜ Science & Technology Museum) You need to do a huge amount of walking to get around this seriously spaced-out museum and some of it is pretty dated, but there are some fascinating exhibits. Kids will love the Robot World section with everything from relentless Rubik's-cube-solving robots to mechanical archers. There's even the chance to take penalty kicks against a computerised goal-keeper.

Four theatres (two IMAX, one 4D and one outer space) show themed films throughout the day (tickets ¥20 to ¥40; 15 to 40 minutes). When you need a break, there's a decent food court for lunch.

CENTURY PARK   PARK

Map p313 (世纪公园, Shìjì Gōngyuán; 1001 Jinxiu Rd; 锦绣路1001号; ¥10; ⏰7am-6pm; Ⓜ Century Park) This modern park at the eastern end of Century Ave is strong on hard edges and synthetic lines, but has an attractive central lake (with boat hire). Children will enjoy themselves, and the spacious paved area between the Science & Technology Museum and the park is great for flying kites (for sale from hawkers) and rollerblading.

 # EATING

Most dining in Pǔdōng is about feasting on priceless views through floor-to-ceiling windows in five-star hotel restaurants. The gargantuan Superbrand Mall in Lùjiāzuǐ has restaurants spread out across 10 floors, and there are several options in the high-end IFC Mall. For hole-in-the-wall dining, try roads such as the eastern end of Dongchang Rd (off South Pudong Rd), where budget *dōngběi* (northeastern) and Xīnjiāng eateries are concentrated.

YANG'S FRY DUMPLINGS   DUMPLING $

Map p312 (小杨生煎馆, Xiǎoyáng Shēngjiān Guǎn; 1406 Lujiazui Ring Rd; 陆家嘴环路1406号; 4 dumplings ¥8; ⏰8am-9pm; Ⓜ Lujiazui) A short walk from the Oriental Pearl TV Tower brings you to a string of restaurants, including the city's best sesame-seed-and-scallion-coated fried dumplings (生煎; *shēngjiān*). It's often hard to get a table but do as the locals do and get a takeaway for snacking on the move around Lujiazui.

SPROUTWORKS   HEALTH FOOD $

Map p312 (豆苗工坊, Dòumiáo Gōngfáng; www.sproutworks.com.cn; B2-06-07, Superbrand Mall, 168 West Lujiazui Rd; 陆家嘴西路168号正大广场B2楼; mains from ¥38, lunch sets from ¥50; ⏰10am-10pm; Ⓜ Lujiazui) For a healthy re-charge, Sproutworks offers a natural and earthy focus on fresh, wholesome food,

in a clean-cut (but rather square) set-ting. Cleanse your insides with delicious smoothies; load up with brown rice, tasty soups and crisp panini sandwiches; try freshly tossed salads, fresh juices, home-made desserts and lunch sets. Most dishes are pre-prepared so are ready to go.

FOOD OPERA   ASIAN $

Map p312 (食代馆, Shídàiguǎn; B2, Superbrand Mall, 168 West Lujiazui Rd; 陆家嘴西路168号B2楼; dishes from ¥15; ⏰10am-10pm; Ⓜ Lujiazui) Grab a card from the booth (¥10 deposit), load up with credits and then spend, spend, spend on a whole host of open kitchens in this hopping food court. There's Korean, teppanyaki, Japanese noodles, pasta and much more. The spicy *shoyu ramen* at **Ramen Play** is a good place to start. Just point at what you want and hand over your card.

SOUTH BEAUTY   SICHUANESE, CANTONESE $

Map p312 (俏江南, Qiào Jiāngnán; ☎021 5047 1917; 10th fl, Superbrand Mall, 168 West Lujiazui Rd; 陆家嘴西路168号正大广场10楼; dishes from ¥20; ⏰11am-10pm; Ⓜ Lujiazui) On the 10th floor of the Superbrand Mall, this branch of South Beauty is a little scuffed around the edges these days but it still cooks up clas-sic dishes from fiery Chóngqìng, Chéngdū and the south. The scorching boiled beef with hot pepper in chilli oil opens the sweat pores, while the piquant *mápō dòufu* (mapo tofu) arrives in a scarlet oily sauce.

Alternatively, if you don't like it hot, go for the delicious pan-fried scallion buns. You'll need to reserve for the coveted Bund-facing window seats on the terrace.

BAKER & SPICE   CAFE $

Map p312 (IFC Mall, 8 Century Ave; 世纪大道8号; sandwiches & salads from ¥50; ⏰10am-10pm; Ⓜ Lujiazui) Small branch in the IFC Mall (p155) with baked pastries, bagels, salad bowls and weekend brunch.

★ SICHUAN FOLK   SICHUAN $$

(☎021 3111 8055; Rm 110, 1368 Shibo Ave; 世博大道1368号110室; mains from ¥22; ⏰11am-2pm & 5-9pm; Ⓜ China Art Museum) Formerly known as Bāguó Bùyī, Sichuan Folk is pretty much the most authentic Sìchuān food in town, cooked up by the diligent chefs at this famous restaurant at the World Expo site, originally founded in Chéngdū. With no concessions to the dainty Shànghǎi palate, prepare for a spicy firecracker of a meal. It's located in a complex opposite the Mercedes-Benz Arena.

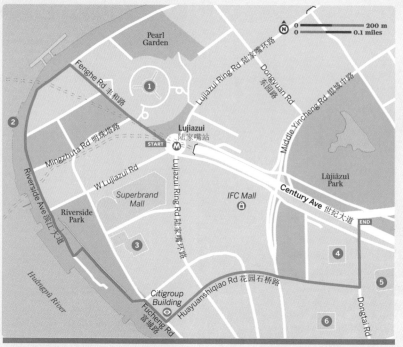

Neighbourhood Walk
Pŭdōng

START LUJIAZUI METRO STATION
END SHÀNGHǍI WORLD FINANCIAL
CENTER
LENGTH 3.5KM; TWO HOURS

Looming above you like a sci-fi control tower, a short walk from the Lujiazui metro station, is the ❶ **Oriental Pearl TV Tower** (p146), one of Lùjiāzuǐ's most opinion-dividing edifices. Make sure you take a walk around the circular overhead walkway above the main intersection south of the tower, especially at night. Inside the tower, the absorbing Shànghǎi History Museum on the basement level is worth exploration.

Walk up Fenghe Rd and turn left onto Riverside Ave to reach a section of the ❷ **Riverside Promenade** (p149) for glorious images of the Bund across the water.

Follow a further stretch of the Riverside Promenade before cutting through River-

side Park and exiting onto Fucheng Rd by the Citigroup Building. Note the dramatic V-form of Tower Two of the ❸ **Pudong Shangri-La hotel** (p213).

Immediately after the Citigroup Building, turn onto Huayuanshiqiao Rd to walk past the twin towers of the International Financial Centre (IFC) on your left; you will see the vast Shànghǎi Tower on your right before reaching the elegant ❹ **Jīnmào Tower** (p148). You're spoiled for high-altitude views all about – you can rocket to the 88th-floor observation deck of the Jīnmào; cross the street to the decks in the ❺ **Shànghǎi World Financial Center** (p145), or top them all with views from the pinnacle of the awesome ❻ **Shànghǎi Tower** (p148). Alternatively, select a bar or restaurant in either tower, but have a table booked for sunset visits. To return to metro line 2, the Lujiazui metro stop is a short walk west along Century Ave.

VINCENT ST. THOMAS/SHUTTERSTOCK ©

1. Jīnmào Tower (p148)
Resembling an art deco take on a pagoda, the tower's crystalline edifice towers over Pǔdōng.

2. Oriental Pearl TV Tower (p146)
The Deng Xiaoping–era design is inadvertently retro, a specific mix of sci-fi meets Soviet brutalist architecture.

3. IFC Mall (p155)
The glamorous mall is home to a coterie of top-name brands, including Armani, Miu Miu and Vuitton.

ZHAO JIAN KANG/SHUTTERSTOCK ©

LEI GARDEN — CANTONESE $$

Map p312 (利苑, Lì Yuàn; ☑021 5106 1688; 3rd fl, 8 Century Ave; 世纪大道8号3楼; dishes from ¥48; ⏱11.30am-3pm & 5.30-9.30pm; Ⓜ Lujiazui) On the 3rd floor of the IFC Mall, Lei Garden is a classy affair serving good-quality Cantonese; perfect for a lunch break during a shopping spree. Be sure to reserve ahead.

PATIO LOUNGE — LOUNGE $$

Map p312 (http://shanghai.grand.hyatt.com; Grand Hyatt, Jīnmào Tower, 88 Century Ave; 世纪大道88号君悦大酒店; afternoon tea for 4 ¥368; ⏱11.30am-11pm Sun-Thu, to midnight Fri & Sat; Ⓜ Lujiazui) Have a drink or indulge in afternoon tea with the spectacular 33-floor atrium of the Grand Hyatt towering above you in the Jīnmào Tower.

★ GRAND CAFÉ — BISTRO $$$

Map p312 (☑021 5047 8838; http://shanghai. grand.hyatt.com; Grand Hyatt, Jīnmào Tower, 88 Century Ave; 世纪大道88号君悦大酒店; buffet lunch/dinner from ¥288/388; ⏱ buffet lunch 11.30am-2.30pm, á la carte 24hr; Ⓜ Lujiazui) On the 54th floor of Jīnmào Tower (in the Grand Hyatt lobby), the Grand Café offers stunning panoramas through its glass walls and an excellent-value lunch buffet; pile your plate with endless crab legs, Peking duck, fresh prawns, mini burgers, dumplings, made-to-order noodles: you name it. Finish it off with gelato, delectable cakes, fruit and French cheeses. Book well in advance for a window table. Service charge 10%.

★ YI CAFE — CAFE $$$

Map p312 (怡咖啡, Yí Kāfēi; ☑021 6882 8888; www.shangri-la.com; 2nd fl, Pudong Shangri-La, 33 Fucheng Rd; 富城路33号2楼; buffet meals from ¥358; ⏱ breakfast 6-10.30am, lunch 11.30am-2.30pm, dinner 5.30-10pm; 🅰; Ⓜ Lujiazui) If you're squabbling over what to eat for lunch, brunch or dinner, settle your differences at smart-casual Yi Cafe. With 12 open kitchens and a walk-through layout, it's a veritable Asian–Southeast Asian–international food fest with endless menus. Be sure to cultivate a real hunger before you stop by. The buffet breakfasts easily match Pŭdōng's sightseeing calorific demands.

ON 56 — INTERNATIONAL $$$

Map p312 (意庐, Yìlú; ☑21 5047 8838; http:// shanghai.grand.hyatt.com; 54th-56th fl, Grand Hyatt, Jīnmào Tower, 88 Century Ave; 世纪大道 88号君悦大酒店; meals from ¥200; ⏱11.30am-2.30pm & 5.30-10.30pm; 🅰; Ⓜ Lujiazui) All the restaurants in this swish selection come with breathtaking views into the Shànghǎi

void from the Grand Hyatt. **Cucina** serves delectable Italian dishes from Campania, with breads and pizzas fresh from the oven; **Grill** does imported meats and seafood; **Kobachi** features excellent sushi, sashimi and yakitori. Sunday brunch is ¥588 per person and includes free-flowing Mumm Champagne (11.30am to 3pm).

Sit in any restaurant of your choosing and order food from another. After dinner, retire to the Patio Lounge.

KITCHEN SALVATORE CUOMO — ITALIAN $$$

Map p312 (☑021 5054 1265; Riverside Ave, 2967 West Lujiazui Rd, near Fenghe Rd; 陆家嘴西路 2967号滨江大道近丰和路; pizza from ¥138; ⏱11.30am-2.30pm & 6-10pm; 🅰; Ⓜ Lujiazui) The hefty price of the wood-fired pizzas will have your eyes as big as the margaritas at this smart riverside restaurant, and the views of fairy-light-festooned boats gliding up and down the night-time Huángpǔ River could keep them that way. The pizzas are sublime, however, and alfresco tables out the front beckon for long summer evenings, with the Oriental Pearl TV Tower rocketing overhead.

🍷 DRINKING & NIGHTLIFE

★ FLAIR — BAR

Map p312 (58th fl, Ritz-Carlton Shanghai Pudong, 8 Century Ave; 世纪大道8号58楼; cocktails from ¥95; ⏱5.30pm-late; 🅰; Ⓜ Lujiazui) Wow your date with Shànghǎi's most intoxicating nocturnal visuals from the outdoor terrace on the 58th floor of the Ritz-Carlton, where Flair nudges you that bit closer to the baubles of the Oriental Pearl TV Tower. If it's raining, you'll end up inside, but that's OK as the chilled-out interior, designed by the firm Super Potato, is very cool. Book well in advance for the terrace.

100 CENTURY AVENUE — BAR

Map p312 (世纪大道100号, Shìjì Dàdào Yībǎi Hào; ☑021 3855 1428; http://shanghai.park.hyatt.com; 91st fl, Park Hyatt, Shànghǎi World Financial Center, 100 Century Ave; 世纪大道100号柏悦酒店91-92 楼; cocktails from ¥95; ⏱ bars 6pm-1am Mon-Thu, to 2am Fri & Sat; 🅰; Ⓜ Lujiazui)) Featuring some of the highest bars in the world, 100 Century Avenue is pretty impressive inside, but the restaurant on the 91st floor has the best views, as you can get up close to the windows. Access is through the lobby of the Park Hyatt, on the south side of the building.

CLOUD 9
BAR

Map p312 (九重天酒廊, Jiǔchóngtiān Jiǔláng; ☎021 5047 8838; http://shanghai.grand.hyatt. com; 87th fl, Jīnmào Tower, 88 Century Ave; 世纪大道88号金茂大厦87楼; ◷5pm-1am Mon-Fri, 2pm-2am Sat & Sun; Ⓜ Lujiazui) Order an espresso martini and watch day fade to night from the 87th floor of the Jīnmào Tower. Access to Cloud 9 is through the lobby of the Grand Hyatt and there is a cover charge of ¥150, redeemable against your bill.

BREW
BAR

Map p313 (酿, Niàng; ☎021 6169 8886; Kerry Hotel, 1388 Huamu Rd; 上海浦东嘉里大酒店花木路1388号; beer half-pint/pint ¥52/70; ◷11am-2am; 🖭; Ⓜ Huamu Rd) Ale connoisseurs can earmark this nifty microbrewery bar in the Kerry Hotel, where resident brew-master Leon Mickelson dispenses six on-tap handmade beers (Skinny Green, pils, White Ant, Indian pale ale, Dugite vanilla stout, Mash) and a cider (Razorback). There's a huge range of other bottled beers. The bar is sleek and cool without being impersonal and the terrace has park views. Target happy hour: buy one and get one free from 3pm to 8pm).

☆ ENTERTAINMENT

ORIENTAL ART CENTER
CLASSICAL MUSIC

Map p313 (上海东方艺术中心, Shànghǎi Dōngfāng Yìshù Zhōngxīn; ☎021 6854 1234; www. shoac.com.cn; 425 Dingxiang Rd; 浦东丁香路425号; Ⓜ Science & Technology Museum) Home of the Shànghǎi Symphony Orchestra, the Oriental Art Center was designed to resemble five petals of a butterfly orchid. Three main halls host classical, jazz, dance and Chinese and Western opera performances. Saturday brunch concerts (10am, held on the first and third Saturday of the month) cost from ¥30 to ¥80. Free tours of the centre are conducted on the first Saturday of the month (from 1.30pm to 4.30pm).

DÀGUĀN THEATER
THEATRE

Map p313 (大观舞台, Dàguān Wǔtái; www .daguantheatre.cn; Himalayas Center, 1188 Fangdian Rd; 喜玛拉雅中心芳甸路1188弄1号; ◷box office 10am-10pm; Ⓜ Huamu Rd) This state-of-the-art 1100-seat theatre in the impressive Himalayas Center, attached to the Jumeirah Himalayas Hotel, stages Chinese opera, other traditional performance arts and Western theatre. The theatre has retractable seating, and also hosts films from the Shanghai International Film Festival.

🛍 SHOPPING

IFC MALL
MALL

Map p312 (上海IFC商场, Shànghǎi IFC Shāngchǎng; www.shanghaiifcmall.com.cn; 8 Century Ave; 世纪大道8号; ◷10am-10pm; Ⓜ Lujiazui) This incredibly glam and glitzy six-storey mall beneath the twin towers of the Shànghǎi International Finance Center hosts a swish coterie of top-name brands (Armani, Prada, Miu Miu, Vuitton) and a host of great dining options including Lei Garden, and branches of Baker & Spice, Simply Thai and Haiku by Hatsune.

SUPERBRAND MALL
MALL

Map p312 (正大广场, Zhèngdà Guǎngchǎng; 168 West Lujiazui Rd; 陆家嘴西路168号; ◷10am-10pm; Ⓜ Lujiazui) Always busy, this gargantuan shopping mall is ultrahandy for its dining options, its supermarket in the basement, a kids' arcade on the 6th floor and a cinema on the 8th floor.

AP XĪNYÁNG FASHION & GIFTS MARKET
GIFTS & SOUVENIRS

Map p313 (亚太新阳服饰礼品市场, Yàtài Xīnyáng Fúshì Lǐpǐn Shìchǎng; ◷10am-8pm; Ⓜ Science & Technology Museum) This mammoth underground market is Shànghǎi's largest collection of shopping stalls. There's tons of merchandise and fakes, from suits to moccasins, glinting copy watches, Darth Vader toys, jackets, Lionel Messi football strips, T-shirts, Indian saris, Angry Birds bags, Bob Marley Bermuda shorts, Great Wall snow globes: everything under the sun.

It includes a branch of the **Shíliùpù Fabric Marke**t and a separate market devoted to pearls, the **Yada Pearl Market** (Yàdà Zhēnzhū Shìchǎng). Shop vendors are highly persistent, sending out scouts to wait at metro exit turnstiles to ensnare shoppers. Haggling is the common language – accompanied by huffing and puffing – so start with a very low offer and take it from there.

🏃 SPORTS & ACTIVITIES

HUÁNGPǓ RIVER CRUISE (PǓDŌNG)
BOATING

Map p312 (黄浦江游览船, Huángpǔjiāng Yóulǎnchuán; Pearl Dock; 明珠码头; per person ¥100; ◷9am-10pm; Ⓜ Lujiazui) Forty-minute cruises departing hourly in Pǔdōng. You can buy tickets at the tourist information office (p270).

Hóngkǒu & North Shànghǎi

Neighbourhood Top Five

❶ Ohel Moishe Synagogue (p159) Getting a history lesson on Jewish Shànghǎi.

❷ Architecture (p162) Taking a self-guided tour of Hóngkǒu's concession-period and art deco build

ings, such as the Broadway Mansions.

❸ 1933 (p162) Getting lost along the labyrinth of concrete walkways.

❹ Duolun Rd (p158) Wandering past historic architecture and curio shops.

❺ Vue (p162) Raising a glass to the Bund and the Pǔdōng skyline at this bar with a view.

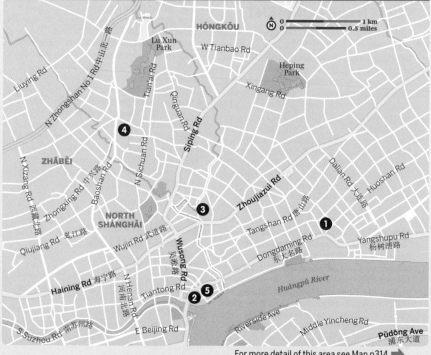

For more detail of this area see Map p314 ➡

Explore: Hóngkǒu & North Shànghǎi

Hóngkǒu and North Shànghǎi (虹口区、北上海) may not have the lion's share of sights in town, but prize chunks of heritage architecture rise up from the swirl of street life and an authentic grittiness survives.

The up-and-coming North Bund area beyond Sūzhōu Creek is worth exploring for its impressive buildings, including the granddaddy of heritage hotels – the Astor House Hotel – looming art deco blocks and noteworthy concession-era classics. The American Settlement was originally here, merging with the British Settlement in 1863 to form the prosperous International Settlement. To the west, Zhábĕi became infamous for its sweatshops and factories and was later flattened by the Japanese in 1932.

A rich vein of Jewish heritage survives towards Yángpǔ in the east, dating from the days when Hóngkǒu was home to thousands of Jewish refugees, mostly from Germany, who transformed 'Little Tokyo' (where 30,000 Japanese lived) into 'Little Vienna'. The Ohel Moishe Synagogue stands as a testament to this era. Wander round this neighbourhood and you'll also find examples of Shànghǎi's trademark terrace-style *shíkùmén* (stone-gate house) architecture, *lòngtáng* (alleyway) houses and narrow alleyways in between.

Close to the Bund, Hóngkǒu has some excellently positioned accommodation options, and while notable restaurants may seem thin on the ground, work your shoe leather and you can track down excellent options from across China.

Local Life

➡ **Snacking** Join locals along North Jiangxi Rd for a profusion of local titbits and hunger-busting bites.

➡ **Hóngkǒu backstreets** Wander the lanes around the Ohel Moishe Synagogue (p159) to soak up the local 'Little Vienna' flavour.

➡ **Park life** Catch the locals performing taichi or honing ballroom-dancing spins in Lu Xun Park (p158).

Getting There & Away

➡ **Metro** Line 10 runs north from East Nanjing Rd to Fùdàn University, passing Tiantong Rd, North Sichuan Rd and Hailun Rd stations. Line 3 also runs north, offering access to Duolun Rd and Lu Xun Park. Lines 4 and 8 loop east–west. Main interchange stations are Baoshan Rd (lines 3 and 4), Hailun Rd (lines 4 and 10) and Hongkou Football Stadium (lines 3 and 8).

Lonely Planet's Top Tip

Basing yourself in south Hóngkǒu – at the Astor House Hotel (p213), Chai Living Residences (p213) or the Bulgari, which is set to open in 2017 – allows you to hang your Shànghǎi fedora within easy reach of the Bund across Wàibáidù Bridge (Garden Bridge) and the nearby concession architecture of the North Bund district.

✕ Best Places to Eat

➡ Guǒyúan (p160)

➡ Xīndàlù (p161)

➡ Yang's Fry Dumplings (p161)

➡ Kathleen's Waitan (p161)

For reviews, see p160 ➡

☕ Best Places to Drink

➡ Vue (p162)

➡ Kathleen's Waitan (p161)

For reviews, see p162 ➡

👁 SIGHTS

SKY RING
FERRIS WHEEL

Map p314 (天空指环, Tiānkōng Zhǐhuán; ☑021 3633-8833; www.shjoycity.com; 8F, North Bldg, Shanghai Joy City, 198 Xizang North Rd; 上海大悦城8楼·西藏北路198号; ¥60; ⊙10am-9.30pm; 🚇; Ⓜ Qufu Rd) Sky Wheel's rooftop location in a rapidly developing neighbourhood is perfect for sweeping views contrasting old Shanghai with new. The 12-minute ride above a neighbourhood of historic *lòng* (里弄) houses offers glimpses of the Huangpu River and, at the very top, Shanghai's newest skyscrapers peeking over even newer riverside construction. When the ride is finished, head to the roof for boutique shopping and a closer look at the wheel itself. Book via smartphone to save time (but not money).

GALLERY MAGDA DANYSZ
GALLERY

(www.magda-gallery.com; 188 Linqing Rd; 临青路188号; ⊙11am-6pm Tue-Sun; Ⓜ Ningguo Rd) Well worth a cultural diversion, this bold and vibrant art space for both emerging and established Chinese and international names is twinned with its Paris gallery, bringing an artistic frisson to Yángpǔ district in north Shànghǎi. Exhibitions range through an inspiring and thoughtful spectrum of visual media – check the website for details. Take metro line 12 to Ningguo Rd and then a taxi (¥14).

SHÀNGHǍI POST MUSEUM
MUSEUM

Map p314 (上海邮政博物馆, Shànghǎi Yóuzhèng Bówùguǎn; 395 Tiantong Rd; 天童 路395号; ⊙9am-5pm Wed, Thu, Sat & Sun, last entry 4pm; Ⓜ Tiantong Rd) **FREE** This fascinating museum in the stunning Main Post Office building explores postal history in imperial China, which dates back to the 1st millennium BC. The system used an extensive pony express to relay messages; Marco Polo estimated there were 10,000 postal stations in 13th-century China. Check out the collection of pre- and post-Liberation stamps (1888–1978) in a special climate-controlled room. You can also inspect a historic mail-train carriage and two old post vans, one horse-drawn, plus a recreation of a Qing dynasty mail room.

DUOLUN ROAD CULTURAL STREET
AREA

Map p314 (多伦文化名人街, Duōlún Wénhuà Míngrén Jiē; Ⓜ Dongbaoxing Rd) This pleasantly restored but sleepy street of fine old houses, just off North Sichuan Rd, was once home to several of China's most famous writers (as well as several Kuomintang generals), when the road was known as Doulean Rd. Today it is lined with art-supply stores, curio and Burmese jade shops, galleries, teahouses and cafes. The main appeal of the street is its galleries and antique shops.

Wander down the street to find the 1928 Hóngdé Temple (p160), its grey-brick interior adorned with pictures of the Stations of the Cross and simple wooden pews; upstairs is a lovely hall with a wooden ceiling. The church was built in a Chinese style as the Great Virtue Church.

The League of Left-Wing Writers was established down a side alley on 2 March 1930. Today the building serves as a **political museum** (左联会址, Zuǒlián Huìzhǐ; Map p314; No 2, Lane 201, Duolun Rd; 多伦路201弄2号), worth a look for the architecture alone.

Duolun Rd ends in another Kuomintang residence, the Moorish-looking, private Kong Residence (p160), built in 1924.

If you need a break, try the Old Film Café (p163), next to the 18.2m-high Xīshí Bell Tower (p159) at the bend in the road. There's a statue of Charlie Chaplin outside.

GÒNGQĪNG FOREST PARK
PARK

(共青森林公园, Gòngqīng Sēnlín Gōngyuán; ☑021 6574 0586; www.shgqsl.com; 2000 Jungong Rd; 军工路2000号; adult/child ¥15/7.5; ⊙6am-5pm, to 6pm in summer; 🚇; Ⓜ Nenjiang Rd, Shiguang Rd) This vast expanse of forested parkland on the western shore of the Huángpǔ River is a leafy, wooded and tranquil slice of countryside in Shànghǎi. This is about as wild as you get in Pǔxī, with acres of willows, luohan pines, magnolias, hibiscus and nary a skyscraper in sight. Aim to spend half if not a whole day picnicking and wandering around this huge area.

For kids, there's a roller coaster, rock climbing, horse riding, paintball and other activities. Nenjiang Rd and Shiguang Lu stations near the northern terminus of metro line 8 will get you close to the western edge of the park; a taxi from the metro station will cost around ¥15. Alternatively, take line 8 to Xiangyin Rd metro station and hop aboard bus 102 from exit 2.

LU XUN PARK
PARK

Map p314 (鲁迅公园, Lǔ Xùn Gōngyuán; 146 East Jiangwan Rd; 江湾东路146号; ⊙6am-6pm; Ⓜ Hongkou Football Stadium) Particularly photogenic in spring and summer when the

TOP SIGHT
OHEL MOISHE SYNAGOGUE

The Ohel Moishe Synagogue was built by the Russian Ashkenazi Jewish community in 1927 and lies in the heart of the 1940s Jewish ghetto.

Today it houses the **Shànghǎi Jewish Refugees Museum**, which offers a moving introduction to the lives of the approximately 20,000 Central European refugees who fled to Shànghǎi to escape the Nazis. Slip a pair of shower caps over your shoes to look at the synagogue itself (in the main building). Then head outside to the exhibition halls in the courtyard.

The exhibition is rounded off with a moving quote from the writer, Nobel Laureate and Holocaust survivor Elie Wiesel: 'The past is in the present, but the future is still in our hands'.

There are English-language tours every hour, from 9.30am to 11.30am and 1pm to 4pm.

DON'T MISS...

➡ Synagogue
➡ Guided tour
➡ Courtyard exhibition halls

PRACTICALITIES

➡ 摩西会堂, Móxī Huìtáng
➡ Map p314, G4
➡ ☎021 6512 6669
➡ 62 Changyang Rd; 长阳路62号
➡ ¥50
➡ ⊙9am-5pm, last entry 4.30pm
➡ Ⓜ Tilanqiao

trees are in blossom, Lu Xun Park is one of the city's most pleasant green spaces. Here you'll find elderly Chinese practising tai-chi or ballroom dancing, and even retired opera singers testing out their pipes. It's a big shame about the fenced-in lawn, but the **Plum Garden** is an attractive diversion.

The English Corner on Sunday mornings is one of the largest in all of Shànghǎi and it's a good place to natter to locals in English. You can take boats out onto the small lake. The park used to be called Hóngkǒu Park but was renamed because it holds Lu Xun's Tomb, moved here from the International Cemetery in 1956, on the 20th anniversary of his death.

LU XUN FORMER RESIDENCE   HISTORIC BUILDING

Map p314 (鲁迅故居, Lǔxùn Gùjū; ☎021 5666 2608; No 9, Lane 132, Shanyin Rd; 山阴路132弄9号; adult/child ¥8/4; ⊙9am-4pm; ⓂEast Baoxing Rd) Lu Xun buffs will adore ferreting around this three-floor domicile on lovely Shanyin Rd, where an excellent English-speaking guide can fill you in on all the period bits and bobs, including the author's tea cosy and the clock that stopped at his time of death. Entry is timed every 20 minutes from 9am.

Don't overlook wandering along Shanyin Rd and peeking into its lovely alleyways and traditional *lòngtáng* houses (for example at Nos 41 to 50, Lane 180, Shanyin Rd; 山阴路180弄41-50号). Around the corner at 2050 North Sichuan Rd (四川北路2050号) is the site of the Uchiyama Bookstore, where Lu Xun used to stock up on literature (it's now a branch of the ICBC bank but there is a plaque).

LU XUN MUSEUM   MUSEUM

Map p314 (鲁迅纪念馆, Lǔ Xùn Jìniànguǎn; Lu Xun Park, 2288 North Sichuan Rd; 鲁迅公园内, 四川北路2288号; ⊙9am-4pm; ⓂHongkou Football Stadium) FREE An excellent museum, this modern hall charts the life and creative output of author Lu Xun with photographs, first editions, videos and waxworks. Detailed English captions throughout.

XĪSHÍ BELL TOWER   HISTORIC BUILDING

Map p314 (夕拾钟搂, Xīshí Zhōnglóu; Duolun Rd; 多伦路; ⓂEast Baoxing Rd) This bell tower at the bend of Duolun Rd is a main feature of the street; it's right next to the Old Film Cafe.

LOCAL KNOWLEDGE

HISTORIC HÓNGKǑU

For a mini walking tour of the streets of the Jewish Quarter – aka 'Little Vienna' – surrounding the Ohel Moishe Synagogue, turn right outside the synagogue, then right again past the former Jewish tenements of Zhoushan Rd (formerly Ward Rd), once the commercial heart of the district. At Huoshan Rd (formerly Wayside Rd), head southwest past the art deco facade of the former Broadway Theatre (p160), to the Ocean Hotel. Turn right up Haimen Rd (Muirhead Rd), past Changyang Rd, to what was once a row of Jewish shops and a kosher delicatessen. Until just a couple of years ago, faded painted signs from the 1940s above the shops declared 'Horn's Imbiss Stube' (Horn's Snack Bar) and 'Cafe Atlantic', but the shops were recently demolished.

At the top of the road (the crossing with Kunming Rd), you'll see the largely rebuilt Xiàhǎi Buddhist Monastery (p160). Take a right turn, then another right, down Zhoushan Rd once again to complete the circle back to the synagogue.

Zhoushan Rd is also home to the British-built **Ward Road Jail** (Map p314; Zhoushan Rd; 舟山路; Ⓜ Dalian Rd), once Shànghǎi's biggest. Used by the Japanese during WWII, it's still functioning as a prison (renamed Tilanqiao Prison) and is probably as close as you'll get, or would want to get, to a Chinese detention facility.

If you're interested in learning more about Hóngkǒu's Jewish heritage, contact Dvir Bar-Gal, an Israeli Shànghǎi resident who offers informative English and Hebrew tours (p163) of the area.

FORMER BROADWAY THEATRE
HISTORIC BUILDING

Map p314 (百老汇大戏院, Bǎilǎohuì Dàxìyuàn; 57 Huoshan Rd; 霍山路57号; Ⓜ Tilanqiao) Admire the magnificent art deco former Broadway Theatre building, located in the Jewish Quarter.

EMBANKMENT BUILDING
HISTORIC BUILDING

Map p314 (河滨大厦, Hébīn Dàshà; 400 North Suzhou Rd; 苏州北路400号; Ⓜ Tiantong Road) Designed by architects Palmer & Turner and dating back to 1935, this art deco landmark was first built for the real estate magnate, Sir Victor Sassoon. Though a little rundown and rough around the edges these days, nevertheless it's still an impressive piece of architecture. It's now home to mostly local Shanghainese, but there are a few stylish holiday apartments rented out by Chai Living Residences (p213).

XIÀHǍI BUDDHIST MONASTERY
BUDDHIST TEMPLE

Map p314 (下海庙, Xiàhǎi Miào; Kunming Rd; 昆明路; ¥5; ⏰ 7am-4pm; Ⓜ Dalian Rd) The name of this large Buddhist temple in Hóngkǒu literally means 'Go to Sea Temple'.

HÓNGDÉ TEMPLE
CHURCH

Map p314 (鸿德堂, Hóngdé Táng; 59 Duolun Rd; 多伦路59号; Ⓜ East Baoxing Rd) This 1928 brick temple was built in a Chinese style as the Great Virtue Church; note the Chinese-style bell tower.

KONG RESIDENCE
HISTORIC BUILDING

Map p314 (孔公馆, Kǒng Gōngguǎn; 250 Duolun Rd; 多伦路250号; Ⓜ East Baoxing Rd) The Moorish-looking Kong Residence, built in 1924, is a former Kuomintang (nationalist political party) house on the Duolun Road Cultural Street (p158).

✖ EATING

★ GUŎYÚAN
HUNANESE $

Map p314 (果园; 524 Dongjiangwan Rd; 东江湾路524号; mains from ¥18; ⏰ 11am-2pm & 5-10pm Mon-Fri, 11am-3pm & 5-10pm Sat & Sun; Ⓜ Hongkou Football Stadium) The cool lime-green tablecloths do little to tame the tempestuous flavours of this fantastic Húnán restaurant. The *tiěbǎn dòufu* (铁板豆腐; sizzling tofu platter) here is a magnificent dish, but its fiery flavours are almost eclipsed by the enticing *xiāngwèi qiézibāo* (湘味茄子煲, Húnán aubergine hotpot) and the lovely *zīrán yángròu* (孜然羊肉; lamb with cumin; ¥32).

Otherwise go for the *málà dòufu* (麻辣豆腐, spicy tofu) or the cracking *tiěbǎn niúròu* (铁板牛肉, sizzling beef platter). Unfortunately there is no English menu;

instead you receive a green paper Chinese menu to tick off what you want, so use the suggestions above or point at what others are eating.

YANG'S FRY DUMPLINGS

DUMPLING $

Map p314 (小杨生煎馆, Xiǎoyáng Shēngjiān Guǎn; 388 W Jiangwan Rd, 江湾西路388号; ⏰10am-10pm; Ⓜ️Hongkou Football Stadium) Hoover up Yang's signature, time-honoured and much-applauded fried *shēngjiān* dumplings at this branch in the Cloud Nine shopping mall (level B2). Order per *liǎng* (两; four dumplings; ¥6). If the dining area is full, get yours to go and enjoy them in the nearby Lu Xun park. Never fear, the soupy goodness inside will still famously scald your mouth by the time you walk there.

It's next to the Hongkou Football Stadium metro station.

KATHLEEN'S WAITAN

FUSION $$$

Map p314 (☎021 6660 0989; www.kwaitan. com; 200 Huangpu Rd; 黄浦路200号; mains ¥198-428; ⏰11am-midnight; Ⓜ️Tiantong Rd) After 10 years located at the top of the Shanghai Art Museum, Kathleen's has set up shop on the north Bund in the Sassoon building – a former opium warehouse. While the fusion fare (roasted duck breast, seafood platters, sushi) can fall flat in some dishes and service can be lacking, focus on the knockout Pudong views and cocktails on the terrace and you can't go wrong.

XĪNDÀLÙ

PEKING DUCK $$$

Map p314 (新大陆; ☎021 6393 1234; www.hyatt onthebundsh.com; 1st fl, Hyatt on the Bund, 199 Huangpu Rd; 黄浦路199号外滩茂悦大酒店1楼; roast duck half/whole ¥218/298, dishes from ¥58; ⏰11.30am-2.30pm & 5.30-10pm; Ⓜ️Tiantong Rd) Although definitive *Běijīng kǎoyā* (Peking

SHÀNGHǍI'S JEWS

Shànghǎi has two centuries of strong Jewish connections. Established Middle Eastern Sephardic Jewish families, such as the Hardoons, Ezras, Kadoories and Sassoons, built their fortunes in Shànghǎi (the Sassoons' fortune came largely from opium and the cotton trade), establishing at least seven synagogues and many Jewish hospitals and schools. It was Victor Sassoon who famously remarked: 'There is only one race greater than the Jews and that's the Derby.'

A second group of Jews, this time Ashkenazi, arrived via Siberia, Hā'ěrbīn and Tiānjīn from Russia after anti-Jewish pogroms in 1906. The biggest influx, however, came between 1933 and 1941, when 30,000 mostly Ashkenazi Jews arrived from Europe by boat from Italy or by train via Siberia. Many had been issued with visas to cross China by Ho Fengshan, Chinese consul general in Vienna, who was recently honoured as the 'Chinese Schindler'.

Shànghǎi was one of the few safe havens for Jews fleeing the Holocaust in Europe, as it required neither a passport nor visa to stay. Gestapo agents followed the refugees and, in 1942, tried to persuade the Japanese to build death camps on Chongming Island. Instead, in 1943, the Japanese forced Jews to move into a 'Designated Area for Stateless Refugees' in Hóngkǒu.

The Jewish ghetto (stateless Russians didn't have to live here) became home to Jews from all walks of life. It grew to shelter a synagogue, schools, a local paper, hospitals and enough cafes, rooftop gardens and restaurants to gain the epithet 'Little Vienna'. Those Jews who held jobs in the French Concession had to secure passes from the Japanese, specifically the notoriously unpredictable and violent Mr Goya. Poorer refugees were forced to bunk down in cramped hostels known as *Heime*, and had to rely on the generosity of others. As the wealthy Anglophile Jewish trading families had left in 1941, the situation was tight. Still, the refugees heard of events in distant Europe and realised perhaps that they were the lucky ones.

Today there are a few remainders of Jewish life in Shànghǎi, such as the Ohel Moishe Synagogue (p159) and the former Jewish Club (1932) in the grounds of the Conservatory of Music, where concerts are still performed. The Ohel Rachel Synagogue was built by Jacob Elias Sassoon in the early 20th century. Unfortunately, it remains closed to the public. Nearby are the remains of the school founded on the grounds by Horace Kadoorie.

HÓNGKǑU ARCHITECTURE

Hóngkǒu has a rich crop of architectural gems, from rundown terraced houses and dilapidated *shíkùmén* (stone-gate houses) to riverside art deco apartment blocks, noble concession-period classics, heritage hotels and converted abattoirs. The lavish Foster + Partners Bulgari Hotel project is proceeding apace on North Suzhou Rd by Sūzhōu Creek and is set to open in 2017, further revitalising the North Bund area.

Examples of *shíkùmén* architecture can be found if you stroll north along Zhapu Rd from Kunshan Rd and pop into the first pinched alley at No 313 (乍浦路313弄) on your left, where a line of typical *shíkùmén* awaits, decorated with distinctively carved lintels. Emerging from the alley, turn right along Baiguan Jie (百官街) for a short walk north to admire a further cluster of *shíkùmén* through the archway on your right. Other areas that are good for *shíkùmén* buildings are on Zhoushan Rd, especially at its southern end. The market street of Dongyuhang Rd (东余杭路), which it crosses, also has some interesting *shíkùmén* entrances. Shanyin Rd is a pleasant tree-lined street with a number of *shíkùmén*-filled alleyways branching off it.

Notable buildings to look out for:

1933 (上海1933老场坊, Shànghǎi 1933 Lǎochǎngfáng; Map p314; 10 Shajing Rd; 沙泾路10号; Ⓜ Hailun Rd) A magnificent concrete slaughterhouse transformed into a shopping complex. The shops themselves are of less interest but the very photogenic 'air bridges' are intact.

Hongkew Methodist Church (景灵堂, Jǐnglíng Táng; Map p314; 135 Kunshan Rd; 昆山路135号; Ⓜ North Sichuan Rd) Dating from 1923, this is the church where Chiang Kaishek, leader of the Republic of China, married Soong Meiling. It's generally closed to the public, but the caretaker may let you in.

Main Post Office (国际邮局, Guójì Yóujú; Map p314; 250 North Suzhou Rd; 苏州北路250号; Ⓜ Tiantong Rd) Overlooking Sūzhōu Creek, this supremely grand building dates from 1924. It is topped with a cupola and clock tower, and ornamented with bronze statues coated in a green patina.

Broadway Mansions (上海大厦, Shànghǎi Dàshà; Map p314; 20 North Suzhou Rd; 苏州北路20号; Ⓜ Tiatong Rd) Looming over Sūzhōu Creek, this classic brick pile (resembling a Ministry of Truth) was built to great fanfare in 1934 as an apartment block and later used to house American officers after WWII. Today it's a hotel.

Astor House Hotel (p213) Bursting with history, this classic old-timer has a yarn or two to tell and a lot of admirers: it's an excellent place to base oneself for swift access to the Bund.

Embankment Building (p160) Designed by architects Palmer & Turner, dating from 1935 and home to Chai Living Residences (p213).

Russian Consulate (p263; 俄罗斯领事馆, Éluósī Lǐngshìguǎn) This grand red-roofed concession building rises up just north of Wàibáidù Bridge.

duck) really needs to be flamed up within quacking distance of the Forbidden City, Shànghǎi's best roast-duck experience imports all the necessary ingredients (including chefs and a special brick oven) direct from Běijīng. In addition to its sleek open kitchen, this place is unusually intimate inside.

You'll need to order the duck at least a few days in advance, and weekend bookings require almost a week's notice.

🍷 DRINKING & NIGHTLIFE

★ **VUE**　　　　　　　　　　　BAR

Map p314 (非常时髦, Fēicháng Shímáo; www.hyatt onthebundsh.com; 32nd & 33rd fl, Hyatt on the Bund, 199 Huangpu Rd; 黄浦路199号外滩茂悦大酒店32-33楼; ⏱ 5.30pm-late; Ⓜ Tiantong Rd) Take in the extrasensory nocturnal views of the Bund and Pǔdōng from Vue bar at the Hyatt on the Bund, complete with outdoor jacuzzi to dip your toes in while you raise your glasses of bubbly. There's a cover charge of ¥100 for those not staying at the hotel, which includes a free drink.

OLD FILM CAFÉ   CAFE
Map p314 (老电影咖啡馆, Lǎodiànyǐng Kāfēiguǎn; ☑021 5696 4763; 123 Duolun Rd; 多伦路123号; coffee/tea from ¥25/35; ⊙9.30am-midnight; Ⓜ Dongbaoxing Rd) Celebrating the golden age of Shànghǎi cinema, this place is not a bad spot for a coffee if you're in the Duolun Rd area. There are some comfy armchairs and photos of Chinese and Western legends of the silver screen.

 **ENTERTAINMENT**

PEARL THEATRE   THEATRE
Map p314 (☑137 6488 9962; www.thepearl.com.cn; 471 Zhapu Rd; 乍浦路471号; Ⓜ North Sichuan Rd) Formerly known as Chinatown, this three-floor place in an old Buddhist temple north of the Bund is set in a magnificent old theatre (with boxes!). It stages drama, cabaret and other shows. Book tickets online.

SHÀNGHǍI CIRCUS WORLD   ACROBATICS
(上海马戏城, Shànghǎi Mǎxìchéng; ☑021 6652 7501; www.era-shanghai.com/era/en/; 2266 Gonghexin Rd; 共和新路2266号; tickets ¥120-600; Ⓜ Shanghai Circus World) Out at the far northern outskirts of town, you'll find this impressive complex. The show – *Era: Intersection of Time* – combines awesome acrobatics with new-fangled multimedia

elements. Shows start at 7.30pm. Tickets are available at the door, but booking ahead is advised.

SHOPPING

DÀSHÀNGHǍI   ANTIQUES
Map p314 (大上海; 181 Duolun Rd; 多伦路181号; ⊙9am-5.30pm, to 6pm in summer; Ⓜ Dongbaoxing Rd) Explore keenly at this Duolun Rd shop, where shelves spill over with all manner of historic collectables from pre-Liberation China: books and catalogues; 1950s maps of Běijīng and Shànghǎi; genuine posters and authentic memorabilia from the Cultural Revolution; black-and-white photos; unopened matchboxes and cigarette packs from the 1960s; Republican-era lipsticks; toothbrushes and more.

SPORTS & ACTIVITIES

HÓNGKǑU'S JEWISH HERITAGE TOURS   WALKING
(☑130 0214 6702; www.shanghaijews.com; half-day tour ¥450) These informative and interesting half-day walking tours run by passionate Israeli expat Dvir Bar-Gal will take you to the landmarks of the Hóngkǒu district, once known as the Jewish ghetto, and give you a lesson on this part of Shanghai's Jewish history. Tours run every day and usually start at 9.30am.

Xújiāhuì & South Shànghǎi

XÚJIĀHUÌ | SOUTH SHÀNGHǍI | WEST BUND

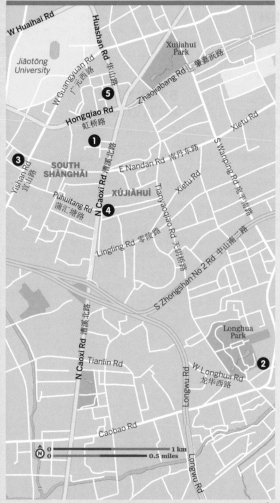

Neighbourhood Top Five

1 **Jesuit heritage** (p168) Exploring the well-preserved architecture of Xújiāhuì.

2 **Lónghuá Temple & Pagoda** (p167) Divining the Buddhist heritage of South Shànghǎi at this pretty, peaceful site.

3 **Xīnjiāng Restaurant** (p170) Going all out for a Uighur lamb feast, complete with dancing and singing performances.

4 **Shanghai Film Museum** (p166) Entering the glamorous world of golden-age cinema at this fascinating museum.

5 **Shop till you drop** (p170) Joining the throngs of wealthy Shanghainese snapping up designer goods in the malls.

For more detail of this area see Map p316 ➡

Explore: Xújiāhuì & South Shànghǎi

Bordering the southwestern end of the stylish French Concession and a zip away on the metro from People's Square, Xújiāhuì (徐家汇) was known to 1930s expats as Zicawei or Sicawei.

Accessed directly on the metro at its namesake station, the area is dominated by giant, glittering shopping malls, circling a five-way intersection that's insanely busy, even by Shànghǎi standards. It's one of the most popular shopping areas in the city, especially for designer gear and electronics, and gets packed at weekends.

The vast majority of people come here today to shop, but a sense of history still clings to the neighbourhood – Xújiāhuì was originally an attractive Jesuit settlement and dates back to the 17th century. The architectural heritage from this period and a clutch of engaging museums make for a rewarding day out, although, as elsewhere in Shànghǎi, you have to explore a bit to pull all the historical threads together.

History, heritage architecture, green lawns and academia converge on the tranquil campus of Jiāotōng University along Huashan Rd, north of the main Jesuit sights, while a host of local dining options offer plenty of cheap eats.

Further out from Xújiāhuì, South Shànghǎi is marked by one of the city's most famous temples, the ancient Lónghuá Temple and its pagoda, while the new West Bund area is rapidly developing into an impressive contemporary art hub.

Local Life

→**Greenery** Join the students relaxing on the lawn of Jiāotōng University (p167).

→**Dumplings** Find out what all the fuss is about – follow Shànghǎi's pernickety local diners to Din Tai Fung (p169).

→**Shopping** See how the Shanghainese spend, spend, spend at Grand Gateway 66 (p170).

Getting There & Away

→**Metro** Lines 1, 4, 9 and 11 run through the district. Xujiahui (lines 1, 9 and 11) and Shanghai Indoor Stadium (lines 1 and 4) are the main interchange stations. Line 1 runs through the French Concession and down to the South Shanghai Railway Station; line 9 can whisk you to Pǔdōng; line 11 stops at Jiāotōng University and heads south to Lónghuá Temple.

Lonely Planet's Top Tip

With its harried shopping hordes and hectic roads, Xújiāhuì can be breathlessly busy. Escape to some of Shànghǎi's best-tended areas of greenery: the peaceful Guāngqǐ Park, and the inviting lawn of Jiāotōng University on Huashan Rd, where students lie down on the grass reading and chatting in warm weather.

✖ Best Places to Eat

→ Din Tai Fung (p169)
→ Xīnjiāng Restaurant (p170)
→ Hóng Làjiāo Xiāngcàiguǎn (p169)
→ Heiseiya (p169)

For reviews, see p169 ➡

☕ Best Places to Drink

→ Harley's Underground (p170)
→ Shanghai Beer Factory (p170)

For reviews, see p170 ➡

◉ Best Sights

→ Shanghai Film Museum (p166)
→ Yuz Museum (p168)
→ Lónghuá Temple & Pagoda (p167)

For reviews, see p166 ➡

XÚJIĀHUÌ & SOUTH SHÀNGHǍI

👁 SIGHTS

👁 Xújiāhuì

ST IGNATIUS CATHEDRAL   CATHEDRAL

Map   p316   (徐家汇天主教堂,   Xújiāhuì
Tiānzhǔjiàotáng; ☎021 6438 4632; 158 Puxi Rd; 蒲
西路158号; Ⓜ Line 1, 9, 11 to Xujiahui, exit 3) The
dignified twin-spired St Ignatius Cathedral
(1904) is a major Xújiāhuì landmark, closed
while undergoing restoration at the time of
writing. Its nave is a long span of Gothic
arches, while the exterior is ornamented
with rows of menacing gargoyles. Note how
the church spires find reflection in much of
the more recently built local architecture.
The original stained glass was destroyed
in the Cultural Revolution, but the vivid
colours of the recent red, azure and purple
replacements (with archaic Chinese inscriptions from the Bible) are outstanding.

TOUSEWE MUSEUM   MUSEUM

Map   p316   (土山湾博物馆,   Tǔshānwān
Bówùguǎn, Tǔshānwān Museum; 55-1 Puhuitang
Rd; 蒲汇塘路55-1号; ¥10; ⏰9am-4pm Tue-Sun;
Ⓜ Line 1, 4 to Shanghai Indoor Stadium; Line 1, 9,
11 to Xujiahui) Alongside a middle school on
Puhuitang Rd, this fascinating museum
is dedicated to the arts and crafts of the
red-brick former Tousewe Orphanage, established here by the indefatigable Jesuits

XU GUANGQI

Xújiāhuì ('the Xu family gathering') is
named after Xu Guangqi (1562–1633),
a Chinese renaissance man. Xu was an
early student of astronomy, agronomy
and the calendar, and he established
a meteorological observatory that
relayed its information to the tower
on the Bund. He was then converted
to Catholicism by Matteo Ricci and
baptised with the name Paul. Xu became a high official in the Ming court
and bequeathed land to found a Jesuit
community, which eventually led to the
construction of St Ignatius Cathedral.
Xu's tomb and memorial hall can still
be visited in nearby Guāngqǐ Park
(p167), next to the historic Xújiāhuì
Observatory, and stands as an inspirational symbol of Shànghǎi's openness
to foreign ideas.

in 1864. The Catholics taught orphans the
techniques of Western art: one of the first
things you see as you enter the museum
is a small, exquisite and exact copy of the
Tiānníng Pagoda in Běijīng and a magnificent wooden *páilou* (decorative arch), the
Tǔshānwān Archway, carved in 1913.

There's a wealth of objects either produced or relating to the orphanage, from
religious ornaments to Jesuit literature.
Woodcraft was particularly productive
at the orphanage, so some splendid items
can be admired; look out for the expertly
carved *Li Kui and his Double*, fashioned
from boxwood, and the Madonna from the
1920s. Filling out the rest of the fascinating
collection are paintings and stained glass.
Audio tours are available.

SHÀNGHǍI FILM MUSEUM   MUSEUM

Map p316 (上海电影博物馆; Shànghǎi Diànyǐng
Bówùguǎn;   ☎021 6426 8666;   www.shfilm
museum.com; 595 North Caoxi Rd; 曹西路595
号; ¥60; ⏰9am-5pm Tue-Sun; Ⓜ Line 1, 4 to Shanghai Indoor Stadium) From the moment you enter the exhibitions via a 'red carpet' corridor
of simulated applause and camera flashes,
this museum is fun-filled and entertaining.
Located on the site of the original Shànghǎi
Film Studio, the museum celebrates the gold-
en ages of Chinese cinema, which were root-
ed in Shànghǎi. The portraits of glamorous
1920s and '30s movie stars, interactive quiz
screens, vintage props and Old Shànghǎi
film sets create an atmospheric experience.
Occasional English-language tours are
on offer – call in advance to confirm.

BIBLIOTHECA ZI-KA-WEI   LIBRARY

Map p316 (徐家汇藏书楼, Xújiāhuì Cángshūlóu;
☎021 5425 9260; www.xjh.sh.cn/pages/cang
shulou; 80 North Caoxi Rd; 漕溪北路80号; Ⓜ Line
1, 9, 11 to Xujiahui) FREE The magnificent St Ignatius Catholic Library, the Bibliotheca Zi-
Ka-Wei is one of several Jesuit monuments
defining historic Xújiāhuì. Established in
1847 by the local Jesuit mission, its priceless
book collection in the main library (大书房;
Dà Shūfáng) can only be seen by application. The collection of antiquarian tomes,
arranged on one floor with a gallery above,
is a rare and astonishing treasure.

Home to 560,000 volumes in Greek,
Latin and other languages, the edifice consists of two buildings, with the main library
itself housed in the lower, two-storey, east-
facing building that partially arches over
the pavement of North Caoxi Rd.

If you can gain access, wander past rare books on ecclesiastical history, Philosophica, Res Sinenses (Things Chinese) and other erudite branches of Jesuit learning. Photography is not allowed.

Visitors can access the atmospheric main reading room of the building, up the stairs on the 2nd floor between the hours of 9am and 5pm, Monday to Saturday. Apply for an access card in advance from Shanghai Library (www.library.sh.cn) for guaranteed entry. Bags must be left in the lockers downstairs

CY TUNG MARITIME MUSEUM   MUSEUM

Map p316 (董浩云航运博物馆, Dǒng Hàoyún Hángyùn Bówùguǎn; ☑021 6293 2403; Jiāotōng University, 1954 Huashan Rd; 华山路1954号交通大学内; ⊙9am-5pm Tue-Sun; Ⓜ Line 11 to Jiaotong University) FREE Named after the Shànghǎi-born shipping magnate, this small but fascinating museum in Jiāotōng University explores Chinese maritime history, with model ships, ancient compasses and early trade-route maps. A large portion of the 1st floor is devoted to Zheng He, the 15th-century admiral and explorer who was born a Hui Muslim in Yúnnán; was later captured and made a eunuch at the Ming court; and eventually went on to command vast Chinese fleets on journeys to east Africa, India and the Persian Gulf.

JIĀOTŌNG UNIVERSITY   UNIVERSITY

Map p316 (交通大学, Jiāotōng Dàxué; http://en.sjtu.edu.cn; 1954 Huashan Rd; 华山路1954号; Ⓜ Line 1, 9, 11 to Xujiahui) Founded in 1896, Jiāotōng University (literally 'Transport University') has a lovely, leafy campus, with well-kept lawns a short walk beyond the main gate and an old library building (图书馆; *túshūguǎn*). Climb to the 3rd floor of the library for a small, two-hall **museum** on the history of the university, complete with English captions. It's a great place to go if the sun's out – make like a student and collapse with a book on the grass among the magnolias.

GUĀNGQĪ PARK   PARK

Map p316 (光启公园, Guāngqǐ Gōngyuán; Nandan Rd; 南丹路; Ⓜ Line 1, 9, 11 to Xujiahui) FREE Dominated by an imposing white marble cross, this serene park is dedicated to 17th-century Christian scholar and scientist Xu Guangqi, whose tomb (a large mound) is also located within the grounds. Locals congregate here to practise taichi and stroll about in the shade of gingko trees, mag-

nolias, palms and bamboo. There's also a decorative archway, and a small **memorial hall** (徐光启纪念馆; Xú Guāngqǐ Jìniànguǎn; ⊙9am-4.30pm Wed-Sun) FREE in a historic Ming dynasty building.

XÚJIĀHUÌ OBSERVATORY   MONUMENT

Map p316 (166 Puxi Rd; 蒲西路166号) The elegant and newly renovated Jesuit-built Xújiāhuì Observatory dates to 1872 and is currently part of the Shànghǎi Meteorological Bureau. Access is only available at weekends as part of a group with prior reservations. Contact Xujiahui Tourist Information Centre (p259) for details.

⊙ South Shànghǎi

LÓNGHUÁ TEMPLE & PAGODA   BUDDHIST TEMPLE

Map p316 (龙华寺、龙华塔, Lónghuá Sì & Lónghuá Tǎ; ☑021 6457 6327; 2853 Longhua Rd; 龙华路2853号; ¥10, incl incense ¥50; ⊙7am-4.30pm; Ⓜ line 11 Longhua) Shànghǎi's oldest and largest monastery is named after the pipal tree (*lónghuá*) under which Buddha achieved enlightenment. Trees are decorated with red lanterns, incense smoke fills the front of the grounds and monks can regularly be heard chanting, making this one of the city's most atmospheric sites. The much-renovated temple is said to date from the 10th century.

The main halls to visit on the complex are **Mile Dian** (Maitreya Hall), **Tianwang Dian** (Hall of Heavenly Kings), **Daxiongbao Dian** (Grand Hall of the Great Sage), **Sānshèng Dian** (Three Sages Hall) and the **Laughing Buddha Hall**; note the four huge Heavenly Kings, each in charge of a compass point. The temple is particularly famed for its 6500kg bell, cast in 1894.

A large effigy of Shakyamuni seated on a lotus flower resides within the main hall (Daxiongbao Dian), while the the Sānshèng Dian holds a golden trinity of Buddhist statues. Also on the complex is the **Thousand Luóhàn Hall**, sheltering a huge legion of glittering arhat.

There's a vegetarian restaurant on-site.

Opposite the temple entrance rises the seven-storey, 44m-high **Lónghuá Pagoda**, originally built in AD 977. Visitors are not allowed to climb it.

The best time to visit is during the Lónghuá Temple Fair, in the third month of the lunar calendar (usually during April or May).

JESUIT XÚJIĀHUÌ

Beyond St Ignatius Cathedral (p166) and the Bibliotheca Zi-Ka-Wei (p166), keep your eyes peeled to unearth a small treasure trove of historical Jesuit architecture around Xújiāhuì.

A tourist information centre can be found on Puxi Rd, in between St Ignatius Cathedral and the Xújiāhuì Observatory; it has a specific focus on the neighbourhood. For more information on the area, head to www.xjh.sh.cn.

SHÀNGHǍI BOTANICAL GARDENS   GARDENS

(上海植物园, Shànghǎi Zhíwùyuán; ☑021 5436 4285; 1111 Longwu Rd; 龙吴路1111号; garden ¥15, garden, tropicarium & conservatories ¥40; ☉7am-5pm; Ⓜ Line 3 to Shilong Rd) The location off a busy road is hardly idyllic, but the spacious Botanical Gardens offer an escape from Shànghǎi's synthetic cityscape. The **Tropicarium** gives you the chance to get close to tropical flora, and once inside you can take the lift to the 5th floor for a bird's-eye view.

Many of the flower beds and gardens here are in need of some TLC, but there are some pleasant routes to walk. The northern side of the gardens has a dusty memorial temple, originally built in 1728. It's dedicated to Huang Daopo, said to have kick-started Shànghǎi's cotton industry by bringing the knowledge of spinning and weaving to the region from Hǎinán.

JĪNJIĀNG ACTION PARK   AMUSEMENT PARK

(锦江乐园, Jīnjiāng Lèyuán; ☑021 5421 6858; 201 Hongmei Rd; 虹梅路201号; 2/6 rides ¥50/80; ☉9am-10pm Jul & Aug, 9am-5.30pm Apr-Jun, Sep & Oct; Ⓜ Line 1 to Jinjiang Park) If the kids are in mutiny against sightseeing, the roller coasters, rides and huge Ferris wheel at this amusement park may mollify them. It's a bit out of town, but easy to get to, as it has its own metro station. Open shorter hours in winter.

MARTYRS MEMORIAL   PARK

Map p316 (龙华烈士陵园, Lónghuá Lièshì Língyuán; Longhua Rd; 龙华路; admission ¥1, memorial hall ¥5; ☉6am-5pm Tue-Sun, museum 9am-4pm; 🚌44 from Xújiāhuì, Ⓜ Line 3, 12 to Longcao Rd) This park marks the site of an old Kuomintang prison, where 800 communists, intellectuals and political agitators were executed between 1928 and 1937. A modern, lamplit tunnel leads to the original jailhouses and the small execution ground. Scattered throughout the manicured lawns are enormous socialist-realist sculptures of workers and soldiers. During WWII this area was a Japanese internment camp and airfield, as depicted in the JG Ballard novel and Spielberg film *Empire of the Sun*.

⊙ West Bund

YUZ MUSEUM   GALLERY

(余德耀美术馆; Yúdéyào Měishùguǎn; www.yuzmshanghai.org; 35 Fenggu Rd; 丰谷路35号近龙腾大道; Tue-Fri ¥120, Sat & Sun ¥150; ☉10am-9pm Sun-Thu, to midnight Fri & Sat; Ⓜ Line 11 to Yun Jin Rd) A huge development for Shànghǎi's contemporary art scene, this enormous gallery is housed in the former hangar of Longhua Airport and sprawls over 9000 sq metres. The temporary exhibitions have been world-class and beautifully curated so far, making an important contribution to the fast-developing West Bund cultural hub. The airy atrium contains a cafe and gift shop. Check in advance what exhibitions and workshops (some held in English) are running.

LONG MUSEUM   GALLERY

(龙美术馆; Lóng Měishùguǎn; ☑021 6422 7636; http://thelongmuseum.org; 3398 Longteng Ave; 龙腾大道3398号; ¥150, 1st Tuesday of month free; ☉10am-7pm Sun-Thu, to 9pm Fri & Sat; Ⓜ Line 7 to Longhua Middle Road) This sister museum to the Pǔdōng venue of the same name is an important part of the movement to create a world-class art hub along the West Bund. The four-storey building shows a mixture of contemporary art, as well as displays of ancient Chinese artefacts. The building itself is tremendous, with an imposing, industrial design created by Chinese architect Liu Yichun. In addition to the exhibitions, there's an onsite restaurant, concert hall, cafe and shop.

SHÀNGHǍI CENTRE OF PHOTOGRAPHY   GALLERY

(上海摄影艺术中心; Shànghǎi Shèyǐng Yìshù Zhōngxīn; 2555 Longteng Ave, near Fenggu Lu; 龙腾达到2555号; ☉10.30am-5.30pm Tue-Sun; Ⓜ Line 11 to Yunjin Lu) **FREE** One of the cluster of galleries making up the new West Bund cultural hub, the Shànghǎi Centre of Photography is a small but effective space displaying rotating exhibitions of portrait, conceptual and documentary photography.

✖ EATING

There are plenty of above-average chain restaurants housed in Xújiāhuì's malls, including some decent Western options. For a more interesting meal, explore the surrounding streets to find eateries that represent cuisines from all corners of China, plus countless small dumpling places. Late in the evening, low-profile street barbecue and stir-fry stalls set up along Wanping South Rd and in the area around Jiāotōng University, offering cheap and often very spicy eats.

✖ Xújiāhuì

★HÓNG LÀJIĀO XIĀNGCÀIGUǍN   HUNANESE $

Map p316 (红辣椒湘菜馆; ☎021 6283 2970; 754 Panyu Rd; 番禺路754号; mains ¥28-58; ⏰11am-midnight; Ⓜ Line 11 to Jiaotong University) There's no shortage of decent Húnán restaurants in Shànghǎi but you won't find much better than this one. Wooden benches and exposed-brick effect make for a rough-and-ready atmosphere, but there's nothing casual about the food: a feast of unforgettably smoky, spicy flavours. Many of the dishes are prepared in the typical 'dry pot' (干锅; gān guō) style, and are served up in an iron pot placed over a burner at the table.

★DIN TAI FUNG   SHANGHAI $

Map p316 (鼎泰丰; Dǐng Tài Fēng; ☎021 3469 1383; 5th fl, Grand Gateway 66, 1 Hongqiao Rd; 虹桥路1号港汇广场5楼; mains ¥38-58; ⏰10am-10pm; Ⓜ Line 1, 9, 11 to Xujiahui) This brightly lit and busy Taiwan-owned restaurant chain may still be peddling its 'Top 10 restaurants of the world' mantra after a two-decades-old review in the *New York Times,* but it does deliver some absolutely scrummy Shànghǎi *xiǎolóngbāo* dumplings. Not cheap perhaps (the pork variety are five for ¥30, or 10 for ¥60), but they're delicate, flavoursome and worth every *jiǎo.*

TSUI WAH   CANTONESE $

Map p316 (翠华; Cuì Huá; ☎021 6427 8550; Novel Plaza, 133 Tianyaoqiao Rd; 天钥桥路133号; mains ¥38-58; Ⓜ Line 1, 9, 11 to Xujiahui) There's a handful of branches of this cheerful Hong Kong chain around the city, and it's always a reliable place for a meal. Cantonese favourites, including plenty of satisfying fried rice and noodle dishes, are done well, while the fish-ball noodle soup is excellent. Don't leave without ordering a couple of fluffy pineapple buns from the on-site bakery.

HEISEIYA   JAPANESE $

Map p316 (平成屋日式料理店; Píngchéng Wū Rìshì Liào Lǐdiàn; ☎021 3368 9577; 323 Tianyaoqiao Rd; 天钥桥路323号; mains ¥30-50; ⏰11.30am-midnight; Ⓜ Line 1, 4 to Shanghai Indoor Stadium) Warm, noisy and pleasantly crowded, every inch of this neighbourhood *izakaya* (Japanese pub) is covered in flags, Japanese posters and decorative liquor bottles. Paper lanterns hang low over wooden tables and the overall effect is one of a cosy, boozy den. There's a solid selection of shochu and sake on the menu, and the tankards of beer are served ice-cold. Bar bites including fried squid, tempura and spring rolls are a good bet for snacking, while noodles and rice bowls are also on offer.

WEST BUND'S ART HUB

No one does urban regeneration quite like Shànghǎi, and the swift transformation of the West Bund from a deserted, industrial stretch of the river into a heartland of contemporary culture is a joy to behold. The two key players – Yuz Museum and the Long Museum – have already raised the bar for modern art in the city, with the Shanghai Centre of Photography and a series of design exhibitions at the nearby **West Bund Arts Centre** also making waves.

It's not just expensive galleries that are making this area a success, however. The surrounding greenery and attractive walkway along this stretch of the Huángpǔ have become a buzzing outdoor public space, drawing Shanghainese at evenings and weekends to jog, cycle, skateboard, clamber up the rock-climbing wall or hang out with friends.

More still is planned for this 'cultural corridor', namely DreamWorks' Shànghǎi DreamCenter, which will feature outdoor event plazas, a 500-seater IMAX cinema and an animation studio, and is expected to open in 2017.

YERSHARI
XINJIANG $

Map p316 (耶里夏丽新疆餐厅; Yēlǐxiàlì Xīnjiāng Cāntīng; 106 East Nandan Rd; 南丹东路106号; mains ¥35-45; ⏰11am-11.30pm; Ⓜ Line 4 to Shanghai Indoor Stadium) Yershari offers a slightly smarter version of the typically raucous Xinjiang dining experience, but this place is still plenty of fun and offers regular live entertainment. Wash down a hearty meal of classic Uighur dishes (including noodles, meat skewers, stews and the particularly excellent lamb chops) with black beer. A great spot for big groups.

XĪNJIĀNG RESTAURANT
UIGHUR $

Map p316 (维吾尔餐厅, Wéiwú'ěr Cāntīng; ☑021 6468 9198; 280 Yishan Rd; 宜山路280号; dishes ¥22-58; ⏰10am-12am; Ⓜ Line 3, 4, 9 to Yishan Rd; Line 1, 9, 11 to Xujiahui) The decor is full-on kitsch at this raucous upstairs Uighur restaurant, but you can feed an army on the whole roast lamb, or simply settle down to some tasty *dàpánjī* (a spicy stew of chicken, peppers and potatoes). There's also fresh yoghurt, *plov* (mutton pilaf), lamb kebabs, onion-laced tiger salad and naan; wash it all down with some Xīnjiāng black beer.

WAGAS
CAFE $

Map p316 (沃歌斯餐饮; Wògēsī Cān Yǐn; www. wagas.com.cn; Room 151, Grand Gateway 66, 1 Hongqiao Rd; 虹桥路1号港汇广场151室; mains ¥55-68; ⏰7am-10pm; 🛜; Ⓜ Line 1, 9, 11 to Xujiahui) This busy Xújiāhuì branch of Wagas is perfect for restorative sandwiches and coffee after shopping at the attached mall. Get there before 11am to take advantage of various breakfast deals. Head next door to sister restaurant Bistrow by Wagas for more substantial mains.

✖ West Bund

SAKURA EDGE
JAPANESE $$

(3268 Longteng Ave; 龙腾大道3268号; mains ¥78-98; ⏰11am-10pm; Ⓜ Line 7 to Longhua Middle Rd) Spectacularly presented sushi, sashimi and grilled fish are the order of the day here. This Japanese venue has a pretty, partly covered terrace overlooking the Bund, while inside booths and private back rooms are decorated with delicate flowers and soft wood tables. A decent selection of sake is on offer.

CAFE DU DRAGON
CAFE $$

(3398 Longteng Ave; 龙腾大道3398号; mains ¥58-78; ⏰9am-9pm; Ⓜ Line 7 to Longhua Middle Rd) For those needing refreshment after a long art appreciation session in the adjoining Long Museum, Cafe du Dragon is just the place. This colourful cafe contains endless shelves of art books for perusing over a cup of coffee and thickly iced slab of rainbow cake. A limited menu of sandwiches, salad and pasta is also available, with beer and wine.

🍷 DRINKING & NIGHTLIFE

HARLEY'S UNDERGROUND
BAR

Map p316 (265 East Nandan Rd; 南丹东路265号; ⏰6pm-2am; Ⓜ Line 1, 9, 11 to Xujiahui) You have to descend into the bowels of Xújiāhuì to access Harley's, but the concrete staircase doesn't seem to put off the punters. This long-running basement dive has recently had a revamp and is now part sports bar, part nightclub. Pool and darts are on offer, and the club runs regular electronic music nights. Drinks are far more reasonably priced than in other parts of town.

SHANGHAI BEER FACTORY
BAR

Map p316 (☑021 3356 5005; No 1 Shanghai Indoor Stadium, 1111 North Caoxi Rd; 曹溪北路1111号; ⏰4pm-1am; Ⓜ Line 1, 4 to Shanghai Indoor Stadium) Shànghǎi's ever-expanding craft-beer scene includes this venue tucked away at Shànghǎi Indoor Stadium. Smart dark-wood decor and large TVs showing sports make it a comfortable place to settle in. There are eight craft beers brewed on-site, and a selection of 'beer cocktails' on offer.

The home brews are not the finest in town by a long way, but prices are lower than elsewhere – a small beer starts at ¥25.

🛍 SHOPPING

GRAND GATEWAY 66
MALL

Map p316 (港汇恒隆广场, Gǎnghuì Hénglóng Guǎngchǎng; ☑021 6407 0111; 1 Hongqiao Rd; 虹桥路1号; ⏰10am-10pm; Ⓜ Line 1, 9, 11 to Xujiahui) Fed by the metro station below ground, Grand Gateway 66 is a vast, airy space and one of Shànghǎi's most high-end malls. It has a wide range of designer and international fashion brands, including Gucci, Calvin Klein and Lacoste, and a constellation of cosmetics and sports-gear outlets.

The complex has a decent range of restaurants on the 5th and 6th floors, an outside food strip, a cinema, and seating for resting weary shopping legs.

West Shànghǎi

CHÁNGNÍNG & GŮBĚI | HÓNGQIÁO AIRPORT AREA

Neighbourhood Top Five

❶ Qībǎo (p173) Squeezing into the narrow alleyways for flavours of traditional China.

❷ Mínshēng Art Museum (p174) Taking in a modern-art exhibit at this often overlooked museum.

❸ Yùyīntáng (p176) Rocking out at one of Shànghǎi's best gritty music venues.

❹ Liu Haisu Art Gallery (p174) Admiring works by prominent Chinese artist Liu Haisu.

❺ Tiānshān Tea City (p176) Sampling countless varieties of tea.

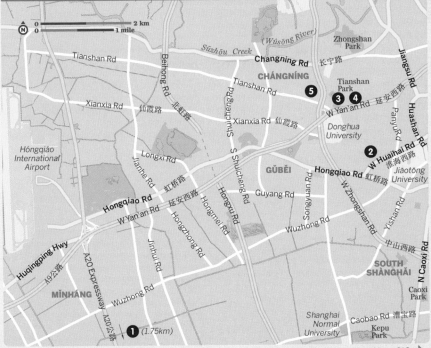

For more detail of this area see Map p318 ➡

Lonely Planet's Top Tip

If you're used to wandering about the French Concession or the Old Town, you'll quickly come to note that West Shanghai's points of interest are really spread out and often a fair walk from any metro station. This is one neighbourhood where taxis come in very handy.

✖ Best Places to Eat

➡ Fú Hé Huì (p175)

➡ 1221 (p175)

➡ Băinián Lóngpáo (p175)

➡ Bellagio Café (p175)

For reviews, see p175 ➡

🍷 Best Places to Drink

➡ Yùyīntáng (p176)

➡ Hongmei Road Entertainment Street (p176)

➡ C's (p176)

For reviews, see p176 ➡

🔒 Best Places to Shop

➡ Tiānshān Tea City (p176)

➡ Hóngqiáo International Pearl City (p176)

For reviews, see p176 ➡

Explore: West Shànghăi

West Shànghăi (长宁、闵行、古北、虹桥) is far more a residential and business zone than a tourist drawcard, though that's not to say you should immediately scratch it from your itinerary. Enveloping a huge swath of land, it's divided into two main districts (Chángníng and Mĭnháng) and is the site of the Hóngqiáo airport and Hóngqiáo Railway Station (Shànghăi's high-speed rail link), as well as the ancient waterside town of Qībăo.

Mĭnháng runs along the southern and western borders of Chángníng district, which includes well-known neighbourhoods such as the middle-class and expat enclave of Gŭbĕi and Hóngqiáo airport. West Shànghăi was once countryside and a playground for the rich to retreat to at weekends, and some of the city's largest parks are found here.

Local Life

➡ **Snacks** From stinky tofu and squid on a stick to sweet black-sesame-paste dumplings, Qībăo has you covered.

➡ **Green space** Escape the relentless concrete sprawl in Zhōngshān Park (p174) or the Song Qingling Mausoleum (p174).

➡ **Art** Head to Red Town (p174) for private art galleries or Liu Haisu Art Gallery (p174) for a culture hit in the West.

Getting There & Away

➡ **Metro** Lines 2 and 10 run east–west through the area (line 10 is more central), converging at Hóngqiáo airport (Terminal 2) and Hóngqiáo Railway Station. Lines 3 and 4 mirror each other, running north–south. Line 9 is to the south, passing through Qībăo and terminating at Sōngjiāng.

CLAUDIO ZACCHERINI/SHUTTERSTOCK ©

TOP SIGHT
QĪBĂO

When you tire of Shànghǎi's incessantly urban overture, tiny Qībǎo is a mere hop, skip and metro ride away. An ancient settlement that prospered during the Ming and Qing dynasties, it's littered with historic traditional architecture, threaded by small, busy alleyways and cut through by a picturesque canal. If you can tolerate crowds, Qībǎo brings you the flavours of old China along with doses of entertainment and some fantastic snacking opportunities.

Sights

Nine sights are included in the through ticket, or you can skip the ticket and pay ¥5 to ¥10 per sight instead. The best include the **Cotton Textile Mill**, **Old Trades House** (a waxworks museum) and the **Shadow Puppet Museum**, where you can catch performances from 1pm to 3pm Wednesdays and Sundays. Half-hour **boat rides** slowly ferry passengers from Number One Bridge to Dōngtángtān (东塘滩) and back. The 1866 Catholic Church (p175), adjacent to a convent off Qibao Nanjie, is south of the canal.

Shopping & Snacking

Wander along **Bei Dajie**, north of the canal, for small shops selling fans, jewellery and wooden handicrafts. South of the canal, **Nan Dajie** has every Chinese snack under the Shànghǎi sun: No 26 cooks up sweet *tāng yuán* (汤圆) dumplings, which steam from bowls, and No 9 is a traditional teahouse with Chinese **storytelling performances**. Beggar's chicken (¥28) can be found at several spots. Also look out for candy floss, glazed strawberries on a stick, jujubes, chestnuts, white rabbit sweets and Qībǎo spirits.

DON'T MISS

➜ Cotton Textile Mill
➜ Bei Dajie souvenirs
➜ Nan Dajie snacks

PRACTICALITIES

➜ 七宝
➜ www.goqibao.com
➜ 2 Minzhu Rd, Mǐnháng district; 闵行区民主路2号
➜ high/low season ¥45/30
➜ ⊙sights 8.30am-4.30pm
➜ Ⓜ Qibao

⊙ SIGHTS

Sights are thin on the ground out in West Shanghai but there are few art galleries definitely worth making the trek out for. Those looking to escape to some green space will find it in Zhōngshān Park. If you don't have plans to visit any canal towns in China, Qibao makes for an easy day trip to experience the waterways.

⊙ Chángníng & Gǔběi

MÍNSHĒNG ART MUSEUM MUSEUM

Map p318 (民生现代美术馆, Mínshēng Xiàndài Měishùguǎn; ☑021 6282 8729; www.minsheng art.com; 570 West Huaihai Rd; 淮海西路570号; ⊙10am-6pm Tue-Sun; MHongqiao Rd) Although sponsored mainly by the Mínshēng Bank, this edgy art space also counts the Tate, Centre Pompidou, MoMA and Guggenheim among its partners, so it should come as no surprise that the exhibits (about three per year) are generally excellent. Adding to its street cred is artistic director Zhou Tiehai, one of Shànghǎi's best-known artists.

RED TOWN GALLERY

Map p318 (红坊, Hóng Fāng; 570 West Huaihai Rd; 淮海西路570号; MHongqiao Rd) FREE The No 10 Steel Factory has come to life again with an enormous display of large-scale sculpture pieces dotting the lawn, offices and studios of this creative cluster. While the majority of the premises is taken over by the so-so Shànghǎi Sculpture Space, there are a couple of other private galleries here, as well as Red Town's main highlight, the Mínshēng Art Museum (p174).

SONG QINGLING MAUSOLEUM MAUSOLEUM

Map p318 (宋庆龄陵园, Sòng Qìnglíng Língyuán; ☑021 6474 7183; 21 Songyuan Rd; 宋园路21号; ⊙9am-5pm, last entry 4.30pm; MSongyuan Rd) FREE Despite the hard-edged communist layout, this green park is good for a stroll. Song Qingling, wife of Dr Sun Yatsen (co-founder of the Republic of China), is interred in a low-key tomb here. She is memorialised in the **Song Qingling Exhibition Hall** (宋庆龄陈列馆; Sòng Qìnglíng Chénlièguǎn) straight ahead from the main entrance, which resembles a Chinese imperial tomb and houses displays of Song memorabilia (including her black *qípáo*, a Chinese-style dress).

There's also a photograph of Marxist Westerners reading from Mao's *Little Red Book* back in the day when it was cool. The **international cemetery** here also contains a host of foreign gravestones, including those of Jewish, Vietnamese and Western settlers of Shànghǎi.

ZHŌNGSHĀN PARK PARK

Map p318 (中山公园, Zhōngshān Gōngyuán; 780 Changning Rd; 长宁路780号; ⊙6am-6pm; ⊞; MZhongshan Park) Called Jessfield Park by the British and today named after 'Father of the Nation' Sun Zhongshan (Sun Yatsen), this lovely park is located in the northeast, in the former 'Badlands' area of 1930s Shànghǎi. On sunny days, you'll find kite flyers, locals playing music, and people picnicking on the lawn.

LIU HAISU ART GALLERY MUSEUM

Map p318 (刘海粟美术馆, Liú Hǎisù Měishùguǎn; 1609 West Yan'an Rd; 延安西路1609号; ⊙9am-4pm Tue-Sun; MWest Yan'an Rd) FREE Moved to a new location in 2016, the impressive Liu Haisu gallery exhibits works of the eponymous painter, as well as displaying international contemporary art from the late artist's private collection. It also hosts visiting exhibitions. There's a brightly coloured 300m graffiti wall surrounding the gallery, featuring works by students from the Fine Arts College at Shanghai University who recreated art they found online (with permission).

LEGOLAND DISCOVERY CENTRE AMUSEMENT PARK

(乐高探索中心, Lègāo Tànsuǒ Zhōngxīn; ☑hotline 4000 988 966; www.legolanddiscovery center.cn; 2nd fl, Parkside Plaza, 168 Daduhe Rd; 大渡河路168号长风景畔广场室内二楼; tickets ¥180, online weekdays/weekend ¥150/¥160; ⊙10am-8pm, last entry 7pm; ⊞; MDaduhe Rd) Plans are in the works for Shànghǎi's own Legoland, but until then the Discovery Centre is more than enough to keep Lego fans happy. Opened to the public in April 2016, this mini amusement park is strictly for kids, no adults allowed entry unless accompanying a child. It features 10 play zones and creative workshops where kids can learn Lego building skills from the masters. The highlight is mini Shànghǎi Land made from millions of Lego pieces, with Pǔdōng airport, Shànghǎi Tower and the Oriental Pearl TV Tower.

There's also a gift shop selling loads of Lego. Try to visit on a weekday afternoon to avoid crowds and book tickets online in advance for discounts and guaranteed entry.

◉ Hóngqiáo Airport Area

QĪBǍO   VILLAGE
See p173.

CATHOLIC CHURCH   CHURCH
(天主教堂, Tiānzhǔ Jiàotáng; 50 Nanjie; 南街 50号) Visit or take part in prayer at this splendid 1866 Catholic church in Qībǎo.

**FORMER SASSOON
MANSION**   HISTORIC BUILDING
Map p318 (Jin Jiang Cypress Hotel; 2419 Hongqiao Rd; 虹桥路2419号; MShanghai Zoo) Set in lush green grounds, this historic house (building No 1 of the Cypress Hotel) was Victor Sassoon's bolthole villa in West Shànghǎi.

✖ EATING

✖ Chángníng & Gǔběi

Hongmei Rd is the main dining hub of West Shanghai, and is often packed with tourists and expats for its collection of mainly Western dining options.

CARREFOUR   SUPERMARKET **$**
Map p318 (家乐福, Jiālèfú; ☑021 6278 1944; www.carrefour.com.cn; 268 South Shuicheng Rd; 水城南路268号; ⊙7.30am-10.30pm; MShuicheng Rd) This French supermarket chain is the epicentre of Gǔběi, and you can find everything from wine and cheese to cheap bikes and crockery. Also here is a popular food court, with a bakery and branches of Wagas and Food Republic.

★1221   SHANGHAI **$$**
Map p318 (Yī Èr Èr Yī; ☑021 6213 6585; 1221 West Yan'an Rd; 延安西路1221号; dishes ¥28-128; ⊙5-11pm; MWest Yan'an Rd) No one has a bad thing to say about this dapper expat favourite, and rightly so: it has never let its standards dip over the years. Meat dishes start at ¥58 for the beef and *yóutiáo* (dough strips), and the plentiful eel, shrimp and squid dishes cost around twice that. Other tempting fare includes the roast duck and braised pork.

Things are backed up by a four-page vegetarian menu, including the sweet-and-sour vegetarian spare ribs, which are out of this world. The setting (tucked away in an alley) is white tablecloths, cream walls and brown leatherette furniture. Service is fantastic. Reserve. It's a bit of a walk from the station; consider a taxi.

BELLAGIO CAFÉ   CHINESE **$$**
Map p318 (鹿港小镇, Lùgǎng Xiǎozhèn; ☑021 6270 6866; 101 South Shuicheng Rd; 水城南路101 号; dishes ¥35-78; ⊙11.30am-midnight; MShuicheng Rd) This popular branch of the Taiwanese restaurant draws crowds of Taiwan expats for its *sānbēijī* (three-cup chicken), fried bean curd and shaved-ice desserts.

★FÚ HÉ HUÌ   VEGETARIAN **$$$**
Map p306 (福和慧; ☑021 3980 9188; 1037 Yuyuan Rd; 愚园路1037号; set menus ¥380, ¥680 & ¥880; ⊙11am-2pm & 5-10.30pm; ✂; MJiangsu Rd) The most recent venture from owner Fang Yuan and chef Tony Lu, the Shànghǎi team behind Fu 1015, Fu 1088 (p139) and Fu 1039 (p175), this is the standout in an amazing bunch. Set in an elegant private room, the strictly vegetarian menu draws on Yuan's Buddhist faith. Choose from three set menus featuring creative and delicate flavours that won it a place in Asia's 50 Best Restaurants 2016.

★FU 1039   SHANGHAI **$$$**
Map p306 (福一零三九, Fú Yào Líng Sān Jiǔ; ☑021 5237 1878; 1039 Yuyuan Rd; 愚园路1039 号; dishes ¥60-108; MJiangsu Rd) Set in a three-storey 1913 villa, Fu attains an old-fashioned charm. Foodies who appreciate sophisticated surroundings and Shanghainese food on par with the decor, take note – Fu is a must. The succulent standards won't disappoint: the smoked fish starter is recommended, with the drunken chicken and the sweet-and-sour Mandarin fish a close second. The entrance, down an alley and on the left, is unmarked and staff speak little English. There's a minimum charge of ¥225 per head here.

✖ Hóngqiáo Airport Area

★BǍINIÁN LÓNGPÁO   DUMPLING **$**
(百年龙袍; 15 Bei Daijie, Qībǎo; 七宝古镇北大街 15号; 8 dumplings from ¥15; ⊙6.30am-8.30pm; MQibao) This tiny spot at the foot of Qībǎo's main bridge has as many dumpling makers

in the kitchen as it does seats. But pay no mind to the cramped premises, as these are by far and away the best *xiǎolóngbāo* ('little steamer buns') on the block. Dumpling fillings include crab, shrimp and pork. For takeaway, the slow-moving queue heads out the door.

CITY SHOP   SUPERMARKET $
Map p318 (城市超市, Chéngshì Cháoshì; ☑400 811 1797; www.cityshop.com.cn; 3211 Hongmei Rd; 虹梅路3211号; ⏰8am-10pm; Ⓜ Longxi Rd) City Shop is great for all those imported goodies you just can't get anywhere else. It also has a range of takeaway sandwiches and baked goods, and groceries can be delivered.

**HONGMEI ROAD
ENTERTAINMENT STREET**   FOOD STREET $$
Map p318 (老外街, Lǎowài Jiē; Lane 3338, Hongmei Rd; 虹梅路3338弄虹梅休闲步行街; Ⓜ Longxi Rd) This strip, popular with expats, has a selection of mostly Western restaurants and bars for those who don't want to head into town. There's not too much to get excited about here, though there are branches of Shànghǎi Brewery, Fat Cow and Simply Thai.

🍷 DRINKING & NIGHTLIFE

Hongmei Rd packs out with revellers on weekends and is a popular spot for a drink with branches of Fat Cow, Shanghai Brewery, The Tap House and Big Bamboo.

MANSION   CLUB
Map p318 (851 Hongjing Rd; 虹井路851号; ⏰24hr weekend parties; Ⓜ Shanghai Zoo) Tucked away in a largely residential area, this club is where Shànghǎi's creative-type expats come to do some serious partying. Open 24 hours on weekends, the basement club hosts local DJs and international artists. Come the summer months, the friendly party atmosphere heads outdoors to the backyard pool and beach. There's always something going on, from silent disco pool parties to dance comps.

C'S   BAR
Map p318 (685 Dingxi Rd; 定西路685号; ⏰7.30pm-late; Ⓜ West Yan'an Rd) The king of all Shànghǎi dives, this graffiti-strewn basement warren won't impress your date, but the echoing music and rock-bottom prices guarantee devoted (student-based) droves of drinkers.

☆ ENTERTAINMENT

★YÙYĪNTÁNG   LIVE MUSIC
Map p318 (育音堂, ☑021 5237 8662; www.yytlive.com; 851 Kaixuan Rd; 凯旋路851号; Ⓜ West Yan'an Rd) Small enough to feel intimate, but big enough for a sometimes pulsating atmosphere, Yùyīntáng has long been one of the top places in the city to see live music. Any Shànghǎi rock band worth its amps plays here, but you can also catch groups on tour from other cities in China, as well as international acts. Rock is the staple diet, but anything goes, from hard punk to jazz.

SHÀNGHǍI FILM ART CENTRE   CINEMA
Map p318 (上海影城, Shànghǎi Yǐngchéng; ☑021 6280 4088; 160 Xinhua Rd; 新华路160号; Ⓜ Jiaotong University) This cinema is the main venue for the Shanghai International Film Festival and usually has at least one movie showing in English at other times.

🛍 SHOPPING

★TIĀNSHĀN TEA CITY   DRINKS
Map p318 (天山茶城, Tiānshān Cháchéng; 520 West Zhongshan Rd; 中山西路520号; ⏰8.30am-8.30pm; Ⓜ Zhongshan Park, West Yan'an Rd) Running low on loose-leaf oolong and aged *pǔ'ěr* cakes? This three-storey sprawl is hands down the largest collection of tea shops in the city. Taste-test a few to see what you like before you purchase. You probably won't need to leave the ground level, but you'll find a decent selection of teaware and porcelain on the 2nd and 3rd floors.

**HÓNGQIÁO INTERNATIONAL
PEARL CITY**   MARKET
Map p318 (虹桥国际珍珠城, Hóngqiáo Guójì Zhēnzhū Chéng; 2nd fl, Hóngqiáo Craft Market, 3721 Hongmei Rd; 虹梅路3721号虹桥市场2楼; ⏰10am-8pm; Ⓜ Longxi Rd) Popular with local expats, the 2nd floor of this market has a selection of freshwater and saltwater pearls that is worth a browse. There's a relaxed atmosphere and you can bargain here.

🏃 SPORTS & ACTIVITIES

MÍNGWǓ INTERNATIONAL KUNGFU CLUB
MARTIAL ARTS

Map p318 (明武国际功夫馆, Míngwǔ Guójì Gōngfu Guǎn; ☑021 6465 9806; www.mingwukungfu.com; 3rd fl, Hongchun Bldg, 3213 Hongmei Rd; 虹梅路3213号红春大厦3楼) This versatile gym offers bilingual classes in a wide range of martial arts, from taichi and qì gōng to *wǔshù* and karate, for both children and adults. There's also a shop on-site, selling clothing and weapons. There's no metro station nearby, so you'll need to jump in a taxi.

DINO BEACH
SWIMMING

(热带风暴, Rèdài Fēngbào; ☑021 6478 3333; www.dinobeach.com.cn; 78 Xinzhen Rd; 新镇路78号; ¥120-¥150; ☺9am-10pm Jun-Sep; 🚼; Ⓜ Xinzhuang, then bus 763 or 173) Way down south in Mǐnháng district, this popular summer place has a beach, a wave pool, water slides and tube hire to beat the Shànghǎi summer heat, and it keeps going late. But it's absolutely heaving at weekends. To get here, take metro line 1 to Xinzhuang, or catch a cab from Qībǎo. Midweek discounts are on offer.

Day Trips from Shànghǎi

Hángzhōu p179
Hángzhōu's gorgeous and placid West Lake sits comfortably among China's top sights.

Sūzhōu p188
China's best-known water town, Sūzhōu is a rewarding bundle of classical gardens, canals, bridges, silk, temples and fab museums.

Tónglǐ p195
One of Jiāngsū's best-looking water towns, with a racy museum dedicated to China's erotic culture.

Zhūjiājiǎo p197
Quaint canal-side town within Shànghǎi municipality, dotted with temples, ancient bridges and pinched lanes.

Zhōuzhuāng p198
Lovely traditional architecture, charming back alleys and bridges make this small Jiāngsū town an eye-catching diversion.

Shěshān p199
Divine views and an imposing hilltop Catholic church, accessible on the metro from Shànghǎi city centre.

Hángzhōu

Explore

One of China's most enduringly popular holiday spots, Hángzhōu (杭州) has dreamy West Lake panoramas and fabulously green hills that can easily tempt you into long sojourns. Eulogised by poets and applauded by emperors, the lake has intoxicated the Chinese imagination for aeons. Kept spotlessly clean by armies of street sweepers and litter collectors, its scenic vistas draw you into a classical Chinese watercolour of willow-lined banks, mist-covered hills and the occasional *shíkùmén* (stone-gate house) and old *lòlòng* (residential lane).

Wonderful as it is, Hángzhōu's charms are by no means limited to West Lake scenery – delve further into the city to climb ancient pagodas and discover blissfully quiet temples. Away from the tourist drawcards exists a charismatic and buzzing city in its own right, with wide pedestrian walkways to wander, an unpretentious and exciting food scene, upbeat nightlife and increasingly cosmopolitan population.

The Best...

→ **Sight** West Lake (p179)

→ **Place to Eat** Green Tea Restaurant (p185)

→ **Place to Drink** JZ Club (p186)

Top Tip

The hills south of West Lake are a prime spot for walkers, cyclists and green-tea connoisseurs.

Getting There & Away

Train The easiest way to travel from Shànghǎi Hóngqiáo Train Station is on the regular high-speed G and D class trains to Hángzhōu East Train Station (55 minutes).

Bus Frequent departures from Shànghǎi's South Station to Hángzhōu's various bus stations (2½ hours). Buses from Shànghǎi's Hóngqiáo airport (two hours) run every 30 minutes between 10am and 9pm. Regular buses also run from Shànghǎi's Pǔdōng International Airport (three hours).

Getting Around

Metro line 1 Runs from the southeast of town, through the Main Train Station, along the east side of West Lake and on to the East Train Station, the Main Bus Station and the northeast of town (first/last train 6.06am/11.32pm).

Metro line 2 Runs south from Chaoyang to Qianjiang Rd.

Need to Know

→ **Area Code** ☑571

→ **Location** 170km from Shànghǎi

→ **Tourist office** (杭州旅游咨询服务中心、Hángzhōu Lǚyóu Zīxún Fúwù Zhōngxīn; ☑0571 8797 8123; Léifēng Pagoda, Nanshan Lu; 雷峰塔南山路; ☺8am-5pm)

◉ SIGHTS

Many of Hángzhōu's sights are set around the West Lake or to the east of it. The best way to fit as many as possible in is by bike, as traffic around the lake can be agonizingly slow. Many venues offer discounted rates for children and the elderly.

WEST LAKE   LAKE

(西湖, Xīhú) The very definition of classical beauty in China, West Lake is utterly mesmerising: pagoda-topped hills rise over willow-lined waters as boats drift slowly through a vignette of leisurely charm. Walkways, perfectly positioned benches, parks and gardens around the banks of the lake offer a thousand and one vantage points for visitors to admire the faultless scenery.

Originally a lagoon adjoining the Qiántáng River, the lake didn't come into being until the 8th century, when the governor of Hángzhōu had the marshy expanse dredged. As time passed, the lake's splendour was gradually cultivated: gardens were planted, pagodas built, and causeways and islands were constructed from dredged silt.

Celebrated poet Su Dongpo himself had a hand in the lake's development, constructing the **Sū Causeway** (苏堤, Sūdī) during his tenure as local governor in the 11th century. It wasn't an original idea – the poet-governor Bai Juyi had already constructed the **Bái Causeway** (白堤, Báidī) some 200 years earlier. Lined by willow, plum and peach trees, today the traffic-free causeways

Hángzhōu

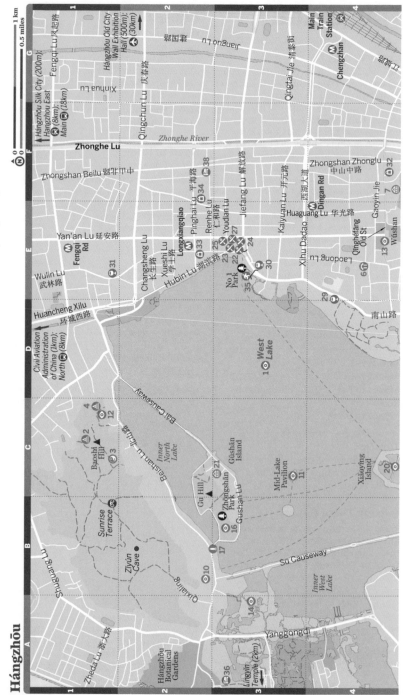

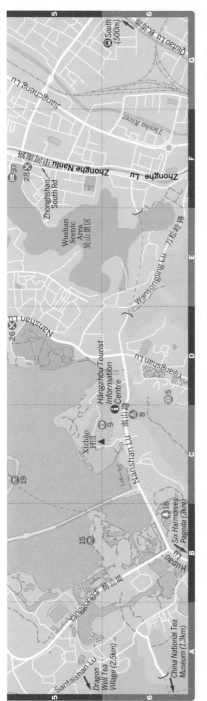

with their half-moon bridges make for restful outings.

Lashed to the northern shores by the Bái Causeway is **Gūshān Island** (孤山岛, Gūshān Dǎo), the largest island in the lake and the location of the **Zhèjiāng Provincial Museum** (浙江省博物馆, Zhèjiāng Shěng Bówùguǎn; 25 Gushan Lu; 孤山路25号; audio guide ¥10; ⊙9am-5pm Tue-Sun) **FREE** and Zhōngshān Park. The island's buildings and gardens were once the site of Emperor Qianlong's 18th-century holiday palace and gardens. Also on the island is the intriguing **Seal Engravers Society** (西泠印社, Xīlíng Yìnshè; ⊙9am-5.30pm) **FREE** (closed for renovations at the time of research), dedicated to the ancient art of carving the name seals (chops) that serve as personal signatures.

The northwest of the lake is fringed with the lovely Qūyuàn Garden (p183), a collection of gardens spread out over numerous islets and renowned for their fragrant spring lotus blossoms. Near Xīlíng Bridge (Xīlíng Qiáo) is **Su Xiaoxiao's Tomb** (苏小小墓, Sū Xiǎoxiǎo Mù), a 5th-century courtesan who died of grief while waiting for her lover to return. It's been said that her ghost haunts the area and the tinkle of the bells on her gown are audible at night.

The smaller island in the lake is Xiǎoyíng Island (p184), where you can look over to **Three Pools Mirroring the Moon** (三潭印月, Sāntán Yìnyuè), three small towers in the water on the south side of the island; each has five holes that release shafts of candlelight on the night of the mid-autumn festival. From Lesser Yíngzhōu Island, you can gaze over to **Red Carp Pond** (花港观鱼, Huāgǎng Guānyú), home to a few thousand red carp.

Impromptu opera singing, ballroom dancing and other cultural activities often take place around the lake, and if the weather's fine don't forget to earmark the east shore for sunset over West Lake photos.

It's hardly needed, but musical dancing fountains burst into action at regular intervals throughout the night and day, close to Lakeview Park.

Crowds can be a real issue here, especially on public days off when it can seem as if every holidaymaker in China is strolling around the lake. Escape the jam of people by getting out and about early in the morning – also the best time to spot the odd serene lakeside taichi session.

The best way to get around the lake is by bike or on foot.

Hángzhōu

LÍNGYǏN TEMPLE   BUDDHIST SITE

(灵隐寺, Língyǐn Sì; Lingyin Lu; 灵隐路; grounds ¥45, temple ¥30; ⊙7am-5pm) Hángzhōu's most famous Buddhist temple, Língyǐn Temple was originally built in AD 326, but has been destroyed and rebuilt no fewer than 16 times. During the Five Dynasties (AD 907–960) about 3000 monks lived here. The Hall of the Four Heavenly Kings is astonishing, with its four vast guardians and an ornate cabinet housing Milefo (the future Buddha). The **Great Hall** contains a magnificent 20m-high statue of Siddhartha Gautama (Sakyamuni), sculpted from 24 blocks of camphor wood in 1956 and based on a Tang dynasty original.

Behind the giant statue is a startling montage of Guanyin surrounded by 150 small figures, including multiple *luóhàn* (arhat), in a variety of poses. The earlier hall collapsed in 1949, crushing the Buddhist statues within, so it was rebuilt and the statue conceived. The Hall of the Medicine Buddha is beyond.

The walk up to the temple skirts the flanks of Fēilái Peak (Fēilái Fēng; Peak Flying from Afar), magically transported here from India according to legend. The Buddhist carvings (all 470 of them) lining the riverbanks and hillsides and tucked away inside grottoes date from the 10th to 14th centuries. To get a close-up view of the best carvings, including the famed 'laughing' Maitreya Buddha, follow the paths along the far (east) side of the stream.

There are several other temples near Língyǐn Temple that can be explored, including Yǒngfú Temple and Tāoguāng Temple.

Behind Língyǐn Temple is the Northern Peak (Běi Gāofēng), which can be scaled by cable car (up/down/return ¥30/20/40). From the summit there are sweeping views across the lake and city.

TÀIZǏWĀN PARK   PARK

(太子湾公园; Nanshan Lu; 南山路) This exquisite and serene park just south of the Sū Causeway off West Lake offers quiet walks among lush woodland, ponds, lakes, rose gardens and lawns along a wooden walkway. Just take off and explore. It's heavenly in spring, with gorgeous beds of tulips and daffodils and flowering trees.

QŪYUÀN GARDEN
GARDENS

(曲院风荷, Qūyuàn Fēnghé) On the northwest shore of West Lake, this lovely collection of gardens spreads out over numerous islets and is renowned for its fragrant spring lotus blossoms.

LÉIFĒNG PAGODA
PAGODA

(雷峰塔, Léifēng Tǎ; Nanshan Lu; 南山路; adult/child ¥40/20; ⊙8am-8.30pm Mar-Nov, to 5.30pm Dec-Feb) Topped with a golden spire, the eye-catching Léifēng Pagoda can be climbed for fine views of the lake. The original pagoda, built in AD 977, collapsed in 1924. During renovations in 2001, Buddhist scriptures written on silk were discovered in the foundations, along with other treasures. There's now an elevator and escalator to help visitors reach the top.

DRAGON WELL TEA VILLAGE
VILLAGE

(龙井问茶; Lóngjǐng Wènchá; ⊙8am-5.30pm) The lush, green scenery around this tea village up in the hills southwest of West Lake (p179) makes for a wonderful break from the bustle of Hangzhou. Visitors can wander through the village and up into the tea plantations themselves. During the spring, which is the best time to visit, straw-hatted workers can be seen picking the tea leaves by hand in the fields and baskets of the fresh leaves are left out to dry in the sun back in the village.

Stop into any of the casual restaurants and teahouses to taste the tea itself, which is renowned throughout China. It's expensive but has a fine, distinctive flavour.

Well-signposted walking trails lead off from the village into the surrounding hills.

JÌNGCÍ TEMPLE
BUDDHIST SITE

(净慈寺, Jìngcí Sì; Nanshan Lu; 南山路; ¥10; ⊙6am-5.15pm summer, 6.30am-4.45pm winter) The serene yet monastically active Chan (Zen) Jìngcí Temple was originally built in AD 954 and is now fully restored. The splendid first hall contains the massive, foreboding Heavenly Kings and an elaborate red and gold case encapsulating Milefo (the future Buddha) and Weituo (protector of the Buddhist temples and teachings). The main hall – known as the **Great Treasure Hall** – contains a vast seated effigy of Sakyamuni (Buddha).

Hunt down the awesome 1000-arm Guanyin (千手观音) in the Guanyin Pavilion, with her huge fan of arms. The temple's enormous bronze bell is struck 108 times for prosperity on the eve of the Lunar New Year. There's a vegetarian restaurant attached.

CHINA SILK MUSEUM
MUSEUM

(中国丝绸博物馆, Zhōngguó Sīchóu Bówùguǎn; 73-1 Yuhuangshan Lu; 玉皇山路73-1号; ⊙9am-5pm Tue-Sun, noon-5pm Mon) **FREE** Closed for renovation at the time of research, this fascinating museum previously housed excellent displays of silk samples, silk-making techniques, a room of looms with workers, a textile conservation gallery where you could watch conservationists in action, a superb gallery devoted to silks from Dūnhuáng, silk embroideries and exhibitions on silkworm anatomy. It is expected to reopen in August 2016.

HÁNGZHŌU OLD CITY WALL EXHIBITION HALL
MUSEUM

(杭州古城墙陈列馆, Hángzhōu Gǔchéngqiáng Chénlièguǎn; 1st fl, Qingchun Men, Qingchun Lu; 庆春路1号庆春门1楼; ⊙9am-4.30pm Wed-Mon) **FREE** Hángzhōu is famed for its lake, but the lake was once only a (glorious) appendage to a flourishing and magnificent city. The historic city of Hángzhōu – directly east of West Lake – has vanished, its monumental city wall long gone. This modest exhibition hall within the reconstructed gate of Qingchun Men celebrates the vanished bastion. For anyone keen to understand what Hángzhōu looked like until the early 20th century, there are photos and testaments to the old city (but no English translations).

The names of the city gates only survive in place names (such as Qingbo Men and Yongjin Men), but the old city of Hángzhōu (and its temples) has been buried beneath department stores and malls, leaving virtually nothing behind. This exhibition hall puts that disappearance in context. You may need to bang on the door to be let in.

CHINA NATIONAL TEA MUSEUM
MUSEUM

(中国茶叶博物馆, Zhōngguó Cháyè Bówùguǎn; http://english.teamuseum.cn; 88 Longjing Lu; 龙井路88号; ⊙8.30am-4.30pm Tue-Sun) **FREE** Not far into the hills of Hángzhōu, you'll begin to see fields of tea bushes planted in undulating rows, the setting for the China Tea Museum – 3.7 hectares of land dedicated to the art, cultivation and tasting of tea. Further up are several tea-producing villages, all of which harvest China's most famous variety of green tea, *lóngjǐng* (dragon well), named after the spring where the pattern in the water resembles a dragon.

Beautiful Tang dynasty tea sets are on display here and staff may invite you for a free tasting. Otherwise you can enjoy one of Hángzhōu's most famous teas at the adjoining restaurant.

Bus 27 will take you to the museum and the village.

QĪNGHÉFĀNG OLD STREET   STREET

(清河坊历史文化街, Qīnghéfāng Lìshǐ Wénhuà Jiē; Hefang Jie; 河坊街) At the south end of Zhongshan Zhonglu is this touristy, crowded and bustling pedestrian street, with makeshift puppet theatres, teahouses and gift and curio stalls, selling everything from stone teapots to boxes of *lóngxūtáng* (龙须糖; dragon whiskers sweets), ginseng and silk. It's also home to several traditional medicine shops, including the **Húqìngyú Táng Chinese Medicine Museum** (中药博物馆, Zhōngyào Bówùguǎn; 95 Dajing Xiang; ¥10; ☉8.30am-5pm), which is an actual dispensary and clinic.

The pedestrianised area continues on the adjoining Southern Song Imperial St (Nan Song Yu Jie; 南宋御街), which runs along one of Hángzhōu's historic thoroughfares and is also packed with shops and cafes.

XIĂOYÍNG ISLAND   ISLAND

(小瀛洲; Xiǎoyíng Zhōu) Wooden cruise boats shuttle visitors from a number of points on the banks of West Lake to the **Mid-Lake Pavilion** (湖心亭, Húxīn Tíng) and Xiǎoyíng Island, which has a fine central pavilion and 'nine-turn' causeway. From the island you can look over at the Three Pools Mirroring the Moon (p181), a string of three small towers in the water, each of which has five holes that release shafts of candlelight on the night of the Mooncake Festival in autumn.

HÁNGZHŌU BOTANICAL GARDEN   GARDENS

(杭州植物园, Hángzhōu Zhíwùyuán; www.hzbg.cn; 1 Taoyuan Ling; 桃源岭1号; ¥10; ☉7am-5pm) With huge tracts of towering bamboo, flowering magnolias and other delightful plants and trees, these vast gardens make for lovely walks to the northwest of West Lake. Sprawling over 610 acres, they're just as well-kept as you'd expect in a city that prides itself on its beautiful environment.

CONFUCIUS TEMPLE   CONFUCIAN TEMPLE

(文庙, Wénmiào; 8 Laodong Lu; 劳动巷8号; ☉9am-4.30pm Tue-Sun) **FREE** A repository of silence and calm, Hángzhōu's Confucius Temple is worth exploring for the main hall and the fabulous painted woodwork of its beams and ceiling. Seated within are imposing figures of Confucius and other Confucian philosophers, including Mencius. Stone sutras with Confucian, Buddhist and Taoist texts are on display.

✕ EATING

Hángzhōu has endless zones dedicated to the art of feasting – try **Gaoyin Jie**, a long sprawl of neon-lit restaurants or Zhongshan South Road Food Street. Many of the smarter restaurants around the West Lake

---

QIÁNTÁNG RIVER TIDAL BORE

An often spectacular natural phenomenon occurs every month on Hángzhōu's Qiántáng River (钱塘江), when the highest tides of the lunar cycle dispatch a wall of water – sometimes almost 9m tall – thundering along the narrow mouth of the river from Hángzhōu Bay, at up to 40km/hr. Occasionally sweeping astonished sightseers away and luring bands of intrepid surfers, this awesome tidal bore (钱塘江潮; *qiántáng jiāngcháo*) is the world's largest and can be viewed from the riverbank in Hángzhōu, but one of the best places to witness the action is on the north side of the river at **Yánguān** (盐官), a delightful ancient town about 38km northeast of Hángzhōu.

The most popular viewing time is during the International Qiántáng River Tide Observing Festival, on the 18th day of the eighth month of the lunar calendar (the same day as the mid-autumn festival), which usually falls in September or October. You can however see it throughout the year when the highest tide occurs at the beginning and middle of each lunar month; access to the park in Yánguān for viewing the tide is ¥25. The Hángzhōu Tourist Information Centre (p179) can give you upcoming tide times. To make it a day trip, a through-ticket (¥100) is available in Yánguān to explore the charming historic temples and buildings of the town.

Take a train (¥92, 35 minutes) fom Hángzhōu East to Hǎiníng (海宁) and change to bus 109 (¥10, 25 minutes) to Yánguān.

itself also offer good-value and interesting meals.

★**GREEN TEA RESTAURANT** HÁNGZHŌU $
(绿茶, Lǜchá; 250 Jiefang Lu, 解放路250号; mains from ¥20; ⏰10.30am-11pm; Ⓜ Longxiangqiao) Often packed, this excellent Hángzhōu restaurant has superb food. With a bare-brick finish and rows of clay teapots, the low-lit dining room is sleek and trendy. Prices are surprisingly low, with the signature fish-head dish the most expensive thing on the menu at ¥48. Eggplant claypot and a Cantonese bread and ice-cream dessert are also sensational.

Ordering can get complicated: scan the QR code on the table and select dishes direct through the menu that will load up on your phone. If you're having trouble, staff are happy to help.

★**GRANDMA'S HOME** HÁNGZHŌU $
(外婆家, Wàipójiā; 3 Hubin Lu; 湖滨路3号; mains ¥15-35; ⏰lunch & dinner; Ⓜ Longxiangqiao) There's no end to the hype about this restaurant, which now has branches across the whole country, with eager diners constantly clustering outside. It almost lives up to its reputation, with low prices and generous portions but dishes do vary enormously in quality. The braised pork and tea-scented chicken are both good bets to get a taste of classic Hangzhou flavours.

Take a paper ticket when you arrive and be prepared to wait a long time for a table.

NAN FANG MI ZONG DUMPLING $
(Youdian Lu; 邮电路; per bun ¥2; ⏰6.30am-6.30pm) Who would have thought the humble *baozi* could taste so good? The fluffy steamed buns served at this small stall near the Renhe Hotel building are simply huge, and come with either pork or a sweet bean filling. The pork ones are sensational, with top-quality meat and a rich gravy. Queues stretch right down the street in the morning.

ZHONGSHAN SOUTH ROAD FOOD STREET MARKET $
(中山南路美食街, Zhōng Shān Nán Lù Diàn; Zhongshan South Rd; 中山南路美食街; ⏰5.30pm-late) Hángzhōu is spoilt for choice when it comes to foodie streets, and this stretch of Zhongshan Nan Rd (starting at the Drum Tower) is an absolute delight. Causal sit-down restaurants line the road and stalls that run along the middle of the road sell everything from fresh seafood and deep-fried insects to Beggar's Chicken and the absolute stinkiest of stinky tofu.

Plastic tables and chairs cover the pavement area, often with giant beer dispensers in the centre.

YÍHÉ ZÁNGXIĀNG BEEF NOODLES NOODLES $
(伊禾藏香牛肉面, Yíhé Zángxiāng Niúròu Miàn; 238 Yan'an Lu; 延安路238号; noodles from ¥19; ⏰6.30am-11.30pm) A superb lunch stop, where the restaurant's namesake – beef noodles – is a must-order. These are done Lanzhou-style (read: magnificently fiery) and the meat is served separately so you can drop it in yourself. Long spacious tables looking out onto bustling Yan'an Lu make this a great stop for families or solo diners, and service is efficient and friendly.

BÌ FĒNG TÁNG CANTONESE $
(避风塘, 256 Jiefang Lu; 解放路256号; mains ¥25-45; ⏰10am-9pm Sun-Thu, to 10pm Fri & Sat; Ⓜ Ding'an Rd or Longxiangqiao) An oldie but a goodie: the dim sum is reliably good at this popular restaurant chain right in the action by West Lake. The menu is wide-ranging, but some of the better Canto classics on offer include fresh prawn crystal dumplings (¥29) and honey-glazed BBQ pork (¥38).

Downstairs is often noisy and busy but it's possible to nab a quieter table upstairs. If the waiting staff hand you a menu chit in Chinese, ask for the picture menu (图片菜单; *túpiàn càidān*).

INNOCENT AGE BOOK BAR CHINESE $
(纯真年代书吧, Chúnzhēn Niándài Shūbā; 8 Baochuta Qian Rd; 保俶塔前山路8号; dishes from ¥22; ⏰9.30am-midnight) You couldn't ask for a prettier setting than this cafe, set just down the slope of Baoshi Hill from Baochu Pagoda. Indoors, there's a quiet reading-room atmosphere and the shelves are full of books. Outside is a glorious terrace overlooking the West Lake. Snacks, cakes, tea and coffee are available or for good-value fuel before you continue your walk, go for a huge and flavoursome bowl of Hangzhou beef noodles.

XIEXIE TEA & COFFEE CAFE $
(谢谢咖啡, Xiè Xie Kā Fēi; 180 Nanshan Rd; 南山路180号; mains ¥47-67; ⏰9am-midnight; 🛜) A beautifully airy three-storey cafe, Xiexie looks out onto the treetops of the park over the road and is a great spot to unwind over a cup of tea or coffee. A young crowd armed with phones, laptops and tablets sprawl on

comfy sofas that are never more than arm's reach from a plug socket.

Salads, pizza and noodles are available, and the cafe also does a slap-up Western breakfast. Grab a seat on the open air roof terrace when weather permits.

🍷 DRINKING & NIGHTLIFE

Hángzhōu's nightlife scene is changing rapidly, with old dives bulldozed and new bars springing up all the time. Many late-night venues offer decent home-brewed and imported beer, wine and cocktails, and there's plenty of live music to enjoy.

⭐ JZ CLUB   CLUB
(黄楼, Huáng Lóu; ☑0571 8702 8298; www.jzclub.cc; 6 Liuying Lu, by 266 Nanshan Lu; 柳营路6号; ☺7pm-2.30am) The folk that brought you JZ Club in Shànghǎi have the live jazz scene sewn up in Hángzhōu with this neat three-floor venue in a historic building near West Lake. There are three live jazz sets nightly, with music kicking off at 9.15pm (until 12.30am). There's no admission charge, but you'll need to reserve a seat on Fridays and Saturdays. Smokers get to go upstairs.

MIDTOWN BREWERY   GASTROPUB
(1st fl, Shangri-la Hotel, 6 Changshou Lu; 长寿路6号杭州城中香格里拉大酒店1楼) The craft-beer craze has certainly hit Hangzhou and the standout place to sample some top-notch craft beers is Midtown Brewery. Housed in the Shangri-La hotel, the beers are brewed on-site and are genuinely outstanding. If you need convincing, order the tasting pad-dle (¥99) of seven samplers, including pale ale, porter and stout. Service is smooth and the setting smart and contemporary.

REGGAE BAR   BAR
(131 Xueyuan Rd; 学院路131号; ☺6.30pm-late) All the staples of a good reggae bar – smoky corners, Jamaican flags, Bob Marley posters and soft tie-dye fabric covering the seats – are present and correct at this boozy outpost. There's regular live music downstairs, shisha pipes upstairs and a surprising drinks menu that lists Beer Laos and Newcastle Brown Ale. The crowd is young and studenty.

EUDORA STATION   BAR
(亿多瑞站, Yìduōruìzhàn; 101-107 Nanshan Lu; 南山路101-107号; ☺9.30am-2am) A fab location by West Lake, roof terrace, outside seating and great happy-hour deals conspire to make this welcoming watering hole a solid choice. There's sports TV, live music, a good range of imported beers, and barbecues fire up on the roof terrace in the warmer months.

🛍 SHOPPING

Hángzhōu is famed for its tea, in particular *lóngjǐng* green tea, as well as silk – both can be snapped up cheaply in the city. The Wushan Lu Night Market, between Youdian Lu (邮电路) and Renhe Lu (仁和路) and Qīnghéfāng Old St are both enjoyable places to wander and pick up cheap souvenirs.

HÁNGZHŌU SILK CITY   SILK
(丝绸城, Sīchóu Shìchǎng; 253 Xinhua Lu; 新华路253号; ☺8am-5pm) Hángzhōu is famous for its silks and there are certainly bar-

---

HÁNGZHŌU BY BIKE

The best way to rent a bike is to use the **Hángzhōu Bike Hire Scheme** (☑0571 8533 1122; www.hzzxc.com.cn; ¥200 deposit, ¥100 credit; ☺6.30am-9pm Apr-Oct, 6am-9pm Nov-Mar). Stations (2700 in total) are dotted in large numbers around the city, in what is one of the world's largest networks. Apply at one of the booths at numerous bike stations near West Lake; you will need your passport as ID. Fill in a form and you will receive a swipe card, then swipe the pad at one of the docking stations till you get a steady green light and can free a bike.

Return bikes to any other station (ensure the bike is properly docked before leaving it). The first hour on each bike is free, so if you switch bikes within the hour, the rides are free. The second hour on the same bike is ¥1, the third is ¥2 and after that it's ¥3 per hour. Your deposit and unused credit are refunded to you when you return your swipe card (check when it should be returned as this can vary). Note you cannot return bikes outside booth operating hours as the swipe units deactivate (you will be charged a whole night's rental).

WEST LAKE HILLS WALK

For a manageable and breezy trek into the forested hills above West Lake, walk up a lane called Qixialing, immediately west of the **Yuè Fēi Temple** (岳庙, Yuè Fēi Mù; Beishan Lu; ¥25; ⊙7.30am-5.30pm). The road initially runs past the temple's west wall to enter the shade of towering trees, with stone steps leading you up. At **Zǐyún Cave** the hill levels out and the road forks; take the right-hand fork towards the Bàopú Taoist Temple, 1km further, and the Bǎochù Pagoda. At the top of the steps, turn left and, passing the **Sunrise Terrace**, again bear left. Down the steps, look out for the tiled roofs and yellow walls of the charming **Bàopú Taoist Temple** (抱朴道院, Bàopú Dàoyuàn; ¥5; ⊙6am-5pm) to your right; head right along a path to reach it.

Exit from the back of the temple and turn left towards the Bǎochù Pagoda; after hitting a confluence of three paths, take the middle track towards and up **Toad Hill** (蛤蟆峰, Hámá Fēng), which affords supreme views over the lake, before squeezing through a gap between huge boulders to meet the **Bǎochù Pagoda** (保俶塔, Bǎochù Tǎ) rising ahead. Restored many times, the seven-storey grey brick pagoda was last rebuilt in 1933, although its spire tumbled off in the 1990s. Continue on down and pass through a **páilou** (牌楼) – or decorative arch – erected during the Republic (with some of its characters scratched off) to a series of stone-carved **Ming dynasty effigies**, all of which were vandalised in the tumultuous 1960s, save two effigies on the right.

Turn left here and walk a short distance to some steps heading downhill to your right past the remarkable weathered remains of a colossal stone **Buddha** by the cliff-face (with square niches cut in him) – all that remains of the **Big Buddha Temple** (大佛寺, Dàfó Sì). Continue on down to Beishan Lu.

---

gains to be found in this seven-storey market. You'll have to work hard to get them, though. Head straight for the 5th and 6th floors (lower levels just sell regular clothes) to find scarves, slinky nightwear, dresses, *qìpáo* (traditional Chinese sheath dresses) and other silk items. If you haggle with persistence vendors will usually let you bargain them down by around 30%.

There's plenty of polyester in the mix at this market, so examine material carefully before you make a purchase.

WUSHAN LU NIGHT MARKET   MARKET
(吴山路夜市, Wúshān Lù Yèshì; Huixing Lu; 惠兴路; ⊙7-10.30pm) Wushan Lu Night Market doesn't have too much to offer by way of interesting souvenirs, but it's still a pleasant place to stroll for half an hour or so. Stalls sell knock-off cosmetics and bags, cheap clothes, shoes, plastic jewellery and other knick-knacks to an excited crowd of mostly teenagers. Get the gloves off and haggle hard if something catches your eye.

Better still, spend your cash at the street-food stalls that line Renhe Lu, where you can pick up skewers of spicy beancurd, seasoned sweetcorn, noodles, fried dumplings and a vast range of other snacks.

The market is located on Huixing Lu (惠兴路), between Youdian Lu (邮电路) and Renhe Lu (仁和路)

LÌ XĪNG PLAZA   MALL
(利星名品广场, Lì Xīng Míngpǐn Guǎngchǎng; 124 Pinghai Lu; 平海路124号; ⊙9am-10pm) One of a number of slick, modern shopping malls to pop up close to the West Lake. Find branches of Watson's, H&M, Muji, Nike, Zara and other international brands here. There are a handful of lacklustre eateries downstairs.

HUÍCHŪN TÁNG   PHARMACY
(回春堂; 117 Hefang Jie; ⊙7.15am-8.30pm) One of the country's oldest traditional Chinese medicine (TCM) clinics, Huíchūn Táng is still a a fully functioning business with TCM doctors on-site and dried herbs, powders and tonics all available to buy. Help yourself to free herbal tea from the dispenser and sip as you browse the intriguing jars. No English is spoken.

🏃 SPORTS & ACTIVITIES

WEST LAKE CRUISE BOATS   BOATING
(游船; Yóuchuán; Hubin Lu; 湖滨路; return adult/child ¥70/35; ⊙7am-5pm) Wooden cruise boats shuttle from a number of points around West Lake (including Gushan Island, Yue Fei Temple, Red Carp Pond and No 1 Park at the south end of Hubin Lu) past

the Mid-Lake Pavilion (p184) to Xiǎoyíng Island (p184), which has a fine central pavilion and 'nine-turn' causeway. Boats depart either every 20 minutes or when full.

From Xiǎoyíng Island you can look over at the Three Pools Mirroring the Moon (p181), a string of three small towers in the water, each of which has five holes that release shafts of candlelight on the night of the Mooncake Festival in mid-autumn. Your ticket allows you to take another boat on to Gushan Island or to any of the other cruise-boat docks.

If you want to contemplate the moon at a slower pace, hire one of the smaller six or 11 person **boats** (小船, *xiǎo chuán*; small/large boats ¥150/180) rowed by a boatsperson for about an hour. Look for them along the causeways. Self-rowing boats are also available, but foreign tourists are not allowed access these without a Chinese escort.

🛏 SLEEPING

HOFANG INTERNATIONAL YOUTH HOSTEL
HOSTEL **$**

(荷方国际青年旅社, Héfāng Guójì Qīngnián Lüshè; ☑0571 8706 3299; 67 Dajing Xiang; 大井巷67号; dm ¥55, s/d ¥188/288; ✳@🛜) Pleasantly tucked away from the noise down a historic alley off Qīnghéfāng Old Street (p184), this hostel has an excellent location and exudes a pleasant and calm ambience, with attractive rooms, the cheapest of which come with tatami. Note that prices go up by between ¥30 and ¥60 on weekends and holidays. The adjoining hostel cafe is a cosy place to check emails with a coffee.

WEST LAKE 7 SERVICE APARTMENTS
APARTMENT **$$**

(西湖柒号酒店公寓, Xīhú Qīhào Jiǔdiàn Gōngyù; 1 Yuewang Lu; 岳王路1号; d ¥320) These large and comfortable serviced apartments offer excellent value for money, with facilities including a washing machine, kitchen and surprisingly speedy wi-fi speeds. The location is not bad, set right next to the Wushan Lu Night Market (p187), and just a few block's walk from the West Lake.

FOUR SEASONS HOTEL HÁNGZHŌU
HOTEL **$$$**

(杭州西子湖四季酒店, Hángzhōu Xīzihú Sìjì Jiǔdiàn; ☑0571 8829 8888; www.fourseasons.com/hangzhou; 5 Lingyin Lu, 灵隐路5号; d

¥3500, ste from ¥6500; ➋✳@🛜🏊) More of a resort than a hotel, the fabulous 78-room, two-pool Four Seasons enjoys a seductive position in lush grounds next to West Lake. Low-storey buildings and three private villas echo traditional China, a sensation amplified by the osmanthus trees, ornamental shrubs, ponds and general tranquillity.

Gorgeously and very spacious ground-floor deluxe premier rooms have access to a garden; rooms have lovely bathrooms, walk-in wardrobes and hugely inviting beds. The infinity pool alongside West Lake is a dream, as is the outstanding spa. Staff are welcoming and helpful.

Sūzhōu

....

Explore

Historically, Sūzhōu (苏州) was synonymous with high culture and elegance, and generations of artists, scholars, writers and high society in China were drawn by its exquisite art forms and the delicate beauty of its gardens. Like all modern Chinese towns, Sūzhōu has unfortunately endured much destruction of its heritage and its replacement with largely arbitrary chunks of modern architecture.

Having said that, the city still retains enough pockets of charm to warrant two to three days' exploration on foot or by bike. And the gardens, Sūzhōu's main attraction, are a symphonic combination of rocks, water, trees and pavilions that reflects the Chinese appreciation of balance and harmony. Adding to the charm are some excellent museums, surviving canal scenes, pagodas and humpbacked bridges. The gardens in particular can get busy, so avoid visiting at the weekend or during public holidays, if possible.

....

The Best...
➡ **Sight** Sūzhōu Museum (p189)
➡ **Place to Eat** Wúmén Rénjiā (p193)
➡ **Place to Drink** Bookworm (p194)

....

Getting There & Away

Train Nánjīng–Shànghǎi express G line trains (26 to 46 minutes) stop at either the centrally located Sūzhōu Train Station (苏州站; Sūzhōu Zhàn) or Sūzhōu North Train Station (苏州北站; Sūzhōu Běizhàn), 12km north of the city centre.

Bus Services from Shànghǎi (1½ hours, every 30 minutes) run to the South Long-distance Bus Station. Buses connect Sūzhōu North Long-distance Bus Station with Shànghǎi's Hóngqiáo Airport (¥53) and Pǔdōng International Airport (¥84) frequently between 6am and 5.30pm.

Getting Around

Bicycle You can rent bikes from most hostels.

Metro Line 1 runs along Ganjiang Lu, connecting Mùdú in the southwest with Zhongnan Jie in the east and running through the Culture & Expo Centre and Times Square, in the Sūzhōu Industrial Park. Line 2 runs north–south from Sūzhōu North Train Station to Baodaiqiao-nan in the south, via Sūzhōu Train Station.

Bus Y5 heads around the western and eastern sides of the city and has a stop at Sūzhōu Museum. Y2 travels from Tiger Hill, Pán Gate and along Shiquan Jie. Y1 and Y4 run the length of Renmin Lu. Bus 80 runs between the two train stations.

Need to Know

➡**Area Code** ☑0512

➡**Location** 85km from Shànghǎi

➡**Tourist office** (苏州旅游咨询中心, Sūzhōu Lǚyóu Zīxún Zhōngxīn; ☑0512 6530 5887; 101 Daichengqiao Lu; 带城桥路101号)

◉ SIGHTS

High-season prices apply from March to early May and September to October. Gardens and museums stop selling tickets 30 minutes before closing, and are best visited early in the mornings before crowds arrive. The gardens were not designed for tour groups, so don't expect too much zen-like tranquillity.

SŪZHŌU MUSEUM   MUSEUM

(苏州博物馆, Sūzhōu Bówùguǎn; 204 Dongbei Jie; 东北街204号; audio guide ¥30; ☺9am-5pm; 🚌Y5) **FREE** This cubist/geometric IM Pei–designed triumph takes a modern interpretation of a Sūzhōu garden, with its

confluence of water, bamboo and straight lines, and mixes it with a fascinating array of jade, ceramics, wooden carvings, textiles and other displays, all labelled with good and informative English captions. Look out for the boxwood statue of Avalokiteshvara (Guanyin), dating from the republican period. No flip-flops.

HUMBLE ADMINISTRATOR'S
GARDEN   GARDENS

(拙政园, Zhuōzhèng Yuán; 178 Dongbei Jie; 东北街178号; high/low season ¥90/70, audio guide free; ☺7.30am-5.30pm) The largest of Sūzhōu's gardens, the Humble Administrator's Garden is often considered to be the most impressive, but its fame draws in constant crowds, so get here early in the morning if you can. First built in 1509, this 5.2-hectare garden is clustered with water features, a museum, a teahouse, zigzagging bridges, bamboo groves and fragrant lotus ponds, along with at least 10 pavilions with poetic names such as 'Listening to the Sound of Rain' and 'Faraway Looking' pavilions.

SŪZHŌU ART MUSEUM   MUSEUM

(苏州美术馆, Sūzhōu Měishùguǎn; 2075 Renmin Lu; 人民路2075号; ☺9am-5pm Tue-Sun; 🚇Sūzhōu Train Station) **FREE** A dazzling use of daylight and design merges in this new museum, hung with contemporary landscapes, calligraphy and modern art that stands out boldly from a seemingly infinite white space. In a nod to the local vernacular, the interior composition includes a lovely courtyard, sprouting bamboo. The museum is an element of a large complex that also includes the Sūzhōu Cultural Center and a theatre.

SŪZHŌU SILK MUSEUM   MUSEUM

(苏州丝绸博物馆, Sūzhōu Sīchóu Bówùguǎn; 2001 Renmin Lu; 人民路2001号; ☺9am-5pm; 🚇Sūzhōu Train Station) **FREE** By the 13th century Sūzhōu was the place for silk production and weaving, and the Sūzhōu Silk Museum houses fascinating exhibitions detailing the history of Sūzhōu's 4000-year-old silk industry. Exhibits include a section on silk-weaving techniques and silk fashion through the dynasties, while you can amble among mulberry shrubs outdoors. You can also see functioning looms and staff at work on, say, a large brocade.

PINGJIANG LU   STREET

(平江路; 🚇Lindun Lu or Xiangmen) While most of the town canals have been sealed

Sūzhōu

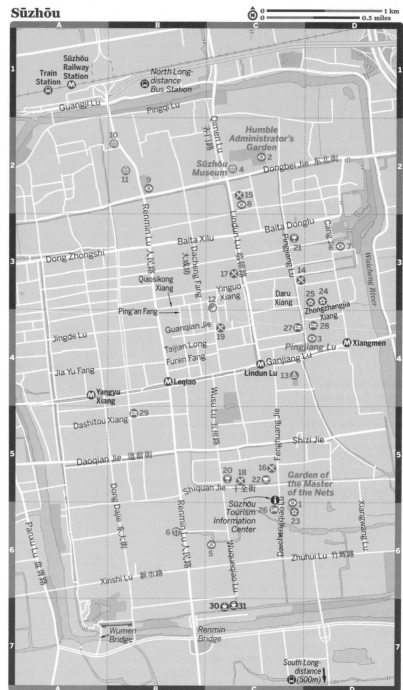

0   1 km
0   0.5 miles

Train Station

Sūzhōu Railway Station

North Long-distance Bus Station

Guangji Lu

Pingqi Lu

Qimen Lu 齐门路

Humble Administrator's Garden

10

11

9

Sūzhōu Museum

4

2

Dongbei Jie 东北街

15
8

Baita Xilu

Lindun Lu 临顿路

Baita Donglu

Pingjiang Lu

Cang Jie

21

7

Watcheng River

Dong Zhongshi

Renmin Lu 人民路

Dacheng Fang 大成坊

14

Qiaosikong Xiang

17

Yinguo Xiang

Daru Xiang

25 24

Zhongzhangjia Xiang

12

Ping'an Fang

Jingde Lu

Guanqian Jie

19

27 28

3

Pingjiang Lu

Xiangmen

Taijian Long

Furen Fang

Ganjiang Lu

Jia Yu Fang

Lindun Lu

Leqiao

13

Yangyu Xiang

Wusu Lu 五卅路

Dashitou Xiang

29

Fenghuang Jie

Shizi Jie

Daoqian Jie 道前街

20 18

16

22

Garden of the Master of the Nets

Dong Dajie 东大街

Renmin Lu 人民路

Shiquan Jie 十全街

Sūzhōu Tourism Information Center

26

1

23

Xiangwang Lu

6

5

Wuquqiao Lu

Daichengqiao Lu

Zhuhui Lu 竹辉路

Xinshi Lu 新市路

Panxu Lu 盘胥路

30 31

Wumen Bridge

Renmin Bridge

South Long-distance (500m)

Sūzhōu

and paved into roads, the pedestrianised Pingjiang Lu offers clues to the Sūzhōu of yesteryear. On the eastern side of the city, this canal-side road has whitewashed local houses, many now converted to guest-houses, teahouses or trendy cafes selling overpriced beverages, sitting comfortably side-by-side. Duck down some of the side streets that jut out from the main path for a glimpse at slow-paced local life. It's a lovely place for a stroll.

Along the main drag it's all rice wine, Tibetan trinkets, cigar sellers, fried potatoes, cake, dumplings and ice-cream vendors.

TWIN PAGODAS   BUDDHIST TEMPLE, PAGODA
(双塔, Shuāng Tǎ; Dinghuisi Xiang; 定慧寺巷; ¥8; ◷8am-4.30pm; Ⓜ Lindun Lu) Beautifully en-hanced with flowering magnolias in spring, this delightful courtyard and former temple contains a pair of sublime pagodas, which don't often come in couples. It's one of the more relaxing, peaceful and composed parts of town, so come here for a break. It's also home to the small and little-visited **Sūzhōu Ancient Stone Carving Art Museum**.

NORTH TEMPLE PAGODA   PAGODA
(北寺塔, Běisì Tǎ; 1918 Renmin Lu; 人民路1918号; ¥25; ◷7.45am-5pm) The tallest pagoda south of the Yangzi is a beauty, dominating the northern end of Renmin Lu. The nine-storey pagoda is an element of Bào'ēn Temple (报恩寺, Bào'ēn Sì) and you can climb it for sweep-ing views of hazy modern-day Sūzhōu.

The temple complex goes back 1700 years and was originally a residence; the current reincarnation dates to the 17th century. Off to one side is **Nánmù Guānyīn Hall** (楠木观音殿, Nánmù Guānyīn Diàn), which was rebuilt in the Ming dynasty with some fea-tures imported from elsewhere.

The Chinese plaque outside the hall intones '一塵不染' ('spotless'), revealing Guanyin's state of unblemished purity. At the rear is a thoughtfully composed **garden and rockery**, with a teahouse. Within the temple compound is also the rather unu-sual **Seven Buddha Hall**.

GARDEN OF THE MASTER OF THE NETS   GARDENS
(网师园, Wǎngshī Yuán; high/low season ¥30/20; ◷7.30am-5pm) Off Shiquan Jie, this pocket-sized garden is considered one of Sūzhōu's best preserved. Laid out in the 12th cen-tury, it went to seed and was later restored in the 18th century as part of the home of a retired official turned fisherman (hence the name). A striking feature is the use of space: the labyrinth of courtyards, with windows framing other parts of the garden, is ingeniously designed to give the illusion of a much larger area.

The central section is the main garden and the western section is an inner garden with a courtyard containing the master's study. Trivia nuts note: the Peony Study was used as the model for the Astor Court and Ming Garden in the Museum of Modern Art, New York.

In the warmer months (March to November), music performances (¥100) are held nightly here from 7.30pm.

There are two ways to the entry gate, with English signs and souvenir stalls marking the way: you can enter from the alley on Shiquan Jie; or via Kuojiatou Xiang (阔家头巷), an alley off Daichengqiao Lu.

TEMPLE OF MYSTERY   TAOIST TEMPLE

(玄妙观; Xuánmiào Guàn; Guanqian Jie; 观前街; ¥10; ⊗7.30am-5pm; M Lindun Lu or Leqiao) Lashed by electronic music from the shops alongside, the Taoist Temple of Mystery stands in what was once Sūzhōu's old bazaar, a rowdy entertainment district with travelling performers, acrobats and actors. The temple dates from 1181 and is the sole surviving example of Song architecture in Sūzhōu. The complex contains several elaborately decorated halls, including the huge **Sānqīng Diàn** (三清殿, Three Purities Hall), which is supported by 60 pillars and capped by a double roof with upturned eaves.

The hall is home to three huge statues of **Yuqing**, **Shangqing** and **Taiqing** (the Three Purities); look out for the **one-horned ox** (独角神牛, *dújiǎo shénniú*) that conveyed Laozi on his travels to the West; there are also shrines to Tianhou (protective Goddess of seafarers), clothed in a pink robe, and the omnipotent Jade Emperor. Note the antique carved **balustrade** around the hall, which dates to the Five Dynasties period (10th century). The blank **Wordless Stele** stands just east of the hall.

BLUE WAVE PAVILION   GARDENS

(沧浪亭, Cānglàng Tíng; Renmin Lu; 人民路; high/low season ¥20/15; ⊗7.30am-5pm) Originally the home of a prince, the oldest garden in Sūzhōu was first built in the 11th century, and has been repeatedly rebuilt since. Instead of attracting hordes of tourists, the wild, overgrown garden around the Blue Wave Pavilion is one of those where the locals actually go to chill and enjoy a leisurely stroll. Lacking a northern wall, the garden creates the illusion of space by borrowing scenes from the outside.

A double veranda leads along a canal from the front pavilion. From the outer path, you'll see green space inside and from the inner path you can see views of the water. Look out for a 'temple' whose dark walls are carved with the portraits of more than 500 sages, and the 'pure fragrance house' has some impressive furniture made from the gnarled roots of banyan trees.

CONFUCIAN TEMPLE   CONFUCIAN TEMPLE

(文庙, Wénmiào; 613 Renmin Lu; 人民路613号; ⊗6.30am-4pm) **FREE** A haven of solitude and an oasis of peace in a busy town, the Confucian Temple is adorned with several ancient (one is 830 years old) gingkos and rows of potted bonsai trees, plus a statue of the temperate sage. The temple highlight is the fabulous stelae carved during the Southern Song dynasty (1137–1279). One features a fascinating map of old Sūzhōu, detailing the canal system (much now paved over and blocked), old roads and the city walls.

There's also an astronomy stele from 1190 – one of the oldest astronomy charts in the world.

COUPLE'S GARDEN   GARDENS

(耦园, Ǒu Yuán; 6 Xiaoxinqiao Xiang; 小新桥巷6号; high/low season ¥20/15; ⊗8am-4.30pm; M Xiangmen) The tranquil Couple's Garden is off the main tourist route and sees slightly fewer visitors than the other gardens, and its pond, courtyards and garden features are quite lovely.

WEST GARDEN TEMPLE   GARDENS

(西园寺, Xīyuán Sì; Xiyuan Lu; 西园路; ¥25; ⊗8am-5pm; 🚌Y1, Y3) This magnificent temple, with its mustard-yellow walls and gracefully curved eaves, was burnt to the ground during the Taiping Rebellion and rebuilt in the late 19th century. Greeting you as you enter the stunning **Arhat Hall** (罗汉堂; Luóhàn Táng) is an amazing four-faced and thousand-armed statue of Guanyin. Beyond lie mesmerising and slightly unnerving rows of 500 glittering *luóhàn* (arhats; monks who have achieved enlightenment and passed to nirvana at death) statues, each unique and near life-size.

Luóhàn usually only appear in two rows of nine on either side of the main temple, equalling 18 in total, but on occasion – and in noteworthy temples – they can appear in a huge multitude. A vegetarian restaurant at the temple serves noodles and other simple meat-free fare. The temple is 400m west

EVENING BOAT TOURS

Evening boat tours wind their way around the outer canal leaving nightly from 6pm to 8.30pm (¥120, 55 minutes, half-hourly). The trips, usually with *píngtán* (singing and storytelling art form sung in the Sūzhōu dialect) performance on board, are a great way to experience old Sūzhōu, passing Pán Gate and heading up to Cháng Gate (in the west of the city wall). Remember to bring bug repellent as the mosquitoes are tenacious. Tickets can be bought at the **Tourist Boat Wharf** (游船码头; Yóuchuán Mǎtóu) down the alley east of Rénmín Bridge, which shares the same quarters with the **Grand Canal Boats** (划船售票处; Huáchuán Shòupiàochù) ticket office. Buses 27 or 94 run to the wharf.

of the Garden to Linger In. Take Y1 or Y3 from the train station.

LION'S GROVE GARDEN
GARDENS

(狮子林, Shīzi Lín; 23 Yuanlin Lu; high/low season ¥30/20; ⊗7.30am-5.30pm) Constructed in 1342 by the Buddhist monk Tianru to commemorate his master, who lived on Lion Cliff on Zhèjiāng's Tiānmú Mountain, this garden's curiously shaped rocks were meant to resemble lions, protectors of the Buddhist faith. This garden can get pretty crowded, so try to get here early if you can.

 EATING

In reflection of its busy and year-round tourist traffic, Sūzhōu has some excellent restaurants, both Chinese and international. The area around Guanqian Jie, especially down the road from the Temple of Mystery, is stuffed with choices, but you'll find good options dotted all over the town.

YĂBA SHĒNGJIĀN
DUMPLING $

(哑巴生煎; 12 Lindun Lu; 临顿路12号; 8 dumplings ¥13; ⊗5.30am-6.30pm) With great clouds of steam rising from the kitchen, this 60-year-old institution mainly flogs noodles but its handmade *shēngjiān bāo* (生煎包; pan-fried dumplings), stuffed with juicy pork, are outstanding and flavour-packed. During lunch hours expect to queue for 30 minutes just to order! Protocol: get a ticket, join the line, snag a table and enjoy.

Head to the side for chilli oil and soy sauce. Watch out for the meat juice, it can fly. There's more room and a breeze through the window upstairs. No English menu.

PINGVON
TEAHOUSE $

(品芳, Pǐnfāng; 94 Pingjiang Lu; 平江路94号; dishes from ¥6) Although often busy, this seriously cute little teahouse finds itself perched beside one of Sūzhōu's most popular canal-side streets, serving up excellent dumplings and delicate little morsels on small plates. The tea rooms upstairs are more atmospheric. There are all sorts of bites, from pine nuts and pumpkin soup (¥6) to crab *xiǎolóngbāo* (steamed dumplings; ¥10 a portion). Picture menu.

Order by ticking what you want on a paper menu and handing it over.

ZHŪHÓNGXĪNG
NOODLES $

(朱鸿兴; Taijian Long; mains from ¥15; ⊗6.45am-8.45pm; ⒨Lindun Lu) Popular with locals, this red-wood-furniture-bedecked eatery, with several branches across town, has a long history and wholesome, filling noodles – try the scrummy *xiàrén miàn* (虾仁面; noodles with baby shrimps) or the *xuěcài ròusīmiàn* (雪菜肉丝面; meat and vegetable noodles).

XĪSHÈNGYUÁN
DUMPLINGS $

(熙盛源; 43 Fenghuang Jie; 凤凰街43号; dumplings from ¥8) Crowds pay and gather near the entrance to wait for the steaming fresh *xiǎolóng bāo* (小龙包; soup dumplings) to come out of the kitchen. If you don't want to jostle, grab a seat and order several other great dishes including assorted *húntūn* (馄饨, dumplings; from ¥8).

WÚMÉN RÉNJIĀ
JIANGSU $$

(吴门人家; ☑0512 6728 8041; 31 Panru Xiang; 潘儒巷31号; dishes from ¥30; ⊗6.30-9.30am, 11am-1.30pm & 5-8.30pm) Hidden in a quiet alley north of Lion's Grove Garden, this lovely traditional courtyard restaurant attracts a mix of locals and visitors for its subtly flavoured Sūzhōu cooking. Service can sometimes be a bit slow, but the setting (with traditional Chinese music) is superlative. Reservations essential.

Try the ever-popular squirrel fish or the kung pao chicken (宫保雞丁, *gōngbăo jīdīng*; spicy chicken with chilli and peanuts).

YÀKÈXĪ   UIGHUR $$

(亚克西酒楼, Yàkèxī Jiŭlóu; 768 Shiquan Jie, 十全街768号; mains from ¥30; ◷10.30am-midnight) The rather gaudy Uighur kitsch atmosphere is entertaining and the Xīnjiāng staples – lamb kebabs (¥2.50) and *nang* bread (flat bread; ¥3) – all tasty. Round it off with a bottle of SinKiang beer (¥10) or a sour milk drink (¥8) and dream of Kashgar. No time to sit down? The lamb kebabs are grilled just outside.

🍷 DRINKING & NIGHTLIFE

There are stacks of trendy cafe-bars scattered along Pingjiang Lu. A gem or two survives, but the nightlife scene on Shiquan Jie has fizzled out as most of the expats' watering holes have moved to the soulless Sūzhōu Industrial Park, 9km east of the centre of town (get there on the metro).

★BOOKWORM   BAR

(老书虫, Lăo Shūchóng; ☑0512 6526 4720; www. suzhoubookworm.com; 77 Gunxiu Fang; 滚绣坊 77号; ◷11am-1am Mon-Fri, 10am-1am Sat & Sun) Běijīng's excellent Bookworm wormed its way down to Sūzhōu, serving as a kind of comfy cultural hub, library, bookshop and cafe. The food is crowd-pleasing (lots of Western options) and the cold beers include Tsingtao and Erdinger. There are readings, live music, an open mic and you can borrow or buy books. Ask about its literary festival, held in March.

★LOCKE PUB   BAR

(240 Pingjiang Lu; 平江路240号; ◷10am-midnight) Any place that plays Tom Waits is good in our book and we're also partial to friendly labradors. This charming spot has ample space, comfy sofas, homemade ice cream, a whole wall of English books, hot whisky, Leffe, Corona and Guinness, all set in a traditional building along Pingjiang Lu.

PINGTAN TEAHOUSE   TEAHOUSE

(评弹茶馆, Píngtán Cháguăn; 2nd fl, 626 Shiquan Jie; 十全街626号2楼) *Píngtán* enthusiasts get together here to keep the traditions alive. The music usually starts between 8pm

and 10pm. Order some tea (the speciality is Yúnnán *pu'er,* unlimited serves from ¥100), and pick songs (from ¥45, some lyrics have English translations) for the master to play.

☆ ENTERTAINMENT

GARDEN OF THE MASTER OF THE NETS   LIVE MUSIC

(网师园, Wăngshī Yuán; tickets ¥100) From March to November, music performances are held nightly from 7.30pm to 9.30pm for tourist groups at this garden. Don't expect anything too authentic.

KŪNQŬ OPERA MUSEUM   CHINESE OPERA

(昆曲博物馆, Kūnqŭ Bówùguăn; 14 Zhongzhangjia Xiang; 中张家巷14号; tickets ¥30) This place puts on performances of *kūnqŭ* at 2pm on Sundays.

PÍNGTÁN MUSEUM   PERFORMING ARTS

(评弹博物馆, Píngtán Bówùguăn; 3 Zhongzhangjia Xiang; 中张家巷3号; admission ¥4, performances ¥6; ◷9.30am-noon & 3.30-5pm) The Píngtán Museum puts on wonderful performances of *píngtán*, a singing and story-telling art form sung in the Sūzhōu dialect. Two-hour shows are at 1.30pm daily.

🛌 SLEEPING

Hotels in Sūzhōu are not cheap, but there's no shortage of choice, from canal-side hostels to comfortable boutique options and professional five-star hotels. Prices can rise across the board at weekends, when rooms can be harder to book, so try to visit from Sunday through to Thursday if possible.

★SŪZHŌU MINGTOWN YOUTH HOSTEL   HOSTEL $

(苏州明堂青年旅舍, Sūzhōu Míngtáng Qīngnián Lüshè; ☑0512 6581 6869; 28 Pingjiang Lu; 平江路28号; 6-bed dm ¥60-65, s/tw ¥200/220; ❄@❄; MXiangmen or Lindun Lu) This well-run youth hostel has a fantastic location on Pingjiang Lu and a charming lobby with rooms and dorms decorated with dark wooden 'antique' furniture. Rooms are not very well soundproofed but there's free laundry and bike rental. Staff speak English and can help with travel tips around town. Rooms are around ¥20 pricier on Friday and Saturday.

SŪZHŌU WATERTOWN YOUTH HOSTEL
HOSTEL $

(苏州浮生四季国际青年旅舍, Sūzhōu Fúshēngsìjì Qīngnián Lǔshè; ☑0512 6521 8885; www.watertownhostel.com; 27 Dashitou Xiang, Renmin Lu; 人民路大石头巷27号; 6-/4-bed dm ¥50/60, s ¥160, d ¥130-220; ❄@❀; Ⓜ Leqiao) Tucked away down Dashitou Xiang ('Big Stone Alley'), a lane off Renmin Lu, this 200-year-old courtyard complex houses an OK hostel. Rooms on the 2nd floor are quieter while ground-floor rooms have better wi-fi reception. Dorms are compact but clean enough. The cosy Sūzhōu-styled patio invites you to chill, and big bottles of Qīngdǎo are cheap. The cheapest twins and the triples are with shared shower. The airport bus station is just a stone's throw away.

★ GARDEN HOTEL
HOTEL $$$

(苏州南园宾馆, Sūzhōu Nányuán Bīnguǎn; ☑0512 6778 6778; www.gardenhotelsuzhou. com; 99 Daichengqiao Lu; 带城桥路99号; r from ¥1558; ❀❀) Within huge, green grounds, the very popular five-star Garden Hotel has elegant, spacious and attractively decorated rooms. Washed over with Chinese instrumental *pípá* music, the lobby is a picture of Sūzhōu, with a clear pond, grey bricks and white walls. Serene stuff and an oasis of calm. It's often possible to get a room here for under ¥800.

PÍNGJIĀNG LODGE
BOUTIQUE HOTEL $$$

(苏州平江客栈, Sūzhōu Píngjiāng Kèzhàn; ☑0512 6523 2888; www.pingjianglodge.com; 33 Niujia Xiang; 钮家巷33号; d ¥988-1588, ste ¥1888-2588; ❄@; Ⓜ Xiangmen or Lindun Lu) Capturing the canal-side Sūzhōu aesthetic, this 17th-century, traditional courtyard building has well-kept gardens and 51 rooms bedecked in traditional furniture. Rooms at the pointy end are very nice suites with split-level living spaces; standard rooms are bit bashed and could do with new carpets. Staff speak (faltering) English. Discounts of up to 50% are available.

Tónglǐ

Explore

Once called Fùtǔ (富土) before changing its name to Tónglǐ (铜里) and then ending up with the name Tónglǐ (同里; different first character), this lovely village is only 18km southeast of Sūzhōu. A leisurely day trip from town (or for those en route to Shànghǎi), Tónglǐ boasts a rich, historical canal-side atmosphere and weather-beaten charm. A restrained carnival atmosphere reigns but the languorous tempo is frequently shredded by marauding tour groups that sweep in, especially at weekends.

The Best...

➡ **Sight** Gēnglè Táng (p196)
➡ **Place to Sleep** Zhèngfú Cǎotáng (p197)

Top Tip

Slow-moving **six-person boats** (¥90 for 25 minutes) ply the waters of Tónglǐ's canal system. The boat trip on Tónglǐ Lake is free, though of no particular interest.

Getting There & Away

Bus From Sūzhōu, take a bus (50 minutes, every 30 minutes) at the South or North Long-distance Bus Station. Electric carts (¥5) run from beside the Tónglǐ Bus Station to the old town, or you can walk it in about 15 minutes. Regular buses leave Tónglǐ Bus Station for Sūzhōu, Shànghǎi and Zhōuzhuāng. There is one bus per day to Hángzhōu. Public bus 263 goes to Zhōuzhuāng.

Need to Know

➡ **Area Code** ☑0512
➡ **Location** 80km from Shànghǎi

◉ SIGHTS

★ CHINESE SEX CULTURE MUSEUM
MUSEUM

(中华性文化博物馆, Zhōnghuá Xìngwénhuà Bówùguǎn; ¥20; ⊙9am-5.30pm) This private museum is quietly housed in a historic but disused girls' school campus with an attractive garden and courtyard. Despite occasionally didactic and inaccurate pronouncements, it's fascinating, and ranges from the penal (sticks used to beat prostitutes, chastity belts) and the penile (Qing dynasty dildos), to the innocent (small statues to the goddess of mercy) and the positively charming (porcelain figures of courting couples).

Founded by sociology professors Liu Da-lin and Hu Hongxia against all odds, the museum's aim is not so much to arouse, but rather to educate and reintroduce an aspect of the country's culture that, ironically, has been forcefully repressed since China was 'liberated' in 1949. The pair have collected several thousand artefacts relating to sex, from erotic landscape paintings, fans and teacups to chastity belts and saddles with wooden dildos used to punish 'licentious' women and some bizarre objects (a pot-bellied immortal with a penis growing out of his head topped by a turtle). This is also one of the only places in the country where homosexuality is openly recognised as part of Chinese culture. Fascinating. The only drawback is that the museum is not included in the through-ticket to the village.

TÓNGLĬ OLD TOWN   VILLAGE

(老城区, Lǎochéngqū; ☑0512 6333 1140; ¥100, after 5.30pm free) This lovely old town, only 18km southeast of Sūzhōu, boasts a rich, historical canal-side atmosphere and weather-beaten charm. Many of the buildings have kept their traditional facades, with stark whitewashed walls, black-tiled roofs, cobblestone pathways and willow-shaded canal views adding to a picturesque allure. The town is best explored the traditional way: aimlessly meandering along the canals and alleys until you get lost.

A restrained carnival atmosphere reigns here but the languorous tempo is frequently upset by marauding tour groups that sweep in, especially at weekends.

The admission fee to the town includes access to the best sights, except the Chinese Sex Culture Museum.

GĒNGLÈ TÁNG   HISTORIC BUILDING

(耕乐堂; ☺9am-5.30pm) Of the three old residences in Tónglǐ that you'll pass at some point, the most pleasant is this elegant, love-ly and composed Ming dynasty estate with 52 halls spread out over five courtyards in the west of town. The buildings have been elaborately restored and redecorated with paintings, calligraphy and antique furniture, while the black-brick paths, osman-thus trees and cooling corridors hung with mǎdēng lanterns (traditional Chinese lanterns) conjure up an alluring charm.

PEARL PAGODA   PAGODA

(珍珠塔, Zhēnzhū Tǎ; ☺9am-5.30pm) In the north of town, this compound dates from the Qing dynasty, containing a spacious residential complex decorated with Qing-era antiques, an ancestral hall, a garden and an opera stage. It gets its name from a tiny pagoda draped in pearls.

TUÌSĪ GARDEN   GARDENS

(退思园, Tuìsī Yuán; ☺9am-5.30pm) This beau-tiful 19th-century garden in the east of the old town delightfully translates as the 'Withdraw and Reflect Garden', so named because it was a Qing government official's retirement home. The 'Tower of Fanning Delight' served as the living quarters, while the garden itself is a meditative portrait of pond water churning with koi, rockeries and pavilions, caressed by traditional Chinese music.

🍴 EATING

Restaurants are everywhere, but food prices here are much higher than Sūzhōu. Some local dishes to try include méigāncàishāoròu (梅干菜烧肉; stewed meat with dried veg-etables), yínyúchǎodàn (银鱼炒蛋, silver fish omelette) and zhuàngyuántí (状元蹄, stewed pig's leg).

🛏 SLEEPING

Most visitors come as day trippers, but guesthouses are plentiful if you'd like to spend the night, with basic rooms starting at about ¥100. The village is much quieter in the evening too, as there's an exodus in the late afternoon as travellers depart.

TONGLI INTERNATIONAL
YOUTH HOSTEL   HOSTEL $

(同里国际青年旅舍, Tónglǐ Guójì Qīngnián Lǚshè; ☑0512 6333 9311; 10 Zhuhang Jie; 竹行街10号; dm ¥55, r from ¥110; ❈@🛜) This youth hostel has two locations. The main one is slightly off Zhongchuan Beilu and near Zhongchuan Bridge. With a charming wooden interior, rooms here have tradition-al furniture (some with four-poster beds) and ooze old-China charm. The lobby area is attractive, decked out with international flags and sofas draped in throws.

The alternative location (234 Yuhang Jie; 鱼行街234号) beside Taiping bridge is simpler, with doubles (¥130) with shared bathroom only.

ZHÈNGFÚ CǍOTÁNG   BOUTIQUE HOTEL **$$**
(正福草堂; ☏0512 6333 6358; 138 Mingqing Jie; 明清街138号; s/d/ste ¥480/680/1380; ✳@☎) *The* place to stay in town. Each one unique, the 14 deluxe rooms and suites are all aesthetically set with Qing-style furniture and antiques, with four-poster beds in some. Facilities like bathrooms and floor heating are modern.

Zhūjiājiǎo

Explore

Thirty kilometres west of Shànghǎi, Zhūjiājiǎo is easy to reach and charming – as long as your visit does not coincide with the arrival of phalanxes of tour buses.

What survives of this historic canal town today is a charming tableau of Ming and Qing dynasty alleys, bridges and *gǔzhèn* (古镇; old town) architecture, its alleyways steeped in the aroma of *chòu dòufu* (stinky tofu).

While first impressions aren't fabulous when you step off the bus – a gritty industrious town – as soon as you hit the old town and its canals (a 10-minute walk from the bus station), you'll be glad you came. The riverside settlement is small enough to wander completely in three hours. Souvenir shops and restaurants line the scenic canal, connected by quaint bridges and narrow laneways that make it genuinely reminiscent of Venice – albeit a very Chinese version.

The Best...
➡**Sight** Fángshēng Bridge
➡**Place to Sleep** Cǎo Táng Inn (p198)

Top Tip

You can tour the canals in one of the Chinese gondola-style row boats (short/long tour ¥80/150 per boat), which seat six people. They depart from the dock out the front of City God Temple.

Getting There & Away

Bus Hop on the frequent direct pink-and-white Hùzhū Gāosù Kuàixiàn bus (沪朱高速快线; one hour) from the Pu'an Rd Bus Station just south of People's Square.

Note local buses also ply this route – these are best avoided and take double the time. Buses also run from Tónglǐ (1½ hours).

Need to Know
➡**Area Code** ☏021
➡**Location** 30km west of Shànghǎi
➡**Tourist office** (旅游办事处; Lǚyóu Bànshì Chù; ☏021 5924 0077; www.zhujiajiao.com/en; Xinfeng Lu; 新丰路; English guide half-/whole day ¥120/200; ◷8.30am-4.30pm)

◉ SIGHTS

If you plan on doing a full day's sightseeing, you can buy a variety of packages from Zhūjiājiǎo's tourist information office. It also has a useful map.

FÁNGSHĒNG BRIDGE   BRIDGE
(放生桥, Fàngshēng Qiáo) Of Zhūjiājiǎo's quaint band of ancient bridges, the standout must be the graceful, 72m-long, five-arched Fángshēng Bridge, first built in 1571 with proceeds from a monk's 15 years of alms-gathering. It passes over a wide expanse of water, reminiscent of sections of Venice's famous waterways.

KÈZHÍ GARDEN   GARDENS
(课植园, Kèzhí Yuán; 109 Xijing St; 朱家角镇西井街109号; ¥20) It's a little pricey, but this Chinese garden established in 1912 is a nice spot for a stroll with pavilions, ponds, quaint bridges and rocky outcrops.

YUÁNJĪN BUDDHIST TEMPLE   BUDDHIST TEMPLE
(圆津禅院, Yuánjīn Chányuàn; 193 Caohe Jie; 漕河街; ¥10; ◷8am-4pm) The Yuánjīn Buddhist Temple is famed for its **Qīnghuá Pavilion** (清华阁; Qīnghuá Gé) at the rear, a towering hall visible from many parts of town. It's located on Caohe St near the distinctive Tài'ān Bridge (泰安桥, Tài'ān Qiáo).

CITY GOD TEMPLE   TAOIST TEMPLE
(城隍庙, Chénghuáng Miào; 69 Caohe Jie; 漕河街; ¥10; ◷7.30am-4pm) Moved here in 1769 from its original location in Xuějiābāng, this temple stands on the west side of the Chenghuang Bridge.

ZHŪJIĀJIǍO CATHOLIC CHURCH OF ASCENSION
CHURCH

(朱家角耶稣升天堂, Zhūjiājiǎo Yēsū Shēngtiāntáng; 27 Caohe Jie, No 317 Alley; 漕河街27号317弄) A gorgeous church dating from 1863 with its belfry rising in a detached tower by the rear gate.

QING DYNASTY POST OFFICE
HISTORIC BUILDING

(清王朝邮局, Qīng Wángcháo Yóujú; 35 Xihu Rd; 西湖路35号; ¥5; ☺8.30am-4.30pm) A historic 1903 outpost of the Qing dynasty postal service, this is not a huge place but it's nice to walk through the old wooden building's interior, with mildly interesting exhibits such as vintage postcards and a postie's uniform dating from the Qing dynasty.

 ## EATING

Plenty of charming teahouses and eateries line the picturesque canal. Aim for the restaurants between Qijia and Yongfeng bridges, which have rooftop terraces full of flowers and English menus. Run the gauntlet of food sellers along Bei Dajie, who flog everything from pig's trotters to plump coconuts and scorpions on skewers.

SLEEPING

Given its proximity to Shànghǎi, there's no real reason to stay in Zhūjiājiǎo; though if you do, you'll get to enjoy it crowd-free once the tourists have gone home.

★CǍO TÁNG INN
HOSTEL $

(草堂客栈, Cǎotáng Kèzhàn; ☎021 5978 6442; 31 Dongjing Jie; 东井街31号; dm ¥80-100, d ¥300-320; ❄@) Not your typical generic backpackers, this friendly and atmospheric hostel is set within a century-old house full of character. Its common area in the lobby has a well-stocked bar and a fire pit to hang out by. There's a lovely courtyard garden too. The rooms are clean and well kept, including dorms and traditionally dressed doubles and twins.

It's popular with travelling musicians around the world, so jams are common.

Turn right after crossing Fángshēng Bridge and head towards another small bridge, cross over the bridge and turn left along the canal where it's 50m along.

Zhōuzhuāng

Explore

The 900-year-old water village of Zhōuzhuāng (周庄) is the best-known canal town in Jiāngsū. Located some 30km southeast of Sūzhōu, it is very popular with tour groups, thanks to Chen Yifei, the late renowned Chinese painter whose works of the once idyllic village are its claim to fame.

It does, however, have considerable old-world charm. Get up early or take an evening stroll, before the crowds arrive or when they begin to thin out, to catch some of Zhōuzhuāng's architectural highlights. The village has 14 stone bridges, dating from the Yuan dynasty through to the Qing.

The Best...
➡ **Sight** Shen's House
➡ **Place to Sleep** Zhèngfú Cǎotáng

Top Tip

Admission to Zhōuzhuāng is ¥100 (access is free after 8pm); make sure you get your photo digitally added to the ticket at purchase, this entitles you to a three-day pass.

Getting There & Away

Bus Frequent departures from Sūzhōu's North Long-distance Bus Station (one hour). Arriving in Zhōuzhuāng, turn left from the station and walk till you see the bridge; cross and you'll see the gated entrance to the village. The walk is about 20 minutes; a taxi should cost no more than ¥10.

Boat Fast boats run to Tónglǐ (20 minutes).

Need to Know
➡ **Area Code** ☎0512
➡ **Location** 60km west of Shànghǎi
➡ **Tourist office** (周庄游客中心, Zhōuzhuāng Yóukè Zhōngxīn; ☎0512 5721 1655; Quanfu Lu near memorial archway; 全福路)

◎ SIGHTS

SHEN'S HOUSE
HISTORIC BUILDING

(沈厅; Shěntīng; Nanshi Jie; 南市街; ☺8am-7pm) Near Fú'ān Bridge, this property of the Shen clan is a lavish piece of Qing-style architecture boasting three halls and over 100 rooms. The first hall is particularly interesting, as it has a water gate and a wharf where the family moored their private boats. You can picture the compound entirely daubed in Maoist graffiti circa 1969 (note the crudely smashed carvings above the doors).

You'll need a separate ticket for the **Zǒumǎ Lóu** (走马楼; ¥10; ⊙8am-4.30pm).

QUÁNFÚ TEMPLE
BUDDHIST TEMPLE

(全福讲寺, Quánfú Jiǎngsì; ⊙8.30am-5.30pm) It's hard to miss this eye-catching amber-hued temple complex. The 'Full Fortune' temple was originally founded during the Song dynasty, but has been repeatedly rebuilt. The structure you see today is an incarnation from 1995, when a handful of halls and gardens were added to the mix. The grounds steal the show, with willow-lined lakes seething with plump goldfish.

ZHANG'S HOUSE
HISTORIC BUILDING

(张厅, Zhāngtīng; ⊙8am-7pm) To the south of the Twin Bridges, this beautiful 70-room, three-hall structure was built in the Ming era and bought by the Zhang clan in early Qing times as their residence. There's an opera stage to keep the ladies entertained (they were not supposed to leave home or seek entertainment outside). Also note the chairs in the magnificently named Hall of Jade Swallows. Unmarried women could only sit on those with a hollow seatback, symbolising that they had nobody to rely on!

Don't overlook the garden, where boats could drift straight up to the house to its own little wharf. Trek back to the road via the 'side lane', a long and narrow walkway for the servants.

TWIN BRIDGES
BRIDGE

A total of 14 bridges grace Zhōuzhuāng, but the most beautiful and iconic are this pair of Ming dynasty bridges (双桥; Shuāngqiáo) gracing the intersection of two waterways in the heart of this canal town. **Shìdé Bridge** (世德桥, Shìdé Qiáo) is a humpbacked bridge while the connecting **Yǒngān Bridge** (永安桥, Yǒngān Qiáo) is the one with a square arch. The bridges were depicted in Chen Yifei's *Memory of Hometown*, which shot the whole town to fame from the 1980s onwards.

✕ EATING

With eateries at almost every corner, you won't starve, but avoid the local *āpó* tea (*āpó chá;* old woman's tea), which is extortionate.

✗ SPORTS & ACTIVITIES

BOAT RIDES
BOATING

It's fun to go under bridge after bridge by boat. There are loads on offer, including an 80-minute boat ride (¥180 per boat; six people) from outside the international youth hostel.

🛏 SLEEPING

ZHŌUZHUĀNG INTERNATIONAL YOUTH HOSTEL
HOSTEL $

(周庄国际青年旅舍; ☑0512 5720 4566; 86 Beishi Jie; 北市街86号; dm ¥45, s/d ¥120/140; ❄@🛜) Near an old opera stage, this efficient youth hostel occupies a converted courtyard. It has tidy rooms and a clean (but dim) dorm, and offers free laundry. The hostel owner is a barista, so enjoy a perfect brew in the ground-floor cafe. When it's slow, dorms go for ¥35; singles go for ¥100 and doubles for ¥120 on weekdays.

ZHÈNGFÚ CĂOTÁNG
BOUTIQUE HOTEL $$

(正福草堂; ☑0512 5721 9333; 90 Zhongshi Jie; 中市街90号; d ¥480-880, ste ¥1080; ❄@🛜) This very attractive and lovingly presented seven-room boutique hotel – a converted historic residence, restored to within an inch of its life – combines antique furniture with top-notch facilities, wood flooring and a lovely courtyard.

Shěshān

Explore

Easily accessed on the Shànghǎi metro, the outer suburb of Shěshān (佘山) is worth a half-day or day trip to get out into nature and to check out its fantastic cathedral and the surrounding views from the hills.

The Best...

➡ **Sight** Shěshan Basilica

Top Tip

Do as the locals do and pack yourself a picnic to enjoy while gazing out over the hills.

Getting There & Away

Metro Take metro line 9 from Shànghǎi to Shéshān station and then take free bus 9 (九号线; *jiǔhào xiàn*), which runs every 20 minutes from 9am, towards Happy Valley amusement park, which drops off at West Hill; alternatively, jump on bus 92. Both depart from the bus stop outside the metro station.

Taxi There are plenty of taxis in the rank out the front of Shéshān station. A taxi from the station to the West Hill entrance takes about 10 minutes and will cost around ¥18.

Getting Around

At the foot of West Hill is one of several bike stations where you can hire green-coloured bikes (from 8am to 4.30pm) to explore the Shěshān area. You will need your passport and a deposit of ¥200; the first hour is free, thereafter ¥1 per hour.

Need to Know

➡ **Area Code** ☑021
➡ **Location** 35km southwest of Shànghǎi

◉ SIGHTS

Sights are contained within the Shěshān National Forest Park, which is divided into two areas: the West Hill area (西景区, Xījǐngqū) and the East Hill area (东景区, Dōngjǐngqū). The most famous historic attractions can be found in the West Hill area. At the time of writing, access to the West Hill was free, while admission to the East Hill (with a forest park, aviary and butterfly garden) was ¥45.

SHÀNGHǍI ASTRONOMICAL
MUSEUM   MUSEUM
(上海天文博物馆, Shànghǎi Tiānwén Bówùguǎn; ¥12; ◷8.15am-5pm, last tickets 4.30pm; ⓂSheshan) The Former Shěshān Observatory is right alongside the Shěshān Basilica) on West Hill, founded by the Jesuits in 1900. The museum contains exhibitions on the history of observatories and astronomical research in China, as well as a collection of ancient telescopes.

SHÉSHĀN
BASILICA   CHURCH
(佘山聖母大殿, Shéshān Shèngmǔ Dàdiàn; ◷8am-4pm; ⓂSheshan) A very pleasant walk up through the trees from the road and the bus drop-off to the top of the hill, this cruciform red-brick and granite church is the highlight of the West Hill area. Decent views range out from the hill over the suburbs of Shànghǎi. The original Holy Mother Cathedral was built here between 1863 and 1866, and the current Basilica of Notre Dame was finished in 1935.

All the stained glass was destroyed during the Cultural Revolution and is being restored; the glass in the church at present is film-coated. Nonetheless, the interior is splendidly illuminated when the sun shines in. Every May sees hordes of local Catholics making a pilgrimage to the church, climbing up the hill along the Via Dolorosa from the south gate.

XIÙDÀOZHĚ
PAGODA   PAGODA
(秀道者塔, Xiùdàozhě Tǎ; ⓂSheshan) Rising from the east flank of West Hill, this graceful 20m-high pagoda dates to the 10th century.

HAPPY VALLEY   AMUSEMENT PARK
(欢乐谷, Huānlè Gǔ; ☑021 3355 2222; http://sh.happyvalley.cn; adult/child/child under 1.2m ¥200/120/free; ◷9am-6pm; ⓂSheshan, Dongjing) Happy Valley is a wildly popular national amusement park with locations around China. This park is separated into different zones (Shanghai Bund, Gold Mine Town, Happy Ocean etc) and features loads of attractions and rides, including the country's first wooden roller coaster, the Fireball.

Sleeping

There's never been a better time to find a bed in Shànghǎi. From ultrachic, carbon-neutral boutique rooms to sumptuous five-star hotels housed in glimmering towers, grand heritage affairs and snappy, down-to-earth backpacker haunts, the range of accommodation in town is just what you would expect from a city of this stature.

Hotels

Top-end stays tend to drop into three categories: chic boutique hotels; historic heritage hotels, where guests can wrap themselves in nostalgia; and top-of-the-range modern tower hotels, bristling with the latest amenities and sparkling with highly polished service (and often glorious views).

The midrange hotel market also offers boutique and heritage choices. The budget end has neat, comfortable but largely soulless express hotels, sometimes offering bigger rooms than hostels, but without the Western-friendly facilities or instant language skills.

Be prepared for surprisingly rudimentary English-language ability, except at the very best hotels (and youth hostels). Almost all the hotels we recommend have air-conditioning, and usually they have wi-fi (sometimes at expensive daily rates or just in the lobby) or broadband.

Hostels

At the budget end, Shànghǎi has a good crop of youth hostels. Usually staffed by versatile English speakers, they offer well-priced dorm beds and private rooms (sometimes better than their hotel equivalent) as well as wi-fi, communal internet terminals, bike hire, kitchen and laundry rooms, and even the odd pool table, table-tennis table or rooftop garden. Most have small and cheap bar-cafe-restaurant areas. Hostels also provide handy travel advice to guests and are exclusively attuned to travellers' needs.

Rates

Expect discounts of up to 50% off standard prices at most hotels, except during national holiday periods or the Formula One grand prix weekend. Rates can be bargained down at many budget and midrange hotels, but not at express hotels or hostels. All hotel rooms are subject to a 10% or 15% service charge; many cheaper hotels don't bother to charge it.

Dorm beds go for around ¥70 to ¥90, but double rooms under ¥200 can be hard to find. Expect to pay at least ¥600 for a midrange room. The fancier boutique hotels will charge more. A standard room in a top-end place will almost certainly top ¥1000, even after discount. Many of the better hotels, especially those aimed at business travellers, have cheaper weekend rates.

Longer-Term Rental

The cheapest way to stay in Shànghǎi is to share a flat or rent local accommodation from a Chinese landlord. Classified ads in listings magazines such as *City Weekend* (www.cityweekend.com.cn/shanghai) are a good place to start. You will need to register with the local Public Security Bureau (PSB, 公安局, Gōng'ānjú) within 24 hours of moving in.

Some hostels and hotels also rent out long-let rooms. Chai Living Residences (p213) is a stylish and recommended option.

NEED TO KNOW

Price Ranges

The following price ranges represent the cost per night of an en suite double room in high season.

$	Less than ¥500
$$	¥500–¥1300
$$$	More than ¥1300

Useful Websites

CTrip (http://english. ctrip.com) An excellent online agency, good for hotel bookings.

eLong (www.elong.net) Hotel bookings.

Lonely Planet (lonely planet.com/china/ shanghai/hotels) Hotel bookings and forum.

Reservations

You'll need to book your room in advance to secure your top choice; avoid the national holiday periods.

Checking In & Out

➡ You need your passport to check in. You'll fill in a registration form, or the hotel may simply scan your passport, a copy of which is sent to the local Public Security Bureau (PSB; 公安局; Gōng'ānjú) office.

➡ A deposit is required at most hotels, paid either with cash or by providing credit-card details.

➡ Check-out is usually by noon.

Lonely Planet's Top Choices

Fairmont Peace Hotel (p206) The grand dame of the Bund: restored, revitalised and renewed.

Mandarin Oriental Pudong (p212) Stunning chic luxury with incredible views.

Kevin's Old House (p209) The three C's: charming, comfortable, competitively priced.

Waterhouse at South Bund (p208) Swish and super-cool boutique style with views to match.

Urbn (p211) Carbon-neutral cool in a former post office.

Best by Budget

$

Le Tour Traveler's Rest (p210) Top-notch hostel in a former towel factory.

Mingtown E-Tour Youth Hostel (p204) Historic alleyway setting.

Mingtown Nanjing Road Youth Hostel (p204) Excellent location and great perks.

$$

Pentahotel Shanghai (p214) Design-savvy boutique hotel.

Kevin's Old House (p209) Charming B&B in an old villa.

Magnolia Bed & Breakfast (p209) Exquisite French Concession guesthouse, with only five rooms.

Quintet (p209) Chic townhouse full of character.

$$$

Langham Xīntiāndì (p210) Luxury choice with all the trimmings.

Waldorf Astoria (p206) Classic NYC style on the Bund.

Mandarin Oriental Pudong (p212) Super stylish with first-class service.

Andaz (p210) Designer digs in Xīntiāndì.

Best Boutique Hotels

Le Sun Chine (p210) French Concession mansion with yesteryear elegance.

Urbn (p211) Carbon-neutral boutique hotel with a hip urban feel.

Waterhouse at South Bund (p208) Industrial chic in a converted warehouse.

Best B&Bs

Quintet (p209) Another reason to bed down in the French Concession.

Kevin's Old House (p209) Top location with character and spacious suites.

Magnolia Bed & Breakfast (p209) Exquisite five-room French Concession guesthouse.

Best Views

Park Hyatt (p212) Awesome panoramas, as standard.

Ritz-Carlton Shanghai Pudong (p212) Beyond a knockout design, the views are breathtaking.

Peninsula Hotel (p207) Five-star views.

Historic Hotels

Fairmont Peace Hotel (p206) Shànghǎi's premier art deco classic.

Waldorf Astoria (p206) Prestigious and grand, in the former Shànghǎi Club on the Bund.

Astor House Hotel (p213) Steeped in concession-era Shànghǎi.

Where to Stay

NEIGHBOURHOOD	FOR	AGAINST
THE BUND & PEOPLE'S SQUARE	Luxury hotels on the Bund; close to the main sights; ubercentral with good transport links; iconic views and exclusive restaurants	Busy; expensive
OLD TOWN	Traditional part of town; river views from stylish and happening South Bund area	Little choice; transport options limited; busy areas; ramshackle parts
FRENCH CONCESSION	Dapper neighbourhood; vibrant, leafy and central; tip-top range of hotels; heritage architecture; standout restaurant choice; fab transport links	Few iconic views; expensive
JÌNG'ĀN	Good transport links; fine range of accommodation choices; shopping zone; central and stylish	Light on sights; spread out
PǓDŌNG	Luxury, stylish and high-altitude hotels; killer views; fantastic restaurants; good transport links	Few sights; spread out; big distances; little character
HÓNGKŎU & NORTH SHÀNGHǍI	Heritage and stylish long-stay options; good transport links; parts close to centre; off the beaten trail	Grittier and less fashionable; sprawling area with spread-out sights
WEST SHÀNGHǍI	Close to Hóngqiáo International Airport; some good-value options	Not much character; far from main sights; huge sprawl; not central

🛏 The Bund & People's Square

★ MINGTOWN E-TOUR YOUTH HOSTEL
HOSTEL $

Map p296 (明堂上海青年旅舍, Míngtáng Shànghǎi Qīngnián Lǚshè; ☏021 6327 7766; www.yhachina.com; 55 Jiangyin Rd; 江阴路55号; dm ¥90, d with/without bathroom ¥300/220; ❄ @ 🛜; Ⓜ Line 1, 2, 8 to People's Square, exit 2) One of Shànghǎi's best youth hostels, E-Tour has fine feng shui, a historic alleyway setting and pleasant rooms. But it's the tranquil courtyard with fish pond and the superb split-level bar-restaurant with cheap cocktails, pool table and comfy sofas that really sell it; plus there's plenty of outdoor seating on wooden decking. Private rooms come with small desks, TV and kettle.

There are both women-only and mixed dorms. YHA members get a small discount, and prices fluctuate slightly between high and low seasons. Reception is only open from 7am to 11pm, so notify the hostel if you're checking in outside these hours.

MINGTOWN PEOPLE'S SQUARE YOUTH HOSTEL
HOSTEL $

Map p296 (明堂青年旅舍人民广场店, Míngtáng Qīngnián Lǚshě Rénmín Guǎngchǎng Diàn; ☏021 3330 1556; www.yhachina.com; 35 Yongshou Rd; 永寿路35号; dm/r from ¥70/220; ❄ @ 🛜; Ⓜ Line 1, 2, 8 to People's Square; Line 8 to Dashijie) Centrally located between People's Square and the Bund; private rooms here have homely touches and Chinese porcelain wash basins, while single-sex dorms have pine-frame bunks with bed lamps, power sockets and large storage lockers. There's a cool bar with pool table and plenty of seating. Its proximity to Yunnan Rd's food street is handy.

There's no hot water from noon to 5pm, and 1am to 7am. Reception closes after 1am so notify staff if you are arriving after hours.

FISH INN BUND
HOTEL $

Map p296 (子鱼居, Zǐyújū; ☏021 3330 1399; www.fishinn.com.cn; 639 Middle Henan Rd; 河南中路639号; r ¥348-450; ❄ 🛜; Ⓜ Line 2, 10 to East Nanjing Rd; Lines 10, 12 to Tianlong Rd) With a handy location about a 10-minute walk from the Bund and East Nanjing Rd, this friendly little place is like a hotel with a vibrant youth hostel energy. Rooms are decent although they are a bit small and dark.

Deluxe rooms come with balcony/patio. Staff are eager to please and the tariff is excellent value for the hotel's position. There are suites for more room and comfort.

PHOENIX
HOSTEL $

Map p296 (老陕客栈, Lǎoshǎn Kèzhàn, Laoshan Hostel; ☏021 6328 8680; www.phoenixhostel shanghai.com; 17 South Yunnan Rd; 云南南路17号; dm ¥80-90, s ¥158-248, d ¥298; ❄ @ 🛜; Ⓜ Line 1, 2, 8 to People's Square; Line 8 to Dashijie) For those looking for a more authentic, local experience, the Phoenix is a good choice right among great street food. Appealingly grungy, rooms are clean and bright; dorms sleep from four to eight people. A rooftop bar, ground-floor Shaanxi restaurant, dumpling cooking classes and Chinese language lessons add to the appeal. Good location close to People's Square.

BLUE MOUNTAIN BUND
HOSTEL $

Map p296 (蓝山国际青年旅舍, Lánshān Guójì Qīngnián Lǚshè; ☏021 3366 1561; www.bmhostel. com; 6th fl, 350 South Shanxi Rd; 山西南路350号6楼; dm from ¥80, d with bathroom ¥240-370, without bathroom ¥180; ❄ @ 🛜; Ⓜ Line 2, 10 to East Nanjing Rd) Though it has a weird location on top of a building block shared by other budget hotels, this hostel gets kudos for its central location. The prized rooms are the deluxe doubles with loft bed and spacious outdoor balconies. Ordinary doubles also get city views, but cheaper rooms have no window. Dorms are smallish but perfectly fine. There's a decent bar with pool table, and a colossal rooftop terrace.

Prices are slightly higher on weekends and in August. Staff are friendly and there's self-service laundry.

MINGTOWN NANJING ROAD YOUTH HOSTEL
HOSTEL $

Map p296 (明堂上海南京路青年旅舍, Míngtáng Shànghǎi Nánjīng Lù Qīngnián Lǚshè; ☏021 6322 0939; www.yhachina.com; 258 Tianjin Rd; 天津路258号; dm/s/d from ¥70/160/260; ❄ @ 🛜; Ⓜ Line 2, 10 to East Nanjing Rd) Just off East Nanjing Rd, this sociable and friendly Mingtown hostel is all about location – halfway between the Bund and People's Square. It's a bit dark and poky, but perks include laundry, kitchen, ground-floor bar-restaurant and pool table. Six-bed dorms have a private bathroom, while doubles are good value with desk and TV. Wi-fi is in public areas only. Discounts for YHA members.

DOCK BUND HOSTEL
HOSTEL $

Map p296 (外滩源青年旅舍, Wàitān Yuán Qīngnián Lǚshě; ☑021 6302 0898; www.bmhos tel.com; 55 Xianggang Rd; 香港路55号; dm/d/ tr from ¥80/280/380; ❄️🛜; Ⓜ️Line 2, 10 to East Nanjing Rd) Sitting on prime real estate a few blocks from the Bund, this backpacker is all about the outstanding location. It's a solid choice with spacious doubles and dorms in configurations of four, six and eight (the latter is mixed sex). The English-speaking staff are friendly and helpful with local info.

ELEGANCE HOTEL
HOTEL $

Map p296 (宜兰贵斯酒店; Yílán Guì Sī Jiǔdiàn; ☑021 6323 0808; www.elegancebund.com; 138 Guangdong Rd; 广东路138号; s/d from ¥380/440; ❄️@🛜; Ⓜ️Line 2, 10 to East Nanjing Rd) Given its central location within striking distance of the Bund and East Nanjing Rd, the Elegance Hotel is remarkable value. While it's more faux elegance – including a sparkling lobby with chintzy chandeliers, Chesterfield lounges and a small bar – it's nicer than most. Rooms have a few rough edges, but are functional with TVs and desk; you'll need to upgrade for a room with a window, however.

HOME INN
HOTEL $

Map p296 (如家酒店; Rújiā Jiǔdiàn; ☑021 6323 9966; www.homeinns.com; Lane 26, Sijing Rd; 泗泾路26弄; d from ¥327; ❄️@🛜; Ⓜ️Line 2, 10 to East Nanjing Rd) Housed in a *lòngtáng* (alleyway), overhung with laundry and accessed from Sijing Rd, this is one of the better branches of the dependable Home Inn chain. The pastel interior may not be everyone's cup of *chá,* but the clean, functional rooms with hot- and cold-water dispensers are nice and bright. There's not much English spoken, but staff are friendly.

MOTEL 268
HOTEL $

Map p296 (莫泰连锁旅馆, Mòtài Liánsuǒ Lǚguǎn; ☑021 3101 2330; www.motel168.com; 50 Ningbo Rd; 宁波路50号; r from ¥319; ❄️@🛜; Ⓜ️Line 2, 10 to East Nanjing Rd) In a 1920s apartment building, this scruffy hotel has a mix of budget and slightly fancier rooms, but when push comes to shove, it's all about location. The wafer-thin walls mean you'll need to be lucky with your neighbours.

METROPOLO HOTEL – PEOPLE'S SQUARE
HOTEL $$

Map p296 (锦江都城上海青年会经典酒店, Jǐnjiāng Dūchéng Shànghǎi Qīngnián Huì Jīngdiàn

Jiǔdiàn; ☑021 3305 9999; www.metropolohotels. com; 123 South Xizang Rd; 西藏南路123号; r ¥939-2039; Ⓜ️Line 8 to Dashijie) Occupying the former Chinese YMCA building (1931) just south of People's Square, this member of the Metropolo chain is one of the city's better midrange hotels. The brown-and-cream rooms offer a reassuring degree of style, and are large and comparable in standard to pricier business hotels. Staff are professional and online discounts can slash room rates by 20%.

The building resembles Běijīng's Southeast Corner Watchtower, with a traditional hammerbeam ceiling. Its lobby has lavish art deco features.

JW MARRIOTT TOMORROW SQUARE
HOTEL $$

Map p296 (明天广场JW万豪酒店, Míngtiān Guǎngchǎng JW Wànháo Jiǔdiàn; ☑021 5359 4969; www.jwmarriottshanghai.com; 399 West Nanjing Rd; 南京西路399号; d from ¥1500; ❄️🛜🏊; Ⓜ️Line 1, 2, 8 to People's Square, exit 11) Victor Sassoon probably would have traded in his old digs in a heartbeat if he could have stayed in the chairman's suite here. Housed across the upper 24 floors of one of Shànghǎi's most dramatic towers, the JW Marriott boasts marvellously appointed rooms with spectacular vistas, coffee-maker, and showers with hydraulic massage functions to soak away the stress.

Service and facilities are top class, with two pools (indoor and outdoor) and an excellent spa. Internet costs ¥120 a day for nonmembers (¥600 per week). Its library is in the *Guinness Book of Records* for the world's highest at 230.9m, but it's only accessible to executive-lounge members.

BUND GARDEN SHANGHAI
HERITAGE HOTEL $$

Map p296 (外滩花园酒店, Wàitān Huāyuán Jiǔdiàn; ☏021 6329 8800; 200 Hankou Rd; 汉口路200号; r ¥980; ☀☎; Ⓜ Line 2, 10 to East Nanjing Rd) Set in a beautiful colonial villa dating from the 1930s, the Bund Garden retains its distinct classic British feel with red-brick Gothic features, chimneys and a beautiful wooden staircase. With only nine rooms, the standard here is more dated B&B than luxury hotel, but all rooms are large with fireplaces and are decorated in period style.

Leading off the lobby is a suitably posh dining room, and a large garden enclosed by heritage buildings, including the charming **Holy Trinity Church** (圣三一教堂, Shèng Sānyī Jiàotáng; Map p296; 219 Jiujiang Rd; 九江路219号). Rates include breakfast.

PARK HOTEL
HISTORIC HOTEL $$

Map p296 (国际饭店, Guójì Fàndiàn; ☏021 6327 5225; http://park.jinjianghotels.com; 170 West Nanjing Rd; 南京西路170号; s/d from ¥800/1068; ☀☎; Ⓜ Line 1, 2, 8 to People's Square, exit 8) The Park Hotel is one of Shànghǎi's most famous art deco heritage spots with a positively supreme location, but it remains stuck in an old-fashioned groove like a scratched record. Staff members are friendly, though, and 10% discounts are common.

PACIFIC HOTEL
HISTORIC HOTEL $$

Map p296 (金门大酒店, Jīnmén Dàjiǔdiàn; ☏021 5352 9898; http://pacific.jinjianghotels.com; 108 West Nanjing Rd; 南京西路108号; d from ¥1000; ☀☎; Ⓜ Line 1, 2, 8 to People's Square, exit 8) Capped by a distinctive clock tower, this historic hotel (1926) is strong on both character and style. The neoclassical entrance leads to a marble lobby with attractive ceiling artwork. However it's a drop in standard from other luxury hotels; the cheaper rooms at the back are distinctly dated (and some smell like stale cigarettes). Those overlooking People's Park have nicer furniture and more space.

It caters mainly to local tourists, so English isn't a strong point here.

SOFITEL HYLAND HOTEL
HOTEL $$

Map p296 (索菲特海仑宾馆, Suǒfēitè Hǎilún Bīnguǎn; ☏021 6351 5888; www.sofitel.com; 505 East Nanjing Rd; 南京东路505号; d ¥1150-2110; ☀☎; Ⓜ Line 2, 10 to East Nanjing Rd) Rising up halfway along East Nanjing Rd, the Sofitel is a solid choice for those insisting on location without breaking the bank. The uncluttered, cool lobby area is dominated by open space and geometric lines. Standard rooms are rather dated, with a crisp, more modern finish in the executive rooms.

Facilities include a spa, two restaurants, a bar and a French bakery.

JINJIANG INN
HOTEL $$

Map p296 (锦江之星, Jǐnjiāng Zhīxīng; ☏021 6322 3223; www.jinjianginns.com; 680 East Nanjing Rd; 南京东路680号; r ¥539-899; ☀@☎; Ⓜ Line 1, 2, 8 to People's Square, exit 19; Line 2, 10 to East Nanjing Rd) Located in the former Shanghai Sincere Department Store (which opened in 1917), the erstwhile East Asia Hotel was grabbed by the folk at Jinjiang Inn and re-presented with smartish rooms with showers. It's often booked out due to its prime location.

★ WALDORF ASTORIA
HOTEL $$$

Map p296 (华尔道夫酒店, Huá'ěr Dàofū Jiǔdiàn; ☏021 6322 9988; www.waldorfastoria shanghai.com; 2 East Zhongshan No 1 Rd; 中山东一路2号; r new/old wing from ¥2500/6000; ☀@☎; Ⓜ Line 2, 10 to East Nanjing Rd) Grandly marking the southern end of the Bund is the former Shànghǎi Club (1910), once the Bund's most exclusive gentlemen's hang-out. The 20 original rooms have been converted to house the Waldorf Astoria's premium suites, six of which look out onto the Huángpǔ River. Behind this heritage building is a new hotel tower, with 252 state-of-the-art rooms.

Each room features touch digital controls, espresso machine, walk-in closet and a TV in the mirror.

There's a pronounced New York–meets–Shànghǎi theme here, from the Peacock Lounge to the cocktail list at the Long Bar.

★ FAIRMONT PEACE HOTEL
HISTORIC HOTEL $$$

Map p296 (费尔蒙和平饭店, Fèi'ěrméng Hépíng Fàndiàn; ☏021 6321 6888; www.fair mont.com; 20 East Nanjing Rd; 南京东路20号; d

¥2500-4000; ⊛🅰🛜🏊; Ⓜ Line 2,10 to East Nanjing Rd) If anywhere in town fully conveys swish 1930s Shànghǎi, it's the old Cathay, rising imperiously from the Bund. One of the city's most iconic hotels, the Fairmont Peace is cast in the warm, subdued tints of a bygone era. Expect all the luxuries of a top-class establishment, with rooms decked out in art deco elegance, from light fixtures down to coffee tables.

Standard rooms come without a view, deluxe rooms with a street view and suites with the coveted river view. Note that wi-fi and broadband access cost an extra ¥99 per day for guests.

The hotel is also home to a luxury spa, two upmarket restaurants and several bars and cafes. Even if you're not staying here, it's worth popping in to admire the magnificent lobby (1929), or taking in an evening show at the jazz bar.

★ YANGTZE BOUTIQUE SHÀNGHǍI
BOUTIQUE HOTEL $$$

Map p296 (朗廷扬子精品宾馆, Lǎngtíng Yángzǐ Jīngpǐn Bīnguǎn; ☑021 6080 0800; www.the yangtzehotel.com; 740 Hankou Rd; 汉口路740号; d¥1200-2000; ⊛🛜; Ⓜ Line 1, 2, 8 to People's Square, exit 14) Dating from the 1930s, this art deco beauty was a famous hang-out for the glitterati in the swinging 1930s. Splendidly refurbished, it features a sumptuous stained-glass oblong and recessed skylight in the lobby, above a deco-style curved staircase. In addition to period decor, rooms feature deep baths, pictureframe TVs, glass-walled bathrooms (with Venetian blinds) and even tiny balconies – a rarity in Shànghǎi.

PENINSULA HOTEL
LUXURY HOTEL $$$

Map p296 (半岛酒店, Bàndǎo Jiǔdiàn; ☑021 2327 2888; http://shanghai.peninsula.com; 32 East Zhongshan No 1 Rd; 中山东一路32号; d incl breakfast from ¥2700; ⊛🅰🛜🏊; Ⓜ Line 2, 10 to East Nanjing Rd) Though built in 2009, this spiffy hotel at the Bund's northern end has a heritage look achieved by combining art deco motifs with Shànghǎi modernity. It's a grade above many other market rivals, with TVs in the tub, well-equipped dressing rooms (with fingernail driers), valet boxes for dirty clothes, Nespresso machines and fabulous views across the river or out onto the gardens of the former British consulate.

Part of the Rockbund development project, it includes an enormous luxury shopping arcade on the ground floor, and a back entrance that leads to the beautifully renovated Yuanmingyuan Rd.

LE ROYAL MÉRIDIEN SHANGHAI
HOTEL $$$

Map p296 (世茂皇家艾美酒店, Shìmào Huángjiā Ài Měi Jiǔdiàn; ☑021 3318 9999; www.leroyal meridienshanghai.com; 789 East Nanjing Rd; 南京东路789号; r ¥1200-1500; ⊛@🛜🏊; Ⓜ Line 1, 2, 8 to People's Square, exit 19) For those who prefer something more contemporary than the old-world hotels nearby, the Méridien is a stylish affair with a Nouvelle Vague soundtrack and art throughout. Rooms have floor-to-ceiling windows with views out to Shànghǎi's skyline, and glassed-in bathrooms with rainshower and standalone bathtubs. The swanky restaurants and bars are counterbalanced by a large, modern gym and lap pool.

The La Vie en Rose Sunday brunch (¥558 with free-flowing champagne) is one of Shànghǎi's best, while the Hu on 65 rooftop bar and club has Bund views.

METROPOLO HOTEL – EAST NANJING
HOTEL $$$

Map p296 (锦江都城外滩经典酒店, Jǐnjiāng Dūchéng Wàitān Jīngdiǎn; ☑021 6321 1666; www.metropolohotels.com; 98 East Nanjing Rd; 南京东路98号; r incl breakfast from ¥1300; ⊛🛜; Ⓜ Line 2, 10 to East Nanjing) One of several Metropolo hotels set up in refurbished historical buildings, this one is just off the Bund. Rooms here take on categories of sassiness, from 'very' sassy to 'super' and 'extreme' sassy. All have a modern, open-plan design with arty touches and standalone bathtubs. The dark-lit foyer with gaudy red velvet won't be to everyone's taste.

Other features include an ostentatious bar and restaurant, and small gym.

GRAND CENTRAL HOTEL SHANGHAI
HOTEL $$$

Map p296 (上海大酒店, Shànghǎi Dàjiǔdiàn; www.grandcentralhotelshanghai.com; 505 Jiujiang Rd; 九江路505号; s/d ¥2500/2600, ste ¥3300-43,000; ⊛🛜🏊; Ⓜ Line 2, 10 to East Nanjing Rd) Grand and fresh, this is a superb choice. The effortlessly elegant lobby areas – with acres of softly burnished marble and a small forest of fairy-light flecked palm trees overlooked by verandah-style balconies – is a congenial prelude to ample and traditionally styled deluxe rooms, furnished to a high degree of comfort. Discounts are usually more than 50%.

LES SUITES ORIENT
HOTEL $$$

Map p296 (东方商旅酒店, Dōngfāng Shānglǚ Jiǔdiàn; ☑021 6320 0088; www.suitesorient. com; 1 East Jinling Rd; 金陵东路1号; r with city/river view from ¥1500/2000; ❄@🖥🏊; MLine 10 to Yuyuan Garden) Located at the southern edge of the Bund, Les Suites Orient is notable as the only hotel on the strip offering standard rooms (Bund Studio) with fantastic river and Bund vistas – in some rooms even the bathtub gets a view. It's housed in a modern 23-storey tower, with hardwood floors and minimalist design adding to the appealingly chic interior. Excellent service.

WESTIN SHANGHAI
HOTEL $$$

Map p296 (威斯汀大饭店, Wēisītīng Dàfàndiàn; ☑021 6335 1888; www.starwoodhotels.com; 88 Middle Henan Rd; 河南中路88号; d from ¥1500; ❄🖥🏊; MLine 2, 10 to East Nanjing Rd) Rooms in the newer tower at the top-notch Westin are sleek and contemporary with capacious bathrooms, some of which have freestanding tubs; rooms in the older tower are the same price, but are a bit more tired and smaller. Service throughout is thoughtful and professional.

There's a gym, a pool, a Thai-style spa and a tempting range of popular restaurants. Expect at least 50% discounts. Wi-fi is free; however, broadband costs ¥100 per night.

JĪNJIĀNG METROPOLO HOTEL
HISTORIC HOTEL $$$

Map p296 (锦江之星新城饭店, Jǐnjiāng Zhī Xīng Xīnchéng Fàndiàn; www.metropolohotels.com; 180 Middle Jiangxi Rd; 江西中路180号; MLine 2,10 to East Nanjing Rd) This magnificent art deco building has been home to a hotel since 1934 and was first established as the Metropole Hotel, owned by the famed Victor Sassoon. While its standards have slipped markedly, it was undergoing a total renovation in 2016 that will hopefully restore some of its former splendour. It overlooks an intersection with similarly imposing grand architecture.

🛏 Old Town

★WATERHOUSE AT SOUTH BUND
BOUTIQUE HOTEL $$

Map p300 (水舍时尚设计酒店, Shuǐshè Shíshàng Shèjì Jiǔdiàn; ☑021 6080 2988; www. waterhouseshanghai.com; 1-3 Maojiayuan Rd, Lane 479, South Zhongshan Rd; 中山南路479弄 毛家园路1-3号; d ¥1100-2800; ❄🖥; MLine 9 to Xiaonanmen) There are few cooler places to base yourself in Shànghǎi than this awfully trendy 19-room, four-storey South Bund converted 1930s warehouse right by the Cool Docks. Gazing out onto supreme views of Pǔdōng (or into the crisp courtyard), the Waterhouse's natty rooms (some with terrace) are swishly dressed. Service can be wanting, though, and it's isolated from the action.

Fittingly for this revived part of town, the ethos is industrial chic, so it best suits design-conscious guests. A lovely rooftop bar caps it all and trim ground-floor Table No 1 (p89) throws in culinary excellence.

HOTEL INDIGO
HOTEL $$$

Map p300 (英迪格酒店, Yīngdígé Jiǔdiàn; www. hotelindigo.com; 585 East Zhongshan No 2 Rd; 中山东二路585号; d ¥1430; ❄🖥🏊; MLine 9 to Xiaonanmen) With its quirky lobby – chairs like birdcages; tree branches trapped in cascades of glass jars; sheets of metal riveted to the wall; modish, sinuously shaped furniture; and funky ceiling lights – towering Hotel Indigo is a stylish South Bund choice. Chic and playful guest rooms feature colourful cushions and whimsical designs, with lovely rugs and spotless bathrooms.

Note that accommodation either looks out onto the Old Town (so-so) or the river (stellar). Service is very helpful and the infinity pool is a dream. Regular discounts tame prices up to 60%.

🛏 French Concession

BLUE MOUNTAIN YOUTH HOSTEL
HOSTEL $

(蓝山国际青年旅舍, Lánshān Guójì Qīngnián Lǚshè; ☑021 6304 3938; www.bmhostel.com; 2nd fl, Bldg 1, 1072 Quxi Rd; 瞿溪路1072号1号甲 2楼; dm ¥85-90, d ¥260-280, tr ¥330; ❄@🖥; MLuban Rd) Although slightly out of the action, this hostel is almost next door to Luban Rd metro station, so transport is sorted. Rooms are clean and simple with pine furniture and flooring, TV and kettle. There are women-only, men-only and mixed four- to eight-bed dorms, and there's a bar-restaurant area with free pool table and free movie screenings. Wi-fi is in the public areas only.

Staff members speak English and are very friendly.

YUÈYÁNG HOTEL
HOTEL $

Map p306 (悦阳商务酒店, Yuèyáng Shāngwù Jiǔdiàn; ☎021 6466 6767; 58 Yueyang Rd; 岳阳路58号; s ¥198, d ¥338-368; ❄; Ⓜ Hengshan Rd) One of the best budget options in the French Concession that's within easy walking distance of a metro station, Yuèyáng has well-kept spacious rooms with big double beds and laminated flooring. Shower rooms are clean and modern, although, annoyingly, the hot water isn't always piping hot. Expect only small discounts, if any.

MOTEL 268
HOTEL $

Map p302 (莫泰连锁旅店, Mòtài Liánsuǒ Lǚdiàn; ☎021 5170 3333; www.motel168.com; 113 Sinan Rd; 思南路113号; d ¥289-399, ste ¥429; ❄ @; Ⓜ Dapuqiao) You can find decent enough rooms at this rather chipped and functional branch of Motel 268, which has a lift and friendly staff. The location on leafy Sinan Rd is ideally located for those wanting to explore the maze of charming alleyways known as Tiánzǐfáng. Note some rooms are windowless. English is limited.

★ QUINTET
B&B $$

Map p306 (☎021 6249 9088; www.quintet-shanghai.com; 808 Changle Rd; 长乐路808号; d incl breakfast ¥850-1100; ❄ ❄ ❄; Ⓜ Changshu Rd) This chic B&B has five homely double rooms in a 1930s townhouse full of character. Some of the rooms are small, but each is decorated with style, incorporating modern luxuries such as large-screen TVs and laptop-sized safes, with more classic touches such as wood-stripped floorboards and deep porcelain bathtubs. The loft room comes with a private rooftop terrace.

Staff members sometimes get a BBQ going in the downstairs restaurant terrace in summer. No sign – just buzz on the gate marked 808 and wait to be let in. Be aware there is no elevator.

★ KEVIN'S OLD HOUSE
B&B $$

Map p306 (老时光酒店, Lǎoshíguāng Jiǔdiàn; ☎021 6248 6800; www.kevinsoldhouse.com; No 4, Lane 946, Changle Rd; 长乐路946弄4号; ste incl breakfast from ¥900; ❄ ❄; Ⓜ Changshu Rd) Housed in a secluded 1927 four-storey French Concession villa, this lovely, quiet place is run by a friendly, English-speaking owner. Six spacious suites are spread throughout the house, featuring wooden floorboards, traditional Chinese furniture and a few antiques, as well as fridges, flat-

screen TVs and washing machines. Suite 328 is the pick of the bunch.

There's an attached Italian restaurant with a long menu of pizza and pasta dishes.

★ MAGNOLIA BED & BREAKFAST
B&B $$

Map p306 (☎021 5403 5306; www.magnoliabnbshanghai.com; 36 Yanqing Rd; 延庆路36号; r ¥702-1296; ❄ @ ❄; Ⓜ Changshu Rd) Opened by Miranda Yao of the cooking school Kitchen at... (p125), this cosy five-room B&B is located in a 1927 French Concession home. It's Shànghǎi all the way, with original art deco features combined with comfort and design; a true labour of love. There are discounts for stays of seven nights or more. There's no front desk, so phone ahead before visiting.

FENYANG GARDEN HOTEL
BOUTIQUE HOTEL $$

Map p302 (汾阳花园酒店, Fényáng Huāyuán Jiǔdiàn; ☎021 5456 9888; www.fenyanggardenhotel.com; 45 Fenyang Rd; 汾阳路45号; r from ¥1100; ❄ ❄; Ⓜ South Shaanxi Rd) Sitting opposite the Shanghai Conservatory of Music (p119), guests at Fenyang Garden are occasionally treated to the sounds of classical music wafting from across the street. This tasteful boutique hotel is set in a Spanish-style villa in a lovely leafy spot, with spacious rooms. Skip the pricey breakfast as there are plenty of options in the area. Some English is spoken by the staff.

ĀNTÍNG VILLA HOTEL
HISTORIC HOTEL $$

Map p306 (安亭别墅花园酒店, Āntíng Biéshù Huāyuán Jiǔdiàn; ☎021 6433 1188; http://anting villahotel.com; 46 Anting Rd; 安亭路46号; r ¥1180-1380, ste ¥1880-5580; ❄ ❄; Ⓜ Hengshan Rd) On a quiet tree-lined street, this pleasant hotel shares its grounds with a 1936 colonial Spanish-style villa. It offers comfortable elegant rooms, with wi-fi and quality furniture including a chaise longue by the window. Some rooms have balconies and fine views over the lovely garden. Discounts of up to 40% are available online.

DŌNGHÚ HOTEL
HISTORIC HOTEL $$

Map p306 (东湖宾馆, Dōnghú Bīnguǎn; ☎021 6415 8158; www.donghuhotel.com; 70 Donghu Rd; 东湖路70号; s/d from ¥450/660; ❄ ❄; Ⓜ South Shaanxi Rd) Once the home of feared Shànghǎi gangster Du Yuesheng, the historic Dōnghú is divided into two hotel offerings on either side of the road. The first, an austere 1934 white concrete building, houses the better rooms with interesting colour scheme and higher prices. The second, newer building is an ugly, white-tiled affair with cheap carpets and tatty furnishings.

Discounts of up to 50% make this a reliable midrange option.

★ HÉNGSHĀN PICARDIE HOTEL HOTEL $$

Map p306 (衡山宾馆, Héngshān Bīnguǎn; ☑021 6437 7050; www.hengshanhotel.com; 534 Hengshan Rd; 衡山路534号; s/d from ¥700/900; ✴@☎; ⓂHengshan Rd) These former Picardie Apartments (1934) still feature impressive art deco charm, most noticeably in the fine exterior and the 1930s touches throughout. Superior rooms are characterful and attractive, with European-style decor, but try to get a corner room for the extra space and views. The location is good, between Hengshan Rd and Xújiāhuì.

★ LANGHAM XĪNTIĀNDÌ LUXURY HOTEL $$$

Map p302 (新天地朗廷酒店, Xīntiāndì Lǎngtíng Jiǔdiàn; ☑021 2330 2288; http://xintiandi.langhamhotels.com; 99 Madang Rd; 马当路99号; r/ste ¥1800/2400; ✴☎✉; ⓂSouth Huangpi Rd) Xīntiāndì has become a magnet for luxury hotels, and they don't come much nicer than this one. Its 357 smart, stylish rooms all feature huge floor-to-ceiling windows, plenty of space to spread out in, and an attention to the minute details that make all the difference: Japanese-style wooden tubs in some suites, heated bathroom floors, Nespresso machines, VPN wi-fi and fresh flowers.

Amenities include the much lauded Cantonese restaurant T'ang Court, an indoor pool and the award-winning stunning Chuan spa.

★ ANDAZ LUXURY HOTEL $$$

Map p302 (安达仕酒店, Āndáshì Jiǔdiàn; ☑021 2310 1234; http://shanghai.andaz.hyatt.com; 88 Songshan Rd; 嵩山路88号; r ¥1800-3300; ✴☎✉; ⓂSouth Huangpi Rd) Housed in a tower with retro 1970s style windows, this fab hotel's design-led lobby – a pronouncement of metal latticework – suggests an art space, a sensation that persists when you hunt for the open-plan reception (it's on the right). Along curving corridors, guest rooms are cool and modern, with basins and bathtubs that glow in different colours, coffee machines and monumental flat-screen TVs.

With room design courtesy of Japanese interior designer Super Potato, all mod cons are operated by iPad, while views of Pǔxī or Pǔdōng – depending on your choice – range out beyond curved and chunky windows.

Extra bonus: free drinks for guests in the bar during happy hour 6pm to 8pm daily. Discounts of up to 35% online.

★ LE SUN CHINE BOUTIQUE HOTEL $$$

Map p306 (绅公馆, Shēn Gōng Guǎn; ☑021 5256 9977; No 6, Lane 1220, Huashan Rd; 华山路1220 弄6号; r ¥999-2999; ✴☎; ⓂJiaotong University) Originally the home of the Sun family, this renovated 1930s mansion has become one of Shànghǎi's most exclusive boutique properties. Seventeen personalised suites – decorated in a choice of four different colours on four floors – combine an antique-strewn style with all the modern comforts of home. A Shanghainese banquet is served in the highly lauded restaurant. You can usually reserve a room for around ¥1300.

MANSION HOTEL HISTORIC HOTEL $$$

Map p302 (首席公馆历史, Shǒuxí Gōngguǎn Lìshǐ; http://mansionhotelchina.com; 82 Xinle Rd; 新乐路82号; r ¥1700-6800; ✴☎; ⓂSouth Shaanxi Rd) This historic mansion was once the residence of notorious gangsters and played host to decadent parties in the 1930s. It's filled with antiques, dark wood and original art deco features, and comes with loads of old-world charm. Suites are apartment-sized with high ceilings and some balcony rooms look out at the Russian Orthodox church. Ask to see rooms first as some are a bit grubby and dated.

INTERCONTINENTAL SHANGHAI RUIJIN HOTEL HISTORIC HOTEL $$$

Map p302 (上海瑞金洲际酒店, Shànghǎi Ruìjīn Zhōujì Jiǔdiàn; ☑021 6472 5222; www.ihg.com; 118 Ruijin No 2 Rd; 瑞金二路118号; standard/executive d from ¥1300/2300; ✴@☎; ⓂSouth Shaanxi Rd) The InterContinental group has acquired this historic 238-guestroom garden estate, which includes Building No 1, a 1919 red-brick mansion and former residence of Benjamin Morris, one-time owner of *North China Daily News*. Dark-wood panelled corridors lead to enormous, pleasantly appointed rooms. The architecture and the park-like gardens are lovely. Staff speak limited English.

🛏 Jìng'ān

★ LE TOUR TRAVELER'S REST HOSTEL $

Map p310 (乐途静安国际青年旅舍, Lètú Jìng'an Guójì Qīngnián Lǚshè; ☑021 6267 1912; www.letourshanghai.com; 319 Jiaozhou Rd; 胶州路319

号; dm ¥100-150, r ¥340-400; ❄ @ 🛈; ⓂLine 2, 7 to Jing'an Temple, exit 2) Housed in a former towel factory, this fabulous youth hostel leaves most others out to dry. You'll pass a row of splendid *shíkùmén* (stone-gate houses) on your way down the alley to get here. The old-Shànghǎi textures continue once inside, with red-brick walls decorated in graffiti, polished concrete floors and reproduced stone gateways above doorways leading to simple but smart rooms and six-person dorms (with shared bathrooms).

Double rooms are not very spacious, but they have flat-screen TVs and they're clean. Rooms are ¥10 to ¥30 pricier on Fridays and Saturdays. The hostel also has small apartments next door for short- and long-term rental. The ground floor has a ping-pong table, a pool table and wi-fi, all of which are free to use, and there's a fine rooftop bar-restaurant with outdoor seating. Bicycles can also be rented for ¥30 per day.

It's down an alley off Jiaozhou Rd.

JINJIANG INN
HOTEL $

Map p310 (锦江之星旅馆, Jǐnjiāng Zhīxīng Lǚguǎn; ☏021 5213 8811; www.jinjianginns.com; 400 Xikang Rd; 西康路400号; r ¥279-409; ❄ 🛈; ⓂLine 7 to Changping Rd, exit 2) Rooms are boxy, but are in excellent condition at this bright and simple chain. It has wi-fi access throughout, but the cheapest rooms don't have windows.

SHANGHAI SOHO INTERNATIONAL YOUTH HOSTEL
HOSTEL $

Map p309 (苏州河畔国际青年旅社, Sūzhōu Hépàn Guójì Qīngnián Lǚshè; ☏021 5888 8817; www.yhachina.com; 1307 South Suzhou Rd; 苏州南路1307号; dm with/without bathroom incl breakfast ¥85/80, d from ¥258-358; ❄ @ 🛈; ⓂLine 1 to Xinzha Rd) Occupying a former warehouse along Sūzhōu Creek next to a park, this spacious hostel has high ceilings, painted murals on the walls and oodles of laid-back common space – including a sunny rooftop deck. It's a bit out of the way, but only a five-minute walk from the Xinzha Rd metro station on line 1, which runs through People's Square and the French Concession. Laundry and some kitchen facilities available. Bicycle hire costs ¥50 per day.

CACHET BOUTIQUE
HOTEL $$

Map p310 (凯世精品酒店, Kǎi Shì Jīngpǐn Jiǔdiàn; ☏021 3302 4990; www.cachethotels.com; 931 West Nanjing Rd; 南京西路931号; r/ste from ¥1300/2300; ❄ @ 🛈; ⓂLine 2, 7 to West Nanjing

Rd) While perhaps falling a tad short of its boutique aspirations, this hotel is a stylish choice – especially given its prime location on West Nanjing Rd. Its dark corridors won't be to everyone's taste, but the rooms themselves are fantastic, with plenty of colour, throw rugs, large mirrors, couches, designer beds and cooking facilities. There's also a small gym.

Reception is on the 3rd floor, which also has an arty open-plan cafe with plenty of lounges. Entrance is along Taixing Rd.

★URBN
BOUTIQUE HOTEL $$$

Map p310 (雅悦酒店, Yǎ Yuè Jiǔdiàn; ☏021 5153 4600; www.urbnhotels.com; 183 Jiaozhou Rd; 胶州路183号; r incl breakfast ¥1400-1700; ❄; ⓂLine 2, 7 to Jing'an Temple, exit 1) 🌿 Within a former post office, China's first carbon-neutral hotel not only incorporates recyclable materials and low-energy products where possible, it also calculates its complete carbon footprint – including staff commutes and delivery journeys – and offsets it by donating money to environmentally friendly projects. The 26 open-plan rooms are beautifully designed using recycled brick and timber from a French Concession *shíkùmén*, with low furniture and sunken living areas that exude space.

Bathtubs are in the bedroom rather than the bathroom (and sometimes right next to the bed!), while grey slate tiling and textured surfaces lend a distinctly urban vibe. Check out the cool wall behind reception arranged with a mosaic of well-travelled suitcases.

Its bar, BeerGrdn (p140), is a good spot to hang out with craft beers on tap.

PÚLÌ
LUXURY HOTEL $$$

Map p310 (璞丽酒店, Púlì Jiǔdiàn; ☏021 3203 9999; www.thepuli.com; 1 Changde Rd; 常德路1号; d from ¥2300; ❄ 🛈 🛈; ⓂLine 2, 7 to Jing'an Temple, exit 9) With open-space rooms divided by hanging silk screens and an understated beige-and-mahogany colour scheme accentuated by the beauty of a few well-placed orchids, the Púlì is an exquisite choice. The Zen calm and gorgeous design of this 26-storey hotel make a strong case for stylish skyscrapers. Other perks are the free minibar and coffee pod machine. Book ahead for discounts of up to 60%.

PEI MANSION HOTEL
HISTORIC HOTEL $$$

Map p310 (贝先大公馆, Bèixuān Dàgōngguǎn; ☏021 6289 7878; www.peimansionhotel.com; 170 Nanyang Rd; 南阳路170号; d incl breakfast from ¥1288; ❄ 🛈; ⓂLine 2, 7 to Jing'an Temple;

Line 2, 12, 13 to West Nanjing Rd) Step back in time to old Shànghǎi at this beautiful heritage hotel (c 1934), which was the former mansion residence of a Shanghainese banker. Its unique architecture incorporates an art deco design with unmistakable Chinese features. Spacious rooms are filled with antique furnishings. Though it's comfortable, don't expect five-star luxury or service – English isn't a strong point – but it does have a very handy central location.

The Cantonese restaurant in a beautiful period dining room and the palatial front garden round out the experience.

PORTMAN RITZ-CARLTON HOTEL $$$
Map p310 (波特曼丽嘉酒店, Bōtèmàn Lìjiā Jiǔdiàn; ☑021 6279 8888; www.ritzcarlton.com; 1376 West Nanjing Rd; 南京西路1376号; r from ¥1800; ✳@🛜🏊; Ⓜ Line 2, 7 to Jing'an Temple; Line 2, 12, 13 to West Nanjing Rd) Impeccable service, excellent facilities and a central location make this one of the best business hotels this side of the Huángpǔ River. While it lacks the gorgeous interior design and architectural pizzazz of Shànghǎi's newest crop of five-star hotels, it's nonetheless a first-rate luxury choice. Selling points include two 7th-floor pools and a gym.

You can access its executive lounge for ¥700: 24 hours of unlimited food and drinks.

🛏 Pǔdōng

BEEHOME HOSTEL HOSTEL $
Map p312 (宾家国际青年旅舍, Bīnjiā Guójì Qīngnián Lǔshè; ☑021 5887 9801; www.beehomehostel.com; 490 Dongchang Rd; 东昌路490号; dm from ¥90, tw/tr ¥298/358, d ¥318-390; ✳@🛜; Ⓜ Dongchang Rd) If you have to live Pǔdōngside, this well-tended hostel is a leafy and homely oasis in an otherwise innocuous housing estate. It offers basic but clean rooms, all with private bathrooms (even the dorms), and excellent communal areas – a bar-restaurant, a balcony seating area and a cute, tree-shaded courtyard garden.

There's wi-fi throughout, a laundry room, kitchen and bar. Go through the gate at 490 Dongchang Rd and the hostel is in a lane on the right.

★ MANDARIN ORIENTAL PUDONG HOTEL $$$
Map p312 (上海浦东文华东方酒店; Shànghǎi Pǔdōng Wénhuá Dōngfāng Jiǔdiàn; ☑021 2082 9888; www.mandarinoriental.com; 111 South Pu-

dong Rd; 浦东南路111号; d ¥1800-2800, ste from ¥3600; ✳@🛜🏊; Ⓜ Lujiazui) Slightly tucked away from the Lùjiāzuǐ five-star hotel melee in a sheltered riverside spot, the 362-room Mandarin Oriental is a visual feast, from the beautiful oval chandeliers and multicoloured glass murals (depicting forests) in the lobby to the excellent dining choices, such as Fifty 8° Grill. All five-star expectations are naturally met, but it's the meticulous service that ices this cake.

Sumptuous rooms aside, there's a 24-hour pool and gym, spa and fantastic views. The address may seem a bit stranded, but it's a short walk to the heart of Lùjiāzuǐ and there's a complimentary shuttle bus within the area.

★ RITZ-CARLTON SHANGHAI PUDONG HOTEL $$$
Map p312 (上海浦东丽思卡尔顿酒店, Shànghǎi Pǔdōng Lìsī Kǎ'ěrdùn Jiǔdiàn; ☑021 2020 1888; www.ritzcarlton.com; Shànghǎi IFC, 8 Century Ave; 世纪大道8号; d from ¥2800; ✳@🛜🏊; Ⓜ Lujiazui) From the stingray-skin-effect wallpaper in the lift to its stunning alfresco Flair bar (p154) and exceptional service, the exquisitely styled 285-room Ritz-Carlton in the Shànghǎi IFC is a peach. The beautifully designed rooms – a blend of feminine colours, eye-catching art deco motifs, chic elegance and dramatic Bund-side views – are a stylistic triumph. Open-plan bathrooms (divided by a screen) feature deep and inviting freestanding bathtubs.

★ PARK HYATT HOTEL $$$
Map p312 (柏悦酒店, Bóyuè Jiǔdiàn; ☑021 6888 1234; www.parkhyattshanghai.com; Shànghǎi World Financial Center, 100 Century Ave; 世纪大道100号世界金融中心; d from ¥2200; ✳@🛜🏊; Ⓜ Lujiazui) Spanning the 79th to 93rd floors of the towering Shànghǎi World Financial Center, this soaring hotel sees Pǔdōng's huge buildings (bar the Shànghǎi Tower) dwarfing into Lego blocks as lobby views graze the tip of the Jīnmào Tower. Smaller than the Grand Hyatt, it's a subdued but stylish 174-room affair with a deco slant, high-walled corridors of brown fabric and grey stone textures.

Rooms are luxurious, with nifty features (mist-free bathroom mirror containing a small TV screen, automatically opening toilet seats). All come with huge TVs, deep bathtubs, leather chaise longues, sumptuous beds and outrageously good views. There are a few dining options including **100 Century**

Avenue with its exceptional views. Access is from the south side of the tower.

GRAND HYATT
HOTEL $$$

Map p312 (金茂君悦大酒店, Jīnmào Jūnyuè Dàjiǔdiàn; ☑021 5049 1234; www.shanghai.grand. hyatt.com; Jīnmào Tower, 88 Century Ave; 世纪大道88号金茂大厦; d ¥1500-2000; ✳@⚡☎; Ⓜ Lujiazui) This classy 548-room hotel, spanning the top 34 floors of the majestic Jīnmào Tower, remains one of Shànghǎi's finest. The neck-craning 33-storey atrium is astonishing, while drinking and dining options, including On 56 (p154) and **Canton**, are outstanding. Tang dynasty poems are inscribed in gold above lovely beds, while espresso machines, smart tan-leather work desks and inviting bathrooms (some with incredible bathtub views) add to the luxury.

Corner rooms are coveted, views are stratospheric, and service remains highly attentive.

JUMEIRAH HIMALAYAS HOTEL
HOTEL $$$

Map p213 (卓美亚喜玛拉雅酒店, Zhuóměiyà Xīmǎlāyǎ Jiǔdiàn; ☑021 3858 0888; www.jumeirah.com; 1108 Meihua Rd; 梅花路1108号; d from ¥2088; ✳@⚡☎; Ⓜ Huamu Rd) Just perusing the lobby landscape, with its traditional Chinese paintings and vast overhead screen swarming with hypnotic patterns, is a diversion in culture-lite Pǔdōng. Feng-shui-arranged rooms are both gorgeous and spacious, and designed with a strong accent on traditional Chinese aesthetics with a modern twist.

Rooms come with lovely bathrooms, hardwood floors and coffee machines. Service is prompt and assuring, and an array of fine restaurants rounds it all out. Discounts are good, but book ahead.

PUDONG SHANGRI-LA
HOTEL $$$

Map p312 (浦东香格里拉大酒店, Pǔdōng Xiānggélǐlā Dàjiǔdiàn; ☑021 6882 8888; www.shangri-la.com; 33 Fucheng Rd; 富城路33号; r old tower/new tower from ¥2200/2500; ✳@⚡☎; Ⓜ Lujiazui) The Shangri-La's two towers – one dated, the other more dramatically modern – house an undisputed elegance. The lobby, corridors, restaurants and rooms are tastefully decorated in natural colours. The beds are sumptuous with pillows galore, and marble bathrooms are exquisite. Rooms in the new tower have floor-to-ceiling windows for full-on views.

🛏 Hóngkǒu & North Shànghǎi

⭐ ASTOR HOUSE HOTEL
HISTORIC HOTEL $$$

Map p314 (浦江饭店, Pǔjiāng Fàndiàn; ☑021 6324 6388; www.astorhousehotel.com; 15 Huangpu Rd; 黄浦路15号; d ¥1880-2580, 'celebrity' r ¥3080, ste from ¥4800; ✳@⚡; Ⓜ Tiantong Rd) Stuffed with history (and perhaps a ghost or two), this old-timer shakes up an impressive cocktail from select ingredients: a location just off the Bund; old-world, Shànghǎi-era charm; great discounts; and colossal rooms. It's played host to the likes of Einstein and Charlie Chaplin, and the original polished wooden floorboards, corridors and galleries pitch the mood somewhere between British public school and Victorian asylum.

CHAI LIVING RESIDENCES
APARTMENT $$$

Map p314 (☑021 5608 6051; www.chailiving.com; Embankment Bldg, 400 N Suzhou Rd; 苏州北路400号; apartments incl breakfast per week ¥7800-¥25,000; ✳⚡; Ⓜ Tiantong Rd) If you need a stylish Shànghǎi address, you can't get much better than one of these 20 luxurious, beautifully appointed and individually styled apartments in the Embankment Building. It is a living, breathing residential Shànghǎi block, and bumping into tenants merely adds authentic charm (although the grotty lift is a real shocker for some).

There's a minimum seven-night stay – just enough time to fully savour the outstanding views (none lower than the 5th floor) and decor of each apartment, each with soundproof German windows. Apartments range from 40 to 220 sq metres, with daily maid service, underfloor heating, kitchens with Nespresso coffee machines and tantalising river views.

🛏 Xújiāhuì & South Shànghǎi

ASSET HOTEL
HOTEL $

Map p316 (雅舍宾馆, Yǎshè Bīnguǎn; ☑021 6438 9900; www.asset-hotel.com; 590 South Wanping Rd; 宛平南路590号; r from ¥420; ✳@; Ⓜ Line 1, 4 to Shanghai Indoor Stadium) Housed in a yellow-and-white building hidden from the main road by apartments, this budget option offers excellent value. Rooms are basic but comfortable, with free broadband, complimentary mineral water, a fridge, TV and kettle. Rates include breakfast, and discounts reach 45%. Staff speaks limited English.

HUATING HOTEL & TOWERS
HOTEL $$

Map p316 (华亭宾馆, Huátíng Bīnguǎn; 1200 North Caoxi Rd;漕溪北路1200号; d from ¥698; ✳️📶🛗🚹; ⓜLines 1, 4 to Shanghai Indoor Stadium) An absolute monolith of a hotel overlooking the Shànghǎi Indoor Stadium, Huating offers good value for a five-star. Book a room on one of the top floors for views over the south of the city – the knots of ring roads with traffic whizzing around look almost charming from a great height. On-site facilities include a fitness centre with pool, hair salon and handful of restaurants.

🛏️ West Shànghǎi

ROCK & WOOD INTERNATIONAL YOUTH HOSTEL
HOSTEL $

Map p318 (老木国际青年旅舍, Lǎomù Guójì Qīngnián Lǚshè; ☎021 3360 2361; No 278, Lane 615, Zhaohua Rd; 昭化路615弄278号; dm ¥75-80, s ¥110-120, d ¥180-190; ✳️@📶; ⓜWest Yan'an Rd) With a serene bamboo-edged pond in its courtyard, and a bright and inviting lounge and bar area, this is an affordable and tranquil choice that sees a steady stream of travellers. Rooms and mixed dorms are clean and quiet, and the deluxe double (¥270 to ¥280) is the nicest of the bunch – basic but clean and comfy with a four-poster pine bed. The staff is very welcoming.

The cheapest single has a shared shower room. There's no kitchen but guests can use the fridge, and the hostel restaurant serves well-priced Western and Chinese cuisine, as well as great coffee.

★PENTAHOTEL SHANGHAI
BOUTIQUE HOTEL $$

Map p318 (上海贝尔特酒店, Shànghǎi Bèi'ěrtè Jiǔdiàn; ☎021 6252 1111; www.pentahotels.com; 1525 Dingxi Rd; 定西路1525号; d from ¥700; ✳️@📶; ⓜZhongshan Park) This youthful hotel is built on a snappy design ethos: the reception doubles as a cool cafe and bar; bright rooms are comfortable and boutique-style without being lavish; and the prices are reasonable. Backing it all up is a helpful staff and efficient management. It's right near Zhongshan Park metro station, and the hotel has free bikes for use with a handy map of the area.

NEW WORLD SHANGHAI HOTEL
HOTEL $$

Map p318 (上海巴黎春天新世界酒店, Shànghǎi Bālíchūntiān Xīnshìjiè Jiǔdiàn; ☎021 6240 8888; www.shanghai.newworldhotels.com; 1555 Dingxi Rd; 定西路1555号; d from ¥1000; ✳️📶🛗; ⓜZhongshan Park) Stylish and excellent value for money, this neat and tastefully presented hotel zeroes in on business travellers, but also appeals to visitors who want more bang for their buck. It seems far out in the west, but it's right by the Zhongshan Park (lines 2, 3 and 4) metro system for quick zips into the centre of things.

Rooms are spacious and modern, and the breakfast buffet is recommended. There's an outdoor swimming pool on the 15th floor and hotel dining options are sound.

XĪJIĀO STATE GUEST HOUSE
HOTEL $$

Map p318 (西郊宾馆, Xījiāo Bīnguǎn; ☎021 6219 8800; www.hotelxijiao.com; 1921 Hongqiao Rd; 虹桥路1921号; r from ¥1280; ✳️🛗; ⓜLongxi Rd) This quiet spot, which has hosted guests as esteemed as Queen Elizabeth II and Mao Zedong, claims to be the largest garden hotel in Shànghǎi. Its 80 hectares include huge lawns, streams, mature trees and a large lake. Standard rooms are nothing special, but facilities include indoor and outdoor tennis courts, a delightful indoor pool and a gym.

Understand
Shànghǎi

Shànghǎi Today

Rapidly becoming a world metropolis, Shànghǎi typifies modern China while being unlike anywhere else in the nation. Awash with cash, ambition and economic vitality, Shànghǎi is, for the movers and shakers of business, the place to be. For all its modernity and cosmopolitanism, however, Shànghǎi is part and parcel of the People's Republic of China, and its challenges are multiplying as fast as cocktails are mixed and served on the Bund.

Best on Film

Shanghai Triad (Zhang Yimou; 1995) Stylish take on Shànghǎi's 1930s gangster scene, starring Gong Li.
Empire of the Sun (Steven Spielberg; 1987) Dramatisation of JG Ballard's account of his internment in WWI Shànghǎi as a child.
Suzhou River (Ye Lou; 2000) A disturbing and obsessive narrative of love in modern Shànghǎi.

Best in Print

Five Star Billionaire (Tash Aw) Compelling tale of four Malaysians trying to make the Shànghǎi big time.
China Cuckoo: How I Lost a Fortune and Found a Life in China (Mark Kitto) Undone by Shànghǎi, Kitto flees to the mountains in this fascinating and charming read.
Life and Death in Shanghai (Nien Cheng) Classic account of the Cultural Revolution, with a Shànghǎi angle.
Shanghai: The Rise and Fall of a Decadent City 1842–1949 (Stella Dong) Rip-roaring profile of the city's good-old, bad-old days.

Money

The Shanghainese may chatter about traffic gridlock and the latest celebrity faux pas or political scandal, but what they really talk about is cash. Labelled *xiǎozī* – 'little capitalists' – by the rest of the land, the Shànghǎi Chinese know how to make *qián* (money) and, equally importantly, how to flaunt it. Ever since Shànghǎi first prospered under foreign control, wealth creation has been indivisible from the Shànghǎi psyche. Whether it's the stock market, apartment price tags or the latest Dior evening bag, money's the talk of the town.

Property

Shànghǎi property prices are talked about at bus stops in the same way British people discuss weather. High prices have ramifications for everyone renting (or owning) floor space, whether poor or wealthy. Amid dark mutterings of a property bubble, the government has repeatedly tried to tame the runaway market with tax and ownership measures to stifle speculation, with limited success, but property prices in relation to income remain higher than in London, New York or Tokyo.

Pollution

In recent years, Shànghǎi has reached record-breaking levels of atmospheric pollutants. In some areas of town, readings climbed to levels that were 28 times World Health Organization safe limits. In response, in 2016 the city pledged to introduce measures to tackle the pollution problem. Plans include building more parks and forest areas, introducing bans on air-polluting vehicles and factories, and monitoring dust emissions from construction sites. It's not just the air that's affected; a 2016 report by the Shanghai Environmental Protection Bureau stated that 50% of Shànghǎi's rivers and lakes were also polluted.

Ageing Shànghǎi

For such a seemingly sprightly city, Shànghǎi is ageing fast. In 2011, 23.4% of the city's population was over 60; by 2030 this will have leaped to more than 30%, with an additional 200,000 people reaching the age of 60 every year. Implemented in 1979, the one-child policy has created a huge bulge of pensioners, around 80% of whom will be looked after by single children. The bulge is set to continue despite new measures, introduced in 2014, permitting Shànghǎi couples to have a second baby if either parent is an only child.

Growth & Urban Density

Over the past two decades, Shànghǎi has grown faster than any other world city and now houses more than 24 million people. To accommodate the vast influx of economic migrants, the city's size has expanded six-fold since the early 1990s. With four times the number of people per sq km living here than in New York, there's not much elbow room. The government is stepping up efforts to control population growth and has set a population cap of 25 million for the city by the end of the decade.

Shànghǎi Versus China

Shànghǎi has a fraught relationship with the rest of China. The city has lured a vast army of labourers who work on the lowest-paid rung of the employment ladder. Although their city has always been a haven for outsiders, the Shànghǎi Chinese tend to look down on other Chinese. A non-Shànghǎi accent automatically flags *wàidìrén* (外地人), who may be considered *tǔ* (literally 'earth', meaning rural). Shànghǎi people conversely see themselves as *yáng* (literally 'sea', but meaning 'Western'). This chauvinism is almost an ideology in itself and, despite the glut of immigrant workers, *wàidì* Chinese have to jump through hoops to become a full 'local'. One such route is to marry a Shànghǎi person, and to stay married for at least 10 years.

Political Uncertainties

The city has been a success story of astonishing proportions, but Shànghǎi is part of a nation facing considerable challenges. The speed of economic growth has slowed, while relations with the East Asia region remain choppy: friction with Japan, Vietnam and the Philippines over contested islands in the East China Sea and South China Sea has steadily grown. In Shànghǎi, as anywhere else in China, the glowing coals of Chinese nationalism are easily stoked. Never far from the surface, anti-Japanese sentiment remains a potent and unpredictable force, occasionally flaring into acrimonious demonstrations such as the 2012 protests in Shànghǎi (and across China) over the Diàoyú (Senkaku) Islands. This uncertainty contributed to a 17% decline in the number of Japanese people living and working in Shànghǎi in 2014.

if Shànghǎi were 100 people

98 would be Han Chinese
1 would be non–Han Chinese
1 would be foreigner

age of population
(% of population by age)

74	16	10
15-64	0-14	65+

population per sq km

SHÀNGHǍI   CHINA

👤 ≈ 145 people

History

In just a few centuries, Shànghǎi went from being an insignificant walled town south of the mouth of the Yangzi River to becoming China's leading and wealthiest metropolis. A dizzying swirl of opium, trade, foreign control, vice, glamour, glitz, rebellion, restoration and money, Shànghǎi's story is a rags-to-riches saga of decadence, exploitation and, ultimately, achievement.

Shànghǎi's Marshy Roots

The online resource Virtual Shanghai (www. virtualshanghai. net) is an intriguing treasure trove of old photos, maps, documents, films and specialist information relating to historic Shànghǎi, and includes a blog.

Up until around the 7th century AD, Shànghǎi was little more than marshland. At that time, the area was known as Shēn (申), after Chunshen Jun, 春申君, a local nobleman from the 3rd century BC; or Hù (沪), after a type of bamboo fishing trap used by fishers. The character *hù* (沪) still identifies the city today – on car number plates, for example – while the city's main football team is known as Shanghai Shenhua (上海申花).

The earliest mention of the name Shànghǎi appears in the 11th century AD and refers to the small settlement that sprang up at the confluence of the Shànghǎi River (long since vanished) and the Huángpǔ River (黄浦江; Huángpǔ Jiāng). Upgraded from village status to market town in 1074, Shànghǎi became a city in 1297 after establishing itself as the major port in the area.

By the late 17th century Shànghǎi supported a population of 50,000, sustained on cotton production, fishing and, thanks to its excellent location at the head of the Yangzi River (长江; Cháng Jiāng), trade in silk and tea.

It All Started with Opium

During the early years of the Qing dynasty (1644–1911), the British East India Company and its later incarnations were trading in the only port open to the West: Canton (now Guǎngzhōu; 广州), south of Shànghǎi. British purchases of tea, silk and porcelain outweighed Chinese purchases of wool and spices, so by the late 18th century the British had decided to balance the books by slipping into India to swap (at a profit)

TIMELINE	453–221 BC	AD 242	960–1126
	Warring States period: the earliest imperial records date from this time, although Neolithic discoveries in Qīngpǔ County suggest human settlement of the region 5900 years ago.	The original Lónghuá Temple is built during the Three Kingdoms Period.	Chinese fleeing the Mongols during the Song dynasty boost the region's population, spurring Shànghǎi on to become the county seat of Jiāngsū in 1291.

silver for opium with which to purchase Chinese goods. The British passion for tea was increasingly matched by China's craving for opium (鸦片; *yāpiàn*), the drug that would virtually single-handedly create latter-day Shànghǎi and earn the city its bipolar reputation as the splendid 'Paris of the East' and the infamous 'Whore of the Orient'.

From a mercantile point of view, the trade in opium – known as 'foreign mud' in China – was an astonishing success, rapidly worming its way into every nook and cranny of Chinese society. Highly addictive and widely available thanks to the prolific efforts of British traders, the drug – smoked via a pipe – quickly became the drug of choice for all sections of the Chinese public, from the lowliest upwards. Jardine & Matheson's highly lucrative trade empire was founded on the opium business.

Opium became the driving force behind Shànghǎi's unstoppable rise and its descent into debauchery; it brought wealth to Shànghǎi's affluent taipans (powerful foreign businesspeople) and lucrative *hongs* (business houses) and fed the city's piercing inequalities. The city became a wanton netherworld of prostitution and vice, violent criminal gangs and corrupt police forces beneath a cartographic constitution of foreign concessions, settlements and Chinese districts.

The Opium War between Great Britain and China was similarly fought in the drug's name and as a pretext to extract the concessions that British opium traders sought from China. The Treaty of Nanking that concluded the First Opium War in 1842 was Shànghǎi's moment of reckoning: its signing spelled the death of old Shànghǎi and the birth of the wild, lawless and spectacularly prosperous endeavour that would rise up over the Huángpǔ River.

By the 1880s, around 10% of the Chinese population smoked opium. No other commodity became so uniquely associated with all of Shànghǎi's spectacular peaks and dismal troughs.

The Illegitimate Birth of Shànghǎi

The Treaty of Nanking in 1842 stipulated, among other things: peace between China and Britain; security and protection of British persons and property; the opening of Canton, Fúzhōu, Xiàmén, Níngbō and Shànghǎi, as well as residence for foreigners and consulates in those cities (for the purpose of trade); fair import and export tariffs; the possession of Hong Kong; and an indemnity of US$18 million. Ironically enough, the trade of opium, legal or otherwise, never entered into the treaty.

Following Great Britain's lead, other countries were inspired to join in, including the US and France. In 1843 the first British consul moved into a local house in the Old Town, signalling a foreign presence in the city that would last for the next 100 years.

Of the five port cities in China, Shànghǎi was the most prosperous due to its superb geographical location, capital edge and marginal interference from the Chinese government. Trade and businesses boomed,

HISTORY THE ILLEGITIMATE BIRTH OF SHÀNGHǍI

1553	1603	1685	1793
The city wall around Shànghǎi's Old Town is constructed to fend off Japanese pirates; 9m high and 5km around, the wall stands until the fall of the Qing dynasty; it's demolished in 1912.	Shànghǎi scientist, astronomer and scholar Xu Guangqi is baptised as a Roman Catholic.	A customs house is opened in Shànghǎi for the first time.	Lord Macartney, George III's envoy to China, is rebuffed by the Qianlong emperor in Chéngdé, sinking British hopes of expanding legitimate trade relations with the 'Middle Kingdom'.

and by 1850 the foreign settlements housed more than 100 merchants, missionaries and physicians, three-quarters of them British. In 1844, 44 foreign ships made regular trade with China. By 1849, 133 ships lined the shores and by 1855, 437 foreign ships clogged the ports.

Foreigners were divided into three concessions. The original British Concession was north of Bubbling Well Rd (now West Nanjing Rd). The American Concession began life in Hóngkŏu District after Bishop William Boone had set up a mission there. These two concessions later joined to form one large area known as the International Settlement. The French, meanwhile, set up their own settlement south of the British one and to the west of the Old Town, in an area that is still referred to by English speakers as the French Concession.

From regulation to sanitation, everything in Shànghăi was vested in the foreign oligarchies of the Municipal Council and the Conseil d'Administration Municipale, a pattern that was to last as long as the settlements. It was not until the early 1920s that Chinese and Japanese residents (eventually the two largest groups in the settlements) were allowed even limited representation on the council.

From the start, Shànghăi's *raison d'être* was trade. Silks, tea and porcelain were still sailing to the West, and 30,000 chests of opium were being delivered into China annually. Soon great Hong Kong trading houses such as Butterfield & Swire and Jardine & Matheson set up shop, and trade in opium, silk and tea gradually shifted to textiles, real estate, banking, insurance and shipping. Banks in particular boomed; soon all of China's loans, debts and indemnity payments were funnelled through Shànghăi. Buying and selling was handled by Chinese middlemen, known as *compradors* (from the Portuguese), from Canton and Níngbō, who formed a rare link between the Chinese and foreign worlds. The city attracted immigrants and entrepreneurs from across China, and overseas capital and expertise pooled in the burgeoning metropolis.

Foreign ideas were similarly imported. By the 1880s, huge numbers of proselytising American Protestants were 'saving souls' in Shànghăi, while the erudite Jesuits oversaw a flourishing settlement in Xújiāhuì (徐家汇), known locally as Siccawei (or Zikawei).

Gradually sedan chairs and single-wheeled carts gave way to rickshaws and carriages, the former imported from Japan in 1874. Shànghăi lurched into the modern age with gaslights (1865), electricity (1882), motorcars (1895), a cinema and an electric tram (1908), and its first bus (1922).

The Manchu in Běijīng gave only cursory glances to the growth of Shànghăi as all eyes focused on the continued survival of the Qing dynasty, under threat from a barrage of insurgencies that arose from within the rapidly radicalising confines of the Middle Kingdom.

By 1934 Shànghăi was the world's fifth-largest city, home to the tallest buildings in Asia, boasting more cars in one city than the rest of China combined, and a haven for more than 70,000 foreigners among a population of three million. Its cosmopolitanism and modernity were encapsulated in the architectural style of art deco.

1823	1839	1842	1843
The British import roughly 7000 chests of opium annually, compared with 1000 chests in 1773. With about 140lb of opium per chest, it's enough to keep one million addicts happy.	Tensions between England and China come to a head when British merchants are arrested and forced to watch three million pounds of raw opium being flushed out to sea.	On 29 August Sir Henry Pottinger signs the Treaty of Nanking aboard the *Cornwallis* on the Yangzi River, prising open China's doors and securing Hong Kong.	A supplement to the Treaty of Nanking, the Treaty of the Bogue regulated trade between Britain and China and the terms under which British people could reside in Shànghăi.

Rebellious Youth

Wreathed in opium, sucked dry by local militia, crippled by taxes, bullied by foreign interests and increasingly exposed to Western ideas, Shànghǎi's population was stirring, and anti-Manchu rebellions began to erupt. The first major rebellion to have an impact on Shànghǎi was the Taiping (太平 – literally, 'Supreme Peace'), led by the Hakka visionary Hong Xiuquan. The uprising, which led to 20 million deaths, went down as the bloodiest in human history.

Hong claimed to have ascended to heaven and received a new set of internal organs by a golden-bearded Jehovah, which he used to battle the evil spirits of the world with his elder brother Jesus Christ. Hong's distorted Christian ideology dates from his contact with Christian missionaries in Canton and an identification of his surname (洪; Hóng, meaning 'flood') with the Old Testament deluge. Believing himself chosen, Hong saw the Manchu as devils to be exterminated and set about recruiting converts to establish a Heavenly Kingdom in China. The rebels burst out of Jīntián village in Guǎngxī (广西) in 1851, swept through Guìzhōu (贵州) and succeeded in taking Nánjīng (南京) three years later, where they established their Heavenly Capital (天京; Tiānjīng).

With the Taiping-inspired Small Swords Society entrenched in the Old Town and fearing the seizure of Shànghǎi, the foreign residents organised the Shanghai Volunteer Corps, a force that would repeatedly protect the interests of foreigners in Shànghǎi.

The Taiping threatened again in 1860 but were beaten back by the mercenary armies of Frederick Townsend Ward, an American adventurer hired by the Qing government who was eventually killed in Sōngjiāng in 1862. British and Qing forces joined to defeat the rebels, the Europeans preferring to deal with a corrupt and weak Qing government than with a powerful, united China governed by the Taiping. The Taiping originally

HISTORICAL READS

→ *In Search of Old Shanghai* (Pan Ling, 1986)

→ *Shanghai 1937: Stalingrad on the Yangtze* (Peter Harmsen, 2014)

→ *Secret War in Shanghai* (Bernard Wasserstein, 2000)

→ *Old Shanghai: Gangsters in Paradise* (Lynn Pan, 2011)

→ *Shanghai* (Harriet Sergeant, 2002)

→ *Shanghai: The Rise and Fall of a Decadent City 1842–1949* (Stella Dong, 2001)

→ *Through the Looking Glass: China's Foreign Journalists from Opium Wars to Mao* (Paul French, 2009)

1846	1847	1849	1850
Richard's Hotel, the first Western hotel in Shànghǎi, opens its doors on the Bund.	Shànghǎi's first library, the Bibliotheca Zi-Ka-Wei in Xújiāhuì, opens.	The French establish their own settlement, known as the French Concession, to the south of the British Concession and beyond the walls of the Chinese Old Town.	The influential English-language weekly newspaper the *North China Herald* is published for the first time (later published in a daily edition as the *North China Daily News*).

banked on the support of the Western powers, but Westerners were ultimately repelled by Hong's heretical concoction.

As rebellions ravaged the countryside, hundreds of thousands of refugees poured into the safety of Shànghǎi's concessions, setting up home alongside the foreigners and sparking a real-estate boom that spurred on Shànghǎi's rapid urbanisation and made the fortunes of many of Shànghǎi's entrepreneurs.

As imperial control loosened, the encroaching Western powers moved in to pick off China's colonial 'possessions' in Indochina and Korea. National humiliation and a growing xenophobia – partly generated by a distrust of Christian missionaries and their activities – spawned the anti-Western Boxer Rebellion, championed in its later stages by the empress dowager, Cixi.

The Boxers were quelled by Western and Japanese troops – who went on to sack Běijīng's Summer Palace – in 1900, but not before the legation quarter in the capital had been devastated. Empress Cixi and her entourage fled to Xī'ān (西安), but returned to Běijīng to face massive indemnities strapped onto the Qing government by the foreign powers.

The weakened state of the country, the death of the empress dowager and the legion of conspiring secret societies marked the end of the tottering Qing dynasty. Shànghǎi renounced the Qing by declaring independence on the wave of public revolt that swept China in 1911, and all men were instructed to shear off their *queues* (long pigtails that symbolised subjection to Manchu authority). But despite the momentous end to China's final dynasty – one that had ruled China for almost 250 years – insular Shànghǎi carried out business as usual, relatively unaffected by the fall of the Qing or the upheavals of WWI. As the rest of China descended into a bedlam of fighting warlords and was plunged into darkness, Shànghǎi emerged as a modern industrial city.

The crossing over Sūzhōu Creek was once undertaken by ferry from three crossing points, until the first proper bridge (Wills' Bridge) was built from wood in 1856, lashing the prosperous British and American settlements together.

'Paris of the East' Reaches Its Peak

By the first decade of the 20th century, Shànghǎi's population had swelled to one million. As the most elite and cosmopolitan of China's cities, Shànghǎi ensnared capitalists and intellectuals alike, with literature and cinema thriving in the ferment as Chinese intellectuals began to ponder the fate of a modern China.

The foreigners had effectively plucked out prime locations and, using their ever-increasing wealth – the fruits of cheap labour – they established exclusive communities designed after their own countries and dovetailing with their requirements. Vice and crime continued to flourish, assisted by the absence of a paramount police force. The multiple jurisdictions, each representing the laws of the various settlements and

1859	1860s	1863	1882
By now half of all British troops stationed in Shànghǎi suffer from venereal disease, introduced to Shànghǎi by Westerners and spread by the city's prostitution industry.	Cotton emerges as Shànghǎi's chief export.	Shànghǎi's first fire engine arrives and enters service, followed by the launch of the Shànghǎi Volunteer Fire Service three years later.	Shànghǎi – and China – is electrified for the very first time by the British-founded Shànghǎi Electric Company. The Bund is illuminated by electric lights the following year.

the Chinese city, meant that criminals could simply move from one area to another to elude arrest.

Exploited in workhouse conditions, crippled by hunger and poverty, sold into slavery and excluded from the city's high life created by the foreigners, the poor of Shànghǎi developed an appetite for resistance. Intellectuals and students, provoked by the startling inequalities between rich and poor, were perfect receptacles for the many outside influences circulating in the concessions. The *Communist Manifesto* was translated into Chinese and swiftly caught on among secret societies.

In light of the intense dislike that many Chinese felt for foreigners, it may seem ironic that fundamental ideals stemmed from overseas inspirations. Shànghǎi, with its vast proletariat (30,000 textile workers alone) and student population, had become the communists' hope for revolution, and the first meeting of the Chinese Communist Party, where Mao Zedong was present, was held in July 1921 in a French Concession house. Elsewhere, political violence was growing.

In May 1925 resentment spilled over when a Chinese worker was killed in a clash with a Japanese mill manager. In the ensuing demonstrations the British opened fire and 12 Chinese were killed. In protest, 150,000 workers went on strike, which was later seen as a defining moment marking the decline of Western prestige and power.

Strikes and a curfew paralysed the city as the Kuomintang under Chiang Kaishek (with the help of communist supporters under Zhou Enlai) wrested Shànghǎi from the Chinese warlord Sun Chaofang.

Kaishek's aim was not focused on the settlements or even the warlords, but rather his erstwhile allies the communists, whom he then betrayed in an act of breathtaking perfidy. Backed by Shànghǎi bankers and armed by Shànghǎi's top gangster Du Yuesheng, Chiang Kaishek armed gangsters, suited them up in Kuomintang uniforms and launched a surprise attack on the striking workers' militia. Du's machine guns were turned on 100,000 workers taking to the streets, killing as many as 5000. In the ensuing period, known as the White Terror, 12,000 communists were executed in three weeks. Zhou Enlai and other communists fled to Wǔhàn (武汉), leaving Shànghǎi in the hands of the warlords, the wealthy and the Kuomintang.

Nestled away safely in a world of selectively structured law and merciless capitalism, by the 1930s Shànghǎi had reached its economic zenith and was soon to begin its fatal downwards slide. Shànghǎi had become a modern city replete with art deco cinemas and apartment blocks, the hottest bands and the latest fashions – a place of great energy where two cultures met. Chinese magazines carried ads for Quaker Oats, Colgate and Kodak, while Chinese girls, dressed in traditional *qípáo* (cheongsam; Chinese-style dresses), advertised American cigarettes.

The first railroad in China was the Woosung Railway, opened in 1876, running between Shànghǎi and Wúsōng (吴淞); it operated for less than a year before being dismantled and shipped to Taiwan.

1891	1895	1908	1910
The Shànghǎi Sharebrokers Association is established, functioning as Shànghǎi's (and China's) first stock exchange.	The Treaty of Shimonoseki (also called the Treaty of Maguan) concludes the First Sino-Japanese War, forcing China to cede territories (including Taiwan) to Japan.	The Shànghǎi–Nánjīng railway is completed. Covering 193 miles of track, the journey takes around 5½ hours.	Shànghǎi is hit by mob disturbances (called the Plague Riots) in response to anti-plague measures.

Shànghăi's modernity was symbolised by the Bund, Shànghăi's Wall Street, a place of feverish trading and an unabashed playground for Western business sophisticates. To this day the bombastic strip alongside the Huángpŭ River remains the city's most eloquent reminder that modern Shànghăi is a very foreign invention.

The 'Paris of the East' and 'Whore of the Orient' became an increasingly exotic port of call. Flush with foreign cash and requiring neither visa nor passport for entrance, Shànghăi became home to the movers and the shakers, the down-and-out and on-the-run. It offered a place of refuge and a fresh start, and rejected no one. Everyone who came to Shànghăi, it was said, had something to hide. The city had become three times as crowded as London, and the cosmopolitan mix of people was unequalled anywhere in the world.

The Death of Old Shànghăi

Following Japan's invasion of Manchuria in 1931, with anti-Japanese sentiment inflamed and Chinese nationalistic fervour on the rise, the Japanese seized the opportunity to protect their interests. Warships brought in tens of thousands of Japanese troops, who proceeded to take on and defeat the Chinese 19th Route army in Zhábĕi (闸北). The Japanese conducted an aerial bombing campaign against the district, levelling most of its buildings.

After Japan's full-scale invasion of China in 1937, Chiang Kaishek took a rare stand in Shànghăi – and the city bled for it. The Japanese lost 40,000 men, the Chinese anywhere from 100,000 to 250,000.

The International Settlement was not immune to the fighting, and after Chinese aircraft accidentally bombed the Bund and Nanjing Rd, most foreign residents reacted not by fighting, as perhaps they would have done for a colony, but by evacuation. Four million Chinese refugees were not so lucky.

After intense house-to-house fighting, the Japanese invaders finally subdued Shànghăi in November 1937, allowing their soldiers to proceed to Sūzhōu before advancing on Nánjīng for their infamous occupation of the

SHANGHAIED

If New York was so good they named it twice, then Shànghăi was so bad they made it an undesirable verb. To shanghai, or 'render insensible by drugs or opium, and ship on a vessel wanting hands', dates from the habit of press-ganging sailors. Men, many of whom were found drunk in 'Blood Alley' (today's Xikou Rd, off modern-day Jinling Rd), were forced onto ships, which then set sail, leaving the comatose sailors no choice but to make up the deficient crew numbers when they sobered up.

1912	1920	1921	1927
Republicans pull down Shànghăi's ancient city walls to break links with the ousted Qing dynasty. The Provisional Republican Government of China is established in Nánjīng.	Built to serve the city's first influx of Jewish immigrants, Shànghăi's first synagogue, the Ohel Rachel Synagogue, opens.	The first meeting of the Chinese Communist Party, formed by Marxist groups advised by the Soviet Comintern, takes place in Shànghăi.	Chiang Kaishek takes control of Shànghăi, followed by his 'White Terror', a slaughter of communists, left-wing sympathisers and labour leaders, also known as the 'Shànghăi Massacre'.

city. Under Japanese rule the easy glamour of Shànghǎi's heyday was replaced by a dark cloud of political assassinations, abductions, gunrunning and fear. Espionage by the Japanese, the nationalists, the British and the Americans for wartime information was rife. The rich were abducted and fleeced. Japanese racketeers set up opium halls in the so-called Badlands in the western outskirts of the city, and violent gangs ran rabid.

By December 1941 the hostilities between Japan and the allied powers had intensified abroad, giving the Japanese incentive to take over the foreign settlements in Shànghǎi. Suspect foreigners were taken off for interrogation and torture in notorious prisons such as the Bridgehouse, where JB Powell, editor of the *China Weekly Review*, lost all his toes to gangrene. Prisoners were forced to sit for hours in the cold, with heads lowered, facing Tokyo.

The British and American troops had abandoned Shànghǎi in 1942 to concentrate their energies elsewhere, and the British and American governments, unable to overtake the Japanese, signed over their rights of the foreign settlements to Chiang Kaishek in Chóngqìng in 1943, bringing to a close a century of foreign influence.

After the Japanese surrender in 1945, a few foreigners, released from their internment, tried to sweep out their Tudor-style homes and carry on as before, but priorities and politics had shifted. The gangs, conmen, dignitaries, merchants and anyone else who could had already made their escape to Hong Kong. Those who remained had to cope with biting inflation of 1100%.

By 1948 the Kuomintang was on the edge of defeat in their civil war with the communists, and hundreds of thousands of Kuomintang troops changed sides to join Mao Zedong's forces. In May, Chen Yi led the Red Army troops into Shànghǎi, and by October all the major cities in southern China had fallen to the communists.

In Běijīng on 1 October 1949, Mao Zedong stood atop the Gate of Heavenly Peace, announced that the Chinese people had stood up, and proclaimed the foundation of the People's Republic of China (PRC). Chiang Kaishek then fled to the island of Formosa (Taiwan), taking with him China's gold reserves and the remains of his air force and navy, to set up the Republic of China (ROC), naming his new capital Taipei (台北, Táiběi).

The People's Republic

The birth of the PRC marked the end of 105 years of 'the paradise for adventurers'. The PRC dried up 200,000 opium addicts; shut down Shànghǎi's infamous brothels and 're-educated' 30,000 prostitutes; eradicated the slums; slowed inflation; and eliminated child labour – no easy task. The state took over Shànghǎi's faltering businesses; the

In the 1920s and '30s, 25,000 White Russians fled their home country for Shànghǎi. By 1935 they formed the city's second-largest foreign community after the Japanese. Ave Joffre (Huaihai Rd) became the heart of the White Russian community. There were Russian cinemas, printing presses and even rival revolutionary and tsarist newspapers.

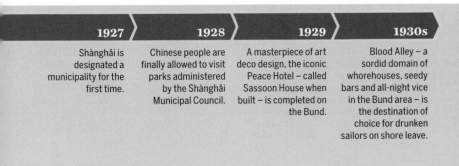

1927	1928	1929	1930s
Shànghǎi is designated a municipality for the first time.	Chinese people are finally allowed to visit parks administered by the Shànghǎi Municipal Council.	A masterpiece of art deco design, the iconic Peace Hotel – called Sassoon House when built – is completed on the Bund.	Blood Alley – a sordid domain of whorehouses, seedy bars and all-night vice in the Bund area – is the destination of choice for drunken sailors on shore leave.

SHÀNGHĂI'S GANGSTERS

In Shànghǎi's climate of hedonist freedoms, political ambiguities and capitalist free-for-all, it was perhaps inevitable that the city should spawn China's most powerful mobsters. Ironically, in 1930s Shànghǎi the most binding laws were those of the underworld, with their blood oaths, secret signals and strict code of honour. China's modern-day triads and snakeheads owe much of their form to their Shanghainese predecessors.

One of Shànghǎi's early gangsters was Huang Jinrong, or 'Pockmarked' Huang, who had the enviable position of being the most powerful gangster in Shànghǎi while at the same time holding the highest rank in the French Concession police force. Now sadly closed, Great World (大世界; Dà Shìjiè) opened in 1917 as a place for acrobats and nightclub stars to rival the existing New World building on Nanjing Rd. It soon became a centre for the bizarre and the burlesque under the seedy control of Huang Jinrong in the 1930s before being commandeered as a refugee centre during WWII.

Another famous underworld figure was Cassia Ma, the Night-Soil Queen, who founded a huge empire on the collection of human waste, which was ferried upriver to be sold as fertiliser at a large profit.

The real godfather of the Shànghǎi underworld, however, was Du Yuesheng, or 'Big-Eared' Du as he was known to anyone brave enough to say it to his face. Born in Pǔdōng, Du soon moved across the river and was recruited into the Green Gang (青帮; Qīngbāng), where he worked for Huang. He gained fame by setting up an early opium cartel with the rival Red Gang, and rose through the ranks. By 1927 Du was the head of the Green Gang and in control of the city's prostitution, drug running, protection and labour rackets. Du's special genius was to kidnap the rich and then to negotiate their release, taking half of the ransom money as commission. With an estimated 20,000 men at his beck and call, Du travelled everywhere in a bulletproof sedan, like a Chinese Al Capone, protected by armed bodyguards crouched on the running boards.

His control of the labour rackets led to contacts with warlords and politicians. In 1927 Du played a major part in Chiang Kaishek's anticommunist massacre and later became adviser to the Kuomintang. He was a fervent nationalist, and his money supplied the anti-Japanese resistance movement.

Yet Du always seemed to crave respectability. In 1931 he was elected to the Municipal Council and was known for years as the unofficial mayor of Shànghǎi. He became a Christian halfway through his life and ended up best known as a philanthropist. When the British poet WH Auden visited Shànghǎi in 1937, Du was head of the Chinese Red Cross.

During the Japanese occupation of Shànghǎi, Du fled to Chóngqìng (Chungking). After the war he settled in Hong Kong, where he died a multimillionaire in 1951. These days you can stay in Du's former Shànghǎi pad, now the Dōnghú Hotel, or in the building once used as offices by him and Huang, now the exquisite Mansion Hotel. Alternatively, seek out Du's one-time summer dwelling in the mountain retreat of Mògānshān in Zhèjiāng province.

1930s	1931	1932	1935
Shànghǎi is the world's fifth-largest city (the largest in Asia), supporting a population of four million. Opium use declines as it goes out of fashion.	In September the Japanese invade Manchuria and by December extend control over the entire area. Shànghǎi's Chinese react with a boycott of Japanese goods.	Japanese naval aircraft bomb Shànghǎi on 28 January.	By now 25,000 White Russians have flocked to Shànghǎi, turning the Frênch Concession into Little Moscow.

racecourse became the obligatory People's Park; and Shànghǎi fell uniformly into step with the rest of China. Under Běijīng's stern hand, the decadence disappeared and the splendour similarly faded.

Yet the communists, essentially a peasant regime, remained suspicious of Shànghǎi. The group lacked the experience necessary to run a big city and they resented Shànghǎi's former leadership, which they always regarded as a den of foreign-imperialist-inspired iniquity, a constant reminder of national humiliation, and the former headquarters of the Kuomintang.

Perhaps because of this, Shànghǎi, in its determination to prove communist loyalty, became a hotbed of political extremism and played a major role in the Cultural Revolution, the decade of political turmoil that lasted from 1966 to 1976 (although its most ferocious period ended in 1969). Sidelined in Běijīng, it was to Shànghǎi that Mao turned in an attempt to reinvigorate the revolution and claw his way back into power. For most of a decade the city was the power base of the prime movers of the Cultural Revolution, the Gang of Four: Wang Hongwen; Yao Wenyuan (editor of *Shanghai Liberation Army Daily*); Zhang Chunqiao (Shànghǎi's director of propaganda); and Jiang Qing, wife of Mao (and failed Shànghǎi movie actress, formerly known as Lan Ping, who used her position to exact revenge on former colleagues at Shànghǎi Film Studios).

Encouraged by Mao, a rally of one million Red Guards marched through People's Square, a force of anarchy that resulted in the ousting of the mayor. Competing Red Guards tried to outdo each other in revolutionary fervour – Shanghainese who had any contacts with foreigners were criticised, forced to wear dunce caps, denounced and sometimes killed.

As the Cultural Revolution unfolded, between 1966 and 1970 one million of Shànghǎi's youth were sent to the countryside. Shànghǎi's industries closed; the Bund was renamed Revolution Blvd; and the road opposite the closed Soviet consulate became Anti-Revisionist St. At one point there was even a plan to change the (revolutionary) red of the city's traffic lights to mean 'go'.

In the revolutionary chaos and in a bid to destroy the 'four olds' (old customs, old habits, old culture and old thinking), Chinese religion was devastated. Temples were destroyed or converted to factories; priests were conscripted to make umbrellas; monks were sent to labour in the countryside, where they often perished; and believers were prohibited from worship. Amid this, Shànghǎi's concession architecture stood largely preserved, its wealthy occupants merely fading memories of a vanished era.

In 1976, after the death of Mao, the Gang of Four was overthrown and imprisoned. Accused of everything from forging Mao's statements to hindering earthquake relief efforts, the gang's members were arrested on 6 October 1976 and tried in 1980. Jiang Qing remained unrepentant,

Between 1931 and 1941, 20,000 Jews took refuge in Shànghǎi, only to be forced into Japanese war ghettos, and fleeing again in 1949. Adding to the mix was an influx of Russians seeking sanctuary from the 1917 Bolshevik Revolution. By 1915 the Japanese had become Shànghǎi's largest non-Chinese group, turning Hóngkǒu into a de facto Japanese Concession.

HISTORY THE PEOPLE'S REPUBLIC

1936	1937	1938	1943
Lu Xun, one of China's finest modern novelists and writers, dies of tuberculosis in Shànghǎi.	In an event known as Bloody Saturday, bombs fall onto the foreign concessions for the first time on 14 August, killing more than 2000.	Twenty thousand Jews arrive in Shànghǎi, fleeing persecution in Europe.	The Japanese round up 7600 allied nationals into eight internment camps as the formal foreign presence in Shànghǎi ends.

When the clean-up of Sūzhōu Creek was finally completed in 2012, a total of more than 100 wartime bombs had been dredged from the muck at the river bottom, many dating to the Japanese occupation.

hurling abuse at her judges and holding famously to the line that she 'was Chairman Mao's dog – whoever he told me to bite, I bit'. Jiang Qing's death sentence was commuted and she lived under house arrest until 1991, when she committed suicide by hanging.

When the Cultural Revolution lost steam, pragmatists such as Zhou Enlai began to look for ways to restore normalcy. In 1972 US president Richard Nixon signed the Shanghai Communiqué at the Jinjiang Hotel. The agreement provided a foundation for increased trade between the US and China, and marked a turning point in China's foreign relations. With the doors of China finally reopened to the West in 1979, and with Deng Xiaoping at the helm, China set a course of pragmatic reforms towards economic reconstruction, which would result in consistently strong annual growth rates.

In communist China, however, the rush of economic reform generated very little in the way of political reform. Corruption and inflation led to widespread social unrest, which in 1989 resulted in the demonstrations in Běijīng's Tiān'ānmén Sq.

The demonstrations overtaking the capital spread to Shànghǎi. In the days leading up to 4 June 1989 tens of thousands of students – holding banners demanding, among other things, democracy and freedom – marched from their universities to People's Square. Hundreds went on hunger strike. Workers joined students to bring chaos to the city by instigating roadblocks across more than 100 Shànghǎi streets. But city mayor Zhu Rongji was praised for his handling of events. In contrast to leaders in Běijīng, he didn't take a heavy-handed approach. According to Lynn T White, author of *Unstately Power* (1999), the only serious incident during the unrest was on 6 June when a train outside Shànghǎi Railway Station ran into demonstrators who were trying to block it. Eight people were killed and 30 were injured.

In 1966 a People's Commune, modelled on the Paris Commune of the 19th century, was set up in Shànghǎi. Led by Zhang Chunqiao from headquarters in the Peace Hotel, it lasted just three weeks before Mao, sensing that the anarchy had gone too far, ordered the army put an end to it.

The Nineties & Noughties

In 1990 the central government began pouring money into Shànghǎi, beginning the city's stunning turnaround. The process was unparalleled in scale and audacity. By the mid-1990s more than a quarter (some sources say half) of the world's high-rise cranes were slowly circling above town. A huge proportion of the world's concrete was funnelled into Shànghǎi as China sucked up a staggering 50% of world production.

Towering over Lùjiāzuǐ, the Oriental Pearl TV Tower was completed in 1994, establishing an architectural template for Pǔdōng that survives today. What followed was a roll-call of skyscraper heavyweights: the Jīnmào Tower (1999), Tomorrow Square (2003), Shimao International Plaza

1945	1949	1966	1972
After the Japanese surrender, the Kuomintang takes back Shànghǎi, closing treaty ports, and revoking foreign trading and self-governing rights.	Hyperinflation means that one US dollar is worth 23,280,000 yuán. Communist forces take Shànghǎi and the establishment of the People's Republic of China (PRC) is proclaimed.	The Cultural Revolution is launched from Shànghǎi; eventually one million Shanghainese are sent to the countryside. St Ignatius Cathedral finds new employment as a grain store.	US President Nixon visits Shànghǎi as China rejoins the world.

(2005) and the Shànghǎi World Financial Center (2008). Shànghǎi's vertical transformation mirrored its growing stature as an international city.

Before the 1990s were spent, the city had already built two metro lines, a light-railway system, a US$2 billion international airport in Pǔdōng, a US$2 billion elevated highway, several convention centres, two giant bridges, several underground tunnels and a whole new city (Pǔdōng).

Always a byword for excess, Shànghǎi had effortlessly outstripped every other city in China by the dawn of the new millennium, bar southern rival Hong Kong. Obsessively comparing itself to Hong Kong, the Huángpǔ River city closed the gap on the ex-British territory with breathtaking rapidity during the noughties. The Chinese government deliberately sought to make Shànghǎi the financial centre of Asia, replacing Hong Kong as China's frontier of the future, swinging the spotlight of attention from the ex-colony on to a home-grown success story.

Served by two airports and the world's first Maglev train, Shànghǎi began to command some of the most dizzying salaries in China, with per capita incomes around four times the national average. The metro system was massively expanded, and is, to date, the world's second longest (running to 14 lines) at 538km in length. Pǔdōng was built from the soles up, forging mainland China's most electrifying skyline. Skyscraping residential towers sprouted across the city while car ownership trebled in the five years from 2007. Swelling numbers of residents dwelled in gated villa communities, rewarding themselves with a desirable middle-class standard of living.

TOP SHÀNGHǍI HISTORICAL BIOGRAPHIES

➠ *Captive in Shanghai,* Hugh Collar (1991) – A fascinating personal account of life in the Japanese internment camps in the early 1940s. It's published by Oxford University Press, but is hard to get your hands on.

➠ *Daughter of Shanghai,* Tsai Chin (1989) – Daughter of one of China's most-famous Běijīng opera stars, Chin left Shànghǎi in 1949 and later starred in the film *The World of Suzie Wong* (as the original 'China doll') and in *The Joy Luck Club*. This memoir bridges two worlds during two different times.

➠ *Life and Death in Shanghai,* Nien Cheng (1987) – A classic account of the Cultural Revolution and one of the few biographies with a Shànghǎi angle.

➠ *Nobody Said Not to Go: The Life, Loves, and Adventures of Emily Hahn,* Ken Cuthbertson (1998) – A look at the unconventional life of Emily Hahn, who passed through Shànghǎi in 1935 (with her pet gibbon), got hooked on opium and became the concubine of a Chinese poet.

➠ *Red Azalea,* Anchee Min (2006) – A sometimes racy account of growing up in Shànghǎi in the 1950s and 1960s amid the turmoil of the Cultural Revolution.

1976	1989	1990	1995
Mao Zedong dies in September – in the same year as the Tángshān earthquake – preparing the way for a rehabilitated Deng Xiaoping to assume leadership of the PRC.	Antigovernment demonstrations in Shànghǎi's People's Square mirror similar protests in Běijīng's Tiān'ānmén Sq; the demonstrations are broken up.	Pǔdōng discovers it will become a Special Economic Zone (SEZ), converting it, over the next decade, from flat farmland into one of the world's most ultramodern urban landscapes.	Line 1 of the Shànghǎi metro commences operation, with line 2 opening five years later.

SHÀNGHǍI VICE

Underneath the glitz and glamour of 1930s Shànghǎi lay a pool of sweat, blood and crushing poverty. According to a British resident, Shànghǎi was violent, disreputable, snobbish, mercenary and corrupt.

The city was often a place of horrific cruelty and brutal violence. After the Small Swords Rebellion, 66 heads, including those of elderly women and children, were stuck up on the city walls. In 1927 striking workers were beheaded and their heads displayed in cages. Up to 80,000 rickshaw pullers worked the littered streets until they dropped, while overcrowded factory workers routinely died of lead and mercury poisoning. In 1934 the life expectancy of the Chinese in Shànghǎi stood at 27 years. In 1937 municipal sanitation workers picked up 20,000 corpses off the streets.

Shànghǎi offered the purely synthetic pleasures of civilisation. Prostitution ran the gamut from the high-class escorts in the clubs of the International Settlement and 'flowers' of the Fuzhou Rd teahouses to the *yějì*, or 'wild chickens', of Hóngkǒu, who prowled the streets and back alleys. The 'saltwater sisters' from Guǎngdōng specialised in foreigners fresh off the boats. Lowest of the low were the 'nail sheds' of Zhapei, so called because their services were meant to be as fast as driving nails. Lists of the city's 100 top-ranking prostitutes were drawn up annually and listed next to the names of 668 brothels, which went by such names as the 'Alley of Concentrated Happiness'.

Prostitution was not the exclusive domain of the Chinese. The traditional roles were reversed when White Russians turned to prostitution and Chinese men could be seen flaunting Western women. An American madam ran Gracie's, the most famous foreign brothel in town, at 52 Jiangsu Rd, in a strip of brothels called 'The Line'.

Linked to prostitution was opium. At the turn of the century Shànghǎi boasted 1500 opium dens (known locally as 'swallows' nests') and 80 shops openly selling opium. Even some hotels, it is said, supplied heroin on room service. Opium financed the early British trading houses and most of the buildings on the Bund. Later it funded Chinese gangsters, warlord armies and Kuomintang military expeditions. It was true that the police in the French Concession kept a close eye on the drug trade, but only to ensure that they got a reasonable slice of the profits. Not that there was much they could do even if they had wanted to; it was said that a wanted man in 1930s Shànghǎi need only pop into the neighbouring concession to avoid a warrant for his arrest.

Feeding much of this growth was a vast, multimillion-strong army of cheap labour and migrant workers from rural areas. The Bund was redesigned and spruced up while other areas – the Old Town, for example – underwent irreversible overdevelopment.

Despite draconian property taxes designed to hit speculators and purchasers of second flats, Shànghǎi property prices went through the roof in the noughties. The authorities were determined to tame the market to avoid a long-term Japanese-style stagnation, but prices continued to soar, bringing untold wealth to homeowners and speculators alike.

2004	2007	2010	2011
The world's first commercially operating Maglev train begins scorching across Pǔdōng. Plans for it to connect Běijīng and Shànghǎi are later put to rest.	World markets crash, slowing down – but not halting – Shànghǎi's previously stratospheric rates of economic growth.	Shànghǎi hosts the 2010 World Expo, drawing 73 million visitors.	The Shànghǎi–Běijīng high-speed rail line enters service, shrinking journey times to 5½ hours.

The Recent Past

After the global financial crisis of 2007 to 2008, the Chinese government's huge fiscal packages, loosening of credit and increased investment in infrastructure protected China and Shànghǎi from economic vicissitudes abroad. The Shànghǎi Tower began construction in November 2008, its concrete form quickly beginning to rise above the sky-high buildings of Pǔdōng.

Some pundits, however, began to see Shànghǎi, and China, at a fork in the road. The formula that served China so well for so long – a cheap workforce, hefty stimulus packages, high investment, endless property price increases and round-the-clock construction – could not go on forever. The Chinese economy continued to grow at a healthy rate, but at a slower clip, growing at 7.8% in 2012, compared to 10.4% in 2010. The breakneck growth patterns of the noughties were clearly unsustainable and a reorientation of the economy became imperative.

The task of the Chinese leadership demanded a more pressing focus on balancing the economy away from its export and high-investment model, rooting out corruption and narrowing the chasm dividing low-wage earners from the wealthy elites. The issue of migrant workers' rights in Shànghǎi and other cities became paramount, as workers sought to bring their rights (education for their children and access to healthcare) closer to native Shanghainese. Meanwhile, atmospheric pollution in Shànghǎi began to occasionally mirror the caustic air of the nation's capital, Běijīng. In December 2013, schoolchildren citywide were ordered indoors and construction was halted as the air quality reached dangerous levels. The burning of coal, car exhaust fumes, factory pollution and weather patterns that confined the smog within the city were all blamed.

Through a bold anticorruption agenda, the new leadership under Xi Jinping appeared determined to seize the nettle, while recognising that the Chinese Communist Party's legitimacy depended heavily on economic growth. Keeping the economy on track while directing it towards increased domestic consumption (and matching the growing expectations of a Chinese middle class pushing for a fairer society), further rooting out corruption, attempting to tame the rampant property market (as apartment prices put home ownership beyond the reach of most) and cleaning up urban air quality became urgent priorities. This new focus and commitment, however, coincided with a period of increased friction with Japan and Vietnam over competing territorial claims in the South China Sea and the East China Sea, a situation that increasingly threatened to lead to maritime conflict.

Having grown faster than virtually any other Chinese city in the past two decades, Shànghǎi remains the pot of gold at the end of the rainbow for China's swarming migrant workers, who now constitute almost four million of the city's total population of more than 24 million, and around 40% of the workforce.

A 2012 survey discovered that fewer than 40% of the city's elementary-school children speak the Shànghǎi dialect (Shànghǎihuà) at home, and even then it may be mixed with Mandarin.

HISTORY THE RECENT PAST

2012	2012	2013	2016
Anti-Japanese demonstrations are held in Shànghǎi and other cities across China in response to Japanese claims to the Diàoyú (Senkaku) Islands.	Thaddeus Ma Daqin is detained and stripped of his title as auxiliary bishop of Shànghǎi.	The Shànghǎi Tower tops out at 632m, making it the world's second-tallest skyscraper.	Disneyland opens on 16 June. Shanghai Shendi Group, Disney's Chinese partner, forecasts it will attract 10 million visitors per year.

Arts

You won't be sidestepping wayfaring buskers, street-side performers or wild-haired poets handing out flyers but there's enough creativity in Shànghǎi to keep you fired up and traditional Chinese arts are well covered.

A well-known graffiti wall at Moganshan Rd (M50) – one of the few places in Shànghǎi where you could see graffiti and wall art – was partially demolished in 2013. It has started to become a canvas for street art once more though and is worth a stroll down.

Visual Arts

Even if the city's artistic output remains limited, a growing gallery and art-museum scene makes Shànghǎi a vibrant place to join the learning curve for contemporary Chinese art. For political and cultural reasons, Shànghǎi has always been creatively rather straight-laced, though this is slowly beginning to change with graffiti walls and street art starting to pop up.

Contemporary & Modern Art

Notable contemporary Shanghainese artists working across a large spectrum of styles include Pu Jie, with his colourful pop-art depictions of Shànghǎi, video-installation artists Shi Yong and Hu Jieming, and Hángzhōu-born Sun Liang. Wu Yiming creates calmer, more impressionistic works, while Ding Yi is a significant abstract artist whose works employ a repetitive use of crosses. Also look out for works by graphic-design artist Guan Chun, and the diverse works of Chen Hangfeng and Yang Yongliang, which draw inspiration from the techniques and imagery of traditional Chinese painting.

After sizing up contemporary directions in art at the Bund-side Rockbund Art Museum (p64) – itself a definitive art deco gem – your next stop should be eclectic M50 (p128), Shànghǎi's most cutting-edge and left-field art zone, housed in warehouses near Sūzhōu Creek. It's the city's equivalent of Běijīng's path-breaking 798 Art District. Standout innovative galleries at M50 include island6 (p134) and ShanghART (p134). In People's Park, the Shànghǎi Museum of Contemporary Art (MOCA Shànghǎi; p66) is a stimulating venue for art-watching. The collection at the China Art Museum (p149) in the former World Expo site in Pǔdōng is colossal, but the permanent collection is largely anodyne, although international exhibitions have been a success. The Shànghǎi Gallery of Art (p65), at well-heeled Three on the Bund, is a spacious venue for cerebral and frequently enticing artworks.

A stroll around the quaint alleys of Tiánzǐfáng rewards with a smattering of galleries, including the excellent photographic gallery Beaugeste (p97), and a host of small art galleries.

The huge art-centre complex known as Red Town (p174), near Jiāotōng University, focuses on contemporary sculpture, and the thought-provoking displays at the Mínshēng Art Museum (p174) are a standout.

Further afield, check out the Liu Haisu Art Gallery (p174) in West Shànghǎi and earmark a trip to the Gallery Magda Danysz (p158) in Hóngkǒu.

In Pǔdōng, the Himalayas Museum (p149), in the organically designed Himalayas Center, is a great environment for showcasing contemporary art trends.

The hulking yet forward-thinking Power Station of Art (p82) – in the 41,000-sq-metre former Nánshì Power Plant – near the Huángpǔ River is the new venue for the Shanghai Biennale, held in November every two years since 1996. Related fringe shows spring up around the same time, and are often of more interest. Outside Biennale years, the China Shanghai International Arts Festival is an event held in November that brings traditional and modern (Western and Chinese) art, artists and galleries together.

A promising arts development seems to be springing up in the West Bund area and includes the West Bund Art Centre and Long Museum (p168), as well as the impressive new Yuz Museum (p168); it exhibits contemporary art in the former hangar of the Longhua Airport and has already hosted the world's largest Alberto Giacometti retrospective – it's an exciting addition to Shànghǎi's art scene.

Pick up a copy of *Shanghai Detour* art map, a guide to the city's commerical art galleries and museums, published every two months. Lots of bars, cafes, hotels and art galleries distribute the map.

ARTS VISUAL ARTS

Traditional Art

The Shànghǎi Museum (p61) puts traditional Chinese art under one roof, with a rare and extensive collection of ancient bronzes, Buddhist sculpture, ceramics, paintings, calligraphy, furniture, ancient jade and ethnic culture. For enthusiasts, an entire day here will only scratch the surface. The Shànghǎi Arts & Crafts Museum (p99) is an entertaining and informative choice, with displays of embroidery, paper cutting, lacquerwork and jade cutting, with skilled craftsmen and women creating pieces on the spot. For iridescent glassware, the Liúli China Museum

AESTHETICS & POLITICS

In reflection of the Chinese character, Chinese aesthetics have traditionally been marked by restraint and understatement, a preference for oblique references over direct explanation, vagueness in place of specificity and an avoidance of the obvious in place of a fondness for the veiled and subtle. Traditional Chinese aesthetics sought to cultivate a reserved artistic impulse, principles that compellingly find their way into virtually every Chinese art form, from painting to sculpture, ceramics, calligraphy, film, poetry, literature and beyond.

As one of the central strands of the world's oldest civilisation, China's aesthetic tradition is tightly embroidered within Chinese cultural identity. For millennia, Chinese aesthetics were highly traditionalist and, despite coming under the influence of occupiers from the Mongols to the Europeans, defiantly conservative. It was not until the fall of the Qing dynasty in 1911 and the genesis of the New Culture Movement that China's great artistic traditions began to rapidly transform. In literature the stranglehold of classical Chinese loosened to allow breathing space for *báihuà* (colloquial Chinese) and a progressive new aesthetic began to flower, ultimately leading to revolutions in all of the arts, from poetry to painting, theatre and music.

It is hard to square China's great aesthetic traditions with the devastation inflicted upon them since 1949. Confucius advocated the edifying role of music and poetry in shaping human lives, but 5th-century philosopher Mozi was less enamoured with them, seeing music and other arts as extravagant and wasteful. The communists took this a stage further, enlisting the arts as props in their propaganda campaigns and permitting the vandalism and destruction of much traditional architecture and heritage. Many of China's traditional skills (such as martial-arts lineages) and crafts either died out or went into decline during the Cultural Revolution. Many of these arts have yet to recover fully from this deterioration, even though 'opening up' and reform prompted a vast influx of foreign artistic concepts.

(p97) has an exquisite collection. Brash propaganda art from the Mao era is the focus of the riveting Propaganda Poster Art Centre (p98), while the foyer of the Jumeirah Himalayas Hotel (p213) in Pǔdōng is a virtual art gallery of traditional Chinese paintings.

More traditional art comes from the southern suburb of Jīnshān, which has its own school of untrained 'peasant' painters who have been producing colourful and vibrant paintings for years. Their works have roots in local embroidery designs and contain no perspective; the themes are mostly rural and domestic scenes full of details of everyday life. You can see a selection of paintings from the Jīnshān area in several shops in the Old Town's Old Street, or you can head out to Jīnshān itself. The Sūzhōu Museum (p189) in Sūzhōu also has a magnificent collection of traditional Chinese art and is one of the highlights of the town. The new Sūzhōu Art Museum (p189) is another impressive space for landscapes, calligraphy and (some modern) Chinese art.

Calligraphy

> Click on www. chineseposters. net for a fascinating collection of Chinese propaganda posters.

Although calligraphy (书法, *shūfǎ*) has a place among most languages that employ alphabets, the art of calligraphy in China is taken to unusual heights of intricacy and beauty. Although Chinese calligraphy is beautiful in its own right, the complex infatuation Chinese people have with their written language helps elucidate their great respect for the art.

Chinese calligraphy is the trickiest of China's arts to comprehend for Western visitors, unless they have a sound understanding of written Chinese. The beauty of a Chinese character may be partially appreciated by a Western audience, but for a full understanding it is also essential to understand the meaning of the character in context.

> The character 永, which means 'eternal', contains the five fundamental brushstrokes necessary to master calligraphy.

There are five main calligraphic scripts – seal script, clerical script, semicursive script, cursive script and standard script – each of which reflects the style of writing of a specific era. Seal script, the oldest and most complex, was the official writing system during the Qin dynasty and has been employed ever since in the carving of the seals and name chops (stamps carved from stone) that are used to stamp documents. Expert calligraphers have a preference for using full-form characters (*fántǐzì*) rather than their simplified variants (*jiǎntǐzì*).

Literature

Energised by a vibrant literary scene, Shànghǎi in the 1920s and '30s cast itself as a veritable publishing-industry hub. Sheltered from the censorship of Nationalists and warlords by the foreign settlements, and stimulated by the city's new-fangled modernity and flood of foreign ideas, Shànghǎi hosted a golden era in modern Chinese literature.

Birth of Modern Literature

> A selection of Lu Xun's books in English, French and German translation can be found in the museum bookshop at the Lu Xun Memorial Hall.

Although born in Shàoxīng, Lu Xun, China's greatest modern writer, lived in Shànghǎi from 1927 until his death of tuberculosis in 1936. One of the first founders of the Shànghǎi-based League of Left-Wing Writers, the highly influential modernist author dragged Chinese literature into the modern era.

Until Lu Xun's radical *Diary of a Madman* in 1918, literary Chinese had been conceived in classical Chinese, a language that represented not Chinese as it was spoken or thought, but as it was communicated by the educated scholarly class. Classical Chinese was a terse, dry and inflexible language that bore little relevance to the real lives of Chinese people. Lu Xun's decision to write his story in vernacular Chinese was a revolutionary act that instantly transformed the literary paradigms of the day, and

SHÀNGHĂI FICTION

➺ *Candy,* Mian Mian (2003) – A hip take on modern Shànghǎi life, penned by a former heroin addict musing on complicated sexual affairs, suicide and drug addiction in Shēnzhèn and Shànghǎi. Applauded for its urban underground tone, but sensational more for its framing of post-adolescent themes in contemporary China.

➺ *Years of Red Dust: Stories of Shanghai,* Qiu Xiaolong (2010) – 23 short stories set against a backdrop of Shànghǎi through the decades and in the context of momentous historic events affecting the city and the inhabitants of Red Dust Lane.

➺ *Empire of the Sun,* JG Ballard (1984) – An astonishingly well-written and poignant tale based on the author's internment as a child in a Japanese prisoner-of-war camp in Shànghǎi, and subsequently made into a film by Steven Spielberg.

➺ *Rules for Virgins,* Amy Tan (2013) – This 42-page e-novella sensuously explores the life of an apprentice courtesan in 1912 Shànghǎi.

➺ *Master of Rain,* Tom Bradby (2003) – Atmospheric, noir-ish detective story set in the swinging Shànghǎi of the '20s. 'Pockmarked' Huang, a brutally murdered Russian prostitute and a naive British investigator come together for a real page-turner.

➺ *Midnight,* Mao Dun (1933) – In the opening scene of *Midnight,* conservative Confucian Old Man Wu visits his son's home in Shànghǎi. The sight of modern women in high-slit skirts and revealing blouses literally shocks him to death. A famed presentation of the social mores of 1920s Shànghǎi.

➺ *Shanghai: Electric and Lurid City,* Barbara Baker (1998) – An excellent anthology of more than 50 passages of writing about Shànghǎi, from its pre-treaty port days to the eve of the 21st century.

➺ *Shanghai Girls,* Lisa See (2010) – A moving novel about two beautiful sisters whose lives as high-flying models in 1930s Shànghǎi are transformed when their father decides to repay his gambling debts by selling the pair to a family in Los Angeles. The book's acclaimed sequel is *Dreams of Joy* (2012).

➺ *Five Star Billionaire,* Tash Aw (2013) – Longlisted for the Man Booker Prize, Malaysian author Tash Aw's third novel explores the fortunes of four ambitious Malaysian new arrivals to Shànghǎi.

➺ *The Distant Land of My Father,* Bo Caldwell (2002) – A moving portrayal of the relationship between a daughter and father, and of betrayal and reconciliation, commencing in 1930s Shànghǎi.

➺ *The Painter from Shanghai,* Jennifer Cody Epstein (2008) – Highly acclaimed debut novel based on the remarkable life of child-prostitute-turned-painter Pan Yuliang.

➺ *The Sing-Song Girls of Shanghai,* Han Bangqing (1892) – Delving deeply into the lives of courtesans and prostitutes in fin-de-siècle Shànghǎi, this absorbing novel was first published in 1892 but only recently translated into English.

➺ *When Red is Black,* Qiu Xiaolong (2004) – A realistic detective story that packs plenty of literary muscle. This is a follow-up Inspector Chen novel (see *Death of a Red Heroine*) and a great snapshot of the changing city seen through Chinese eyes.

➺ *When We Were Orphans,* Kazuo Ishiguro (2000) – Subtle and absorbing portrayal of an English detective who sets out to solve the case of his parents' disappearance in Shànghǎi, climaxing in war-shattered Hóngkǒu.

helped underpin the New Culture Movement (新文化运动, Xīn Wénhuà Yúndòng), which sought to challenge traditional Chinese culture.

Lu Xun's most famous work, the 1921 novella *The True Story of Ah Q* (阿Q正传, *Ā Q Zhèngzhuàn*) – a satirical look at early-20th-century China – is considered a modern masterpiece and was the first piece of literature to entirely utilise vernacular Chinese. Admirers of Lu Xun can visit his Shànghǎi residence.

Writers were not immune to political dangers; Lu Xun's friend Rou Shi was murdered by the Kuomintang in February 1931.

Mao Dun (real name Shen Yanbing), an active leftist writer in the 1930s, penned *Midnight* (Zǐyè), one of the most famous novels about Shànghǎi. *Rainbow* (1929), by the same author, tells the tale of a young girl from a traditional family background who travels to Shànghǎi on a journey of political awakening.

Ding Ling, whose most famous work is *The Diary of Miss Sophie*, lived in Shànghǎi, as did for a time the writers Yu Dafu and Ba Jin.

Eileen Chang (Zhang Ailing; 1920–95) is one of the writers most closely connected to Shànghǎi, certainly among overseas Chinese. She lived in the city only from 1942 to 1948 before moving to Hong Kong and then the USA. Seeped in the city's details and moods, her books capture the essence of Shànghǎi. Chang's most famous books include *The Rouge of the North, The Faded Flower, Red Rose and White Rose, The Golden Lock* and *Love in a Fallen City*. Her 1979 novella *Lust, Caution* was made into an award-winning film directed by Ang Lee (director of *Crouching Tiger, Hidden Dragon* and *Brokeback Mountain*) in 2007.

For a great selection of books on China and Shànghǎi – everything from historical novels and art hardbacks to books dedicated to tea – check out the shop at the Shànghǎi Museum, or Garden Books in the French Concession.

Contemporary Directions

Contemporary voices are more sparse. The most respected Shànghǎi writer today is Wang Anyi, whose bestselling novels (in China) include *Love on a Barren Mountain, Baotown* and *Song of Everlasting Sorrow,* the last following a Shanghainese beauty-pageant winner through four decades from the 1940s. Wang also co-wrote the script for Chen Kaige's film *Temptress Moon.*

More recently, several high-school drop-outs gained notoriety, beginning with Mian Mian, who vividly described the marginalised underbelly of China in *Candy*. To date this remains her only novel translated into English.

Increasingly known in the West is writer/rally-driver/musician/blogger Han Han, who skyrocketed to fame before his 18th birthday with his novel *The Third Gate,* a searing critique of China's educational system. He inspired awe and disgust simultaneously by turning down a scholarship to the prestigious Fùdàn University in order to race cars in Běijīng. Today, Han Han's highly influential blogs are among the most widely read in China.

Sprinkled with snippets from the Shànghǎi dialect (but as yet untranslated), Wang Xiaoying's *Song of a Long Street* (2010) is a vivid portrait of the textures and grain of everyday life in a Shànghǎi backstreet.

Translated into English, *Vicissitudes of Life* (2010) is a collection of stories from contemporary Shànghǎi writers, including Wang Xiaoying, Qiu Maoru and Wang Jiren.

As with Chinese film, fiction dealing with contemporary Shànghǎi is far less successful at filling bookstore shelves than historically set novels. Historical fiction is a safer and far more popular publishing choice, meaning voices on contemporary issues are more marginalised.

Shànghǎi writers today share a common despair about the loss of the Shànghǎi dialect while having to compose in Mandarin (Shanghainese is not written down).

Disappearing Shanghai by Howard W French and Qiu Xiaolong atmospherically captures a vanishing way of life in Shànghǎi's old quarters through thoughtful and tender images and poetry.

Music

Shànghǎi had a buzzing live-music scene in the 1930s, featuring everything from jazz divas to émigré Russian troubadours, but the contemporary scene has been long dominated by Filipino cover bands and saccharine-sweet Canto-pop. Things are changing, though, and while Shànghǎi's live-music scene still lags behind Běijīng's, there are some cracking venues in town where you can catch local bands, the best of which are Yùyīntáng (p176) and MAO Livehouse (p118). The sci-fi-styled Mercedes-Benz Arena in Pǔdōng is the venue for big-name international and Chinese solo artists and bands, including Taylor Swift, the Rolling Stones, Jennifer Lopez, Jessie J, Iron Maiden and Jacky Cheung. Look out for the JUE Festival, a music and art festival held in Běijīng and Shànghǎi in March. The Shànghǎi Midi Festival is three days of live music and DJs held in Pǔdōng in April.

Rock & Punk

Local bands worth checking out include Nonplus of Color, a psychedelic shoegaze rock band formed in 2014; gritty punk rockers Dirty Fingers; popular indie garage rock band Banana Monkey, often compared to the Strokes; rockers Da Bei; and all-girl band Bigger Xifu. Torturing Nurse, meanwhile, is China's leading hardcore noise band. Top Floor Circus, who sang and wrote in Shanghainese and played anything from folk to punk, were legendary on the Shànghǎi music scene. Sadly, they announced their split in early 2016.

Jazz

Shànghǎi's once world-famous jazz scene isn't quite as snappy as it was, but there are still a number of places around town where you can sample the sounds of the 1930s. Cotton Club (p118) is the best choice.

The Fairmont Peace Hotel Jazz Bar has been serenading punters for decades; the band has an average age of 80.

Traditional Chinese Music

The *èrhú* is a two-stringed fiddle that is tuned to a low register, providing a soft, melancholy tone. The *húqín* is a higher-pitched two-stringed viola. The *yuèqín,* a sort of moon-shaped four-stringed guitar, has a soft tone and is used to support the *èrhú.* Other instruments you may come across are the *shēng* (reed flute), *pípá* (lute), *gǔzhēng* (zither) and *xiāo* (vertical flute). A good place to hear free traditional music performances is at the Shànghǎi Gǔqín Cultural Foundation (p125) or at a performance of Chinese opera.

Classical Music

The Shànghǎi Conservatory of Music (p119) is a prestigious clearing house of Chinese talent. One of its most famous former students is Liao Changyong, a world-class baritone who has performed with Plácido Domingo, among others. Other famous classical-music venues include the Shanghai Symphony Orchestra Hall (p118), the Shànghǎi Concert Hall (p76) and the Oriental Art Center (p155).

To pick up a traditional Chinese musical instrument such as the *pípá* (lute), *èrhú* (two-stringed fiddle) or *gǔzhēng* (zither), pop down to Parsons Music on Fenyang Rd near the Shànghǎi Conservatory of Music.

Chinese Opera

Chinese opera, best known for Běijīng opera (京剧, Jīngjù), has a rich and continuous history of some 900 years. Evolving from a convergence of comic and ballad traditions in the Northern Song period, the art brought together a disparate range of forms: acrobatics, martial arts, poetic arias and stylised dance.

Operas were usually performed by travelling troupes, who had a low social status in traditional Chinese society. Chinese law forbade mixed-sex performances, forcing actors to act out roles of the opposite sex. Opera troupes were frequently associated with homosexuality in the public imagination, contributing further to their lowly status.

Formerly, opera was performed mostly on open-air stages in markets, streets, teahouses or temple courtyards.

More than 100 varieties of opera coexist in China today, including Shanghainese opera (沪剧, Hùjù), sometimes called flower-drum opera, which is sung in the local dialect and has its origins in the folk songs of Pǔdōng. Yueju opera (越剧, Yuèjù) was born in and around Shàoxīng County in neighbouring Zhèjiāng (the ancient state of Yue) province in the early 20th century. Yuèjù roles are normally played by women. Kunju opera (昆剧, Kūnjù) or Kunqu opera (昆曲, Kūnqǔ) originates from Kūnshān, near Sūzhōu in neighbouring Jiāngsū.

Actors portray stylised stock characters who are instantly recognisable to the audience. Most stories are derived from classical literature and Chinese mythology and tell of disasters, natural calamities, intrigues or rebellions. The musicians usually sit on the stage in plain clothes and play without written scores.

China's most legendary 20th-century opera star was Mei Lanfang, who allegedly performed privately for several of Shànghǎi's gangland bosses in the 1930s. The most central venue for appreciating Chinese opera in Shànghǎi is the Yìfū Theatre (p76) on Fuzhou Rd.

The lower Yangzi region has a long tradition of storytelling, farce, comic talk and mimicking, all of which were traditionally performed in teahouses. Hángzhōu and Sūzhōu have their own variants. *Píngtán* balladry is a mix of *pínghuà* (Sūzhōu-style storytelling) and *táncí* (ballad singing), accompanied by the *pípá* (lute) and *sānxián* (banjo). You can hear samples of various Chinese operas and *píngtán* at the Shànghǎi History Museum (p148) in Pǔdōng, or at the Píngtán Museum (p194) in Sūzhōu.

> The shrill singing and loud percussion of Chinese opera were designed to be heard over the public throng, prompting American writer PJ O'Rourke to compare it to a truck loaded with wind chimes crashing into a set of empty oil drums during a bird-call contest.

Cinema

Early Film

The first screening of any film in China illuminated the garden of a Shànghǎi teahouse in 1896, when Spanish entrepreneur Galen Bocca showed a series of one-reel films to astonished audiences. The city's first cinema opened up in 1908, but before films could reach their glamorous peak in the 1930s, film-makers had to convince the distrustful Shanghainese that it was worth their hard-earned cash. Soon hooked, the city boasted more than 35 cinemas and more than 140 film companies by 1930. Shànghǎi's teahouse culture began to feel the pinch, along with a host of traditional performing arts.

The Golden Age

The 1932 Japanese bombing of the Shànghǎi district of Hóngkǒu had a big effect on the industry, prompting a patriotic fervour epitomised by films coming out of the Lianhua Studio, with its close connections to Chiang Kaishek's Nationalist Party.

> The Old Film Café in Hóngkǒu, housed in a beautiful three-storey brick building with charming wooden interior, shows old Shànghǎi films on demand, although few have English subtitles.

Shànghǎi's golden age of film-making reached its peak in 1937 with the release of *Street Angel,* a powerful drama about two sisters who flee the Japanese in northeast China and end up as prostitutes in Shànghǎi, and *Crossroads,* a clever comedy about four unemployed graduates. There was still time, however, after WWII and before the Chinese Communist Party (CCP) took over in 1949, for a final flowering. *A Spring River Flows East,* dubbed the *Gone with the Wind* of Chinese cinema, and *Springtime in a Small Town,* another wartime tear jerker, remain popular films today.

Shànghǎi Cinema Today

China's film industry was stymied after the Communist Revolution, which sent film-makers scurrying to Hong Kong and Taiwan, where they played key roles in building up the local film industries that flourished there. Chinese film-makers need to work against a system of censorship that famous director Feng Xiaogang has termed 'ridiculous'.

Today's movie-goers are scarce, as DVD piracy and internet downloads upset the economics of domestic film-making.

More innovative film studios in Xī'ān and Běijīng have captured much of the international acclaim of contemporary Chinese film. Co-productions have been more successful for the Shànghǎi Film Studios, which in 2001 moved from its central location in Xújiāhuì to the far-western city district of Sōngjiāng.

One critical success was *The Red Violin*, a coproduction between Canada and Shànghǎi. Shànghǎi-born Vivian Wu (Wu Junmei; *The Last Emperor*, *The Pillow Book*) returned to her native city with her husband, director Oscar L Costo, in order to focus on their production company, MARdeORO Films. It produced the well-received *Shanghai Red*, starring Wu and Ge You *(Farewell My Concubine, To Live)*, in 2006. Another actress hailing from Shànghǎi is Joan Chen (Chen Chong), who started her career at the Shànghǎi Film Studios in the late 1970s.

Shànghǎi's independent films are scarce. Look out for Ye Lou's *Suzhou River* (Sūzhōu Hé) and Andrew Chen's *Shanghai Panic* (Wǒmen Hàipà). Both were shot with digital cameras and are notable for showing a decidedly unglamorous and more realistic side of the city.

Peng Xiaolian's *Shanghai Story*, released in 2004, follows the fortunes of a wealthy family in Shànghǎi who were torn apart by the Cultural Revolution. It was the winner of Best Picture in the Golden Rooster Awards (China's film awards) where it beat *House of Flying Daggers*. Surprisingly, it was not touched by the censors despite its references to the Cultural Revolution.

Chen Yifei's 1920s period drama *The Barber* (aka *The Music Box*) was released posthumously in 2006, while Taiwanese-born Oscar-winning director Ang Lee *(Crouching Tiger, Hidden Dragon* and *Brokeback Mountain)* released *Lust, Caution* in 2007. A controversial tale of sex and espionage set in WWII Shànghǎi, based on the 1979 novella by Eileen Chang, the award-winning film was heavily censored for its mainland China release. Wayne Wang's 2011 release *Snow Flower and the Secret Fan* is partly set in contemporary Shànghǎi, with scenes set in the Peninsula Hotel, among other locations.

The Shanghai International Film Festival (www.siff. com) celebrates international and locally produced films in June every year.

Fashion

The Shanghainese have the reputation of being the most fashionable people in China. 'There's nothing the Cantonese won't eat', one version of a popular Chinese saying goes, 'and nothing the Shanghainese won't wear'. The generation gap is perhaps starker here, though, than anywhere else: you're still quite likely to see locals wandering around their neighbourhood dressed in very comfortable (but extremely uncool) pyjamas and slippers, but Shànghǎi has breathtaking, voguish pockets and young Shànghǎi women ooze glamour in even the cheapest skirts and blouses.

On the street, Chinese-language lifestyle magazines such as *Shanghai Tatler*, *Elle*, *Vogue*, *Harper's Bazaar* and *Marie Claire* crowd every corner newsstand. Christian Dior, Gucci and Louis Vuitton shops glut Shànghǎi's top-end malls, while hip boutiques line French Concession streets such as Changle Rd, Xinle Rd and Nanchang Rd.

Shànghǎi still has a long way to go just to catch up with its own 1930s fashion scene, however, when images of Chinese women clad in figure-hugging *qípáo* (cheongsam) gave rise to its epithet as the 'Paris of the East'.

Shanghai Fashion Week (www.shanghaifashionweek.com) is a bi-annual event showcasing the work of local, national and international designers. There is also the city-sponsored, month-long International Fashion Culture Festival in March or April.

Martial Arts

China lays claim to a bewildering range of martial-arts styles.

As well as being an annual gay pride festival, Shanghai Pride (www.shpride.com) is a week-long celebration of creativity across all media.

Some pugilists stress a mentalist approach while others put their money on physical power. On the outer fringes are the esoteric arts, abounding with metaphysical feats, arcane practices and closely guarded techniques.

Many fighting styles were once secretively handed down for generations within families and it is only relatively recently that outsiders have been accepted as students. Some schools, especially of the more obscure styles, have been driven to extinction partly due to their exclusivity.

Unlike Western fighting arts – such as savate, kickboxing, boxing, wrestling etc – Chinese martial arts are deeply impregnated with religious and philosophical values. Closely linked to martial arts is the practice of *qì gōng*, a technique for cultivating and circulating *qì* around the body. *Qì* can be developed for use in fighting to protect the body, as a source of power, or for curative and health-giving purposes.

Shànghǎi's parks are good places to go to look for teachers of taichi and *wǔshù* (martial arts), although language may be a barrier. Check the listings of entertainment magazines such as *That's Shanghai* or *City Weekend* for classes, or check for courses at the Lóngwǔ Kung Fu Center (p124), the HongWu Kungfu Centre (p125) or the Míngwǔ International Kungfu Club (p177).

Architecture in Shànghǎi

Jaw-dropping panoramas of glittering skyscrapers are its trump card, but Shànghǎi is no one-trick pony: the city boasts a diversity of architectural styles that will astound most first-time visitors. Whether you're an art deco hound, a neoclassical buff, a fan of English 1930s suburban-style villas, 1920s apartment blocks or Buddhist temple architecture, Shànghǎi has it covered.

Modern Architecture

Charm and panache may ooze from every crevice of its concession-era villas, *shíkùmén* (stone gate) buildings, *lòng* lanes and art deco marvels, but for sheer wow factor, look to the city's modern skyline. Shànghǎi's tall towers get all the media attention, but many of the city's most iconic and noteworthy contemporary buildings are low-rise.

Above: Grand Hyatt hotel (p242)

High-rise Shànghǎi

Like Hong Kong before it, Shànghǎi has filled its horizons with forests of soaring towers that capture a brash and sophisticated zeitgeist. The grandiose Bund may forever recall the indignity of foreign control, but Pǔdōng – and more specifically Lùjiāzuǐ – concerns itself with the future, and that's a future made in and by China.

Pǔdōng only dates to the early 1990s, so don't expect the sheer variety of New York skyscraper architecture. But some of the world's very tallest buildings erupt from Shànghǎi's notoriously boggy terrain, including the astonishing Shànghǎi Tower (p148) in Lùjiāzuǐ, the world's second-tallest building. To carry the load of the glass skin around the tower, an innovative curtain wall was devised, which is suspended from floors above and then stabilised with struts and hoop rings. In mid-2016, however, a panel of glass fell from the 76th floor, smashing to the ground and injuring the foot of a driver getting out of his car.

The 632m-high Gensler-designed Shànghǎi Tower's spiralling glass-coated form is the dominant structure of a triumvirate of skyscraping towers that also includes the breathtaking Shànghǎi World Financial Center (SWFC; p145), another of the world's tallest buildings since its 2008 completion. Metallic and glass, uncompromising and audaciously designed, the SWFC tower is a further brash testament to money and ambition. The original design incorporated a circle at its top, where the 'bottle-opener' trapezoid aperture (which reduces wind pressure) sits, but this design was shouted down by local fears that it would recall the Japanese flag.

The most attractive and elegant of the three towers is the smallest: but it's no lightweight. Replete with Chinese symbolism, the pagoda-like 421m-high Jīnmào Tower (p148) has 88 floors (eight is a Chinese lucky number), while its 13 stepped bands allude to Buddhist imagery. Designed by Adrian Smith of Skidmore, Owings & Merrill, the Jīnmào Tower remains one of Shànghǎi's most interesting and notable buildings. On floors 53 to 87, the Grand Hyatt contains the world's highest atrium, a breathtaking architectural feat, while the world's longest laundry chute runs dirty sheets and pillowcases down the length of the tower.

Don't overlook Pǔxī on the far side of the river, where there's a vigorous collection of modern architecture, including claw-like Tomorrow Square (p66), rocketing nefariously over People's Square. The fifth-tallest building in Shànghǎi and completed in 2003, the tower begins as a square before morphing into a diagonal square, topped with a pincer-like formation. On the other side of People's Square rises the slightly taller, but not as architecturally interesting, Shimao International Plaza.

With such a meteoric construction agenda and an anything-goes attitude, designs can occasionally cause divided opinions. The Oriental Pearl TV Tower (p146) is one of the most iconic buildings in the city and looks dazzling at night when lit up, though not everyone is a fan of its Soviet retro-style design with cheesy Chinese characters. Others include the curious crown atop the Bund Center (88 Middle Henan Rd) and the Radisson Blu Hotel Shanghai New World (88 West Nanjing Rd).

Low-rise Shànghǎi

In the Pǔdōng-side former World Expo site, the staggering flying-saucer shaped Mercedes-Benz Arena (p149) looks like it's refuelling after a warp-speed voyage from Alpha Centauri. It's well worth seeing at night, but it looks like it might actually take off in a tornado. The nearby up-turned red-pyramid design of the China Art Museum (p149; the former China Pavilion) is another distinctive architectural icon of the site. In 2012 the pavilion was reinvented as a modern-art museum, guaranteeing it a second wind. Unfortunately, most of the other World

Shànghǎi's notoriously boggy firmament – a clay-based, river-delta type – meant the Shànghǎi Tower had to be built upon 831 reinforced concrete bores buried deep in the ground.

Pǔdōng's looming skyscrapers: Jīnmào Tower, Shànghǎi World Financial Center and Shànghǎi Tower

ARCHITECTURE IN SHÀNGHǍI MODERN ARCHITECTURE

Expo pavilions – including the staggeringly inventive UK Pavilion – were dismantled after the event, but a few are still standing. On the other side of the river, the Nánshì Power Plant has found a dramatic new interpretation as the Power Station of Art (p82).

Also in Pǔdōng, the Arata Isozaki–designed Himalayas Center – attached to the Jumeirah Himalayas Hotel (p213) – is a highly complicated, organic-looking and challenging form in an otherwise uniform neighbourhood of Shànghǎi.

A stroll around People's Square in Pǔxī introduces you to three of the city's most eye-catching designs. The Shànghǎi Urban Planning Exhibition Hall (p66) is capped with a distinctive roof with four 'florets'.

A TALL STOREY

Shànghǎi's tallest buildings (in order of height):

Shànghǎi Tower (p148) Brand-new and rising supreme over Lùjiāzuǐ; 121 storeys.

Shànghǎi World Financial Center (p145) A colossal, shimmering bottle-opener at the heart of Lùjiāzuǐ; 101 storeys.

Jīnmào Tower (p148) Crystalline, art deco–inspired pagoda and Shànghǎi's most attractive tower; 88 storeys.

Plaza 66 Tower One (恒隆广场, Hénglóng Guǎngchǎng; Map p310; ☏021 6279 0910; 1266 West Nanjing Rd; 南京西路1266号; ◔10am-10pm; Ⓜ Line 2, 12, 13 to West Nanjing Rd, exit 1) One of Pǔxī's tallest buildings, best known for its exclusive mall slung out below; 66 storeys.

Tomorrow Square (p66) Dramatically futuristic aluminium-and-glass tower climbing into the skies above People's Square; 55 storeys.

Pǔdōng International Airport Terminal

The nearby Shànghǎi Grand Theatre (p75) combines Chinese sweeping eaves with a futuristic employment of plastic and glass. Opposite this pair is the uniquely designed Shànghǎi Museum (p61), resembling an ancient Chinese vessel known as a *dǐng*.

Other low-rise modern Shànghǎi structures with spectacular interiors and exteriors include Pǔdōng International Airport Terminal 1 and Shànghǎi Hóngqiáo Railway Station.

Elsewhere, conversions of industrial buildings have breathed new life into disused structures. 1933 (p162) in Hóngkǒu is a highly photogenic modern structure, given a new and invigorating lease of life. This former slaughterhouse has been converted to boutiques, galleries and restaurants, among its silent, concrete overture of flared columns, skybridges and ramps. Its only disadvantage is that it's a bit isolated and the shops and restaurants are of little interest, but it's one of the top architectural highlights of Shànghǎi.

Don't also overlook hotels, where funky modern architecture and snappy interior design find a creative harmony. While making a groundbreaking push into sustainability among Shànghǎi's hotels, Urbn (p211) also captures a unique take on Shànghǎi's local aesthetic, with a highly modern and trendy finish. All steel, exposed concrete and brickwork, the Waterhouse at South Bund (p208) presents cutting-edge work from Shànghǎi's architectural firm NHDRO, combining industrial and modern aesthetics in this former Japanese army headquarters and warehouse near the river. The 40-floor Bulgari Hotel (due to open in 2017) north of Sūzhōu Creek won't exactly be low-rise, but it won't be in chart-topping high-rise territory either. Set to transform this part of Zhábĕi, the tower is designed by Foster + Partners, with interior design from architectural firm Antonio Citterio Patricia Viel and Partners. The former Chinese

Chamber of Commerce is a notable historic building incorporated into the Bulgari design for the area.

Shànghǎi shopping malls can also be showstoppers in their own right. The interior design of the superduper IAPM Mall (p120) on Middle Huaihai Rd is fantastic and worth a look, even if you're not out to buy anything.

Shànghǎi's vast bridges, including the enormous Lúpǔ Bridge, which combine length and height in equal measure, are also sights in their own right.

Concession Architecture

For many foreign visitors, Shànghǎi's modern architectural vision is a mere side salad to the feast of historic architecture lining the Bund and beyond. Remnants of old Shànghǎi, these buildings are part of the city's genetic code, inseparable from its sense of identity as the former 'Paris of the East'.

Neoclassical

Although the Bund contains the lion's share of Shànghǎi's neoclassical designs, among the most impressive is the Shànghǎi Race Club Building (till recently the Shànghǎi Art Museum) in People's Square. It's a beautiful building with a clock tower and once formed part of the main stand at the old racecourse. Another standout building is the British-designed General Post Office, home of the Post Office Museum, completed in 1924.

In the 1920s the British architectural firm of Palmer & Turner designed many of Shànghǎi's major buildings (13 structures on the Bund alone), including the neoclassical Hongkong and Shanghai Banking Corporation (HSBC) building (p60), the Yokohama Specie Bank, the Custom House (p60) and other gems.

The Shànghǎi Exhibition Centre (p130) is a triumphant example of Soviet neoclassical architecture.

Villa Architecture

The tree-lined streets of the French Concession house a delightful collection of magnificent residential early-20th-century villa architecture, much of which has been well preserved. Standout examples include the Mansion Hotel (p210), InterContinental Shanghai Ruijin Hotel (p210), and Āntíng Villa Hotel (p209).

Art Deco

The late 1920s saw the Shànghǎi arrival of art deco and its sophisticated, modish expressions of the machine age. It was one of Shànghǎi's architectural high-water marks, with the city boasting more art deco buildings than any other city in the world. For a comprehensive lowdown on the style, turn to *Shanghai Art Deco* by Deke Erh and Tess Johnston.

An art deco classic, the Paramount Ballroom is said to be haunted by the ghost of a young girl who refused to dance with a Japanese soldier (although others say it was gangster Du Yuesheng), who shot her dead.

ARCHITECTURE IN SHÀNGHǍI CONCESSION ARCHITECTURE

BUILDING THE BUND

The Bund – Shànghǎi's most famous esplanade of concession buildings – was built on unstable foundations due to the leaching mud of the Huángpǔ River. Bund buildings were first built on concrete rafts that were fixed onto wood pilings, which were allowed to sink into the mud. Because of the lack of qualified architects, some of the earliest Western-style buildings in Shànghǎi were partially built in Hong Kong, shipped to Shànghǎi, then assembled on-site.

Top: Architectural detail,
Xīntiāndì (p95)
Bottom: *Shíkùmén*
(stone-gate house)
architectural style

Art deco buildings of note include the Fairmont Peace Hotel (p206), the Paramount Ballroom at 218 Yuyuan Rd, Broadway Mansions (p162), the Cathay Theatre (p119), the Liza Building at 99 East Nanjing Rd, the Savoy Apartments at 209 Changshu Rd, the Picardie Apartments (now the Héngshān Picardie Hotel (p210)) on the corner of Hengshan Rd and Wanping Rd, the Embankment Building (p160; housing Chai Living Residences), the Bank of China building (p57) on the Bund and the French Concession building that contains the James Cohan art gallery. There are also dozens of others.

Strongly associated with art deco (although he also used earlier styles), Ladislaus Hudec (1893–1958) was a Hungarian who came to Shànghǎi in 1918 after escaping en route to a Russian prisoner-of-war camp in Siberia. The Park Hotel, Grand Theatre, China Baptist Publication Society, Green House and other art deco buildings all owe their creation to Hudec.

The Rockbund Art Museum (p64) is a further magnificent example of art deco architecture, complete with Chinese design motifs, such as the eight-trigram windows. The museum is on Yuanmingyuan Rd, itself a long gallery of art deco classics.

Shanghai's Art Deco Master by Spencer Dodington is a terrific read documenting the life and work of French architect Paul Veysseyre, whose architectural firm transformed the former French Concession in the 1920s and 1930s with projects such as the Okura Garden Hotel.

Lòngtáng & Shíkùmén

Even though Shànghǎi is typified by its high-rise and uniform residential blocks, near ground level the city comes into its own with its low-rise *lòngtáng* and *shíkùmén* architecture. Here, both Western and Asian architectural motifs were synthesised into harmonious, utilitarian styles that still house a large proportion of Shànghǎi's residents.

Lòngtáng

In the same way that Běijīng's most authentic features survive among its homely (but far older and entirely non-European) *hútòng* alleyways, so Shànghǎi's *lòngtáng* (or *lĭlòng*) lanes are the historic city's principal indigenous urban architectural feature. *Lòngtáng* (弄堂) are the back alleys that form the building blocks of living, breathing communities, supplying a warm and charming counterpoint to the abstract and machine-like skyscrapers rising over the city. Sadly, these alleys and their signature buildings, the *shíkùmén* (stone-gate houses), have offered little more than a feeble resistance against developers who have toppled swaths of *shíkùmén* to make way for more glittering projects. But if you want to find Shànghǎi at its most local, community-spirited, neighbourly and also at its quietest, more than enough *lòngtáng* survive off the main drag for you to savour their slow-moving tempo.

Shíkùmén

Following the devastation of the Taiping Rebellion in 1853, some 20,000 Chinese fled into the International Settlement. Sensing a newly arrived cash cow, the British decided to scrap the law forbidding Chinese from renting property in the concessions, and foreigners from developing real estate. British and French speculators built hundreds of houses in what became Shànghǎi's biggest real-estate bonanza. The result was *shíkùmén* (石库门) – literally 'stone gate' – referring to the stone porticoes that fronted these buildings and the alleys that led to them.

Shànghǎi *shíkùmén* architecture is a unique mixture of East and West, a blend of the Chinese courtyard house and English terraced housing. Typical *shíkùmén* houses were two to three storeys tall and fronted by an imposing stone-gate frame topped with a decorated lintel enclosing two stout wooden doors (frequently black), each decorated with a bronze handle. The lintel was sometimes elaborately carved with

Chronicling the changing face of Shànghǎi and its impact on the people who live here, Shanghai Street Stories (www.shanghai streetstories. com) is a terrific resource for anyone interested in the architectural heritage of the city.

Jade Buddha Temple (p130), Jìng'ān

a dictum in Chinese, usually four characters long. At the entrance to the alley there was often a *yānzhǐdiàn* (烟纸店) – literally a 'tobacco and paper shop' – where residents could pick up provisions round the clock.

Shíkùmén were originally designed to house one family, but Shànghǎi's growth and socialist reorientation led to them being sublet to many families, each of which shared a kitchen and outside bathroom to complement the *mǎtǒng* (chamber pot). For the Shanghainese, a single-family kitchen and separate bedrooms remained a dream until the 1990s.

Such buildings made up 60% of Shànghǎi's housing between the 1850s and the 1940s; they can be found across historical Shànghǎi, but are most prevalent in the French Concession, Jìng'ān, Hóngkǒu and parts of the Old Town. One of the most charming *shíkùmén* areas is in the boutique-littered Tiánzǐfáng area in the French Concession. Xīntiāndì is a restored, but more synthetic, *shíkùmén* area housing the absorbing Shíkùmén Open House Museum (p96).

Two other *shíkùmén* areas well worth exploring are Zhāng Garden (p130) east of the intersection between West Nanjing Rd and Shimen No 1 Rd, and Cité Bourgogne (p97) on the northeast corner of the crossing between West Jianguo Rd and South Shaanxi Rd.

Religious Architecture

Following the tumultuous destruction of religious beliefs, practices and architecture that characterised the Mao era, religion has enjoyed a powerful resurgence in Shànghǎi (as it has nationwide) from the 1980s to the present day. The city's standout buildings may serve Mammon, but many of Shànghǎi's most impressive religious buildings are once again active places of worship.

SHÀNGHĂI'S BEST TEMPLES, CHURCHES & SYNAGOGUES

Jade Buddha Temple (p130) Shànghăi's best-known shrine, housing a serene effigy of Sakyamuni (Buddha).

Jìng'ān Temple (p129) Impressively restored, this Buddhist temple is a major Jìng'ān landmark.

Chénxiānggé Monastery (p82) One of the Old Town's most sacred sites.

Shĕshān Basilica (p200) Standing sublimely atop a hill just outside town.

Ohel Moishe Synagogue (p159) Jewish Shànghăi's most significant chunk of religious heritage.

Temples

The place of prayer for Buddhist, Taoist or Confucian worshippers, Chinese *sìmiào* (寺庙; temples) tend to follow a strict, schematic pattern. Most importantly, all are laid out on a north–south axis in a series of halls, with the main door of each hall facing south.

One striking difference from Christian churches is the open-plan design of temples, with buildings interspersed with breezy open-air courtyards. This allows the climate to permeate; seasons therefore play an essential role in defining the mood. The open-air layout furthermore allows the *qì* (气; vital energy) to circulate, dispersing stale air and allowing incense to be burned liberally.

Buddhist temples of architectural note include the Jade Buddha Temple (p130), with its striking yellow-and-red walls; the Jìng'ān Temple (p129), a recent rebuild of one of Shànghăi's first temples; and the Old Town's lovely Chénxiānggé Monastery (p82).

An important Taoist temple is the Temple of the Town God (p82) in the Old Town, a neighbourhood that's also home to the large Confucius Temple (p86), lovingly restored in the 1990s.

Churches

Churches in Shànghăi reflect the long Christian presence in this historically cosmopolitan city. After St Ignatius Cathedral (p166) and Shĕshān Basilica (p200), other churches of note are the beautiful Russian Mission Church (p99), with its blue domes; the pretty Dǒngjiādù Cathedral (p87), Shànghăi's oldest church (c 1853); the disused St Nicholas Church (p96; 1934); and the delightful St Joseph's Church (c 1862; 36 South Sichuan Rd), with its Gothic spires, now located within the grounds of a school.

Mosques

The main active mosque in Shànghăi is the Peach Garden Mosque (p87), built in the Old Town in 1917. While not particularly impressive architecturally, it is nevertheless an interesting mix of styles with its neoclassical-like facade, Islamic green domes and mixture of Arabic lettering and Chinese characters.

Synagogues

Of the seven synagogues once built in Shànghăi, only two remain. The renovated Ohel Moishe Synagogue (p159) now houses the absorbing Jewish Refugees Museum. Of more authentic charm is the rather neglected, ivy-cloaked Ohel Rachel Synagogue (p130) in Jìng'ān, which was Shànghăi's first synagogue (1920), but it is generally not open to visitors.

Shànghăi is not an ancient city like Bĕijīng. The city's oldest house is a courtyard home called Shū Yín Lóu (书隐楼) in the Old Town, dating to the 18th century and named after a library. It's located at 77 Tiandeng Nong.

Religion & Belief

Religious belief may not dominate contemporary Shànghǎi life, but faith still exercises a powerful hold over the spiritual imagination, and the city is home to a large and disparate brood of temples, churches and mosques.

Buddhism

During the Cultural Revolution, many Christian churches in Shànghǎi and around China served as warehouses or factories and were gradually rehabilitated in the 1980s. St Ignatius Cathedral was enlisted for the storage of grain.

Although Buddhism (Fójiào) originated in India, so is not an indigenous Chinese faith, it is the religion most deeply associated with China, Tibet and Chinese culture. Its influence today may be a mere shadow of its Tang dynasty apogee, and the religion was heavily bruised by the Cultural Revolution (1966–76), but Buddhism is widely practised in today's Shànghǎi, where several notable Buddhist temples can be visited.

As with many church-goers in the West, many Shànghǎi Buddhists are 'cultural Buddhists' rather than devout believers who live their lives according to strict rules.

Shànghǎi temples may lack the history and scale of their counterparts elsewhere in China (take Běijīng, for example), but they can be fascinating places to watch local people light *shāo xiāng* (incense) to worship Buddha, Guanyin and other deities. For more impressive Buddhist temples, head to Hángzhōu's fabulous Língyǐn Temple (p182) or Sūzhōu's huge West Garden Temple (p192).

Taoism

The home-grown philosophy-cum-religion of Taoism (Dào Jiào) is entirely Chinese, but exercises less of an influence over the minds of modern-day people in Shànghǎi and China than Buddhism.

In its simplest, purest and most philosophical form, Taoism draws from *The Classic of the Way and its Power* (Taote Jing; Daode Jing), penned by the sagacious Laotzu (Laozi; c 580–500 BC), who left his writings with the gatekeeper of a pass as he headed west on the back of an ox. Some Chinese believe his wanderings took him to a distant land in the west where he became Buddha.

Taoists seek to live by bringing their lives into harmony with the 'Way' (道, *dào*) and in so doing attain fulfilment. In its more religious manifestations, Taoism is fused with superstitious beliefs in a domain

---

MONEY, TRADE & REBELLION

Born of money and trade and for so long a byword for exploitation, ill-gotten gains and vice, Shànghǎi is a city whose most prominent buildings – both historically and today – were shrines and temples to Mammon. Conversely, however, the city has also served as a crucible for newfangled – and often potent – ideas, many imported from overseas. For starters, the Chinese Communist Party was conceived here in 1921 and went on to stridently undermine religious belief during the zealous Mao Zedong years.

NATIONALISM

In today's Shànghǎi, '-isms' (主义, zhǔyì or 'doctrines') are often frowned upon. 'Intellectualism' is suspect as it may clash with political taboos. 'Idealism' is nonpragmatic and potentially destructive, as Maoism showed.

Some argue that China's one-party state has reduced thinking across the spectrum via propaganda and censorship. This has, however, helped spawn another '-ism': nationalism.

Nationalism is not restricted to Chinese youth but it is this generation – with no experience of the Cultural Revolution's terrifying excesses – that most closely identifies with its message. The fènqīng (angry youth) have been swept along with China's rise; while they are no lovers of the Chinese Communist Party (CCP), they yearn for a stronger China that can stand up to 'foreign interference'.

The CCP actively encourages strong patriotism, but is nervous about its sublimation into nationalism and its potential for disturbance. With China's tendency to get quickly swept along by passions, nationalism has become an often unseen but quite potent force, with anti-Japanese disturbances occurring in Shànghǎi and other cities.

overseen by myriad deities, including the Money God, the Fire God and Guandi.

Taoist temples are similar to Buddhist temples in layout, and although the pantheon of deities differs, the main hall in each type of temple is usually dominated by a trinity of large statues. Taoist monks wear squarish trousers and jacket, with their hair grown long and twisted into a topknot, while Buddhist monks wear robes and shave their heads.

As with Buddhist temples, Shànghǎi has far fewer examples of Taoist temples than elsewhere in China, and none of any great age or heritage, apart from the Temple of the Town God (p82) in the Old Town.

Confucianism

A mainstay of Chinese civilisation for the past 2000 years, Confucianism (Rújiā Sīxiǎng) is a humanist philosophy (rather than a religion) based upon the teachings of Confucius (Kǒngzǐ), a 6th-century-BC philosopher who lived during a period of incessant warfare and strife. Confucius' disciples gathered his ideas in the form of short aphorisms and conversations, forming the work known as the *Analects* (Lúnyǔ).

In its quest for social harmony and the common good, Confucianism advocated codes of conduct and systems of obedience with an emphasis on the five basic hierarchical relationships: father-son, ruler-subject, husband-wife, elder-younger and friend-friend. Confucius believed that if each individual carried out his or her proper role in society (ie a son served his father respectfully while a father provided for his son, a subject served his ruler respectfully while a ruler provided for his subject, and so on) social order would result.

Confucianism eventually permeated every level of society, and an intimate knowledge of the Confucian classics was a prerequisite to a life in officialdom.

What started off as a fresh and radical philosophy later became conservative, reactionary and an obstacle to change. Confucius' thinking came under vitriolic attack during the Cultural Revolution; however, the sage has been officially rehabilitated into modern Chinese society, and even though his influence and prestige has waned, Confucius' social ethics have resurfaced in government propaganda, where they lend authority to the leadership's emphasis on 'harmony' (héxié).

Confucius Institutes around the world aim to internationally promote Chinese language and culture, while simultaneously developing China's cultural influence abroad.

SHÀNGHǍI'S CHRISTIANS

Christianity is the fastest-growing faith in China, and Shànghǎi alone has at least 140,000 Catholics, largely due to its history of Jesuit communities. St Ignatius Cathedral is the largest church in the city proper but Shěshān Basilica, in the suburbs, is even larger. Relations between the government and the Holy See are uneasy, as the state-run overseeing Chinese Patriotic Catholic Association does not acknowledge the authority of the Vatican and appoints its own bishops. China's one-child policy does not sit well with the Catholic stand on abortion either. For these reasons, the Vatican maintains diplomatic relations with Taiwan, much to China's consternation.

To see or take part in prayer, Catholics can visit the Christ the King Church (p98) in the French Concession, St Ignatius Cathedral (p166) or the splendid Catholic Church (p175) in Qībǎo. Protestants can visit the lively Community Church (p100), near South Wulumuqi Rd in the French Concession, which has a Sunday school for children and a small nursery for toddlers. There is also a growing flock of modern, newly built churches throughout Shànghǎi, including in Pǔdōng. Other historic Catholic churches can be found in Zhūjiājiǎo and Hángzhōu.

Shànghǎi's historic Confucius Temple (p86) is, like many other temples, in the Old Town, a quiet and unruffled corner of the city.

Christianity

Christianity (Jīdū Jiào) first arrived in China with the Nestorians, a sect from ancient Persia that split with the Byzantine Church in AD 431 and who travelled to China via the Silk Road in the 7th century. Much later, in the 16th century, the Jesuits appeared and were popular figures at the imperial court, although they made few converts; they were later very active in Shànghǎi, especially in Xújiāhuì. Large numbers of Catholic and Protestant missionaries established themselves in China in the 19th century, but bore the brunt of much antiforeigner feeling during the Boxer Rebellion and other anti-Western spasms.

David Aikman's *Jesus in Beijing: How Christianity is Transforming China and Changing the Global Balance of Power* (2003) predicts almost one-third of Chinese turning to Christianity within the next few decades.

In today's Shànghǎi (and China), Christianity is a burgeoning faith, perhaps uniquely placed to expand due to its industrious work ethic, associations with economically developed nations, and its emphasis on human rights and charitable work. Some estimates point to as many as 100 million Christians in China; however, the exact number is hard to calculate as many groups – outside the four official Christian organisations – lead a strict underground existence in what are called 'house churches'.

Islam

Islam (Yīsiïlán Jiào) in China dates to the 7th century, when it was first brought to China by Arab and Persian traders along the Silk Road. Later, during the Mongol Yuan dynasty, maritime trade increased, bringing new waves of merchants to China's coastal regions. It is estimated that 1.5% to 3% of Chinese today are Muslim. Shànghǎi's most famous mosque is the Peach Garden Mosque (p87) in the Old Town.

Judaism

Although Shànghǎi was never a base for Chinese Judaism (Yóutài Jiào) like Kāifēng in north China's Hénán province, the city has a long and splendid history of Jewish immigration. Hóngkǒu contains several reminders of the Jewish Quarter there, especially around Zhoushan Rd, including the Ohel Moishe Synagogue (p159).

Survival Guide

Transport

ARRIVING IN SHÀNGHĂI

Most international passengers reach Shànghǎi by air. The city has two airports: Pǔdōng International Airport to the east and Hóngqiáo International Airport on the other side of the city to the west, with most international passengers arriving at the former. Shànghǎi is China's second-largest international air hub (third-largest including Hong Kong) and if you can't fly direct, you can go via Běijīng, Hong Kong or Guǎngzhōu (and a host of lesser international airports in China).

➜ From the US west coast, figure on a 13- to 14-hour flight to Shànghǎi or Běijīng, and an additional hour or more to Hong Kong.

➜ From London Heathrow it's about an 11-hour flight to Běijīng and 12 to 13 hours to Shànghǎi and Hong Kong.

➜ Daily (usually several times a day) domestic flights connect Shànghǎi to every major city in China.

➜ Shànghǎi is linked to the rest of China by an efficient rail network (with numerous high-speed lines) and, to a far lesser extent, long-distance buses.

➜ Shànghǎi can be reached by ferry from Osaka, Kobe and Nagasaki in Japan.

Flights, cars and tours can be booked online at lonely planet.com/bookings.

Pǔdōng International Airport

Pǔdōng International Airport (PVG; 浦东国际机场, Pǔdōng Guójì Jīchǎng; ☎021 6834 7575, flight information 96990; www.shairport.com) is located 30km southeast of Shànghǎi, near the East China Sea. Most international flights (and some domestic flights) operate from here. If you're making an onward domestic connection from Pǔdōng International Airport, it's crucial that you find out whether the domestic flight leaves from Pǔdōng or Hóngqiáo, as it will take at least an hour to cross the city.

There are two main passenger terminals (with a new satellite terminal under construction), which are easy to navigate. Departures are on the upper level and arrivals on the lower level, where there is a tourist information counter.

➜ Banks and ATMS are located throughout the airport, on both sides of customs.

➜ The **Dazhong Merrylin Airport Hotel** (大众美林阁空港宾馆; Dàzhòng Měilín Gékōng Gǎng Bīnguǎn; ☎021 3879 9999; www.dazhongair porthotel.com; r from ¥320; ❋ ❂) is located between Terminals 1 and 2, in front of the Maglev ticket office.

➜ Left luggage is located in the arrival and departure halls and open from 6am to 11pm. Charges are from ¥10 to ¥45 depending on luggage size (up to four hours), or ¥50 per day.

➜ Shuttle buses connect the terminals, stopping at doors 1 and 8 (Terminal 1) and doors 23 and 27 (Terminal 2), running every 10 minutes.

➜ Wi-fi is available but tends to be out of service quite frequently.

Maglev

The warp-speed **Maglev** (磁浮列车, Cífú Lièchē; www. smtdc.com; economy one way/ return ¥50/80, with same-day air ticket ¥40, children under/ over 1.2m free/half price) runs from Pǔdōng International Airport to Longyang Rd metro stop (just south of Century Park) on metro line 2 in eight minutes, running every 20 minutes in both directions. Trains from Pǔdōng International Airport run from 6.45am to 9.40pm. Trains to the airport run from 7.02am to 10.40pm.

Metro

Metro line 2 zips from Pǔdōng International Airport to Hóngqiáo International Airport, passing through central

TAKING THE SHÀNGHǍI MAGLEV

If you need to reach or depart Pǔdōng International Airport quick, Shànghǎi's futuristic **Maglev** (磁浮列车, Cífú Lièchē; www.smtdc.com; economy one way/return ¥50/80, with same-day air ticket ¥40, children under/over 1.2m free/half price) train comes with a top speed of 430km/h. Launched in 2003, it's the world's sole Maglev (magnetic levitation) train in commercial operation. In place of conventional wheels, the Sino-German train's carriages are supported above the tracks by a magnetic field. Carriages have simple interiors with ample legroom and, perhaps tellingly, no seatbelts. LED meters notch up the rapidly escalating velocity, although the train starts to decelerate around five minutes into its eight-minute cruise, in preparation for arrival. When it hits peak velocity, taxis heading in the same direction in the adjacent freeway fast lane appear to be driving backwards.

The Maglev train takes you as far as the terminus at Longyang Rd station in Pǔdōng, from where you'll have to disembark and lug your bags onto the metro system to continue your journey. Nonetheless, a trip on the train is thrilling and a return trip to the airport is a fun outing for kids and the family. From a transportation point of view, the Maglev has competition from metro line 2, which travels all the way into town from Pǔdōng International Airport and on to Hóngqiáo Airport Terminal 2, via the city centre.

Shànghǎi. You will, however, need to disembark at Guanglan Rd station and transfer to another train on the same platform to continue your journey. Pǔdōng International Airport is a long way out: it takes about 45 minutes to People's Square (¥7).

Airport Bus

Airport buses take between 60 and 90 minutes to reach destinations in Pǔxī, west of the Huángpǔ River. Buses drop off at all departures halls and pick up outside arrivals, at both Terminals 1 and 2, leaving the airport roughly every 15 to 30 minutes from 7am to 11pm and heading to the airport from roughly 5.30am to 9.30pm (bus 1 runs till 11pm). The most useful buses:

Airport bus 1 (¥30) Links Pǔdōng International Airport with Hóngqiáo International Airport (Terminals 1 and 2)

Airport bus 5 (Map p309; ¥16 to ¥22) Links Pǔdōng Airport with Shànghǎi Railway Station via People's Square.

Airport bus 7 (¥20) runs to Shànghǎi South Railway Station.

Midnight line (¥16 to ¥30) Operates from 11pm to the last arrival, running to Hóngqiáo Airport Terminal 1 via Longyang Rd metro station to Shimen No 1 Rd and Huashan Rd.

Taxi

Rides into central Shànghǎi cost around ¥160 and take about an hour; to Hóngqiáo airport it costs around ¥200. Most Shànghǎi taxi drivers are honest, but ensure they use the meter. Avoid monstrous overcharging by using the regular taxi rank outside the arrivals hall.

Hotel Shuttle Bus

Most top-end and some mid-range hotels operate shuttle buses to and from their hotels at fixed times (roughly ¥40 to Pǔdōng International Airport). Enquire at the rows of hotel desks in the arrivals hall or contact your hotel beforehand.

Long-Distance Bus

Regular buses run to Sūzhōu (苏州; ¥84, three hours, 18 per day) and Hángzhōu (杭州; ¥100, three hours, 12 per day) from the long-distance bus stop at the airport.

Hóngqiáo International Airport

Hóngqiáo International Airport (SHA; 虹桥国际机场, Hóngqiáo Guójì Jīchǎng; ☎021 5260 4620, flight information 021 6268 8899; www.shairport.com; Ⓜ Hongqiao Airport Terminal 1, Ⓜ Hongqiao Airport Terminal 2), 18km west of the Bund, has two terminals: the older and less-used **Terminal 1** (east terminal; halls A and B), and the new and sophisticated **Terminal 2** (west terminal; attached to Shànghǎi Hóngqiáo Railway Station), where most flights arrive. If flying domestically within China from Shànghǎi, consider flying from here; it is closer to central Shànghǎi than Pǔdōng International Airport. If transferring between Hóngqiáo and Pǔdōng International Airports, note they are a long way apart and it will take at least an hour.

➡ ATMs are located at most exits; accept international cards.

➡ **Information counter** (虹桥国际机场咨询服务处, Hóngqiáo Guójì Jīchǎng Zīxún Fúwùchù; ☉5.30am-11pm) staff can assist by booking discounted

CLIMATE CHANGE & TRAVEL

Every form of transport that relies on carbon-based fuel generates CO_2, the main cause of human-induced climate change. Modern travel is dependent on aeroplanes, which might use less fuel per kilometre per person than most cars but travel much greater distances. The altitude at which aircraft emit gases (including CO_2) and particles also contributes to their climate change impact. Many websites offer 'carbon calculators' that allow people to estimate the carbon emissions generated by their journey and, for those who wish to do so, to offset the impact of the greenhouse gases emitted with contributions to portfolios of climate-friendly initiatives throughout the world. Lonely Planet offsets the carbon footprint of all staff and author travel.

accommodation, providing free maps, offering advice on transport into town and writing the Chinese script for a taxi.

➜ Luggage storage is available in the departure and arrivals hall of both terminals, operating between 7am and 8.30pm. Bags must be locked and a passport or ID is required.

➜ Shuttle buses run frequently (from 6am to 11pm) between Terminals 1 and 2, taking 13 minutes.

➜ Wi-fi is accessed by using the password provided at an information counter.

Terminal 2
METRO
Terminal 2 is connected to downtown Shànghǎi by lines 2 and 10 (30 minutes to People's Square) from Hóngqiáo International Airport Terminal 2 metro station; both lines run through East Nanjing Rd station (for the Bund). Line 2 runs to Pǔdōng and connects with Pǔdōng International Airport (¥8; 1¾ hours) and Longyang Rd metro station, south of Century Park, from where you can hop aboard the Maglev. The next stop west from Hóngqiáo Airport Terminal 2 is Hóngqiáo Railway Station (connected to the airport and accessible on foot).

TAXI
A taxi to the Bund will cost around ¥100; to Pǔdōng International Airport, around ¥200.

BUS
Airport bus 1 (¥30; ⊘6am-9.30pm) Runs to Pǔdōng International Airport.

Bus 941 (Map p309; ¥6; ⊘5.30am-11pm) Runs to the main Shànghǎi Railway Station.

Night buses 316 & 320 (⊘11am-5pm) and **320** Run to East Yan'an Rd near the Bund.

LONG-DISTANCE BUS
The long-distance bus station at Terminal 2 runs to myriad destinations, including Sūzhōu, Nánjīng, Qīngdǎo, Túnxī (for Huángshān), Hángzhōu and Dēngfēng (for the Shaolin Temple).

TRAIN
Attached to Terminal 2, Shànghǎi Hóngqiáo Railway Station has high-speed G-class trains to Hángzhōu, Sūzhōu, Nánjīng and Běijīng.

Terminal 1
METRO
Hóngqiáo Airport Terminal 1 is the next stop east on line 10 from Hóngqiáo Airport Terminal 2 metro station. Change to line 2 for the metro to Pǔdōng International Airport (¥8).

BUS
Airport bus 1 (¥30; ⊘6am-9.30pm) Runs to Pǔdōng International Airport.

Airport shuttle bus (¥4; ⊘7.50am-11pm) Runs from Hóngqiáo Airport Terminal 1 to the largely defunct Airport City

Terminal in Jìng'ān; it's useful for accessing the Jìng'ān area.

Bus 925 (¥4; ⊘5.30am-10.30pm) Runs to People's Square via Hongmei Rd and Shimen No 1 Rd.

Bus 938 (¥7; ⊘6am-midnight) Runs to Yángjiādù in Pǔdōng via Hongxu Rd, North Caoxi Rd and South Xizang Rd.

Bus 941 (Map p309; ¥6; ⊘5.30am-11pm) Links Hóngqiáo International Airport with the main Shànghǎi Railway Station.

Bus 806 (¥5; ⊘6am-11pm) Runs to Lùpǔ Bridge in the south of Pǔxī.

TAXI
Taxi queues can be long at Terminal 1; it can be quicker to take the metro or the bus.

Bus
As trains are fast, regular and efficient, and traffic on roads unpredictable, travelling by bus is not a very useful way to leave or enter Shànghǎi, unless you are visiting local water towns. Buses to Běijīng take between 14 and 16 hours: it is far faster and more comfortable (but more expensive) to take the 5½-hour high-speed G-class trains to the capital, or even the eight-hour D-class trains.

The huge **Shànghǎi South Long-Distance Bus Station** (上海长途客运南站, Shànghǎi Chángtú Kèyùn Nánzhàn; ☑021 5436 2835;

www.ctnz.net; 666 Shilong Rd; Ⓜ Shanghai South Railway Station) has buses largely to destinations in south China. Destinations include Sūzhōu (苏州; ¥38, very frequent), Nánjīng (南京; ¥96, four per day), Hángzhōu (杭州; ¥68, very frequent) and Níngbō (宁波; ¥127, very frequent).

Although it appears close to Shànghăi Railway Station, the vast **Shànghăi Long-Distance Bus Station** (上海长途汽车客运总站, Shànghăi Chángtú Qìchē Kèyùn Zǒngzhàn; Map p309; ☑021 6605 0000; www.kyzz.com.cn; 1666 Zhongxing Rd; 中兴路1666号; Ⓜ Shanghai Railway Station) is a pain to get to (taxi is easiest), but has buses to everywhere, including regular buses to Sūzhōu (¥38, two hours) and Hángzhōu (¥68, 2½ hours), as well as two buses to Nánjīng (¥105, 4½ hours, 9.30am and 2.50pm), Zhōuzhuāng (¥29, six daily, two hours) and Běijīng (¥354, 4pm, 18 hours).

Regular buses also depart for Hángzhōu (¥100, two hours) and Sūzhōu (¥84, two hours) from Pǔdōng International Airport. Buses for Hángzhōu, Sūzhōu and a host of destinations also leave from the **Hóngqiáo Long-Distance Bus Station** (虹桥长途客运站, Hóngqiáo Chángtú Kèyùn Zhàn) at Hóngqiáo Airport Terminal 2.

From the **Shànghăi Sightseeing Bus Centre** (上海旅游集散中心, Shànghăi Lǚyóu Jísàn Zhōngxīn; Map p316) at Shànghăi Stadium, you can join tours to Sūzhōu, Hángzhōu, Tónglǐ, Zhōuzhuāng, Zhūjiājiǎo and other destinations around Shànghăi.

Car & Motorcycle

Most visitors arrive in Shànghăi by plane or train. It's not really advisable to hire a car, due to the bureaucratic nightmare of the whole process; you will need a temporary or long-term Chinese driving licence.

Train

China's rail service is gargantuan, excellent and more than a little mind-boggling, and colossal investment over recent years has pumped up the high-speed network. The only 'international' train to arrive in Shànghăi is the T99 from Kowloon in Hong Kong. The train is, however, an excellent way to arrive in Shànghăi from other parts of China. The railway to Lhasa in Tibet began running in 2006, despite scepticism that it could ever be laid, so you can climb aboard a train in Shànghăi and alight in Tibet's capital.

Train information is available by phone in Chinese only (☑800 820 7890).

Railway Stations

The new and sophisticated **Shànghăi Hóngqiáo Railway Station** (上海虹桥站, Shànghăi Hóngqiáo Zhàn; Ⓜ Hongqiao Railway Station) is Asia's largest train station. It is located at the western end of metro line 10 and on line 2, near Hóngqiáo International Airport. It's the terminus for the high-speed G-class trains and other trains, and includes services to Běijīng (from ¥555, very regular), Hángzhōu (from ¥73, very regular), Nánjīng South (from ¥95, frequent) and Sūzhōu (from ¥25, regular).

The vast, hectic and sprawling **Shànghăi Railway Station** (上海火车站, Shànghăi Huǒchē Zhàn; ☑in Chinese 12306; 385 Meiyuan Rd; 梅园路385号; Ⓜ Shanghai Railway Station), located in the north of town, is easily reached by metro lines 1, 4 and 3 and has G-class, D-class and express trains to Běijīng (¥309, three daily), Hángzhōu (¥95, four daily), Hong Kong (¥226, 6.20pm), Huángshān (¥93, two daily), Nánjīng (¥144, frequent),

---

SHÀNGHĂI BY BOAT

Shànghăi Port International Cruise Terminal (上海港国际客运中心, Shànghăi Găng Guójì Kèyùn Zhōngxīn; Map p314; Gaoyang Rd; 高阳路) Located north of the Bund and mostly serving cruise ships. A few international passenger routes serve Shànghăi, with reservations recommended in July and August. Passengers must be at the harbour three hours before departure to get through immigration.

China-Japan International Ferry Company (中日国际轮渡有限公司, Zhōngrì Guójì Lúndù Yǒuxiàn Gōngsī; Map p314; ☑021 6325 7642; www.shinganjin.com/index_e.php; 18th fl, Jin'an Bldg, 908 Dongdaming Rd, 东大明路908号金岸大厦; tickets from ¥1300, plus ¥150 fuel surcharge) Has staggered departures every week to either Osaka or Kobe (46 hours) in Japan on Saturdays at 12.30pm. Fares range from ¥1300 in an eight-bed dorm to ¥6500 in a deluxe twin cabin.

Shànghăi International Ferry Company (上海国际轮渡, Shànghăi Guójì Lúndù; Map p314; ☑021 6537 5111; www.shanghai-ferry.co.jp/english/; 15th fl, Jin'an Bldg, 908 Dongdaming Rd; 东大明路908号金岸大厦; ⊗8.30am-5pm Mon-Fri) Has departures to Osaka (46 hours) on Tuesdays at 11am. Fares range from ¥1300 in an eight-bed dorm to ¥6500 in a deluxe twin cabin.

Sūzhōu (¥40, frequent) and Xī'ān (¥180, frequent).

Modern **Shànghǎi South Railway Station** (上海南站, Shànghǎi Nánzhàn; ☎021 9510 5123; 200 Zhaofeng Rd) is easily accessed on metro lines 1 and 3. It has trains largely to southern and southwestern destinations including Guìlín (¥190, four daily) and Hángzhōu (¥29, frequent).

A few trains also leave from the renovated West Station (上海西站, Shànghǎi Xīzhàn), including trains to Nánjīng; however, it's less convenient.

Tickets

Although procuring tickets for nearby destinations (such as Sūzhōu and Hángzhōu) and high-speed train tickets is often straightforward, buying rail tickets in Shànghǎi and China can be very troublesome.

WHERE TO BUY TICKETS

There are several options for purchasing train tickets in Shànghǎi.

➡ Queue at the ticket offices (售票厅, shòupiàotīng) at train stations, but brace for a long wait. Shànghǎi Railway Station has two halls: one in the main building (same-day tickets) and another on the east side of the square (advance tickets). One counter should have English-speakers.

➡ Ask your hotel to obtain a ticket for you. Note, a surcharge may be levied.

➡ Purchase tickets for a small surcharge from travel agencies.

➡ Book tickets online using **CTrip** (http://english.ctrip. com), **China Highlights** (www. chinahighlights.com) or **China DIY Travel** (www.china-diy-travel.com). CTrip tickets will be delivered to your address in China; you cannot buy e-tickets, print your own tickets or collect them. China Highlights offers a similar service, and can also deliver e-tickets by email.

➡ Use the small train ticket offices dotted around town to avoid the queues at Shànghǎi Railway Station. **Advance Train Ticket Office** (Map p309; 824 Hengfeng Rd; 恒丰路; ⊙8am-7pm), under the bridge a short walk west in Jìng'ān, and **Jìng'ān Train Ticket Office** (静安火车售票处, Jìng'ān Huǒchē Shòupiào Chù; Map p310; 77 Wanhangdu Rd; 万航渡路77号; ⊙8am-6pm), located to the west of Jìng'ān Temple, are useful.

TIPS FOR BUYING TICKETS

➡ Foreigners need their passports when buying a ticket at all train ticket offices. The number gets printed on your ticket.

➡ Never aim to get a hard-sleeper (or, increasingly, a soft-sleeper) ticket on the day of travel – plan a few days ahead.

➡ Most tickets can be booked in advance between two and 18 days (and sometimes longer) prior to your intended date of departure.

➡ Automated ticket machines at Shànghǎi Railway Station and other train stations require Chinese ID and your passport will not work; you will need to queue at the ticket window.

➡ Ticket purchases at stations and ticket offices can only be made in cash.

➡ Tickets for travel around Chinese New Year and during the 1 May and 1 October holiday periods can be very hard to find, and prices increase on some routes.

➡ Tickets on many routes (such as to Lhasa, Tibet) can be very hard to find in July and August, so prepare to fly instead.

➡ Avoid black-market tickets – your passport number must be on the ticket.

➡ There are no refunds for lost train tickets, so hold on to them tightly.

➡ You can get refunds on returned tickets before your train departs, but you will be charged between 5% and 20% depending on how late you leave it till you return your ticket. Most train stations have a ticket-returns window.

Classes

The most comfortable way to get to destinations around Shànghǎi (such as Sūzhōu and Hángzhōu) is by high-speed train, which assures you a comfortable seat and regular and punctual departures.

On swish high-speed G-class, D-class and C-class trains seating classes are straightforward:

➡ 1st class (一等, yīděng)
➡ 2nd class (二等, èrděng)
➡ Business class (商务座, shāngwù zuò)
➡ VIP class (特等座, tèděng zuò)

For most other slower (T-class, K-class, some Z-class and other) Chinese trains, you have the following choice of ticket types:

➡ Hard seat (硬座, yìngzuò)
➡ Hard sleeper (硬卧, yìngwò)
➡ Soft seat (软座, ruǎnzuò)
➡ Soft sleeper (软卧, ruǎnwò)

On non-high-speed trains, numbered soft seats are more comfortable than hard seats. Hard-seat class is not available on the high-speed C-, D- and G-class trains, and is only found on T- and K-class trains, and trains without a number prefix; a handful of Z-class trains have hard seats. Hard-seat class generally has padded seats, but it's often unclean and noisy, and painful on the long haul. Since hard seat is the only class most locals can afford, it's packed to the gills.

For overnight trips to further destinations, hard sleepers are easily comfortable enough, with only a fixed number of people allowed in the sleeper carriage. They serve very well as an overnight hotel.

The hard-sleeper carriage consists of doorless compartments with half-a-dozen bunks in three tiers and fold-away seats by the windows. Sheets, pillows and blankets are provided. Carriages are nonsmoking, although smokers congregate between carriages. Competition for hard sleepers is keen, so reserve early. Prices vary according to the berth: upper (cheapest), middle or lower berth.

Soft sleepers cost twice as much, and are four comfortable bunks in a closed, carpeted compartment.

Timetables & Useful Websites

China DIY Travel (www.china-diy-travel.com)

China Highlights (www.china highlights.com)

CTrip (http://english.ctrip.com)

Seat 61 (www.seat61.com/china.htm)

Travel China Guide (www.travelchinaguide.com)

GETTING AROUND SHÀNGHǍI

➡ **Metro** The rapidly expanding metro and light railway system works like a dream; it's fast, efficient and inexpensive. Rush hour on the metro operates above capacity, however, and you get to savour the full meaning of the big squeeze.

➡ **Taxis** Ubiquitous and cheap, but flagging one down during rush hour or during a rainstorm requires staying power of a high order.

➡ **Bus** With a wide-ranging web of routes, buses may sound tempting, but that's before you try to decipher routes and stops or attempt to squeeze aboard during the crush hour. Buses also have to contend with Shànghǎi's traffic, which can slow to an agonising crawl.

➡ **Bicycles** Good for small neighbourhoods but distances are too colossal for effective transport about town.

➡ **Walking** This is only really possible within neighbourhoods, and even then the distances can be epic and tiring.

Bicycle

If you can handle the fumes and menace of Shànghǎi's intimidating traffic, cycling can be a good way to get around town, but you will need to link it in with public transport.

➡ Bikes are banned from some major roads, so cyclists often surge down the pavements (sidewalks) of busy streets.

➡ Cars will give you little room; if you're new to Shànghǎi, allow a few days to adjust.

➡ Make sure that you have your own bicycle cable lock and try to leave your bike at bike parks.

➡ Cyclists never use lights at night and Chinese pedestrians favour dark clothing, so ride carefully.

Several hostels around town, including **Le Tour Traveler's Rest** (乐途静安国际青年旅舍, Lètú Jìng'ān Guójì Qīngnián Lǚshè; Map p310; ☑021 6267 1912; www.letour shanghai.com; 319 Jiaozhou Rd; 胶州路319号; dm ¥100-150, r ¥340-400; ❄@🛜; Ⓜ Line 2, 7 to Jing'an Temple, exit 2), can rent you a bike. **BOHDI** (☑021 5266 9013; www.bohdi.com.cn; Bldg 15, 271 Qianyang Rd; 千阳路271号; ☺8am-5pm Mon-Fri; Ⓜ Zhenbei Rd) also sells and rents quality bikes.

The city has a public bike-hire scheme called Forever Public Bike Hire Scheme (bikes per hour ¥4), launched for the World Expo in 2010. It's far more limited than the fantastic system in Hángzhōu (the world's largest) and has not proved a success, especially for visitors, due to registration difficulties, a lack of docking stations in tourist areas and a Chinese-language-only website (www.chinarmb.com). To register for a card (¥300 deposit and ¥100 credit), you will need to take your passport to the **Xújiāhuì Tourist Information Centre** (徐家汇旅游咨询中心, Xújiāhuì Lǚyóu Zīxún Zhōngxīn; Map p316; ☑021 5425 9260; www.xjh.sh.cn; 166 Puxi Rd; 蒲西路166号; ☺9am-5pm) or the **Wukang Road Tourist Information Centre** (武康路旅游咨询中心, Wǔkāng Lù Lǚyóu Zīxún Zhōngxīn; Map p306; 393 Wukang Rd; 武康路393号; ☺9am-5pm; Ⓜ Shanghai Library).

Boat

Ferries cross the Huángpǔ River between Pǔxī on the west bank and Pǔdōng on the east. Most useful is the **Shanghai Ferry** (Map p296; 127 East Zhongshan No 2 Rd; 中山东二路127号; one way ¥2; Ⓜ Line 2, 10 to East Nanjing Rd, exit 1), which operates between the southern end of the Bund and Dongchang Rd in Pǔdōng, running every 15 minutes from 7am to 10pm. Tickets are sold at the kiosks out the front. The **Fuxing Road Ferry** (复兴路轮渡站, Fùxīng Lù Lúndùzhàn; Map p300; one way ¥2) runs from Fuxing Rd north of the Cool Docks in the South Bund to Dongchang Rd. Ferries run every 10 to 20 minutes from 5am to 11pm.

Bus

Although sightseeing buses can be extremely handy, the huge Shànghǎi public bus system is unfortunately very hard for foreigners who don't speak or read Chinese to use. Bus-stop signs and routes are in Chinese only. Drivers and conductors speak little, if any, English, although onboard announcements in English will alert you to when to get off. The conductor will tell you when your stop is arriving, if you ask. Bus stops are widely spaced and your bus can race past your destination and on to the next stop up to a kilometre away. Suburban and long-distance buses don't carry numbers – the destination is in characters.

➡ Air-con buses (with a snow-flake motif and the characters 空调 alongside the bus number) cost ¥2 to ¥3. The far rarer buses without air-con cost ¥1.5.

➡ On buses without conductors, drop your cash into the slot by the driver. Always carry exact money; no change is given.

➡ The swipe-able Transport Card works on many but not all bus routes.

➡ Try to get on at the terminus (thus guaranteeing yourself a seat), avoid rush hours, and stick to a few tried-and-tested routes.

➡ If you can't speak Chinese, have your destination written down in Chinese to show the driver, conductor or even a fellow passenger.

➡ Be alert to pickpockets, especially during the rush-hour squeeze.

➡ Buses generally operate from 5am to 11pm, except for 300-series buses, which operate all night.

➡ For English-language bus routes in town, go to http://msittig.wubi.org/bus.

Car

It is possible to hire a car in Shànghăi, but the bureau-cratic hurdles are designed to deter would-be foreign drivers – you can't simply pick up a car at Pǔdōng International Airport and hit the road. You will need a temporary or long-term Chinese driving licence.

For most visitors, it is more advisable to hire a car and a driver. A Volkswagen Santana with driver and petrol starts at around ¥600 per day; it is likely to be cheaper to hire a taxi for the day. Ask for more information at your hotel.

Metro

The Shànghăi metro (www. shmetro.com) is fast, cheap, clean and easy, though hard to get a seat on at the best of times (unless you get on at a terminus). The rush hour sees carriages filled beyond capacity, but trains are frequent and the system has been rapidly expanded to envelop more and more of the city.

➡ There are 14 lines serving more than 366 stations over 617km.

➡ There are plans to extend the network with nine new lines and 250km of track, starting in 2017, with a 2025 completion date.

➡ Metro maps are available at most stations. The free tourist maps also have a small metro map printed on them, and there's an English section on the metro website.

➡ Metro station exits can be confusing, so look for a street map (usually easy to find) in the ticket hall before exiting to get your bearings.

➡ To find a metro station look for the red M.

➡ The *Explore Shanghai* app helps you calculate how long your journey will take, how much it will cost and where the nearest metro station is.

➡ In 2016 wi-fi was rolled out to most metro lines and platforms. To access the internet, users need to download an application on their phones and register.

Key Metro Lines

The most useful lines for trav-ellers are 1, 2 and 10. Lines 1 and 2 connect at People's Square interchange, the city's busiest station. TV screens at stations count down the wait to the next train.

Line 1 (一号线, *yīhào xiàn*) Runs from Fujin Rd in the north, through Shànghăi Railway Sta-tion and People's Square, along Middle Huaihai Rd, through Xújiāhuì and Shànghăi South Railway Station to Xīnzhuāng in the southern suburbs.

Line 2 (二号线, *èrhào xiàn*) Runs from East Xujing in the west via Hóngqiáo Railway Sta-tion and Hóngqiáo International Airport Terminal 2, passing through Jìng'ān, People's Square, East Nanjing Rd (and the Bund district) in the centre of town, going under the Huángpǔ River and on to Long-yang Rd, the site of the Maglev terminus, before terminating at Pǔdōng International Airport in the east.

Line 10 (十号线, *shíhào xiàn*) Runs from Hóngqiáo Railway Station in the west through Hóngqiáo International Airport Terminal 2 and Terminal 1 be-fore zipping through the French Concession, the Old Town, the Bund area and Hóngkǒu before terminating at Xinjiang-wancheng.

Fares & Tickets

➡ Tickets range from ¥3 to ¥15, depending on the distance.

➡ Tickets are generally only sold from coin- and note-operated machines.

➡ Service counters will provide you with change if your bills are not accepted.

➡ Keep your ticket until you exit.

➡ When entering the metro, swipe your Transport Card across the turnstile sensor for access; when exiting, enter it into the slot, where it will be retained.

➡ The rechargeable Transport Card can be used on the metro, some buses, ferries and all taxis.

➡ One-day (¥18) and three-day travel passes (¥45) for use on the metro are available from service counters in stations.

➡ There can be huge distances between different lines at interchange stations, such as between line 9 and 1 at Xújiāhuì station, so factor this into your journey time.

➡ A growing number of stations have coin-operated toilets.

Operating Hours

There's one main shortcoming to the metro system: it stops running relatively early in the night. Most lines begin their final run between 10pm and 10.30pm (some earlier), so anyone out later than 11pm will need to catch a cab home.

Taxi

Shànghǎi has around 45,000 taxis. Most are Volkswagen Santanas, some are Volkswagen Passats; there's a fleet of Mercedes-Benz taxis and a 4000-strong fleet of spacious and comfortable white Volkswagen Touran taxis. Shànghǎi's taxis are reasonably cheap, hassle-free and generally easy to flag down except during rush hour and in summer storms.

➡ Drivers can be inept at navigating, even to obvious places. Some stick to main roads and have little grasp of shortcuts. Avoid total novices by examining the number of stars below the driver's photo on the dashboard; stars range from one to five in order of expertise (and English-language skills).

➡ Taxi drivers (mostly male) are mostly honest, but you should always go by the meter. The driver should push the meter down to start it when you get in the cab.

➡ Taxis may not have rear seatbelts, in which case sit in the front.

➡ Taxis can't take the tunnel to Lùjiāzuǐ in Pǔdōng from 8am to 9.30am and 5pm to 6.30pm.

➡ Fares are metered. Flag fall is ¥14 for the first 3km, and ¥2.5

TRANSPORT CARDS & TOURIST PASSES

If you are making more than a fleeting trip to Shànghǎi, it's worth getting a Transport Card (交通卡; *Jiāotōng Kǎ*). Available at metro stations and some convenience stores, cards can be topped up with credit and used on the metro, some buses and ferries, and all taxis. Credit is electronically deducted from the card as you swipe it over the sensor, at metro turnstiles and near the door on buses; when paying your taxi fare, hand it to the taxi driver, who will swipe it. Cards don't save you money, but will save you from queuing for tickets or hunting for change. A refundable deposit of ¥20 is required.

per km thereafter; there is no need to tip.

➡ A night rate operates from 11pm to 5am, when the flag fall is ¥18, then ¥3.10 per km.

➡ Pay by cash (*xiànjīn*) or use a Transport Card.

➡ At night you can tell if a taxi is empty by the red 'for hire' sign on the dashboard of the passenger side.

➡ Ask for a printed receipt, which gives the fare and the driver and car number, the distance travelled, waiting time and the number to call if there are any problems or if you left something in the taxi.

➡ If you don't speak Chinese, take a Chinese-character map, have your destination written down in characters or carry your destination's business card. Alternatively, download the handy *Shanghai Taxi Guide and Offline Maps* app to show the driver your destination.

➡ Use your mobile to call your local contact (or the 24-hour tourist hotline – ☑ 962 288) in Shànghǎi and ask him or her to give instructions to the driver.

➡ It also helps if you have your own directions and sit in the front with a map, looking knowledgable (to deter circuitous, looping detours).

➡ Shànghǎi's main taxi companies include turquoise-coloured **Dàzhòng** (大众; ☑ 021 96822), gold **Qiángshēng** (强

生; ☑ 021 6258 0000) and green **Bāshì** (巴士; ☑ 021 96840).

TOURS

The following provide a good introduction to Shànghǎi, particularly if you're short on time:

Big Bus Tours (上海观光车, Shànghǎi Guānguāngchē; ☑ 021 6351 5988; www.bigbustours.com; adult/child ¥300/200) & **City Sightseeing Buses** (都市观光, Dūshì Guānguāng; ☑ 021 40082 06222; www.springtour.com; tickets ¥30; ⏰ 9am-8.30pm summer, to 6pm winter) Double-decker open-bus tours around town.

Insiders Experience (☑ 138 1761 6975; www.insidersexperience.com; from ¥800) Fun motorbike-sidecar tours.

Newman Tours (新漫, Xīnmàn; ☑ 138 1777 0229; www.newmantours.com; from ¥190) Themed guided walks around Shànghǎi.

BOHDI (☑ 021 5266 9013; www.bohdi.com.cn; Bldg 15, 271 Qianyang Rd; 千阳路271号; ⏰ 8am-5pm Mon-Fri; Ⓜ Zhenbei Rd) Night-time cycling tours on Tuesdays from March to November and trips around the region.

China Cycle Tours (☑ 021 6384 7772; www.chinacycletours.com; half-/full-day tours from ¥400/¥850) City and rural tours in Shànghǎi and Sūzhōu.

Directory A–Z

Business Cards

Business name cards are absolutely crucial, even if you're not in China on business. Don't be left high and dry when name cards are being dealt around. Try to get your name translated into (simplified) Chinese and printed on the reverse of the card. Chinese pay particular attention to the quality of business cards, so aim for a good finish. When proffering and receiving business cards, emulate the Chinese method of respectfully using the thumb and forefinger of both hands. Buying a name-card wallet is also recommended.

Cultural Centres

The following offer useful resources and can be a good place to meet internationally minded Shanghainese.

Alliance Française (上海法语培训中心, Shànghǎi Fǎyǔ Péixùn Zhōngxīn; Map p314; ☑021 6357 5388; www. afshanghai.org; 5th & 6th fl, 297 Wusong Rd; 吴淞路297号 5; ☑8.30am-8.30pm Mon-Thu, to 7pm Fri, to 6.30pm Sat, to 5pm Sun; Ⓜ North Sichuan Rd) On hand is a large French library with magazines, newspapers, DVDs and music CDs; exhibitions, music concerts and literary events are also held here. The centre offers French-

and Chinese-language courses. There is another branch in the west of town and another in Sōngjiāng.

Goethe Institute (歌德学院, Gēdé Xuéyuàn; Map p296; ☑021 6391 2068; www.goethe. de/china; Room 102a, Cross Tower, 318 Fuzhou Rd; 福州路318号102A室; Ⓜ Line 2, 10 to East Nanjing Rd) Has a useful library, film screenings, internet access and German courses.

Customs Regulations

Chinese customs generally pay tourists little attention. There are clearly marked green channels and red channels. Importation of fresh fruit or cold cuts is prohibited. Pirated DVDs and CDs are illegal exports from China as well as illegal imports into most other countries. If they are found they will be confiscated.

Objects considered to be antiques require a certificate and a red seal to clear customs when leaving China. Anything made before 1949 is considered an antique, and if it was made before 1795 it cannot legally be taken out of the country.

Duty-free allowances:
➡ 400 cigarettes (or 100 cigars or 500g of tobacco)
➡ 1.5L of alcoholic beverages

➡ 50g of gold or silver
➡ ¥20,000 in Chinese currency; there are no restrictions on foreign currency but declare any cash that exceeds US$5000 or its equivalent in another currency.

Electricity

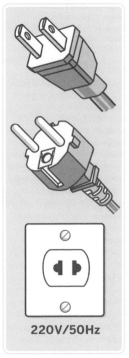

220V/50Hz

220V/50Hz

Embassies & Consulates

Most consulates defer to their embassies in Běijīng, but have efficient websites with useful information about doing business in Shànghǎi, cultural relations, events and also downloadable maps.

Australian Consulate (澳大利亚领事馆, Àodàlìyà Lǐngshìguǎn; Map p310; ☎021 2215 5200; www.shanghai. china.embassy.gov.au; 22nd fl, CITIC Sq, 1168 West Nanjing Rd; 南京西路1168号22楼; ⊗8.30am-5pm Mon-Fri; Ⓜ Line 2, 12, 13 to West Nanjing Rd)

Canadian Consulate (加拿大领事馆, Jiānádà Lǐngshìguǎn; Map p310; ☎021-3279 2800; www.shanghai.gc.ca; 8th fl, 1788 West Nanjing Rd; 南京西路1788号8楼; ⊗8.30am-noon & 1-5pm; Ⓜ Line 2, 7 to Jing'an Temple)

French Consulate (法国领事馆, Fǎguó Lǐngshìguǎn; Map p318; ☎021 6010 6050; www. consulfrance-shanghai.org; 8th fl, Bldg A, Soho Zhongshan Plaza, 1055 West Zhongshan Rd; 中山西路1055号中山广场A座18楼; ⊗8.15am-12.15pm Mon, 8.45am-12.15pm Tue-Fri)

German Consulate (德国领事馆, Déguó Lǐngshìguǎn; Map p306; ☎021 3401 0106; www. shanghai.diplo.de; 181 Yongfu Rd; 永福路181号)

Irish Consulate (爱尔兰领事馆, Ài'ěrlán Lǐngshìguǎn; Map p310; ☎021 6010 1360; www. embassyofireland.cn; 700a Shànghǎi Centre, 1376 West Nanjing Rd; 南京西路1376号700a室; ⊗9.30am-4.30pm Mon-Fri; Ⓜ Line 2, 7 to Jing'an Temple; Line 2, 12, 13 to West Nanjing Rd)

Japanese Consulate (日本领事馆, Rìběn Lǐngshìguǎn; Map p318; ☎021 5257 4766; www.shanghai.cn.emb-japan. go.jp; 8 Wanshan Rd; 万山路8号; ⊗9am-12.30pm & 1.30-5.30pm Mon-Fri)

Dutch Consulate (荷兰领事馆, Hélán Lǐngshìguǎn; Map p318; ☎021 2208 7288; http:// china.nlembassy.org; 10th fl, Tower B, Dawning Center, 500 Hongbaoshi Rd; 红宝石路500号东银中心东塔10楼; ⊗9am-noon & 1-5.30pm Mon-Fri)

New Zealand Consulate (新西兰领事馆, Xīnxīlán Lǐngshìguǎn; Map p302; ☎021 5407 5858; www.nzembassy.com; 2801-2802A & 2806B-2810, 5 Corporate Ave, 150 Hubin Rd; 湖滨150号; ⊗8.30am-noon & 1-5pm Mon-Fri)

Russian Consulate (俄罗斯领事馆, Èluósī Lǐngshìguǎn; Map p314; ☎021 6324 2682; www.rusconshanghai.org.cn; 20 Huangpu Rd; 黄浦路20号; ⊗9.15am-noon Mon, Wed & Fri)

Singaporean Consulate (新加坡领事馆, Xīnjiāpō Lǐngshìguǎn; Map p318; ☎021 6278 5566; www.mfa.gov.sg/shanghai; 89 Wanshan Rd; 万山路89号; ⊗8.30am-noon & 1-5pm)

Thai Consulate (泰王国领事馆, Tàiwángguó Lǐngshìguǎn; Map p318; ☎021 5260 9899; www.thaishanghai.com; 18 Wanshan Rd; 万山路18号; ⊗visa office 9.30-11.30am Mon-Fri; Ⓜ Yili Rd)

UK Consulate (英国领事馆, Yīngguó Lǐngshìguǎn; Map p310; ☎021 3279 2000; http:// ukinchina.fco.gov.uk; 17th fl Garden Sq, 968 West Beijing Rd; 京西路968号花园广场17楼; ⊗8.30am-5.30pm Mon-Fri, consular service 9am-noon & 2-4pm Mon, Wed & Thu, 9am-noon Tue & Fri; Ⓜ Line 2, 7 to Jing'an Temple; Line 2, 12, 13 to West Nanjing Rd)

US Consulate (美国领事馆, Měiguó Lǐngshìguǎn; Map p306; ☎021 6433 6880; http://shanghai.usembassy-china.org.cn; 1469 Middle Huaihai Rd; 淮海中路1469号乌鲁木齐路) Consulate general.

US Consulate (美国领事馆, Měiguó Lǐngshìguǎn; Map p310; ☎after-hour emergency for US citizens 021 3217 4650; http:// shanghai.usembassy-china. org.cn; 8th fl, Westgate Tower, 1038 West Nanjing Rd; 南京西路1038号8楼; ⊗8.15-11.30am & 1.15-2.30pm Mon-Fri; Ⓜ Line 2, 12, 13 to West Nanjing Rd, exit 1) For US citizen services and visas.

Emergency

Ambulance	☎120
Fire	☎119
Police	☎110

Health

Health concerns for travellers to Shànghǎi include worsening atmospheric pollution, traveller's diarrhoea and winter influenza. You can find a more than adequate standard of medical care in town, providing you have good travel insurance.

PRACTICALITIES

Magazines

Stacked up in bars, restaurants and cafes, free expat entertainment and listings magazines cover all bases:
➡ **City Weekend** (www.cityweekend.com.cn/shanghai) Glossy bimonthly.
➡ **That's Shanghai** (http://online.thatsmags.com/city/shanghai) Info-packed monthly.

Newspapers

➡ Imported English-language newspapers can be bought from five-star-hotel bookshops and some read online. The Shànghǎi-published English-language newspaper the *Shanghai Daily* (www.shanghaidaily.com) is a better read than the insipid national *China Daily* (www.chinadaily.com.cn), but is nevertheless censored.

Radio

Websites can be jammed but it's possible to listen to the following:
➡ **BBC World Service** (www.bbc.co.uk/worldserviceradio/on-air)
➡ **Voice of America** (www.voa.gov)

Smoking

➡ From 2010, antismoking legislation in Shànghǎi required a number of public venues (including hospitals, schools, bars and restaurants) to have designated nonsmoking areas and to install signs prohibiting smoking. However, you'll often find this rule flouted in bars and some restaurants.

TV

➡ Your hotel may have ESPN, Star Sports, CNN or BBC News 24. You can also tune into the (censored) English-language channel CCTV9 (Chinese Central TV).

Weights & Measures

➡ China officially subscribes to the international metric system, but you will encounter the ancient Chinese weights and measures system in markets. The system features the *liǎng* (*tael*, 50g) and the *jīn* (*catty*, 0.5kg). There are 10 *liǎng* to the *jīn*.

If you have arrived from South America or Central Africa you are required to show proof of a yellow-fever vaccination within the last 10 years.

Health Insurance

Be sure to purchase travel insurance before you depart; medical care in Shànghǎi can be expensive. Worldwide travel insurance is available at www.lonelyplanet.com/travel-insurance. You can buy, extend and claim online anytime – even if you're already on the road.

Recommended Vaccinations

There are no special vaccination requirements for visiting Shànghǎi, but you should consider vaccination against hepatitis A and B. Other vaccinations to consider are for diphtheria, tetanus, influenza, Japanese encephalitis, polio and typhoid. It's best to see your doctor three months in advance of your trip.

Common Diseases

Traveller's diarrhoea is the most common disease that a traveller will encounter in Shànghǎi. Many different types of organisms, usually bacteria (eg *E. coli*, salmonella), are responsible and the result is sudden diarrhoea and vomiting, or both, with or without fever. Hepatitis A and B are both common in the Shànghǎi area. Japanese encephalitis, which is transmitted by mosquitoes, is also present but restricted to more rural areas, particularly near rice fields. Typhoid fever is common throughout China and is caught from faecally contaminated food, milk and water. It manifests as fever, headache, cough, malaise and constipation or diarrhoea. Treatment is with quinolone antibiotics, and a vaccine is recommended before you travel.

Tap Water

Don't drink tap water or eat ice. Bottled water is readily available. Boiled water is OK.

Pollution

The air quality in Shànghǎi can be appalling, and can ruin your holiday, especially if you are sensitive to impurities in the air. If you suffer from asthma or other allergies you should anticipate a worsening of your symptoms in Shànghǎi and may need to increase your medication. Eye drops can be a useful addition to your travel kit; contact-lens wearers can experience discomfort here. Check pollution levels before you fly; click on http://aqicn.org/city/shanghai for the latest reading.

Website Resources

There is a wealth of travel-health advice on the internet. Lonelyplanet.com is a good place to start. The **World Health Organization** (WHO) publishes a book called *International Travel & Health,* which is revised annually and is available for free online at www.who.int/publications/en.

It's also a good idea to consult your own government's official travel-health website before departure.

Australia (www.dfat.gov.au/travel)

Canada (www.travelhealth.gc.ca)

New Zealand (https://mfat.govt.nz)

UK (www.gov.uk/foreign-travel-advice/china) Search for travel in the site index.

USA (www.cdc.gov/travel)

Internet Access

Getting internet access will be one constant source of frustration on your visit to China if you rely heavily on being connected, and are used to a lightning-fast service. The Chinese authorities remain mistrustful of the internet, and censorship is heavy-handed. Around 10% of websites are blocked; sites such as Google may be slow while Google Maps and Gmail is blocked; social-networking sites such as Facebook, Instagram and Twitter are blocked (as is YouTube). Media such as the *New York*

Times and *Bloomberg* are also blocked. Users can get around blocked websites by using a VPN (Virtual Private Network) service such as Astrill (www.astrill.com) or Vypr (www.goldenfrog.com/vyprvpn).

Occasionally email providers can go down, so having a back-up email address set up before you leave home is advised.

The majority of hostels and hotels have broadband internet access, and many hotels, cafes, restaurants and bars are wi-fi enabled. The wi-fi icon is used in Lonely Planet reviews where it is available.

Remember that wi-fi is generally unsecured, so take care what kind of information you enter if you're using a wireless connection.

If you don't have your own computer, try the following spots for internet and wi-fi access:

Goethe Institute (歌德学院, Gēdé Xuéyuàn; Map p296; ☑021 6391 2068; www.goethe.de/china; Room 102a, Cross Tower, 318 Fuzhou Rd; 福州路318号102A室; Ⓜ Line 2, 10 to East Nanjing Rd)

Shanghai Library (上海图书馆, Shànghǎi Túshū Guǎn; Map p306; ☑021 6445 5555; www.library.sh.cn; 1555 Middle Huaihai Rd; 淮海中路1555号; ⊗8.30am-8.30pm; ☎; Ⓜ Shanghai Library)

Wukang Road Tourist Information Centre (武康路旅游信息, Wǔkāng Lù Lǚyóu Xìnxī; Map p306; 393 Wukang Rd; 武康路393号; ⊗9am-5pm)

Legal Matters

China does not officially recognise dual nationality or the foreign citizenship of children born in China if one of the parents is a PRC (People's Republic of China) national. If you have Chinese and another nationality you may, in theory, not be al-

lowed to visit China on your foreign passport. In practice, Chinese authorities are not switched on enough to know if you own two passports, and should accept you on a foreign passport. Dual-nationality citizens who enter China on a Chinese passport are subject to Chinese laws and are legally not allowed consular help. If over 16 years of age, carry your passport with you at all times as a form of ID.

China takes a particularly dim view of opium and all its derivatives; trafficking in more than 50g of heroin can lead to the death penalty. Foreign-passport holders have been executed in China for drug offences.

The Chinese criminal justice system does not ensure a fair trial and defendants are not presumed innocent until proven guilty. China conducts more judicial executions than the rest of the world combined, up to 10,000 per year according to some reports. If arrested, most foreign citizens have the right to contact their embassy.

Gambling is officially illegal in mainland China.

Distributing religious material is illegal in mainland China.

LGBT Travellers

Local law is ambiguous in its attitude to LGBT people; generally the authorities take a dim view of same-sex couples but there's an increasingly confident scene, as indicated by gay bars and the annual event-stuffed Shanghai Pride (www.shpride.com). Shànghǎi heterosexuals are not, by and large, particularly homophobic, especially the under-40s. Young Chinese men sometimes hold hands; this carries no sexual overtones.

For up-to-date information on the latest gay and lesbian hot spots in Shànghǎi and elsewhere throughout China, try Utopia (www.

utopia-asia.com/chinshan. htm). For further tips, check out Travel Gay Asia (www. travelgayasia.com).

Medical Services

Shànghǎi is credited with the best medical facilities and most advanced medical knowledge in mainland China. The main foreign embassies keep lists of the English-speaking doctors, dentists and hospitals that accept foreigners.

Huádōng Hospital (华东医院外宾门诊, Huádōng Yīyuàn Wàibīn Ménzhěn; Map p306; ☑6248 3180 ext 63208; Foreigners Clinic, 2nd fl, Bldg 3, 221 West Yan'an Rd; 延安西路221号3号楼2层; ◷24hr emergency) Foreigners' clinic on the 2nd floor of building 3.

Huàshān Hospital (华山医院国际医疗中心, Huàshān Yīyuàn Guójì Yīliáo Zhōngxīn; Map p306;☑021 5288 9998; www.sh-hwmc.com.cn; 12 Middle Wulumuqi Rd; 乌鲁木齐中路12号; ⋈Changshu Rd) Hospital treatment and outpatient consultations are available at the 8th-floor foreigners' clinic, the **Huashan Worldwide Medical Center** (华山医院国际医疗中心, Huáshān Yīyuàn Guójì Yīliáo Zhōngxīn; Map p306;☑021 6248 3986; www.sh-hwmc.com.cn; 12 Middle Wulumuqi Rd; 乌鲁木齐中路12号; ◷8am-10pm; ⋈Changshu Rd), and there's 24-hour emergency treatment on the 15th floor in building 6.

International Peace Maternity Hospital (国际妇幼保健院, Guójì Fùyòu Bǎojiànyuàn; Map p316;☑021 6407 0434; www. ipmch.com.cn/en/about us_en.html; 910 Hengshan Rd; 衡山路910号; ⋈Line 1, 9, 11 to Xujiahui) Specialist hospital providing maternal care and child health care.

Parkway Health (以极佳医疗保健服务; Yíjíjiā Yīliáo Bǎojiàn

Fúwù;☑24hr hotline 021 6445 5999; www.parkwayhealth. cn; 2258 Hongqiao Rd; 虹桥路2258号; ◷9am-7pm Mon-Fri, 9am-5pm Sat & Sun) Numerous locations around town, including at **Jìng'ān** (以极佳医疗保健服务, Yíjíjiā Yīliáo Bǎojiàn Fúwù; Map p310;☑24hr 021 6445 5999; Suite 203, Shànghǎi Centre, 1376 W Nanjing Rd; 南京西路1376号203室; ⋈Line 2, 7 to Jing'an Temple). Offers comprehensive private medical care from internationally trained physicians and dentists. Members can access after-hours services and an emergency hotline.

Ruìjīn Hospital (瑞金医院, Ruìjīn Yīyuàn; Map p302;☑021 6437 0045; www.rjh.com.cn/ chpage/c1352/; 197 Ruijin No 2 Rd; 瑞金二路197号) Teaching hospital under the Shànghǎi Jiāotōng University School of Medicine.

Shànghǎi Children's Hospital (上海儿童医院, Shànghǎi Er Tóng Yīyuàn; Map p310;☑021 6247 4880; www.shchildren. com.cn; 1400 West Beijing Rd; 北京西路1400号; ⋈Line 2, 7 to Jing'an Temple) Centrally located children's hospital.

Shànghǎi United Family Hospital (上海和睦家医院, Shànghǎi Hémùjiā Yīyuàn; ☑24hr emergency 021 2216 3999, appointments 400 639 3900; http://shanghai.ufh. com.cn; 1139 Xianxia Rd; 仙霞路1139号) This complete private hospital is Western-owned and managed, and staffed by doctors trained in the West. Medical facilities run to inpatient rooms, operating rooms, an intensive-care unit, birthing suites and a dental clinic.

Pharmacies

The handy Hong Kong store **Watson's** (屈臣氏, Qūchénshì; Map p302; ☑021 6474 4775; 787 Middle Huaihai Rd; 淮海中路787号; ◷24 hr) can be found

in the basements of malls all over town (there's a branch in Westgate Mall). It sells imported toiletries and a limited range of simple, over-the-counter pharmaceuticals.

For harder-to-find foreign medicines, try any pharmacy (药房, yàofáng), easily identified by a green cross outside; some have service through the night (via a small window). Nearly all pharmacies stock both Chinese and Western medicines. You may not need a doctor's prescription for some medicines that you need a prescription for at home (eg antibiotics), especially outside Shànghǎi, but check at the pharmacy.

Traditional Chinese Medicine

Traditional Chinese medicine (TCM) is extremely popular in Shànghǎi, both for prevention and cure. There are many Chinese medicine shops, but English is not widely spoken. Chiropractic care, reflexology and acupuncture are popular, but check that disposable needles are used.

Body and Soul TCM Clinic (Map p300;☑021 5101 9262; www.tcm-shanghai.com; Suite 5, 14th fl, Anji Plaza, 760 South Xizang Rd; 西藏南路760号安基大厦14层5室; ◷9am-6pm Mon, Wed, Fri & Sat, 9am-8pm Tue & Thu,) International staff integrating TCM and Western medical practices. There are three clinics in town. Acupuncture and tuīná (traditional) massage available.

Lónghuá Hospital Shanghai University of Traditional Chinese Medicine (龙华中医院, Lónghuá Zhōngyīyuàn; Map p316;☑021 6438 5700; www. longhua.net; 725 South Wanping Rd; 零陵路725号; ⋈Line 4 to Shanghai Indoor Stadium) A kilometre northeast of Shànghǎi Indoor Stadium. A full range of TCM therapies and treatments.

Shànghǎi Qìgōng Institute (上海气功研究所, Shànghǎi

TRADITIONAL CHINESE MEDICINE

Traditional Chinese Medicine (TCM) views the human body as an energy system in which the basic substances of *qì* (气; vital energy), *jīng* (精; essence), *xuè* (血; blood) and *tǐyè* (体液; body fluids, blood and other organic fluids) function. The concept of *yīn* (阴; yin) and *yáng* (阳; yang) is fundamental to the system. Disharmony between yin and yang or within the basic substances may be a result of internal causes (emotions), external causes (climatic conditions) or miscellaneous causes (work, exercise, stress etc). Treatment includes acupuncture, massage, herbs, diet and *qì gōng* (气功), which seeks to bring these elements back into balance. Treatments can be particularly useful for treating chronic diseases and ailments such as fatigue, arthritis, irritable bowel syndrome and some chronic skin conditions.

Be aware that 'natural' does not always mean 'safe'; there can be drug interactions between herbal medicines and Western medicines. If using both systems, ensure you inform both practitioners what the other has prescribed.

Qìgōng Yánjiūsuǒ; Map p302; ☑021 6439 4141; top fl, 218-220 Nanchang Rd; 南昌路218-220号; ⊘8am-4.30pm; Ⓜ South Shaanxi Rd) Part of Shànghǎi's TCM school, the Qìgōng Institute offers *qì gōng* (*qì*-energy development) treatments and massage, as well as acupuncture sessions. No English is spoken; appointments necessary.

Shǔguāng Hospital (曙光医院, Shǔguāng Yīyuàn; Map p302; ☑021 6385 5617; 185 Pu'an Rd; 普安路185号; Ⓜ South Huangpu Rd) Situated next to Huaihai Park, this hospital has a full range of TCM health care. The hospital is affiliated with the Shanghai University of Traditional Chinese Medicine.

Money

The Chinese currency is known as rénmínbì (RMB), or 'people's money'. Officially, the basic unit of RMB is the yuán (¥), which is divided into 10 jiǎo, which again is divided into 10 fēn. In spoken Chinese the yuán is referred to as *kuài* and jiǎo as *máo*. The fēn has so little value that it is rarely used these days. It's generally a good idea to keep ¥1 coins on you for the metro (some ticket machines frequently take only coins) and buses.

The Bank of China (中国银行, Zhōngguó Yínháng) issues RMB bills in denominations of one, two, five, 10, 20, 50 and 100 yuán. Coins come in denominations of one yuán; one and five jiǎo; and one, two and five fēn (the last are rare). Paper versions of the coins circulate, but are disappearing.

ATMs

ATMs are widespread and generally accept Visa, MasterCard, Cirrus and Maestro cards. Most operate 24 hours. Bank of China and the Industrial & Commercial Bank of China are the best bets.

Changing Money

You can change foreign currency at money-changing counters at almost every hotel and at many shops, department stores and large banks such as the Bank of China and HSBC, as long as you have your passport; you can also change money at both Pǔdōng International Airport and Hóngqiáo International Airport. Some top-end hotels will change money only for their guests. Exchange rates in China are uniform wherever you change money, so there's little need to shop around.

Whenever you change foreign currency into Chinese currency you will be given a money-exchange voucher recording the transaction. You need to show this to change your yuán back into any foreign currency. Changing Chinese currency outside China is a problem, though it's quite easily done in Hong Kong.

Counterfeit Bills

Very few Chinese will accept a ¥50 or ¥100 note without first checking to see if it's a fake. Many shopkeepers will run notes under an ultraviolet light, looking for signs of counterfeiting. Visually checking for forged notes is hard unless you are very familiar with bills, but be aware that street vendors may try to dump forged notes on you in large-denomination change.

Credit Cards

Credit cards are more readily accepted in Shànghǎi than in other parts of China. Most tourist hotels will accept major credit cards (with a 4% processing charge) such as Visa, Amex, MasterCard, Diners and JCB, as will banks, upper-end restaurants and tourist-related shops. Credit hasn't caught on among most Chinese, and most local credit cards are in fact debit cards. Always carry enough cash for buying train tickets and for emergencies.

Check to see if your credit-card company charges a foreign transaction fee (usually between 1% and 3%) for purchases in China.

Call your card's emergency contact number in case of loss.

Travellers Cheques

As ATMs are so plentiful and easy to use in Shànghǎi, travellers cheques are far less popular than they once were. Stick to the major companies such as Thomas Cook, American Express and Citibank.

Opening Hours

Businesses in China close for the week-long Chinese New Year (usually in February) and National Day (beginning 1 October).

Bank of China Branches 9.30am–11.30am and 1.30–4.30pm Monday to Friday. Some also open Saturday and Sunday. Most have 24-hour ATMs.

Bars Around 5pm–2am (some open in the morning).

China Post Most major offices 8.30am–6pm daily; sometimes open until 10pm. Local branches closed weekends.

Museums Most open weekends; a few close Monday. Ticket sales usually stop 30 or 60 minutes before closing.

Offices and Government Departments Generally 9am–noon and 2–4.30pm Monday to Friday.

Restaurants Most 11am–10pm or later; some 10am–2.30pm and 5–11pm or later.

Shops Malls and department stores generally 10am–10pm.

Post

The larger tourist hotels and business towers have convenient post offices from where you can mail letters and small packages. China Post (中国邮政; Zhōngguó Yóuzhèng) offices and post boxes are green.

Useful branches of China Post:

Main China Post Office (中国邮政, Zhōngguó Yóuzhèng; Map p314; ✆021 6393 6666; 276 North Suzhou Rd; 苏州北路276号; ◷7am-10pm)

China Post Xīntiāndì (中国邮政, Zhōngguó Yóuzhèng; Map p302; Xingye Lu; 兴业路) Opposite the Site of the 1st National Congress of the CCP.

Shànghǎi Centre (中国邮政, Zhōngguó Yóuzhèng; Map p310; ✆021 6279 8044; 3rd fl East Office, Shànghǎi Centre, 1376 West Nanjing Rd; 南京西路1376号上海商城; Ⓜ Line 2, 7 to Jing'an Temple)

Letters and parcels take about a week to reach most overseas destinations; Express Mail Service (EMS) cuts this down to three or four days. Courier companies can take as little as two days. Ubiquitous same-day courier companies (快递, kuàidì) can express items within Shànghǎi from around ¥6 within the same district.

Public Holidays

Many of the following are nominal holidays and do not qualify for a day off work.

New Year's Day (Yuándàn) 1 January.

Spring Festival (Chūn Jié) 28 January 2017, 16 February 2018, 5 February 2019. Also known as Chinese New Year. Officially three days, but generally a week-long break.

Tomb Sweeping Day (Qīngmíng Jié) Held on 4 or 5 April in any given year.

International Labour Day (Láodòng Jié) 1 May. Three-day holiday.

Dragon Boat Festival (Duānwǔ Jié) 30 May 2017, 18 June 2018, 7 June 2019.

Mid-Autumn Festival (Zhōngqiū Jié) 4 October 2017, 24 September 2018, 13 September 2019.

National Day (Guóqìng Jié) 1 October. Officially three days, but often morphs into a week-long vacation.

Safe Travel

Shànghǎi feels very safe, and crimes against foreigners are rare. If you have something stolen, you need to report the crime at the district Public Security Bureau (PSB, 公安局, Gōng'ānjú) office and obtain a police report.

Scams

Preying on visitors to the Bund, East Nanjing Rd, People's Square and elsewhere, Shànghǎi's number one scam ruins the holidays of hundreds of foreigners. One or a pair of English-speaking girls approach single men and ask to be photographed using their mobile phone, then insist on taking the victim to a traditional Chinese teahouse, where he is left to pay eye-watering and heart-stopping bills (hundreds of dollars, usually payable by credit card).

Some of the massage services offered to visitors on East Nanjing Rd will similarly scam you out of large chunks of your holiday budget in the presentation of a huge bill. Just say no.

Watch out for taxi scams, especially at Pǔdōng International Airport and outside the Maglev terminal at Longyang Rd metro station. Aim for larger taxi firms and insist on using the meter to avoid taxi sharks.

Taxes

All four- and five-star hotels and some top-end restaurants add a service charge of 10% or 15%, which extends to the room and food; all other consumer taxes are included in the price tag.

VAT refunds can be claimed at the airport when leaving Shànghǎi, for single

TRAFFIC & STREET HAZARDS

➡ Crossing the road is probably the greatest danger: develop avian vision and a sixth sense to combat the shocking traffic. Don't end up in an ambulance: Chinese drivers never give way.

➡ The green man at traffic lights does not mean it's safe to cross. Instead, it means it is *slightly safer* to cross, but you can still be run down by traffic allowed to turn on red lights.

➡ Bicycles and scooters regularly flout all traffic rules, as do many cars. Bicycles, scooters, mopeds and motorbikes freely take to the pavements (sidewalks), as occasionally do cars.

➡ Older taxis only have seatbelts in the front passenger seat. Watch out for scooters whizzing down Shànghǎi roads – especially on unlit streets – without lights at night.

➡ Be careful when taking a taxi alone late at night, as foreigners have been sexually assaulted and robbed. Stick to the larger taxi firms, such as the turquoise **Dàzhòng** (大众; ☎021 96822), gold **Qiángshēng** (强生; ☎021 6258 0000), green **Bāshì** (巴士; ☎021 96840) or white **Jǐnjiāng** taxis, and avoid black-market cabs. A registered taxi should always run on a meter and have a licence displayed on the dashboard.

➡ Other street hazards include spent neon-light tubes poking from litter bins, open manholes with plunging drops, and welders showering pavements with burning sparks. Side streets off the main drag are sometimes devoid of street lights at night, and pavements can be crumbling and uneven.

purchases over ¥500 in a tax-free store.

Telephone

Using a mobile phone is naturally most convenient. If you have the right phone and are in a wi-fi zone, Skype (www.skype.com) and Viber (www.viber.com) can make calls either very cheap or free. You won't get far communicating with anyone in China unless you have the WeChat app (also known as Weixin in China).

Calling Codes

Long-distance phone calls can be placed from hotel-room phones, though this is expensive without an internet phonecard. You may need a dial-out number for a direct line. Local calls should be free.

Note the following country and city codes:

Běijīng	☎010
People's Republic of China	☎00 86
Shànghǎi	☎021

If calling Shànghǎi or Běijīng from abroad, drop the first zero.

The following numbers are useful:

Enquiry about international calls	☎106
Local directory enquiries	☎114
Weather	☎12121

Mobile Phones

You can certainly take your mobile phone to China, but ensure it is unlocked, so you can use another network's SIM card in your phone. Purchasing a SIM card in Shànghǎi is straightforward: pick one up from a branch of China Mobile (中国移动; Zhōngguó Yídòng); branches are widespread.

Mobile-phone shops (手机店; shǒujīdiàn) can sell you a SIM card, which will cost from ¥60 to ¥100 and will include ¥50 of credit. SIM cards are also available from newspaper kiosks (报刊亭; bàokāntíng). When credit runs out, you can top up

the number by buying a credit-charging card (充值卡; chōngzhí kǎ) for ¥50 or ¥100 worth of credits. The main networks are China Mobile, China Unicom and China Telecom, with branches throughout the city.

The Chinese avoid the number four (sì; which sounds like but has a different tone from the word for death – sǐ) and love the number eight (bā). Consequently, the cheapest numbers tend to contain numerous fours and the priciest have strings of eights.

Buying a mobile phone in Shànghǎi is also an option as they are generally inexpensive. Cafes, restaurants and bars in larger towns and cities usually have wi-fi.

Phonecards

The internet phonecard (IP card; IP卡) connects via the internet and is much cheaper than dialling direct. You can use any home phone, some hotel and some public phones (but not card phones), or a mobile phone to dial a special telephone number and follow the

SMARTPHONE & TABLET APPS

Handy Android and iPhone apps for Shànghǎi for your smartphone or tablet include the following:

Air Quality China Check the China Air Quality Index for major cities in China, including Shànghǎi. Free.

Baidu Maps Even if you can't read Chinese, this is a very handy map app.

City Weekend The app with an ever-updated database of Shànghǎi restaurant, bar and club listings. Free.

Pleco Fantastic and resourceful app for making sense of Chinese with OCR (Optical Character Recogniser) function: point your smartphone camera at a Chinese character and it will translate it for you. Also has flashcards, handwriting recogniser and audio pronunciation. Free.

Shanghai Toilet Guide When you need one, pronto. Free.

WeChat Chinese people largely use this app to send voice messages, texts and pictures at no cost. Free.

---

instructions (there is usually an English option).

Phonecards can be bought at newspaper kiosks, but are far less available than they used to be. Cards come in denominations of ¥50, ¥100, ¥200 and ¥500 – but they are always discounted, with a ¥100 card costing in the region of ¥35 to ¥40.

Check that you are buying the right card. Some are for use in Shànghǎi only, while others can be used around the country. Check that the country you wish to call can be called on the card.

Generally, a safe bet is the CNC 10-country card (国际十国卡, *guójì shíguókǎ*), which can be used for calls to the USA, Canada, Australia, New Zealand, Hong Kong and Macau, Taiwan, England, France, Germany and some East Asian countries.

Remember to check the expiry date.

If travelling around China, check the card can be used outside the city or province you buy it in.

Time

Time throughout China is set to Běijīng local time, which is eight hours ahead of GMT/UTC. There is no daylight-saving time.

Toilets

Shànghǎi has plenty of public toilets. Often charging a small fee, they run from the sordid to coin-operated portaloos and modern conveniences. The best bet is to head for a top-end hotel, where someone will hand you a towel, pour you some aftershave or exotic hand lotion and wish you a nice day.

➡ Fast-food restaurants can be lifesavers.

➡ Always carry an emergency stash of toilet paper, as many toilets are devoid of it.

➡ Growing numbers of metro stations have coin-operated toilets.

➡ Toilets in hotels are generally sitters, but expect to find squatters in many public toilets.

➡ Remember the Chinese characters for men (男) and women (女).

Tourist Information

For competent English-language help, call the **Shànghǎi Call Centre** (☏021 962 288), a free 24-hour English-language hotline that can respond to cultural, entertainment or transport enquiries (and

even provide directions for your cab driver).

Other branches of tourist information offices:

The Bund (旅游咨询服务中心,Lǚyóu Zīxún Fúwù Zhōngxīn; Map p296;☏021 6357 3718; 518 Jiujiang Rd; 九江路518号; ⏱9.30am-8pm; Ⓜ East Nanjing Rd) Beneath the Bund promenade, opposite the intersection with East Nanjing Rd.

French Concession (旅游咨询服务中心; Lǚyóu Zīxún Fúwù Zhōngxīn; Map p302;☏021 5386 1882; 138 S Chengdu Rd; 成都南路138号; ⏱9am-9pm; Ⓜ South Huangpi Rd)

Jìng'ān (旅游咨询服务中心, Lǚyóu Zīxún Fúwù Zhōngxīn; Map p310;☏021 6248 3259; Lane 1678, 18 West Nanjing Rd; 南京西路1678弄18号; ⏱9.30am-5.30pm Mon-Fri; Ⓜ Line 2, 7 to Jing'an Temple)

Old Town (旅游咨询服务中心, Lǚyóu Zīxún Fúwù Zhōngxīn; Map p300;☏021 6355 5032; 149 Jiujiaochang Rd; 旧校场路149号; ⏱9am-7pm; Ⓜ Line 10 to Yuyuan Garden) Southwest of Yùyuán Gardens.

Pǔdōng (旅游咨询服务中心; Lǚyóu Zīxún Fúwù Zhōngxīn; Map p312; Base of Oriental Pearl TV Tower; 东方明珠广播电视塔1楼; ⏱9am-5pm; Ⓜ Lujiazui)

The **Tourist Hotline** (☏021 962 020) offers a limited English-language service.

Travel Agencies

The following agencies can help with travel bookings.

CTrip (http://english.ctrip.com) Excellent online agency, good for hotel and flight bookings.

eLong (www.elong.net) Hotel and flight bookings.

STA Travel (Map p314; ☏021 2281 7723; www.statravel.com.cn; Room 1609, Shanghai Trade Tower, 188 Siping Rd; ◷9.30am-6pm Mon-Fri; Ⓜ️Hailun Rd)

Travellers with Disabilities

Shànghǎi's traffic and the city's overpasses and underpasses are the greatest challenges to travellers with disabilities. Many metro stations have lifts (elevators) to platforms but escalators may only go up from the ticket hall to the exit, and not down. Pavements on lesser roads may be cluttered with obstacles.

That said, an increasing number of modern buildings, museums, stadiums and most new hotels are wheelchair accessible. Try to take a lightweight chair for navigating around obstacles and for collapsing into the back of taxis. Top-end hotels have wheelchair-accessible rooms but budget hotels are less well prepared.

China's sign language has regional variations, as well as some elements of American Sign Language (ASL), so foreign signers may have some problems communicating in sign language.

Download Lonely Planet's free *Accessible Travel* guide from http://lptravel.to/AccessibleTravel.

Visas

For residents of most countries, a visa is required for visits to the People's Republic of China, although 144-hour visa-free transit in Shànghǎi (and Běijīng, plus five other cities with international airports) is available.

Visas are easily obtainable from Chinese embassies, consulates or Chinese Visa Application Service Centres abroad. Getting a visa in Hong Kong is also an option. Most tourists are issued with a single-entry visa for a 30-day stay, valid for three months from the date of issue. Your passport must be valid for at least six months after the expiry date of your visa (nine months for a double-entry visa) and you'll need at least two entire blank pages in your passport for the visa. For children under the age of 18, a parent must sign the application form on their behalf.

The visa application process has become more rigorous; applicants are required to provide the following:

➡ A copy of your flight confirmation showing onward/return travel.

➡ For double-entry visas, flight confirmation showing all dates of entry and exit.

➡ If staying at a hotel in China, confirmation from the hotel (this can be cancelled later if you stay elsewhere).

➡ If staying with friends or relatives, a copy of the information page of their passport, a copy of their China visa and a letter of invitation from them.

Prices for a standard single-entry 30-day visa (not including Chinese Visa Application Service Centre administration fees):

➡ £85 for UK citizens

➡ US$140 for US citizens

➡ US$30 (approximately) for all other nationals

In many countries, the visa service has been outsourced from the Chinese embassy to a Chinese Visa Application Service Centre (www.visaforchina.org), which levies an extra administration fee.

When asked about your itinerary on the application form, if you are planning on travelling from Shànghǎi, list standard tourist destinations. Many travellers planning trips to Tibet or western Xīnjiāng leave them off the form as the list is nonbinding, but their inclusion may raise eyebrows; those working in media or journalism often profess a different occupation to avoid having their visa refused or being given a shorter length of stay than requested.

A growing number of visa-arranging agents can do the legwork and deliver your visa-complete passport to you. In the US, many people use the **China Visa Service Center** (☏in the US 800 799 6560; www.mychinavisa.com), which offers prompt service. The procedure takes around 10 to 14 days. CIBT (www.uk.cibt.com) offers a global network and a fast and efficient turnaround.

A 30-day visa is activated on the date you enter China, and must be used within three months of the date of issue. Longer-stay visas are also activated upon entry into China. Officials in China are sometimes confused over the validity of the visa and look at the 'valid until' date. On most 30-day visas, however, this is actually the date by which you must have *entered* the country, not left.

Although a 30-day length of stay is standard for tourist visas, 60-day, 90-day, six-month and 12-month multiple-entry visas are also available. If you have trouble getting more than 30 days or a multiple-entry visa, try a local visa-arranging service or a travel agency in Hong Kong.

COMMON VISA CATEGORIES

The most common categories of ordinary visas are as follows:

TYPE	DESCRIPTION	CHINESE NAME
C	flight attendant	*chéngwù*
D	resident	*dìngjū*
F	business or student (less than 6 months)	*fǎngwèn*
G	transit	*guòjìng*
J1	journalist (more than 6 months)	*jìzhě1*
J2	journalist (less than 6 months)	*jìzhě2*
L	travel	*lǚxíng*
M	commercial & trade	*màoyì*
Q1	family visit (more than 6 months)	*qīnshǔ1*
Q2	family visit (less than 6 months)	*qīnshǔ2*
R	needed skills/talents	*réncái*
S1	visit to foreign relatives/private (more than 6 months)	*sīrén1*
S2	visit to foreign relatives/private (less than 6 months)	*sīrén2*
X1	student (more than 6 months)	*xuéxí1*
X2	student (less than 6 months)	*xuéxí2*
Z	working	*rènzhí*

Note that if you go to China, on to Hong Kong or Macau and then to Shànghǎi, you will need a double-entry visa to get 'back' into China from Hong Kong or Macau, or you will need to reapply for a fresh visa in Hong Kong.

Shànghǎi Visa-Free Transit

Citizens from a number of countries including the USA, Australia, Canada, New Zealand, Germany, Sweden and France can transit through Shànghǎi via Pǔdōng International Airport and Hóngqiáo International Airport for up to 144 hours without a visa as long as they have visas for their onward countries and proof of seats booked on flights out of China. Your departure point and destination should not be in the same country. Note also that you are not allowed to visit other cities in China during your transit.

Residence Permit

Residence permits can be issued to English teachers, businesspeople, students and other foreigners who are authorised to live in the PRC. They range from one to five years – depending on certain criteria the applicant must be able to meet – and allow unlimited exits and re-entries. In addition to this, as of July 2015, high-earning foreigners who have lived in Shànghǎi for four straight years and have paid their taxes will be eligible for permanent residence permits (previously only open to top-level business executives or professors). International students who graduate from a Chinese university are now eligible to apply for a residence permit valid for two years.

To get a residence permit you first need to arrange a work permit (normally obtained by your employer), health certificate and temporary visa ('Z' type visa for most foreign employees).

If your employer is organised, you can arrange all of this before you arrive in Shànghǎi.

You then go to the **Public Security Bureau** (PSB, 公安局, Gōng'ānjú; Map p272; ☏021 2895 1900; 1500 Minsheng Rd; 民生路1500号; ⏰9am-5pm Mon-Sat) with your passport, health certificate, work contract or permit, your employer's business registration licence or representative office permit, your employment certificate (from the Shanghai Labour Bureau), the temporary residence permit of the local PSB where you are registered, passport photos, a letter of application from your employer and around ¥400 for a one-year permit. In all, the process usually takes two to three weeks. Expect to make several visits and always carry multiple copies of every document. In most cases, your employer will take care of much of the process for you.

Travel in China

Most of China is accessible on a standard Chinese visa. A small number of restricted areas in China require an additional permit from the PSB. In particular, permits are required for travel to Tibet, a region that the authorities can suddenly bar foreigners from entering.

Visa Extensions

Extensions of 30 days are given for any tourist visa. You may be able to wrangle more with reasons such as illness or transport delays, but second extensions are usually only granted for a week, on the understanding that you are leaving. Visa extensions take three days and cost ¥160 for most nationalities and ¥940 for Americans (reciprocity for increased US visa fees). The fine for overstaying your visa is up to ¥500 per day.

To extend a business visa, you need a letter from a Chinese work unit willing to sponsor you. If you're studying in China, your school can sponsor you for a visa extension.

Visa extensions in Shànghǎi are available from the Public Security Bureau and can be completed online.

Work

It's not too difficult to find work in Shànghǎi, though technically you will need a work visa. Being able to speak Chinese is increasingly an important string to your bow. Examine the classified pages of the expat magazines and websites for job opportunities. Modelling and acting can be quite lucrative – especially if you find a decent agent – and teaching English is perennially popular. Bear in mind that most big companies tend to recruit from home, offering comfortable expat packages.

Language

Discounting its many ethnic minority languages, China has eight major dialect groups: Pǔtōnghuà (Mandarin), Yue (Cantonese), Wu (Shanghainese), Minbei (Fuzhou), Minnan (Hokkien-Taiwanese), Xiang, Gan and Hakka. Each of them also divides into subdialects.

Mandarin, which the Chinese themselves call Pǔtōnghuà (meaning 'common speech') is considered the official language of China. Most of the population speaks Mandarin, so you'll find that knowing a few basics in Mandarin will come in handy in Shànghǎi (as well as in many other parts of the country) which is why we've included it in this chapter.

For some more information about Shanghainese, see the boxed text, p277.

Writing

Chinese is often referred to as a language of pictographs. Many of the basic Chinese characters are highly stylised pictures of what they represent, but around 90% are compounds of a 'meaning' element and a 'sound' element.

A well-educated, contemporary Chinese speaker might use between 6000 and 8000 characters. To read a Chinese newspaper you need to know 2000 to 3000 characters, but 1200 to 1500 would be enough to get the gist.

Theoretically, all Chinese dialects share the same written system. In practice, Cantonese adds about 3000 specialised characters and many dialects don't have a written form at all.

WANT MORE?

For in-depth language information and handy phrases, check out Lonely Planet's *China Phrasebook* and *Mandarin Phrasebook*. You'll find them at **shop.lonelyplanet.com**.

Pinyin & Pronunciation

In 1958 the Chinese adopted Pinyin, a system of writing Mandarin using the Roman alphabet. The original idea was to eventually do away with Chinese characters, but over time this idea was abandoned.

Pinyin is often used on shop fronts, street signs and advertising billboards. However, in the countryside and the smaller towns you may not see a single Pinyin sign anywhere, so unless you speak Chinese you'll need a phrasebook with Chinese characters.

In this chapter we've provided Pinyin alongside the Mandarin script. Below is a brief guide to the pronunciation of Pinyin letters.

Vowels

a	as in 'father'
ai	as in 'aisle'
ao	as the 'ow' in 'cow'
e	as in 'her' (without 'r' sound)
ei	as in 'weigh'
i	as the 'ee' in 'meet' (or like a light 'r' as in 'Grrr!' after c, ch, r, s, sh, z or zh)
ian	as the word 'yen'
ie	as the English word 'yeah'
o	as in 'or' (without 'r' sound)
ou	as the 'oa' in 'boat'
u	as in 'flute'
ui	as the word 'way'
uo	like a 'w' followed by 'o'
yu/ü	like 'ee' with lips pursed

Consonants

c	as the 'ts' in 'bits'
ch	as in 'chop', with the tongue curled up and back
h	as in 'hay', articulated from further back in the throat
q	as the 'ch' in 'cheese'
sh	as in 'ship', with the tongue curled up and back
x	as the 'sh' in 'ship'
z	as the 'ds' in 'suds'
zh	as the 'j' in 'judge', with the tongue curled up and back

The only consonants that occur at the end of a syllable are n, ng and r. In Pinyin, apostrophes are occasionally used to separate syllables in order to prevent ambiguity, eg the word píng'ān can be written with an apostrophe after the 'g' to prevent it being pronounced as pín'gān.

Tones

Mandarin is a language with a large number of words with the same pronunciation but a different meaning. What distinguishes these homophones (as these words are called) is their 'tonal' quality – the raising and lowering of pitch on certain syllables. Mandarin has four tones – high, rising, falling-rising and falling, plus a fifth 'neutral' tone that you can all but ignore. Tones are important for distinguishing meaning of words – eg the word ma has four different meanings according to tone: mā (mother), má (hemp, numb), mǎ (horse), mà (scold, swear). Tones are indicated in Pinyin by the following accent marks on vowels: ā (high), á (rising), ǎ (falling-rising) and à (falling).

Basics

When asking a question it is polite to start with qǐng wèn – literally, 'May I ask?'.

Hello.	你好。	Nǐhǎo.
Goodbye.	再见。	Zàijiàn.
How are you?	你好吗?	Nǐhǎo ma?
Fine. And you?	好。你呢?	Hǎo. Nǐ ne?
Excuse me.	劳驾。	Láojià.
Sorry.	对不起。	Duìbùqǐ.
Yes./No.	是。/不是。	Shì./Bùshì.
Please ...	请……	Qǐng ...
Thank you.	谢谢你。	Xièxie nǐ.
You're welcome.	不客气。	Bù kèqi.

What's your name?
你叫什么名字?   Nǐ jiào shénme míngzi?
My name is ...
我叫……   Wǒ jiào ...
Do you speak English?
你会说英文吗?   Nǐ huìshuō Yīngwén ma?
I don't understand.
我不明白。   Wǒ bù míngbái.

Accommodation

Do you have a single/double room?
有没有(单人/   Yǒuméiyǒu (dānrén/
套)房?   tào) fáng?
How much is it per night/person?
每天/人多少钱?   Měi tiān/rén duōshǎo qián?

KEY PATTERNS

To get by in Mandarin, mix and match these simple patterns with words of your choice:

How much is (the deposit)?
(押金)多少?   (Yājīn) duōshǎo?
Do you have (a room)?
有没有(房)?   Yǒuméiyǒu (fáng)?
Is there (heating)?
有(暖气)吗?   Yóu (nuǎnqì) ma?
I'd like (that one).
我要(那个)。   Wǒ yào (nàge).
Please give me (the menu).
请给我(菜单)。   Qǐng gěiwǒ (càidān).
Can I (sit here)?
我能(坐这儿)吗?   Wǒ néng (zuò zhè'er) ma?
I need (a can opener).
我想要(一个   Wǒ xiǎngyào (yíge
开罐器)。   kāiguàn qì).
Do we need (a guide)?
需要(向导)吗?   Xūyào (xiàngdǎo) ma?
I have (a reservation).
我有(预订)。   Wǒ yǒu (yùdìng).
I'm (a doctor).
我(是医生)。   Wǒ (shì yīshēng).

air-con	空调	kōngtiáo
bathroom	浴室	yùshì
bed	床	chuáng
campsite	露营地	lùyíngdì
guesthouse	宾馆	bīnguǎn
hostel	招待所	zhāodàisuǒ
hotel	酒店	jiǔdiàn
window	窗	chuāng

Directions

Where's a (bank)?
(银行)在哪儿?   (Yínháng) zài nǎr?
What's the address?
地址在哪儿?   Dìzhǐ zài nǎr?
Could you write the address, please?
能不能请你   Néngbunéng qǐng nǐ
把地址写下来?   bǎ dìzhǐ xiě xiàlái?
Can you show me where it is on the map?
请帮我找它在   Qǐng bāngwǒ zhǎo tā zài
地图上的位置。   dìtú shàng de wèizhi.
Go straight ahead.
一直走。   Yìzhí zǒu.
Turn left/right.
左/右转。   Zuǒ/Yòu zhuǎn.

Question Words

What?	什么?	Shénme?
When?	什么时候	Shénme shíhòu?
Where?	哪儿?	Nǎr?
Which?	哪个?	Nǎge?
Who?	谁?	Shéi?
Why?	为什么?	Wèishénme?

at the traffic lights	在红绿灯	zài hónglǜdēng
behind	背面	bèimiàn
far	远	yuǎn
in front of ...	……的前面	... de qiánmian
near	近	jìn
next to	旁边	pángbiān
on the corner	拐角	guǎijiǎo
opposite	对面	duìmiàn

Eating & Drinking

What would you recommend?
有什么菜可以
推荐的? — Yǒu shénme cài kěyǐ tuījiàn de?

What's in that dish?
这道菜用什么
东西做的? — Zhèdào cài yòng shénme dōngxī zuòde?

That was delicious.
真好吃。 — Zhēn hǎochī.

The bill, please!
买单! — Mǎidān!

Cheers!
干杯! — Gānbēi!

I'd like to reserve a table for ...	我想预订一张……的桌子。	Wǒ xiǎng yùdìng yīzhāng ... de zhuōzi.
(eight) o'clock	(八) 点钟	(bā) diǎn zhōng
(two) people	(两个) 人	(liǎngge) rén

I don't eat ...	我不吃……	Wǒ bùchī ...
nuts	果仁	guǒrén
pork	猪肉	zhūròu
red meat	牛羊肉	niúyángròu

Key Words

bar	酒吧	jiǔbā
bottle	瓶子	píngzi
bowl	碗	wǎn
breakfast	早饭	zǎofàn
cafe	咖啡屋	kāfēiwū
(too) cold	(太)凉	(tài) liáng

dinner	晚饭	wǎnfàn
food	食品	shípǐn
fork	叉子	chāzi
glass	杯子	bēizi
hot (warm)	热	rè
knife	刀	dāo
local specialties	地方小吃	dìfang xiǎochī
lunch	午饭	wǔfàn
market	菜市	càishì
menu (in English)	(英文) 菜单	(Yīngwén) càidān
plate	碟子	diézi
restaurant	餐馆	cānguǎn
(too) spicy	(太)辣	(tài) là
spoon	勺	sháo
vegetarian food	素食食品	sùshí shípín

Meat & Fish

beef	牛肉	niúròu
chicken	鸡肉	jīròu
duck	鸭	yā
fish	鱼	yú
lamb	羊肉	yángròu
pork	猪肉	zhūròu
seafood	海鲜	hǎixiān

Fruit & Vegetables

apple	苹果	píngguǒ
banana	香蕉	xiāngjiāo
carrot	胡萝卜	húluóbo
celery	芹菜	qíncài
cucumber	黄瓜	huángguā
fruit	水果	shuǐguǒ
grape	葡萄	pútáo
green beans	扁豆	biǎndòu
mango	芒果	mángguǒ
mushroom	蘑菇	mógū
onion	洋葱	yáng cōng
orange	橙子	chéngzi

Signs

入口	Rùkǒu	**Entrance**
出口	Chūkǒu	**Exit**
问讯处	Wènxùnchù	**Information**
开	Kāi	**Open**
关	Guān	**Closed**
禁止	Jìnzhǐ	**Prohibited**
厕所	Cèsuǒ	**Toilets**
男	Nán	**Men**
女	Nǚ	**Women**

pear	梨	lí
pineapple	凤梨	fènglí
plum	梅子	méizi
potato	土豆	tǔdòu
radish	萝卜	luóbo
spring onion	小葱	xiǎo cōng
sweet potato	地瓜	dìguā
vegetable	蔬菜	shūcài
watermelon	西瓜	xīguā

Other

bread	面包	miànbāo
butter	黄油	huángyóu
egg	蛋	dàn
herbs/spices	香料	xiāngliào
pepper	胡椒粉	hújiāo fěn
salt	盐	yán
soy sauce	酱油	jiàngyóu
sugar	砂糖	shātáng
tofu	豆腐	dòufu
vinegar	醋	cù
vegetable oil	菜油	càiyóu

Drinks

beer	啤酒	píjiǔ
coffee	咖啡	kāfēi
(orange) juice	(橙)汁	(chéng) zhī
milk	牛奶	niúnǎi
mineral water	矿泉水	kuàngquán shuǐ
red wine	红葡萄酒	hóng pútáo jiǔ
rice wine	米酒	mǐjiǔ
soft drink	汽水	qìshuǐ
tea	茶	chá
(boiled) water	(开)水	(kāi) shuǐ

SHANGHAINESE

Shanghainese has around 14 million speakers. As one of the dialects of Wu Chinese, it is similar to the dialects of Níngbō, Sūzhōu and Kūnshān. It is not mutually intelligible with other Wu dialects nor with Standard Mandarin. Nonetheless, it is infused with elements of Mandarin. The younger generation of Shànghǎi residents uses Mandarin expressions and, with government campaigns to encourage the use of Mandarin only, some fear for the future of the dialect. However, while it is rarely heard in schools or in the media, it remains a source of pride and identity for many Shànghǎi natives. Travellers will be perfectly fine using Mandarin in Shànghǎi.

| white wine | 白葡萄酒 | bái pútáo jiǔ |
| yoghurt | 酸奶 | suānnǎi |

Emergencies

Help!	救命!	Jiùmìng!
I'm lost.	我迷路了。	Wǒ mílù le.
Go away!	走开!	Zǒukāi!

There's been an accident.
出事了。 Chūshì le.

Call a doctor!
请叫医生来! Qǐng jiào yīshēng lái!

Call the police!
请叫警察! Qǐng jiào jǐngchá!

I'm ill.
我生病了。 Wǒ shēngbìng le.

Where are the toilets?
厕所在哪儿? Cèsuǒ zài nǎr?

Shopping & Services

I'd like to buy ...
我想买…… Wǒ xiǎng mǎi ...

I'm just looking.
我先看看。 Wǒ xiān kànkan.

Can I look at it?
我能看看吗? Wǒ néng kànkan ma?

I don't like it.
我不喜欢。 Wǒ bù xǐhuān.

How much is it?
多少钱? Duōshǎo qián?

That's too expensive.
太贵了。 Tàiguì le.

Can you lower the price?
能便宜一点吗? Néng piányí yīdiǎn ma?

There's a mistake in the bill.
帐单上有问题。 Zhàngdān shàng yǒu wèntí.

ATM	自动取款机	zìdòng qǔkuǎn jī
internet cafe	网吧	wǎngbā
post office	邮局	yóujú
tourist office	旅行店	lǚxíng diàn

Time & Dates

What time is it?
现在几点钟? Xiànzài jǐdiǎn zhōng?

It's (10) o'clock.
(十)点钟。 (Shí) diǎn zhōng.

Half past (10).
(十)点三十分。 (Shí) diǎn sānshífēn.

Numbers

1	一	yī
2	二/两	èr/liǎng
3	三	sān
4	四	sì
5	五	wǔ
6	六	liù
7	七	qī
8	八	bā
9	九	jiǔ
10	十	shí
20	二十	èrshí
30	三十	sānshí
40	四十	sìshí
50	五十	wǔshí
60	六十	liùshí
70	七十	qīshí
80	八十	bāshí
90	九十	jiǔshí
100	一百	yībǎi
1000	一千	yīqiān

morning	早上	zǎoshang
afternoon	下午	xiàwǔ
evening	晚上	wǎnshàng
yesterday	昨天	zuótiān
today	今天	jīntiān
tomorrow	明天	míngtiān
Monday	星期一	xīngqī yī
Tuesday	星期二	xīngqī èr
Wednesday	星期三	xīngqī sān
Thursday	星期四	xīngqī sì
Friday	星期五	xīngqī wǔ
Saturday	星期六	xīngqī liù
Sunday	星期天	xīngqī tiān

Transport

boat	船	chuán
bus (city)	大巴	dàbā
bus (intercity)	长途车	chángtú chē
plane	飞机	fēijī
taxi	出租车	chūzū chē
train	火车	huǒchē
tram	电车	diànchē

I want to go to ...
我要去…… — Wǒ yào qù ...

Does it stop at ...?
在……能下车吗? — Zài ... néng xià chē ma?

At what time does it leave?
几点钟出发? — Jǐdiǎnzhōng chūfā?

At what time does it get to ...?
几点钟到……? — Jǐdiǎnzhōng dào ...?

I want to get off here.
我想这儿下车。 — Wǒ xiǎng zhè'er xiàchē.

When's the first/last (bus)?
首班/末班 (车) — Shǒubān/Mòbān (chē)
几点走? — jǐdiǎn zǒu?

A ... ticket to (Dàlián).	一张票到 (大连)。	Yī zhāng piào dào (Dàlián).
1st-class	头等	tóuděng
2nd-class	二等	èrděng
one-way	单程	dānchéng
return	双程	shuāngchéng
aisle seat	走廊的 座位	zǒuláng de zuòwèi
ticket office	售票处	shòupiàochù
timetable	时刻表	shíkè biǎo
window seat	窗户的 座位	chuānghù de zuòwèi
bicycle pump	打气筒	dǎqìtóng
child seat	婴儿座	yīng'ér zuò
helmet	头盔	tóukuī

I'd like a taxi to depart at (9am)
我要订一辆出租车, (早上9点钟)出发。 — Wǒ yào dìng yīliàng chūzū chē, (zǎoshàng jiǔ diǎn zhōng) chūfā.

I'd like a taxi now.
我要订一辆出租车, 现在。 — Wǒ yào dìng yīliàng chūzū chē, xiànzài.

I'd like a taxi tomorrow
我要订一辆出租车, 明天。 — Wǒ yào dìng yīliàng chūzū chē, míngtiān.

Where's the taxi rank?
在哪里打出租车? — Zài nǎli dǎ chūzū chē?

Is this taxi free?
这出租车有人吗? — Zhè chūzū chē yǒurén ma?

Please put the meter on.
请打表。 — Qǐng dǎbiǎo.

How much is it (to this address)?
(到这个地址) 多少钱? — (Dào zhège dìzhǐ) duōshǎo qián?

Please take me to (this address).
请带我到 (这个地址) — Qǐng dàiwǒ dào (zhège dìzhǐ).

GLOSSARY

arhat – Buddhist, especially a monk who has achieved enlightenment

běi – north

biéshù – villa

bīnguǎn – tourist hotel

bówùguǎn – museum

cāntīng – restaurant

CCP – Chinese Communist Party; founded in Shànghǎi in 1921

cheongsam – see *qípáo*

Chiang Kaishek – (1887–1975) leader of the Kuomintang, anticommunist and head of the nationalist government from 1928 to 1949

chop – carved name seal that acts as a signature

Confucius – (551–479 BC) legendary scholar who developed the philosophy of Confucianism, which defines codes of conduct and patterns of obedience in society

Cultural Revolution – a brutal and devastating purge of the arts, religion and the intelligentsia by Mao's *Red Guards* and later the *PLA* from 1966 to 1970, it officially ended in 1976.

dàdào – boulevard, avenue

dàfàndiàn – large hotel

dàjiē – avenue

dàjiǔdiàn – large hotel

dàshà – hotel, building

Deng Xiaoping – (1904–97) considered to be the most powerful political figure in China from the late 1970s until his death; Deng's reforms resulted in economic growth, but he also instituted harsh social policies and authorised the military force that resulted in the Tiān'ānmén Square incident in Běijīng in 1989

dōng – east

fàndiàn – hotel, restaurant

fēn – one-tenth of a *jiǎo*

fēng – peak

fēng shuǐ – geomancy, literally 'wind and water'; the art of using ancient principles to maximise the flow of *qì* (universal energy)

Gang of Four – members of a clique, headed by Mao's wife, Jiang Qing, who were blamed for the *Cultural Revolution*

gé – pavilion, temple

gōngyuán – park

gùjū – house, home, residence

gǔzhèn – ancient town

hé – river

hú – lake

huā – flower tea

jiāng – river

jiǎo – unit of currency, one-tenth of a *yuán*

jiē – street

jié – festival

jīn – unit of measurement (500g)

jìniànguǎn – memorial hall

jiǔdiàn – hotel

jū – residence, home

kuài – in spoken Chinese, colloquial term for the currency, *yuán*

Kuomintang – *Chiang Kaishek's* Nationalist Party; the dominant political force after the fall of the Qing dynasty

liǎng – unit of measurement (50g)

lǐlòng – alleyway

lòngtáng – narrow alleyway, or *lǐlòng*; lòngtáng is the preferred term used in Shànghǎi

lóu – tower

lǜchá – green tea

lù – road

luóhàn – see *arhat*

máo – in spoken Chinese, colloquial term for the *jiǎo*

Mao Zedong – (1893–1976) leader of the early communist forces, he founded the *PRC* and was party chairman until his death

mǎtou – dock

mén – gate

miào – temple

nán – south

PLA – People's Liberation Army

pǔ'ěr – post-fermented, dark tea from Yúnnán (pu-erh)

PRC – People's Republic of China

PSB – Public Security Bureau; the arm of the police force set up to deal with foreigners

qiáo – bridge

qípáo – the figure-hugging dress worn by Chinese women (also called a cheongsam)

Red Guards – a pro-Mao faction that persecuted rightists during the *Cultural Revolution*

renminbi – literally 'people's money', the formal name for the currency; shortened to RMB

RMB – see *Renminbi*

shān – mountain

shì – city

shìchǎng – market

shíkùmén – stone-gate house; a blend of Chinese courtyard housing and English terraced housing

sì – temple, monastery

Sun Yatsen – (1866–1925) first president of the Republic of China; loved by republicans and communists alike

tǎ – pagoda

taichi – slow-motion shadow-boxing

Taiping Rebellion – rebellion (1850–64) that attempted to overthrow the Qing dynasty

tíng – pavilion

wūlóng – oolong tea

xī – west

yuán – Chinese unit of currency, the basic unit of RMB; garden

zhōng – middle

Zhou Enlai – an early comrade of Mao's, Zhou exercised the most influence in the day-to-day governing of China following the *Cultural Revolution*

MENU DECODER

bīng 冰 ice

bīngqílín 冰淇淋 ice cream

cù 醋 vinegar

dòufu 豆腐 tofu

hànbǎobāo 汉堡包 hamburger

huángguā 黄瓜 cucumber

huángyóu 黄油 butter

hújiāofěn 胡椒粉 pepper

jiàngyóu 酱油 soy sauce

jīdàn 鸡蛋 egg

jīròu 鸡肉 chicken

làjiāo 辣椒 chilli

lāmiàn 拉面 pulled noodles

miànbāo 面包 bread

niúròu 牛肉 beef

pángxiè 螃蟹 crab

qiézi 茄子 aubergine

qíncài 芹菜 celery

qīngcài 青菜 green vegetables

sèlā 色拉 salad

shāokǎo 烧烤 barbecue

shǔtiáo 薯条 chips

sùcài 素菜 vegetables

tāng 汤 soup

táng 糖 sugar

tǔdòu 土豆 potato

wèijīng 味精 MSG

xīhóngshì 西红柿 tomato

yán 盐 salt

yángròu 羊肉 lamb

yángròuchuàn
羊肉串
lamb kebab

yāzi 鸭子 duck

yóuyú 鱿鱼 squid

zhōu 粥 rice porridge
(congee)

zhūròu 猪肉 pork

Rice Dishes 米饭

báifàn 白饭
steamed white rice

chǎofàn 炒饭 fried rice

jīdàn chǎofàn 鸡蛋炒饭
fried rice with egg

Soup 汤

húntun tāng 馄饨汤
won ton (dumpling) soup

jīdàn tāng 鸡蛋汤
egg drop soup

sānxiān tāng 三鲜汤
three kinds of seafood soup

suānlà tāng 酸辣汤
hot and sour soup

xīhóngshì jīdàntāng
西红柿鸡蛋汤
tomato and egg soup

Vegetable Dishes 素菜

báicài xiān shuānggū
白菜鲜双菇
bok choy and mushrooms

cuìpí dòufu 脆皮豆腐
crispy skin bean curd

dìsānxiān 地三鲜
cooked potato, aubergine
and green pepper

háoyóu xiāngū 蚝油鲜菇
mushrooms in oyster sauce

hēimù'ěr mèn dòufu
黑木耳焖豆腐
bean curd with mushrooms

jiǔcài jiǎozi 韭菜饺子
chive dumplings

shāo qiézi 烧茄子
cooked aubergine (eggplant)

tángcù ǒubǐng
糖醋藕饼
lotus root cakes in sweet-and-
sour sauce

Seafood 海鲜

chāngyú 鲳鱼 pomfret

chǎo huángshàn 炒黄鳝
fried eel

cōngsū jìyú 葱酥鲫鱼
braised carp with onion

dàzhá xiè 大闸蟹
hairy crabs

fúróng yúpiàn
芙蓉鱼片
fish slices in egg white

gānjiān xiǎo huángyú
干煎小黄鱼
dry-fried yellow croaker

guōbā xiārén 锅巴虾仁
shrimp in sizzling rice crust

héxiāng báilián 荷香白鲢
lotus-flavoured silver carp

hóngshāo shànyú
红烧鳝鱼
eel soaked in soy sauce

huángyú 黄鱼
yellow croaker

jiāng cōng chǎo xiè
姜葱炒蟹
stir-fried crab with ginger
and scallions

jiǔxiāng yúpiàn 酒香鱼片
fish slices in wine

mìzhī xūnyú 蜜汁熏鱼
honey-smoked carp

níngshì shànyú 宁式鳝鱼
stir-fried eel with onion

qiézhī yúkuài 茄汁鱼块
fish fillet in tomato sauce

qīngzhēng guìyú
清蒸鳜鱼
steamed Mandarin fish

sōngjiānglúyú 松江鲈鱼
Songjiang perch

sōngshǔ guìyú 松鼠鳜鱼
squirrel-shaped Mandarin fish

sōngzǐ guìyú 松子鳜鱼
Mandarin fish with pine nuts

suānlà yóuyú 酸辣鱿鱼
hot-and-sour squid

yóubào xiārén 油爆虾仁
fried shrimp

zhá hēi lǐyú 炸黑鲤鱼
fried black carp

zhá yúwán 炸鱼丸
fish balls

Home-Style Dishes 家常菜

biǎndòu ròusī 扁豆肉丝
shredded pork and green beans

fānqié chǎodàn 番茄炒蛋
egg and tomato

hóngshāo qiézi 红烧茄子
red-cooked aubergine

huíguō ròu 回锅肉
double-cooked fatty pork

jiācháng dòufu 家常豆腐
'home-style' tofu

jīngjiàng ròusī 精酱肉丝
pork cooked with soy sauce

níngméng jī 柠檬鸡
lemon chicken

niúròu miàn 牛肉面
beef noodles in soup

páigǔ 排骨 ribs

sùchǎo biǎndòu 素炒扁豆
garlic beans

sùchǎo sùcài 素炒素菜
fried vegetables

tiěbǎn niúròu 铁板牛肉
sizzling beef platter

yángcōng chǎo ròupiàn
洋葱炒肉片
pork and fried onions

yúxiāng qiézi 鱼香茄子
fish-flavoured aubergine

Shanghainese Dishes 上海菜

hǔpíjiānjiāo 虎皮尖椒
tiger skin chillies

jīngcōng ròusī jiá bǐng
京葱肉丝夹饼
soy pork with scallions in
pancakes

jīngdū guō páigǔ 京都锅排骨
Mandarin-style pork ribs

sōngrén yùmǐ 松仁玉米
sweet corn and pine nuts

sōngzǐ yā 松子鸭
duck with pine nuts

xiāngsū jī 香酥鸡
crispy chicken

xiánjī 咸鸡
cold salty chicken

xiǎolóngbāo 小笼包
little steamer buns

xièfěn shīzitóu 蟹粉狮子头
lion's head meatballs with crab

yóutiáo niú ròu 油条牛肉
fried dough sticks with beef

zuìjī 醉鸡 drunken chicken

Hángzhōu Dishes 杭州菜

dōngpō bèiròu 东坡焙肉
Dongpo pork

héyè fěnzhēng ròu
荷叶粉蒸肉
steamed pork wrapped
in lotus leaf

jiào huā jī 叫化鸡
beggar's chicken

lóngjǐng xiārén 龙井虾仁
Longjing stir-fried shrimp

shāguō yútóu dòufu
沙锅鱼头豆腐
earthenware-pot fish-head tofu

xīhú chúncài tāng
西湖纯菜汤
West Lake water shield soup

xīhú cùyú 西湖醋鱼
West Lake fish

Cantonese Dishes 粤菜

chǎomiàn 炒面 chow mein

chāshāo 叉烧 cha siu

diǎnxīn 点心 dim sum

guōtiē 锅贴 fried dumplings

háoyóu niúròu 蚝油牛肉
beef with oyster sauce

kǎo rǔzhū 烤乳猪
crispy suckling pig

mìzhī chāshāo
蜜汁叉烧
roast pork with sweet syrup

tángcù lǐjí/gǔlǎo ròu
糖醋里脊/古老肉
sweet-and-sour pork fillets

xiāngsū jī 香酥鸡
crispy chicken

Sichuanese Dishes 川菜

dàndànmiàn 担担面
Dandan noodles

gōngbào jīdīng 宫爆鸡丁
spicy chicken with peanuts

málà dòufu 麻辣豆腐
spicy tofu

mápó dòufu 麻婆豆腐
tofu and pork crumbs in a spicy
sauce

shuǐ zhǔ niúròu 水煮牛肉
fried and boiled beef, garlic
sprouts and celery

suāncàiyú 酸菜鱼
boiled fish with pickled
vegetables

yuānyāng huǒguō
鸳鸯火锅
Yuanyang hotpot

yúxiāng ròusī 鱼香肉丝
fish-flavoured meat

Běijīng & Northern Dishes 京菜和北方菜

běijīng kǎoyā 北京烤鸭
Peking duck

jiǎozi 饺子 dumplings

mántou 馒头 steamed buns

ròu bāozi 肉包子
steamed meat buns

shuàn yángròu huǒguō
涮羊肉火锅 lamb hotpot

sùcài bāozi 素菜包子
steamed vegetable buns

Drinks 饮料

báijiǔ 白酒 white spirits

dòunǎi 豆奶 soya milk

hóngchá 红茶
Western (black) tea

júhuā chá 菊花茶
chrysanthemum tea

lǜ chá 绿茶 green tea

mǐjiǔ 米酒 rice wine

nǎijīng 奶精 coffee creamer

yēzi zhī 椰子汁 coconut juice

zhēnzhū nǎichá 珍珠奶茶
bubble tea

Behind the Scenes

SEND US YOUR FEEDBACK

We love to hear from travellers – your comments keep us on our toes and help make our books better. Our well-travelled team reads every word on what you loved or loathed about this book. Although we cannot reply individually to your submissions, we always guarantee that your feedback goes straight to the appropriate authors, in time for the next edition. Each person who sends us information is thanked in the next edition – the most useful submissions are rewarded with a selection of digital PDF chapters.

Visit **lonelyplanet.com/contact** to submit your updates and suggestions or to ask for help. Our award-winning website also features inspirational travel stories, news and discussions.

Note: We may edit, reproduce and incorporate your comments in Lonely Planet products such as guidebooks, websites and digital products, so let us know if you don't want your comments reproduced or your name acknowledged. For a copy of our privacy policy visit lonelyplanet.com/privacy.

OUR READERS

Many thanks to the travellers who used the last edition and wrote to us with helpful hints, useful advice and interesting anecdotes: Daniëlle Wolbers, Darryl Campbell, Fred Dobruszkes, Johannes Voit, Marina Ma and Sue Helme.

WRITER THANKS

Kate Morgan

Thanks to Megan Eaves for commissioning me for this great project. Big thanks to Pat Rogers and Chris Rogers for some excellent Shànghǎi suggestions, and thanks very much to my parents, Heather and Gary, for all their support. The most important thank you goes to my favourite person and travel partner, Trent, for always being there and for all the laughs along the way.

Helen Elfer

A huge 谢谢 to everyone I met on this trip who patiently answered questions and offered advice. Also to friends past and present who made my time in China so memorable. Particular gratitude to bona fide China Hands Casey and Mike Hall for all sorts of logistical, technical and moral support in Shànghǎi, plus heaps of fun. And, finally, thanks to Orlando for coming along for the ride, to China and in general.

Trent Holden

Firstly a huge thanks to Megan Eaves for giving me the opportunity to work on one of my all-time fav cities. A truly fantastic experience. Also a big thumbs-up to the in-house production team for their hard work putting this together. Likewise a big shout-out to my co-authors Kate Morgan and Helen Elfer, and locals and travellers who helped with input. Finally, as always, lots of love to my family and friends back home.

ACKNOWLEDGEMENTS

Cover photograph: The Bund at twilight, Shànghǎi, 123ArtistImages/Getty ©

Illustration pp58–9 by Michael Weldon.

THIS BOOK

This 8th edition of Lonely Planet's *Shanghai* guidebook was researched and written by Kate Morgan, Helen Elfer and Trent Holden. The 7th edition was written by Damian Harper and Dai Min, and the 6th edition by Damian Harper and Christopher Pitts. This guidebook was produced by the following:

Destination Editor Megan Eaves
Product Editors Susan Paterson, Sandie Kestell
Senior Cartographer Julie Sheridan
Book Designers Virginia Moreno, Mazzy Prinsep
Assisting Editors Imogen Bannister, Janice Bird, Nigel Chin, Carly Hall, Kellie Langdon, Lauren O'Connell
Cartographer Valentina Kremenchutskaya

Cover Researcher Naomi Parker
Thanks to Cheree Broughton, Jennifer Carey, Neill Coen, Daniel Corbett, Jane Grisman, Victoria Harrison, Corey Hutchinson, Liz Heynes, Kate James, Andi Jones, Lauren Keith, Claire Naylor, Karyn Noble, Tom O'Malley, Kirsten Rawlings, Alison Ridgway, Wibowo Rusli, Ellie Simpson, Lyahna Spencer, Dora Whitaker

See also separate subindexes for:

✖ **EATING P288**

🍷 **DRINKING & NIGHTLIFE P289**

☆ **ENTERTAINMENT P290**

🛍 **SHOPPING P290**

🏃 **SPORTS & ACTIVITIES P290**

🛏 **SLEEPING P291**

Index

NOTES

Shànghǎi Maps

Sights

- Beach
- Bird Sanctuary
- Buddhist
- Castle/Palace
- Christian
- Confucian
- Hindu
- Islamic
- Jain
- Jewish
- Monument
- Museum/Gallery/Historic Building
- Ruin
- Shinto
- Sikh
- Taoist
- Winery/Vineyard
- Zoo/Wildlife Sanctuary
- Other Sight

Activities, Courses & Tours

- Bodysurfing
- Diving
- Canoeing/Kayaking
- Course/Tour
- Sento Hot Baths/Onsen
- Skiing
- Snorkelling
- Surfing
- Swimming/Pool
- Walking
- Windsurfing
- Other Activity

Sleeping

- Sleeping
- Camping

Eating

- Eating

Drinking & Nightlife

- Drinking & Nightlife
- Cafe

Entertainment

- Entertainment

Shopping

- Shopping

Information

- Bank
- Embassy/Consulate
- Hospital/Medical
- Internet
- Police
- Post Office
- Telephone
- Toilet
- Tourist Information
- Other Information

Geographic

- Beach
- Gate
- Hut/Shelter
- Lighthouse
- Lookout
- Mountain/Volcano
- Oasis
- Park
- Pass
- Picnic Area
- Waterfall

Population

- Capital (National)
- Capital (State/Province)
- City/Large Town
- Town/Village

Transport

- Airport
- Border crossing
- Bus
- Cable car/Funicular
- Cycling
- Ferry
- Metro/MRT/MTR station
- Monorail
- Parking
- Petrol station
- Skytrain/Subway station
- Taxi
- Train station/Railway
- Tram
- Underground station
- Other Transport

Note: Not all symbols displayed above appear on the maps in this book

Routes

- Tollway
- Freeway
- Primary
- Secondary
- Tertiary
- Lane
- Unsealed road
- Road under construction
- Plaza/Mall
- Steps
- Tunnel
- Pedestrian overpass
- Walking Tour
- Walking Tour detour
- Path/Walking Trail

Boundaries

- International
- State/Province
- Disputed
- Regional/Suburb
- Marine Park
- Cliff
- Wall

Hydrography

- River, Creek
- Intermittent River
- Canal
- Water
- Dry/Salt/Intermittent Lake
- Reef

Areas

- Airport/Runway
- Beach/Desert
- Cemetery (Christian)
- Cemetery (Other)
- Glacier
- Mudflat
- Park/Forest
- Sight (Building)
- Sportsground
- Swamp/Mangrove

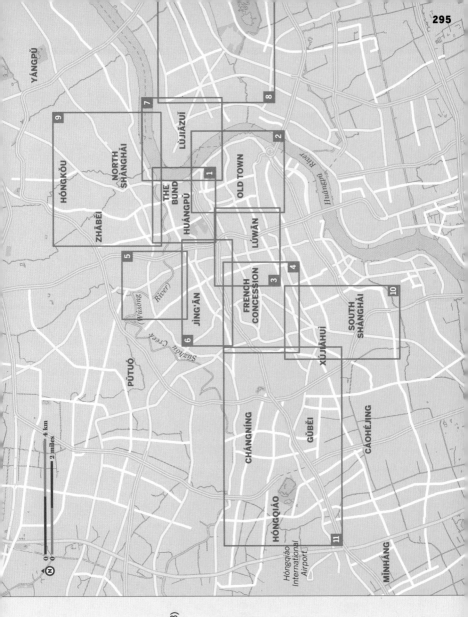

MAP INDEX

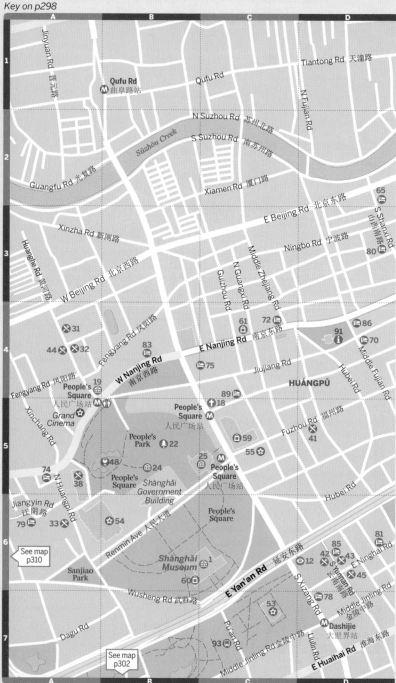

See map p310

See map p302

THE BUND & PEOPLE'S SQUARE

See map p314

Tiantong Rd
天潼路站

N Henan Rd

N Suzhou Rd 苏州北路
S Suzhou Rd 南苏州路

Huangpu Rd

Wàibáidù Bridge
(Garden Bridge)

Middle Jiangxi Rd
Middle Sichuan Rd
Jiangxi Rd
Yuanmingyuan Rd
圆明园路

Huángpǔ
Park

Bund Sightseeing Tunnel

E Beijing Rd 北京东路

Middle Henan Rd

THE
BUND

Dianchi Rd

Huángpǔ
River
黄浦江

See map
p312

E Nanjing Rd 南京东路

E Zhongshan No 1 Rd 中山东一路

The Bund

Tianjin Rd

East Nanjing Rd
南京东路站

East Yan'an Rd Tunnel

Hankou Rd

Middle Shandong Rd
Middle Henan Rd

Shanxi Rd

Fuzhou Rd 福州路

Sichuan Rd 四川中路

Sijing Rd

Guangdong Rd 广东路

E Yan'an Rd 延安东路

E Zhongshan No 2 Rd

S Fujian Rd 福建南路
福建中路

E Jinling Rd 金陵东路
S Sichuan Rd
Yong'an Rd
Xinyongan Rd 新永安路

Renmin Rd

Yongshou Rd

Zhonghua Rd

Yuyuan
Garden
豫园站

Fuyou Rd

OLD TOWN

New Yuyuan Rd
Jiujiaochang Rd

Yùyuán
Gardens &
Bazaar

Anren St
Wutong Rd
Danfeng Rd

See map
p300

Dajing Rd
Zihua Rd
Houjia Rd
Middle Fangbang Rd

0 500 m
0 0.25 miles

THE BUND & PEOPLE'S SQUARE *Map on p296*

OLD TOWN

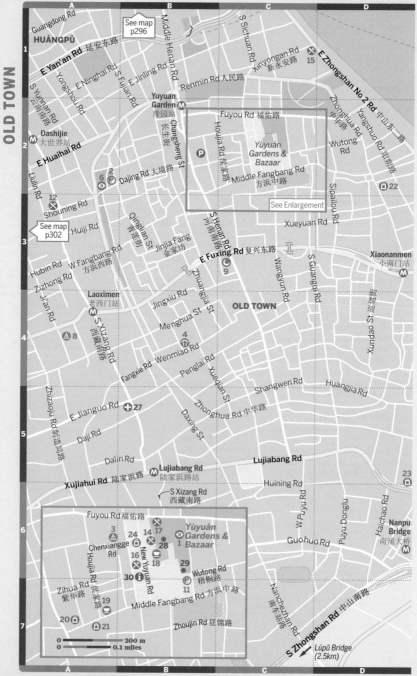

Guangdong Rd

HUÁNGPǔ

E Yan'an Rd 延安东路

See map
p296

S Sichuan Rd

Xinyongan Rd
新永安路

E Zhongshan No 2 Rd 中山东二路

15

S Yunnan Rd 云南南路

Yongshou Rd

E Ninghai Rd

S Fujian Rd

E Jinling Rd

Middle Henan Rd

Renmin Rd 人民路

Zhonghua Rd

Yangshuo Rd 羊朔路

Dashijie
大世界站

E Huaihai Rd

Liulin Rd

Dajing Rd 大境路

Changsheng St 长生街

Yuyuan Garden
豫园站

Fuyou Rd 福佑路

Houjia Rd 侯家路

Yùyuán Gardens & Bazaar

Wutong Rd

Sipailou Rd

22

6   2

Middle Fangbang Rd
方浜中路

See Enlargement

Shouning Rd

See map
p302

Huiji Rd

Qinglian St 青莲街

Jinjia Fang 金家坊

S Henan Rd 河南南路

Xueyuan Rd

Xiaonanmen
小南门站

12

Hubin Rd

W Fangbang Rd 方浜西路

Zizhong Rd

Ji'an Rd

E Fuxing Rd 复兴东路

9

Zhuangjia St

Wangyun Rd

S Guangqi Rd

Laoximen
老西门站

S Xizang Rd 西藏南路

Jingxiu Rd

Menghua St

OLD TOWN

8

4

Wenmiao Rd

Penglai Rd

Xueqian St

Shangwen Rd

Huangjia Rd

Fangxie Rd

E Jianguo Rd

27

Daji Rd

Zhonghua Rd 中华路

Daxing St

Zhizaoju Rd 制造局路

Dalin Rd

Xujiahui Rd 陆家浜路

Lujiabang Rd
陆家浜路站

Lujiabang Rd

Huining Rd

23

S Xizang Rd
西藏南路

W Puyu Rd

Puyu Donglu

Nanpu Bridge
南浦大桥

Guohuo Rd

Nanchezhan Rd 南车站路

Haichao Rd

S Zhongshan Rd 中山南路

*Lúpǔ Bridge
(2.5km)*

Fuyou Rd 福佑路

3

24 14 17

*Yùyuán
Gardens &
Bazaar*

**Chenxiangge
Rd**

16

28

1

18

New Yuyuan Rd

30

29

Wutong Rd
梧桐路

11

Zihua Rd
紫华路

19

Houjia Rd 侯家路

Middle Fangbang Rd 方浜中路

20   21

Zhoujin Rd 昼锦路

0   200 m
0   0.1 miles

0   500 m
N
0   0.25 miles

See map
p312

LÙJIĀZUĬ

Huángpǔ River

Fucheng Rd 富城路
Dongchang Rd 东昌路

25

Fuxing Road
Ferry

E Fuxing Rd
夏兴东路

Baidu Rd 白渡路

S Zhongshan Rd

26
10

Maojiayuan Rd
毛家园路

13 5

Dongjiadu Rd

7

Nancang St

S Zhongshan Rd 中山南路

Nanpu
Bridge

Power Station
of Art (800m)

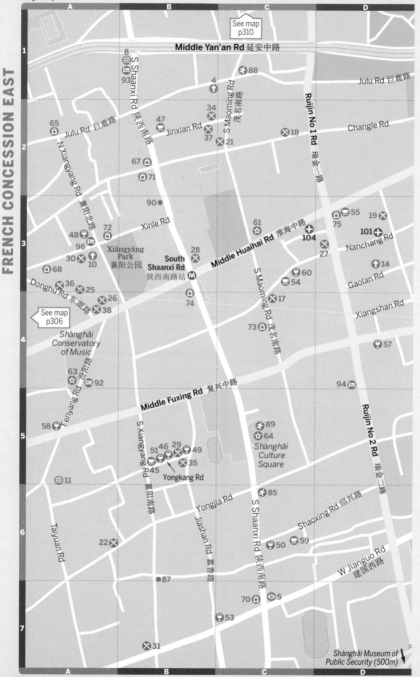

See map
p310

See map
p306

Middle Yan'an Rd 延安中路

Julu Rd 巨鹿路

S Shaanxi Rd 陕西南路

Julu Rd 巨鹿路

N Xiangyang Rd 襄阳北路

Jinxian Rd

S Maoming Rd 茂名南路

Changle Rd

Ruijin No 1 Rd 瑞金一路

Xinle Rd

Middle Huaihai Rd 淮海中路

Nanchang Rd

Xiāngyáng
Park
襄阳公园

**South
Shaanxi Rd**
陕西南路站

Gaolan Rd

Xiangshan Rd

Donghu Rd 东湖路

Shànghǎi
Conservatory
of Music

S Maoming Rd 茂名南路

Fenyang Rd 汾阳路

Middle Fuxing Rd 复兴中路

Ruijin No 2 Rd 瑞金二路

S Xiangyang Rd 襄阳南路

Yongkang Rd

Shànghǎi
Culture
Square

Taiyuan Rd

Yongjia Rd

Jiashan Rd 嘉善路

S Shaanxi Rd 陕西南路

Shaoxing Rd 绍兴路

W Jianguo Rd 建国西路

*Shànghǎi Museum of
Public Security (500m)*

N
0 — 500 m
0 — 0.25 miles

See map p296

Guǎngchǎng Park
广场公园

Middle Jinling Rd
金陵东路

S Huangpi Rd

Middle Huaihai Rd 淮海中路

Times Square

South Huangpi Rd
黄陂南路站

Songshan Rd
嵩山路

40

Huáihǎi Park
淮海公园

102

Middle Huaihai Rd 淮海中路

103

41

Xing'an

95
32
91
86
Taicang Rd
太仓路
78

Chongde Rd 崇德路

Dongtai Rd
东台路

Jinan Rd

Hubin Rd

Zizhong Rd
自忠路

Ji'an Rd
吉安街

Danshui Rd

Yandang Rd 雁荡路

Xīntiāndì

2
42
39

69
82
13
98
100

12

Tàipíngqiáo Park
太平桥公园

Xingye Rd 兴业路

83 76 56

6
Fùxīng Park
复兴公园

Zizhong Rd 自忠路

Madang Rd 马当路

23

81

S Huangpi Rd

E Fuxing Rd 复兴东路

See map p300

15

Xintiandi
新天地站

44

Middle Fuxing Rd 复兴中路

Hefei Rd 合肥路

20

Shunchang Rd

Zhizaoju Rd 制造局路

16

Sinan Rd 思南路

S Chongqing Rd 重庆南路

LÚWĀN

E Jianguo Rd

Yongnian Rd
永年路

99

Middle Jianguo Rd 建国中路

62

Madang Rd
马当路站

Xujiahui Rd 徐家汇路

52
43
66
33
3
24
84
9
79
77 80
7

97

Jumen Rd

Tiánzǐfáng

Taikang Rd
泰康路

Dapuqiao
打浦桥站

Xujiahui Rd

W Mengzi Rd

Liyuan Rd

Xīngguāng Photography Equipment (250m)

FRENCH CONCESSION EAST *Map on p302*

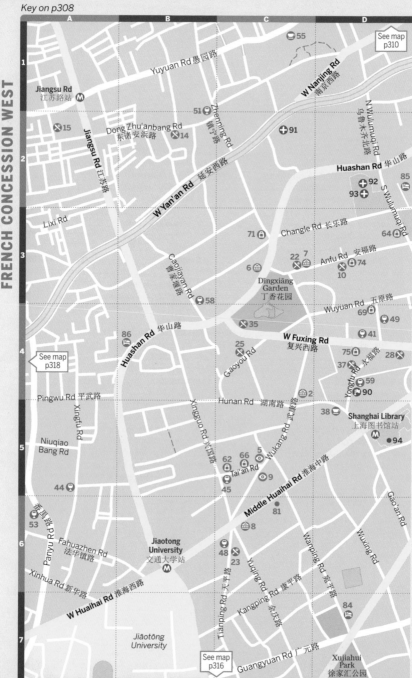

FRENCH CONCESSION WEST

See map p310

Yuyuan Rd 愚园路

55

W Nanjing Rd 南京西路

Jiangsu Rd 江苏路站

15

Dong Zhu'anbang Rd 东诸安浜路

14

51

Zhenning Rd 镇宁路

91

N Wulumuqi Rd 乌鲁木齐北路

Huashan Rd 华山路

92

93

85

S Wulumuqi Rd

W Yan'an Rd 延安西路

Lixi Rd

Jiangsu Rd 江苏路

Changle Rd 长乐路

71

64

Caojiayan Rd 曹家堰路

6

22 7

Anfu Rd 安福路

10

74

58

Dīngxiāng Garden 丁香花园

Wuyuan Rd 五原路

69

49

35

W Fuxing Rd 复兴西路

41

Huashan Rd 华山路

86

See map p318

25

Gaoyou Rd

75

37

Yongfu Rd 永福路

28

59

90

Pingwu Rd 平武路

Hunan Rd 湖南路

Xingfu Rd

Xinguo Rd 兴国路

Wukang Rd 武康路

2

38

Shanghai Library 上海图书馆站

94

Niuqiao Bang Rd

62 66 5

44

Tai'an Rd

9

45

Middle Huaihai Rd 淮海中路

81

Panyu Rd

53

Fahuazhen Rd 法华镇路

8

Gao'an Rd

Jiaotong University 交通大学站

48

23

Wanping Rd 宛平路

Wuxing Rd

84

Xinhua Rd 新华路

W Huaihai Rd 淮海西路

Tianping Rd 天平路

Yuqing Rd 余庆路

Kangping Rd 康平路

Guangyuan Rd 广元路

Xujiahui Park 徐家汇公园

Jiāotōng University

See map p316

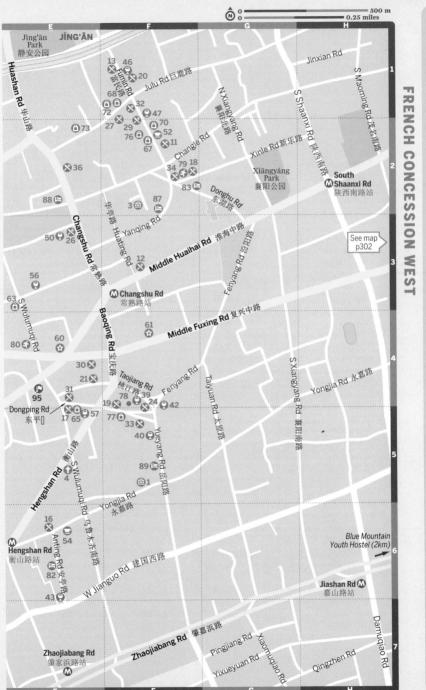

Jìng'ān Park
静安公园

JÌNG'ĀN

Huashan Rd 华山路

13 46
68 新民路
72
27 29
76
67

32
47
70
52
11

Julu Rd 巨鹿路

Changle Rd

N Xiangyang Rd 襄阳北路

36

88

50 26

56

63

S Wulumuqi Rd

80

60

30

21

31

95

Dongping Rd
东平路

17 65 57

16

54

Hengshan Rd
衡山路站

82

43

Zhaojiabang Rd
肇家浜路站

Changshu Rd 常熟路

Baoqing Rd 宝庆路

Hengshan Rd 衡山路

S Wulumuqi Rd 乌鲁木齐南路

Anting Rd 安亭路

华亭路 Huating Rd

Yanqing Rd

3

87

12

Middle Huaihai Rd 淮海中路

Changshu Rd
常熟路站

61

Middle Fuxing Rd 复兴中路

Taojiang Rd
桃江路

78
19
77

39
24 42
33
40

89

1

4

Yongjia Rd
永嘉路

W Jianguo Rd 建国西路

Zhaojiabang Rd

Zhaojiabang Rd
肇家浜路

Julu Rd 巨鹿路

34 79 18

83

Donghu Rd
东湖路

S Shaanxi Rd 陕西南路

Xinle Rd 新乐路

Xiāngyáng
Park
襄阳公园

South
Shaanxi Rd
陕西南路站

Fenyang Rd 汾阳路

Fenyang Rd

Taiyuan Rd 太原路

Yueyang Rd 岳阳路

Pingjiang Rd

Yixueyuan Rd

S Xiangyang Rd 襄阳南路

Jinxian Rd

S Maoming Rd 茂名南路

See map
p302

Yongjia Rd 永嘉路

Blue Mountain
Youth Hostel (2km)

Jiashan Rd
嘉山路站

Xiaomuqiao Rd

Qingzhen Rd

Damuqiao Rd

1
2
3
4
5
6
7

FRENCH CONCESSION WEST *Map on p306*

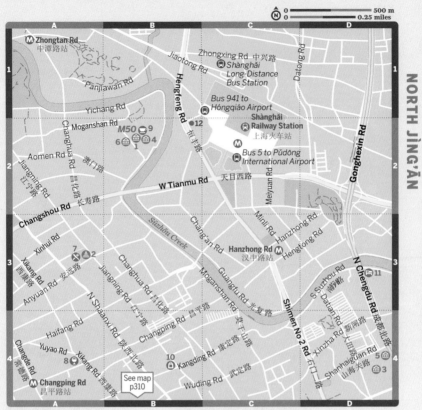

SOUTH JÌNG'ĀN

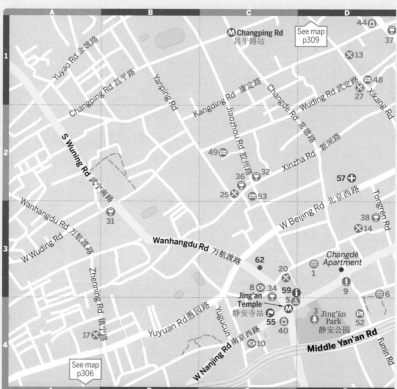

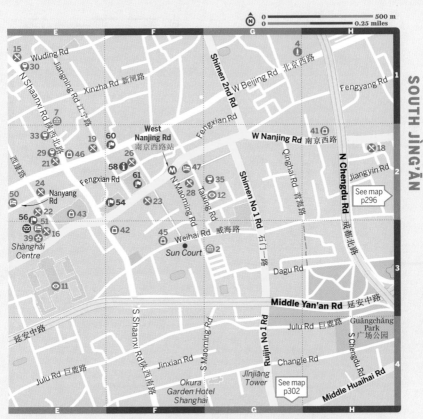

PŬDŌNG

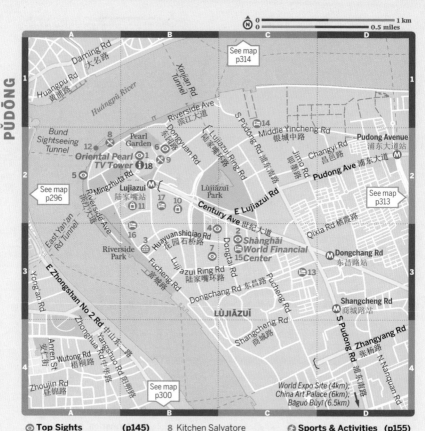

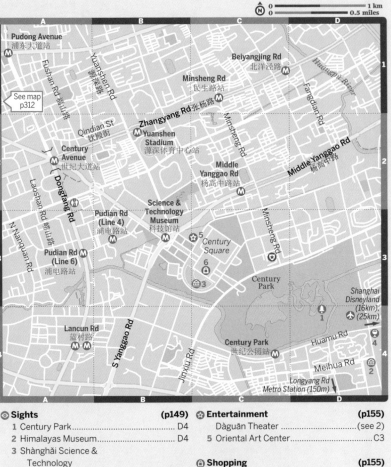

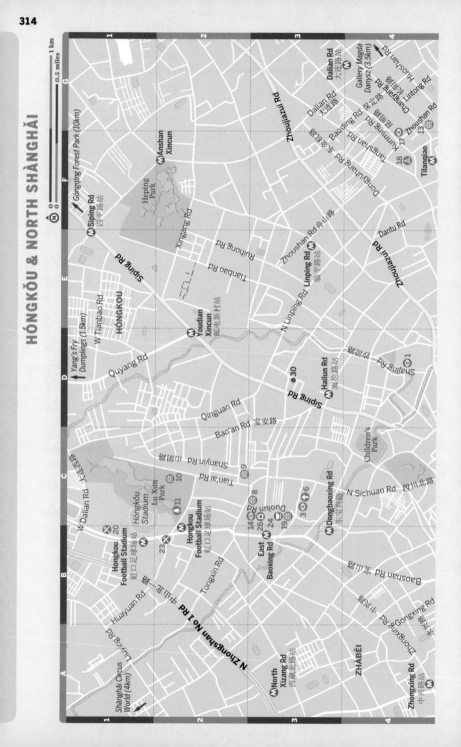

0 0
0 0.5 miles
0 1 km

G
F
E
D
C
B
A

1
2
3
4

Gallery Magda
Danysz (3.5km)

Dalian Rd 大连路站

Huoshan Rd
Lintong Rd
Changyang Rd 长阳路
Zhoushan Rd

17
13
Tilanqiao

18

Baoding Rd 保定路
Dalian Rd 大连路
Kunming Rd
Tangshan Rd 唐山路站

Dongyuhang Rd 东余杭路

Zhoujiazui Rd 周家嘴路

Zhoujiazui Rd

Dantu Rd

Zhoushan Rd 舟山路

N Linping Rd Linping Rd 临平路站

Anshan
Xincun

Heping
Park

Xingang Rd

Tianbao Rd

Ruihong Rd

Siping Rd 四平路站

Siping Rd

W Tianbao Rd

HÓNGKŎU

Quyang Rd

Youdian
Xincun 凯虹新村站

Hailun Rd 海伦路站

Shajing Rd 沙泾路

1

30

Siping Rd

Qinguan Rd

Bao'an Rd 宝安路

Shanyin Rd 山阴路

Tian'ai Rd

Children's
Park

Lu Xün
Park

Hóngkŏu
Stadium

11

10

9

8

N Sichuan Rd 四川北路

6

Dongbaoxing Rd

3

19

24

26

14

Duolun Rd

Hongkou
Football Stadium
虹口足球场站

Hongkou
Football Stadium
虹口足球场

20

23

East
Baoxing Rd

Tongxin Rd

Baoshan Rd 武进路

N Zhongshan No 1 Rd 中山北一路

Huáyuán Rd

Lùxùng Rd

Shànghǎi Circus
World (4km)

North
Xizang Rd
西藏北路站

ZHÁBĚI

Zhongxing Rd
中兴路站

Zhongxing Rd

Gongxing Rd

Yang's Fry
Dumplings (1.5km)

Gōngqìng Forest Park (10km)

N

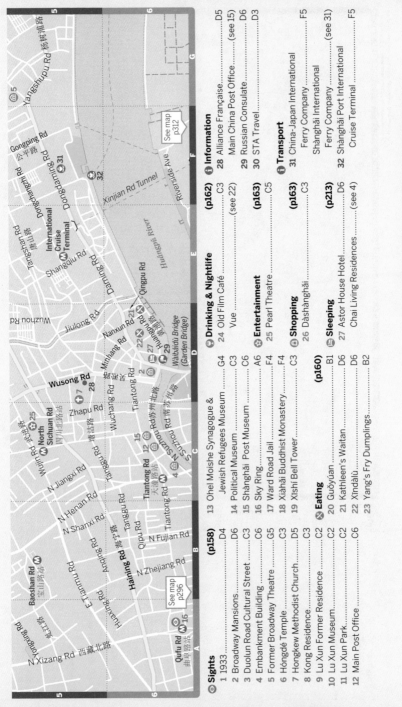

◎ **Sights** (p158)
1 1933...D4
2 Broadway Mansions.....................D6
3 Duolun Road Cultural Street C3
4 Embankment Building C6
5 Former Broadway Theatre...........G5
6 Hóngdé Temple C3
7 Hongkew Methodist Church.........D5
8 Kong Residence C3
9 Lu Xun Former Residence............C2
10 Lu Xun Museum..............................C2
11 Lu Xun Park.....................................C2
12 Main Post Office............................C6

13 Ohel Moishe Synagogue &
    Jewish Refugees Museum G4
14 Political Museum..............................C3
15 Shànghǎi Post Museum.................C6
16 Sky Ring...A6
17 Ward Road Jail.................................F4
18 Xiàhǎi Buddhist Monastery..........F4
19 Xīshì Bell Tower..............................C3

✘ **Eating** (p160)
20 Guóyúan...B1
21 Kathleen's Waitan..........................D6
22 Xīndàlù...D6
23 Yang's Fry Dumplings.....................B2

◉ **Drinking & Nightlife** (p162)
24 Old Film Café..................................C3
   Vue..(see 22)

✪ **Entertainment** (p163)
25 Pearl Theatre...................................C5

◎ **Shopping** (p163)
26 Dàshànghǎi......................................C3

⌂ **Sleeping** (p213)
27 Astor House Hotel...........................D6
   Chai Living Residences ....(see 4)

ℹ **Information**
28 Alliance Française...........................D5
   Main China Post Office.........(see 15)
29 Russian Consulate..........................D6
30 STA Travel.......................................D3

☀ **Transport**
31 China-Japan International
    Ferry Company...............................F5
   Shànghǎi International
   Ferry Company.......................(see 31)
32 Shànghǎi Port International
    Cruise Terminal.............................F5

XÚJIĀHUÌ & SOUTH SHÀNGHĂI

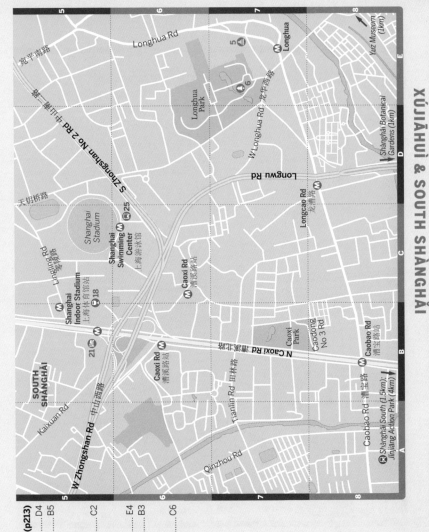

Sleeping (p213)

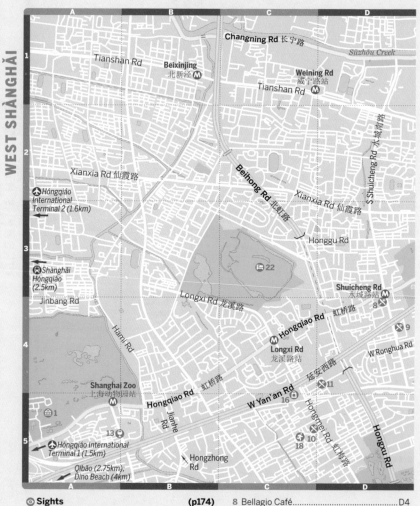

Our Story

A beat-up old car, a few dollars in the pocket and a sense of adventure. In 1972 that's all Tony and Maureen Wheeler needed for the trip of a lifetime – across Europe and Asia overland to Australia. It took several months, and at the end – broke but inspired – they sat at their kitchen table writing and stapling together their first travel guide, *Across Asia on the Cheap*. Within a week they'd sold 1500 copies. Lonely Planet was born.

Today, Lonely Planet has offices in Franklin, London, Melbourne, Oakland, Dublin, Beijing and Delhi, with more than 600 staff and writers. We share Tony's belief that 'a great guidebook should do three things: inform, educate and amuse'.

Our Writers

Kate Morgan

Plan Your Trip, French Concession, Pǔdōng, West Shànghǎi, Hóngkǒu & the North, Shěshān, Understand, Survival Guide Having lived and travelled extensively in North Asia, Kate was keen for the chance to again explore Shànghǎi. Days were spent shooting to the top of Pǔdōng skyscrapers, hunting out the best boutiques in the French Concession, tracing Jewish history in Hóngkǒu, taste-testing oolong tea and dining on dumplings. Kate has worked for Lonely Planet for over a decade now on destinations including Japan, India, Melbourne and Zimbabwe.

Read more about kate at:
https://auth.lonelyplanet.com/profiles/Kmorgantravels

Helen Elfer

Old Town, Xújiāhuì & South Shànghǎi, Hángzhōu Helen Elfer made Shànghǎi her home between 2007 and 2010, so she was delighted to be able to return and contribute to the latest *Shanghai* guide. After a two-year stint in Abu Dhabi, she moved back to London, working as a travel writer for various newspapers and magazines. She's currently Lonely Planet's destination editor for the Middle East and North Africa.

Read more about Helen at:
https://auth.lonelyplanet.com/profiles/planethelen

Trent Holden

The Bund & People's Square, Zhūjiājiǎo Trent has worked for Lonely Planet since 2005. He's covered 30-plus guidebooks across Asia, Africa and Australia. With a penchant for megacities, Trent's in his element when assigned to cover a nation's capital – the more chaotic the better – to unearth cool bars, art, street food and underground subculture. On the flipside he also writes about idyllic tropical islands across Asia, in between going on safari to national parks in Africa and the subcontinent. When not travelling, Trent works as a freelance editor, reviewer and spends all his money catching live gigs. Catch him on Twitter: @hombreholden

Read more about Trent at:
https://auth.lonelyplanet.com/profiles/hombreholden

Published by Lonely Planet Global Limited
CRN 554153
8th edition – May 2017
ISBN 978 1 78657 521 0
© Lonely Planet 2017   Photographs © as indicated 2017
10 9 8 7 6 5 4 3 2 1
Printed in China